WHO'S WHO
IN VENTURE CAPITAL

WHO'S WHO IN VENTURE CAPITAL
THIRD EDITION

A. David Silver

JOHN WILEY & SONS
New York • Chichester • Brisbane • Toronto • Singapore

Copyright © 1987 by John Wiley & Sons, Inc.

All rights reserved. Published simultaneously in Canada.

Reproduction or translation of any part of this work
beyond that permitted by Section 107 or 108 of the
1976 United States Copyright Act without the permission
of the copyright owner is unlawful. Requests for
permission or further information should be addressed to
the Permissions Department, John Wiley & Sons, Inc.

This publication is designed to provide accurate and
authoritative information in regard to the subject
matter covered. It is sold with the understanding that
the publisher is not engaged in rendering legal, accounting,
or other professional service. If legal advice or other
expert assistance is required, the services of a competent
professional person should be sought. *From a Declaration
of Principles jointly adopted by a Committee of the
American Bar Association and a Committee of Publishers.*

Library of Congress Cataloging in Publication Data:

Silver, A. David (Aaron David), 1941-
   Who's who in venture capital.

   Includes bibliographies and indexes.
    1. Venture capital—United States—Directories.
2. Venture capital—Great Britain—Directories.
3. Venture capital—Canada—Directories.   I. Title.
HG4963.S56   1987   332.66   86-28974
ISBN 0-471-85639-8

Printed in the United States of America

10 9 8 7 6 5 4 3 2 1

To Albert Frank

PREFACE

The search for venture capital can be exasperating, time consuming, and costly. Frequently, elegant entrepreneurial solutions to large problems die on the vine due to the absence of capital. This should not happen.

This directory of venture capitalists and venture capital funds is prepared the way I would like to see a directory put together. It has biographical data on more than 1,100 venture capitalists to help an entrepreneur match his or her business plan to the venture capitalists who are most likely to understand the plan. You may even find a venture capitalist whom you once worked with or attended school with. This kind of connection may help you establish credibility with the venture capital community.

In addition, the directory includes a fairly complete listing of the active funds: those with capital to invest. Information on many of the more than 600 funds in this directory includes a listing of the companies in which venture capitalists have invested. This information will show you venture capitalists' industry preferences, the kinds of companies they like to invest in, and their geographical preferences.

Finally, *Who's Who in Venture Capital: Third Edition* has a very affordable price tag. Many entrepreneurs are put off by high-priced directories, preferring to save their precious capital for internal needs. This directory is one-third the price of previous editions, but it contains 100 percent of the information of previous editions, all of it updated.

The reader must realize that there is a gestation period of almost nine months between the time information is gathered and a book is available. While we make every effort to ensure that information is correct, venture capital is a volatile market and there are changes everyday. Also, we are limited in that we must accept information given to us by those filling out questionnaires, and can make no guarantee as to its accuracy.

The data for this directory was gathered by the staff of Alembic Press, Inc. who, incidentally, manage the Association of Venture Capital Clubs. The venture capital club movement is becoming an important networking system to aid entrepreneurs in making their business plans presentable to venture capitalists. The knowledge base at Alembic Press helps to make this directory the most useful of its kind.

A. DAVID SILVER

Santa Fe, New Mexico
January 1987

CONTENTS

	Introduction	1
1.	Marketing and Innovation	7
2.	Five Categories of Generic Entrepreneurial Opportunities	37
3.	The Investment Criteria of Venture Capitalists	69
4.	The Contribution of Venture Capitalists to the Entrepreneurial Economy	93
5.	Directory of Venture Capital Funds: U.S., U.K., Canada; Including Biographies of Leading Venture Capitalists	101
	Index	465

INTRODUCTION

In order to make the best use of our time, we strive to use it effectively rather than efficiently. Let us say I wish to knock down a brick wall. To do so, I might beat my head against it repeatedly in the weakest spot until I knock loose some bricks. That might be an efficient method of making one hole in the wall, but I risk serious head injury and a lessened desire to complete the task. A more effective method would be to loosen several bricks by rubbing a stick in the mortar between them and removing them one at a time by hand, perhaps even stacking them up for reuse at another time. The second method requires more planning and more up-front labor until the bricks begin to come loose, but it is more effective than banging one's head against the wall. There are greater rewards in using one's time effectively than in using it efficiently.

The same applies to raising capital to finance one's dreams. The efficient way to raise capital is to provide a generous, guaranteed return for the lender or investor in a relatively short period of time. For example, in the name of efficiency, you might borrow $250,000 at an interest rate of 20 percent, with one quarter's interest prepaid, a closing fee of 5 percent, and a finder's fee of 5 percent, collateralized with a second mortgage on your house, personally guaranteed by you, a monthly consulting fee of $2000 payable to the lender, two seats out of five on your board of directors and the right to elect a third (and fire you) if you fail to meet sales projections, plus warrants to purchase 25 percent of your company's common stock for one cent per share with additional warrants if you fail to meet earnings projections.

The financial forests are full of wolves in sheep's clothing ready to pounce on unsuspecting entrepreneurial lambs seeking financing for the first time. You may think that the entrepreneurial lamb has not been born who would accept a $250,000 loan with terms as oppressive as those just described. Do not be surprised to learn that, to an entrepreneur who has had bank and investor doors slammed in his or her face repeatedly for six months while the savings account has shrunk to zero and the family is pushing the panic button, any offer of financing, no matter how odious, is taken seriously. Since start-up financing is a very precious commodity, the efficient entrepreneur might accept these oppressive terms in order to launch his or her new company. Now let's look at how far the money will go. First of all, the $250,000 is actually $213,000, after closing fees and expenses, with additional first-year fixed charges of $22,000 in consulting fees and $45,000 in interest, or net proceeds of $146,000. After deducting the first year's salaries for two people, rent, utilities, and consumables, there is not much capital available for the launch. This $250,000 financing, which at first appeared "better than nothing," will probably cost the entrepreneur his or her company, and possibly the house and the spouse and kids as well. The efficient way to raise capital is certainly not the best way.

How can one raise capital effectively? The first step is to determine whether or not one's new company requires capital. Instead, can it leverage customers, suppliers, marketing representatives, the local community, a grant program, or a combination of several of these sources of leverage plus a few thousand dollars from the family rainy day fund? Certain kinds of companies are launched with leverage and a very small amount of capital—under $25,000—while others require large sums of capital. Electronic Data Systems Corporation, acquired by General Motors Corporation in 1984 for $2.5 billion, was launched with $24,000 plus customer financing in 1964; whereas Federal Express Corporation, with a current market valuation of approximately $1.5 billion, was launched in the mid-1970s with approximately $96 million in venture capital. Why did Electronic Data Systems (EDS) need $95,876,000 less than Federal Express to get launched? Is H. Ross Perot, the founder of EDS, a much more clever enterpreneur than Frederick E. Smith, the founder of Federal Express? Did inflation in the 10-year period between the founding of the two companies play a role? The answer to the last two questions is "no." EDS addressed an opportunity that enabled the entrepreneur to use almost 100 percent customer financing in order to launch his company. This opportunity, called perfect DEJ, will be described in Chapter 1, "Marketing and Innovation." For an entrepreneur who has identified a perfect DEJ opportunity—and there are hundreds of them—there is no need to read the biographies of venture capitalists. These entrepreneurs will never have to break bread with venture capitalists.

There are eight DEJ factors, perfect DEJ representing all eight. Entrepreneurs who identify opportunities with seven of the eight DEJ factors, known as a nearly perfect DEJ condition, will require capital, but a relatively small amount. An example of a nearly perfect DEJ company is Automatic Data Processing, Inc., which has grown to a market value of approximately $750 million on an initial capital injection of $300,000. Henry Taub and Frank Lautenberg, the principal founders of Automatic Data Processing (ADP) along with Henry's younger brother, Joe, would not have needed a directory of venture capitalists either. They tapped the new issues market for ADP's initial $300,000.

Having six of the DEJ factors will reduce the entrepreneur's need for venture capital as well, but if the new company has five DEJ factors or fewer the entrepreneur is wasting his or her time and any capital he or she might raise, because the new business lacks validity. It may attract

INTRODUCTION

venture capital—particularly if the entrepreneur hits some of the venture capitalist's areas of greatest vulnerability—but it will probably end in disaster and unhappiness for all concerned. Venture capitalists are most vulnerable in productivity-improving capital equipment manufacturers and airline start-ups, tending to overinvest in new companies in these two areas. In the first instance this is because they like companies that sell products to other companies rather than to consumers, because selling to consumers is a more difficult task. In the second instance, investors are drawn in because they become directors of the new airline companies and are thus entitled to fly for free on all airlines in the United States. Because venture capitalists travel about 50 percent of their working days, free travel is an important contribution to the bottom line.

Outside of these two sensitive areas, venture capitalists have no particular industry preferences. As you will discover in Chapter 2, however, it is possible to categorize venture capitalists in terms of their preferred generic entrepreneurial opportunities. There are five generic entrepreneurial opportunities, or GEOs:

Major social and medical problems
Industrial problems
Niche problems
Elegant solutions
Leveraged buyouts

Major social and health problems are the GEOs most favored by experienced venture capitalists, those with more than 10 years of experience and a surplus of entrepreneurial achievements, peer recognition, and personal net worth. These angels of capitalism are truly evolved men and women who fulfill Walter Lippman's dreams in his 1943 masterpiece *The Good Society* that America's capitalist system provides its citizens "a way of producing wealth in which the good fortune of others multiplies their own."* Investing in entrepreneurial solutions to major social and health problems typically requires a longer wait for a payoff and the assumption of additional risks. Relatively few venture capitalists are willing to assume additional risks and a greater strain on their patience; hence many entrepreneurial solutions to major social and health problems are launched by means other than professional venture capital.

Industrial problems are the GEOs most favored by venture capitalists. These include products and services that reduce costs or increase profits for industrial corporations. Venture capitalists invested excessively in personal computer software packages in the early 1980s, which resulted in an advertising blitz in an effort to distinguish between the packages, a cascade of new computer-oriented magazines to accommodate the demand for advertising space, and the coining of a new word, *vapor-

---

*Walter Lippman, *The Good Society* (Boston: Little, Brown & Co., 1943), p. 124.

ware, as the software companies and magazines began to fail. Vaporware is software that evaporates upon receiving venture capital. Industrial problems such as computer-assisted design of semiconductors, office automation, transmitting price changes to numerous branch offices simultaneously, and improving quality control via automatic test instruments are the favored GEOs of venture capitalists. Arguably these kinds of companies produce smaller returns than do entrepreneurial companies that solve major problems, but many venture capitalists prefer to assume less risk and concomitantly lower returns in order to keep coming to bat. Although home run hitters make more money than singles hitters, they strike out more frequently as well. Babe Ruth struck out more than 3000 times in his career.

Niche problems entice a large number of venture capitalists because they appear to represent a quick-in-and-out, low-risk, modest return. A window opens briefly in a large market, say, computer printers with three or four features overlooked by Dataproducts or Qume, or an inexpensive medical instrument that emulates some of the features of larger, more costly instruments and is sold to smaller hospitals. Niche product companies must get rolling quickly at high speeds in order to leap through the window of opportunity that is temporarily open for them.

Frequently, however, the window slams shut before the company can leap through it. The entrepreneur blames the venture capitalists for dragging their feet, and the venture capitalists blame the entrepreneur for reacting too slowly. The company either folds up or merges into one of the market leaders. Quite a large number of business software companies were launched in 1983 to address vertical markets, such as accountants, doctor's office automation, travel agents, and so forth. Each company offered a niche investment opportunity to the venture capital community. Hundreds of these companies received financing, and only a handful survived. Niche opportunities seem to be 99 percent promise and 1 percent delivery. There is a means of taking advantage of niche opportunities that rely on venture capital, but it requires more creativity and individual effort on the part of the entrepreneur.

The fourth GEO is the elegant solution in search of a problem. At an earlier stage in the evolution of entrepreneurship, from 1937 to 1968, or the period between the founding of Xerox and Polaroid Corporation and the founding of Intel Corporation, many entrepreneurs were inventors. They did not, as a rule, understand or care to learn about the entrepreneurial process. Rather than formulate a large problem, conceive certain solutions to mitigate or solve it, and then test those ideas prior to developing solutions, the inventor develops solutions and then looks for problems that they can solve. It is a roundabout and substantially longer process.

Chester Carlson, the inventor of xerography, believed that his invention would assist other inventors in filing patents, a process that required a considerable amount of mimeographing at the time. Carlson told his story for 12 years until xerography finally attracted capital and sponsorship.

INTRODUCTION

Edwin H. Land, the inventor of a means of polarizing light, believed that his invention would reduce the glare of automobile headlights. He worked on this application for seven years before the Detroit automobile manufacturers finally rejected it. It was quite by accident that Dr. Land then stumbled upon instant photography, the product that made Polaroid a major success.

Carlson, Land, and a handful of other inventors have been able to convert elegant solutions into major companies, but the hands of fate had more to do with their success than knowledge of the entrepreneurial process. Many inventors are unable to convert their ideas to wealth because their ideas cannot be applied to useful purposes. They fare about as well financially as other artisans. Most venture capitalists are able to gainsay the elegant solutions GEO without remorse.

There is a growing body of interest in the fifth GEO, known as the leveraged buyout. This GEO is tailor-made for the entrepreneur who wants to own his or her own business but has no money nor insight into problems nor elegant solutions. The leveraged buyout attracts venture capitalists as well, because it does not require laborious audits of market size or technical audits. If the numbers work, and if the venture capitalists trust the entrepreneur, they will fund the buyout. When leveraged buyouts were initially discovered in the early 1970s, they were relatively inexpensive, and interesting businesses could be acquired by borrowing 100 percent of the purchase price on the assets of the target company. By the mid-1980s, an excessive number of leveraged buyout funds were created and the prices of the target companies were bid up accordingly. With the institutionalizing of leveraged buyouts, an entrepreneur who does not seek to save the world, solve a serious problem, fix a minor problem, or push his or her elegant solution into an unsuspecting marketplace can now be his or her own boss in less than 90 days without robbing a bank. The entrepreneur need only share ownership with a venture capitalist.

These five categories of generic entrepreneurial opportunities are of interest to venture capitalists to a greater or lesser extent. In Chapter 2 you will discover which GEO may be best for you, which GEO venture capitalists are most likely to fund, and how to use the directory to locate them.

The subject of Chapter 3 is the investment criteria of venture capitalists. I express these criteria through four laws, summarized as follows:

1. $V = P \times S \times E$, where V = valuation or wealth, the object of the game, P = the size of the problem the entrepreneur says he or she can solve, S = the elegance or uniqueness of the entrepreneur's solution or solution delivery system, and E = the quality of the entrepreneurial team.
2. The law of the big P, briefly stated, is that entrepreneurs and venture capitalists are able to achieve financial success—high values of V—without delivering S to P in a competent manner (i.e., "commercial success") if the entrepreneur attempts to solve

a very large *P*. For example, Genentech Corporation, a company that claims it can solve problems associated with diabetes and cancer, has achieved valuations in the range of $350 million to $800 million since 1981, despite the fact that its aggregate sales since 1981 have been less than 10 percent of that amount.

3. The law of risk aversion explains the five risks of investing in early-stage companies and tells which of the two risks venture capitalists are most comfortable accepting.
4. The "law of the hockey stick" is a pricing formula used by most venture capitalists in determining how much ownership they will need in order to invest in various GEOs.

The entrepreneurial economy is a subject of great interest lately. The most precious component in the entrepreneurial economy is cash. Economists and some government officials are gatekeepers on the highway between entrepreneurs in search of cash and venture capitalists and their investors who have the cash. Most of our laws encourage nonproductive investment, such as real estate, and discourage productive or job-creating investment. The venture capitalist represents an increasingly important voice in Washington. William G. Draper, a founder of Sutter Hill Capital, a highly regarded venture capital fund founded in the early 1970s, is currently the director of the Export-Import Bank. The venture capital trade association, National Venture Capital Association, is an effective lobbying organization on behalf of all investors, public and private, in start-up and early-stage companies. There are many pressures on Congress to create legislation that would, if enacted into law, seriously impede the ability of entrepreneurs and small businesspersons to obtain cash. The venture capital industry is developing a voice that effectively expresses opposition to these pressures. There is much more that the industry could do in terms of collecting data, reviewing peers, and making information available to entrepreneurs and others, but the need has not been identified that would force these changes.

Chapter 5 provides a biographical sketch of more than 1000 venture capitalists from the United States, United Kingdom, and Canada. The primary intent of this directory is to assist entrepreneurs in matching their company or dream with the venture capitalists most likely to be interested. For example, a veteran venture capitalist with some accumulated personal wealth and peer recognition would be the most likely to invest in a unique cancer therapy. A young venture capitalist, on the other hand, with neither personal wealth nor peer recognition, would not be willing to take on high-risk put-your-career-on-the-line deals. A productivity-improving capital equipment manufacturer with sales and low risk of failure would be more this venture capitalist's cup of tea.

A complete directory of the venture capital industry from the United States, the United Kingdom, and Canada is provided in Chapter 6. Here you will find the names, addresses, telephone numbers, and GEO preferences of 683 venture capital funds.

1

MARKETING AND INNOVATION

If you grew up in the 1950s or 1960s, you have probably heard of Goose Tatum and Marques Haynes. They were the principal basketball players on the Harlem Globetrotters. Tatum was marketing and Haynes was innovation. Although Tatum is dead and Haynes has slowed down considerably now that he has reached the age of 60, the Globetrotters and their spin-off, the Harlem Magicians, continue to barnstorm the country as they have done for 35 years, each team playing about 250 games per year. The sound of the Globetrotters' warm-up song "Sweet Georgia Brown" forewarns the sellout crowds that they are going to see a couple of hours of a hilarious and unique form of basketball.

Tatum played comedy basketball. One night he dressed in a hula skirt for a game in Hawaii. Tatum walked out into the pivot position and began swiveling his hips, popping his eyes, swishing his skirt, and making arm movements that were so hilarious that the players on the opposing team began laughing and falling over each other. The Globetrotters fed the ball to Tatum, who easily dunked it for two fast points.

Haynes was the first basketball player to dribble a basketball inches from the floor, between his legs, behind his back, while lying down, while sliding between an opponent's legs, and in a manner that caused the opposing team members to dive frantically for the ball, grabbing for the dribbler and coming up empty-handed and embarrassed.

Marketing and innovation. Goose Tatum and Marques Haynes. More staying power than other organizations that launched new products in the early 1950s but have crumbled since then. The companies' products were protected by patents and supported by millions of dollars of advertising. The Globetrotters had no patents and did not advertise. Polaroid Corporation, Sperry Corporation, and Xerox Corporation have proven themselves inferior to the Globetrotters and Magicians at marketing and innovation. "Sweet Georgia Brown" should have been played more frequently at corporate strategy sessions throughout the country. The validity of any business rests on its ability to market and remain innovative. Benjamin Franklin's better-mousetrap dictum to the contrary, marketing and innovation justify a company's existence.

MOST SUCCESSFUL COMPANIES OF THE LAST 25 YEARS

I have learned through the process of losing and making money in the venture capital business that certain kinds of companies succeed and other kinds of companies fail. Moreover, those that succeed frequently require less capital than those that fail. There is an inverse relationship between commercial success and venture capital. To examine this hypothesis I studied 100 of the most successful companies of the last 25 years, paying particular attention to the amount of start-up capital they required. I excluded companies in the extractive industries—oil, gas, coal, uranium, and other minerals—and real estate development companies because neither industrial category has successfully mitigated the problems of energy and shelter. Problem solving is part of the definition of entrepreneurship.

The 100 companies created, on average, approximately $1 billion in wealth for their founders and early investors on an initial average capital investment of approximately $150,000 (including outside investors), in an average time span of 16 years. Of the 100 companies, 75 were low tech and 25 were high tech. Moreover, 78 were bootstrapped with the founders' sweat equity and a few thousand dollars of savings and 22 raised venture capital. The companies are listed in Exhibit 1.1.

Electronic Data Systems Corporation (EDS) was acquired by General Motors Corporation for $2.5 billion in 1984. Twenty years had passed since H. Ross Perot launched EDS with $24,000. Sam Walton launched Wal-Mart Stores, Inc., in 1962 with sweat equity, and its market value is more than $5.2 billion in 1985.

CHANGES IN THE HEALTH CARE FIELD

Several different entrepreneurial teams have launched hospital management companies with sweat equity, leverage, and a timely initial public offering, including Charter Medical Corporation, Community Psychiatric Centers, Inc., Hospital Corporation of America, Humana Corporation, and National Medical Enterprises Corporation. In Exhibit 1.2, you can see that the average wealth created in the hospital management industry has been $2.1 billion in 20 years on an average initial investment per entrepreneur of less than $100,000.

With the creation of health maintenance organizations in 1973, and their momentum in selling prepaid health insurance policies to employee groups and individuals, hospitals have become increasingly less able to compete on a cost basis with other health care delivery organizations, such as free-standing medical centers (referred to as "doc-in-a-box"), mobile medical services, and in-home medical products and services. Hospital occupancy rates nationwide declined from over 70 percent in 1983 to 65 percent in 1984. Several hospital management companies have responded by acquiring other sources of cash flow, including health maintenance organizations and doc-in-a-box services.

Exhibit 1.1 The 100 Most Successful New Companies of the Last 25 Years

Name	Year Incorporated	Average Market Valuation in 1984	Initial Capital
Adelson, Sheldon The Interface Group, Inc.	1971	$200 million[a]	$10,000[b]
Allen, Martin A. Computervision Corp.	1969	1.3 billion	10,000
Alpert, Martin Tecmar, Inc.	1974	150 million	10,000
Anderson, J. Reid Verbatim Corp.	1969	460 million	10,000
Ash, Mary Kay Mary Kay Cosmetics	1963	450 million	5,000
Bloch, Henry W. & Richard A. H & R Block, Inc.	1955	522 million	10,000
Blount, Winton Malcom Blount, Inc.	1946	138 million	10,000
Blumkin, Rose Nebraska Furniture Mart	1937	60 million	500
Buffett, Warren E. Berkshire Hathaway, Inc.	1965	1 billion	10,000
Burr, Donald C. People Express Airlines, Inc.	1980	408 million	250,000
Cape, Ronald E. Cetus Corp.	1971	330 million	14 million
Carlson, Curtis L. Carlson Companies	1938	500 million	50
Carney, Frank L. Pizza Hut, Inc.	1958	300 million	10,000
d'Arbeloff, Alexander V., & DeWolf, Nicholas Teradyne, Inc.	1960	666 million	300,000
Day, Cecil B., & Kessler, Richard C. Days Inns of America, Inc.	1970	180 million	350,000
Dion, C. Norman Dysan Corp.	1973	250 million	2.5 million
Dotts, Richard Pedus International, Inc.	1979	35 million	200,000
Farley, William Francis Farley Industries, Inc.	1976	150 million	10,000
Fatjo, Tom J., Jr. Browning-Ferris Industries, Inc.	1970	1.2 billion	7,500
Fickling, William Arthur, Jr. Charter Medical Corp.	1969	500 million	10,000

Exhibit 1.1 (*Continued*)

Name	Year Incorporated	Average Market Valuation in 1984	Initial Capital
Fields, Debbi Mrs. Fields Cookies, Inc.	1977	50 million	50,000
Finegold, Aryeh Daisy Systems Corp.	1981	413 million	10,000
Frist, Dr. Thomas F., Sr., & Dr. Thomas F., Jr. Hospital Corp. of America	1968	3.4 billion	10,000
Fuqua, John Brooks Fuqua Industries, Inc.	1964	225 million	10,000
Gates, William Microsoft Corp.	1975	300 million	10,000
Gibbons, Fred Software Publishing Corp.	1981	67 million	1 million
Green, Robert L. Community Psychiatric Centers	1962	570 million	10,000
Grove, Andrew, Moore, Gordon, & Noyce, Robert Intel Corp.	1968	2 billion	2 million
Hambrecht, William Hambrecht & Quist, Inc.	1968	460 million	1 million
Hanson, John K. Winnebago Industries, Inc.	1958	250 million	10,000
Hirsch, Neil S. Telerate, Inc.	1969	792 million	30,000
Honda, Soichiro Honda Motor Co., Ltd.	1948	4.4 billion	10,000
Horchow, Roger The Horchow Collection	1973	50 million[a]	10,000
Hwang, K. Philip TeleVideo Systems, Inc.	1975	460 million	10,000
Ibuka, Masaru, & Morita, Akio Sony Corp.	1946	3.5 billion	500
Jackson, David Altos Computer Corp.	1977	150 million	100,000
Jeanloz, Claude & Donna Renovator's Supply, Inc.	1978	60 million[a]	50,000
Jobs, Steven, & Wozniak, Steven Apple Computer, Inc.	1975	1.5 billion	10,000
Kauffman, Ewing Marion Marion Laboratories, Inc.	1950	655 million	10,000

Exhibit 1.1 (*Continued*)

Name	Year Incorporated	Average Market Valuation in 1984	Initial Capital
Kelly, Thomas L., Jr. TIE/Communications, Inc.	1971	610 million	500,000
Khoury, Amin J. Delmed, Inc.	1974	113 million	500,000
Klein, Raphael Xicor, Inc.	1978	165 million	10,000
Knight, Phillip H. Nike, Inc.	1972	437 million	10,000
Kosowsky, David I. Damon Corp.	1961	100 million	10,000
Kroc, Raymond A. McDonald's Corp.	1961	4.2 billion	10,000
Kurtzig, Sandra L. ASK Computer Systems, Inc.	1974	200 million	2,000
LaBrecque, Francis American Discount Auto Parts	1975	28 million	10,000
Lazarus, Charles Toys 'R' Us, Inc.	1978	2.2 billion	10,000
Levy, Lawrence F. The Levy Organization, Inc.	1976	25 million	10,000
Lewis, Sydney Best Products Co., Inc.	1957	405 million	10,000
Little, Royal Textron, Inc.	1954	1 billion	10,000
Lucas, George Lucasfilms, Inc.	1975	500 million	10,000
Manoogian, Alex Masco Corp.	1929	1.6 billion	10,000
McGovern, Patrick J. International Data Group, Inc.	1964	375 million	10,000
McGowan, William G. MCI Communications Corp.	1968	2.8 billion	50,000
McLean, Malcolm P. Sea-Land Services, Inc.	1961	525 million	6 million
Merns, Sy Syms Syms Corp.	1959	228 million	10,000
Millard, William H. ComputerLand Corp.	1976	700 million	10,000
Moffitt, Phillip, & Whittle, Christopher 13-30 Corp.	1969	100 million	10,000

Exhibit 1.1 (*Continued*)

Name	Year Incorporated	Average Market Valuation in 1984	Initial Capital
Montgomery, Parker G. Cooper Laboratories, Inc.	1958	205 million	1 million
Murphy, Thomas S. Capital Cities Communications, Inc.	1954	1.9 billion	10,000
Nemeth, Lane Discovery Toys	1977	40 million[a]	25,000
Norris, William C. Control Data Corp.	1957	1.4 billion	10,000
Olsen, Kenneth H. Digital Equipment Corp.	1956	5.7 billion	70,000
Ortenberg, Elisabeth Claiborne Liz Claiborne, Inc.	1976	347 million	250,000
Oshman, M. Kenneth, & Maxfield, Robert R. Rolm Corp.	1969	1.5 billion	200,000
Packard, David Hewlett-Packard, Inc.	1939	9.9 billion	538
Park, Roy Hampton Park Communications, Inc.	1962	230 million	2.5 million
Parkinson, Joseph C., & Parkinson, Ward Micron Technology, Inc.	1978	513 million	10,000
Paulson, Allen E. Gulfstream Aerospace Corp.	1970	1.1 billion	10,000
Paulucci, Luigino F. Jeno's, Inc.	1967	200 million	10,000
Perot, H. Ross Electronic Data Systems Corp.	1962	2.5 billion	24,000
Petrie, Milton S. Petrie Stores Corp.	1932	672 million	10,000
Poduska, John William Apollo Computer, Inc.	1980	600 million	15 million
Price, Sol The Price Company	1976	828 million	10,000
Proctor, Barbara Gardner Proctor & Gardner Advertising, Inc.	1970	15 million	$—
Rouse, James W. Rouse Company	1939	495 million	20,000
Sanders, W. Jeremiah III Advanced Micro Devices, Inc.	1969	1.6 billion	1.5 million

Exhibit 1.1 (*Continued*)

Name	Year Incorporated	Average Market Valuation in 1984	Initial Capital
Schwab, Charles Charles Schwab & Co.	1971	53 million	10,000
Shakarian, David B. General Nutrition, Inc.	1955	300 million	10,000
Shoen, Leonard Samuel U-Haul Systems, Inc.	1945	600 million[a]	5,000
Siegel, Morris J. Celestial Seasonings, Inc.	1970	25 million	10,000
Sikora, Robert F. Bobby McGee's U.S.A., Inc.	1971	30 million	10,000
Simplot, Jack R. J. R. Simplot Corp.	1927	500 million	7,800
Singleton, Henry E. Teledyne, Inc.	1960	2.7 billion	1 million
Smith, Frederick W. Federal Express Corp.	1973	1.7 billion	103 million
Stata, Raymond Analog Devices, Inc.	1965	500 million	100,000
Swanson, Robert A., & Boyer, Herbert W. Genentech, Inc.	1976	490 million	250,000
Tandon, Sirjang Lal Tandon Corp.	1975	600 million	65,000
Tandy, Charles Tandy Corp.	1963	2.7 billion	10,000
Taub, Henry, Lautenberg, Frank, & Taub, Joseph Automatic Data Processing Corp.	1949	1.2 billion	10,000
Tauscher, William Y. FoxMeyer Corp.	1978	154 million	10,000
Treybig, James G. Tandem Computers, Inc.	1974	1.1 billion	3.1 million
Turner, Robert Edward III Turner Broadcasting System, Inc.	1969	400 million +	10,000
Ueltschi, Albert L. FlightSafety International, Inc.	1951	375 million	10,000
Vollum, Howard Tektronix, Inc.	1946	1.2 billion	10,000
Walton, Sam Moore Wal-Mart Stores, Inc.	1962	5.4 billion	10,000

Exhibit 1.1 (*Continued*)

Name	Year Incorporated	Average Market Valuation in 1984	Initial Capital
Wang, An Wang Laboratories, Inc.	1955	4.1 billion	1.3 million
Weill, Sanford I. Shearson Loeb Rhoades	1960	930 million	30,000
Wilson, Charles Kemmons Holiday Inns	1952	3.7 billion	10,000

Source: A. David Silver, *Entrepreneurial Megabucks: The 100 Greatest Entrepreneurs of the Last 25 Years* (New York: Wiley, 1985).

*a*Indicates an estimate comparing the company's value with that of similar companies for which public information is available.

*b*If the amount of capital with which the entrepreneur launched the company is unknown, it is estimated to have been $10,000 in personal savings.

The hospital management companies have emerged rapidly—indeed, they are still very entrepreneurial, their large revenues notwithstanding—yet they face the immediate and growing problem of a decline in occupancy rates brought about by a highly cost-conscious marketplace. Hospital management companies must become innovative in order to survive.

The health maintenance organizations (HMOs) have become tollgates on the highway between those who require health care and those who provide health care. Figure 1.1 portrays the role of the HMO as "gatekeeper" in the U.S. health care delivery market.

To survive in the face of declining occupancy rates, the hospital management companies will doubtless trade some of their stock for cash flow in other less volatile sectors of the health care market. Pharmaceutical and disposable suppliers may begin to appear attractive. Doc-in-a-box chains will certainly make sense. The next few years will test the ability of the hospital management companies to remain valid through marketing and innovation.

Exhibit 1.2 Wealth Creation Among U.S. Hospital Management Companies

Name	Year Incorporated	Market Valuation in 1985
Charter Medical Corp.	1969	$ 590,000
Community Psychiatric Centers	1962	1,025,000
Hospital Corp. of America	1960	4,600,000
Humana Corp.	1964	2,320,000
National Medical Enterprises	1968	1,740,000

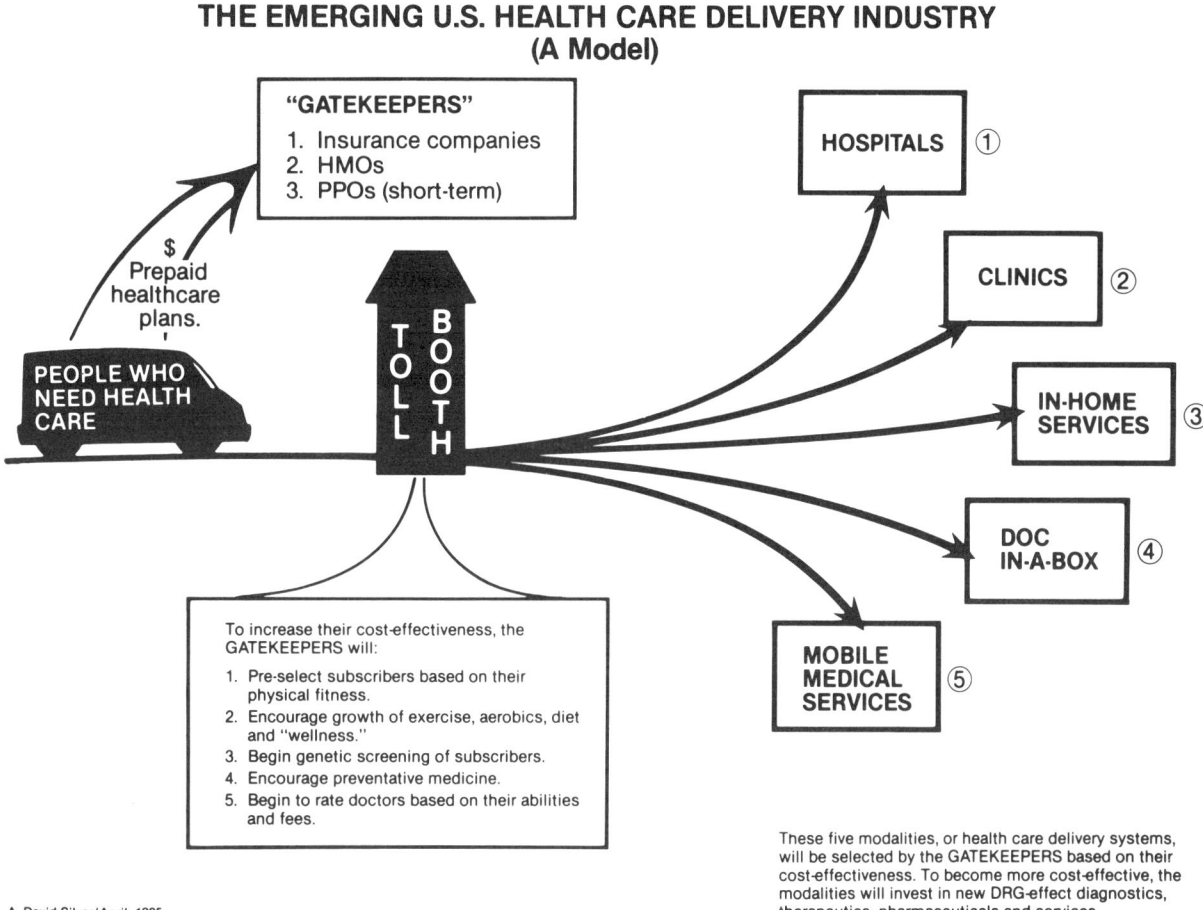

FIGURE 1.1. A model of the emerging U.S. Health care delivery industry.

The HMOs rocketed onto the health care delivery highway right under the noses of the logical providers of prepaid health insurance plans, the health insurance industry. There is some scrambling among the health insurance companies to get onto the HMOs' playing fields. But the market values of the HMOs have risen to great heights, making the entrance fee very steep—more than $1000 per subscriber. Were the initial capital requirements of the HMOs so high that the health insurance industry could not afford the diversification? On the contrary, the average initial capital requirement of the 7 largest HMOs was $762,400, whereas their average market valuation by mid-1985 had risen to $294 million in an average time period of five years. Exhibit 1.3 provides the comparative data on the largest members of this 10-year-old industry.

The HMOs have not attracted much professional venture capital. Their founders, like the hospital management company founders before them, used sweat equity, leverage, and customer financing to bootstrap their way to an initial public offering where cash could be raised to repay patient lenders. The HMO industry derives its validity through mar-

Exhibit 1.3 Historic Rates of Return Among U.S. HMOs ($ in thousands)

Name	Year Incorporated	Initial Capital	Market Valuation in 1985	Return on Investment
Bay Pacific Health Corp.	1984	$3,250	$ 40,000	12×
HealthAmerica Corp.	1980	10	539,000	53,900×
HealthGroup International	1979	1,300	19,000	15×
HealthWays Systems, Inc.	1984	40	15,500	388×
Maxicare Health Plans, Inc.	1973	37	565,800	15,292×
U.S. Health Care Systems, Inc.	1982	100	797,200	7,972×
Western Health Plans	1979	600	83,100	139×

keting and innovation and the federal legislation that fathered it in 1983, as a governmental response to rising costs of health care.

The newer providers of health care—doc-in-a-box, in-home products, and mobile medical services—are in a relatively early stage of evolution. A significant number of companies in these industry subsectors have attracted professional venture capital. Doc-in-a-box includes specialty medical services offered on an outpatient basis by doctors associated with the providers in retail establishments that are typically located in shopping malls. Some have referred to the trend toward retail medical establishments as the "McDonaldizing" of medicine. The doc-in-a-box establishments offer lower-cost health care alternatives in areas such as elective surgery and the kind of care one typically finds in a hospital emergency room.

In-home products represent perhaps the least expensive health care modality. Here the patient purchases an inexpensive disposable device at a pharmacy, takes it home, and at the appropriate time diagnoses himself, herself, or a child for strep throat, urinary tract infection, pregnancy, fertility, or other conditions. A considerable amount of time and expense is saved thereby.

Mobile medical services arose in response to the need for small medical practices or medical practitioners in small towns to gain access to the large, sophisticated medical equipment of the urban hospitals. For example, if a doctor in a small town feels that several of his or her patients require imaging of their brains, other organs, or arteries, the doctor in most instances must recommend that they take a day off from work and travel to the nearest large hospital in order to have a CAT scan, NMR image, or ultrasound diagnostic test performed. The doctor might lose his or her patient to the hospital or clinic, and it is an inconvenience for the patient and the doctor. With the availability of mobile medical services, the equipment can be driven to the small-town doctor's office, and with the assistance of the technicians who come with the equipment the doctor can keep his or her patient and earn a portion of the fee charged by the mobile medical service.

These companies have been unable to grow by bootstrapping because

MARKETING AND INNOVATION

of the up-front capital equipment and real estate financing requirements in the case of mobile medical and doc-in-a-box services and because of the up-front product development requirements in the case of in-home products. The venture capital industry has been a principal supplier of launch capital to these three subsectors, and in the absence of venture capital, the new issue market has come to entrepreneurs' aid.

The companies in these subsectors have yet to evolve into relatively mature, well-managed businesses. Thus, it is unfair to compare their returns to investors with those of hospital management companies and HMOs. The market valuations of these new modalities may grow dramatically over the next few years, but it is doubtful that they will provide the returns to investors that hospital management companies and HMOs have achieved. In Exhibit 1.4, the returns for this subsector are defined.

ENTREPRENEURIAL MASTERPIECES

The returns on investment to venture capitalists have never achieved—indeed, can never achieve—the dramatic heights reached by the returns on investment to the founding entrepreneurs of companies that do not

Exhibit 1.4 Historic Rates of Return Among New Health Care Modalities ($ in thousands)

Name	Year Incorporated	Initial Capital	Market Valuation in 1985	Return on Investment
Medical Care International (formerly Surgicare + Medical 21) (O/S)	1984	$1,000	$49,913	50×
Readicare, Inc. (O/D) (formerly Urgent Care Centers)	1982	400	29,580	74×
Surgical Care Affiliates (O/S)	1982	1,000	39,774	40×
Occupational Medical Corp. (O/E)	1980	100	9,975	100×
U.S. Medical Enterprises, Inc. (O/D)	1984	250	10,000	40×
John O. Butler Co. (I)	1949	5	68,000	13,600×
Continental Health Affiliates (I)	1981	10	54,600	5,460×
Pancretic, Inc. (I)	1983	105	11,431	109×
MMI Medical, Inc. (M)	1981	149	19,228	129×
American Shared Hospital Services (M)	1980	70	9,625	138×

Key: O/S, outside medical care centers/surgical; O/E, outside medical care centers/emergency care; O/D, outside medical care centers/doc-in-a-box; I, in-home products and services; M, mobile medical centers.

require venture capital. A company that can emerge, grow, and generate profits without venture capital is a rather pure and beautiful entity. Like a painting by one of the great masters, or a symphony by Mozart, a new company that does not need venture capital is a masterpiece. It tells its story, yields its beauty, sings its song without the need of a supporting cast of producers, directors, and other fellow travelers. Among the more beautiful entrepreneurial masterpieces of the last 25 years are the following 10 companies:

1. Capital Cities Communications Corporation
2. Chun King Corporation
3. Flight Safety International, Inc.
4. Mary Kay Cosmetics Corporation
5. McDonald's Corporation
6. Microsoft Corporation
7. Renovator's Supply Corporation
8. 13-30 Corporation
9. U-Haul System
10. Wal-Mart Stores, Inc.

These 10 companies were launched with sweat equity, customer financing, secured bank financing, the entrepreneurs' piggy banks, the labor of the spouse and children, and every other conceivable kind of launch capital except selling a piece of the equity to venture capitalists.* There are hundreds of other companies like these whose marketing, innovation, and use of leverage created sufficient validity to obviate the need for professional venture capital. Let us look more closely at each of these museum pieces.

Capital Cities Communications Corporation

Thomas Sawyer Murphy is a tall, athletic, shy, and intensely private individual. He was born in Brooklyn, New York, in 1926 and raised in a devoutly Catholic home by a strong-willed mother from whom, it is said, Mr. Murphy gained much of his optimism and faith in individual achievement. Mr. Murphy's father, Charles, an attorney, was appointed a justice of the New York Supreme Court in 1947. He served in that capacity until his death in 1959.

Tom enrolled in Cornell University and earned a B.S.M.E. degree in 1945. After serving in the armed forces and then selling oil for Texaco

---

*For a description of the various methods of financing a start-up see A. David Silver, *Up-Front Financing* (New York: Wiley, 1982).

for a year, he entered Harvard University and earned an M.B.A. degree in 1949.

After Harvard, Murphy worked for the Kenyon & Eckhardt advertising agency as an account executive for several years and then moved on to Lever Brothers as a product manager. When a group of investors formed Capital Cities Communications in 1954 to purchase Hudson Valley Broadcasting Company in Albany, New York, Murphy joined the company as general manager of the Albany television station. Capital Cities also bought WTVD, a Raleigh-Durham, North Carolina, station (hence its corporate name). In 3 years, Murphy became a director, and in 10 years he was president of Capital Cities.

Under his leadership, the company has grown by acquisition to include 19 television and radio stations in major markets throughout the United States, 54 cable television systems in 16 states, 10 daily newspapers in eight markets, 36 business and specialized newspapers and magazines, and 36 weekly community publications, and it is an electronic distributor of information and data bases. Three of the company's electronic data bases include financial information sold to the investment community, medical supplies information sold to hospitals and other health care providers, and a data base of electronic components, complete with technical specifications, prices, and delivery schedules, sold to electronic designers and partially supported by advertising.

Murphy's diversification into electronic data bases makes him every bit the high-technology entrepreneur, as much as his acquisition of more than 100 broadcasting and publishing companies makes him one of the preeminent leverages buyout entrepreneurs. When Fairchild Publications, publisher of *Women's Wear Daily, Daily News Record, Electronic News,* and many other trade newspapers, was seeking to be acquired 15 years ago, John Fairbanks contacted Tom Murphy. Fairchild instantly liked him, as do most people who meet Murphy. He liked his optimism and his willingness to consider new ideas. Mr. Fairchild told the *New York Times*, "He has big blue eyes . . . and when he gets excited about an idea, they roll."*

Thus, when Leonard S. Goldenson, founder of ABC, began to face the issue of management succession, he looked outside his company to Capital Cities. ABC television provides programming for more than 200 affiliates and owns five television stations. ABC radio has 1596 affiliates and owns five FM and seven AM radio stations. Until the FCC decides which of the TV and radio stations must be sold in order to meet its guidelines, Capital Cities-ABC's combined stations will serve one-fourth of the nation's population. Goldenson saw in Murphy perhaps the same management abilities that attracted Warren S. Buffett, Capital Cities' largest individual investor. Capital Cities has consistently earned more than 15 percent on revenues over the last 10 years, and more than 20 percent on stockholders' equity. Indeed, to finance the purchase of ABC, Buffett invested over $517 million in Capital Cities.

*Pamela G. Hollie, *New York Times*, March 20, 1985, p. 38.

Chun King Corporation

Jeno F. Paulucci, born in 1918, has driven himself and others to succeed since he was a child. There does not appear to be any way to slow him down, even though Paulucci is a centimillionaire many times over. He is an incurable successful entrepreneur. According to his autobiography, the Paulucci family was poor even by depression standards. Paulucci's father, Ettore, had migrated to Aurora, Minnesota, to work in the iron mines. The work, however, was irregular, and food for the family of four was available only when everyone scrounged. Young Jeno walked along the railroad tracks looking for fallen lumps of coal, pulling a little red wagon held together by discarded parts. He gathered cardboard boxes to sell for a penny each to the Pauluccis' landlord, who burned them for fuel.

By age 12, Paulucci figured that there was more to work than muscles. He peddled iron ore samples in glass vials to tourists who came to visit the iron ore mines, and he conducted guided tours of the mines. Paulucci's father abandoned the family shortly thereafter, though he returned when Paulucci was successful. In 1933 his hardworking mother opened a grocery store in the family's living room, and Paulucci took a job at a downtown grocery. He displayed a willingness to put in 16-hour days and a gift for sales that the small chain's owner, David Persha, admired. Always combative, Paulucci led two strikes at high school, one against long homework assignments for students who held jobs and the other against learning poetry. At 16 he became the Minnesota sales representative for a food wholesaler after negotiating a 50 percent profit split.

During World War II, fresh vegetables were in short supply, and Paulucci observed that Oriental families in Minnesota were growing their own bean sprouts in hydroponic gardens. Paulucci experimented with growing soybeans, and he and David Persha became partners in the new venture. Persha was an experienced businessman, reasonable, and cautious. Paulucci was young, energetic, abrasive, combative, and full of ideas. He was only five feet, five inches tall, but he was known to take on an entire barroom; later, when Chun King had management meetings, he would jump onto the conference table, stare down at his vice presidents, and terrorize them.

Chun King toughed it out through the late 1940s, and Paulucci's marriage tempered his pugnacity somewhat. It was for pure spite that Paulucci started Northland Foods, predecessor to Jeno's, Inc. In the book *Self-Made* by Carol Pine and Susan Mundale, the beginning of Northland Foods is described thus:

> It was 1947, and Jeno owed everybody money—his packers, his suppliers, even some of his customers who had credit memos. A federal investigator, moreover, determined that Paulucci owed his employees $15,000 in back pay for time-and-a-half over 40 hours instead of 48 as stated in their union contract. Jeno bid on a government contract to pack boned turkey on the basis of a verbal loan agreement from a Duluth bank. When the bank

backed out, he had to tell the government to take the next lowest bit. Finally, a small Duluth bank granted him a loan.

In an effort to settle one debt, Jeno made an agreement with the packer who had won the lawsuit. Jeno would act as a field broker, selling the packer's canned pie fillings at a low brokerage rate. But the packer, who had been so prompt about collecting payments on the settlement, proved slow to pay the brokerage fee. Again Jeno took matters into his own hands. He telephoned the packer's company with a fictitious order for $9,000 worth of pie filling. When the cans were in the truck and on their way to Duluth, he phoned the packer again. "If I don't get $5,000 by tomorrow, I'm going to dump this stuff in the Twin Cities for bargain prices," he said. "Furthermore, I'm going into the pie-filling business myself, and it's a vendetta." Northland Foods, later Jeno's Inc., was thus born.*

Chun King began to attract acquisition interest in the 1960s. Paulucci rejected a Chef Boy-Ar-Dee offer for $4 million. But in 1966 R. J. Reynolds Industries bought the company for $63 million, freeing Paulucci to work on the expansion of Jeno's. He certainly was not going to stay at Chun King, with the new corporate regime in place. Paulucci says: "When I showed up for work at my usual time the first morning, the guard wouldn't let me into the building. I suddenly realized that I was in a different world! These people came to work at *nine* in the morning. I thought I was late walking in at *six*!"**

FlightSafety International

Albert L. Ueltschi was born on a dairy farm in Frankfort, Kentucky, in 1915, one of seven children. Life on the farm was difficult, and Al had to milk the cows before school, bottle the milk, and sell it in town for a nickel a quart. He attended a one-room school and graduated from high school in the mid-1930s with a burning desire to fly. He told reporter Jerry Wakefield of the *Frankfort State Journal,* "I always had a feeling I'd like to fly. I remember Lindbergh crossing the Atlantic and when I was in grammar school I always read all the aviation books I could." He learned to fly when he was 16 on an old airstrip. "A fellow named Charlie Black had a farm out on the Georgetown Pike where he had built a hangar for me. So I ran some ads in the paper for the Frankfort Flying School. We'd put on a little air show and charge everybody about $3.00 or something like that."†

Ueltschi ran a restaurant during his college years, and then he became a barnstorming pilot until World War II, briefly serving as Juan Trippe's (Pan Am's founder) pilot. With the growth in commercial aviation after the war, Ueltschi observed that industrial corporations were having trouble finding trained pilots, and aircraft manufacturers were getting

---

*Carol Pine and Susan Mundale, *Self-Made: The Story of 12 Minnesota Entrepreneurs* (Minneapolis: Dorn Books, 1982), p. 28.
**Ibid., p. 29.
†Jerry Wakefield, "Al Ueltschi," *Frankfort State Journal,* July 30, 1984, p. 75.

out of the pilot-training business in order to concentrate on aircraft manufacture.

In 1951, Ueltschi jumped into the pilot-training gap by renting space at LaGuardia Airport's Marine Air Terminal and renting flight simulators. In 1954, when the business appeared viable, he mortgaged his house to buy a $10,000 training simulator from Link. A cautious man, Ueltschi remained a Pan Am pilot until 1968, running FlightSafety during his off-hours. He took the company public in 1968 and began to give it his full-time attention.

The company owns and operates approximately 75 flight simulators, which duplicate nearly every flight experience and are identical in instrumentation and appearance to the cockpits of actual aircraft.

The simulators cover a broad range of aircraft, with an emphasis on smaller, business aircraft as opposed to commercial airlines. FlightSafety has an estimated 30 percent market share of the general aviation training market. It is the authorized training organization for 17 aircraft manufacturers. Some might say Ueltschi has a lockup.

A $2.5 billion grant has said just that. Singer Company has asked a federal court to nullify FlightSafety's agreement with major aircraft manufacturers including McDonnell Douglas, Lockheed, and the Sikorsky division of United Technologies. These manufacturers steer their customers to FlightSafety, and Singer says the practice is anticompetitive; they want easier access into the market. Ueltschi is defending his position vigorously. He recently told *Forbes*: "I built this damn thing from nothing and I did it clean. Nobody can take that away from me."*

Mary Kay Cosmetics Corporation

Mary Kay Ash founded her own company in 1963, about three months after retiring from another direct sales company where she had worked for 25 years. She entered the direct sales business as a divorced mother of three. She wanted to create a company in which being a woman would not be a hindrance to upward mobility and financial rewards and in which motivation was based on goals and objectives important to women. Her entrepreneurial genius was in creating a unique motivational system that would attract, hold onto, motivate, and reward an all-woman marketing organization. The unique product, or elegant solution to a large problem, was not part of Mary Kay's initial formulation, although clearly the product would have to possess economic validity for her company to be successful.

She chose a cosmetic that she had been using for years, a skin-care line based on formulas developed by a hide tanner that had been sold only by the tanner's granddaughter. She rented a storefront in a Dallas office building and began selling the products to generate revenues. She pulled her son, Richard, age 20, out of college to assist her. Mary Kay

---

*Anne Bagamery, "Dogfight," *Forbes*, July 30, 1984, p. 68.

immediately began recruiting and training beauty consultants to begin home demonstrations. Although practically every male friend, adviser, and counselor tried to dissuade her, Mary Kay claims to have been given the courage to succeed by her previous successes in direct sales and her mother's encouragement.

Revenues grew slowly in the 1960s as the foundation was being laid, but they reached $31 million in 1974 and have grown tenfold since. The company has consistently earned more than 20 percent before taxes, and its stockholders' equity exceeds $140 million, of which cash ($26 million) is approximately 20 percent. The company has virtually no long-term debt. Mary Kay Ash has built a cash-generating machine that, moreover, has transformed a quarter of a million women into self-employed businesswomen with lots of ability and handsome bank accounts. As in many party-plan companies, the wives begin outearning the husbands.

How did Mary Kay Ash accomplish this? She created a feeling of family in her company, a hierarchical organization chart that had a system of rewards and penalties. Through frequent seminars attended by the independent beauty consultants, Mary Kay "preaches" to her women like a tent meeting evangelist. Typical of her gospel is the following: "If you are here today, you are too smart to go home and scrub floors. You are spending one dollar time on a one penny chore." This admonition not only gives the women pride, but encourages them to get housekeepers so that they can spend more time recruiting additional beauty consultants and selling more cosmetics. "I created this company for you," she tells them. This and similar pronouncements enhance the spirit of family and create the excitement of a crusade.

Mary Kay Cosmetics depends for its success on the continual attraction of new independent beauty consultants. After training they purchase their initial inventory and are sent on their way. The company does not advertise for women; rather, it relies on word of mouth. Thirty percent of its 200,000 direct sales personnel are college graduates. When the economy is weak and inflation is strong, women flock to Mary Kay in greater numbers than when the economy is buoyant. To counter this situation, the company has introduced the Mr. K line of male cosmetics. Can this vibrant lady and her talented son enter a second line as successfully as they did the first? Only time will tell. But, win or lose on Mr. K, Mary Kay Ash is one of the most valuable entrepreneurs in the country.

McDonald's Corporation

Raymond A. Kroc, who died in 1984 at the age of 82, was raised by his mother after his father "worried himself to death." He attended public school with Ernest Hemingway and dropped out of high school to become a musician. Later he served in World War I with Walt Disney, who enlisted at the age of 16. While in his early twenties, Kroc got a job as a musical director of a Chicago radio station and discovered the singing comedy team of Sam and Henry, later to be known as Amos 'n' Andy.

In the 1920s he drove to Florida to try to make a fortune in real estate. He drove back "stone broke." He was a failure by his thirtieth birthday. He bounced around, finally becoming a milkshake machine salesman. Orders frequently came from a drive-in restaurant in San Bernardino, California, owned by the McDonald brothers. Like so many crazes, the drive-in began in California. The McDonald brothers had so many hungry adolescents clamoring for their 15-cent burgers stuffed into paper bags that the day Kroc visited the restaurant security guards were needed to quell the mob. Kroc saw an opportunity to sell franchises, so he asked for the job. Kroc gave the brothers 0.5 percent of the gross receipts of franchise fees and royalties. After six years of paying the brothers, and 300 franchises, Kroc found the brothers "were beginning to get on my nerves." He bought them out for $2.7 million in cash.

Kroc was a self-taught businessman with numerous one-line prescriptions for success. For example, to select sites, he recommended flying over neighborhoods to count church steeples and schools. He believed service personnel who deal with customers should not have long hair, sideburns, moustaches, bad teeth, severe skin blemishes, or tattoos. A vicious competitor, Kroc is remembered as having said: "It's dog-eat-dog and if anyone tries to get me I'll get them first. It's the American way of survival of the fittest."*

For all his toughness in business, Kroc and his third wife Joan are reknowned for their charitable contributions. Ronald McDonald House is an extremely important "giving" institution. Kroc never gave money to colleges; he helped trade schools instead. He valued hard work rather than "phony intellectuals." As one economist once wrote about Kroc, "his enterprise expresses the prosaic idea on which American prosperity rests: things add up."† Kroc's entrepreneurial genius was acting boldly on the obvious and never stopping to rest.

Microsoft Corporation

William Gates was born in 1954 and raised in an upper-middle-class home in Seattle. In the seventh grade, he learned how to program a computer. By his senior year in high school, TRW Corporation had pulled him to Vancouver, Washington, to write programs for one of its divisions. Gates entered Harvard University at 17, but he dropped out and moved to Albuquerque, New Mexico, with Microsoft Corporation cofounder Paul Allen. There a small company called MITS had put Intel's 8080 microchip on a board and soldered wires to the board leading to the keyboard and a monitor. Many of the early microcomputer

---

*Tom Robbins, "Ray Kroc Did It All for You," *Esquire*, December 1983, p. 344.
†Ibid.

entrepreneurs had read about the MITS computer in *Popular Science* magazine and had descended on Albuquerque.

Gates and Allen rented a cheap motel room in Albuquerque and adapted the popular BASIC language to create an operating system for the first microcomputer. There were other operating systems of equal or greater popularity in the late 1970s—CP/M being the most widely used—but MS DOS was selected by IBM when it built its IBM PC in 1981, and, as the sportscasters say, the rest is history.

Gates is generally acknowledged in the personal computer industry as a man of brilliance and perspicacity beyond his years. David Bunnell, publisher of *PC World,* was also a resident of Albuquerque during the birth of the personal computer; he says of Gates: "When the history of the microcomputer industry is written, Bill Gates will be remembered as the guy who wrote the first successful program for the mass market."*

A single-product company less than 10 years old would not qualify for a list of successful new businesses. As a measure of Gates's maturity, he has been diversifying Microsoft Corporation rapidly and vertically. The company has a highly successful spreadsheet package called *Multiplan* and released a windowing package in 1985. As for horizontal diversification, Gates recently wrote an operating system for the Japanese personal computer manufacturers called MSX, which is expected to become the principal system in Europe.

Renovator's Supply Corporation

Claude and Donna Jeanloz were tossed out of an African country in 1974 by a dictator who hated the United States and its Peace Corps. They returned to their home in Massachusetts and for lack of something better to do began restoring their colonial house in Northfield. Like many other restorers, the Jeanlozes ran up against a wall. Many of the authentic fixtures they were looking for were just not made any longer. And when items were available, getting them took infinite patience and dogged pursuit. Sheer desperation finally drove them to manufacturers' directories where they hunted down sources for the things no one else could supply.

Four years later the couple had completely restored their house in Massachusetts and another in Canada. In the process, they had answered dozens of inquiries from people who wondered where they had found their supplies. This prompted the Jeanlozes to start a mail-order business, a clearinghouse for exactly the kinds of electrical and plumbing fixtures, hardware, and ornaments that had so many house restorers over a barrel. Their basic catalog offers necessities for fixing up old houses of any period or region. Supplementary catalogs offer specialty products to add finishing touches, nostalgia, and whimsy.

As the business grew, the Jeanlozes moved it into an old garage, which,

---

*David Bunnell, *Esquire*, December 1984, p. 29.

of course, they restored. Then in December 1983 they moved down the street into a large factory, which went through a renovation. Sales grew from $34,000 in 1978 to $12 million in 1983. The introduction of a computer early on to collect subscriber names and inquiries and to store product information has been critical to the company's rapid growth. To generate additional revenues, the Jeanlozes permitted manufacturers to advertise in their catalog.

A stunning cash flow has permitted the couple to diversify rapidly into a chain of retail stores called Renovator's Supply. The first was opened in Flemington, New Jersey, a historic town with a restored old town section; the other 13 stores are situated primarily in New England.

In March 1984 the company purchased the publisher of *Aristera*, a catalog of products for left-handed people, and *Country Notebook*, a catalog of country-inspired home decoration items. Other diversifications included an on-premises blacksmith shop that produces wrought iron items for the home and Play for Growth, a toy line for children.

The Jeanloxes and Renovator's Supply are an excellent example of what dissatisfaction, insight into the problem, and energy in presenting the solution can achieve.

13-30 Corporation

Phillip Moffitt and Christopher Whittle, both born in the mid-forties, are the H. Ross Perots of magazine publishing. They are in the facilities management segment of publishing, a niche that Perot nailed down for himself in data processing. Moffitt and Whittle approach a large advertiser such as Nissan Motor Corporation, R. J. Reynolds Industries, or Ralston Purina Company and say, "We'll publish a magazine targeted at college students [or moviegoers or veterinarians] and you'll be the principal advertisers." Nissan Motor Corporation then hires 13-30 to publish *America*, R. J. Reynolds Industries hires them for *Moviegoer*, and Ralston Purina Company signs up for *Veterinary Practice Management*. They have repeated this scenario more than a dozen times and have used the ample cash flow therefrom to purchase *Esquire*, whose revenues they increased to $35 million in 1984 from just a couple of million when they bought it in 1979. Moffitt and Whittle are a very private publishing team that has come up with an idea one would expect out of a Rupert Murdoch or some other Madison Avenue publishing guru. But Moffitt and Whittle did their problem formulating in a very unlikely spot, Knoxville, Tennessee. Is it really so unlikely a place? It's my hometown. I should know.

Approach 13-30 Corporation, as it was first called, got into business with *Knoxville in a Nutshell*, a primer for students entering the University of Tennessee. Even then Moffitt and Whittle were thinking target audiences. The expansion phase came early, as *Nutshell* was produced for other campuses. Writing for students was easy and cheap; the team hired student writers.

A commercial banker played venture capitalist to 13-30. Moffitt's economics teacher, Tony Spiva, put his personal guarantee on the line, but Valley Bank officer Lawrence Frierson, who died in 1973, made loans in excess of Spiva's net worth. Total borrowings reached $1 million by 1973, the first time 13-30 began to show profits. In 1974, the company made $300,000 and began paying down the loans.

Moffitt explained his feelings when 13-30 owed $1 million and was unprofitable to Jane Gibbs DuBose of the Knoxville News Sentinel: "I never saw on any logical level any reason that it would not work, and that has turned out to be a tremendous asset for the company. We are strategic people and the reason it is so instinctive to use is because of those early days. The only thing we could go on was the soundness of the strategy."*

The founders of the single-sponsor magazines keep rolling. They signed Seagram Company, Ltd., to a multimillion-dollar contract to publish a magazine for waiters called Tables. The U.S. Army signed up for a magazine for high school seniors called On Your Own. There seems to be no end to target publishing on a single-sponsor basis. When Whittle predicts sales of $250 million by 1984, the Madison Avenue gurus who chortled when the hillbillies bought Esquire do not scoff anymore.

U-Haul System

Leonard S. "Sam" Shoen, 69, has built one of America's best-known businesses using sale–leaseback techniques and customer financing. When an entrepreneur doesn't use equity financing, he or she holds onto most of the company's common stock. Shoen owns 92 percent of the U-Haul System, whose revenues are in excess of $750 million. I called on Shoen in the late 1960s to sell him the investment banking services of my employer, Kuhn, Loeb & Co. After reviewing his exquisite use of financial leverage, I realized that Shoen knew more about investment banking than did most of us on Wall Street.

He would purchase trailers and trucks and sell them to employees, family members, friends, and investors who would then lease them back to AMERCO, the parent company of U-Haul. The equipment had tax advantages and generated income for the trailer owners from their continual rental. The equipment was eventually packaged, and the offerings became larger and more popular and were registered with the SEC. But they were never equity linked.

While leveraging the capital equipment needs at one end, Shoen leveraged the customer at the other. He made gasoline stations into U-Haul dealers, thus eliminating his need for retail outlets and the cost of carrying labor. The advertising was largely paid for by the person who drove a U-Haul trailer down the highway. It was a moving billboard

---

*Jane Gibbs DuBose, "2 Ol' East Tennessee Boys Teach Publishing World a Thing or Two," Knoxville News-Sentinel, October 21, 1984, p. C1.

seen by thousands. The general and administrative costs were also largely borne by the dealers, who handled the paperwork at the rental and receiving ends. You would have to look long and hard to find a more elegant service business than the U-Haul System.

Sam Shoen was born on a farm near McGrath, Minnesota, in 1916, the second of seven children. "I owe much of my understanding of a business operation to my father who can best be characterized as a 'jack of all trades'. . . . He is not awed by the new and the different," Shoen said in his book, *You and Me*, written in 1980. "My father moved his family from Minnesota to Oregon in . . . 1923. Because I was the oldest boy, he secured my help in all his business ventures and was quite free with his advice and with the details of the business operations."* Many of the elder Shoen's ventures were unsuccessful, and Sam worked on nearby farms and in local stores throughout his teens. Finding business to be unrewarding, Sam registered in the premedical program at Oregon State University in 1937. To pay for medical school, he learned how to be a barber.

In his sophomore year in college, Shoen leased the barber shop in a hotel in Corvallis, and within six months he had four barbers operating for him. With cash from this barber shop, Shoen opened a three-chair barber shop in Albany, Oregon. He expanded with two shops later in the year. When World War II began, Shoen lost his barbers to the draft. He closed his shops and put the equipment into storage.

In spite of his business distractions, Shoen's grades were good. Yet in his senior year of medical school Shoen was suspended for answering in class for his lab partner. Shoen enlisted in the U.S. Navy but in 1944 contracted scarlet fever and was hospitalized for five months. It was the first time in his life that he had not been active. But his mind was. Shoen conceived the business plan for the U-Haul System while on his back in the hospital.

Shoen had seen trailers in Los Angeles made out of parts of old automobiles. Rental lots were renting 20 to 40 of these "junkers" per day for $2.00. The trailers would usually fall apart and the tires would go flat before 100 miles of use. Besides, the trailers had to be returned to the rental lot. Servicemen were the primary customers. Shoen saw the enormity of the need for one-way rentals and more substantial trailers.

Upon his release from the hospital, Shoen did some extensive market research. He examined the reasons that the trailer rental industry had not developed: poor materials, tire shortage, weak bumpers, and a lack of convenience. Trailers were so inexpensive to make that people could afford to buy them instead of renting.

It was necessary that Shoen think big: He would have to produce his own trailers, design the entire system, and put it into place quickly and efficiently. With $5000 in personal savings and newly married, Shoen decided to chase his dream rather than buy a house. He writes: "Since my fortune was just about enough to make the down payment on a home

---

*Leonard S. Shoen, *You and Me* (Las Vegas: AMERCO, 1980), p. 2.

and furnish it, and knowing that if I did this we would be sunk, we started the life of nomads by putting our belongings in a trailer and living between in-laws and parents for the next six months. I barbered part-time and bought trailers of the kind I thought we needed to rent from anybody who happened to have one at the price I thought was right. By the fall of 1945 I was in so deep into the trailer rental deal economically that it was either make it or lose the whole thing."*

U-Haul has been the dominant firm in the one-way trailer rental business for more than 30 years with very little effective competition. As Shoen says: "I believe in luck. The harder I work the luckier I get." By the way, Shoen thought an understanding of the law might be useful. Thus, while building the U-Haul System, he earned a legal degree in 1955 by going to night school at Lewis and Clark College in Portland. He graduated at the head of the class.

Wal-Mart Stores, Inc.

Sam Moore Walton was a J.C. Penney trainee after graduating from college, and he admires James Cash Penney a great deal. In 1945, at the age of 27, he opened his first Ben Franklin store, in Newport, Arkansas. In 1950 Walton's store folded. He reopened another Ben Franklin five-and-dime in Bentonville, Arkansas, immediately, and by 1962 he had 16 of them. His brother James gave Walton the idea for discount stores, and the Ben Franklins were converted to form the base for what has become one of the greatest family fortunes in America. Walton owns 39 percent of a business valued at $5.4 million. What did he see 22 years ago that others overlooked?

Walton knows small towns. With a twin-engine Piper Aztec, he flies from small town to small town, often visiting four stores per day, and spending a couple of hours with the store managers, the associates who run the various departments, and the customers. He told *Forbes:* "We like to let folks know we're interested in them and that they're vital to us. 'Cause they are. Those department heads are the ones who *really* know what's going on out there in the field, and we've got to get them to tell us."†

Walton carries an idea that works in one town to another town. He will ask the manager if the idea will work and discuss its pros and cons. Walton knows the names of thousands of employees, and he has their loyalty.

There is often a Penney's store in town, but he does not worry about it. Wal-Marts have a wider merchandise mix with more hard goods. His real competitors are K-Mart Corporation, Gibson's (a southern chain), and TG&Y stores (a division of Household Finance). They find Wal-Mart Stores very tough competitors. Often when they find an attractive town

---

*Ibid.
†Harold Seneker, "A Day in the Life of Sam Walton," *Forbes*, December 1, 1977, p. 47.

a Wal-Mart is already there. When it is not, Wal-Mart is not above putting a bigger, brighter store in wherever competitors show the slightest vulnerability. Some of them have been run out of town.

Wal-Mart's boundaries are set by one-day truck routes from six warehouses. Eighty percent of its goods pass through these huge company distribution complexes for transshipment. That way, volume discounts and its own trucking save 2 to 5 percent on cost, no small matter to a company with a 7 percent pretax margin.

Success for Wal-Mart is the result of caring. The stores are big and attractive and they say to the customers, "You may be small-town people, but you have big-town taste!" Walton pays his customers a compliment, and they have paid him back many times over.

THE EIGHT DEJ FACTORS

There is an explanation for the fact that certain new companies do not require venture capital to be transformed from a dream to a reality, while others require the continual sale of equity securities to atavistic venture capitalists. Microsofts and Wal-Marts do not happen accidentally. Bill Gates and Sam Walton were not, to refute Peter F. Drucker,* "Look Ma, no hands" types. Their achievements in two entirely different industries can be predicted, duplicated, and replicated by entrepreneurs who choose to find and execute the "perfect DEJ."

For some time, I have been writing about the eight characteristics of a new company that will ensure its success. These are known as demonstrable economic justification (DEJ) factors. If a new company possesses all eight DEJ factors, it has a very high probability of success and will require very small if any amounts of venture capital. The 10 companies cited above required very little venture capital; neither do the HMOs, nor the hospital management companies. They are *entrepreneurial masterpieces*.

The requirement for venture capital is in indirect proportion to the number of DEJ factors possessed by the company. The potential for success, on the other hand, correlates with the number of DEJ factors.

When a new company is missing four or more DEJ factors, it will probably fail, usually after it raises venture capital. The absence of certain DEJ factors—number eight, for example, which means there is a need to advertise a product heavily—is appealing to many venture capitalists, who, I sometimes believe, receive a psychic reward upon seeing one of their companies' advertisements in print. It is not just the young venture capitalists who back companies whose products need to be advertised, but the retreads as well. Rothschild's, Inc., an experienced venture capital firm, hired Archie McGill, formerly the president of

---

*In *Entrepreneurship and Innovation: Principles and Practice* (New York: Harper & Row, 1985, p. 267) Peter F. Drucker says: "Most of the literature on entreneurship is anecdotal and of the 'Look, Ma, no hands' variety." He has not read the mountains of literature on the subject of the entrepreneurial process from myriad sources, many of which are cited herein.

AT&T, to direct its investment activities in 1983. He championed an investment of more than $5 million in Knoware, Inc., in 1984, a start-up software company without a product line, with most of the capital going toward advertising. When the company vaporized in early 1985, so did Mr. McGill.

The experienced venture capitalist Fred R. Adler said it first and best: "I am not in the venture capital business to act as an intermediary between the pension funds who back me and Madison Avenue." You will see in the following descriptions of the eight DEJ factors that the reliance on advertising is proof positive of the absence of one of them.

DEJ 1. Existence of Qualified Buyers. The persons to whom the product must be sold know that they require the product. Buyers do not have to be *educated*, that is, told they have a problem. Buyers know they have a problem and know they must pay for a solution. Buyers are able to pay for a solution. A minimal amount of buyer education is required.

DEJ 2. Existence of Competent Sellers. The entrepreneurs, and the people they hire to join them, are competent at providing the solution to the problem. They are competent at marketing. The root word of *competent, competere*, is the same as the root word of *competitive*. To be competent in marketing is to be competitive.

DEJ 3. Homogeneity of Buyers. The problem that the entrepreneurial company solves is essentially the same for all buyers, with minor differences in degree or severity. The solution does not have to be tailor-made or customized for each buyer. Selling off the racks is cheaper and provides more rapid cash flow than selling custom-made.

DEJ 4. Large Number of Buyers. The number of potential buyers sharing essentially the same problem is very large. One test is to multiply the number of potential buyers (sometimes referred to as the universe of selling sites) times the price they would pay for the solution. If the number exceeds $1 billion, the business plan should be undertaken.

DEJ 5. Lack of Institutionalized Barriers to Entry. The buyers are not organized. They do not belong to an association. There is no regulatory body to which they are responsible for their activities, such as the American Medical Association or Federal Aviation Administration. Scaling institutional barriers to entry can be as difficult as seeking Federal Drug Administration approval of a new drug—several years and over $5 million in costs—or as simple as obtaining a state license to sell a product or service, as in the case of HMOs.

DEJ 6. "Hey, It Really Works!" The solution is passed along from buyer to buyer by word-of-mouth advertising. Not only is word of mouth the cheapest form of advertising, it is also the most effective. A solution that is passed along from buyer to buyer has far greater credibility than one that must be advertised in order to attract buyers.

DEJ 7. Optimum Cost/Price Relationship. The price of the solution is approximately equal to the cost of the problem. The price of a solution cannot be questioned as being excessively high or unwarranted if the buyers are paying the same price for their problem that they are asked to pay to have it solved. If the same $100 that brings the buyer problems now brings solutions, he or she is $100 ahead. As they say in *The Godfather*, the entrepreneur must make buyers an offer they cannot refuse.

DEJ 8. Invisibility of the New Company. The new company operates quietly and without fanfare. It does not advertise or promote heavily. It does not gain attention so that it could be copied by competitors. When a company goes public very early it risks allowing potential competitors to gain information about its business plan and financial statements. Exposing a business plan to a large number of venture capitalists can also sacrifice one's invisibility.

Possession of all eight DEJ factors ensures the entrepreneur of a major success without having to raise start-up venture capital, unless, of course, the entrepreneur fails to carry through the launch in a competent manner. The launch includes building a skilled management team, designing an intelligent business plan, and remaining market driven and innovative. There have been instances in which entrepreneurial teams have screwed up perfect DEJ companies, but they are too few to count.

HMOs: AN INDUSTRY OF NEARLY PERFECT DEJs

Health maintenance organizations, or HMOs, possess seven out of eight DEJ factors. The missing DEJ factor is the institutional barrier to entry, the scaling of which requires venture capital. Now let's look at HMOs in terms of their DEJ factors.

Existence of Qualified Buyers (DEJ 1). Large employers, small employers, and individuals alike are aware of the problem of dramatically increasing health care costs. The second most expensive component of a Detroit-made car is the health insurance of the employees who assemble it. Rising health care costs and health insurance costs were capped in 1983 by the federal government's DRG (diagnostic related group) law, and this made physicians and hospitals look with favor at HMOs.

Existence of Competent Sellers (DEJ 2). HMOs hire independent insurance agents to sell their prepaid insurance plans. There is very little training involved and a modest learning curve to climb. These salespeople are commission merchants who generally find the logic of HMOs to be very persuasive.

Large Number of Buyers (DEJ 3). The universe of selling sites includes every man, woman, and child in the United States, with the exception of a small group of the very elderly and the very ill. The buyers are approached through their employer in most cases, thus reducing the cost of making sales.

Homogeneous Buyers (DEJ 4). Prepaid health insurance is a standardized product. It does not have to be tailor-made for each customer. One size fits all.

No Institutional Barriers to Entry (DEJ 5). There is an institutional barrier to entry: Federal and state licensing are required and, in most states, a bond must be posted. This could require an expenditure of $500,000 to $1 million per state, which generally must be raised by selling equity interests in HMOs to investors. After obtaining a license to operate an HMO, the door slams on potential competitors who seek to serve a particular region.

"Hey, It Really Works!" (DEJ 6). Word-of-mouth advertising is the least expensive way to get the word spread around. One corporation that lowers its health insurance costs quickly tells another, and it tells another, until demand spreads in a multiplier fashion.

Optimum Cost/Price Relationship (DEJ 7). The cost of an HMO health insurance plan is generally lower than indemnity plans, because there is a zero deductibility in an HMO plan. For the typical employee of a large corporation when a medical emergency occurs, a deductible of $500 to $1000 that requires an out-of-pocket payment can be a financial hardship.

Invisibility of the Company (DEJ 8). The HMO does not have to go public in a financial or euphemistic sense and thus reveal its profit margins and operating ratios to a curious public. In this manner, it is able to operate quietly and efficiently. Potential competitors are none the wiser.

EDS: A PERFECT DEJ

An example of perfect DEJ is Electronic Data Systems Corporation, or EDS, as it is known. H. Ross Perot launched EDS in 1963 with $24,000 to solve data-processing problems of large corporations. EDS did so via facilities management contracts: It agreed to operate the data-processing facilities of large corporations at their budgets by assuming all of their costs and obligations—equipment and payroll—and agreeing to deliver processed data. The customers at the time were paying $1 million per annum and not receiving satisfaction. EDS convinced them to pay it the same $1 million per annum and it would satisfy. As EDS added more and more customers, it did not need all of their equipment and all of their staffs, so it let them go, to the benefit of its cash flow. Approximately 20 years after it was launched, EDS was acquired by General Motors Corporation for $2.5 billion. The perfect DEJ of EDS is described as follows.

Existence of Qualified Buyers (DEJ 1). Corporate data-processing inefficiency was a very real problem. Buyers did not have to be *educated*, that is, told they had a problem. Buyers knew they had a problem and knew they had to pay for a solution. Buyers were able to pay for a solution. A minimal amount of buyer education was required.

Existence of Competent Sellers (DEJ 2). Ross Perot, the Electronic Data Systems entrepreneur, hired managers who were skilled in providing solutions to the problems of the EDS customers. Mr. Perot was a skilled former IBM salesman, and he hired personnel in his image. He was competitive, and so were his employees.

Homogeneity of Buyers (DEJ 3). The problem that EDS solved was essentially the same for all buyers, with minor differences in degree or severity. The solution did not have to be tailor-made or customized for each buyer.

Large Number of Buyers (DEJ 4). The number of potential buyers sharing essentially the same problem was in excess of 3000 corporations and institutions. Assuming each one had an annual data-processing budget of $1 million total potential, the market size of EDS's solution was $3 billion per annum, and no other competitor was within two years of sharing a piece of the pie. (More than any other single factor, this explains why EDS's initial public offering was at a common stock price in excess of the then-unheard-of 115 times earnings.) Facilities management, five years after EDS began operations, became the fastest growing segment of the data-processing industry.

Lack of Institutionalized Barriers to Selling (DEJ 5). The buyers were not organized. They belonged to no association. There was no regulatory body to which they were responsible for their activities, such as the American Medical Association or Federal Aviation Administration. Their buyers were new to their problem. Their purpose in seeking a solution was to save money, and there was no requirement for them to seek permission or clarification from an outside or collective institution.

"Hey, It Really Works!" (DEJ 6). EDS's solution was passed along from buyer to buyer by word-of-mouth advertising.

Optimum Cost/Price Relationship (DEJ 7). The price of the solution was equal to the cost of the problem, that is, the buyer's data-processing budget.

Invisibility of the New Company (DEJ 8). EDS operated quietly and without fanfare. It did not advertise or promote heavily. It did not gain attention so that it could be copied by competitors. In 1973, 10 years after the formation of EDS, the first company larger than EDS (General Electric) entered the facilities management business. By that time Mr. Perot had banked hundreds of millions of dollars in capital gains.

SOME PERFECT DEJs AWAITING DISCOVERY

From time to time entrepreneurs will discover perfect DEJs. HMOs represent a nearly perfect one. Facilities management of data-processing departments of large corporations, or data-processing departments of divisions within large corporations, was a perfect DEJ of the 1960s and 1970s. There are dozens of perfect DEJs in the universe of GEOs, just awaiting exploitation by entrepreneurs. Some that come to mind are the following:

1. Facilities management of prisons
2. Facilities management of toxic and urban waste
3. Marketing of chemical abuse mitigation programs utilizing the Weight Watchers International plan
4. Direct-mail marketing of devices that effectively treat male sexual impotency
5. Party-plan-type marketing of educational software using schoolteachers as the sales force
6. Leveraged buyout of colleges and implementation of hospital management practices in order to reduce the high cost of tuition
7. A high-technology means to reduce recidivism and overcrowding in prisons: braceleting good-behavior and nonviolent criminals with a semiconductor-based signal transmitter and installing receivers in police stations and parole officers' homes, to alert them if the parolee has not gone to work or returned home.

This list of major and minor problems that are solvable through the entrepreneurial process and without significant amounts of venture capital is very long. We must learn to think in terms of perfect DEJs if our hearts drive us to solve these costly kinds of problems. For some of us, the GEOs of major social problems may not be too appealing. They may not be to the venture capitalists' liking either. In Chapter 2, let's learn about the preferences of venture capitalists by examining the five generic entrepreneurial opportunities, or GEOs.

2

FIVE CATEGORIES OF GENERIC ENTREPRENEURIAL OPPORTUNITIES

All entrepreneurial opportunities fall into one of the following five generic entrepreneurial opportunities (GEOs):

1. Big problem
2. Second-stage problem
3. Small problem
4. Elegant solution
5. Leveraged buyout

You might ask where we would put the small businessperson whose goal is to open and manage a neighborhood store. This person is not an entrepreneur, at least within my definition of the word. A small businessperson seeks to become his or her own boss, which is a similar motivation to one of the entrepreneurial drives. However, the small businessperson typically selects a form of retail business or personal service activity with fairly convenient working conditions. The small business person *goes into business for himself;* entrepreneurs *go into business for others.* The small businessperson frequently selects a franchise to represent locally or a neighborhood mall or strip center in which to locate a store or office. The other critical steps in the entrepreneurial process are not required by the small businessperson. Thus, he or she does not locate a problem in need of a solution, formulate it in terms of how best and where to penetrate it, develop a solution that mitigates or solves the problem, and build an entrepreneurial team, including the selection of a corporate achiever as a manager–partner to assist in launching and managing the business. Small businesspersons in most instances do not aspire to become wealthy, and in fact, very few do so.

THE LAWS OF VENTURE CAPITAL

The five GEOs are best understood when set against the backdrop of the laws of venture capital. This is helpful because it explains to the entrepreneur the goals and objectives of the venture capitalist. The four laws or guideposts of venture capital, then, are the following:

1. $V = P \times S \times E$, where V = valuation or wealth, and it is achieved through creating high values for P, S, and E, where P = the size of the problem, S = the elegance of the solution, and E = the quality of the entrepreneurial team.
2. Invest in big-P companies, because the public market will accord to them an unreasonably high V, irrespective of S and E.
3. Accept no more than two risks per investment.
4. Calculate ownership required using the hockey stick method.

Now let us look more closely at each law.

V = P × S × E. The second law of venture capital, $V = P \times S \times E$, where P = problem, S = solution, E = entrepreneurial team, and V = solution, defines the components of high valuation. The law says that the selection of companies with high quantitative values for the components P, S, and E will result in high valuations, or wealth. The most important of the three components is P, because if there is no problem, then a good solution conveyed by an outstanding entrepreneurial team will not generate revenues. Over the last three years, start-up genetic engineering companies have carried extraordinarily high valuations because of the enormity of the problems they were addressing. However, the values are exponentially greater if the scientific team includes a Nobel laureate. One Harvard medical school instructor turned investment banker structured a new interferon deal—using recombinant DNA techniques, of course, plus a member of the Nobel nominating committee for her entrepreneur-scientist—at an initial, postfinancing valuation of $100 million. Thus, the greater the problem and the team assembled to solve it, the higher the start-up valuation.

The Law of the Big *P*. The third law of venture capital is the law of the Big P. The law is as follows:

> *In big-P companies, the valuation is equal to the size of the problem, rather than its solution.*

One is able to achieve financial success with big-P companies before one achieves commercial success.

The Law of Risk Aversion. There are typically five risks in a start-up or early-stage company. It is up to the venture capitalist to accept no more than two of these risks, and the two that the venture capitalist can control most effectively are the third and fourth: marketing and management. The five risks are as follows:

1. *The Development Risk.* Can we develop the product?
2. *The Manufacturing Risk.* If we can develop it, can we produce it?
3. *The Marketing Risk.* If we can make it, can we sell it?
4. *The Management Risk.* If we can sell, can we sell it at a profit?
5. *The Growth Risk.* If we can manage the company, can we grow it?

The acceptable risks are marketing and management, because they are the most controllable. The development and production risks should be borne by the entrepreneur prior to the seeking of venture capital. The growth risk is typically borne by public investors after the venture capitalist has liquidified his or her investment. To remain an investor in a company after one has nursed it through its start-up, first stage, second stage, and initial public offering is to assume the noncontrollable risk of the company's stock price declining and having to give back much of the hard-earned profit.

The Law of the Hockey Stick. To determine the amount of ownership that the venture capitalist requires in order to make a given investment, which is another way of measuring valuation, many venture capitalists rely on the hockey stick method. It derives its name from the observation that all financial statements look like hockey sticks. The present undercapitalized company is at the toe and the rosy future is up at the handle.

In an article that I wrote for *Venture* magazine in August 1981, a descriptive drawing was created that amplifies the hockey stick method of pricing early-stage investment opportunities. In this diagram, the need for venture capital is $1.5 million and third-year projected net profits after taxes are $2 million. The formula is:

$$\frac{\text{amount of venture capital} \times 5}{\text{third-year net profit after taxes} \times 10 \text{ or } 12} = \begin{array}{c}\text{percentage ownership required}\\\text{by the venture capitalist to}\\\text{meet a convention ROI goal}\end{array}$$

The illustrative diagram from *Venture* is reprinted in Figure 2.1.

Now that we have covered the four laws of venture capital investing, the philosophy and objectives of venture capital investing are better understood. All venture capitalists do not practice all four laws all of the time. After all, venture capital investing is not a religious or ritualistic affair, although some venture capitalists seem to have a holier-than-thou aura from time to time. The law most frequently disobeyed is the law of the big P. Only the most confident and financially secure venture capitalists attack big problems. The other three laws are practiced in one form or another by most venture capitalists, although they

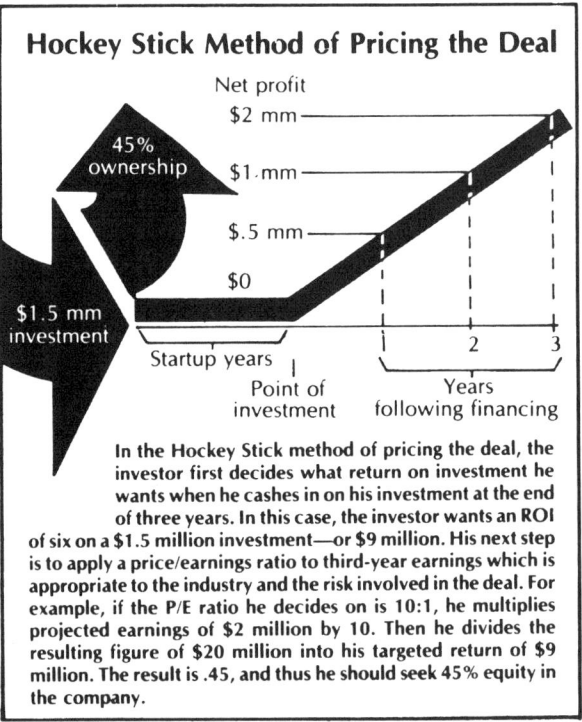

FIGURE 2.1. Hockey stick method of pricing the deal. Compound Growth Rates. (Reprinted from the August, 1981 issue of *VENTURE, The Magazine for Entrepreneurs,* by special permission. © 1981 Venture Magazine, Inc., 521 Fifth Avenue, New York, N.Y. 10175)

will describe their methods in their own terms and rarely if ever admit that they subscribe to mine, or those of another of their tribe. That is to be expected. I was one of Milton Friedman's lucky students when he said: "You can always pick out a professional from a pack of people. He is the one who when he must compliment another member of his profession, such as a fellow economist, will usually heap effusive praise on all of his skills and hobbies, except the very one that he practices professionally." So it goes in the venture capital profession. Friendly competition prevents our heaping praise on another of our persuasion.

Thus it is with temerity that I suggest that entrepreneurial opportunities can be neatly pigeonholed into five categories.

BIG PROBLEMS

Entrepreneurs who create companies to solve the world's largest problems frequently have global-sized egos. It takes quite a bit of chutzpah to believe one can make a positive contribution in the race to cure serious diseases, mitigate hunger, eliminate terrorism, reduce inner-city crime, increase literacy, and ease emotional distress. Yet big problems are tempting to an increasing number of entrepreneurs. Disease and hunger are being attacked with the tools of genetic engineering, as the stories of the founders of Genentech Corporation and Cetus Corporation reveal.

Genentech Corporation

Robert A. Swanson and Herbert W. Boyer have formed the most potent entrepreneurial team in biotechnology acceptable to investors, the scientific community and the large pharmaceutical companies. When the mission is to conquer life-threatening diseases, the ingredients are capital, great scientists, and outstanding marketing companies, such as Eli Lilly & Company. Genentech has won the hearts, minds, and pocketbooks of all three. It has raised over $125 million—much more aggregate capital than its aggregate revenues since 1976 of $98 million—and licensed Eli Lilly & Company, Hewlett-Packard Company, Boehringer Mannheim Corporation, Miles Laboratories (subsidiary of Bayer A.G.), and others to market its products or codevelop new ones. How did Swanson, who left Kleiner & Perkins at 28, and Boyer, a scientist, pull off this miracle, where so many others have failed?

Boyer had agreed to leave academia, a difficult step for a distinguished scientist to take. Swanson had telephoned him out of the blue, but Swanson had a record of impetuousness. When he completed his undergraduate work at Massachusetts Institute of Technology (MIT) in chemical engineering in three years rather than four, Swanson had convinced the Sloan School of Management to let him begin graduate school early. Later Citicorp Venture Capital hired him and, although he was just 25, sent him to San Francisco to open an office for them. A year later, Kleiner & Perkins hired him. Swanson was an entrepreneur, however, not a venture capitalist, so his next step was to find a problem that he could be happy solving.

After learning about Cetus Corporation, a 1971 biotechnology startup, Swanson focused his investigations at the local library on the infant science of bioengineering. He compiled lists of authors and started telephoning the scientists one by one for their opinions on commercializing gene splicing. Each call would give Swanson more and more data, but none of the scientists believed that recombinant DNA could be bottled and sold as a remedy. Then he called Boyer to find out whether this technology could be commercialized. Boyer replied that it could.

The two repaired to a local saloon and several beers later agreed to invest $1000 in exploiting recombinant DNA technology through a new company called Genentech: genetic engineering technology. Their strategy violated several implicit rules of high-tech entrepreneurship, as promulgated in Silicon Valley during the 1970s. Instead of raising millions of dollars through an offering to plow into huge expenditures for plant and equipment, and instead of going on a hiring binge, Swanson and Boyer acted on Tom Perkins's advice and contracted out their early research to university labs. Rather than attempting to bring a product to market immediately (which was, after all, the goal), they opted simply to demonstrate that the technology would actually work—that through genetic engineering a microorganism could be made to produce a substance that it ordinarily does not make. In the original experiments by Boyer and Cohen, an artificially created gene had simply been replicated or cloned. Now they were trying not only to create and clone a gene in a laboratory, but also to place it inside a bacterium and cause the bacterium in turn to manufacture a useful protein. This had never before been accomplished. This certification of the technology, the principals believed, would generate the excitement and money necessary to finance a continuing operation.

For their experiments, Boyer selected somatostatin, a hormone found in the brain. It has no market to speak of, but Boyer felt certain it could be synthesized. Its structure is simple, consisting of four amino acids. They would synthesize the DNA fragments at City of Hope National Medical Center, recombine the DNA, insert it in a bacterium (in this case *E. coli*, a fast-reproducing bacterium found in the human intestine), and then assay the "molecular soup" back at City of Hope to detect somatostatin.

The first test, which took seven months, was unsuccessful. Swanson was worried. Then one of the scientists thought of protecting somatostatin from some proteins in *E. coli* that might be attacking it. Says Robert Crea, a chemist at City of Hope, "We found that by playing this genetic trick of protection, there was really that thing in the soup."* Swanson and Boyer had the beginnings of a new pharmaceutical company: Recombinant DNA was a replicatable technology.

Swanson and Boyer then decided on a first product: synthetic human insulin. For this they needed to raise capital and recruit scientists. Swanson went after the best molecular biologists, protein chemists, and fermentation experts he could find. It was like compressing at least 10 years of new product development at a major pharmaceutical company, because Genentech was only two people.

Manufacturing synthetic insulin was integral to Swanson's business strategy. Immediately after the somatostatin synthesis, Swanson informed Eli Lilly & Company, the $3 billion pharmaceutical giant, of their insulin plan. Eli Lilly had begun marketing insulin in 1923; by 1979 it held 85 percent of the American insulin market. Swanson had no intention of competing with Eli Lilly & Company; it would have been futile, perhaps suicidal, to challenge its advanced sales and marketing staff.

But Swanson knew that the mere existence of synthetic human insulin would seem a threat to the giant. Swanson wanted to license Lilly to market insulin to raise capital.

In early summer of 1978, the final breakthrough occurred—the recombination and the expression of the insulin gene. Genentech was at last a company. It had the credibility to attract major financing, and to find scientists to join it. Like Luke Skywalker hiring Han Solo to join

---

*Randall Rothenberg, "Robert A. Swanson, Chief Genetic Officer," *Esquire*, December 1984, p. 372.

in attacking the *Empire*, Swanson and Boyer have found their own Force—interferon—to attack the big *P*'s of cancer, diabetes, and other serious diseases.

Cetus Corporation

Ronald E. Cape has raised more capital from corporate venturers, the public stock market, and tax shelter–oriented investors by selling the "problem" than any other entrepreneur in recent memory. The problems are cancer and hunger. The solutions, to hear Cape and other genetic engineering entrepreneurs talk, lie with recombinant DNA; with the ability to transfer DNA from one form of life to another, making it possible to produce in great quantities substances whose natural availability is very limited.

Human insulin produced through genetic engineering is already on the market; the Food and Drug Administration is expected to approve a genetically engineered growth hormone within the next two years. In the works are vaccines against hepatitis and herpes. The market is looking for, hoping for, effective substances for treating cancer and heart disease, and for genetically engineered seeds that will permit food to grow in desert lands.

To solve these multibillion-dollar problems requires millions of dollars of capital to pay for scientific research. Those dollars are attracted by painting a picture of a disease-free world, as Cape recently described to a visitor:

> This is our interferon pilot unit. In this one vessel we can make ten thousand patient-doses of interferon overnight. We take a human gene, stick it into a bacterium and say: "Do it!" And the project is real human interferon, not a close animal relative to it. Interferon is a hot prospect for the treatment of cancer, and possibly for other "autoimmune" diseases—diseases in which your body's own chemicals are destroying you: muscular dystrophy, maybe multiple sclerosis, probably rheumatoid arthritis . . . Tay-Sachs disease and sickle-cell anemia. . . . Almost everything that kills people except heart attacks and car accidents potentially can be attacked by these methods.*

That is hard selling, but quite effective. The speaker, Ron Cape, was born in Canada and earned a B.A. degree summa cum laude in chemistry from Princeton University in 1953 and an M.B.A. degree from Harvard University with distinction in 1955. After working for Merck & Company (1955–1956), Professional Pharmaceutical Corporation, and his family's Montreal cosmetics business, Cape saw a research study about DNA and enrolled in McGill University, which awarded him a Ph.D. in biochemistry in 1967. Cape then moved to the University of California at Berkeley

---

*Gerald K. O'Neill, *The Technology Edge: Opportunities for America in World Competition* (New York: Simon & Schuster, 1983), p. 120.

to further his studies in molecular biology, whereupon he met Dr. Peter Farley and they launched Cetus Corporation. Its purpose then as now is "the innovative use of microorganisms in the profitable production of materials to fill human needs."

Although Cetus has thus far not delivered solutions, Cape has been a terrific raiser of capital. Look at the statistics:

Year	Approximate Amount Raised ($ in millions)	Investor	Post-Financing Valuation ($ in millions)
1973	$ 2	Venture capitalists	$ 10
1974	3	Venture capitalists	37.5
1977	5	Standard Oil Indiana	17.8
1978	14	Chevron	70
1979	14	National Distillers	70
1981	115	Public Market	500
1983	75	R & D Ltd. Partnership	—
	$228		

To have raised $228 million on the strength of pulling together a team of brilliant scientists to address a variety of genetic engineering solutions is a monumental achievement. Because it is the best-financed biotechnology company, the market expects a great deal from Cetus Corporation.

When entrepreneurs attack big problems, those affecting millions of people, they are certainly heroes. The word *hero* defines someone who is great; someone who has achieved an authentic instance of greatness. A hero is someone who has intentionally taken a large step, one far beyond the capacities of most humans, in solving a problem that affects a large number of people. A hero brings about something that is unlikely to happen by the mere force of events, by the trends or tendencies of the time, that is, something that is unlikely to occur without his or her intervention.

The peculiar quality of greatness stems from a delight in being alive at "the right time" and in control of events at a critical moment in history. The new American heroes thrive on change and the instability of things, on the infinite possibilities the future offers for spontaneous moment-to-moment improvisation and large, imaginative, bold strokes that they can make to cause important events to occur that will change the course of history. Strength comes to our heroes from a clear, brightly colored vision of and passionate faith in their view of the future, in their power to mold it. They know where they are going and by what means and why.

Big-problem, or big-P, entrepreneurs generate wealth for themselves and their investors of heroic proportions as well. Exhibit 2.1 lists the market values from 1982 through mid-1985 of the 10 most widely held biotechnology companies. Although their aggregate annual revenues during this period were less than $450 million (including interest in-

Exhibit 2.1 Market Values and Revenues of the 10 Largest Biotechnology Companies from 1982 to mid-1985 ($ in thousands)

Company Name	(Fiscal Year End)	Revenues			Average Market Values[a] from 1982 to mid-1985
		1982	1983	1984	
AmGen Corp.	(3/31)	2,715	1,511	6,115	77,825
Cetus Corp.	(6/30)	32,889	28,853	46,221	267,416
Chiron Corp.	(4/30)	1,718	3,754	7,392	46,133
Damon Biotech Inc.	(8/31)	1,692	3,038	5,045	172,619
Genentech Inc.	(12/31)	32,603	47,003	69,786	275,086
Genetic Systems	(12/31)	2,234	3,915	5,416	137,213
Genex Corp.	(12/31)	6,115	11,091	34,819	161,647
Immunex Corp.	(12/31)	1,095	1,713	3,471	42,894
Mentor Corp.	(3/31)	6,096	8,946	27,737	55,746
Monoclonal Antibodies	(3/31)	260	1,615	5,041	30,454

[a]Based on quarterly high/low stock price averages and average common stock shares outstanding.

come on idle funds), their aggregate market values for the same period were approximately $1.3 billion.

Wealth creation is not the objective of big-P entrepreneurs. Surely they prefer BMWs over less comfortable cars and they prefer not having to worry about money. But the motivation for big-P entrepreneurs, as it is for others, is to solve a problem very well. The entrepreneurial drive is to realize a dream. The chase is more important than the capture.

In *Wealth and Poverty*, George Gilder writes:

> Capitalists are motivated not chiefly by the desire to consume wealth or indulge their appetites, but by the freedom and power to consummate their entrepreneurial ideas. . . . whether piling up coconuts or designing new computers, they are movers and shakers, doers and givers, obsessed with positive visions of change and opportunity. They are men with an urge to understand and act, to master something and transform it, to work out a puzzle and profit from it, to figure out a part of nature and society and turn it to the common good. They are inventors and explorers, boosters and problem solvers; they take infinite pains and they strike fast.*

The big-P entrepreneur strives for the "Good Society," as espoused in 1943 by Walter Lippmann. He writes:

> Until the division of labor had begun to make men dependent on the free collaboration of other men, the worldly policy was to be predatory. The

---

*George Gilder, *Wealth and Poverty* (New York: Basic, 1981), p. 30.

claims of the spirit were otherworldly. So it was not until the industrial revolution had altered the traditional mode of life that the vista was opened at the end of which men could see the possibility of the Good Society on this earth. At long last the ancient schism between the world and the spirit, between self-interest and disinterestedness, was potentially closed.*

In the ruins of the great depression and in the midst of a great war, Lippman identified the problem-solving nature of entrepreneurship and the fundamental role that it plays in capitalism. About the capitalist system, he wrote: "For the first time in human history [it gave people] a way of producing wealth in which the good fortune of others multiplied their own."**

The stock-buying public has an incurable love affair with companies that have targeted major social and medical problems as their raison d'être. More than ever, and particularly among younger investors, the public puts its money on common stocks issued by companies that are addressing serious social and medical problems. Some analysts have inaccurately called these "yuppie" stocks, on the theory that yuppies express their social concerns with their billfolds. There may be something to this hypothesis, but it remains to be seriously investigated. I have expressed it elsewhere as the law of the big P:†

> In big-P companies, the valuation is equal to the size of the problem, rather than its solution.

This law helps to explain certain prices of publicly held stocks, unjustified by earnings. It also explains, perhaps, why our stock market is vibrant while stocks languish in other countries that lack the optimism of the U.S. stock-buying public.

Just as Americans love movies that have important "chase" scenes—*Star Wars*, *The Empire Strikes Back*, and *Chariots of Fire*—so too do they love new publicly held companies who claim to be chasing disease, hunger, and illness with weapons such as interferon, monoclonal antibodies, and breakthroughs in medical technology. Cetus Corporation fights the big P of hunger by genetically engineering seeds that will affix to the sandy soil of the Sudan. It has a market value in excess of $300 million, with the prospect for earnings many years off into the future. Genentech, armed with gene-splicing and recombinant DNA skills, chases diabetes, cancer, hoof-and-mouth disease, and dwarfism. Its market value once reached $800 million, and significant earnings are very much into the future. Cetus, Genentech, and other biotechnology companies are chasing big Ps with elegant S's and experienced managers. They are able to go to the public market and to R&D limited partnerships for bales of capital, because the typical investor loves a good chase.

---

*Walter Lippman, *The Good Society* (Boston: Little, Brown & Company, 1943), p. 36.
**Ibid.
†David Silver, *Venture Capital: The Complete Guide for Investors* (New York: Wiley, 1984), p. 113.

Thus, an entrepreneur can usually become wealthier more quickly in a big-P company than in a lower-P company. It is possible to achieve financial success in big-P companies before they are commercially successful. All the more reason for venture capitalists to invest in big-P companies. Yet very few actually do so. In Exhibit 2.2 appear the names of the venture capital funds that have invested in two or more big-P companies.

An understanding of *giving* as the basis of the validity and vitality of capitalism is required in order for a capitalist to invest in big-P companies. The venture capital funds that do so are highly evolved, mature, and comfortable with their role in society. It is more satisfying to launch a new company to solve the problems of serious disease and hunger than it is to raid a tired old rust-belt corporation and hold it up for "greenmail." Furthermore, there is more money to be made in solving big problems than in greenmail, as is clearly shown in Exhibit 2.3, in which the largest greenmail winners are compared with the largest big-P start-ups.

With the continued evolution of the entrepreneur and the growth and development of the network of agents and agencies that assist and service the entrepreneur, our society can look forward to the emergence of dozens of new industries in the latter half of the 1980s that address

Exhibit 2.2 Venture Capital Funds That Have Invested in Big-*P* Companies

ABS Ventures	Interwest Partners
Adler & Co.	The Lambda Funds
Advanced Technology Ventures	MarketCorp Venture Associations, L.P.
Allstate Insurance Co.	Matrix Partners, L.P.
Cable, Howse & Cozadd, Inc.	Nazem & Co.
Cambridge Venture Partners	New Enterprise Associates
Citicorp Venture Capital, Ltd.	Norwest Venture Capital Mgmt. Inc.
Clarion Capital Corp.	Oak Investment Partners
Columbine Venture Fund, Ltd.	Pathfinder Venture Capital Fund
Continental Capital Ventures	Pioneer Ventures Co.
Continental Illinois Venture Corp.	Plant Resources Venture Fund
The Early Stages Co.	Regional Financial Enterprises
Fairfield Venture Partners	Robertson, Coleman & Stephens
Frontenac Venture Co.	Santa Fe Private Equity Fund
GeoCapital Ventures	Southwest Venture Partners
Golder, Thoma & Cressey	Sprout Group
Greater Washington Investor	Sutter Hill Ventures
Hambrecht & Quist	Technology Venture Investors
Hambro International Venture Fund	Vista Ventures
The Hillman Co.	Whitehead Associates

Exhibit 2.3 Is the Payoff in Solving Big Problems Entrepreneurially Greater Than It Is for Greenmail?

	Payoff Before Tax ($ in thousands)
Largest Greenmail Hits[a]	
Walt Disney Productions/Saul Steinberg	$ 76,417
Occidental Petroleum Corp./David Murdock	57,329
Texaco/Bass Brothers Enterprises	137,665
Warner Communications, Inc./Rupert Murdoch	53,478
Cities Service/Nu-West Group	88,789
Largest Big-P Hits	
Genentech, Inc./Robert Swanson	490,000
Cetus Corp./Ronald E. Cape	330,000
Hospital Corp. of America/Dr. Thomas Frist	4,600,000
Humana Corp.	2,320,000
Community Psychiatric Centers/Robert L. Green	1,025,000

[a]Taxable at short-term capital gains rates.

major social and medical problems. Several of the candidates for entrepreneurial successes in this area include low-cost, nontoxic cancer therapies, an absolutely perfect AIDS detector, and eventually an AIDS cure via genetic engineering, the mitigation of teenage urban crime via creative employment schemes, stress reduction, reduction of chemical abuse, elimination of drunk driving via a microchip-based sensor implanted on automobile dashboards, and reduction of recidivism among prisoners via the marriage of telecommunications to work rehabilitation programs and the facilities management of prisons.

SECOND-STAGE PROBLEMS

The primary area of interest among venture capitalists is that of industrial problems. The rapid rise of the information industry reflects, in large measure, the willingness of capitalists to launch companies that have developed data or word processing, transmitting and manipulating systems for industry. The systems do it better, faster, and cheaper than the previous year's models, do it in foreground or background to permit other functions to be handled or multiple terminals to be linked, do it double fail-safe or triple fail-safe, and do it for specific industries, known as vertical market solutions. To give you a feeling for just how many companies have been formed and taken public in the information industry, Value Line, a leading stock market research firm, follows approximately 3000 information industry companies compared with approximately 300 publicly held health care companies.* The use of computers to generate more information and to present it in cleverer and more useful ways is unquestionably of value to industry, and to the several million individuals who have home computers and modems to dial up data from several hundred data banks. There is an excessive number of companies in the information industry. Rather than getting the whole loaf, these companies are competing with each other for crumbs from IBM's table and the tables of other hardware and software leaders such as Apple Computers, Inc., Microsoft Corporation, Intel Corporation, and Tandem Computers, Inc. The effect on the venture capital industry is very serious. Fewer than five venture capital funds, out of a total of over 400, earned positive returns on investment for their investors in 1984. The seriousness of the problem is such that some venture capital funds will probably fail in 1986. To correct the investment mistakes of overindulging in the information industry, a number of venture capitalists began forming health care–oriented funds in mid-1985. By July 1985, David Glickstein, who manages the venture capital fund investments for New York Life Insurance Company, reported having seen nine new health care venture capital fund proposals.

Understandably, the majority of venture capital funds prefer productivity-improving capital equipment manufacturers. Among the ideas that have recently captured the hearts and minds of numerous venture capital funds are the following:

1. Artificial intelligence software applications for horizontal and vertical markets
2. Computer-assisted engineering software bundled with workstations to speed the design and development stages in new product development
3. Supermicrocomputers that operate with the speed and memory size of minicomputers but are priced like microcomputers
4. Productivity tools for programmers and system developers to accelerate the debugging step in software development
5. Devices that control access to computerized information, including data protection and software security
6. Winchester disk drives for desktop, portable and lap personal computers
7. Streaming tape-drive subsystems that provide backup in the data storage process to prevent loss of data if the floppy disk is destroyed or misplaced

---

*At the Santa Fe Private Equity Funds, we maintain an on-line data base of 634 publicly-held health care delivery companies.

8. Data-capturing systems that input engineering information more rapidly into computer-aided design systems
9. Telecommunications peripheral products that store telephone numbers in memory, redial them automatically, and route incoming calls more efficiently
10. Microwave signal-generating and signal-processing components, principally for the defense and aerospace industries

These entrepreneurial opportunities are identical in the sense that a product or system is designed, developed, and produced, and then it is marketed to industrial and service corporations, who make their decision on a comparative basis. The products are not clearly differentiated from one another, and the sale is frequently made by lowering the price and/or increasing the after-sale support. Venture capitalists, like other kinds of investors, act somewhat like penguins. If one of their leaders invests in a personal computer company, as Don Valentine did in 1976 with Apple Computer, Inc., 30 other venture capitalists follow routinely by launching that many Apple clones. If another leader spots an opportunity in fail-safe computers, as Tom Perkins did in 1977 with Tandem Computers, Inc., 12 other venture capitalists feel compelled to launch double-fail-safe computer manufacturers. This manner of behavior is both expected and disastrous. Following the leader appears at first blush to be risk averse and intelligent. On the other hand, it leads to overcrowding, price-cutting, thinning of margins, and mass bankruptcies. As the information industry continues its course of gastroenteritis, its supply of blood and oxygen from venture capital funds will peter out. The more penguinlike venture capital funds will lose their investors and cease to operate. In 1986, the financial press will cover the "surprise" reversals and setbacks in the venture capital industry. The industry will be compared with other gold-into-dross financial fiascoes such as REITs (real estate investment trusts) and savings and loans. There may be calls for (perish the thought) tighter regulation.

Like other professions composed of private companies, the venture capital industry does not have a scoreboard. We cannot judge which venture capitalists are doing well and which are doing less well, or losing money for their investors. It is somewhat of a club, with barriers to entry in the form of established track records. As a result it is impossible to rank the track records of venture capital funds. Suffice it to say that better track records are owned by the venture capital funds that address big-P companies than by those that address second-stage problems. These are more tempting as a rule, but less rewarding in the long run.

Using data published by the *Venture Capital Journal,* a monthly newsletter that gathers data on the investments of many of the country's venture capital funds, it is possible to list the venture capital funds that have invested largely in companies that manufacture products or provide services that solve industrial problems. Admittedly based on data gathered on a second-source basis, this list follows:

Battery Ventures
Berry Cash Southwest Partnership
Boettcher Venture Capital Partners, L.P.
Colorado Venture Capital Corporation
Ferranti High Technology, Inc.
The Hill Partnership
Hutton Venture Investment Partners, Inc.
Investech, L.P.
Investments Orange Nassau
The Masters Fund
Mayfield Fund
Merrill Pickard Anderson & Eyre
New England Capital Corporation
Palmer Partners
Sevin Rosen Management Company

There have been a number of stunning successes in the productivity-improving capital equipment industry sectors. Apollo Computer Corporation, Tandem Computers Corporation, Daisy Systems, Inc., and Intel Corporation come immediately to mind. But these were leaders, not followers. Their products were and remain clearly differentiated from the pack that has followed them. The venture capital community must back away from its tendency to follow the leader or suffer the consequences of running out of capital and credibility.

SMALL PROBLEMS

The average investment size at Santa Fe Private Equity Fund, where I hang my hat, is $1 million. Our minimum acceptable P level is $1 billion per annum, and if we seek to earn at least $10 million for every $1 million we invest, and if our average ownership percentage is 25 to 30 percent (but after several private and public financing dilutions the ownership would become 10 percent), we need our investments to achieve market valuations of $100 million (10 percent of $1 billion). It is not necessarily the case that companies have a market valuation equal to 100 percent of their revenues, but that is a reasonable approximate. Hence, the revenue test of $100 million and the P test of $1 billion.

In practice, it works this way. A business plan is submitted to the Santa Fe Private Equity Fund, and it is logged in by an assistant. We have a log in which are entered the name of the company, the date of its receipt, a brief description, and its disposition. Exhibit 2.4 shows the Santa Fe Private Equity Fund's log.

Exhibit 2.4 Santa Fe Private Equity Fund's Incoming Deal Log

Date Received: _____

Name of Company: _____

Address: _____
_____

Telephone No: _____

Stage of Development: _____

Capital Invested to Date: _____

Capital Requirement: _____

Description of Business: _____
_____
_____
_____

Entrepreneur, Name: _____

Age, Background: _____

Manager(s), Name(s): _____

Age(s), Background(s): _____

Recommendation:		
	Turndown	___/___/___
	Market Size Audit	___/___/___
	Technical Audit	___/___/___
	Entrepreneur Audit	___/___/___
	Request Meeting	___/___/___

Disposition: _____

Reviewed by: _____

After the deal is logged in, an associate reads the business plan to measure the size of the P. This is done by counting the number of selling sites for the solution and multiplying them times the price people would pay for the solution. For example, assume that an entrepreneur has developed a computer-aided design (CAD) system for the semiconductor industry. A bit of searching (frequently the business plan does not calculate the size of the opportunity that the company is addressing) reveals that there are approximately 900 potential selling sites for the CAD system. The entrepreneur intends to price the system at $250,000 per unit, which makes the overall market size $225 million. We do not believe that any company will capture more than a 10 percent share of its market, or in this instance $22.5 million. As our minimum-size P at the Santa Fe Private Equity Fund is $1 billion, we return the CAD business plan explaining that it does not meet our criteria.

Let's assume that the entrepreneur of the CAD system realizes that venture capitalists prefer markets with more than 900 selling sites and modifies the business plan in order to service not only semiconductor manufacturers but also manufacturers of printed circuit boards, manufacturers of computers, and manufacturers of input–output devices for computers. Further, the entrepreneur modifies the CAD system so that it is sold with a maintenance agreement requiring the payment of $2000 per month for 12 months following the installation. With the addition of 2800 potential selling sites and $24,000 in cash flow per sale, the CAD system entrepreneurial opportunity would meet our minimum P requirement:

$$3700 \times \$274,000 = \$1014 \text{ million}$$
$$\times \ 10 \text{ percent} = \$100 \text{ million}$$

Alas, the majority of entrepreneurs focus their energies on small problems, or niche markets, as they are referred to, and their companies end in disappointment. They choose to address a narrow market with perhaps 900 selling sites rather than multiple markets that add up to 9000 to 90,000 selling sites.

One of the most successful entrepreneurs of the last several years, Sam Walton, opened large discount stores in towns of 10,000 or fewer people. Wal-Mart has grown to over 900 stores and $6 billion in revenues and a V of more than $5 billion in less than 16 years. An Wang, another billionaire entrepreneur, developed a small computer system targeted at the office automation problem, a P with more than 100,000 selling sites. Wang Laboratories' sales exceeded $2 billion in 1984 and its V was more than $5 billion. Other discount store chains—W. T. Grant, E. J. Korvette, Montgomery Ward—opened stores in and around larger cities, and they have been squeezed out by swifter competitors. Other small computer manufacturers did not have a problem in mind for which their computers offered a solution—Columbia Data, Victor, Osborne, Xerox, Franklin—and they got trampled on by IBM and Apple.

Niche market entrepreneurs occasionally surprise everyone and build revenues to $20 million or so, then merge into a larger company. Fortunately, there are a number of venture capital firms that enjoy small, local niche market companies. In the directory that follows, the venture capital funds that say they prefer to invest in companies in their geographic region are the ones to call on for niche markets. Because they are regional funds, it is incumbent upon them to invest in the businesses located near them. Many of these businesses are niche market companies. Venture capital funds that prefer to invest in the states in which they are located are listed in Exhibit 2.5.

Exhibit 2.5 Regional Venture Capital Funds

Name of Fund	Geographical Preference
Private Capital Corp. Birmingham, AL	Southeast
Alpha Partners Menlo Park, CA	San Francisco Bay Area
South Atlantic Capital Corp. Tampa, FL	Southeast
North American Capital Group Lincolnwood, IL	Midwest
White River Capital Corp. Columbus, IN	Midwest
Maine Capital Corp. Portland, ME	Maine only
Aegis Fund Limited Partnership Boston, MA	Within 75 miles of Boston
Granite State Capital, Inc. Concord, NH	New England
Heritage Capital Corp. Charlotte, NC	Southeast
Primus Capital Fund Cleveland, OH	Midwest
Tennessee Venture Capital Corp. Nashville, TN	Within two hours of office
Reedy River Ventures, Inc. Greenville, SC	Southeast
The Woodlands Venture Capital Co. The Woodlands, TX	Southwest
Impact Seven, Inc. Turtle Lake, WI	Wisconsin only
Capital Corp. of Wyoming, Inc. Casper, WY	Wyoming only

ELEGANT SOLUTIONS

In the early stages of the present entrepreneurial revolution, most entrepreneurs were more "inventor" than problem solver. They did not possess the single-mindedness of the entrepreneur, the drive *to do one thing very well.* They believed that they could develop an elegant solution and that the people with the problems would step forth and proclaim, "I will buy that solution for my problem." That is the better-mousetrap notion first espoused by Benjamin Franklin. It is incorrect, and the inventor–entrepreneurs who have swallowed the line have suffered deeply in the pocketbook time and time again.

Venture capitalists are continuously approached by inventor–entrepreneurs, but they are almost always turned down. The penny stock market is very much attracted to better mousetraps, or solutions in search of problems, as they are known. Inventor–entrepreneurs and the penny stock market have a long-standing love affair. Some of my favorite better mousetraps of the last few years are the following:

1. Solar collectors built into shutters, slightly tilted to catch the sun's rays and store electricity.
2. A chain of Bunny Hut fast-food restaurants selling (a) bunny burgers, (b) rabbits' feet, (c) pet rabbits, (d) hutches, and (e) Bunny Hut franchises.
3. Sidewalks converted to steel plates under which are springs that press levers when pedestrians walk on the plates. The levers turn gears converted to turbines that generate electricity to light and heat and provide power to buildings that stand alongside the sidewalks. Another system, where there are more cars and fewer pedestrians, would replace paved roads with steel plates.
4. A device sold to plastic surgeons and other physicians who use it to tattoo eyeliner on ladies who do not like to put on mascara every day. Operating room nurses represent a major market for the product.
5. An improved sawhorse that can be easily assembled and taken apart, with adjustable heights and compartments to store nails and tools.

A number of western European countries are in their early stages of evolution in the current entrepreneurial revolution. As such, their entrepreneurs are more inventor–entrepreneurs than problem solvers. The venture capitalists who fund the European entrepreneurs are in many cases affiliated with more experienced United States funds. Thus, it is not likely that they will place their bets on the inventors, and that this inventor phase will quickly pass. If, however, the inventor–entrepreneurs receive funding in quantity, in all likelihood they will fail en masse and delay the evolution of the entrepreneurial revolution in those countries.

Why do inventor–entrepreneurs fail? Because their product or service has not found a problem that it can solve. The entrepreneur must go through months, perhaps years, of trial and error in order to locate the problem for which he or she has the solution. Time is money. In most cases the inventor–entrepreneur runs out of one or the other. A few get lucky. Chester Carlson, the inventor of xerography, required 12 years to find his first customer, and his patent law activities fed his entrepreneurial need. Edwin H. Land, the founder of Polaroid Corporation, required 14 years to find his first customer, but his manager–partner, Herbert Silver, kept Land's dream alive with capital.

Another way to consider the plight of the inventor of a solution in search of a problem is to examine the DEJ factors in which these kinds of entrepreneurial opportunities are remiss:

1. The problems are not large.
2. The buyers are not qualified.
3. The buyers are not homogeneous.
4. The sellers are not competent.

As was mentioned in Chapter 1, if a company has four DEJ factors or fewer, it is highly likely to fail. But to start a company that is clearly missing the first four DEJ factors is to invite a quick demise. DeLorean Motor Company is a perfect example of an insufficiency of DEJ factors. The Infomart concept—large buildings full of showrooms in which computer manufacturers can rent permanent exhibit space—appears to be another insufficient-DEJ situation. There are numerous tales of woe that could be related in agonizing detail, but suffice it to say that there probably is not an experienced venture capitalist alive still funding solutions to nonproblems.

LEVERAGED BUYOUTS

For the entrepreneur who has not spotted the problem or built an elegant solution, but who wants to run a company, there is the leveraged buyout. A leveraged buyout is the purchase of a company using its assets to secure loans that are used to pay the seller. If the assets are inadequate to attract the full amount of the sales price, the seller must be persuaded to take notes or the buyer must attract equity capital. The more equity capital required, the smaller the percentage of ownership the entrepreneur is able to keep. If the company's asking price is too high or the cost of debt financing too dear, then more equity capital is required to the point of diluting the entrepreneur's interest, and at some point he or she will have to walk away from the deal.

The best candidates for leveraged buyouts are divisional spin-offs from large industrial corporations. These giants periodically go through a housecleaning exercise in which they discard small divisions or subsidiaries that were appendages of larger companies that were acquired or that were themselves acquired many years ago when the corporation's goals and objectives were perceived differently. These small divisions are frequently not attractive to other corporations because of their size, thus making them candidates for entrepreneurial purchase. Private or family-owned companies are less attractive leveraged buyout candidates because the record keeping is usually sloppier, and there is no assurance that the family is truly a willing seller. Sometimes they will put their company on the market merely to establish a value for estate planning purposes. In a divisional spin-off, the board has authorized the president to sell, and he or she is instructed to get the best price with the most cash. Further, the division is usually audited every year, and the key general ledger items are normally maintained on computer.

FIVE CATEGORIES OF GENERIC ENTREPRENEURIAL OPPORTUNITIES

Exhibit 2.6 presents the financial statements of a wholesale distributor of electronic components offered for sale by a large corporation at a price of net worth plus $1 million.

From this financial information, an entrepreneur can raise approximately $4 million in debt, collateralized by the assets of the company, and the balance of $1.8 million to $2 million in the form of venture capital or a combination of venture capital and notes held by the seller. With very little of his or her own money at risk, an entrepreneur could own between one-fourth and one-third of the company described in Exhibit 2.6.

The accounts receivable and inventory of a wholesale distributor are very attractive collateral to a secured lender. The customers that make up the accounts receivable are generally retail organizations or manufacturers who pay their bills within 90 days and who can be located and usually collected from if their bill is unpaid in 90 days. The in-

Exhibit 2.6 Leveraged Buyout Candidate—Electronic Parts Distributor

Balance Sheet
(fiscal year ending 1984)

Assets		Liabilities and Net Worth	
Cash	$ 67,800	Accounts payable	$ 425,000
Accounts receivable	2,203,600	Accrued expenses	504,000
Inventories	2,881,200		
Total current assets	5,152,600	Total liabilities	929,000
Equipment and leasehold improvements—net	582,900	Net worth	4,778,900
Other assets—net	(27,600)		
Total assets	$5,707,900	Total liabilities and net worth	$5,707,900

Operating Statement
(fiscal year ending 1981)

Sales	$15,999,000
Cost of goods sold	10,159,000
Gross profit	5,840,000
Selling general and administrative expenses	4,159,000
Net operating income	1,681,000
Corporate interest charge	263,000
Corporate rent	279,000
Corporate management fee	141,000
Net profit before taxes	$ 998,000

ventory is in a finished goods stage, usually labeled, easily counted, and readily disposed of at an auction or to a competitor if the lender has to liquidate the company to repay his or her loan.

Turning next to the operating statement, we see that the division earns about $1 million per annum, which at today's high interest rates could support comfortably about $3 million of borrowing (i.e., 22 percent × $3 million = $660,000, which can be paid by the company's earnings and have a margin of safety). But how much money does the division make when we deduct corporate charges and the expensive overhead allocation that divisions of large corporations are saddled with? This is the more important number, and it is known as adjusted net income. The adjusted net income of the division, $1,681,000, represents the earnings of the division on a stand-alone basis, free of corporate charges for capital and services. This relatively high level of income could support the entire purchase price of $5.8 million at an interest rate of 22 percent per annum (i.e., $5,800,000 × 0.22 = $1,276,000 in annual interest, which is less than $1,681,000 in adjusted net income).

We are in the comfortable position of having a strong cash flow to support borrowing. Now we return to the balance sheet to see how much we can borrow. The most tangible asset is accounts receivable. If the seller guarantees the collectibility of 100 percent of the accounts receivable, then a secured lender will loan $2.2 million with the receivables as collateral. The maximum loan ratio on finished goods inventory is probably not more than 60 percent, which in this case would generate just under $1.8 million. The two current assets are able to provide an aggregate loan of $4 million. There is probably some collateral value in the shelves, office furniture, and equipment as well as in the customer list, particularly if rented to others. This additional collateral could yield another $200,000 of loan value. Thus, the entrepreneur has found $4.2 million in capital to buy the division, and so far the entrepreneur owns 100 percent of it.

Now the balancing act begins. The entrepreneur will normally shoot for perfect leverage and ask the seller to take a note for the balance of the purchase price, or in this case, $1.6 million. Clearly the division's income will support interest on additional debt of that amount and leave several hundred thousand dollars to spare, but will it support a fast repayment? Large corporations are not inclined to loan money to entrepreneurs to help them buy their divisions and to pile on so much debt that they will get the division back upon foreclosure. In this case, a loan from the corporation could not be repaid inside of five years, assuming no material improvement in the company or material reduction in interest rates. The seller might be willing to take back a $500,000 note for one year secured by an important asset, such as the division's name or catalog mailing list (if the secured lender will release it), and then only if the seller saw a substantial equity investor in the company.

To lure an equity investor into the deal, the entrepreneur will have to persuade the best members of the division's management team to stay—normally by offering raises and stock and additionally by developing a business plan that shows why this division will grow faster and earn more money when managed by the entrepreneur and the division managers. For investing substantially all of the risk money in the deal, the equity investor will certainly seek control, and usually there are intense negotiations with several different venture capital funds to see which one will ask for the smallest equity participation and the easiest stock repurchase or equity bonus plan.

In the meantime, the seller has given the entrepreneur a fixed time to come up with $5.8 million, after which time he or she will take one of the other offers that always seem to be there. The secured lender cannot leave his or her commitment outstanding for more than a short time, as well, because of other demands for funds. Further, the division management who have been called on to do a tap dance for the investors are beginning to realize that they don't need the entrepreneur to pull off the buyout. There are several other forces at work creating delays that the entrepreneur must counterbalance, such as lawyers, accountants, appraisers, committees, and their other time commitments, and the entrepreneur's ability to prioritize events and balance the various players is critical to consummating a leveraged buyout.

The division just described is an attractive company with outstanding cash flow. The purchase price is less than four times cash flow, which is cheap for this level of quality. The entrepreneur and his or her managers would probably be able to own one-third of the company if they fully leveraged the buyout, after which their percentage of ownership could increase through performance or options. A mature entrepreneur with 10 to 15 years of toil remaining in his or her business career might reasonably expect to make a couple of million dollars on this deal. An empire builder might need to own more of the buyout. To own more of a buyout, the entrepreneur has to find a less attractive company to buy. Here the time constraints will not be as severe, the threat of competitive bids will be a smaller factor, and the entrepreneur will end up owning more of the company. There are degrees of unattractiveness ranging from the small, no-growth manufacturing company to the bankrupt situation that needs a workout plan acceptable to creditors and the court. In the first instance the company may never be able to grow sufficiently to retire the debt used to purchase it; in the second instance the factors that led to the bankruptcy may creep back into the picture after the acquisition.

An example of the financial statements of a less attractive company—a typical small urban manufacturer of metal stampings—appears in Exhibit 2.7.

Assume that a family owns this small metal stamping business and that it is seeking $450,000 in cash. The adjusted net income includes net profits before taxes of $114,000, plus the seller's salary of $80,000 and various perquisites aggregating $25,000, for total adjusted net income of $219,000. If the full $450,000 is borrowed at an interest rate of

Exhibit 2.7 Financial Statements of a Typical Small Manufacturer

Balance Sheet
(fiscal year ending 1984)

Assets		Liabilities and Net Worth	
Cash	$ 12,000	Accounts payable	$112,000
Accounts receivable	218,000	Accrued expenses	62,000
Inventory	306,000	Taxes payable, other	24,000
Total current assets	536,000	Total liabilities	198,000
Equipment—net	85,000	Net worth	450,000
Other assets	27,000		
Total assets	$648,000	Total liabilities and net worth	$648,000

Operating Statement
(fiscal year ending 1981)

Sales	$1,200,000
Cost of goods sold	840,000
Gross profit	360,000
S, G&A expenses	256,000
Net profit before taxes	$114,000

22 percent, annual interest charges would be $100,000, or ample coverage, even after adding back the entrepreneur's salary of $60,000 per annum.

Commercial finance companies are eager to assist in financing the transfer of ownership by way of the leveraged buyout method. In this instance they would be prepared to advance 80 percent of the value of the good (less than 90 days old) accounts receivable and 50 percent of the value of finished goods and raw material inventory. In this example those loan ratios would generate about $280,000. Where does the balance of the purchase price, or $270,000, come from?

Frequently in older manufacturing companies, the machinery and equipment, tools, dies, jigs, molds, blueprints, and drawings have been depreciated to extremely low levels. In this example the assets are carried on the books for $85,000, whereas their replacement value is probably 10 times that and their market value perhaps 4 times larger. In the old days, walls were built two feet thick, floors of solid concrete went down three and four feet, the metal stamping and cutting machinery was oiled and cleaned every day, and the replacement value of these assets is frequently 40 to 50 times their book value.

Secured lenders make loans on equipment using neither replacement nor book value. Rather, they rely on something known as liquidation value, or quick-sale value. This is the estimate by a skilled appraiser of how much cash the lender could raise if he had to sell the machinery and equipment at auction within 60 days. In most instances the entrepreneur will be required to pay for the appraisal, but it is advisable to ask the secured lender to recommend several appraisers whom he or she trusts. Prior to paying the appraiser to visit the plant and inspect the equipment, the entrepreneur should submit detailed information on the equipment and have the appraiser estimate the liquidation value. This is known as a desk appraisal, and it is free. If the desk appraisal is too low to proceed, then the deal can be broken off before any expenses are incurred.

Secured lenders are generally willing to loan as much as 75 percent of the liquidation value of machinery and equipment. Thus, in the metal stamping company example, the needed $270,000 would be available if the liquidation value of the machinery and equipment is appraised for at least $360,000. In the event that it is appraised for less, the entrepreneur has at least four alternative ways to raise the difference: (1) Convince the sellers to hold a note for the difference, possibly securing it with second liens on all assets; (2) obtain a 90 percent guarantee on the equipment loan from the Small Business Administration to increase the lender's advance; (3) raise venture capital by offering a portion of the company's common stock to others; and (4) sell the equipment to a limited partnership of wealthy individuals for a price sufficient to close the gap, thus providing them with a tax shelter, and lease the equipment back over 7 to 10 years, with low rental payments in the early years. Usually one of these methods will work if it is doggedly pursued. These negotiations and financial arrangements must be done quickly because sellers can get nervous and back out of a deal, as can lenders.

More time is available to the entrepreneur who purchases a company that has filed for protection under Chapter XI of the bankruptcy act, otherwise known as voluntary bankruptcy. This is so because the bankruptcy court freezes the company's obligations at the time of the bankruptcy filing (these are called the prepetition debts) and allows the company a period of time—usually around six months—to develop a plan to pay the prepetition debts and get back on its feet. If no plan is offered, the company is liquidated for the benefit of creditors. In Chapter X, or involuntary bankruptcy, the six months shrinks to about two, because the creditors have gotten angry at the company and have put it into bankruptcy, feeling that in liquidation they will fare better than in reorganization.

One of the more interesting and exciting entrepreneurial challenges is to purchase a company in Chapter XI utilizing nothing more than verbal communication skills. Frequently in these situations the company is more viable than its owners believe. Many Chapter XIs result from the inheritance of a business by the incompetent children of a dynamic father. The father ran it with instincts, timing, contacts, friends among the suppliers and customers, and other important assets not available to the children. Moreover, in his day the prime rate of interest was not more than 6 percent. He would not have been as successful with prime at 20 percent.

Thus the children or their appointed managers see that sales are higher (inflation), but profits are lower. They are borrowing more than ever; the suppliers are demanding payment in 30 days, whereas Dad could hold them off for 90; and the customers are paying in 60 days, whereas they used to pay in 30. One or two creditors ask to see the company's financial statements, notice that the goods they supply are pledged to the bank, that net worth is shrinking or at least not growing, and they put the company on C.O.D. or credit limits until there is a balance sheet improvement. The children no longer have a friend at the bank. Dad's banker friend has died, and the children now deal with a 22-year-old upstart who must channel all loan requests to central credit or some other committee of credit officers. To the bank, which has to make money, the company's balance sheets look sick also. Not only does central credit turn down the request for more money, but it also asks the children to begin reducing the loan and have it "cleaned up" within six months. The children panic and go downtown to the law firm they have used for contracts, leases, rents, and commercial collections to discuss the problem. In the flicker of a gnat's eyelash, the lawyers file for protection under Chapter XI to buy six months' time. Everyone believes the situation is much worse than it is, completely ignoring the asset values that the father created, but focusing on the tightness of credit. This company becomes a fattened calf for the hungry, wolfish entrepreneur.

Dozens of these companies exist. You can receive numerous submittals by placing an ad that says you are a buyer of companies in Chapter XI in the *Wall Street Journal* or newspapers read by lawyers and bankers. The obvious one to go after has the following characteristics:

1. Numerous suppliers (prepetition creditors) owed relatively small amounts of money (i.e., less than $2500)
2. Relatively few major suppliers owed large sums of money (i.e., over $25,000)
3. A large customer list, made up of corporate purchasers, not governments or individuals
4. Relatively more finished goods and raw material inventory than work in process
5. Substantially fully depreciated property, plant, and equipment with no or minor amounts of loans outstanding against them
6. Preferably a wholesale distributor or a manufacturer of an industrial component sold to several industries such as construction, aerospace, transportation, or restaurants, hotels, and housing
7. Sufficient profits to pay you a salary that compensates you for alternatives foregone, after reducing the family's salaries and prerequisites

A first step is to meet with the worried owners and their advisers and ask every question you can think of about the nature of the company's operations. Do not tip your hand by being pointed in your questioning. For example, do not say: "Do you have many suppliers owed small amounts?" Rather, ask to see the list of prepetition creditors submitted to the court. Or, if the company is on the precipice of Chapter XI, ask to see the complete list of trade debt. Find out who in the company talks to the credit managers of the suppliers. Frequently it is a clerk whose quavering voice has done the company more harm, without the owners' knowledge, than any other single factor. A firmer, more positive voice can relax the creditors for several months, even if payments to them become slower while cash is bundled into larger packages to deal with more pressing problems such as the Internal Revenue Service (IRS), telephone company, and utilities, as well as larger creditors.

It is best to gather all of the material after the initial meeting and take it to your hotel room for a long, careful analysis. Inform the owners that you will make up your mind in the morning. Practically every detail is important in analyzing a potential workout situation, because the difference between a comatose and a salvageable company is marginal. The key is cash flow. "Cash before pride," the workout experts will tell you, as they hack away at bloated personnel rosters, excess inventory, unused equipment. What assets can be liquidated or used creatively as collateral and what expenses can be slashed to generate cash? Assuming there is enough cash to keep the company afloat, given an acceptable payout plan to creditors and lenders, is it worth it? Or asked another way, assuming that you risk personal assets and work an 18-hour day for 12 months to turn around a sick company, is the ownership of that company worth the effort?

Further, are there any variables beyond your control that, if unleashed, would surprise you and jeopardize the turnaround? For example, measure the effect of a 20 percent interest rate increase on the cost of capital during the workout. Is there a better–faster–cheaper competitive product ready to come onto the market? Has some once-considered-harmless litigation been swept under the rug? If there is a union, could it strike midway through the recovery?

Once you have considered as many negative occurrences as you can, and if you believe that sufficient cash can be generated on the company's assets, given a reasonable payout schedule to trade creditors and lenders, then it is time to return to the conference room and make the offer to the beleaguered owners. You must set the tone of this meeting as serious–dramatic. An opening sentence might be, "Gentlemen, you have 60 days to survive at most." Or, "The condition of your company is critical, and I do not know if I or anyone else can save it."

The objective from their point of view is to come out of the trouble with some ownership and their pride—the wrong objective with which to enter negotiations with an entrepreneur. Your objective is to obtain as much ownership as possible for the least amount of personal risk. The most practical offer you can make is an option to obtain voting control of the common stock subject to your increasing the company's working capital or net worth at stated intervals: 30, 90, 180 days, for example. As the benchmarks are met, additional shares are issued to you until you reach 80 percent, or 67 percent, or whatever number you can get through negotiation. It is also important to have the proxy to vote 51 percent of the common stock while effecting the workout, so that you may sell material assets, make stretch-out deals with creditors, and move quickly without requiring a board action.

Let us walk through a workout situation to see how an entrepreneur might use the company's assets plus creditor responsiveness to stretch-outs to obtain majority ownership.

By practically every measure of efficiency, the company portrayed in the financial statements of Exhibit 2.8 is headed for bankruptcy. On the surface, of course, it has a deficit working capital and an inadequate equity base to support its current level of sales. But a more detailed investigation shows average accounts payable of 90 days; accounts receivable of 74 days; and 4.7 inventory turns per annum. The company employs 200 people who receive $145,000 every two weeks, yet there is only $35,000 cash on hand. Every asset is pledged to secure a loan. Who would want this company? Any management decision seemingly would amount to no more than rearranging the deck chairs on the *Titanic*.

An entrepreneur would want this company because in those financial statements there is cash than can be brought to the surface. And the reward for saving this company is control of a $20 million manufacturing company—an event that would take 10 years to accomplish from a standing start.

First of all, there are personnel inefficiencies, but not many. The product has a low labor content, as indicated by the high sales-per-employee ratio of $100,000. Nonetheless, the company can be put through a shake-up with 10 percent fired and others doubling up while the company works itself out. That is a savings of $29,000 per month plus $6000 per month in obligations to the Federal Insurance Contributions Act (FICA).

The bank has underloaned on accounts receivable and inventory, and it should be replaced with a commercial finance company that is more comfortable with asset-based loans. The current assets can support a revolving credit of $5 million, assuming that only 15 percent of the receivables are over 90 days old and that two-thirds of the inventory is in raw materials and finished goods. A commercial finance company would respond favorably to an overall business plan rather than on the strength of the assets alone. This would generate $900,000 in cash after paying off the bank.

Appraisals of the plant and equipment should indicate some improvement in their value as collateral. Let us assume that the chattel and real estate mortgage can be refinanced to yield $500,000 more.

Finally, the accounts payable can yield the necessary working capital to meet the first 30-day test of the option period. At least $1.5 million

Exhibit 2.8 Financial Statements of a Company Candidate for Leveraged Buyout

Balance Sheet
(most recent date)

Assets		Liabilities and Stockholders' Equity	
Current assets:		Current liabilities:	
Cash	$ 35,000	Accounts payable	$ 4,860,000
Accounts receivable	4,080,000	Accrued expenses[a]	665,000
Inventories	4,260,000	Notes payable[b]	3,975,000
Total current assets	8,375,000	Total current liabilities	9,500,000
Equipment—net	1,130,000	Mortgages payable[c]	450,000
Plant, real estate	875,000		
Other assets	115,000	Total liabilities	9,950,000
		Stockholders' equity:	
		Common stock	75,000
		Retained earnings	470,000
		Total stockholders' equity	545,000
Total assets	$10,495,000	Total capitalization	$10,495,000

Operating Statement

	Most Recent 12 Months	Most Recent Month
Sales	$20,000,000	$1,650,000
Cost of goods sold	15,000,000	1,250,000
Gross profit	5,000,000	400,000
Selling expenses	1,585,000	107,000
General and administrative expenses	1,360,000	110,000
Net operating income	2,055,000	183,000
Interest expenses	1,325,000	145,000
Depreciation	240,000	20,000
Net profit before taxes	490,000	18,000
Provision for taxes	245,000	8,000
Net profit after taxes	$ 245,000	$ 10,000

[a] Includes payroll for approximately 200 employees (145,000 every two weeks) and unpaid, overdue withholding taxes of $375,000, plus overdue payments to representatives.
[b] Note payable to local bank secured by accounts receivable and inventories, plus owners' personal signatures.
[c] Note payable to local bank secured by chattel on equipment and mortgage on real estate.

of accounts payable can be shifted to long-term debt and paid out over two years including a 90-day grace period. Remember, the old assistant controller had the suppliers' credit departments in a state of near panic by the time the entrepreneur arrived. The entrepreneur may have to guarantee some or all of these term notes.

The increase in interest expenses of $300,000 per year is offset largely by the personnel reductions. Further, the products that the company sells probably have not had a price rise in a few years—now is an excellent time.

The cash raised should be used to pay overdue withholding taxes and representative commissions, to reward key people who assist in the turnaround, to introduce production efficiencies, and to accomplish other entrepreneurial goals.

Raising money by way of the purchase of an existing company, using its assets to borrow on, and stretching out its debts to gain time and ownership is not a new method. However, it has become increasingly popular and, indeed, systematized by managers of leveraged buyout investment companies. These people are skilled at identifying companies whose stocks trade publicly at prices less than book value and whose assets are substantially written down, hence further deflating their value. They offer the control block a price above market value, which is typically at or near book value but less than appraised or liquidation value, obtain the block, and tender for the balance of the shares. Buyouts of relatively large publicly held companies are occurring with greater frequency as leveraged buyouts become part of the lexicon of entrepreneurs.

On a smaller scale, for example, in buyouts of companies with sales up to $20 million, the first acquisition in many cases is the springboard to building a major company. Teledyne, Gulf + Western, and LTV, three of *Fortune's* top 50 companies, were each begun with a small leveraged buyout. Charles Bluhdorn, the founder of Gulf + Western, after buying a small, troubled auto parts distributor, picked up New Jersey Zinc, E. W. Bliss, a Dominican Republic sugar refiner and approximately one-fifth of that country's real estate, Paramount Pictures, and several other companies. Frequently an entrepreneur will go after a distributor initially because the receivables are from corporations, the inventory is all finished goods, and there is a considerable amount of real estate and plant suitable for refinancing. The automobile and truck parts industries make particularly good waters to fish because the suppliers to these fields will be unusually helpful to an entrepreneur. One shock absorber manufacturer might offer 90-day terms if its line is stocked and a competitor's line is removed.

For entrepreneurs who merely want to have their own business, set their own hours, and pay themselves whatever they feel like paying, there are numerous leveraged buyout candidates under $20 million in sales. Attracting a supply of them to review and select from is not particularly difficult, although it does require time, systematization, and a war chest of $15,000 to $25,000 to permit a six-month effort that involves travel, investigation time, telephone, and postage. The best sources of sellers are merger and acquisition brokers, many of whom are listed in the Yellow Pages of the telephone book. The First National Bank of Maryland publishes a monthly list of companies for sale. The *Wall Street Journal* also lists companies for sale under the business opportunities column in the classified advertising section.

There are several ways to get hurt doing leveraged buyouts. The first is to fall in love with the company. This affliction could lead to overpaying, overborrowing, or overguaranteeing loans in order to sit at the president's desk. The second most common way to get hurt is to have an insufficient audit, which can lead to buying a company that is too sick to turn around. The company's financial statements must be carefully audited as well as its personnel, its contracts, its supplier relationships, its customer relationships, and then, last but not least, its industry and its competition. Just because a company is inexpensive or financeable does not mean it should be bought. The third most common error in doing buyouts is to rely on anyone but yourself to accomplish anything. Hire a sharp accountant to help you understand the financial statements and not a trainee. In analyzing the company, use first-class, top-flight, experienced people, avoid the advice of management insiders, sellers, and sellers' lawyers, and, above all, avoid free advice.

3

THE INVESTMENT CRITERIA OF VENTURE CAPITALISTS

It is critical in the money-raising process that entrepreneurs have a full and complete understanding of the investment criteria of venture capitalists. Although they may prefer different GEOs and different industries, venture capitalists are similar in certain other regards:

1. Venture capitalists are risk averse.
2. Venture capitalists follow the law of $V = P \times S \times E$, in one form or another.
3. Venture capitalists seek an annual compound rate of return of approximately 60 percent.

To understand better the five risks in a start-up or early-stage company, first referred to in Chapter 2, see Figure 3.1.

RISK AVERSION

The Development Risk. It is the function of the venture capitalist to provide capital and management assistance to the start-up company after the product development and manufacturing risks have been eliminated. The development risk is normally assumed by the entrepreneur upon his or her having identified a large problem in need of a solution. The solution is the product or service that the entrepreneur has developed. If venture capitalists could conceive of solutions to large problems they would be entrepreneurs (or their equivalents, i.e., artists, writers, scientists) rather than venture capitalists. There have been venture capitalists who funded on a regular basis companies in their development stage, but they are no longer making investments.

The development risk is typically assumed by one or more of the following providers of capital:

1. Wealthy individuals who hire tax attorneys to structure their investments in a manner that generates a reduction or elimination of their income taxes.

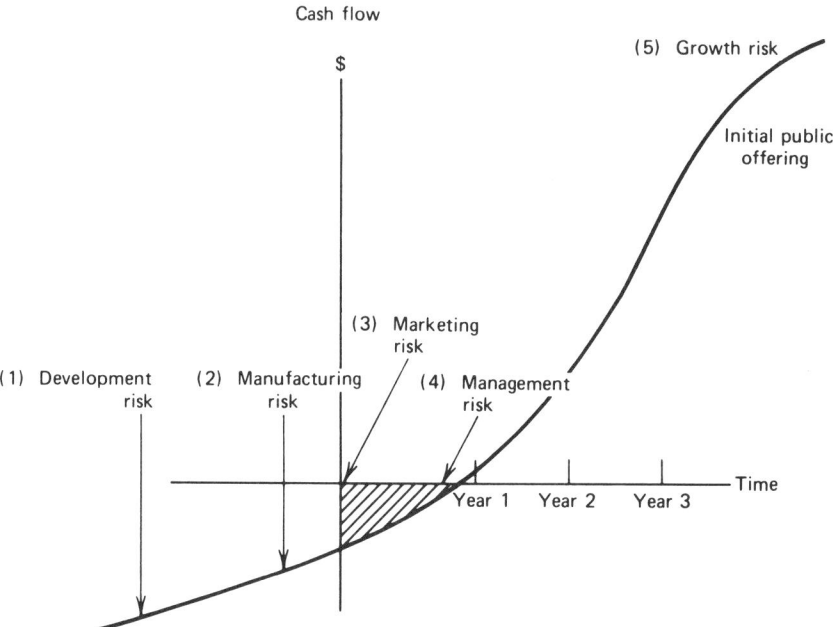

FIGURE 3.1. The five risks in a start-up company.

2. State and federal governments via grant programs the intent of which is job creation.
3. Customers, such as large corporations, who invest in consideration for an ownership position plus the rights to market the product once it is developed.
4. Suppliers who see a large market for certain of their products if the product is successfully developed.
5. Family and friends who, because of emotional ties, are willing to invest in the entrepreneur's dream.

Rarely is it appropriate for a venture capitalist to invest in a company prior to the development of a new product or service. However, every rule has its exceptions. A development risk may be assumed with not more than 5 percent of a venture capital fund's assets in the very earliest years of its life, and then only with a corporate customer or suppliers as an investing partner. The reason for corporate coinvestors is that the product, if developed, will have to be manufactured. The coinvesting corporate partners are most likely to know how to produce the product, once developed. For example, Chester Carlson, the inventor of xerography, was funded by the Haloid Corporation, which engaged Battelle Memorial Laboratories to develop the xerography process that Xerox Corporation (née Haloid) then produced.

The Manufacturing Risk. The manufacturing or production risk is also inappropriate for venture capital. What if the solution to a large problem cannot be produced at a price low enough to make it more attractive than (a) continuing to live with the problem or (b) competitive solutions? What can the venture capitalist do to lower the production costs? Not a thing.

What if the solution can be manufactured at a low enough cost to attract customers, but for a component that resists all attempts to produce it? What can the venture capitalist do to produce it? Not a thing.

Venture capital should not seek companies that are unable to demonstrate a completely operative product or service. Clearly, the product or service can be in prototype form, and it frequently is. But can it be demonstrated, tested, and placed on a potential customer's site for testing? The venture capitalist can inquire of the potential customer: "Did it solve your problem? Would you purchase it? How much would you pay for it?"

There are exceptions to averting the manufacturing risk, which are similar to those for averting the development risk. If the venture capital fund is in its formative years and if a coinvestor exists that is able to manufacture the product, then a small amount of the venture capital fund may be used to invest in companies at this stage of their development. The product, of course, must be absolutely proprietary, protected by a bullet-proof patent filed in the key countries, in order to make adding a third risk acceptable.

The Marketing Risk. In service companies, the delivery system must be very difficult to duplicate in a short period of time and heavily underrated by existing competition using other delivery systems. For example, Federal Express Corporation introduced a new means of delivering small packages overnight. Among its more unique features was that it "absolutely, positively" guaranteed next-day delivery. The competition relied on commercial airlines to deliver their freight. Before Federal Express could attract venture capital, they hired two management consulting firms to measure the demand for the service, the size of the demand and price elasticity, the key cities to begin in, and every other factor they could think of. In this manner, the production risk was mitigated and venture capital was raised.

The Management Risk. It is one thing to achieve a compound annual return of 70 to 90 percent over three years or over five years. But to maintain it beyond that requires the continual introduction of products and services that solve a continual group of problems for a large number of people. Very few companies can develop a succession of managers who are capable of maintaining near miraculous growth records. IBM comes the closest to achieving that kind of performance, and it is often hailed as the only megabillion-dollar entrepreneurial company in the United States. The exception proves the rule. The entrepreneurial period in a person's life is a stage of development lasting about five years, after which, if one succeeds, he or she enters a time period of being a manager. In this period, the entrepreneur is more cautious, because there are assets to protect. The same is true of companies. When they mature from an entrepreneurial to a managed state, their growth slows down, because they are more cautious. There are assets to protect. This is the primary reason that companies in this stage address a certain kind of risk better understood by public investors than by venture capital investors.

In summary, venture capitalists usually accept only two of the five risks addressed by start-up and early-stage companies: the marketing and the management risk. The three other risks—development, production, and growth—are best understood by other kinds of investors.

The Growth Risk. One could argue that venture capitalists are as equipped as anyone and perhaps better equipped to measure and deal with the growth risk, since they know the company from its infancy and are familiar with its products, markets, and management team. The other side of the coin is that the investors who hire the venture capitalists do not engage their services to invest in publicly held companies; rather, it is their task to distribute to their investors the shares of publicly held companies, which the investors can determine to hold or sell as they choose. It would seem that the more reasonable approach is to sell the companies once they are public or distribute them to the fund's investors to hold or sell. The overriding issue it seems is how long a company can continue to grow at a rate acceptable to a venture capitalist. The target rate of return of most venture capital funds is approximately 5 times in 3 years or 10 times in 5 years, which works out to a compound return on investment of approximately 70 to 90 percent per annum (see Figure 3.2).

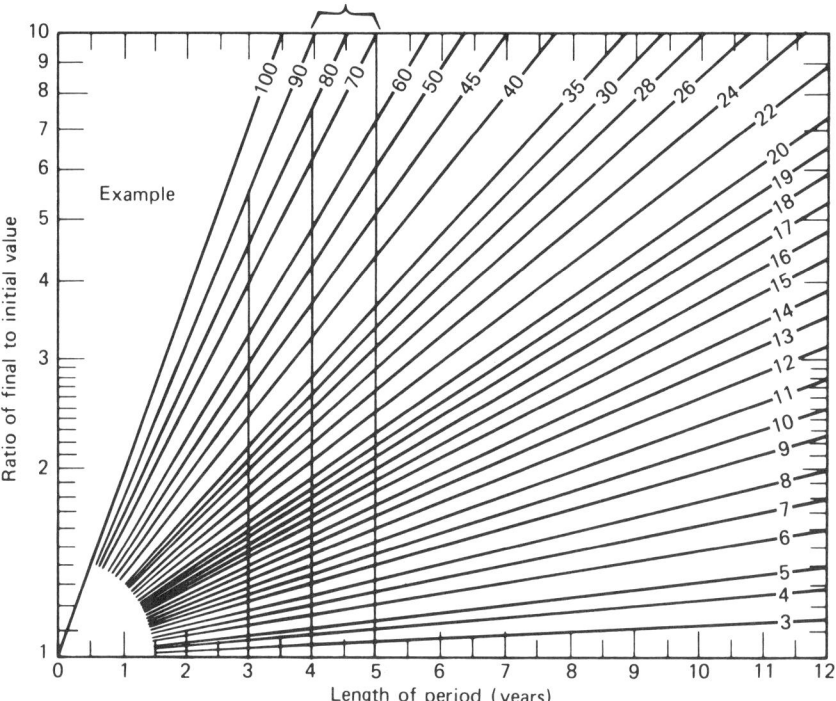

FIGURE 3.2. Target rates of return of a typical venture capital fund.

By minimizing the number and kind of risks that they are willing to accept, venture capitalists are risk averters rather than risk takers. Although this may make the breed less attractive to the financial press, who would prefer to think of them as "gunslingers," it is axiomatic. The most successful venture capitalists understand when to get into and when to get out of deals, that is, which risks to accept and which ones to avoid.

The Problem. In the law of $P \times S \times E = V$, described in Chapter 2, P, the problem, is the most important. Examples of non-P industries in the 1970s have included feminine deodorant sprays, safer automobiles, automated voting systems, wind power, electric cars, and a variety of food products that appear on supermarket shelves one month only to vanish the next. It is impossible, of course, to avoid investing in non-P and low-P industries and companies, because one person's valuation of P is different from another's. However, there are certain methods for identifying big-P investment opportunities. And if one attempts diligently to place venture capital into big-P opportunities, the amount of capital wasted because the P is low rather than high will become less. When venture capitalists run penguinlike into the same industry over and over again, as they did into disk drives, workstations, portable computers, entertainment software, and integrated software in 1982 and 1983, and as they did 15 years before that in computer time-sharing and day-care center franchisors, they are not addressing the solution to large problems. Rather, they are trying to succeed by copying others and trying to catch a trend.

The problems of our society are addressed by problem indexers. The best of these are the *New York Times* and *Washington Post*. Of the two, the *New York Times* is the more thorough—they don't waste any space on cartoons. The day's events in our world are not humorous to the *New York Times*. It describes social, industrial, and physical problems on most of its pages. A venture capitalist, or any other investor, can be made aware of big P's in search of solutions by a careful reading of the *New York Times*.

The technique of measuring a society's concerns has been used successfully by John Naisbitt, author of *Megatrends*, whose firm counts lines of print devoted to various topics in hundreds of local newspapers. In so doing, Naisbitt spots the things that concern large numbers of people, or megatrends. Pollution, civil rights, women's liberation, energy, AIDS, and other topics are indexed by Naisbitt, the *New York Times*, and other serious problem locators.

In *Megatrends*, Naisbitt sees the transformation from an industrial to an "information economy" as a megatrend. He writes: "The transition times between economies are the times when entrepreneurship blooms. We are now in such a period."* There seems to be a Naisbitt every few years who summarizes the forces that drive our society forward and the

---

*John Naisbitt, *Megatrends: Ten New Directions Transforming Our Lives* (New York: Warner, 1982), p. 16.

obstacles that stand in its way. It is these obstacles that create entrepreneurial opportunities.

The venture capitalist should assign numerical values to the factors P, S, and E and accept only those business plans whose product of the equation $P \times S \times E$ exceeds a predetermined minimum acceptable level. For example, an efficient rating system is 0 to 3, where 3 is the highest possible value for P, S, or E and 0 is the lowest possible value. The highest valuation or V factor that an incoming deal could have then is 27, or:

$$P \times S \times E = V$$
$$3 \times 3 \times 3 = 27$$

The existence of a high-P factor in an incoming deal of more than 2.5 on a scale of 0 to 3 is extremely critical for success in venture capital investing. It seems obvious, and not in need of reiteration, that solutions for which there are no problems result in a waste of time and money. Without a large problem in search of a solution, a new business is doomed to failure. Big P's change over time, and one must not lock in on the obvious big P's of disease, hunger, and cost of health care. For example, in the mid-1960s, fast-food chains addressed the large problem of women entering the work force and the consequent need for a fast, reliable family dinner. In the mid-1980s, there is probably only the smallest justification to launch a new restaurant chain, no matter how unusual its menu or other features.

The staff of the venture capital fund manager should decide among themselves and their advisers which problems they consider greater than 2.5, or their minimum acceptable level; or, stated more conventionally, which problems they would like to solve with their capital. The values assigned to the various problems can be altered every year. When a company or group of companies begins earning a profit, by definition it has begun solving a problem for its market, which reduces the size of the problem and makes it a less interesting investment area for venture capitalists. Some of the big P's are:

Hunger
Disease (cancer, heart attack, diabetes)
Increasing size of elderly population
Chemical abuse
Computer literacy for adults
Computer literacy for children
Selecting efficient software quickly
Rising cost of government
Costs associated with criminal justice

These problems easily warrant values of P in excess of 2.5 on several scales: number of lines of print devoted to the subjects in the *New York Times*, dollars raised to research the problems annually, and the number of people willing to pay for a solution times the price they would pay for a solution.

It is undeniable that cancer is one of the biggest problems in the United States, with upward of 400,000 deaths attributed to it each year. According to the American Cancer Society, 855,000 Americans became cancer victims in 1983 for cancers they had gotten earlier. Multiply 3.4 million cancer patients times the market price for the solution and it is readily apparent that cancer nets a value of 3. Heart disease, diabetes, and other killing diseases are not far behind.

To attempt to solve the problem of AIDS, for example, a venture capitalist might invest $1 million at a $10 million valuation, while an equally competent entrepreneurial team that addresses a problem in office automation would have its start-up company valued at less than $2 million by the same venture capitalist. In mid-1984, the aggregate market valuation of the five leading publicly held U.S. genetic engineering companies was equal to the market valuation of the nation's third largest bank, Chase Manhattan. These five companies—Biogen, Cetus, Genentech, Genex, and Molecular Genetics—had no material revenues and negligible earnings, but their dreams and plans were viewed as being worth in the public marketplace an aggregate of nearly $2 billion.

Experienced venture capitalists know that they can take big-P companies public before they have achieved earnings because of the public's desire to invest in companies that chase after real-life Darth Vaders: cancer, hunger, diabetes, and other killing diseases.

The Solution. The values of S are more difficult to calibrate, because S is composed of two factors, B and T:

$$B \times T = S$$

where T = the existence of low-priced technology and B = the business plan or the solution-delivery mechanism. Let's assume the range of values for two factors of S is from 0 to 3. Thus, the technology factor, or T, might warrant a 3 if it involves microprocessors, state-of-the-art software algorithms, or recombinant DNA techniques. The value of T might drop to 1 if the technology involves relatively expensive photovoltaic cells, or to 0.5 if the government could block or delay entry.

Experienced venture capitalists look for an "elegant S." This means that if the solution is a product it should be proprietary, and if it is a service it should have a distribution system that cannot be duplicated. Anything short of these requirements makes the S factor fall under minimum acceptable levels. The P and E factors would have to be relatively high to cause an experienced venture capitalist to invest in a nonelegant-S company. Venture capitalists call these kinds of companies JA deals, as in JAWS or JAISP, which mean "just another workstation" and "just another integrated software package" company.

The T, or technology, component of the S factor is important in achieving an elegant S. New technologies can be protected via basic patents, process patents, or lead time, and these three kinds of protection are of great importance to the investor. There is an axiom in the company-launching business:

Anything worth doing is worth duplicating.

This means that if an investment opportunity is attractive to one group of investors or to one entrepreneurial team it will surely be attractive to several others. A better–faster–cheaper system or device, no matter how thoroughly protected by patents or an elegant, nonduplicatable delivery system, will very shortly be copied, duplicated, and simulated; in short, it will attract significant competition. Natural monopolies simply do not last more than three years, unless protected by the government; thus the emphasis placed on the T subfactor by venture capitalists.

In the case of nonproprietary companies, such as one frequently finds in the service industries, venture capitalists tend to prefer delivery systems that are either nonduplicatable or very expensive for the second or third company in the industry to copy or emulate. Perhaps the best example is Federal Express, which identified an opportunity to deliver time-sensitive small packages overnight on a guaranteed basis. The established freight forwarders were using commercial airlines to carry their packages. If the commercial airlines were delayed due to weather or strikes, the packages simply would not be taken. If the destination was off the main route of the commercial carriers, they didn't get there next day; maybe not for three days. To fill this gap, Federal Express's founding entrepreneur, Fred Smith, conceived of a delivery system that involved flying all packages into Memphis, Tennessee, a city with an airport rarely closed due to bad weather and located near the center of the country. The packages were sorted between 1:00 A.M. and 4:00 A.M. and then flown to their destination for next-day delivery. The start-up costs of this unique delivery system were high, and Federal Express nearly died several times before it lived. The competition—Airborne Freight, Emery, and Purolator—merely scoffed at the upstart. But by the time Federal Express was passing them by, and passing the U.S. Postal Service by as well, the cost of duplicating Federal Express's unique delivery system would have been several hundred million dollars. Thus the entrepreneurial company beat the established competition with a difficult-to-duplicate delivery system.

Weight Watchers International, Inc., the first of the weight-loss service companies, had an extremely easy-to-duplicate delivery system. However, no competitor bothered to attack Weight Watchers using the same or similar delivery system until Weight Watchers was the established leader in the field of weight-loss systems; then it was too late. At the time it was acquired by H. J. Heinz, Weight Watchers had a recognition factor of 92 percent; that is, more than 9 persons out of 10 questioned knew the name Weight Watchers and what the company did. Heinz, on the other hand, had a recognition factor of 17 percent. The advertising budget of Heinz exceeded that of Weight Watchers by tens of millions of dollars. Among other things, this fact shows that entrepreneurial achievements can come quickly and capture the awareness of money; but when they mature, such as Heinz, they are more or less forgotten—another reason for venture capitalists to avoid the "growth" risk discussed previously.

Jean Neditch, the founding entrepreneur of Weight Watchers, conceived a rather simplistic business plan that read something like the following: "I will invite overweight ladies to come to a hotel conference room once or twice a week and pay $2.00 for the privilege of standing up in front of other overweight ladies and saying how fat they are. At the end of the session I will sell them books, tapes, and diet plans in the back of the room as they leave." This business plan was so simplistic that many investors turned Mrs. Neditch down when she sought venture capital in the late 1960s. Thus, when she sold Weight Watchers to H. J. Heinz for $120 million in 1979, she kept most of the proceeds.

On reflection, Weight Watchers' business plan is relatively complex. And the delivery system for the service, when it is launched simultaneously in several dozen metropolitan markets, is difficult to duplicate. A similar system would be deemed a copycat, a "number 2," and probably not "the genuine article." The Weight Watchers delivery system required (1) effective newspaper advertising, (2) renting convenient, attractive conference rooms, (3) positioning a knowledgeable person in the conference rooms to greet the customers and lead them in a weight-loss program, (4) having products available at the conference room, (5) taking the cash and accounting for it properly, and most important, (6) making sure that the system worked. Indeed, a careful reading of the Weight Watchers business plan would indicate that the conveyance system, if done well, would obviate competition for a number of years. Once Weight Watchers gained sufficient size, it began marketing food products under its own brand name. The conversion to a proprietary company came immediately thereafter.

If, therefore, the service company's delivery system is believed to be safe from duplication to the point of eventually becoming unique and *sui generis*, then it qualifies for the same quantitative valuation as a proprietary technology, or T-factor company.

The B subfactor, or business plan component, of the S factor is quite another matter. It is important for entrepreneurs to take the time and make the effort to develop a thorough and competently presented business plan. The venture capitalist ultimately makes his or her investment decision on the *credibility of the operating statement projections*—sometimes referred to as the hockey stick—in the business plan. If there is no business plan, then the venture capitalist must request that one be prepared in order to determine (1) how much capital is required, (2) the projected profitability of the enterprise, and (3) the valuation to be placed on the business at the time of the venture capital investment.

The solution, or S factor, that the entrepreneurial team claims that it can convey to the problem must be investigated thoroughly in terms of the uniqueness of the solution and the difficulty of duplication of the conveyance system. An investigation of these components, and their expression in a well prepared business plan, are the most time-consuming activities in the venture capitalist's review process.

The Quality of the Entrepreneurial Team. The E factor—placing a value on it between 0 and 3—is the final component in the second law of venture capital: $V = P \times S \times E$. The venture capitalist has more control over this factor after he or she has invested, if the terms and conditions of the venture capital investment permit changing members when the company defaults on the terms. Regardless of its ability to change the E factor after financing, the investment should not be made unless the entrepreneur and his or her manager partner meet minimum acceptable characteristics to justify an investment. However, the venture capitalist is able to effect the greatest amount of change in a deal via the E factor. It is not possible for a venture capitalist to change the P factor, and modifying the S factor is done usually via a committee appointed by the board of directors, a consulting organization, or the contracting of a production job to another firm to design a new T. The component of a new company that can be changed by the venture capitalist is the entrepreneurial team: the entrepreneur or his or her manager partner. The mechanism that permits the venture capitalist to change members of the management team is the purchase agreement. If the entrepreneurial team is in default under the terms of the purchase agreement, the venture capitalist can bring to bear a number of changes to protect the capital entrusted to his or her partnership to invest wisely. A venture capitalist who fails to change members of the entrepreneurial team quickly and as necessary is abdicating his or her fiduciary responsibility. For, indeed, to invest mostly in early-stage, unique companies without benefit of controls over the entrepreneurial team is irresponsible. It is the equivalent of locking yourself into a room without doors.

It is necessary to have the ability to make changes in the entrepreneurial team, but it is possible to select entrepeneurs and managers based on certain criteria that suggest the likelihood of their achieving success. Potentially successful entrepreneurs and managers can be weeded out before the investment is made. If the values of P and S are extremely high, but the entrepreneur and his or her manager partner do not get high marks for their potential to launch a new company successfully, they can be asked if they would mind stepping aside or out. Chairmanship of a board of scientific advisers is one possible and frequently used innocuous position; technical consultant is another. If the company's board of directors is large enough, the entrepreneur and/or the manager can be hidden thereon.

If moving them to the side is not acceptable, it may be necessary to buy their interest. This can be effected by offering them a certain dollar amount—perhaps 5 percent of the amount to be invested, as if the founders were finders or brokers. A carried interest in the equity of 1 or 2 percent may be required to sweeten the offer. If the removal of the founders to a more passive position cannot be effected by persuasion or compensation, then the deal should be rejected. Random events, it should never be forgotten, will continually collide with a new company and knock it off its business plan. It takes an excellent entrepeneurial team to get the company back onto its path. On the other hand, an inferior entrepreneurial team will be unable to maintain the company on its business plan. It will lead it off the path without the provocation of random events. Whereas a superior entrepreneurial team can overcome low values for P and S and achieve a fine success, an inferior entrepreneurial team virtually ensures failure.

RATE OF RETURN ON INVESTMENT

There are several means by which venture capitalists set a valuation on companies they invest in. Many of them use the hockey stick method (see Chapter 2, Figure 2.1) or a variation thereof.

The venture capitalist completes his or her due diligence and accepts the credibility of a given set of three-year operating statement projections. He multiplies three-year projected net profits after taxes by a conservative price/earnings ratio, normally 10 to 15, or the price/earnings ratio of the composite DJIA stocks, which has hovered around 12 for the last decade. The venture capitalist, in so doing, says: "I believe that this company should earn $1 million [or whatever the number is] after three years and have a value of at least 12 times $1 million, or $12 million."

The venture capitalist's target return on investment is approximately five times in three years to 10 times in five years, which translates logarithmically into a compound return on investment of between 60 and 70 percent per annum. See Figure 3.3 for a logarithmic scale that connects ratios of final to initial values over time to compound annual returns on investment.

The amount of venture capital that must be invested is then multiplied by the ratio of final to initial value: say, 5, because in this example the projections were only for three years. Assume the company requires $800,000. That amount is multiplied by 5, and the multiplicand of $4 million is the amount the venture capitalist expects to make on his or her investment.

The target of $4 million is then divided by the company's projected third-year value, which in this example is $12 million. The result, or 33 percent ($4 million/$12 million), is the percentage of ownership that the investor requires. He or she may ask the entrepreneur for 37.5 percent or 40 percent, but the required ownership level is 33 percent. If 0.33 is divided into $800,000, one can see that the company's postfinancing valuation is $2.4 million. It was worth, in the eyes of the investor, $1.6 million before the venture capital, and $2.4 million after financing.

The entrepreneur's idea of valuation is nearly always too high, reflecting his or her optimism but not the possibility of the operating

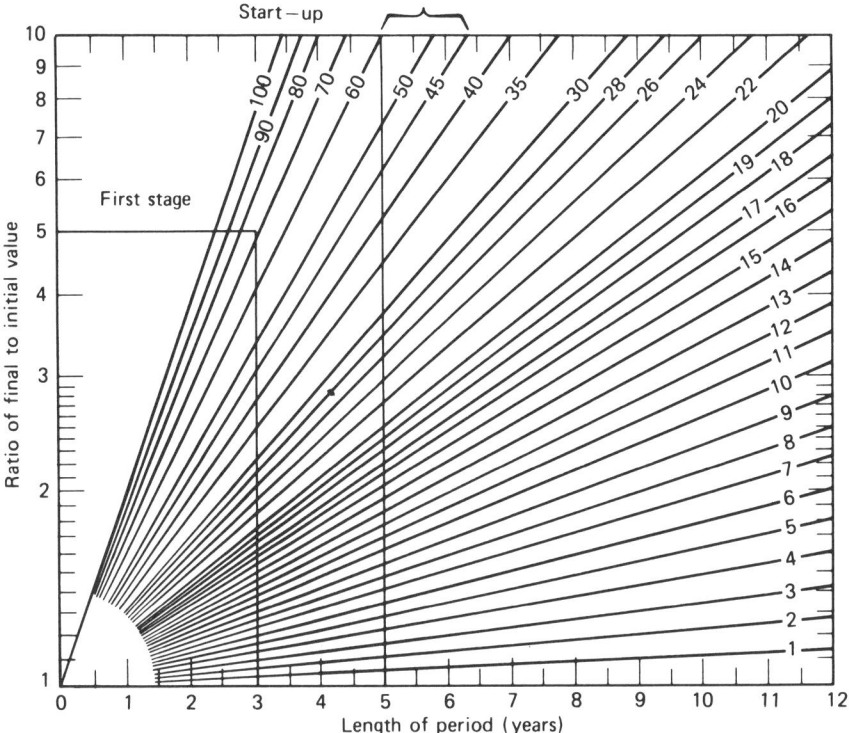

FIGURE 3.3. Logarithmic scale of ratios: final to initial values over time.

statement projections not being realized. One can always increase the price of the stock and the company's valuation in subsequent rounds of financing if the increases are warranted. However, achieving price or valuation reductions means that the company is in very difficult circumstances. Conditional prices that fall one way if the entrepreneur achieves a certain goal or another way if the goal is not achieved make opponents out of partners. It is best to agree on a single price and valuation and not conditional prices. If a price cannot be agreed to, at least you can leave the room as friends.

TERMS OF INVESTMENT

When the venture capitalist completes his or her due-diligence process, obtains approval for the investment in committee, and forms a syndicate with other venture capitalists to invest the full amount of money that is required, it is the duty of the lead venture capitalist to prepare a term sheet and submit it to the entrepreneur. The entrepreneur must approve all of the terms of investment listed on the term sheet, sometimes referred to as a "laundry list." When that occurs, the term sheet is presented by the venture capitalist to his or her attorney to draw up the closing documents.

The Term Sheet. The laundry list is worked on by the entrepreneur and the lead venture capitalist. The deal can fall apart at this point if there is a misunderstanding about terms or a failure to agree on price. There are dozens of items that can kill an investment when it is in a contract stage, so it is better to hammer it out on the laundry list before the lawyers are involved, in order to save money. The most traditional subjects covered in the laundry list are summarized as follows:

1. *Amount of the Investment.*
2. *Securities.* Generally they are convertible preferred stock, or common stock in the case of venture capital funds and subordinated convertible debentures in the case of SBICs.
3. *Conversion Price and Terms of the Preferred Stock (debentures).* Valuation is established as well as the dividend (interest) rate, if any, and the date the money is repayable if the company has not done well enough to encourage conversion into common stock.
4. *Representations and Warranties.* These terms require the entrepreneur to prepare a list of documents, normally exhibits to the contracts, which prove various statements that he or she put into the business plan or made to the investors during the due-diligence process. These include evidences of incorporation, trademarks, patents, indebtedness, leases, contracts, capital equipment, and other items, evidence of which might give the investors greater comfort. The entrepreneur, on the other hand, may ask the investors to represent and warrant that they are able to provide the time of their senior people, an additional round of financing if necessary, or other items that might give the entrepreneur greater comfort.
5. *Affirmative Covenants.* This is a listing of "do's"—a variety of actions that the entrepreneur agrees regularly to do so long as any of the preferred stock (debentures) is outstanding. These include making dividend (interest) and principal payments in a timely manner and tax payments and insurance payments when due, submitting financial statements, unaudited and audited, voting enough of the entrepreneur's shares to elect the agreed-upon number of venture capitalists or their representatives to the board of directors, calling board meetings regularly, maintaining properties, books, and records in good order, and meeting other reasonable requests.
6. *Negative Convenants.* This is a listing of "don'ts"—a variety of actions that the entrepreneur will not take or permit to occur without the consent of all or some of the preferred stockholders (debenture holders). This list can be relatively long or relatively short, depending on several things, including the mutual trust of the parties, the financial health of the company, the number

of investors in the syndicate, and the tautological desires of the investors' counsel. A typical listing consists of the following:

(a) Don't change the type of business engaged in.
(b) Don't pay any common stock dividends.
(c) Don't incur liens on the company's assets.
(d) Don't make any loan or guarantee any loan to any person or entity above a minimum dollar amount; same for investment.
(e) Don't acquire or merge with any other company.
(f) Don't change the company's capital structure.
(g) Don't increase officers' salaries above agreed limits.
(h) Don't incur lease liabilities above certain minimums.
(i) Don't pay employees more than agreed amounts.
(j) Don't permit dealings with insiders (e.g., an officer or director selling a service to the company).

7. *Default.* In the event that the company fails to comply with one or more affirmative or negative covenants, the company is in default and the amount invested by the venture capitalists becomes immediately due and payable. However, there is usually a "cure" period of 30 to 120 days, which can be extended by mutual agreement, to permit the company to take whatever steps are necessary to cure the default.

8. *Registration.* This section deals with the investors' right to have the company register its shares of common stock for an initial public offering when it registers the company's shares. If the company's founders do not choose to make the company public, the investors are able to seek their own underwriter. This would indicate considerable friction, and no underwriter would leap at the opportunity to make public the shares of a quarreling company. Thus, though these terms and conditions appear harsh, they have never been enforced by a venture capitalist in recent memory.

9. *Cosale and "Take Me Along."* This section deals with offers by outsiders to buy the stock of management and how the entrepreneur must have the offer made to the investors as well. Should they receive a similar offer, they must take the entrepreneurial team along. This prevents either group from bailing out without the other.

10. *Additional Provisions.* This section includes methods of modifying the agreements, means of notifying one another who will pay legal fees, and other primarily legal items.

The venture capitalist should take the time to review the term sheet with the entrepreneur very carefully until he or she fully understands the terms and the venture capitalist's reasons for the terms. In this manner, possible misunderstandings may be avoided.

**Exhibit 3.1 High-Tech Start-up Corporation
(hereinafter referred to as HTSU)**

Summary of Terms

1.	Amount	$500,000	

			Approximate Purchase Price
2.	Investors	Lead Venture Capital Fund	$250,000
		Follower Venture Capital Co.	$250,000

3. Instrument — Series A Cumulative Convertible Preferred Stock (Preferred Stock or Shares), convertible on a share-for-share basis into the number of common shares that would represent 25 percent of the fully diluted equity shares of HTSU as of the closing of this private placement.

4. Dividends — Subsequent to October 31, 1987 (three years hence), the annual dividend rate payable on Preferred Stock will be 10 percent of the liquidation value of the Preferred Shares, payable quarterly thereafter on June 30, September 30, December 31, and March 31 of each year. Dividends will be cumulative on Preferred Stock.

5. Voting Rights — Holders shall be entitled to receive notice of the shareholders' meetings and to vote for the election of directors. These rights exist as if each share of Preferred Stock had been converted into the number of shares of Common Stock into which it is then convertible.

6. Preference in Liquidation — The liquidation value (Liquidation Value) shall initially be the Holders' original cost per Preferred Share. The Liquidation Value of the Preferred Stock increases on each quarterly dividend date by the amount of any dividend not paid on such date (subject to reduction if thereafter paid). In case some Preferred Stock is redeemed, Liquidation Value of such Holders' remaining shares shall increase on the date of such redemption by the amount of any unpaid dividends transferred from shares redeemed.

In the event of liquidation or redemption, Liquidation Value also increases by an amount equal to a dividend of 10 percent for each full year from date of issuance until liquidation. Preferred Shares, plus unpaid dividends, have preference over all Common Shares in liquidation. The Series A Preferred Shares shall rank on a parity with any other series of Preferred Stock subsequently issued and distributions will be made pro rata among the Holders of all series of Preferred Stock.

7. Conversion Privileges — A holder of shares may, at any time prior to the mandatory redemption dates, elect to convert, in

EXHIBIT 3.1 (*Continued*)

		whole or in part, into Common Shares. A Holder may convert, at any time, without notice to HTSU by (and upon) delivering to HTSU the shares it intends to convert. The company shall reserve a sufficient number of Common Shares for the transaction and will promptly deliver the appropriate number of Common Shares to said Holder.
8.	Mandatory Redemption	HTSU must redeem the Preferred Shares equally in years seven, eight, nine, and ten.
9.	Voluntary Redemption Privileges	HTSU may make voluntary redemptions of the Preferred Shares at any time after March 31, 1987, provided:

    a. HTSU gives the Holders 90 days' written notice via registered or certified mail, return receipt requested, of its intent to redeem such Preferred Shares.

    b. HTSU sends to the Holders, via registered or certified mail, return receipt requested, a certified or cashier's check at least 15 days prior to the date on which HTSU intends to redeem such Preferred Shares for an amount equal to all accrued dividends (to date of voluntary redemption), plus the Liquidation Value of the Preferred Shares which it intends to voluntarily redeem.

    c. Voluntary redemptions are in multiples of $50,000 of Preferred Shares; and

    d. Any optional redemptions must be offered pro rata to all Holders and will be applied in inverse order of the regular redemption schedule.

HTSU's ability to make voluntary redemptions will in no way abrogate any of the Holders' rights to convert into Common Shares prior to redemption. If, at any time, HTSU notifies the Holders that it intends to redeem, the Holders reserve the right, prior to the expiration of the 90 days' notice, to convert any portion or all of their Preferred Stock into Common Shares.

10.	Preconditions to Closing	All patent rights owned by the entrepreneur shall be transferred to HTSU. In exchange for the patents, the entrepreneur will own at least 70 percent of the fully diluted Common Stock of the company immediately prior to closing. In addition, the company must forego its Subchapter S status, converting to a conventional corporation.
11.	Antidilution Provisions	If HTSU sells any of its Common Shares at net prices less than the then existing underlying conversion price per share (hereinafter called the ex-

EXHIBIT 3.1 (*Continued*)

isting conversion price), or if it sells or grants any options (convertible securities, warrants, etc.) to purchase Common Shares at less than the existing conversion price, then the lowest net price per share shall become the new price per share for which all of the Preferred Shares may be converted or exercised into Common Shares. In the case of a time sale of HTSU Common Shares, for the purpose of this Section, the price per share shall be determined by discounting the price to be paid over time (including interest based on a simple interest calculation) by the prime rate at the time the transaction is closed.

HTSU is encouraged to extend employee stock options, employee stock purchase plans, and similar compensation plans to key employees. Such plans, to be limited to an aggregate of 10 percent of the Common Stock of HTSU on a fully diluted basis immediately after the time of closing, will not affect these antidilution provisions. When granting such options, however, the minimum exercise price per share shall be the greater of (a) 90 percent of the market value of the Common Shares, or (b) one-half of the conversion price of the Preferred Shares.

12. Adjustment for Stock Splits and Dividends

In the event of stock splits and dividends, a pro rata adjustment in conversion price and number of Common Shares into which the Preferred Shares may be converted will be made.

13. Demand Registration Rights

At the earlier of 36 months from the date of closing, or any sale of Common Stock to the public, the Holders will have the right to demand *two* free registrations of their (to be converted) Common Shares; registration costs and filing fees for these demand registrations will be paid for by HTSU. Holders of 75 percent of the unregistered Common Shares of this private placement may elect to demand such registrations. HTSU will not be obligated to register its Common Shares for the Holders during any period within six months of a prior registration, offering, and sale of its primary or secondary Common Shares (other than a shelf registration). If the holders request, then HTSU, at its own expense, must keep a shelf registration active for six months after each demand registration prompted by the Holders. At the Holders' option, the shelf registration may be further extended at their expense.

In addition to the two free demand registrations,

EXHIBIT 3.1 (*Continued*)

		the Holders will be entitled to two demand registrations for which the Holders will pay their pro rata shares of all the registration expenses, such as employees, rent, telephone, etc. If a demand registration does not become effective, then such a demand registration will not be counted as a demand registration. The Holders shall have preference in any Holder-called-for demand registration. In the event that there may be other Holders who may exercise rights to demand registration of their Common Shares simultaneously with the Holders exercising their rights to demand registrations, then all Holders wishing to register and sell Common Shares shall do so on a pro rata basis. HTSU shall bear the entire cost of such registrations under such circumstances, and such registrations shall only be counted as free provided that the Holders are able to register and sell at least 90 percent of those shares requested to be registered.
14.	Rights to Choose Investment Bankers, Underwriters, Managers, and Comanagers	The Holders reserve the right to select the investment banker(s), manager(s), and/or comanager(s) for each of their demand registrations or for any shared demand registrations (those in which other institutions or persons participate). The Holders reserve the right to veto or approve of HTSU's selection of investment banker(s), manager(s), and/or comanager(s) for all primary registrations and public sales of HTSU securities or private placement thereof; such approval by the Holders may not be unreasonably withheld.
15.	"Piggyback" Rights	The Holders will have "piggyback" registration rights for their Common Shares and will not have to pay any registration expenses or filing fees so long as HTSU offers primary shares in connection with such registrations. If, however, the underwriters determine that a "piggyback" registration or a secondary sale may be detrimental to a primary offering and selling primary shares, they must pay their pro rata expenses.
		In case of underwriting limitation, HTSU will have registration and sale priorities for primary shares, and the Holder will have preference over the sale of any other secondary shares. HTSU will provide at least 90 days' notice to the Holders of its intent to file a registration statement.
16.	Affirmative Covenants	HTSU will furnish to the Holders the following: (a) Monthly financial and operating statements (with comparisons to budgets and to corresponding periods of the preceding year)

EXHIBIT 3.1 (*Continued*)

       within 30 days after the end of the first 11 months of each fiscal year, prepared on a long-form, consolidated, and consolidating basis.

  (b) Accompanying the monthly statements, certificates of compliance from HTSU's Chief Executive Officer stating it is or it is not in compliance with the Preferred Purchase Agreement and any other material agreements.

  (c) Within 90 days after the end of each fiscal year, an unqualified certified audit report consisting of long-form, consolidated, and consolidating financial statements prepared by a nationally recognized certified public accounting firm (also to be included with these reports are the CPA's management letter and their statement with reference to HTSU's compliance with all of its material agreements).

  (d) Sixty days prior to the fiscal year-end, a detailed operating budget (prepared on a monthly basis) for the subsequent fiscal year. This budget should be prepared on a long-form, consolidated, and consolidating basis. The budget should also include detailed balance sheets, profit and loss statements, and cash flow statements.

  (e) Within 10 days of issuance, duplicate copies of any general written communications with shareholders, directors, executive committee(s), or with the financial community, and any reports filed by HTSU with any security exchanges or with the SEC.

  (f) Within five days after the discovery or notification that HTSU is not in compliance with the Purchase Agreement or any other material agreement, a detailed statement outlining such noncompliance(s) or default(s).

17. Negative Covenants

HTSU may not do any of the following without the prior written consent of the Holders.

  (a) Pay any dividends except those related to the Preferred Shares for three years.

  (b) Issue any security or note that has any equity-type feature, profit participation feature, or may be purchased as part of an investment unit if such security ranks superior to the Preferred Shares.

  (c) Have any partially owned subsidiaries.

  (d) Create any subsidiary outside of the United States or its territorial possessions.

EXHIBIT 3.1 (*Continued*)

		(e) Cause any reverse splits in any of its equity securities.
		(f) Change its fiscal year.
		(g) HTSU will comply in all respects with, and will not amend without Holders' approval, the provisions in its Certificate of Incorporation and Bylaws that affect, directly or indirectly, these Preferred Shares.
		(h) Without the consent of the Holders, no merger, consolidation, or disposition of all or substantially all of HTSU's assets shall occur, except:
		(i) A merger under which HTSU is the surviving corporation and its Common Stock is not changed; or
		(ii) Other than in the normal course of business, a sale of assets that represent more than 10 percent of its total assets.
		(i) Enter into or engage in businesses other than those presently engaged in or proposed to be engaged in.
		(j) Repurchase any Common Shares.
		(k) Create any other class of Common Stocks.
		(l) Engage in any insider transactions.
18.	Inspection Rights	The Holders may inspect HTSU's properties, books, and other records (and make copies thereof and take extracts therefrom) and may interview HTSU's directors, officers, and any employees regarding HTSU's affairs, provided such interviews are held during any regular business hours and at such other times as may be reasonably requested.
19.	Right to Attend Board of Directors' Meetings	Representatives of two venture capital funds may attend all board of directors' meetings and committee meetings of the board, and/or may be elected to the board of directors at their option. HTSU will pay all such Holders' representatives travel and out-of-pocket expenses for attending such board and committee meetings. There will be no less than four board of directors' meetings per year, at least 60 days apart. HTSU will give the Holders at least 10 business days notice of each meeting.
20.	Life Insurance Policy	So long as any Preferred Shares are outstanding, HTSU will maintain insurance on the life of the entrepreneur, aggregating $500,000, and assign the proceeds of such insurance to the Holders. Such insurance will be obtained and the assignment made prior to the closing of this private placement. The amount of this coverage may decline to coin-

EXHIBIT 3.1 (*Continued*)

cide with Preferred Shares outstanding at HTSU's option. Any insurance proceeds payable by reason of death shall, at the option of the Holders, first be used to redeem any outstanding Preferred Shares. The balance of any insurance proceeds not used to redeem the Preferred Shares shall accrue to HTSU. The respective Holder must decide whether the insurance proceeds will be used to redeem its Preferred Shares within 60 days from time of receipt of such proceeds.

21.	Ownership Retention	The entrepreneur shall not sell or transfer more than 20 percent of his Common Shares (as of the date of closing and as adjusted by any subsequent stock splits and stock dividends) until the Holders have recovered their cost either through the redemption of the Preferred Shares or sale of securities.
22.	Future Agreements That May Affect Dividend and Redemption Payments	After the closing, HTSU will not become a party to any agreement that by its terms may restrict HTSU's ability and obligation to pay dividends on the Preferred Shares or to make mandatory redemption payments on such Preferred Stock.
23.	Taxes and Debts	HTSU will pay all taxes and debts, unless contested in good faith.
24.	Auditor	HTSU will retain a nationally known auditing firm.
25.	Patents, Licenses, and Trademarks	HTSU will possess and maintain all necessary patents, trademarks, trade names, copyrights and licenses to conduct its business as now operated, without any known conflict with the valid patents, trademarks, trade names, copyrights, and licenses of others.
26.	Amendments and Waivers	The Purchase Agreement may be amended or waived by unanimous consent of the Holders of the Preferred Shares.
27.	Assignments	All of the terms, convenants, and undertakings contained in the Purchase Agreement will be binding upon and inure to the benefit of the Holder's respective successors and assigns and may be assigned by them at their discretion to any financial institutions and/or any corporations, trusts or individuals. In the event of any assignment, the new assignee must "legend" the transferred shares to comply with securities laws or regulations and obtain a letter of opinion from transferer's counsel that such transfer does not violate security laws or regulations.

EXHIBIT 3.1 (*Continued*)

28.	Indemnification for Finder's Fees	HTSU will, at closing, give the Holders a letter listing any finder's or broker's fees that will be incurred in connection with this private placement and agrees promptly to indemnify the Holders and their assigns against any claims (including legal, travel, and out-of-pocket expenses for defending such claims) that may arise for any such fees and expenses.
29.	Attorneys' Fees	HTSU will pay, on the date of closing, all of the Holders' legal fees and expenses, as invoiced by its attorneys, in connection with its attorneys' efforts to prepare the Purchase Agreement, to a maximum of $10,000.
30.	Other Terms and Severability	Other terms traditionally contained in purchase agreements of this type, including representations, warranties, etc., shall be contained in the Purchase Agreement. There will be a standard severability clause and the governing law of the Purchase Agreement for the Preferred Shares will be of the state in which HTSU is located.
31.	Events of Noncompliance	An event of noncompliance by HTSU will occur if: (a) HTSU breaches any of the covenants or fails to comply with other provisions of this Summary of Terms and Conditions. (b) Any cumulative preferred dividend is unpaid or HTSU fails to make any mandatory redemption payment when due. (c) All of HTSU's representatives and warranties are not substantially true as of the closing. (d) Any current or future debt holder demands payment of a material debt prior to its stated maturity. (e) HTSU files or fails to have dismissed within 90 days a bankruptcy or receivership proceeding, makes an assignment for the benefit of creditors, attempts materially to compromise debts with creditors, or suffers acceleration of a material third-party obligation.
32.	Remedies for Events of Noncompliance	Immediately upon the occurrence of any noncompliance described in Section 31(c), (d), or (e), or after 15 days of continuous noncompliance described in Section 31(a) or (b): (a) The conversion price shall be decreased by 10 percent for each six weeks that HTSU is in continuous noncompliance. Notwithstanding the above, the conversion price shall not fall below 65 percent of the original conversion price, as adjusted by splits and antidilution provisions.

EXHIBIT 3.1 (*Continued*)

    (b) At the option of the Holders, acceleration of the mandatory redemptions may be made.

    (c) The foregoing remedies are not exclusive, and other available legal remedies may be pursued.

Preferred Stock. Venture capitalists should endeavor to own a security that is senior to common stock. Venture capitalists need to hold securities senior to those held by the entrepreneurial team in order to "monitor" the portfolio companies in a fiduciary manner. *Monitor* is a complex word. It means to watch closely and influence the decisions of management. Without senior securities, it would be difficult for the investors to maintain their board seats or have other privileges not shared by common stockholders. And if venture capitalists were unable to exert leverage on their portfolio company managers, many of the advantages indigenous to venture capital investing would be eliminated. If a venture capitalist cannot make or influence management changes when things go wrong in his or her portfolio companies, then venture capital investing loses its leverage.

As G. Felda Hardymon, a partner in Bessemer Venture Partners, New York, says, "Venture capitalists put in all or most of the money and don't ask for a key to the company's offices. What other kind of investor would be so relaxed?"

Before resuming the analysis of typical terms and conditions that venture capitalists have their lawyers prepare for submission to the entrepreneur, it would be useful to review a sample laundry list, a summary of terms and conditions with the laundry list items fully described. Exhibit 3.1 is such a summary. These terms and conditions apply to a high-technology, early-stage company whose revenues were approximately $20,000 per month at the time of the investment. The company, managed by a 27-year-old entrepreneur and in search of a corporate achiever, needed the addition of a marketing plan and the people to implement it, especially in marketing and finance. The terms and conditions are typical for many high-technology start-up businesses.

Senior securities enable venture capitalists to demand that management remain in close contact with them after the investment. They also provide early warning signals, hooks, and handles that enable the investors to make changes in management or take other steps necessary to protect their investment when it begins to decline in value. There is on occasion an additional reason for using senior securities: to ensure some income on the investment.

As the company grows and prospers, the senior securities may no longer be needed, or may be replaceable on more advantageous terms, for example, at a lower interest or preferred dividend rate. In recognition of this, it is customary for senior securities to be "callable" or "redeemable" at the option of the corporation. Sinking-fund provisions in senior securities, both debt and preferred stock, are in effect provisions for compulsory repayment at stated intervals.

The other side of the coin is provisions for the convertibility of senior securities into common stock, so that the venture capitalist willing to give up prior claims and hooks and handles necessary for proper monitoring may share in the growth and prosperity of the company through ownership of the common stock.

4

THE CONTRIBUTION OF VENTURE CAPITALISTS TO THE ENTREPRENEURIAL ECONOMY

There are three types of lenders: no risk, calculated risk, and risk. No-risk lenders are banks; calculated-risk lenders are commercial finance companies; risk lenders are venture capitalists. Many new companies raise money from all three sources either at various times in their growth or at the same time as a packaged financing (sometimes called a "blended-rate") deal. It is imprudent and a waste of everyone's time to seek risk capital from a bank without offering the bank collateral, cash flow, and secondary collateral, or as it is sometimes referred to, belt, suspenders, and safety pins. No matter how well you talk, the obstacles to your success are overpowering, even with a government loan guarantee.

The entrepreneur must understand his or her company and assets, both hidden and visible, to know from which of the three sources to raise capital and at what magnitude. For example, a manufacturer seeking to purchase machinery and equipment might be able to borrow on an unsecured basis from a bank if the present cash flow exceeds the pro forma loan repayment schedule. The situation might require a commercial finance loan secured by the machinery and equipment if the ability to repay is unquestionable—for example, if the company has experienced a loss year or had too brief a track record of positive cash flow. Venture capital would be the solution if there are doubts about the ultimate productivity of the machinery and equipment. There are, of course, variations and exceptions to all of these rules, but exceptions are usually the result of extraordinary circumstances.

An agent of the lender is the guarantor, generally government guarantor, generally federal but occasionally state, and generally in the person of a local civil servant manning an area office and trying just as hard as you to understand the guidelines under which he or she can approve a loan guarantee for your company. Clearly no equity is given up to the government. In speaking with civil servants an entirely different orientation is required. You must realize that they have been somewhat depersonalized by their monolithic client and no matter what you say at the first meeting they will feel compelled to find a reason to turn down your application. No matter how perfectly applications have been filled out, civil servants feel that if they do not turn them down at least once, they have not executed their duties properly.

Therefore, entrepreneurs should make their conversation especially pleasant and attempt to personalize civil servants. They should find like experiences to share and strive to discover common interests. Entrepreneurs should be self-effacing. They should make the government guarantors feel that their turndown of the application is actually (1) a search for information and (2) an opportunity to visit with each other again. Civil servants have the opportunity to assist entrepreneurs in achieving wealth, which is a commodity they may not have and may be envious of. Thus it is important to make civil servants feel an important part of the process. The same applies to unsecured and secured lenders.

LENDERS' POLICIES VARY

The rules of selling a credit are the same whether the entrepreneur is raising money from a no-risk, calculated-risk, or risk lender. The rules apply, however, only if the entrepreneur is selling to the appropriate lender. No matter how outstanding the verbal presentation, a credit cannot be sold to a lender if granting the loan violates his or her policies and objectives. In summary, these policies are as follows:

Commercial Bank. The ability to repay the loan must be absolutely certain and protected in three ways: cash flow, asset coverage, and side collateral. These are made up, for example, of historical cash flow that exceeds the pro forma repayment schedule, accounts receivable substantially in excess of the value of the loan, and a guarantor willing to pledge liquid collateral in support of the loan.

Commercial Finance Company. The ability to repay the loan must be highly profitable and supported by assets—accounts receivable, inventories, or plant and equipment—that in liquidation would aggregate more than the value of the loan. In addition, the commercial finance company must be familiar with the kinds of assets used to secure the loan so that it will know to whom they might be sold in the event of liquidation. Personal guarantees usually are required to show good faith and to keep the entrepreneurs from running off to some other company.

SBIC or MESBIC. The loan must have a high profitability of repayment, but it is not supported by assets pledged to secure the loan. Rather, the venture capitalist generally takes a full risk on the principal amount of the loan, in consideration for which he or she purchases a significant minority equity position in the borrowing company. The venture capital company will sell its equity position at a profit to the public, a larger company, or back to the entrepreneur at some future date, when and if it has increased in value.

Government Guarantor. The loan must have a high probability of repayment, which the government believes is more likely to occur if the entrepreneurs invest approximately 10 to 20 percent of the total proceeds in the form of equity, or if the borrower's net worth is equal to a similar percentage of the loan. The government whenever possible seeks to collateralize its loans with "negative incentive" assets, such as a lien on the entrepreneur's house or other hard assets. When this is not possible, the borrower must present overriding social benefits as a reason for granting the guarantee.

Using the foregoing guidelines, an entrepreneur in many cases will be able to determine which type of lender to attempt to sell to. It is pointless to seek risk money from a bank or commercial finance company, and it is costly to seek no-risk money from a venture capitalist.

GETTING THE MEETING

Before meeting the lender or investor the entrepreneur should bear in mind the plight of the first person ever to have eaten a crab. Although he or she may have enjoyed the taste, communicating this pleasure to others must have been a difficult assignment. I can hear the people saying, "But it crawls on the bottom of the sea," and "It is so terrible looking," and, perhaps, "How did you prevent it from grabbing your nose with its pinchers?"

There are parts of a business plan that need quite a bit of explaining as well. Although the entrepreneur may understand the nuances of market and product, a lender or investor may not understand them all. Consider the small business computer industry. Few are the lenders who understand words and phrases such as *Mbyte, floppy disk,* and *vertical market software.* The entrepreneur who expects to accomplish anything at the meeting should be prepared to begin at the beginning.

Many entrepreneurs use intermediaries to submit their business plans and arrange meetings. Sponsorship is the best means of getting the meeting. Naturally, there is a fee, but it is usually worthwhile to pay 5 percent if the chance of raising capital depends on it. Without the services of a financial intermediary, however, it is advised that the entrepreneur deliver the business plan in person and attempt to sell the credit at the first meeting while the lender skims the material. In order to get the appointment, the entrepreneur should ask the lender or investor if he may "come by and drop off the material." At that point, the lender or investor will probably reply with: "Why don't you just mail it and I'll give you a call after I have read it." Persistence and tenacity are appreciated by lenders and investors, and the entrepreneur should rebut with:

"I have to be near your office tomorrow anyway, and it would not be out of my way to drop it off." This proposal might fit neatly into the lender's or investor's schedule, but assuming it does not, the entrepreneur can choose one of several other options:

1. "If the afternoon is not good for you, I can change my other appointment and see you in the morning."
2. "If tomorrow is not acceptable, I need to be back your way in one or two days."
3. "If your schedule is tight right now, why don't we get together for breakfast?"
4. "Perhaps you could squeeze me in after work one day this week."

I firmly believe that lenders and investors are more interested in tenacious entrepreneurs than in relaxed or casual entrepreneurs. Intimidation mixed with charm is an excellent initial impression to make on an investor or lender. For example, if the person absolutely will not see you, you might laughingly say something like, "Gee, you guys must have a lot of good deals in there now."

In attempting to arrange the meeting, the entrepreneur must be careful to modulate his or her persistence so as not to appear "pushy" but to create a busy, important image—running off to meetings with other lenders, customers, suppliers, lawyers, and advertising agencies. If nothing seems to be working, but the lender or investor still has not hung up the telephone, the entrepreneur might take a few minutes to explain the key ingredients, entrepreneurial team, market size, and product niche. If these are indeed interesting, then the lender or investor will try to find time for a meeting.

MAKING THE PITCH

Selling the credit begins the moment you enter the room. I suggest entering quickly and confidently with a glowing smile, an extended hand, and an unexpected remark such as "Thank you for seeing me. Sorry to be late, but we've just completed our biggest month in history . . .," or ". . . we've just received a major order from _____. . .," or ". . . we were having a session with our patent counsel. . . ." Thus the first impression is that you are a "doer."

One entrepreneur I know always says "It's done" as he enters the lender's or investor's office for the first time. "It's done" is a surprising remark. My entrepreneur friend claims that it is the single best opener because it is completely unexpected, it makes you look like a doer—an accomplisher—and it causes the lender to want to do something with you also. If yours is an entrepreneurial team, the two of you could enter the room one saying to the other "It's done!" and then gleefully introduce yourselves to the lender. Chances are the lender will ask, "What's done?"

Then you can lead into the proverbial presentation with a positive tone of accomplishment. The "What's done?" question could elicit a response from the lender in the form of writing something in the margin of a page.

Dress is a topic that is important in selling a credit. When a lender decides to grant a loan, in the back of his or her mind there is a nagging concern that the entrepreneur may lack the judgment to spend the money wisely. This concern is definitely not major once a positive decision has been reached, but the entrepreneur's appearance could affect the positive decision just enough to skew it from slightly bullish to slightly bearish. Hence the entrepreneur's clothing should suggest conservatism more than liberalism, risk aversion more than risk taking, caution rather than devil-may-care optimism. They dress for their superiors (to whom they sell their brains, hearts, and souls daily), who expect them to be judicious with the institution's money. Roe Stamps, a partner in the venture capital fund of Summit Partners, says that successful entrepreneurs usually speak Yiddish for terms of commerce, of which there are many, while dressing like a Savile Row banker.

Colors of clothing may reflect conservatism in one part of the country and liberalism in another. The following dress code for men was given to me by a colorful, spicy entrepreneur who kept pulling out different attire as we traveled from city to city raising venture capital.

1. *New England.* Dark blue suit, blue shirt, semiwide paisley tie, lace-up shoes.
2. *New York.* Gray pinstriped suit, blue shirt, red and blue striped tie, lace-up shoes or conservative loafers.
3. *Chicago and Industrial Midwest.* Gray or dark brown suit, dark tie, lace-up shoes. Give appearance of being ready to slap a hard hat on your head and tramp through a foundry right after the meeting.
4. *South and Southwest.* Light gray or light brown suit, any color shirt except white, bright tie, lace-up shoes or conservative loafers.
5. *Los Angeles.* Similar to the south and southwest except colors should be coordinated and loafers may be tassled.
6. *San Francisco.* Dark blue suit, white shirt, bright tie, lace-up shoes or conservative loafers.

Women should follow the color guidelines stated above, translating suits and ties to simply tailored suits and scarves worn with conservative shoes. If jewelry is worn it should be plain and understated.

Lenders derive some of their personality characteristics from the entrepreneurs to whom they lend money and whose plans, dreams, and aspirations become their own plans, dreams, and aspirations. It is inevitable that the lender will ask himself or herself, "Do I see a part of myself in that entrepreneur? Could I possibly share common goals with him [or her]? Are we at all alike?" It is in this area that dress plays a role. Of course, it is secondary to the substance of the conversation, but the entrepreneur should provide an appearance more appropriate for handling money wisely than for going to a ball game.

Select the most comfortable seat nearest the lender and at all times sit forward but straight. Never lean back or become relaxed. If the lender sits behind his or her desk, you should sit in front of the desk and place your material on the desk in a folder in front of you. The entrepreneur should never appear at ease. The subject is money, and that is not a casual topic. One entrepreneur with whom I have worked believes that the entrepreneur should act very ill at ease and uncomfortable, even if he or she is not.

One of the best credit selling meetings I attended involved a commercial bank officer and an entrepreneur whose company, in bankruptcy proceedings at the time, had just completed its second year of operations with revenues of $75,000. The entrepreneur was a skilled salesperson, and he pulled out all the stops in the empathy game. He pretended he was too hot and asked if he might remove his jacket. It was the south, so jacket removal was acceptable. He put the jacket over the arm of his chair and then tugged at his collar, still looking like a fully dressed man in a steam room. All the while, he was describing his business and its prospects once it obtained financing. In the meantime, he coordinated collar tugs with knocking his jacket down to the floor, picking it up, pushing it down, picking it up, shifting around, folding and unfolding it, and finally letting it fall to the floor and stepping on it. At that point, the lender left his seat and came over to the entrepreneur, obstensibly to see his material more closely.

There's another entrepreneurial style that is fascinating to watch. Let's say our entrepreneur's name is Susan. She is so excited about the prospects for her company that she has to stand up and walk around. The excitement, if you will, causes her to leave her seat. While standing, Susan employs two basic moves: the grip and the stroll. The grip involves holding tightly to the back of a chair for support and reassurance, and the stroll is simply an animated walk around the office of the lender, one hand in a jacket pocket, the other moving furiously to stress various points. Susan stops in midsentence to offer an apology: "I'm sorry but I get so excited sometimes I can't keep my seat." Sound corny? It would be if everyone did it. But many entrepreneurs are so frightened in meetings with lenders that they curl up in a fetal position in a womblike corner of the office, praying silently that the lending community is like Monopoly and this particular office is "Free Parking."

Hands are fascinating to watch. The best entrepreneurs use their hands in syncopation with their voices. Billy Graham slices the air up and down and from side to side. Oral Roberts, while saying, "Let me help you, Let me give you," rolls his hands outward to his audience. Reverend Ike shoots his bejeweled hands skyward. Johnny Carson, who sells shyness, leaves his hands in his pockets and brings them out Jack Benny style to underscore surprise. The list of "hand talkers" is endless, and much can be learned from watching them. For entrepreneurs who are poor speakers, I recommend hiring a speech tutor or coach.

There are dozens of body language signs to watch for in meetings with lenders. If arms and legs are folded or crossed, you're not reaching your target; his or her mind is closed to your proposal. If the arms and legs unfold, the lender is beginning to show interest. A person leaning back with hands behind head, legs spread apart is saying, "Sell me, I'm yours."

It is possible to effect a positive change in body language in the listener by a number of actions on your part. For example, you can push things toward the lender's hands that he or she has to reach for in order to receive and examine them. If the product you manufacture is small enough to bring with you, you can place it in easy reach of the lender. You can push the product off the desk, and he or she will have to get up in order to retrieve it.

If you are an entrepreneurial team, one of you should take out a pencil and write during the meeting. This encourages the listener to take notes also, opening up the hands and arms. Excessive body movement on your part will tend to open up the lender in the same way that the sight of a high jumper makes people raise their legs as the athlete kicks up to the bar. It is instinctive to want to move with someone who is in motion.

Never, but never, use the word *problem* in a meeting with a lender. Never say anything like "Here's our problem," "Our problem is this," or "We have a cash flow problem." Most lenders have problems in their portfolios, and they don't want more of them. If they think you will become a problem, they will turn you down. Always bring lenders solutions, not problems.

Avoid street terms such as *con,* as in "We were conned by a supplier." Avoid inferences to crime, fraud, felony, and dishonesty, and if possible, avoid discussing litigation or government action regarding your business. These topics raise the specter of uncertainty and business interruption or the possible loss of the lender's money and embarrassment to him or her.

I have vivid memories of a lender's face turning from smiles to frowns when an entrepreneur, who was just about to get financed, launched into a crime story replete with an impersonation of a thug. Although it was humorous, it placed the lender in the same category by association and gave the impression that the entrepreneur was stupid enough or hard up to have had that kind of meeting in the first place. The lender wants to deal with Rockefellers, Watsons, and Phippses, but since they do not need money, he wants to deal with people who act like them: proud, self-reliant, honest, competent, and absolutely right.

Finally, the lender or investor wants answers to at least five questions at the meeting:

1. How much can I make?
2. How much can I lose?

3. How do I get my money out?
4. Who else is in the deal?
5. Who says you are any good?

These questions refer to other points covered, including upside potential, areas of risk, future public offering potential, names of suppliers, customers, investors, and lenders who are involved, and the track record of the entrepreneurial team. While speech, dress, posture, and body language are important, these questions are even more so, and they must be dealt with clearly and carefully.

5

DIRECTORY OF VENTURE CAPITAL FUNDS: U.S., U.K., & CANADA; INCLUDING BIOGRAPHIES OF LEADING VENTURE CAPITALISTS

ABBOTT CAPITAL CORP.
9933 Rawler
Suite 125
Skokie, IL 60077
(312) 982-0404

Richard E. Lasser

Average Size of Investment	$100K
Size of Fund	Undisclosed
Investment Criteria	Manufacturing, location important
Portfolio Companies	Undisclosed

ABINGWORTH p.l.c.
26 St. James's Street
London, SW1A1HA, England
01-839-6745

Hon. A. T. S. Montagu
Chairman and Chief Executive Officer

Directorships

Garfunkels Ltd., Restaurants
C & S Exploration, Inc., Oil and gas exploration
Internet, Software for international banking systems

P. F. Dicks
Director

Directorships

Standard Microsystems Corp.
Whiting Petroleum Corp.
CXC Corp.
Sphinx Ltd.
Dellfield Digital Ltd.

David W. Quysner
Director

Directorships

Research Machines Ltd., Microcomputers for education
Charcoal Cloth, Ltd., Advanced filtration materials

Prior Position

Manager, Industrial and Commercial Finance Corp., Ltd.

Education

MA, Selwyn College, Cambridge, 1969

Average Size of Investment	$500K–$1.5M
Size of Fund	$125M
Investment Criteria	High-quality proven management
Portfolio Companies	Acuson, San Francisco, CA, Ultrasound; Bridge Communications, San Francisco, CA, Communications; Convex, Dallas, TX, Supercomputers; Digital Communications, Atlanta, GA, Communications; Microsource, Santa Rosa, CA, YIG oscillators; Standard Microsystems, Long Island, NY, Semiconductors; Whiting Petroleum, Denver, CO, Oil and gas; CXC Corp., Orange Co., CA, PBX manufacturer

ABS VENTURES LIMITED PARTNERSHIPS
135 East Baltimore Street
Baltimore, MD 21202
(301) 727-1700

Bruns H. Grayson
Partner

Directorships

Panoramic, Software applications
Crop Genetics International, N.V., Agricultural biotechnology
International Laser Machines, Industry lasers
Quad Systems Corp., Surface mounting devices
Anadigics, Gallium arsenide
Polygen Corp., Integrated molecular design system

Prior Positions

Associate, Adler & Co.
Consultant, McKinsey & Co.

Education

JD, University of Virginia, 1980
MA, Oxford University, 1976
BA, Harvard College, 1974

Arthur H. Reidel
Partner

Directorships

Aries Technology, Engineering workstations
Audio Visual Laboratories, Presentation graphics systems
Weitek Corporation, Application specific ICs
Multiflow Computer, High performance parallel processing
Polygen Corporation, Integrated molecular design system
Soft-Switch Corporation, Software computer automation

Prior Positions

Vice President, Engineering and Operations, Interactive Training Systems, Inc.
Vice President, Technology, Schlumberger CAS
Director, Software Development, Entrex, Inc.

Education

BS, Massachusetts Institute of Technology, 1973

Edward T. Anderson
Partner

Directorship

Incepts, Inc., Life insurance applications software
Amnet, Inc., Packet switching networks
Percom, Inc., Communications gateways
ADCAD, Computer-aided software

Prior Positions

Director of Business Planning, Phelps Dodge Industries
General Manager, Phelps Dodge Solar Enterprises
Management Consultant, The Michael Allen Co.

Education

MS, Columbia University Graduate School of Business, 1977
BA, University of Denver, 1971

Robert B. Bank
Partner

Directorships

Aetna Shirt Co., Men's and women's apparel manufacturing & retailing
Casey & Osh, Retail sportswear

Prior Positions

Consultant, Hasbro Industries, Hartmax Corp., Land's End, U.S. Shoe Corp., Kirk-Steiff Co.
Principal, Executive Vice President, Joseph A. Bank Clothiers

Education

MA, Johns Hopkins University, 1971
AB, Princeton University, 1969

Robert Walkingshaw
Partner

Directorships

Aetna Shirt Co.
Retail Shirt Manufacturing
Sensormedics Corp.
Medical Instrument

Prior Positions

Principal, Vice President, Morgan Stanley, Inc.
Vice President, Corporate Finance, Salomon Brothers

Education

MBA, Dartmouth's Amos Tuck School of Business Administration, 1976
AB, Economics, Princeton University, 1974

John H. N. Fisher
Associate

Directorships

Software Corporation of America
Decision Support Systems

Prior Positions

Corporate Finance, Alex. Brown & Sons
Account Officer, Bank of America

Education

AB, Harvard University, 1981
The Phillips Exeter Academy, 1977

Average Size of Investment	$1M
Size of Fund	$108M
Investment Criteria	Technology-based, specialty retailing, start-ups; will act as lead investor
Portfolio Companies	57

ACCEL PARTNERS
One Palmer Square
Princeton, NJ 08542
(609) 683-4500

One Embarcadero Center
Suite 2102
San Francisco, CA 94111
(415) 989-5656

2020 Hogback Road
Ann Arbor, MI 48104
(313) 971-4451

Arthur C. Patterson
Managing Partner, San Francisco

Directorships

Xyvision, Inc.
Applied MicroCircuits Corp.
MicroGenics Corp.
Synercom Technology, Inc.
Telesoft
Tolerant Systems
Viasoft
Walker Interactive Products
Zoran Corp.

Prior Positions

General Partner, Adler & Co., 1979–83
Vice President, Citicorp Venture Capital Ltd., 1971–79

Education

MBA, Harvard Business School, 1968
AB, Harvard College, 1966

James R. Swartz
Managing Partner, NJ

Directorships

The DMW Group, Inc., Information system and telecommunications consulting firm
Elcam, Inc.

Fleming Ventures, Private venture capital firm
International TeleManagement Corp., Network management
Managed Care Corp.
Netlink Technology, Inc.
Perceptron, Inc.
Physical Acoustics Corp.
Sports Medicine Systems, Inc.
Ungermann-Bass, Inc., Local area networks
United Jersey Bank, N.A.
WaferScale Integration, Inc.

Prior Positions

General Partner, Adler & Co., 1978–83
Vice President, Citicorp Venture Capital Ltd., 1974–78

Education

MS, Carnegie-Mellon University, 1966
AB, Harvard College, 1964

Dixon R. Doll
Managing Partner, MI

Directorships

Bridge Communications Inc.
Doelz Networks, Inc.
DMW Group, Inc.
International TeleManagement Corp.
NetLink Technology, Inc.
Network Equipment Technologies

Prior Position

Adjunct Faculty Member, IBM Systems Research Institute

Education

MSE and PhD, University of Michigan, 1965, 1969
BSEE, Kansas State University, 1964

Average Size of Investment	$1M
Size of Fund	$100M
Investment Criteria	Will function either as deal originator or investor in deals created by others
Portfolio Companies	Aida Corporation, Santa Clara, CA, High performance CAE workstation; Applied MicroCircuits, San Diego, CA, Gate array ASIC semiconductors; Doelz Networks, Inc., Irvine, CA, Data communications networking; Education Systems Technology Corp., San Diego, CA, Computer based education laboratories; Elcam Inc., Waltham, MA, CIM terminals; Health Data Sciences Corp., San Bernardino, CA, Software/health care; Managed Care Corp., Boston, MA, Health maintenance organization; Microgenics, Concord, CA, Bioengineered immunodiagnostic system; Micro Linear, San Jose, CA, Analog ASIC; NetLink Technology, Inc., Raleigh, NC, SNA network products; Network Equipment Technologies, Menlo Park, CA, Network bypass equipment; Perceptron, Inc., Farmington Hills, MI, Machine vision systems; Phoenix Telecom, Inc., Rochester, NY, OSS systems; Physical Acoustics Corp., Princeton, NJ, Test instrumentation; Sports Medicine Systems, Inc., Wellesley Hills, MA, Sports medicine centers; Synercom Technology, Inc., Sugar Land, TX, Mapping industry software; Telesoft, San Diego, CA, ADA computer products; Tolerant Systems, San Jose, CA, High performance transaction processor; TSB International, Etobiocoke, Ontario, Network information management; Viasoft, Phoenix, AZ, COBOL maintenance tools; WaferScale Integration, Fremont, CA, Standard cell semiconductors; Walker Interactive Products, San Francisco, CA, Mainframe financial software; Xyvision, Inc., Woburn, MA, Computerized typesetting systems; Zoran Corp., Santa Clara, CA, DSP processors

JIM ACKERMAN & ASSOCIATES
1800 North Meridian Street
Suite 610
Indianapolis, IN 46202
(317) 923-2353

James F. Ackerman
President

Directorships

TCA Cable, Inc., Cable television operator
Communication Equities, Inc., Cable television broker
Cardinal Communications, Cable television operator
Midwest Bank Fund

Prior Positions

Executive Director and Partner, Becker Communications Associates, 1973–85
Senior Vice President, A. G. Becker Paribas, 1973–84

DIRECTORY AND BIOGRAPHIES

Education

BS, Purdue University, 1947

Average Size of Investment	$500K
Size of Fund	Undisclosed
Investment Criteria	Cable television
Portfolio Companies	Undisclosed

ACKLEY CAPITAL CORP.
58 North Main Street
Honeoye Falls, NY 14472
(716) 624-2024

Edward J. Ackley
President

Directorships

Consler Corp., Macrofiltration manufacturer
Micron Separations, Inc., Microfiltration membrane manufacturer

Education

MBA, University of Rochester, 1964
BSc, Engineering, University of Rochester, 1953

Bruce W. Marche
J. William Reeves
Ronald P. Hotte
James S. Johnson
John M. Greenwood
Judith D. Harris

Average Size of Investment	$100K
Size of Fund	$1M
Investment Criteria	Prefer role as deal originator but will invest in others; prefer manufacturing-based seed or start-up
Portfolio Companies	Undisclosed

ACORN VENTURES, INC.
2401 Fountainview
Suite 950
Houston, TX 77057
(713) 977-7421

Stuart Schube
President
(713) 977-7401

Directorships

Custom MOS Arrays, Inc., Manufacturers/marketers of semicustom/custom integrated circuits utilizing computer design tools
Digital Pathways, Manufacturers of timing devices for computers, robotic communicators, remote/automatic measurement/control systems, modem security systems
The Software Express, Inc., Specializes in software sector of information processing industry; worldwide distribution of "Appgen" application software
Test Systems Strategies, Inc., Automated test systems for electronic components and assemblies

Prior Positions

Assistant to the President, Telecom Corp.
Vice President, Intermedco, Inc.

Education

MS, Industrial Administration, Purdue University, 1964
Bachelors, Industrial Engineering, Pratt Institute, 1963

Average Size of Investment	$500K–$600K
Size of Fund	$8M
Investment Criteria	Second- or third-stage companies, high-technology oriented
Portfolio Companies	Advanced Clinical Products, VA, Research, development, production, and marketing of new health care products; Advanced Manufacturing Systems, Houston, TX, Factory automation; Custom MOS Arrays, Inc., Milpitas, CA, Manufactures/markets semicustom integrated circuits; The Software Express, Inc., Houston, TX, Specializes in software sector of information processing industry/"appgen" distribution; Test Systems Strategies, Beaverton, OR, Automated test systems for electronic components and assemblies

ACQUIVEST GROUP, INC.
Ten Speen Street
Framingham, MA 01701
(617) 875-3242

S. John Loscocco
President

Directorships

Bio-scale-up, Inc., Bioprocessing
Dietz Art Ltd., Art replicas
Exercycle Corp., Fitness equipment

Prior Positions

Chairman, Cell Products Inc., 1983
Director, Sanitas Service Corp., 1983
Various professional corporate development assignments including Mooney Chemicals, Taracorp Inc., and Media General

Education

MBA, Harvard Business School, 1949
BS, Boston College, 1947

Hans A. Reinecker
Chairman, NY and Germany

Directorships

Hermitage Group, Inc., Art Products
Pittsburgh Environmental Systems, Inc.
E-Tron Corp.
European Trade Development Co.

Prior Positions

President, investment management, Pallas A 6, Dusseldorf
Managing Director, Ecology Patent A 6, Zug and Zurich, Switzerland

Education

Stuttgart City College for Commerce & Trade

Average Size of Investment	$3M
Size of Fund	Undisclosed
Investment Criteria	Leveraged buy-out projects $4M–$40M; provides sponsorship for qualified managers; any field where new or continuing management has relevant experience
Portfolio Companies	Undisclosed

ACTIVEST CAPITAL & RESOURCES CORP.
P.O. Box 76
Cornwall Bridge, CT 06754
(203) 672-6651

Susan Bohlen
William N. Vitalis

Average Size of Investment	$100K
Size of Fund	Undisclosed
Investment Criteria	Leveraged buy-outs are of interest; diversified company preferences
Portfolio Companies	Undisclosed

ADLER & COMPANY
375 Park Avenue
Suite 3303
New York, NY 10152
(212) 759-2800

1245 Oakmead Parkway
Sunnyvale, CA 94086
(408) 720-8700

Frederick R. Adler
Partner, NY

Directorships

International Health Care, Inc.
Biotechnology General, Inc.
Control Automation, Inc.
Daisy Systems Corp.
Data General Corp.
Integrated Measurement Systems, Inc.
Life Technologies
Research Corp. of America
Sci-Tex Corp. Ltd.
Sit Investment Associates
Zoran Corp.
Memorial Sloan-Kettering Cancer Center

DIRECTORY AND BIOGRAPHIES

Prior Position

Editor, *Harvard Law Review*, 1949–51

Education

JD, Harvard Law School, 1951
BA, Brooklyn College, 1948

Joy London
Partner, New York

Directorships

Synercom Technology, Inc. (OTC)
Xyvision, Inc. (OTC)
Polytel Computer Products Corp. (Private)

Prior Positions

Vice President, Alan Patricof Associates, 1979–83
Vice President, Associate Publisher, Human Nature Magazine, Harcourt Brace, 1976–79

Education:

MA, New York University, 1976
AB, Vassar College, 1963

Yuval Binur
Partner, New York

Directorships

Elcam, Inc.
Hypres, Inc.
Comstron Corporation
Yipkon Corp.
Zoran Corp.
Simulog

Prior Position

Vice President, Elron Electronic Industries Ltd., 1976–82

Education

PhD, Tel Aviv University, 1974

Les Strauss
Chief Financial Officer, New York

Directorships

Perceptron Corp.
Tolerant Systems Corp.
Printek, Inc.
Spectrum Digital Corp.

Prior Positions

Chief Financial Officer, Cadmus Computer Systems, 1983–85
Chief Financial Officer, Savin Corp., 1982–83
Chief Financial Officer, AES Data, Ltd., 1980–82
Group Controller, Digital Equipment Corp., 1972–80

Education

MS, Accounting, Bentley College, 1976
MBA, Columbia University, 1967
BS, Chemistry, The Citadel, 1965

Daniel C. O'Neill
Associate, CA

Directorships

XCAT Inc.
IXYS, High-voltage ICs
Applied Micro Circuits Corp.
Health Data Sciences
Micro Linear Corp.
CAECO
Viasoft
Culler Scientific Systems
Panoramic Technologies Inc.

Prior Positions

Director, Anicon, 1983–84
Associate, A. D. Little, 1981–83
Senior Member, Technical Staff, Hughes Aircraft Co., 1980–81

Education

MBA, University of California at Berkeley, 1980
MSEE, University of California at Davis, 1978
BSEE, BS, University of California at Davis, 1976

David J. Blumberg
Venture Manager, New York

Directorship

Myrias Research Corp.

Prior Positions

Alan Patricof Associates, Paris, 1984
Securities Analyst, T. Rowe Price Associates, 1981–83
Analyst, Export-Import Bank, 1980

Education

MBA, Stanford Graduate School of Business, 1985
AB, Harvard College, 1981

Gill Cogan
Venture Manager, New York

Directorship

Inter Basic Resources

Prior Positions

Chairman, Chief Financial Officer, Formtek, 1982–84
Vice President, Fostin Capital, 1980–82

Education

MBA, University of California, Los Angeles, 1977
BA, California State University at Los Angeles, 1975

Gari M. Grimm
Venture Manager

Directorship

Anicon

Prior Positions

President, Second Source Corp., 1984–86
President, Chief Financial Officer, Modular Integration, Inc., 1981–84
Operating Officer, Casey & Pruzan, 1974–83

Education

School of Law, University of Washington, 1970
Post graduate, Harvard University, 1960
BA, University of Colorado, 1956

John R. Hamann
Venture Manager, New York/Sunnyvale

Prior Positions

Manager, Tenant Services Venture, General Electric
Marketing and Engineering Management, General Electric
Design Engineer, General Electric

Education

MSEE, University of Wisconsin, Madison, 1974
BSEE, Michigan State University, 1973

John Weber
Venture Manager, New York

Prior Position

Chief Executive Officer, The Monchik-Weber Corp., 1970–84

Education

BA, Economics, St. Vincent College, 1958

Average Size of Investment	$1.5M–$2M
Size of Fund	$250M
Investment Criteria	Diversified preferences, technology-based companies preferred; start-ups; leveraged buy-outs
Portfolio Companies	Undisclosed

ADVANCED TECHNOLOGY DEVELOPMENT FUND
430 Tenth Street, N.W.
Suite N–114
Atlanta, GA 30318
(404) 875-4393

Daniel D. Ross
General Partner

Directorships

T-Bar, Inc., High-tech supplier of proprietary hardware/software switching and control equipment for computer and data communications users
Syntellect, Inc.

HealthServ Corp.
IMX, Inc.
LanTel Corp.
Omni Eye Services
Redi-Med, Inc.

Prior Positions

Vice President and Chief Operating Officer, Timex Computer Corp.
Executive Vice President, Memorex Finance Co.

Education

BS, Math and Computer Science, Louisiana Institute of Technology

Ronald W. White
General Partner

Directorships

AmeriCom Corp.
Computest, Inc.
Comsell, Inc.
Digital Transmission Systems
GMD Systems
Learning Resources, Inc.

Prior Positions

Managing Director, Investors Equity, Inc.
President, Alarmco, Inc.

Education

MBA, Harvard, 1967
BES, Brigham Young University, 1965

Average Size of Investment	$458K
Size of Fund	$11.2M
Investment Criteria	The primary concentration of the partnership's investment opportunity analysis is on four areas: management, markets, product, and financial return
Portfolio Companies	Americom Corporation, Norcross, GA, Provides integrated mobile communications network for the specialized mobile radio (SMR) market; Broadway & Seymour, Inc., Charlotte, NC, Provides professional consulting service and turn-key mainframe packages to the banking industry; Choice Computer Corporation, Marietta, GA, Supplies turn-key hardware and software systems for the retail merchandiser, linking the cash register, computer and other peripherals to provide a total information system; COIN Financial Systems, Inc., Norcross, GA, Turnkey hardware/software systems to facilitate sales of automobiles and related finance and insurance packages by automotive dealerships; Computest, Inc., Titusville, FL, Provides automatic test equipment for in-circuit assemblies; Comsell, Inc., Atlanta, GA, Interactive video disk systems for training, catalog and sales applications; Digital Transmission Systems, Inc., Norcross, GA, Develops high-data-rate, all-digital modems for satellite and terrestrial microwave communications; GMD Systems International, Inc., Atlanta, GA, Supplies software products in support of IBM's Manufacturing, Accounting and Production Information Control System; Healthserv Corporation, Atlanta, GA, Provides electronic claims processing, cash management, accounts receivable and practice management service to the healthcare industry; Integrated Computer Graphics, Inc., Atlanta, GA, Provides CAD/CAM systems that apply graphics and data management to wood-frame construction applications; Interactive Financial Services, Inc., Marietta, GA, Provides hardware and software for the financial planning and investment banking community; International Medical Exchange, Inc., Louisville, KY, Provides marketing, financial, and information management service to the healthcare industry; Lantel Corporation, Norcross, GA, Produces two-way voice/data modems for the local area network marketplace; Learning Resources, Inc., Raleigh, NC, Provides an "information utility" for the college admissions market and interactive video systems/productions for training and point-of-sale; Natural MicroSystems Corp., Natick, MA, Uses signal processing technology to implement integrated voice and data telephone management systems; Omni Eye Services, Atlanta, GA, Provides ophthalmic services and performs specialized cataract and retinal surgery; Redi-Med, Inc., Social Circle, GA, Repackages prescription drugs and sells directly to doctors who dispense directly to their patients; Syntellect, Inc., Phoenix, AZ, Provides robotic telephone operations designed to replace CRT operators performing telephone data entry or inquiry functions

ADVANCED TECHNOLOGY VENTURES
Ten Post Office Square
Suite 1230
Boston, MA 02109
(617) 423-4050

1000 El Camino Real
Suite 210
Menlo Park, CA 94025-4327
(415) 321-8601

Ralph J. Nunziato
Managing Partner, Menlo Park

Directorships

Quidel, Biotechnology
Vestar Research, Inc., Biotechnology

Prior Positions

President, Rodenstock Instrument Co., 1978–82
President, Optics Technology, Inc., 1972–77
Vice President, Emerson Electric, 1967–70
Associate, Lawrence S. & David Rockefeller, 1960–65

Education

United States Air Force, Pilot Training Program, 1944
Bachelor of Aeronautical Engineering, Daniel Guggenheim School of Aeronautics, New York University, 1942

Albert E. Paladino
General Partner, Boston

Directorships

Advanced Energy Dynamics, Coal cleaning and refining
Theta-J Corp., Optically coupled interface devices
Laser Science, Inc., Advanced molecular gas lasers
MilliTech Corp., Millimeter wave components and systems
Mosaic Systems, Inc., Wafer scale integrated circuits

Prior Positions

Deputy Director, Office of Energy Programs, U.S. Dept. of Commerce, NBS
Assistant Director, Telephone Operations Technology Center, GTE Laboratories, Inc.
Program Manager, Materials, U.S. Congress, Office of Technology Assessment
Manager, Electronic Materials Group, Raytheon Co., Microwave Power Tube Division

Education

PhD, Massachusetts Institute of Technology, 1962
BS, MS, Alfred University, 1954, 1956

Ivan E. Sutherland
Robert G. Loewy
General Partner
Rensselaer Polytechnic Institute
J.E.C. 4010
Troy, NY 12181
(518) 266-6594

Directorship

Mohasco Corp., Home furnishings

Prior Positions

Dean of Engineering, University of Rochester, 1967–74
Chief Scientist, United States Air Force, 1965–66

Education

PhD, University of Pennsylvania, 1962
MS, Massachusetts Institute of Technology, 1948
BAE, Rensselaer Polytechnic Institute, 1947

William R. Sutherland
Robert F. Sproull
Special Limited Partner
4419 Schenley Farms Terrace
Pittsburgh, PA 15213
(412) 687-2855

Prior Positions

Associate Professor, Carnegie-Mellon University, 1980–84
Member Research Staff, Xerox Corp., 1973–77

Education

PhD, Stanford University, 1977
AB, Harvard College, 1969

Jos C. Henkens
General Partner, Menlo Park

Directorship

Semiconductor Test Solutions, Inc., ATE

Prior Position

Product Marketing Manager, Spectra-Physics, Inc.

DIRECTORY AND BIOGRAPHIES

Education

MS, EES, Stanford University, 1979
MBA, Stanford University, 1979
MS, Physics, University Leyden (Netherlands), 1977

Robert C. Ammerman
General Partner, Boston

Directorships

Millitech Corp., Millimeter wave devices
Ideaware, Inc., Microcomputer software

Prior Positions

Vice President, BT Capital Corp., SBIC
Vice President, Bankers Trust Co.

Education

MSIA, Carnegie-Mellon University
BS, Mathematics, Carnegie-Mellon University
BA, History, Carnegie-Mellon University

Average Size of Investment	$500K
Size of Fund	$73M
Investment Criteria	Early-stage ventures with a high degree of proprietary technology
Portfolio Companies	Advanced Energy Dynamics, Natick, MA, Dry coal-cleaning systems; Tartan Laboratories, Pittsburgh, PA, Software compilers; Valid Logic Systems, Mountain View, CA, Computer-aided engineering; Vestar Research, Pasadena, CA, Microencapsulation technology; VLSI Technology, San Jose, CA, Design and manufacture of custom software chips

ADVENT CAPITAL COMPANIES
45 Milk Street
Boston, MA 02109
(617) 574-6719

David D. Croll
Richard H. Churchill, Jr.
Stephen F. Gormley
William P. Collatos
James F. Wade

Average Size of Investment	$6M
Size of Fund	$100M+
Investment Criteria	Leveraged buy-outs are of interest, especially in media
Portfolio Companies	Undisclosed

ADVENT LTD.
25 Buckingham Gate
London, SWIE 6LD
England
01-630-9811

David J. S. Cooksey
Managing Director

Directorships

Advent International Corp., Venture fund management
Agricultural Genetics Co., Ltd.
Electra Management PLC, Fund management
Macro 4 P.L.C., Systems software
Xenotron Holdings PLC, Comp. hard/software
European Silicon Structures S.A.

Education

MA, Oxford University, 1963

John A. S. Nash
Director

Directorships

Advance Power Supplies Ltd.
Advance Bryans Ltd.
Biomedical Sensors Ltd.
Borland International Inc.
Computer Recognition Systems Ltd.
Computer Security Ltd.
National Telephones Ltd.

Prior Positions

Corporate Finance Assistance Director, Lazard Brothers & Co., Ltd.

Education

MA, Corpus Christi, Oxford, 1971
Barrister–at–Law, 1972

Colin M. Amies
Director

Directorships

Seima Consultants Ltd., Consultancy
Pearce Technology Ltd., Videotex and software systems
Computer Security Ltd.

Prior Positions

Corporate Finance Director, Midland Bank plc, 1980–85
Managing Director, Exacta Circuits Ltd., 1968–77

Education

MA (honors), Christs College, Cambridge, 1962

Average Size of Investment	£ 350,000
Size of Fund	£ 68 million
Investment Criteria	High-technology companies with proprietary products
Portfolio Companies	Over 50 investments made

AEA INVESTORS, INC.
640 Fifth Avenue
New York, NY 10020
(212) 757-0333

C. Stephen Clegg
Paul N. Leitner
MacDonell Roehm, Jr.
David M. Thomas

Average Size of Investment	$20M–100M
Size of Fund	Undisclosed
Investment Criteria	Interested in leveraged buy-outs; will act as lead investor
Portfolio Companies	Undisclosed

ALBRIGHT VENTURE CAPITAL CORP.
8005 Rappahannock Avenue
Jessup, MD 20794
(301) 799-7935

William A. Albright
President

Average Size of Investment	$70K
Size of Fund	Undisclosed
Investment Criteria	Interested in diversified company preferences; construction and manufacturing included; MESBIC; Eastern U.S.
Portfolio Companies	Undisclosed

ALIMANSKY VENTURE GROUP INC.
605 Madison Avenue, Suite 300
New York, NY 10022-1901
(212) 832-7300

Burt Alimansky
Executive Managing Director

Directorships

VOIS Inc.
Women's Travel Connections Inc.
Auretina Patent Management Co. Inc.
New York Venture Group

Prior Positions

Dow Jones & Co. Inc.
Doyle Dane Bernbach Inc.

Education

MBA, Harvard University, 1977
MA, Claremont Graduate School, 1966
BA, Dartmouth College, 1964

Philip N. Sussman
Managing Director

DIRECTORY AND BIOGRAPHIES

Directorships

The Planning Forum Inc.
New York Venture Group

Prior Positions

International Paper Co.
Equitable Life Assurance Society of the U.S.
M.I.T. Energy Laboratory
National Bureau of Economic Research

Education

MBA, M.I.T., 1974
BS, SUNY Stony Brook, 1972

Average Size of Investment	$1M+
Size of Fund	Undisclosed
Investment Criteria	Start up, first stage, second stage, third stage, buy-out or acquisition financing; must have background of the business, description of its products and services, resumes of the principals, and whatever data are available; communications, computer related, consumer, distribution, electronic components and instrumentation, genetic engineering, industrial products and equipment, medical/health related, and others such as agriculture, forestry, fishing, finance and insurance, specialty retailing, and transportation
Portfolio Companies	Vois Inc., New York, NY, Speech recognition technology; Peoples Telephone Co., Miami, FL, Private telephone network; Knowledge Products Inc., Nashville, TN, Audio publishing; Retail Opportunities Inc., New York, NY, Specialty retailing; Anasco Inc., Danvers, MA, Electronic components distribution; C Tek Software Inc., New York, NY, Financial services software

ALLIANCE BUSINESS INVESTMENT CO.

One Shell Plaza
Suite 3990
Houston, TX 77002
(713) 224-8224

One Williams Center
Suite 2000
Tulsa, OK 74172
(918) 584-3581

Leon Davis
Chairman of the Board, Houston

Directorships

Verna, Drilling company
Specific Equipment Company, Oil supply

Education

BA, Economics, University of Oklahoma, 1940

Barry M. Davis
President, Tulsa

Directorships

Energy Minerals, Inc.
First Development Corp.
Titan Rig Corp.

Education

BBA, Corporate Finance

Average Size of Investment	$1M
Size of Fund	Undisclosed
Investment Criteria	Will act as lead investor in diversified companies, oil development companies preferred; geographic proximity important
Portfolio Companies	Undisclosed

ALLIANCE ENTERPRISE CORP.

1801 Market Street
Third Floor
Philadelphia, PA 19103
(215) 977-3714

William B. Priestley
Terrence Hicks

Average Size of Investment	$150K
Size of Fund	$6M
Investment Criteria	Varies
Portfolio Companies	Undisclosed

ALLIED BANCSHARES CAPITAL CORP.
1000 Louisiana
P.O. Box 3326
Houston, TX 77253
(713) 226-1625

Philip A. Tuttle
President

Directorships

Allco Chemical, Specialty chemical
Corporate Valuations, Inc.
Pancretec, Inc., Ambulatory infusion pumps
OMNA Corp., Health-care services
Pasar, Inc., Electrical testing units
Chardonnol, Inc.

Prior Positions

Chairman of Executive Committee, OMNA Corp., 1972–present
Vice President, Flint Capital Corp., 1971–74
Vice President, Cardio-Pulmonary Instruments Corp., 1970–71
President, Ventilation Associates, Inc.

Education

MBA, Northwestern University, 1965
BA, Rice University, 1963

Mary D. Bass
Investment Officer
(713) 221-4875

Directorship

MIT Enterprise Forum of Texas

Prior Positions

Internal Auditor, Mississippi Chemical Corp., 1981–83
Assistant Agent, State Farm Insurance, 1979–81

Education

MBA, Mississippi State University, 1979
BS, Mississippi State University, 1978

Average Size of Investment	$700K
Size of Fund	$20M
Investment Criteria	Undisclosed
Portfolio Companies	Undisclosed

ALLIED CAPITAL CORP.
1625 I Street
Suite 603
Washington, DC 20006
(202) 331-1112

George C. Williams
Chairman of the Board

Directorships

Pandick, Inc., Financial printing
Riggs National Bank

Prior Positions

President, Allied Capital Corp., 1964–84
Special Agent, Federal Bureau of Investigation, 1950–53

Education

BS, Commerce, University of Virginia, 1950

David Gladstone
President

Prior Positions

Management Consultant, Price Waterhouse & Co., 1972–74
Internal Consultant, IT&T (Europe)

Education

MBA, Finance and Marketing, Harvard Business School, 1972
MA, Computer Science and Government, American University, 1969
BA, Government and Economics, University of Virginia, 1967

Brooks H. Browne
Senior Vice President

Prior Positions

Managing Director, Overseas Private Investment Corp., 1976–84
Commercial Loan Officer, Citibank, N.A., 1972–74

DIRECTORY AND BIOGRAPHIES

Education

MBA, International Business, Harvard Business School, 1976
BA, Political Science, Williams College, 1972

Jonathan J. Ledecky
Vice President

Prior Positions

Deferred Admit Assoc., Kidder Peabody & Co., Inc., 1979–81
Account Executive, Barmmer Elliott Public Relations
Summer Associate, Morgan Stanley & Co.

Education

MBA, Harvard Business School, 1983
BA, Government, Harvard College, 1979

Average Size of Investment	Up to $1M
Size of Fund	$117M
Investment Criteria	Will consider either loans or investments; diversified industry preference; second or third stage preferred
Portfolio Companies	AmQuest Corp., Texas, Gas exploration; Atlantic Research Corp., Alexandria, VA, Propulsion and telecommunications; CAMAC Corp., Virginia, Solution dyed fiber; Central Florida Utilities, Inc., Florida, Utility company; Computer Terminal Systems, Hauppauge, NY, Manufacturing terminals; Consumer Health Services, Inc., Medical/dental consumer info service; Cruiseship Information Systems, Florida, Data base services; Dixie Yeast Corp., North Carolina, Manufacturing yeast; DMI Furniture, Inc., Kentucky, Furniture manufacturing; Educational Direction, Inc., New York, Educational films; Financial News Network, Inc., California, National network; Florida Crafts, Inc., Florida, Craft stores; International Signal & Control Group PLC, Lancaster, PA, Manufacturing components; Interstate Communications, Inc., Maryland, Radio station; Ionia Corp., Washington, D.C., Real estate; Robert F. Koch, Maryland, Real estate; Marline Oil Corp., New York, Oil exploration; Meadowbrook Utility Systems, Inc., Florida; Miller Shoe Industries, Inc., Ohio, Orthopedic shoes; Nav-Tec Industries, Inc., New York, Reactor manufacturing; ND Resources, Inc., Arizona, Energy exploration; Nexus Communications, Inc., North Carolina, Radio station; Northeast Broadcasting Co., Inc., Massachusetts, Radio station; Pandick, Inc., New York, NY, Financial printer; Pinewood Mills Joint Venture, Virginia, Real estate development; Primedical, Inc., Maryland, Medical service; Howard Sanders, Communications Corp., Washington, DC, Radio station; Smith Laboratories, Northbrook, IL, Pharmaceutical manufacturing; Southern Broadcasting, Florida, Television station; Southern Systems, Inc., Florida, Manufacturing computer printer; SPA Lady Corp., Virginia, Women's health spa; E. J. Stewart, Inc., Pennsylvania, Video productions; Storall Place, Virginia, Real estate development; Summit Oilfield Services, Texas, Oil servicing; TGIF Texas, Texas, Restaurants; Unison Industries, Illinois, Magnetos; Yellow Book Corp., New York, Telephone directories

R. W. ALLSOP & ASSOCIATES
2750 First Avenue, N.E.
Suite 210
Cedar Rapids, IA 52402
(319) 363-8971

815 East Mason Street
Suite 1501
Milwaukee, WI 53202
(414) 271-6510

35 Corporate Woods
Suite 244
9101 West 110th Street
Overland Park, KS 66210
(913) 451-3719

111 West Port Plaza
Suite 600
St. Louis, MO 63146
(314) 434-1688

Robert W. Allsop
General Partner, IA

Directorships

Gray & Company, Processor of maraschino cherries, glace fruit and filberts
Met-Coil Systems Corporation, Manufacturer of sheet metal processing equipment
Crane Electronics, Inc., Manufacturer of electronic connectors
Phoenix Venture Acquisitions, Inc., Holding company for LBO opportunities

Prior Positions

President, MorAmerica Capital Corporation

Education

University of Illinois, 1950

Gregory B. Bultman
General Partner, WI

Directorships

ATM Network Management Corporation, Computerized transaction switching service for ATM's
Disc Technology Corporation, Develops and produces disc media
Servlite, Inc., Develop and operate franchised restaurants
Wrought Washer Manufacturing, Inc., Manufactures washers and stampings

Prior Position

Vice President, MorAmerica Capital Corp.

Education

BBA, University of Wisconsin, 1970

Robert L. Kuk
General Partner, MO

Directorships

CR Technology, Machine vision systems
ProfitKey International, Inc., Management information systems
Quintron Corp., Telecommunication equipment
ProNet, Inc., Digital paging, telephone answering services to medical field

Prior Position

Vice President, MorAmerica Capital Corp., 1974–80

Education

MBA, Northern Illinois University, 1974
BA, University of North Dakota, 1965

Larry C. Maddox
General Partner, KS

Directorships

Graphic Technology, Design and manufacture labels and custom label materials
Smith & Loveless, Inc., Manufacturer of water and waste transfer and treatment equipment
Titan Rig Corporation, Holding company for acquisition candidates
Ceramic Research, Inc., Research on ceramic material
Softyme, Inc., Provides electronic distribution and support of software

Prior Positions

Vice President, MorAmerica Capital Corporation

Education

MBA, University of Iowa, 1969
BS, Texas Tech, 1964

Paul D. Rhines
General Partner, IA

Directorships

The Indiana Railroad Co., Operates short-line railroad
Teleconnect Co., Communications systems and services, long distance telephone service
ALC Communications Corp., Long-distance telephone service
Direct Sales Tire Co., Retailer of tires, gasoline, and related accessories
Sate-Lite Holdings, Inc., Designs and manufactures reflector kits

Prior Position

Executive Vice President, MorAmerica Capital Corp.

Education

BA, Accounting, University of Northern Iowa, 1965

James D. Thorp

Average Size of Investment	$700K
Size of Fund	$45M
Investment Criteria	Industry preferences are communications, computer-related technology, industrial products, automation, medical/health care; no geographical preference
Portfolio Companies	Undisclosed

ALLSTATE INSURANCE CO.
Allstate Plaza
Suite E2
Northbrook, IL 60062
(312) 291-5335

Leonard A. Batterson

Directorships

Atlantic American Cablevision
Contemporary Communications
Synthetic Blood Corp.
Advisor, Montgomery Medical Ventures

DIRECTORY AND BIOGRAPHIES

Prior Positions

President, Chief Executive Officer, Director, Lamb Enterprises
Executive Vice President, Barry-Wehmiller Electronics
Assistant Treasurer, General Steel Industries

Education

JD, Washington University Law School
MBA, Harvard University
BA, Washington University

Oliver M. Darden
Donald R. Johnson
Robert L. Lestina
Sharri E. Marcin
Paul J. Renze
Marc S. Sandroff
Marcy H. Shockey

Average Size of Investment	$1M
Size of Fund	$200M
Investment Criteria	Interested in technology-based, manufacturing, specialty retail, and communication companies; start-ups; will act as lead investor
Portfolio Companies	Undisclosed

ALPHA CAPITAL VENTURE PARTNERS
Three First National Plaza
Suite 1400
Chicago, IL 60602
(312) 372-1556

Andrew H. Kalnow
Managing Partner

Directorships

Citizens Financial Corp., Data processing
Calg Corp., Investments
National Machinery Co., Machinery producer
Commercial National Bank, Commercial banking

Prior Positions

Vice President, Calg Corp.
Vice President, First Chicago

Education

MBA, Babson College, 1977
BA, Lawrence University, 1974

Daniel W. O'Connell
Managing Partner

Directorships

R. W. Allsop & Associates, Venture capital
Target Corp., Manufacturing

Prior Position

Vice President, First Chicago Investment Advisors

Education

MS, DePaul University, 1983
MBA, Harvard Business School, 1974
BS, University of Illinois, 1968

Average Size of Investment	$350K
Size of Fund	Undisclosed
Investment Criteria	Diversified by industry and stage of company development
Portfolio Companies	Undisclosed

ALPHA PARTNERS
2200 Sand Hill Road
Suite 250
Menlo Park, CA 94025
(415) 854-7024

Wallace F. Davis
General Partner

Prior Positions

General Partner, Mayfield Funds I, II, III, 1969–82
Vice President, Research and Development, Itek Corp., 1963–68
President, Vidya, Inc., 1958–63
Research Engineer, Engineering Manager, National Advisory Committee for Aeronautics, 1941–58

Education

MS, BA, Stanford University, 1939

Brian J. Grossi
General Partner

Prior Positions

Research engineer, Project Leader, SRI International, 1976–82
Design and Development Engineer, Hewlett-Packard Labs, 1973–76

Education

MS, BS, Stanford University, 1973

Glenn E. Penisten
General Partner

Prior Positions

Executive Vice President, Chairman, Electronics Components Business Section, Gould, Inc., 1982–83
Chairman, American Electronics Association, 1982
Chairman, Chief Executive Officer, President, American Microsystems Inc., 1976–84
Chief Executive Officer, Datran, 1972–76
Corporate Vice President, Texas Instruments, 1956–72
Bell Labs, 1955–56

Education

BS, Oklahoma State University, 1953

Samuel Urcis
General Partner

Prior Positions

President, Dover Capital Corp., 1979
Senior Vice President, Operations, Geosource, Inc., 1972–79
Director, Earth Resources Operations, Rockwell International, 1968–72
Assistant Laboratory Manager, Hughes Aircraft Co., 1964–68
Director of Engineering, Aerolab Development Co., 1959–64
Project and Design Engineer, Sundberg-Serrill Corp., 1955–59

Education

BS, University of California, Los Angeles, 1955

A. Larry Tannenbaum
Business Manager

Prior Positions

Manager, Corporate Planning, Tandem Computers, 1985
Manager, Corporate and Financial Planning, Senior Financial Analyst, Gould AMI, 1981–83
Financial Analyst, Intel Corp., 1979–81

Education

MBA, University of Utah, 1979

Average Size of Investment	Undisclosed
Size of Fund	$40M
Investment Criteria	Seed financing; willing to start with innovative idea for high technology products, if idea has ingredients to support launching of a new company
Portfolio Companies	Vitaphore, Materials technology for control of infection; Tokos Medical Corp., Home health care devices and services; High Yield Technology, Particulate monitoring for process control; Cochlea, Inspection by acoustics; Ikos Systems, Inc., ASIC functional verification workstation; Pindar Development Corp., Large screen color projector for video and digital communication; Enhansys, Software tools and support for manufacturing productivity; Analog Design Tools, Computer aided engineering; Quintus Computer Systems, Prolog language implementation in artificial intelligence; Star Microwave, High power traveling wave tubes; Inova Microelectronics, Wafer scale integration; Altera Corp., User programmable logic devices

ALTA-CAN TELECOM INC.
26th Floor, 411 - 1 Street S.E.
Calgary, Alberta T2G 4Y5
Canada
(403) 231-8535

Archibald A. Mackinnon
President, Chief Executive Officer

Directorships

President, Association of Canadian Venture Capital Companies (ACVCC)

Prior Positions

Vice President, CDC Ventures, Inc.

Education

BS, Electrical Engineering, University of British Columbia, 1960
MBA, York University, 1969

Norman W. Clark
Vice President

Prior Positions

Principal, Touche Ross & Partners, Management Consultants, 1980–85

Education

Master's, Computer Science, University of Calgary, 1971
Certified Management Accountant, 1982
Certified Management Consultant, 1983

David F. Campbell
Director of Finance

Prior Positions

Controller, Oil & Gas Division, Bralorne Resources Ltd.

Education

MBA, Queen's University, 1974
Chartered Accountant, 1977

Terrance L. Umbach
Director of Technology

Prior Positions

Manager, Planning and Special Projects, NOVA, An Alberta Corp.
Technical and marketing positions, IBM Canada

Education

BM, Computer Science, University of Waterloo, 1968

Average Size of Investment	$1.05M
Size of Fund	$10M
Investment Criteria	High technology telecommunications and information processing
Portfolio Companies	Cybernex Limited, Ottawa, Ontario, Designs, manufactures, and markets video display terminals; Idacom Electronics Ltd., Edmonton, Alberta, Manufactures and markets test equipment for digitized data networks; Innovage Microsystems Inc., Calgary, Alberta, Manufactures and markets testing device for microprocessor-based products; Telematic Products, Inc., Redmond, WA, Designs, manufactures and markets teleprocessing products

AMERICAN RESEARCH & DEVELOPMENT, INC.
45 Milk Street
Boston, MA 02109
(617) 423-7500

Charles J. Coulter
President

Directorships

Adage
Fusion
Scan-Tron
Xylogics

Prior Positions

Contracts Manager, Laboratory for Electronics
Sales Manager, Honeywell Datamatic
Director, Honeywell Computers, Europe
Vice President, Boston Capital

Education

Harvard Business School
Harvard College

R. Courtney Whitin
Senior Vice President

Directorships

ImagiTex
Summagraphics
Logos

Prior Positions

Financial Management, Booz, Allen & Hamilton
Vice President and Treasurer, Boston Capital
Founding President, Urban National

Education

Harvard Business School
Williams College

A. Wade Blackman
Vice President

Directorships

ANA Tech
Autoclave

Prior Positions

Chief Executive Officer, Binational Industrial R & D Foundation
Manager, New Ventures Analysis, Stone and Webster

Education

Graduate degrees, Engineering and Management, Massachusetts Institute of Technology
Sloan Fellow, Massachusetts Institute of Technology

Francis J. Hughes, Jr.
Vice President

Directorships

Commterm
Lan-Tel
Raycom

Prior Positions

Designer, RCA's Astro-Electronics Division
Consultant, Boston Consulting Group

Education

MBA, Harvard Business School
SB, MS, Electrical Engineering, Massachusetts Institute of Technology

George W. McKinney III
Vice President

Directorships

Karyon
Ceramics Process Systems
Tipnis
Validec

Prior Positions

Manufacturing, Engineering, Finance, and Corporate Management, Corning Glass
Director of Business Development and Corporate Planning, Corning Glass
Founder and Chief Executive Officer, Corning Designs

Education

PhD, Stanford University
SB, Massachusetts Institute of Technology

Luc Beaubien
Assistant Vice President

Directorships

Cadre Technologies, Inc.
data recording systems, inc.

Prior Position

Senior Engineer, Bell Canada

Education

SM, Management Science, Massachusetts Institute of Technology
BSEE, McGill University

Average Size of Investment	$500K
Size of Fund	$60M under management
Investment Criteria	Technology oriented companies in the Northeast; LBO's, seed, startups, etc.
Portfolio Companies	Adage, Inc., Billerica, MA, Interactive computer graphics workstations and systems for CAD/CAM and image processing applications; Adra Systems, Inc., Lowell, MA, Low-cost, high-performance interactive CAD/CAM systems; ANA Tech Corp., Littleton, CO, Design and manufacture of proprietary systems that convert existing graphic materials into an electronic format; Autoclave Engineers, Inc., Erie, PA, Design and manufacture of components and systems for high-pressure and high-temperature technology; AVL, Tinton Falls, NJ, Self-contained desk-top computer graphics presentation systems; Cadre Technologies, Inc., Providence, RI, Software development tools that integrate computer-aided design, interactive graphics and software system development methodologies; Canadian Enterprise Development Corp. Ltd., Toronto, Canada, Venture capital; Ceramics Process Systems Corp., Lexington, MA, Design of controlled integrated processing systems for high-performance ceramics; Commterm, Inc., Billerica, MA, Digitized voice messaging systems for corporate environments, original equipment manufacturers and service provider networks; Computer Controls Corp., Wilmington, MA, Design, manufacture, installation, and servicing of sophisticated environmental control systems; Computer Identics Corp., Canton, MA, Bar code scanning equipment; data recording systems, inc., Melville, NY, High-resolution plain

paper laser printer for original equipment manufacturers in the printing, publishing, engineering and medical markets; Dorman Bogdonoff Corp., Andover, MA, Design and manufacture of flat panel keyboards and touchscreens for the instrumentation, computer, and business equipment markets; Envoy Systems Corp., Waltham, MA, Portable information systems for increasing the sale productivity of field sales organizations; Fusion Systems Corp., Rockville, MD, Systems built around patented microwave lamps for the instantaneous curing of ultraviolet inks and coatings; ImagiTex, Inc., Nashua, NH, Microprocessor-based scanners and interactive image workstations; Karyon Technology, Inc., Norwood, MA, Innovating cell technology with a proprietary gel entrapment process for biomedical and industrial markets; Lan-Tel, Inc., Orleans, MA, Modular voice/data digital key telephone systems and private branch exchanges incorporating local area networks; Logos Corp., Waltham, MA, Sophisticated software for the computer-aided translation of natural language; Aquidneck Energy Limited Partnership, Oxford, MA, Co-generation power based on fluidized bed technology; Maze Technology Corp., Lawrence, MA, Full-custom, CMOS, microelectronic integrated circuits; SmartNames, Inc., Waltham, MA, System to enhance selectivity of mailing lists used by direct marketers; Tegra, Inc., Billerica, MA, Electronic printing and imaging systems for the graphic arts industry; Navigation Sciences, Inc., Bethesda, MD, Design and manufacture of a computerized navigation system with full-color electronic charts; Prentice Corp., Sunnyvale, CA, Modem and statistical multiplexer equipment for data communications networks; Raycom Systems, Inc., Boulder, CO, Fiber-optic transceivers and hubs for local area networks; RF Monolithics, Inc., Dallas, TX, Surface acoustic wave filters and resonators used in cable TV converters, satellite TV receivers, wireless security and garage door transmitters, radar synthesizers, and cellular mobile telephones; Scan-Tron Corp., Rancho Dominguez, CA, Optical mark reading equipment and specialized form for testing and computer data entry; Summagraphics Corp., Fairfield, CT, Data tablets, digitizers, and computer-aided design and drafting systems; Symbolics, Inc., Cambridge, MA, and Chatsworth, CA, Development and manufacture of symbolic computing systems; Tipnis, Inc., Cincinnati, OH, Software systems for manufacturing preproduction; blueprint to part production within 24 hours; Validec Inc., San Carlos, CA, Point-of-origin remote communication systems for table service restaurants; Visual Technology, Inc., Tewksbury, MA, Microprocessor-based alphanumeric and graphics video display terminals, intelligent workstations, personal computers, and multiuser systems; Xylogics, Inc., Burlington, MA, High-performance, intelligent peripheral controllers for leading mini- and microcomputer systems

AMERICAP CORPORATION/AMERIWAY VENTURE PARTNERS I
7575 San Felipe
Houston, TX 77063
(713) 780-8084

Ben B. Andrews
Vice President

Directorships

Mini Base Systems, Microprocessor applications in metering and measuring

Prior Position

Partner, Ash Exploration, 1980–84

Education

BBA, University of Texas, 1976

James L. Hurn
President

Directorships

Prentice Colour, Inc., Color separations processor
Boyce Engineering Intl. Inc., Turbine monitoring systems
Positron Corp., Medical research/diagnostic imaging

Prior Positions

Investment Analyst, Bowlane Capital Corp., 1981–82
Senior Account Officer, Citicorp, 1979–81
Assistant Secretary, Manufacturers Hanover Trust Co., 1976–79

Education

JD, University of Houston, 1976
MA, Human Relations, University of Oklahoma, 1974
BA, English, University of Texas at Austin, 1970

Average Size of Investment	$200K
Size of Fund	$5M
Investment Criteria	Undisclosed
Portfolio Companies	Undisclosed

AMEV CAPITAL CORPORATION/AMEV VENTURE ASSOCIATES
One World Trade Center
Suite 5001
New York, NY 10048-0024
(212) 775-9100

Martin S. Orland
President

Prior Positions

Executive Vice President, Treasurer, Director, The Franklin Corp., 1965–79
CPA, Arthur Young & Co., 1959–65

Education

BS, Accountancy, Long Island University, 1959
AAS, Retailing, State University of New York, 1952

Emmett P. Bonner III
Vice President

Prior Positions

Ventures Management Company, 1984–86
Chief Operating Officer, Acquisition Funding Corporation, 1981–84
Assistant Vice President, Citicorp Industrial Credit, Inc., 1976–81

Education

MBA, Finance, The American University, 1976
BA, Villanova University, 1968

Bruce Bromberg
Assistant Vice President

Prior Positions

Assistant Vice President, Laidlaw Adams & Peck, Inc., 1983–85
Associate, W. H. Newbolds' Sons & Co., Inc., 1982–83

Education

MBA, The Wharton School, 1983
BS, Economics, The Wharton School, University of Pennsylvania, 1982

Average Size of Investment	$750K
Size of Fund	Undisclosed
Investment Criteria	Expansion financings, leveraged buy-outs in diversified industries; will act as lead investor
Portfolio Companies	Undisclosed

AMOCO VENTURE CAPITAL CO.
200 East Randolph
Chicago, IL 60601
(312) 856-6523

Gordon E. Stone

Average Size of Investment	$250K
Size of Fund	Undisclosed
Investment Criteria	Diversified company preferences, either technology oriented or able to supply goods or services to Amoco Corp.; must be owned by a racial minority
Portfolio Companies	Undisclosed

AMPERSAND MANAGEMENT CO.
265 Franklin Street, #1501
Boston, MA 02110
(617) 439-8300

Richard A. Charpie
William C. Mill, III

Average Size of Investment	$500K
Size of Fund	Undisclosed
Investment Criteria	Technology-based companies
Portfolio Companies	Undisclosed

ANALOG DEVICES ENTERPRISES
Two Technology Way
P.O. Box 280
Norwood, MA 02062
(617) 329-4700

Lawrence T. Sullivan
Senior Vice President, Corporate Development, General Manager

Directorships

Memory Devices Ltd., Synchrodigital products
International Imaging Systems, Image processors
Numerix Corp., Array processors
Quantitative Technology Co., Signal processing software
Bipolar Integrated Technology, High-speed integrated circuits
Jupiter Systems, Inc., Graphic terminals

Prior Positions

Senior Vice President, Corporate Development and Finance, Analog Devices, Inc., 1976–80
Vice President/General Manager, Modular Instrument Division, Analog Devices, Inc., 1973–76
Vice President/Marketing, Analog Devices, Inc., 1971–72

Education

MBA, Harvard School of Business, 1959
MSEE, University of Southern California, 1957
BSEE, University of Vermont, 1955

Robert A. Boole
Director, Venture Analysis

Directorships

Charles River Data Systems, 32-Bit microcomputers
Photodyne, Inc., Fiber-optic test equipment
Testsystems, Inc., Automatic test equipment
Micro Control Systems, Inc., 3-D Graphic software for PCs

Prior Positions

Corporate Director, Marketing, Analog Devices, Inc.
Product Director, Digital Panel Instrument Operation, Analog Devices Inc.

Education

MBA, Boston University, 1958
BSEE, Massachusetts Institute of Technology, 1952

John J. Hudson
Controller, Venture Capital

Prior Positions

Manager, Financial Planning, Analog Devices, Inc., 1982–85
Corporate Planning, Data General Corp., 1979–82

Education

MBA, Babson College, 1978
BS, Northeastern University, 1973

Pierre Dogan
Manager, Venture Analysis

Prior Positions

System Marketing Manager, Europe, Analog Devices
International Marketing Manager, Analog Devices
Product Group Manager, Analogic Corp.
Division Manager, Draper Labs
Director, Corporate Development, Draper Labs

Education

MBA, Harvard Business School, 1973
PhD, Massachusetts Institute of Technology, 1967
MS, Civil Engineering, University of Louvain (Belgium), 1963

Average Size of Investment	$1M
Size of Fund	$50M
Investment Criteria	High technology
Portfolio Companies	Bipolar Integrated Technology, Beaverton, OR, High-speed ICs; Charles River Data Systems, Framingham, MA, 32-bit microcomputers; GigaBit Logic, Inc., Newbury Park, CA, Gallium arsenide ICs; Imagerie Industrie Systeme, Bordeaux, France, Machine vision cameras; International Imaging Systems, Milpitas, CA, Image processors; Jupiter Systems, Inc., Alameda, CA, Graphic terminals; Numerix Corp., Newton, MA, Array processors; Photodyne, Inc., Newbury Park, CA, Fiber-optic test equipment; Quantitative Technology, Beaverton, OR, Signal processing software; Testsystems, Inc., Tempe, AZ, Automatic test equipment

ANDROCAN INC.
50 Bartor Road
Weston, Ontario M9M 2G5
Canada
(416) 745-3333

Barrie D. Rose
Chairman and Chief Executive Officer

Directorships

Clayson, Inc., Management and investment holding company
Autrex, Inc., Manufacturer of housewares and outdoor lighting
Harris Steel Group, Inc., Fabricates and distributes steel, manufacturer of wire products
Noma Industries Ltd., Manufacturer of electrical and mechanical products

Prior Position

President, Acme Paper Products

Education

Chartered Accountant, Ontario, British Columbia, England, and Wales
Fellow of Chartered Accountants of Ontario
MBA, Northwestern University, 1955
B. Com., University of London, 1953

Frederick E. Ross
President

Directorships

Clayson, Inc., Management and investment holding company
Autrex, Inc., Manufacturer of housewares and outdoor lighting

Prior Positions

Various senior positions, Acme Paper Products, 1970–72
General Manager, Quebec Containers, 1966–68

Education

BASc, University of Toronto, 1954
Professional Engineer (P. Eng.), 1954

Bruce S. McCubbin
Executive Vice President

Directorships

Clayson, Inc., Investment and management holding company
Autrex, Inc., Manufacturer of housewares and outdoor lighting

Prior Position

President, Imasco Retail Ltd.

Education

B. Eng., Nova Scotia Technical College, 1965
Eng. Diploma, Mount Allison University, 1963

Average Size of Investment	$1M–$7.5M
Size of Fund	Undisclosed
Investment Criteria	Consumer housewares, do-it-yourself, hardware, specialty industrial, and chemical manufacturers and distributors are desired for acquisition
Portfolio Companies	Adjusta-Post Manufacturing, Co., Norton, OH, Manufacturer of exterior lighting products and metal posts; Autrex, Inc., Weston, Ontario, Holding company and manufacturer of housewares and outdoor lighting; Bison Instruments Inc., Minneapolis, MN, Manufacturer of seismological, resistivity, and other geotechnical equipment; Canbar, Inc., Kitchener-Waterloo, Ontario, Manufacturer of industrial containers, wooden and plastic pipelines; Gem, Inc., Byhalia, MS, Manufacturer of housewares, cleaning and food products; Ingredients International Inc., Los Angeles, CA, Distributor of specialty chemicals; Kelstan Plastic Products Ltd., Kitchener-Waterloo, Ontario, Manufacturer of corrosion-resistant drainage systems for laboratories, etc.

APPLIED TECHNOLOGY PARTNERS, L.P.
55 Wheeler Street
Cambridge, MA 02138
(617) 354-4107

180 Maiden Lane, 29th Floor
New York, NY 10038
(212) 797-3877

Frederick B. Bamber
Managing Director, MA

Directorships

Interleaf, Electronic publishing and office automation
Sphere Technology, MIS productivity and speech technology
Aurora Systems, Videographics

Prior Position

Vice President, Data Resources, Inc., 1970–79

Education

MBA, Wharton School, University of Pennsylvania, 1969
BA, Yale College, 1966

Thomas L. Flaherty
Michael I. Mayers

Average Size of Investment	$300K–$500K
Size of Fund	Undisclosed
Investment Criteria	Telecommunications, software, industrial automation, computer hardware
Portfolio Companies	Aurora Systems, San Francisco, CA, Videographics systems; Microvertics, Mountain View, CA, Information systems for hospitality industry; Pacific Monolithics, Palo Alto, CA, Gallium arsenide integrated circuits; Dama Telecommunications, Parsippany, NJ, Communication services; Imagen, Santa Clara, CA, Graphic arts; Inference, Los Angeles, CA, Artificial intelligence; Interleaf, Cambridge, MA, Electronic publishing and office automation; Solomon Design Automation, Santa Clara, CA, Computer-aid engineering, electronics engineering; Sphere Technology, Providence, RI, MIS productivity and speech technology

ARSCOTT, NORTON & ASSOCIATES
375 Forest Avenue
Palo Alto, CA 94301
(415) 853-0766

David G. Arscott
Dean C. Campbell
Leal F. Norton

Average Size of Investment	$1M
Size of Fund	Undisclosed
Investment Criteria	Interested in technology-based companies, will act as lead investor, also interested in start-ups
Portfolio Companies	Undisclosed

ASSET CAPITAL & MANAGEMENT CO.
608 Ferry Boulevard
Stratford, CT 06497
(203) 375-0299

Ralph Smith

Average Size of Investment	$100K
Size of Fund	Undisclosed
Investment Criteria	Communications, start-ups are desirable
Portfolio Companies	Undisclosed

ASSET MANAGEMENT CO.
2275 East Bayshore Road
Palo Alto, CA 94303
(415) 494-7400

Craig C. Taylor
John F. Shoch
Franklin P. Johnson, Jr.

Average Size of Investment	$1M
Size of Fund	$50M
Investment Criteria	Technology-based companies are of interest; geographic proximity is important; will act as lead investor; start-ups are welcome
Portfolio Companies	Amgen; Applied Biosystems; Coherent; Tandem; Teradyne; Ross Stores

ASSOCIATED SOUTHWEST INVESTORS, INC.
2400 Louisiana N.E., #4
Albuquerque, NM 87110
(505) 881-0066

John R. Rice
President, Chief Executive Officer

Directorship

Connection Communications, Cable television

Prior Positions

President, Chief Executive Officer, Crest Ultrasonics (Crestek)
Vice President, Overseas Operations, Mohawk Recreation Products, Inc.

Education

BA, Harvard University, 1968

Average Size of Investment	$100K–$1M
Size of Fund	Undisclosed
Investment Criteria	Return on investment
Portfolio Companies	Undisclosed

ASSOCIATES VENTURE CAPITAL CORP.
425 California Street
Suite 2203
San Francisco, CA 94104
(415) 956-1444

Walter P. Strycker
President

Directorships

Associates Venture Capital, Venture funds
Si Fab, Semiconductor devices
Superphone, Telecommunications
Western Energy Inc., Alternate energy
Marine Coastal Co., Consulting

Prior Positions

Vice President, Treasurer, Wheelaerator Frye, Inc.
Senior Vice President, Signal Energy Systems, Inc.

Education

BS, University of California at Berkeley, 1952

Harold T. McCormick

Average Size of Investment	$150K
Size of Funds	Venture: $1.5M
	MESBIC: $1.2M
Investment Criteria	Start-up and second-stage financing
Portfolio Companies	Farm Information Machinery, Denver, CO, Farm management software; H.D.B. Inc., Denver, CO, Beverage marketing; Physis Inc., San Francisco, CA, Corporate health evaluation/maintenance; Superphone, Inc., Fremont, CA, Telecommunications; V.O.P. USA Inc., San Francisco, CA, Home video player

ATLANTA CAPITAL CORP.
450 Park Avenue
New York, NY 10022
(212) 832-1104

L. Mark Newman
Victor Hecht
Robert C. Vitale
Linda S. Newman

Average Size of Investment	$1M
Size of Fund	Undisclosed
Investment Criteria	Diversified company preferences; will act as lead investor; start-ups are welcome
Portfolio Companies	Undisclosed

ATLANTIC AMERICAN CAPITAL, LTD.
Lincoln Center, Suite 851
5401 West Kennedy Boulevard
Tampa, FL 33609
(813) 877-8844

J. Patrick Michaels, Jr.

Average Size of Investment	$100K
Size of Fund	$1M
Investment Criteria	Communications and technology-based companies
Portfolio Companies	Undisclosed

ATLANTIC VENTURE PARTNERS
701 East Franklin Street, Suite 815
Richmond, VA 23219
(804) 644-5496

801 N. Fairfax Street, Suite 404
Alexandria, VA 22314
(703) 548-6026

Robert H. Pratt
General partner, Richmond

Directorships

Pandick, Inc.

Prior Positions

President, Virginia Capital Corporation

Education

LLB, University of Pennsylvania, 1950
BA, Princeton University, 1944

Wallace L. Bennett
General Partner, Alexandria

Directorships

CTI Data Corp.
Concord Management Systems
Nappe Babcock

Prior Positions

Vice President, Merrill Lynch White Weld Capital Markets Group

Education

MBA, Washington University of St. Louis, 1972
AB, University of Virginia, 1965

Average Size of Investment	$700K
Size of Fund	$2M
Investment Criteria	Rapidly growing companies with optimum combination of: 1. Highly competent and motivated management with past record of success; 2. Market with favorable mix of size, growth potential, and competitive objectives; 3. Adequate capital being raised to achieve operating objectives; and 4. Predisposition to work with outside investors toward common goals.
Portfolio Companies	Concord Management Systems, Inc., Software; Consumer Health Services, Health services marketing; Executive Courier Network, Grand courier; Genicom Corporation, Computer printers; Ladd Furniture, Furniture manufacturer

ATLANTIC VENTURES TRUST
1246 Hollis Street
Halifax, Nova Scotia B3J 1T6
Canada
(902) 421-1595

Thomas J. Hayes
President

Directorships

Video Atlantic
Atlantic Fish Specialties
Internav, Ltd.
Fundy Aquaculture

Prior Position

Director, Fisheries Development, Government of Canada

Education

BBA, St. Francis Xavier University, 1971

William M. Jones

Average Size of Investment	$250K
Size of Fund	$6M
Investment Criteria	Existing business requiring funds to expand, introduce new product line
Portfolio Companies	Atlantic Fish Specialties, Charlottetown, P.E.I., Smoked fish; Internav, Ltd., Sydney, N.S., Marine navigational aids; Fundy Aquaculture, Grand Manan, N.B., Salmon farming; Video Atlantic, Charlottetown, P.E.I., Video equipment rental

ATLAS CAPITAL CORP.
55 Court Street
Boston, MA 02108
(617) 482-1218

C. Gerard Drucker
Herbert Carver

Average Size of Investment	$300K
Size of Fund	Undisclosed
Investment Criteria	Diversified company preferences
Portfolio Companies	Undisclosed

AVALON VENTURES
1020 Prospect Street, Suite 405
La Jolla, CA 92037
(619) 454-3803

Kevin J. Kinsella
Managing General Partner

Directorships

Spectragrapics Corp.
NeoRx Corp.
Synaptics Corp.

Education

MS, International Economics, Johns Hopkins
BS, Management and Electrical Engineering, MIT, 1967

Average Size of Investment	Undisclosed
Size of Fund	Undisclosed
Investment Criteria	Must be a start-up, preferably in a high tech area
Portfolio Companies	Spectragraphics Corp., San Diego, CA, Computer graphics workstations; Landmark Graphics Corp., Houston, TX, Computer graphics workstations; Network Switching Systems, Andover, MA, Computer digital switches; NeoRx Corp., Seattle, WA, Cancer diagnosis and therapy; Ansa Software Corp., Belmont, CA, Database software for PC; Synaptics, Inc., San Jose, CA, Artificial intelligence; GourMate, Inc., La Jolla, CA, Gourmet healthfood restaurant

AVF INVESTMENTS LTD.
300 Mount Royal Village
1550 Eighth Street, S.W.
Calgary, Alberta T2R 1K1
Canada
(403) 228-9152

Clifford M. James
President

Directorships

AVF Management Ltd., Management services
Deltx Windpump Corp. Ltd., Wind energy technology
Prime Energy Ltd., Oil and gas explorer/developer
AVF Resources Inc., Oil and gas explorer/developer
Primary Exploration Ltd., Oil and gas explorer/developer
Avestan Resources Inc., Oil and gas explorer/developer
Huntec (70) Limited, Geoscientific instrumentation and technological services
Enertec Geophysical Services Ltd., Geophysical services
AVF Minerals Ltd., Mining
Mercator Resource Corp., Mining
Dawson Gold Exploration Ltd., Mining

Prior Positions

Founded and managed a group of consulting companies which provided highly technical services to the petroleum and mining industries, 1976–80
Exploration Geologist & Exploration Supervisor, Tenneco Oil Co., 1972–76

Education

PhD Studies, Geology, University of Western Ontario, 1971–72
MSc, Geology, Carleton University, 1971
BSc (honors), Geology, University of Western Ontario, 1969

Robert W. Ruff
Vice President of Finance and Administration

Directorships

AVF Management Ltd., Management services
Deltx Windpump Corp., Ltd., Wind energy technology
Prime Energy Ltd., Oil and gas explorer/developer
AVF Resources Inc., Oil and gas explorer/developer
Avestan Resources Inc., Oil and gas explorer/developer
Huntec (70) Ltd., Geoscientific instrumentation and technological services
Petroleum Recycling Service Ltd., Mobile recycling of lubricating oils
Enertec Geophysical Services Ltd., Geophysical services
AVF Minerals Ltd., Mining
Mercator Resource Corp., Mining

Prior Positions

Manager, Finance and Administration, Franklin Supply Co. Ltd.
Manager, Accounting, Alberta Energy Co. Ltd.

Education

Chartered Accountant, 1970
B. Comm., University of Alberta, 1968

Average Size of Investment	$1.25M
Size of Fund	$13.25M
Investment Criteria	Natural resource field preferred; all investments to be in some manner technologically unique or to have potential to be unique
Portfolio Companies	Avestan Resources, Inc., Canada, Oil and gas explorer and developer; AVF Management Ltd., Canada, Management services; AVF Minerals Ltd., Canada, Mining; AVF Resources Inc.,

Canada, Oil and gas explorer and developer; Dawson Gold Exploration Ltd., Canada, Mining; Deltx Windpump Corp. Ltd., Canada, Wind energy technology; Enertec Geophysical Services Ltd., Canada, Geophysical services including state-of-the art vibroseis; Huntec (70) Ltd., Canada, Development and sale of geoscientific instrumentation and technological services including marine survey systems; Mercator Gold Corp. Inc., U.S., Mining; Mercator Resource Corp., Canada, Mining; Petroleum Recycling Services Ltd., Canada, Mobile recycling of lubricating oils; Primary Exploration Ltd., Canada, Oil and gas explorer and developer; Prime Energy Ltd., Canada, Oil and gas explorer and developer

AVI MANAGEMENT INC.
3000 Sand Hill Road
Building 3, Suite 280
Menlo Park, CA 94025
(415) 854-4470

Peter L. Wolken
President

Directorship
Cadmation, Inc.

Prior Position
General Manager, Page Mill Investment Co.

Education
BSME, University of California, 1958

David Sturdevant
Vice President

Directorships
Valley Bank of Nevada; Channelmark Corp., Unity Systems

Prior Position
Vice President, Bank of America

Education
MBA, Golden Gate University, 1980
BA, University of Denver, 1971

Chuck K. Chan
Vice President

Directorships
Optotech, 5¼" Optical disk drive
Elantec, Linear IC
Newport Electro-Optic Systems, Electro-optic/laser subsystems
Photon Dynamics
Aurora Systems
Alta Group
Parallel Computers

Prior Position
Division Marketing Manager, Spectra-Physics

Education
MBA, Harvard University, 1977
BS, MS, PhD, Physics, Massachusetts Institute of Technology, 1975

Average Size of Investment	$500K
Size of Fund	$20M
Investment Criteria	Seed, start-up, first round; will act as lead investor; technology-based Silicon Valley firms
Portfolio Companies	Alta Group, San Jose, CA, Video editing equipment; Aurora Systems, San Francisco, CA, Electronic artist's workstations; Cadmation, Inc., Santa Clara, CA, CAE workstations/peripherals; Channelmark Corp., San Mateo, CA, Software/accessories marketing; Sierra Semiconductor, Sunnyvale, CA, Semiconductors; Photon Dynamics, Cupertino, CA, Laser testing IC's; Unity Systems, Redwood City, CA, Home management computer systems; Data Technology Corp., Sunnyvale, CA, Disk storage sub-systems; Elantec, Inc., Milpitas, CA, Linear integrated circuits; Metheus Corp., Hillsboro, OR, Computer graphics; Micronix Inc., Los Gatos, CA, X-ray lithography systems; Optotech, Inc., Colorado Springs, CO, Optical disk drives; Parallel Computers, Santa Cruz, CA, Fault-tolerant computers

ROBERT W. BAIRD & CO., INC.
Box 672
Milwaukee, WI 53201
(414) 765-3889

J. S. Anderson

Average Size of Investment	Undisclosed
Size of Fund	Undisclosed
Investment Criteria	Midwest, over $1M
Portfolio Companies	Undisclosed

BANCAP CORP.
155 East 42nd Street
New York, NY 10017
(212) 687-6470

William L. Whitely

Average Size of Investment	$300K
Size of Fund	Undisclosed
Investment Criteria	Diversified industry preferences
Portfolio Companies	Undisclosed

BANCBOSTON VENTURES
100 Federal Street
Boston, MA 02110
(617) 434-2442

Paul F. Hogan
President
(617) 434-5700

Prior Positions

Vice President, First National Bank of Boston, 1974–84
Chemist, McCord Corp., Detroit, MI, 1970–72

Education

MBA, Amos Tuck School of Business, 1974
MS, Chemistry, Massachusetts Institute of Technology, 1968
BS, Chemistry, Boston College, 1966

Jeffrey W. Wilson
Vice President and Treasurer
(617) 434-2428

Prior Position

Senior Accounting Officer, Bank of Boston

Education

MBA, Suffolk University, 1977
BSBA, Boston University, 1967

Diana H. Frazier
Vice President
(617) 434-5398

Prior Positions

Research Associate, Temple Barker & Sloane, 1978–80
Consultant, Washington, D.C., France, West Africa, England, 1969–77

Education

MS, Sloan Massachusetts Institute of Technology, 1981
BA, Wellesley College, 1969

Robert M. Freedman
Investment Associate
(617) 434-4060

Prior Positions

Producer, Director, Boston Broadcasting, Inc.
Senior Producer, WGBH Educational Foundation (PBS)

Education

MBA, Harvard University, 1984
MPP, Kennedy School of Government, Harvard, 1979
SB, Massachusetts Institute of Technology, 1972

Stephen J. O'Leary, III
Investment Associate
(617) 434-4634

Prior Position

Lieutenant, United States Navy, 1977–82

Education

MBA, Harvard University, 1984
BS, United States Naval Academy, 1977

Cheryl Krane
Investment Associate

Prior Positions

Marketing Training, Analog Devices, 1985
Research Associate, Center for Strategic Research, 1980
Computer Sales, Texas Instruments, 1979

Education

MS, Finance and Strategy, Sloan School of Management, 1984
BS/BA, Finance and Marketing, Boston University, 1979

Average Size of Investment	$500K initial investment, up to $2M on subsequent financings
Size of Fund	$35M
Investment Criteria	Technology-based companies with above-average growth potential; areas of special interest are computer and peripherals, software, biotechnology, and medical products
Portfolio Companies	Undisclosed

BANDO-MCGLOCKLIN INVESTMENT CO.
13555 Bishops Court
Suite 225
Brookfield, WI 53005
(414) 784-9010

George Schonath
Salvatore L. Bando
Jon McGlocklin

Average Size of Investment	$600K
Size of Fund	Undisclosed
Investment Criteria	Interested in manufacturing companies, real estate; will act as lead investor
Portfolio Companies	Undisclosed

BANKERS CAPITAL CORP.
4049 Pennsylvania Street
Kansas City, MO 64111
(816) 531-1600

Raymond E. Glasnapp

Average Size of Investment	$100K
Size of Fund	Undisclosed
Investment Criteria	Diversified industry preferences
Portfolio Companies	Undisclosed

BANKIT FINANCIAL CORP.
111 East Wisconsin Avenue
Suite 1900
Milwaukee, WI 53202
(414) 271-5050

Gary R. Placek

Average Size of Investment	$300K
Size of Fund	Undisclosed
Investment Criteria	Diversified company interests including manufacturing; leveraged buy-outs also
Portfolio Companies	Undisclosed

BARTLESVILLE INVESTMENT CO.
P.O. Box 548
Bartlesville, OK 74003
(918) 333-3022

J. L. Diamond

Average Size of Investment	$100K
Size of Fund	Undisclosed
Investment Criteria	Diversified company preferences, also interested in natural resources and construction areas
Portfolio Companies	Undisclosed

BASIC INVESTMENT CORPORATION
6723 Whittier Ave., Office 201
Mclean, VA
(203) 356-4300

Frank Lewis
President

Directorship
Edward Sandler

Average Size of Investment	$15–50K
Size of Fund	$500K
Investment Criteria	MESBIC; loans to economically and socially disadvantaged only
Portfolio Companies	Undisclosed

BASIC SEARCH COMPANY
Park Place
10 West Streetsboro Street
Hudson, OH 44236
(216) 650-4321

Burton D. Morgon
President

Directorships

Top Roc
Morgan Adhesives/Chase Transcriptions
Method Systems
10 others

Prior Positions

President, Morgan Adhesives
President, Fasson
Chief Engineer, Behr Manning

Education

BSME, Purdue, 1938

Average Size of Investment	$100K
Size of Fund	Group of private investors
Investment Criteria	Start-ups; must meet the entrepreneur; must have national potential
Portfolio Companies	B. J. Davis, Cleveland, OH, Electronic components; Method Systems, Cleveland, OH, Computer translators; Centrak, Cleveland, OH, Lasers; Multicolor, Cincinnati, OH, Labels; Vickery Chem., Hudson, OH, Films; Chase Transportation, Hudson, OH, Limousine service; Midwest Biological, Mansfield, OH, Laboratory supplies; Park Place Travel, Hudson, OH, Travel agency; Freeport Farms, Shalesville, OH, Corn farms; Hatch Inc., Hudson, OH, Start-up business service; Chase, Hudson, OH, Medical transcription; Giangarlo, Pittsburgh, PA, Instruments; Medi Max, Cleveland, OH, Medical service; Power Pad, Akron, OH, Brake linings; Top Roc, Erie, PA, Prestress concrete; Western Reserve Furniture, Barberton, OH, Furniture

BATTERY VENTURES
200 Portland Street
Boston, MA 02114
(617) 367-1011

Howard Anderson
General Partner

Prior Position

President and Founder, The Yankee Group

Education

MBA, Harvard Business School, 1966–68
BA, University of Pennsylvania, 1962–66

Robert G. Barrett
General Partner

Prior Position

Vice President and Regional Office Manager, The First National Bank of Chicago

Education

MBA, Harvard Business School, 1966–68
BA, Harvard College, 1962–66

Richard D. Frisbie
General Partner

Prior Position

Vice President and Partner, Urban National Corp.

Education

JD, Harvard Law School, 1971–74
BA, Harvard College, 1967–71

Oliver D. Curme
Associate

Prior Positions
Officer, High tech lending division, First National Bank of Boston
Laboratory Manager, Environ Electronic Labs

Education
MBA, Harvard Business School, 1982
BS, Brown University, 1976

Allen H. Alley
Associate

Prior Positions
Marketing Director, Mechanical Computer-Aided Engineering, Computervision Corp.
Senior Product Manager, Geometric Modeling, Computervision Corp.
Lead Engineer, Boeing Commercial Airline Co.

Education
BS, Purdue University, 1976

Average Size of Investment	$750K–1M
Size of Fund	$34M
Investment Criteria	High-technology, factory, and office automation, information systems, and communication; start-up, first and second round
Portfolio Companies	Fifteen investments in the following areas: high-end local area network software; computer based integrated test instrumentation system; network processors; file transfer software for IBM mainframes; distributed data base systems; satellite communications; advanced signal processing; transmission products and systems for the special services segment of the telecommunications area; optical digitizing systems; software tools for automating design of custom integrated circuits; software for control of order processing, distribution logistics, and warehouse management; COBOL restructuring program in mainframe software renewal business

BAY AREA WESTERN VENTURE GROUP, INC.
383 Diablo Road
Suite 100
Danville, CA 94526
(415) 820-8079

Jack Wong

Average Size of Investment	$200K
Size of Fund	Undisclosed
Investment Criteria	Diversified industry preferences; geographic proximity important
Portfolio Companies	Undisclosed

BAY PARTNERS II/III
10600 N. DeAnza Blvd.
Suite 100
Cupertino, CA 95014
(408) 725-2444

John Bosch
John Friedenrich
W. Charles Hazel

Average Size of Investment	$1M
Size of Funds	$60M
Investment Criteria	Start-ups are desirable; will act as lead investor; technology-based companies are preferred
Portfolio Companies	Undisclosed

BAY VENTURE GROUP
One Embarcadero Center
Suite 3303
San Francisco, CA 94111
(415) 989-7680

William R. Chandler
General Partner
(415) 989-7682

Directorships

Alphasil, Inc., Flat panel displays
Biovation, Inc., Hospital info systems
Everest Solutions, Software
Kelsius, Inc., Remote fiber sensors
SiScan Systems, Laser scanners
Alar Systems Corp., Departmental computers
Current Networks, Desktop communications
Ocean Genetics, Inc., Marine biotech

Que Systems, Industrial process computers
On Target Tech., Ink jet printers

Prior Positions

Venture Analyst, Western Growth Fund, 1971–76
Assistant President, Veriflo Corp., 1965–71

Education

ABFT, American Graduate School of International Business, 1959
BS, Oregon State University, 1956

Charles Slutzkin

Average Size of Investment	$200K–$500K
Size of Fund	$7M
Investment Criteria	Start-up, seed financings; San Francisco Bay Area only
Portfolio Companies	Undisclosed

BEACON PARTNERS LIMITED
3 Landmark Square
Suite 400
Stanford, CT 06902
(203) 348-8858

Leonard Vignola, Jr.
Managing Director

Directorship

Bridgeport Chapter, Connecticut Venture Group

Prior Positions

Vice President, Director, Venture Association of New Jersey
Director of Support Center of New Jersey
Director, Accountants for Public Interest/Support Center of NY

Education

MBA, Case Western Reserve
BS, Northwestern

Richard C. Burcaw
Managing Director

Prior Positions

President, E.A.B. Venture Corp., 1980–85
Senior Vice President, European American Bank, 1975–80
Vice President, Auerbach Pollak & Richardson, 1969–74
Investment Officer, Chase International Investment Corp., 1966–69
Officer, Chase Manhattan Bank, 1961–66

Education

BA, Houghton College, 1961

Jack Katzen
Managing Director

Prior Positions

Vice President, AVCO Corp., 1978–85
Manager, Business Development, Far East, G.E. Co., 1972–78
Manager, Strategic Planning & Review, G.E. Co., 1971–72
General Manager, Worldwide, G.E. Information Systems, 1968–71
General Manager, Military Space, 1963–68

Education

BS, Carnegie Tech, 1942
Master's-level work, MIT, 1942

Charles W. Murphy
Managing Director

Prior Positions

President, Integration Planning Corp., 1984–85
President, AMBI Corporation, 1982–84
Group Director, Exxon Enterprises, 1977–82
General Manager, Bunker Romo Corp., 1973–77

Education

BS, Eastern Illinois University, 1963
Master's-level work, University of California, Los Angeles, 1963–66

Arnold Greenhut
Managing Director

Directorships

Trans World Music, Inc.

Prior Positions

President, Regas Diversified Investors, 1974–86
President, Parsons Brinckerhoff Development Group, 1982–85
Executive Vice President, Transcontinental Investing Corp., 1970–73

Education

MSIE, New York University, 1961
BSIE, New York University, 1958

Average Size of Investment	$500K
Size of Fund	Undisclosed
Investment Criteria	Management team and market niches; troubled companies
Portfolio Companies	Undisclosed

BENSON INVESTMENT CO.
504 South Commerce Street
Geneve, AL 36340
(205) 684-2824

W. T. Benson

Average Size of Investment	$200K
Size of Fund	Undisclosed
Investment Criteria	Interested in construction, real estate, grocery industries; will act as lead investor; geographic proximity is important
Portfolio Companies	Undisclosed

BESSEMER VENTURE PARTNERS, L.P.
3000 Sand Hill Road
Menlo Park, CA 94025
(415) 854-2200

630 Fifth Avenue
New York, NY 10111
(212) 708-9300

83 Walnut Street
Wellesley Hill, MA 02181

Neill H. Brownstein
General Partner, CA

Directorships

BusinessLand, Inc., Business systems distributor
ICOT, Inc., Communications controllers
VMX, Inc., Voice messaging systems
Ungermann-Bass, Inc., Local area network
Circadian, Inc., Medical instruments

Education

MBA, Northwestern University, 1968
AB, Columbia University, 1966

William T. Burgin
Partner, NY

Directorships

CompuScan, Inc.
Galileo Electro-Optics Corp.
James River Corp.
Numerax, Inc.
Midway Airlines, Inc.

Education

MBA, Harvard University, 1967
AB, Harvard University, 1965

Robert B. Field
G. Felda Hardymon
Robert H. Buescher

Average Size of Investment	$1M
Size of Fund	Undisclosed
Investment Criteria	First-round high technology
Portfolio Companies	Undisclosed

BIDDINGER INVESTMENT CAPITAL CORP.
9012 North Meridian
Suite 500
Indianapolis, IN 46260
(317) 844-7390

John W. Biddinger
President

Directorships

SunGroup, Broadcasting
City Securities Corp.
Diamond Electronics
Lesbury Management Corp.
Crime Control, Security monitoring
Media Omaha, Broadcasting
USA Vault Corp., Security storage

Prior Positions

Vice Chairman, Anacomp, Inc.
President, City Securities, Inc.

Education

BS, Indiana University, 1962

William Muirhead
Financial Consultant

Directorships

Diamond Electronics, Inc.

Education

BS, University of Illinois, 1957

Marilyn G. Hinkle
Accountant, Secretary/Treasurer

Prior Positions

Bookkeeper, Lewis & Konezny, CPAs, 1980–81
Teller, State Bank Chanhassen, 1977–81

Education

BA, Academy of Accountancy, 1981
AS, Normandale College, 1975

Charles Koehler

Average Size of Investment	$1M
Size of Fund	Undisclosed
Investment Criteria	Broadcasting, medical, fast food, communications, security, light manufacturing electronics
Portfolio Companies	Undisclosed

BIOTECH CAPITAL CORP.
600 Madison Avenue
New York, NY 10022
(212) 758-7722

Earl W. Brian
Chairman

Directorships

Questech Capital Corp., SBIC
Clinical Sciences, Inc.
Financial News Network
Hadron, Inc.
Data Broadcasting, Inc.

Prior Positions

Director, Center for Health Research, University of Southern California
President Reagan's Cabinet Secretary of Health and Welfare when Reagan was governor of California

Education

Duke University, Medical School, 1966

John Koonce
President

Directorships

Hadron Inc.
Clinical Sciences, Inc.
American Biometrics Inc.

Prior Positions

Director of Financial Analysis, Hertz Corp., 1979–81

Education

BA, Duke University, 1964

Barbara T. Hann
Vice President

Directorships

American Biometrics
HSC/Bias, Inc.
Medical Magnetics
Guest Business Agency

Prior Positions

Vice President, Charterhouse Group International, 1984
Senior Accountant, Citicorp, 1983
Business Development Officer, Barclays Bank, 1981–83

Education

Masters, Bridgewater College, 1975
BS, Salem College, 1968

Carolyn C. Lewis
Vice President

Directorship

American Cytogenetics, Inc.

Prior Position

Tax Senior, Price Waterhouse & Co., 1977–80

Education

MBA, Columbia University, 1977
MA, Duke University, 1965
BA, Florida State University, 1963

Connie Harrison

Average Size of Investment	$250K–$1M
Size of Fund	$35M available capital
Investment Criteria	Start-ups, turnarounds or expansion/mezzanine capital
Portfolio Companies	American Bio-Nuclear, Inc., Emeryville, CA, Supplier of DNA and DNA-related biological materials; American Cytogenetics, Inc., Los Angeles, CA, and Teaneck, NJ, Cancer screening and diagnostic genetic screening tests (i.e., pap smears and amniocentesis); Clinical Sciences, Inc., Whippany, NJ, Researches, manufactures, and markets immunodiagnostic test kits and reagents for detection of infectious diseases; Data Broadcasting, Vienna, VA, Stock market quotes and financial data direct to personal computers without telephone lines via TV signal; Environmental Processing, Inc., Richardson, TX, Testing and conditioning of semiconductor circuits; Medical Magnetics, Ramsey, NJ, Manufactures and markets orthodontic devices using magnetic for a technology; Contex Scientific Corp., Stamford, CT, Developer and electronic publisher of business news and information databases with exclusive rights to UPI's database; Quest Business Agency, Houston, TX and NY, Advertising Agency specializing in business to business marketing communication; Saturn Chemicals, Philadelphia, PA, Automated chemical facility with a proprietary process used in manufacturing hydrocarbon resins, acrylates and construction chemicals; The Learning Channel, Washington, DC, Cable network broadcasting learning informational and enrichment programs to over 7 million homes nationwide; Financial News Network, Inc., New York, NY, and Santa Monica, CA, 13 hours daily of financial and business news to cable TV systems and television broadcasting stations via communications satellite; Hadron, Inc., Vienna, VA, Technical consulting service in engineering and computer technology to both government agencies and communications organizations; HSC/Bios, Inc., Valhalla, NY, Cardiac probe for early detection of coronary artery disease; Immucor, Inc., Atlanta, GA, Market blood bank and hospital laboratory reagents used for donor and patient processing; TI Industries, Inc., Vienna, VA, Specialty software, electronic mail, computerized financial data service, translating work processor, data processing management services

WILLIAM BLAIR VENTURE PARTNERS
135 South LaSalle Street
Chicago, IL 60603
(312) 853-8250

James E. Crawford III
General Partner

Directorships

Internet Systems Corp., Computer software
Micro Capital Corp., Microcomputer leasing

Prior Positions

Vice President, MCC Powers, Unit of Mark Controls, 1978–83
Associate, McKinsey & Co., 1974–78

Education

BSEE, Princeton University, 1968

Samuel B. Guren
General Partner

Directorships

Amherst Associates, Health care information systems
Sanford Corp., Manufactures and markets brand name markers, pens, ink pads, adhesives and other related products

Prior Position

Vice President, Continental Illinois Venture Corp.

Education

MBA, Wharton School, University of Pennsylvania, 1974
BA, University of Wisconsin, 1969

Scott F. Meadow
General Partner

Directorship

D'Lites of America, Restaurant company

Prior Positions

Consultant, Booz Allen & Hamilton
Assistant to President, Phillips Industries

Education

MBA, Harvard Business School, 1980
BA, Harvard College, 1977

Average Size of Investment	$500K–$2M ($750K avg.)
Size of Fund	$50M
Investment Criteria	Health care, general, growth equity, leveraged buy-outs
Portfolio Companies	Undisclosed

BLAKE, BRUNELL, LEHMANN & CO.
1101 30th Street, N.W.
Suite 101
Washington, DC 20007
(202) 833-9031

Carl W. Blake
David D. Brunell
Managing Director

Prior Positions

Management Consultant, self-employed, 1982–83
Project Director, Union of Concerned Scientists, 1981–82
Vice President, International Development, Trans Century Corp., 1976–81

Education

MBA, Harvard University, 1962
BA, Chemical Engineering, Rensselaer Polytechnic Institute, 1957

Russell F. Smith

Average Size of Investment	$500K–$10M
Size of Fund	Undisclosed
Investment Criteria	Current business plan
Portfolio Companies	Undisclosed

BLALACK-LOOP, INC.
696 East Colorado Boulevard
Suite 220
Pasadena, CA 91101
(818) 449-3411

Charles M. Blalack
Chairman of the Board

Directorships

Interdyne Co., Memory device
Discflo Corp., New slury pump
Monolithic Memories, Semiconductors
Transducer Technologies, Transducers
William J. Purdy Co., Electronics distributors
Systonetics, Inc., Software company

Prior Position

Chairman and CEO, B/W/A, Inc., 1953–69

Clavin L. Loop
M. Rosemary Lyons

Average Size of Investment	$500K–$10M
Size of Fund	Undisclosed
Investment Criteria	Large potential growth
Portfolio Companies	Discflo Corp., Santee, CA, New slurry pump; Interdyne Company, Milpitas, CA, Memory device; Monolithic Memories, Santa Clara, CA, Semiconductors; Systonetics, Inc., Fullerton, CA, Software company; Transducer Technologies, Pasadena, CA, Transducers

BNP VENTURE CAPITAL CORPORATION
3000 Sand Hill Road, Bldg. 1, Suite 125
Menlo Park, CA 94025
(415) 854-1084

Claude Ossart
Director

Prior Positions

Computer consultant, Banque Nationale de Paris
Retail and distribution manager, Logabax
Retail and distribution manager, Electronique Serge Dassault
Retail and distribution manager, Snecma

Education

Ecole Polytechnique, 1961

Edgerton Scott II
President

Directorships

Quantel International

Prior Positions

Vice President, Bank of the West
Vice President, Wells Fargo Bank

Education

BA, University of California at Berkeley, 1965

Average Size of Investment	$300K
Size of Fund	$9M
Investment Criteria	Prefer high technology companies, West Coast, all stages
Portfolio Companies	Priam, Santa Clara, CA, Disk drives; Sun Microsystems, Workstation, Mountain View, CA; Calgene Biotechnology, Davis, CA; Aret & Systems, Transaction processor, San Jose, CA; Maxim Integrated Products, Analog circuits, Sunnyvale, CA; Optigraphics, CAD/CAM, San Diego, CA; Protype, Office automation, Los Angeles, CA; Read-Rite, Disk drive heads, Milpitas, CA; Quantel, Lasers, Santa Clara, CA; Cohesive Networks, Telecommunications, Los Gatos, CA; ELANTEC, Analog semiconductors, Milpitas, CA; Robinton Products, Industrial meters, Sunnyvale, CA SOREP Technology Hybrid circuits, Houston, TX

BOETTCHER VENTURE CAPITAL PARTNERS, L.P.
828 17th Street
Denver, CO 80201
(303) 628-8333

Foye F. Black, Jr.
Senior Vice President/Manager

Directorships

Ford/Higgins, Ltd.
Barcus-Berry Electronics, Inc.

Prior Positions

Vice President, Capital Management Services Inc., 1971–76
Vice President, Midland Capital Corp., 1963–71

Education

BS, Banking and Finance, University of North Carolina

Michael C. Franson
Vice President

Directorships

Micro Decisionware, Inc.

Prior Positions

Vice President, Boettcher-Equity Research, 1983–84
Equity investment analyst, Pacific Mutual Life, 1981–83

Education

BMA, Finance, University of Oregon, 1981
BS, Marketing, California State University, 1977

Larry R. Wonnacott
Vice President

Directorships

Intelligent Medicine, Inc.
Venture Capital Association of Colorado

Prior Positions

Vice President and Manager, Norwest Venture Capital Management, 1978–85
Credit Officer, Central Bank of Denver, 1974–78

Education

MA, Economics, Florida Atlantic University, 1972

Average Size of Investment	$500K
Size of Fund	$10.7M
Investment Criteria	Later stage; companies beyond product development with key management in place
Portfolio Companies	Amcodyne, Inc., Minicomputer disk drives, Longmont, CO; Barcus-Berry Electronics, Inc., Commercializes Load Reactance Compensation (LRC), Huntington Beach, CA; Computer Accessories Co., Support products for office computer market, San Diego, CA; Ford/Higgins, Ltd., Multiuser computer system for minicomputer market, Longmont, CO; McDATA Co., Information sytems products for data processing market, Broomfield, CO; Medical Imaging Centers of America (MICA), Outpatient medical diagnostic imaging centers, San Diego, CA; Micro Decisionware Inc. (MD), Microcomputer software, Boulder, CO

BOSTON CAPITAL VENTURES, INTERNATIONAL

1 Devonshire Place, Suite 2913
Boston, MA 02109
(617) 227-6550

1 Seaport Plaza
New York, NY
(212) 214-1000

A. Dana Callon Jr.
General Partner, Boston

Directorships

Parexel

Prior Positions

Vice President, Braxton Capital Corp.
Associate, Braxton Inc.
Consultant, Tymshare Inc.

Education

MBA, Dartmouth-Tuck, 1979
BA, Tufts University, 1974

H. J. von der Goltz
General Partner, Boston

Directorships

Logos Corp.
Hospital Efficiency Corp.

Education

PMD, Harvard
BS, M.I.T., 1960

Donald J. Steiner
General Partner

Directorships

Grand Circle Travel

Prior Positions

Director, New Business Development, The Gillette Co.

Average Size of Investment	$500K
Size of Fund	$30M
Investment Criteria	Emerging growth companies believed capable of achieving near-term competitive success and profitability; concentrating in data communications, design and manufacturing automation, health care products and services, and selected service-oriented opportunities
Portfolio Companies	Parexel Int.; Health care services, Boston, MA; Camex Inc., Electronic publishing, Boston, MA; HEC, Inc., Energy services, Boston, MA; Logos, Artificial intelligence, Wellesley, MA; CTL Inc., Raleigh, NC

BRADFORD ASSOCIATES
22 Chambers Street
Princeton, NJ 08540
(609) 921-3880

Bradford Mills
Managing Partner

Directorships

OPG Holdings, Inc., Tempered safety glass
Filtration Sciences, Inc., Low-density paper and synthetic products used as filter media
Overseas Princeton Placements, N.V.
Overseas Private Equities, N.V.
CST Group, Inc.
SPEX Group, Inc.
Central Sprinkler Corp.
HWC Holding Corp.
Overseas Private Investors
Ampad Corp.
The Coca Cola Bottling Co. of Southern Florida, Inc.

Prior Positions

President, Overseas Private Investment Corp.
Managing Partner, New York Securities Co., 1962
Partner, F. Eberstadt & Co., 1960

Education

Postgraduate work, Oxford University
Bachelors, Princeton University

Winston J. Churchill
Managing Partner

Directorships

CST Group, Inc.
Central Sprinkler Corp.
Bangor America, Inc.
Prime Cable Corp.
Filtration Sciences, Inc.

Prior Position

Lawyer, Saul, Ewing, Remick & Saul

Education

JD, Yale Law School
MA, Economics, Oxford University (Rhodes scholar)
BS, Physics (summa cum laude), Fordham University
University of Paris

Barbara L. Mills
General Partner

Directorships

Central Sprinkler Corp.
OPG Holdings, Inc.
HWC Holding Corp.

Prior Position

President, Bradford Ventures Ltd.

Education

Bachelors, Princeton University

Herbert Salzman
General Partner

Directorships

Bangor America Inc.
CST Group, Inc.

Prior Position

Ambassador, Organization for Economic Cooperation and Development

Education

Yale

Average Size of Investment	$15M
Size of Fund	Unlimited
Investment Criteria	Minimum after-tax earning of $500K, preferably over $1M; profitable operations for at least 3 years; top management team; sound financial condition; P/E ratio offering appropriate protection and potential of appreciation; equity investment of between $1M and $50M; significant or controlling equity position; yield is secondary to potential for capital preservation and appreciation

Portfolio Companies — American Healthcorp, Inc., Hospital management; Ampad Corp., Holyoke, MA, Ruled and printed pads, office forms, calendars, notebooks, art papers; The Coca-Cola Bottling Co. of Southern Florida, Inc., Production, packaging, and distribution of soft drinks; Central Sprinkler Corp., Manufacturer of sprinkler heads and automatic warning valves for fire control systems; Bangor America Inc., Designer, manufacturer, and seller of men's and women's sweaters and knitwear; Filtration Sciences, Inc., Low-density paper and synthetic products used as filter media; OPG Holdings, Inc., Manufacturer of tempered safety glass; Prime Cable Corp., Cable TV systems and franchises; Spex Group, Inc., Manufacturer of optical spectrometers, reagent chemicals, and spectroscopic standards; CST Group, Inc., Computer stock continuous forms; HWC Holding Corp., Master distributor of specialized wire and cable products

BRAINTREE MANAGEMENT LTD.
Penthouse 7
59 South Greeley
Chappaqua, NY 10514
(914) 238-5221

G. C. Newlin

Average Size of Investment	$200K
Size of Fund	Undisclosed
Investment Criteria	Interested in manufacturing, construction, and real estate companies
Portfolio Companies	Undisclosed

BRENTWOOD ASSOCIATES
11661 San Vicente Boulevard
Suite 707
Los Angeles, CA 90049
(213) 826-6581

Roger C. Davisson
General Partner

Directorships

Altus Corp.
Atkis, Inc.
Doelz Networks, Inc.
Protype Corp.

Prior Position

Vice President, Treasurer, U.S. Filter Corp.

Education

MBA, Stanford University, 1968
MS, Engineering Science, California Institute of Technology, 1966
BS, Engineering, California Institute of Technology, 1965

B. Kipling Hagopian
General Partner

Directorships

Censtor Corp.
Lanx Corp.
Maxim Integrated Products
Performance Semiconductor
Quidel
Teradata Corp.

Prior Position

Vice President, Westland Capital Corp.

Education

MBA, University of California at Los Angeles, 1966
BA, Business Administration, University of California at Los Angeles, 1964

G. Bradford Jones
General Partner

Directorships

Edge Computer
Adaptive Data Systems, Inc.
Interpore International
California Devices

Education

MBA, JD, Stanford University, 1981
MA, Physics, Harvard University, 1978
BA, Chemistry and Physics, Harvard University, 1977

DIRECTORY AND BIOGRAPHIES

Timothy M. Pennington, III
General Partner

Directorships

System Industries, Inc.
Cardiovascular Devices, Inc.
Infodetics Corp.
Greyhawk Systems Corp.
View Engineering, Inc.

Prior Position

Vice President, Corporate Finance, Blyth & Co.

Education

MBA, University of California at Los Angeles, 1966
BS, Engineering, University of Arizona, 1963

Frederick J. Warren
General Partner

Directorships

C P G International
Digital Sound Corp.
Ideal School Supply
Optical Associates, Inc.
University Technology Transfer, Inc.

Prior Position

President, Westland Capital Corp.

Education

MBA, Wharton School, University of Pennsylvania, 1961
BS, Engineering, University of Pennsylvania, 1960

William M. Barnum, Jr.
Principal

Prior Position

Associate, Morgan Stanley & Co.

Education

MBA, JD, Stanford University, 1981
AB, Economics, Stanford University, 1976

William M. Matthes
Associate

Prior Positions

Financial Analyst, Morgan Stanley & Co., Inc.

Education

MBA, Harvard University, 1986
AB, Economics, Stanford University, 1982

Average Size of Investment	$2M
Size of Fund	$275M
Investment Criteria	High-technology-based start-ups and early-stage companies; leveraged buy-outs; West Coast preference if leading role
Portfolio Companies	Actel Corporation; ByVideo, Inc.; Acme General Corporation; CPG International, Inc.; California Devices, Inc.; Catheter Technology Corp.; Cirrus Logic, Inc.; Edge Computer Corp.; Ideal School Supply; Liposome Technology; Network Equipment Technologies; System Industries, Inc.; Acton Computer; Technology, Inc.; Adaptive Data Systems, Inc.; Altus Corp.; Atkis, Inc.; Cardiovascular Devices, Inc.; Censtor Corp.; Digital Sound Corp.; Doelz Networks Inc.; Greyhawk Systems Corp.; Infodetics Corp.; Interpore International; Lanx Corp.; Maxim Integrated Products; Megatape Corp.; Molecular Computer; Optical Associates, Inc.; Performance Semiconductor Protype Corp.; Quidel; Teradata Corp.; University Technology Transfer Inc.,; Via Visuals Inc.; View Engineering, Inc.

BRIDGE CAPITAL ADVISORS, INC.
50 Broadway
29th Floor
New York, NY 10004
(212) 514-6700

Hartford, CT
(203) 275-6700

Donald P. Remey
Managing Director

Prior Positions

Managing Director, Rothschild, 1980–82
Vice President, Citibank, NA, 1974–80

Education
MBA, Harvard Graduate School of Business, 1966
BA, Colgate University, 1964

Hoyt J. Goodrich
Managing Director

Prior Position
Vice President, Aetna Life & Casualty, 1963–83

Education
BA, Dartmouth College, 1958

Geoffrey H. Wadsworth
Managing Director

Prior Positions
Vice President, Rothschild Asset Management, 1981–84
Vice President, Citibank, 1979–81

Education
MBA, New York University, 1971
BA, Middlebury College, 1965

J. Barton Goodwin
Managing Director, NY

Prior Position
Director, Private Placements, Kidder Peabody, 1981–86
Various positions, Kidder Peabody, 1974–81

Education
MBA, Columbia University, 1974
BA, Washington & Lee University, 1969

Average Size of Investment	$3–7M
Size of Fund	Bridge Capital Investors: $50M
	Bridge Capital Investors II: $100M
Investment Criteria	Skilled management team; well-conceived business plan; financial results and projections sufficient to meet debt service requirements of existing and new debt levels; identifiable exit for the equity element; potential returns from the equity portion of an investment that are 1 to 3 times the fixed coupon rate
Portfolio Companies	Undisclosed

BRISTOL INVESTMENT TRUST
842A Beacon Street
Boston, MA 02215
(617) 566-5212

Bernard G. Berkman

Average Size of Investment	$300K
Size of Fund	Undisclosed
Investment Criteria	Interested in diversified companies, including recreation; start-ups are encouraged and will act as lead investor; geographic proximity is important
Portfolio Companies	Undisclosed

BRITTANY CAPITAL COMPANY
1525 Elm Street
2424 LTV Tower
Dallas, TX 75201
(214) 954-1515

Robert E. Clements
General Partner

Directorships
Diagnostic Services, Inc., Oil field service
Cumberland Beverage Co., Beer distributor

Prior Position
Vice President, Dean Witter

Education
BA, University of Texas, 1962

Steven S. Peden
Partner

Directorships
B H & G, Inc.
Ennis Asphalt, Inc.
Dallas Petroleum Co., Inc.

DIRECTORY AND BIOGRAPHIES

Prior Position

Emerging Business Services, Coopers & Lybrand, 1978–80

Education

MBA, Tulane University, 1978
BA, Economics, Tulane University, 1975

Average Size of Investment	$100K
Size of Fund	$3M
Investment Criteria	None
Portfolio Companies	Undisclosed

BROAD ARROW INVESTMENT CORP.
P.O. Box 2231-R
Morristown, NJ 07960
(609) 924-8646

C. N. Belim

Average Size of Investment	$100K
Size of Fund	Undisclosed
Investment Criteria	Diversified interests, especially technology based, construction, or real estate; will consider start-ups
Portfolio Companies	Undisclosed

BROVENTURE CAPITAL MANAGEMENT
16 West Madison Street
Baltimore, MD 21201
(301) 727-4520

Harvey C. Branch
General Partner

Directorships

Samna Corp., Software
Allied Data Communications, Inc., Local area networks

Prior Positions

Venture Capital, Business and Corporate Development, Inco Ltd., 1970–82
Marketing, Manufacturing, Engineering, Various companies, 1958–69

Education

MBA, Xavier University, 1965
BS, Engineering, University of Michigan, 1958

William M. Gust
Partner

Directorships

Conferex, Teleconferencing
Display Data, Turnkey computer systems
Phoenix Digital, Process control systems/factory networks
Computest, Automatic test equipment
Logisticon, Material handling systems

Prior Positions

Vice President, First Boston Corp.
Securities Analyst, L. F. Rothschild
Assistant Media Director, Benton & Bowles, Inc.

Education

BA, Northwestern University, 1964

Edward F. Hummer
General Partner

Prior Positions

Associate, Nazem & Co. (venture capital), 1984–85
Counsel, Surrey & Morse (law firm), 1980–81
Associate, Cahill Gordon & Reindel (law firm), 1972–80

Education

MBA, Stanford University Graduate School of Business, 1983
JD, Georgetown University Law Center, 1970
BA, Princeton University, 1967

Average Size of Investment	$750K–$1M
Size of Fund	$40M
Investment Criteria	Undisclosed
Portfolio Companies	Undisclosed

BRYAN & EDWARDS
3000 Sand Hill Road
Suite 2-215
Menlo Park, CA 94025
(415) 854-1555

600 Montgomery Street
35th Floor
San Francisco, CA 94111
(415) 421-9990

John M. Bryan
Partner, San Francisco

Directorships

Acurex Corp.
American Insurance Management
Blue Diamond Oil
Pacific Bank
Storables U.S.A.
Trust Co. of the West
Worldwide Special Fund

Prior Position

Account Executive, Blyth & Co.

Education

AB, Economics, Stanford University, 1947

Alan R. Brudos
Partner, San Francisco

Directorship

Cutler-Williams, Inc., Computer services and software products

Prior Position

Tax Manager, Deloitte Haskins & Sells

Education

MS, University of Colorado, 1959
AB, Economics, Luther College, 1955

Guy H. Conger
Partner, Menlo Park

Directorships

Domestic Automation Corp., Electric meter micro-computer
Visual Engineering, Inc., UNIX graphics software
NLP, Inc., Natural language software

Prior Positions

Venture Capitalist, G.E. Venture Capital Corp.
Investment Manager, Stanford University

Education

MBA, Stanford University, 1977
MSEE, Stanford University, 1976
BS, Physics, Stanford University, 1973

William C. Edwards
Partner, Menlo Park

Directorships

Acurex Corp., Provides and services in the aerospace, electronics, and energy industry
Avantek, Inc., Vertically integrated microwave and telecommunications company
Boole & Babbage, Inc., Develops and markets computer software for large IBM mainframe systems
Hambrecht & Quist Group, Investment banking firm servicing both technology based and special situation companies exhibiting substantial growth potential and investors interested in such companies
Therma-Wave, Inc., Engaged in development, manufacturing, and marketing of sophisticated thermal-wave microscope systems for materials inspection and process monitoring
Opportunity Capital Corp., Minority Enterprises Small Business Investment
Imperial Automation, Inc., Manufactures banking and financial data-processing equipment
Summit Information Systems, Inc., Credit union automation systems

Prior Positions

Vice President and Investment Counselor, Lionel D. Edie & Co.

Education

MBA, Harvard University, 1953
BS, Petroleum Engineering, Stanford University, 1951

Robert W. Ledou
Partner, San Francisco

DIRECTORY AND BIOGRAPHIES

Prior Positions

Vice President, Portfolio Manager and Analyst, Bank of America Investment Management Corp.
Investment Analyst, Title Insurance & Trust Co.

Education

MBA, Boston University, 1970
BA, Economics, University of New Hampshire, 1964

Average Size of Investment	$500K
Size of Fund	Undisclosed
Investment Criteria	Undisclosed
Portfolio Companies	Undisclosed

BT CAPITAL CORPORATION
280 Park Avenue
New York, NY 10017
(212) 850-1916

James G. Hellmuth
Chairman
P. O. Box 318
Church Street Station
New York, NY 10015
(212) 850-1916

Directorships

Multi Metal Wire Cloth, Inc., Manufacturer of filtration screens and devices
Alsy Corp., Manufacturer of lamps
Management Assistance, Inc., Computers

Education

LLD, George Washington, 1953
BS, Yale University, 1948

Noel E. Urben
Michael E. Nugent
Vice President
P. O. Box 318
Church Street Station
New York, NY 10015
(212) 850-1778

Prior Positions

Vice President, Heizer Corp., 1983–84
President, Carvern International Industries Ltd., 1981–82
President, Keds Corp., 1979–81

Education

MBA, University of Chicago, 1966
MA, Cambridge University, England, 1958

Keith R. Fox
Vice President/Director
P.O. Box 318
Church Street Station
New York, NY 10015
(212) 850-1905

Directorships

Funk & Wagnalls, Inc.
Carter Furniture
Capital Controls
The Sercim Corp.

Prior Position

Financial Analyst (A.C.M.A.), Whitbread & Co., Ltd., London, England, 1976–79

Education

MBA, Harvard University, 1981
MA, BA, Oxford, 1976

B. Martha Cassidy
Assistant Vice President
(212) 850-1465

Directorship

Pilling Co., Surgical instruments

Education

MBA, Wharton School, 1982
BA, Wellesley, 1977

Adrienne R. Halper
Assistant Vice President
P. O. Box 318
Church Street Station
New York, NY 10015
(212) 850-1997

Directorship

Manhattan Toy Co., Toy manufacturer

Prior Position

Audit Senior, Coopers & Lybrand, 1979–81

Education

MBA, University of Chicago, 1983
BS, Economics, University of Pennsylvania, 1979

Melanie Okun
Assistant Vice President
P. O. Box 318
Church Street Station
New York, NY 10015
(212) 850-1804

Prior Positions

Assistant Treasurer, 1984
Associate, 1983

Education

MBA, Stanford University, 1983
BA, Mathematics, Wesleyan University, 1981

Average Size of Investment	$3M–$5M
Size of Fund	$75M
Investment Criteria	Leveraged buy-outs; no high technology and no start-ups
Portfolio Companies	Alsy Corp., New York, NY, Manufactures lamps; Anitec Image Technology, Binghamton, NY, Manufactures film; B&B Holdings, St. Paul, MN, Manufactures calendars; Capital Holdings, Inc., Philadelphia, PA, Water purification; Carter Industries, Salisbury, NC, Manufactures furniture; Century Glove, Albany, NY, Manufactures gloves; $CRYO_2$, Ft. Pierce, FL, Liquid oxygen system; Holiday House Corp., Deland, FL, Restaurant chain; Ideal Industries, La Jolla, CA, Plastics; International Signals & Control, Lancaster, PA, Military hardware; Yellow Book Corp., Oceanside, NY, Telephone directories

BUFFALO CAPITAL CORP.
(an affiliate of The Hickman Corp. and Arthur Taylor & Co. Saudi Arabian Investment Company)
Mount Morris Road
Geneseo, NY 14454
(716) 243-4310

John H. Hickman III
Chairman

Directorships

National Health Care Affiliates, Inc., Extended care nursing home chain
American Family Pizza, Inc., Food services
Interco Systems, Inc., Buying services
Dissen & Juhn Corp., Marine construction
Multinational Computer Models, Inc., Computer systems, international treasury and foreign exchange management

Prior Positions

Chairman and Chief Executive Officer of Seilon, Inc.;
First Bancorporation; Lockwood Corp.; Foster, Hickman & Zaeglein
Investment Banker, McConnell & Co.

Education

JD, Yale Law School, 1962
Certificate in Chinese, Yale School of Far Eastern Languages, 1960
AB, Brown University, 1959

Arthur R. Taylor
John H. Hickman IV
Michael Palmer

Average Size of Investment	$1M
Size of Fund	$5M+
Investment Criteria	Start-up through third stage including management buy-outs
Portfolio Companies	American Family Pizza, Inc., Hollywood, FL, Fast food; Interco Systems, Inc., Rochester, NY, Buying services

DIRECTORY AND BIOGRAPHIES

BUILDERS CAPITAL CORP.
2716 Ocean Park Boulevard
Santa Monica, CA 90406
(213) 450-0779

Victor Indiek

Average Size of Investment	$500K
Size of Fund	Undisclosed
Investment Criteria	Construction
Portfolio Companies	Undisclosed

MALCOLM BUND & ASSOCIATES
2000 L Street, N.W., Suite 200
Washington, DC 20036
(202) 293-2910

Malcolm Bund
President

Education

MBA, Wharton, 1974
BA, University of New South Wales, 1969

Average Size of Investment	$1M
Size of Fund	$3 to $5M
Investment Criteria	No industry preference; investment will be made in companies with experienced managers
Portfolio Companies	Undisclosed

BURR, EGAN, DELEAGE & CO.
Three Embarcadero Center
Suite 2560
San Francisco, CA 94111
(415) 362-4022

One Post Office Square
Suite 3800
Boston, MA 02109
(617) 482-8020

South Coast Metro Center
575 Anton Blvd., Suite 440
Costa Mesa, CA 92626
(714) 557-9250

Craig L. Burr
General Partner, Boston

Directorships

Codon
Genesys Software Systems, Inc.
Softsel Computer Products, Inc.

Prior Position

Partner, T.A. Associates

Education

MBA, Harvard Business School
Cum Laude in Economics, Harvard College

William P. Egan
General Partner, Boston

Directorships

Broderbund Software, Inc.
National Demographics and Lifestyles, Inc.
Silicon Valley Group, Inc.

Prior Positions

Partner, T. A. Associates
Manager of Venture Capital, Bank of New England

Education

MBA, Wharton School, University of Pennsylvania
BA, Fairfield University

Jean Deleage
General Partner, San Francisco

Directorships

Chiron Corp.
International Genetic Engineering, Inc.
Syquest Technology

Versaflex Deliver Systems
Paradise Systems, Inc.
Tandon Corp.

Prior Positions

Director, Western Association of Venture Capitalists
Founder, Sofinnova, inc.

Education

PhD, Economics, Sorbonne
Master's, Electrical Engineering, École Supérieure d'Electricité

Brion B. Applegate
General Partner, San Francisco

Directorships

Anaheim Broadcasting Corp.
The Narragansett Clothing Co., Inc.
Southland Communications Corp.

Prior Position

Corporate Office, Manufacturers Hanover Trust Co.

Education

MBA, Harvard Business School, 1980
Colgate University

Shirley Cerrudo
General Partner, San Francisco

Directorships

Optical Specialties, Inc.
Telco Systems, Inc.
Virtual Microsystems, Inc.

Prior Positions

Vice President and Treasurer, Wells Fargo Investment Co.
Research Associate for McKinsey & Co. and the Bank of America
Assistant to Director of Long Range Planning, University of California Medical School

Education

BA, Economics, Bucknell University

Johnathan A. Flint
Boston

Prior Position

Associate, Testa, Hurwit & Thibeault

Education

JD, University of Virginia, 1979
BA, Hobart College, 1973

Frank J. Kenny
Boston

Directorships

Aegis, Inc.
Solutions By Computer, Inc.

Prior Positions

Partner, J.B. Management, Dublin
General Manager, General Tire Co.

Education

MBA, University of Chicago
Master's degree, Economics, University College, Dublin

Jean-Bernard Schmidt
General Partner, San Francisco

Directorships

Paradise Systems, Inc.
Telelearning Systems, Inc.

Prior Positions

SEMA, Management consulting firm, Paris
President, Sofinnova, Inc.

Education

MBA, Columbia University
Degrees in Business and Economics, Essec (Paris)

Esther Sharp
Boston

Prior Positions

EDP Department Administrator, Browning Ferris Industries
Assistant to the President, Harvard Real Estate, Inc.

Education

Master's, Management, Simmons Graduate School of Management
BA, University of South Carolina

Thomas E. Winter
General Partner, Costa Mesa

Directorships

D.A.V.I.D. Systems, Inc.
Elantec, Inc.
Western Data Systems

Prior Positions

Vice President, Finance and Administration, and Director, Burroughs Corp.
Vice President, Operations, for Information Products Group, Corporate Controller, Director of Distribution, Director of Pricing, Xerox Corp.

Education

MS, Industrial Management, Georgia Institute of Technology
BS, Aeronautical Engineering, Georgia Institute of Technology

Annette Bianchi

Average Size of Investment	$1–2M, depending on the state of the company
Size of Fund	$250 M
Investment Criteria	Start-up, early stage, expansion, mainly in electronics, communication, and health-related companies; subordinated debt financing in established companies
Portfolio Companies	Continental Cablevision, Inc., Boston, MA; Optical Specialties, Inc., Fremont, CA; Silicon Valley Group, San Jose, CA; Softsel Computer Products, Inc., Inglewood, CA; Telco Systems, Inc., Menlo Park, CA; Chiron Corp., Emeryville, CA; Paradise Systems, Inc., S. San Francisco, CA; Broderbund Software, Inc., San Rafael, CA

BUSINESS CAPITAL CORP.
P.O. Drawer 57329
New Orleans, LA 70157
(504) 581-4002

David R. Burrus

Average Size of Investment	$150K
Size of Fund	Undisclosed
Investment Criteria	Diversified company preferences
Portfolio Companies	Undisclosed

BUSINESS DEVELOPMENT CORP. OF NORTH CAROLINA
P.O. Box 10665
Raleigh, NC 27605
(919) 755-7040

Gary M. Underhill

Average Size of Investment	$100K
Size of Fund	Undisclosed
Investment Criteria	Diversified company preferences; geographic proximity important
Portfolio Companies	Undisclosed

BUSINESS EQUITY & DEVELOPMENT CORP.
1411 West Olympic Boulevard
Los Angeles, CA 90015
(213) 385-0351

Ricardo J. Olivarez

Average Size of Investment	$300K
Size of Fund	Undisclosed
Investment Criteria	Interested in diversified company preferences including movies; will act as lead investor; will look at start-ups; geographic proximity is important
Portfolio Companies	Undisclosed

BUSINESS RESEARCH CO.
205 Worth Avenue
P.O. Box 2137
Palm Beach, FL 33480
(305) 832-2155

George B. Kilborne
President

Directorships

Diversified Communications Co., Radio, TV, cable
Bay Street Corp., Investments

Prior Positions

Chairman/President, First Citizen Bank, 1970–74
Partner, Comac Co., 1968–70
President, Business Research Co., 1961–74
Vice President, William Skinner & Sons, 1955–60

Education

BA, Yale University, 1952

A. Donald Grosset, Jr.

Average Size of Investment	$750K
Size of Fund	Undisclosed
Investment Criteria	Prefer established firms; engineered hard goods
Portfolio Companies	Undisclosed

BUSINESS VENTURES, INC.
20 North Wacker Drive
Suite 550
Chicago, IL 60606
(312) 346-1580

Milton G. Lefton
President

Directorship

Asset Leasing Corp., Equipment leasing

Prior Positions

President, David Berg & Co., 25 years
President, King Kold Frozen Food, 10 years
President, Asset Leasing Corp., 5 years

Terry G. Chapman
Secretary

Directorships

Abrams & Chapman, Law firm
Meat Land Industries, Food processing

Prior Positions

Partner, Abrams, Rifkin & Chapman
Treasurer, Meat Land Industries

Education

Law School (cum laude), Northwestern University Law School, 1976
Certified Public Accountant, 1973
Masters, Accounting, Wharton School of Business, 1973
BS, Economics (cum laude), University of Pennsylvania, 1973

Marc B. Grayson
Chairman

Directorships

South Central Bank & Trust Co.
Business Ventures, Inc.
American Institute of Banking (on faculty)

Prior Positions

Executive Vice President, South Central Bank & Trust Co.
Vice President, Harvey Lumber Co.

Education

BA (honors), Economics, University of Michigan, 1958

Average Size of Investment	$50K–$350K
Size of Fund	$600K
Investment Criteria	Chicago metropolitan area
Portfolio Companies	Six companies

BUTLER CAPITAL CORPORATION
767 Fifth Avenue
New York, NY 10025
(212) 980-0606

DIRECTORY AND BIOGRAPHIES

Charles M. Sukenik
Managing Director

Average Size of Investment	Undisclosed
Size of Fund	$400M
Investment Criteria	Profitable, leading market position in sub-market; $3M pre-tax, pre-interest profits
Portfolio Companies	Pamill Knitting Co., Apparel, VA; Ithaca Industries, Apparel, NC; Sun Media, Printing, OH; Alford Industries, Packaging, NJ; Golden State Foods, Food, CA

CABLE, HOWSE & COZADD, INC.
999 Third Avenue
Suite 4300
Seattle, WA 98104
(206) 583-2700

1800 One Main Place
101 Southwest Main
Portland, OR 97204
(503) 248-9646

3000 Sand Hill Road
Building 1, Suite 190
Menlo Park, CA 94025
(415) 845-3340

Thomas J. Cable
General Partner, WA

Prior Positions

Vice President, Director, Foster & Marshall, Inc., 1975–77
Robertson, Colman & Siebel, 1969–75
Smith Barney & Co.

Education

MBA, Stanford University School of Business, 1968
BA, Physical Sciences, Harvard University, 1961

Elwood D. Howse, Jr.
General Partner, WA

Prior Positions

Vice President, Corporate Finance, Foster & Marshall, Inc., 1976–77
Chief Financial Officer, Seattle Stevedore Co., 1974–76
Corporate Treasurer, Data Science Ventures, Inc., 1970–74

Education

MBA, Stanford University Graduate School of Business, 1970
BS, Engineering, Stanford, 1961

Michael A. Ellison
General Partner, WA

Prior Positions

Vice President, General Manager, Ellison Cattle Co., 1972–75
Territory Manager, John Deere Co.

Education

MBA, Stanford University Graduate School of Business, 1980
BS, Engineering Management, United States Air Force Academy, 1968

Wayne C. Wager
General Partner, WA

Prior Positions

Venture Capital Associate, Intern, Hambrecht & Quist, 1982
Hewlett-Packard, 1978–81

Education

MBA, Stanford University Graduate School of Business, 1983
BS, Mechanical Engineering, Stanford University, 1978

L. Barton Alexander
General Partner, OR

Prior Positions

Consultant, 1979–83
Vice President, Finance, Electro Scientific Industries, 1975–79

Education

MBA, University of Santa Clara, Graduate School of Business, 1975
MS, Systems Science, Carnegie-Mellon University, 1963
BS, Electrical Engineering, Carnegie-Mellon University, 1960

Gregory H. Turnbull
General Partner, Menlo Park

Prior Positions

First Vice President, White, Weld & Co., 1969–78
Principal, Morgan Stanley, 1978–83

Education

MBA, Stanford Graduate School of Business, 1962
BS, Chemical Engineering, Oregon State University, 1960

James B. Glavin

Average Size of Investment	$1.5M
Size of Fund	$153.5M
Investment Criteria	(1) Ten times investment in 5 years minimum; (2) liquidity; (3) proprietary product; (4) opportunity for scale; (5) early stage and losses acceptable
Portfolio Companies	As of June 1986, over 75 portfolio companies are listed

CADDO CAPITAL CORP.
3010 Knight
Suite 240
Shreveport, LA 71105
(318) 869-1689

Thomas L. Young, Jr.

Average Size of Investment	$100K
Size of Fund	Undisclosed
Investment Criteria	Diversified company preferences; will act as lead investor; geographic proximity important
Portfolio Companies	Undisclosed

CALIFORNIA CAPITAL INVESTORS, LTD.
11812 San Vicente Boulevard
Los Angeles, CA 90049
(213) 820-7222

Arthur H. Bernstein
General Partner

Directorships

Ryder System, Inc., Transportation
Redken Laboratories, Inc., Cosmetics
Great Western Capital Corp., Finance

Prior Positions

Senior Vice President, Finance and Administration, Max Factor & Co.
Vice President, Finance, Norton Simon, Inc.
Sr. Associate, Lasard Frires & Co.

Education

LLD/JD, Cornell Law School, 1950
BS, Chemical Engineering, Cornell University, 1947

Stephen D. Moses
General Partner

Directorships

National Investment Development Corp., Real estate
Tennessee Resources Corp., Energy
Brentwood Bank

Prior Positions

President, Land Development Subsidiary, Boise Cascade Corp.
President, City Reconstruction Co.

Education

LLD, Harvard Law School
BS, Franklin & Marshall College

Katherine Keck Moses
General Partner

Directorships

Pitzer College
Claremont Graduate School
Center for National Policy

Education

BS, University of Southern California

Average Size of Investment	$250K
Size of Fund	$6M+
Investment Criteria	No start-ups or seed financing
Portfolio Companies	Undisclosed

DIRECTORY AND BIOGRAPHIES

CALIFORNIA PARTNERS
3000 Sand Hill Road
Building 4, Suite 210
Menlo Park, CA 94025
(425) 854-7472

Timothy C. Draper
General Partner

Directorships

Unity Systems, Inc.
PLX Technology
Home Security Center

Prior Positions

Associate, Alex Brown & Sons, Inc., 1984–85
Assistant to the President, Apollo Computer, 1983
Marketing Engineer, Hewlett Packard, 1980–82

Education

MBA, Harvard Business School, 1984
BSEE, Stanford University, 1980

William C. Edwards

Average Size of Investment	$500K
Size of Fund	Undisclosed
Investment Criteria	Interested in technology-based companies and other diversified areas; start-ups considered
Portfolio Companies	Undisclosed

CAMBRIDGE RESEARCH & DEVELOPMENT GROUP
21 Bridge Square
Westport, CT 06880
(203) 226-7400

Sean O'Connor
Deborah Gardner

Average Size of Investment	$1M
Size of Fund	Undisclosed
Investment Criteria	Technology-based companies are of interest; start-ups considered
Portfolio Companies	Undisclosed

CAMBRIDGE VENTURE PARTNERS
88 Steele Street
Suite 200
Denver, CO 80206
(303) 393-1111

Bruce B. Paul
Managing Partner

Directorships

Innotron Diagnostics, Medical technology
Zicomp, Inc., Computer system manufacturer
Bankland Company, Bank

Prior Positions

President, Key Investment Corp., 1968–present
Lawyer

Education

JD, Harvard Law School, 1958
BS, History, Harvard, 1956

Oscar (Ozzie) Malek
General Partner, Chief Financial Officer

Directorships

Zicomp, Inc., Computer systems manufacturer
Automated Microbiology Systems, Inc., Medical technology

Prior Position

Secretary/Treasurer, Midwest Liquor & Wine

Education

BS, Science, Michigan State University, 1958

Average Size of Investment	$250K
Investment Criteria	Advanced medical, computer, and communications technology; geographic preference: West Coast and Rocky Mountain regions

Portfolio Companies Automated Microbiology Systems Inc., San Diego, CA, Medical technology; Innotron Diagnostics, Inc., Irvine, CA, Medical technology; Zicomp, Inc., Scotts Valley, CA, Computer systems

CAMELBACK CAPITAL CORP.
123 North Centennial Way
Suite 103
Mesa, AZ 85201
(602) 834-4954

John G. Bartol
Chairman

Directorships

Hunt Manufacturing Co., Office and art supplies
Utah Research and Development Co., Airborne electrical/electronic equipment
Rockford Corp., Car stereo amplifiers and speakers

Prior Positions

General Partner, CountrieTowne Investors, Ltd.
Director, Okidata Corp.

Education

JD, University of Pennsylvania, 1952
BA, Princeton University, 1948

Robert F. Pothier

Average Size of Investment	$247.5K
Size of Fund	Ca. $1M
Investment Criteria	None except private introduction
Portfolio Companies	Undisclosed

CANADIAN ENTERPRISE DEVELOPMENT CORP.
880-1100 Melville Street
Vancouver, BC V6E 4A6
Canada
(604) 684-3271

Daniel R. Nixon
Vice President

Directorships

Applied Microsystems Corp., Microprocessor test and measurement company
Hicomp Technology Corp., Nonvolatile memories for microcomputers

Prior Positions

Market Consultant, Westmills Ltd., 1978–80
Manager, O'Connor's Mens Wear Ltd., 1970–73

Education

MBA, University of Western Ontario (London), 1980
B. Comm., University of Calgary, 1977

Richard Burke
Senior Vice President

Directorships

Digitech Ltd., Earth sciences data acquisition and processing
Tangram Resources Ltd., Oil and gas exploration
Mil Industries Ltd., Diesel engine repair
Slocam Forest Products Ltd., Lumber production

Prior Position

Director of Research and Customer Engineering, Wire Rope Industries of Canada

Education

MBA, Stanford University, 1969
BASc, University of B.C., 1953

Average Size of Investment	$500K
Size of Fund	$25M
Investment Criteria	Technology investments in Canada and U.S.; management must be first-rate and product must have some proprietary technology
Portfolio Companies	Undisclosed

CANADIAN ENTERPRISE DEVELOPMENT CORP., LTD.
199 Bay Street
Suite 1100
Toronto, Ontario M5J 1L4
Canada
(416) 366-7607

DIRECTORY AND BIOGRAPHIES 157

Gerald D. Sutton
President and Chief Operating Officer

Directorships

Bay Mills Ltd., Industrial products manufacturer
Corod Manufacturing Ltd., Petroleum exploration and development company
Cassidy's Ltd., Institutional and retail china, glassware, etc.
Unican Security Systems Ltd., Manufacturer of security and furniture hardware
Taurus Computer Products, Inc., Data acquisition and control functions

Prior Positions

Director of Research, Nesbitt Thomson Bongard Inc., 1958–64
Assistant Economic Adviser, Bank of Montreal, 1949–58
Junior Economist, Clerk, Bank of Montreal, 1941–49

Education

Pilot, R.C.A.F., 1943–45
Master of Commerce, B. Com. Queen's University, approx. 1947

Richard Burke
William J. Brown
Vice President

Directorships

Taurus Computer Products, Inc., Automated data collection
Attic Records, Record company

Prior Positions

Corporate Planning, Bank of Nova Scotia, 1982–84
Partner, Thorne Stevenson and Kellogg, 1977–82

Education

PhD, O.R., Case Western Reserve University, 1973
MS, O.R., Case Western University, 1969
MA, Economics, University of Manitoba, 1967
BA (honors), Economics, University of Manitoba, 1966

Daniel Nixon
Barbara Atchie

Average Size of Investment	$450K
Size of Fund	$21M
Investment Criteria	It is not CED's policy to control or manage the companies with which it becomes associated; our preference is to invest on a minority basis and through board representation, assist people to achieve their goals, not to direct them
Portfolio Companies	Alphacom, Inc., Campbell, CA, Designs, develops and markets printers, printer control boards, and printer mechanisms for home and personal computer applications; Amnet, Inc., Watertown, MA, Manufactures microprocessor-driven private network packet switching systems and switching "modules"; Applied Microsystems Corp., Redmond, WA, Leading independent supplier of dedicated microprocessor support products including emulators and board testing systems; Attic Records Ltd., Toronto, Ontario, Independent record publisher promoting Canadian musical groups at home and abroad and foreign acts in Canada; Bay Mills Ltd., Toronto, Ontario, Manufactures a range of industrial products from synthetic fibers at six plants in Canada and the U.S.; Central Dynamics Ltd., Pointe Claire, Quebec, Manufactures studio and video equipment at plants in Montreal and Huntsville, AL; Corod Manufacturing, Ltd., Nisku, Alberta, Manufactures and installs proprietary continuous pumping rods for oil wells; Digitech Ltd., Calgary, Alberta, The largest Canadian-owned commercial earth science computer processing company; Exalloy Metals, Inc., Mississauga, Ontario, Processes aluminum scrap into powder for use in industrial explosives and metallurgical applications; Finlay Navigation Ltd., Victoria, BC, Operates a marine towing, booming, and barging operation on Williston Lake in north-central British Columbia; Hicomp Computer Corp., Redmond, WA, Satellite-based company manufactures reliable disk-replacement memory systems utilizing bubble technology; Marcus Information Systems, Inc., Los Angeles, CA, Manufactures board and disk-level hardware/software devices to expand the capability of the IBM and other personal computers through increased ease of use and programing, and powerful data manipulation capabilities; Orcatech, Inc., Ottawa, Ontario, Manufactures low-cost but powerful CAD/CAM workstations with high-resolution graphic systems; Quantum Medical Technology, Inc., Issaquah, WA, Developing high-resolution medical diagnostic equipment for cardiology, neurology, and vascular medicine markets; Seattle Silicon Technology, Inc., Bellevue, WA, Developing and marketing silicon compiler software; Sensor Diagnostics, Inc., Pocasset, MA, Developing new processing equipment for measuring the constituents of fluids, including body fluids; Slocan Forest Products Ltd., Richmond, BC, Produces lumber and wood chips at its sawmills in Slocan and Quesnel, BC; Tangram Resources Ltd., Calgary, Alberta, Petroleum exploration company with holdings in Canada and the U.S.; Taurus Computer Products, Inc., Ottawa, Ontario, Manufactures industrial-quality microprocessor-driven systems for data acquisition and control functions in industry and science; Thousand Trails, Inc., Seattle, WA, Owns and operates private membership campground resorts in the U.S. and BC.; Trilog, Inc., Irvine, CA, Manufactures doubleheaded printers with bar code and color capability; Ulstein Maritime Ltd., Burnaby, BC, Manufactures steerable marine propulsion units and owns Headhunters Diesel, which

repairs and remanufactures major components of large diesel engines; Unican Security Systems Ltd., Montreal, Quebec, Manufactures mechanical and electronic security hardware, furniture hardware, and other metal products at three plants in Canada and the U.S., with distribution worldwide

CAPITAL CORPORATION OF AMERICA
225 South 15th Street
Suite 920
Philadelphia, PA 19102
(215) 732-1666

Martin M. Newman
President

Directorship

Vanguard Savings and Loan, Savings and Loan

Prior Position

General Manager, Gulf Resources, 1967–69

Education

Candidate MBA, University of Missouri, 1966
BS, ME, Rose Hullman Institute, 1949

Henry Ginsberg
Chairman of the Board
880 El Camino del Mar
San Francisco, CA 94121
(415) 221-8700

Directorships

Quantech Electronics Corp., Electronic parts and service
The Ginsberg Collection, Interior design imports

Prior Positions

President, Scott Publishing, 1975
Senior Vice President, Cantor Fitzgerald & Co.

Education

New York University, 1947
City College of New York, 1946

Barton M. Banks
Secretary
c/o Banks and Banks
1521 Walnut Street
Philadelphia, PA 19102
(215) 204-2840

Directorships

Vanguard Savings and Loan, Thrift
Philadelphia Investment Exchange, Brokerage and Management
Realty Management Inc., Leasing

Prior Position

President, Capital Corporation of America

Education

LLB, Temple University Law School, 1955
BA, Temple University, 1952

Average Size of Investment	$200K
Size of Fund	$3M
Investment Criteria	Expansion capital, second-stage financing, bridge financing, buy-outs and acquisitions
Portfolio Companies	Container Transport, Philadelphia, PA, Specialty trucking; Media Concepts, Inc., Philadelphia, PA, Video communications; Urgent Medical Care, Haverford, PA, Immediate-care clinic

CAPITAL CORP. OF WYOMING, INC.
145 South Durbin Street
Suite 201
P.O. Box 3599
Casper, WY 82602
(307) 234-5438

Larry McDonald
President

DIRECTORY AND BIOGRAPHIES

Directorships
IAP, Inc., Publishing
WIDC, Financial and real estate
Sweetwater Investments, Investments
Capital Corp., SBIC
University of Wyoming, College of Business Administration
Trans American Cold Storage, Warehousing

Education
BSBA, University of Denver, 1963

Scott Weaver
Lue Kremer

Average Size of Investment	$100K
Size of Fund	$2M
Investment Criteria	Diversified; Wyoming area only
Portfolio Companies	Undisclosed

CAPITAL FOR BUSINESS, INC.
11 South Meramec
Suite 800
St. Louis, MO 63105
(314) 854-7427

1000 Walnut
18th Floor
Kansas City, MO 64106
(816) 234-2357

James B. Hebenstreit
President and Director, St. Louis

Directorships
Continental Disc Corp.
Commerce Bank of St. Louis
Sorkins Directories

Prior Position
President, Terra-Light Division of Butler Manufacturing Co., 1980–82

Education
MBA, Harvard Business School
BA, Harvard University

Bart Bergman
Vice President, Kansas City

Prior Position
Investment Officer, Commerce Bank

Education
BA, Illinois State University, 1977

William O. Cannon
Vice President, St. Louis

Prior Positions
President, Aragorn Investments, 1983
Director of Data Services, CEMPROC, 1978–83

Education
MBA, Washington University, 1983
BA, Cornell College, 1974

Timothy P. Nolan
Senior Investment Officer, St. Louis

Prior Position
Kirk Organization

Education
AB, Economics, Harvard College, 1983

Average Size of Investment	$500K
Size of Fund	$15M
Investment Criteria	Prefer later stage venture funding and leverage buy-out of manufacturing companies; will consider exceptional early stage or service companies
Portfolio Companies	Undisclosed

CAPITAL FORMATION CONSULTANTS, INC.
P.O. Box 798
Diablo, CA 94528
(415) 820-8030

1720 Ala Moana Boulevard
Suite 1506-B
Honolulu, HI 96815
(808) 949-0544

P.O. Box 8045
Incline Village, NV 89450

John H. Rohan
President, CA

Directorship

Zemco, Inc., Electronics

Prior Position

Vice President, Consolidated Capital, Inc.

Average Size of Investment	$2M–$5M
Size of Fund	Undisclosed
Investment Criteria	Profitable venture
Portfolio Companies	Undisclosed

CAPITAL FOR TERREBONNE, INC.
1613 Barrow Street
P.O. Box 1868
Houma, LA 70361
(504) 868-3933

Hartwell A. Lewis

Average Size of Investment	$100K
Size of Fund	Undisclosed
Investment Criteria	Diversified company interests; geographic proximity is important
Portfolio Companies	Undisclosed

CAPITAL INVESTMENTS, INC.
744 North Fourth Street
Suite 400
Milwaukee, WI 53203
(414) 273-6560

Frank Norris, President
Robert Banner, Vice President
Steve Rippl, Secretary/Treasurer

Average Size of Investment	$100K
Size of Fund	$13M
Investment Criteria	Interested in diversified companies; will act as lead investor
Portfolio Companies	Undisclosed

CAPITAL RESOURCE CORP.
1001 Logan Building
Seattle, WA 98101
(206) 462-7248

T. Evans Wyckoff
President

Directorships

First Interstate Bank of Washington, Full-service bank
Savings Bank of Puget Sound, Savings and loan bank
Aero-Go, Inc., Manufactures pneumatic lifts, etc.

Prior Positions

President, Johnny Appleseed Co., 1968–84
President and Chief Executive Officer, Seaboard Lbr. Co., 1965–75

Education

BA, History, University of Virginia

Average Size of Investment	$100K
Size of Fund	$2M
Investment Criteria	Proven product; multi-investors; no dormant inventory; non-service business; non-labor intensive; good management in place

DIRECTORY AND BIOGRAPHIES

Portfolio Companies Centigram Corp., Sunnyvale, CA, Computerized voice technology; Circadian, Inc., San Jose, CA, Holter monitors, etc.; Cyborg Corp., Newton, MA, Data acquisition and control; Dealer Information Systems, Bellingham, WA, Software for farm equipment dealers; Elantec, Inc., San Jose, CA, Linear integrated circuits; Inference Corp., Los Angeles, CA, Artificial intelligence; Lin Data Corp., Santa Clara, CA, Sputtered media; Mouse Systemes, Santa Clara, CA, Optical mice; Pearlsoft, Wilsonville, OR, Data base software; Photec Diagnostics, Inc., Little Falls, NJ, Color immunoassay; Plains Resources, Inc., Oklahoma City, OK, Oil and gas exploration; Porta-Printer, Inc., Largo, FL; Portable meter reading computer; Techmedica, Inc., Camarillo, CA, Artificial joints; Thos. E. Wolfe Co., San Francisco, CA, Men's trousers; Interconnect Technology, Inc., Los Angeles, CA, Advanced, dense circuit boards; Output Technology Corp., Spokane, WA, 3-headed computer printers; 700 cps

CAPITAL RESOURCE CORPORATION OF CONNECTICUT (L.P.)
699 Bloomfield Avenue
Bloomfield, CT 06002
(203) 243-1114

I. Martin Fierberg
General Partner

Directorships
Boca Raton First National Bank

Prior Positions
Director, Colonial Bank of Connecticut, 1973–86

Education
BS, Engineering, University of Connecticut, 1948

Janice M. Romanowski
General Partner

Average Size of Investment	Equity, $75K; Secured Loan, $150K
Size of Fund	$5.5–6M
Investment Criteria	Undisclosed
Portfolio Companies	Undisclosed

CAPITAL SERVICES & RESOURCES INC.
5159 Wheelis Drive
Memphis, TN 38117
(901) 761-2156

Charles Y. Bancroft

Average Size of Investment	$150K
Size of Fund	Undisclosed
Investment Criteria	Diversified company interests, especially in manufacturing; leveraged buy-outs are of interest
Portfolio Companies	Undisclosed

CAPITAL SOUTHWEST CORP.
12900 Preston Road
Suite 700
Dallas, TX 75230
(214) 233-8242

William R. Thomas
President

Education
MBA, Harvard Business School, 1956
BS, Chemical Engineering, Texas A & M, 1949

J. Bruce Duty
Vice President, Secretary, and Treasurer

Prior Position
Accountant (CPA), Alford Meruney & Co., 1976–79

Education
BBA, University of Texas at Austin, 1972

Patrick F. Hamner
Vice President

Education
MBA, University of Texas at Austin, 1981
BS, Southern Methodist University, 1979

Average Size of Investment	$750K
Size of Fund	$85M
Investment Criteria	Diversified
Portfolio Companies	A-1 Cal Leasing Corp., Burlingame, CA, Daily rental and long-term leasing of automobiles in SF and LA, CA areas; ALC Communications Corp., Birmingham, MI, Long distance telephone services; DBC Capital Corp., Dallas, TX, Medical research and development activities; Dow B. Hickam, Inc., Sugar Land, TX, Specialty pharmaceutical products marketed through nationwide hospital-oriented sales force; Steffen Dairy Foods Co., Inc., Wichita, KS, Processing and distribution of dairy food products; U.S. Funds Express, Inc., Dallas, TX, Money transfer, regulatory permits and fuel purchase programs primarily for the trucking industry; United Telecommunications, Inc., Kansas City, MO, Operation of telephone system; telecommunications and electrical products; other communications and computer-related businesses; USALAMO Inc., San Antonio, TX, Heavy-duty mowing equipment for highway right-of-ways and other large areas; steel foundry castings for industrial and oil field equipment; Varix Corp., Richardson, TX, Software-driven universal integrated circuit programmers; Vista Chemical Co., Houston, TX, Petrochemicals including surfactants and polyvinylchloride (PVC); Western Tele-Communications, Inc., Englewood, CO, Microwave relay systems in Western U.S.; The Wholesale Club, Inc., Indianapolis, IN, Self-service, membership-only wholesale warehouses located in Indianapolis, Cleveland, and Milwaukee; American Nursery Products, Inc., Tahlequah, OK, Wholesale nurseries growing a wide variety of trees, shrubs, and plants; Balco International Inc., Wichita, KS, Specialty architectural products used in the construction and remodeling of commercial and institutional buildings; Columbia Scientific Industries Corp., Austin, TX, Analytical instruments for laboratory measurements, air pollution monitoring instruments, and intercom equipment; FMC Corp., Chicago, IL, Machinery and chemicals in diversified product areas; Hercules Offshore Drilling Co. and Hercules L.P., Houston, TX, Workover and drilling services on oil and gas production platforms in the Gulf of Mexico using modular rigs; Houston Oil Fields Co., Houston, TX, Oil and gas exploration and production; Humac Co., Dallas, TX, Royalty interests in underdeveloped coal deposits in Wyoming; Modular Computer Systems, Inc., Ft. Lauderdale, FL, Minicomputer systems used primarily in measurement and control of industrial processes and in data communications applications; Oak Creek Homes, Inc., Dallas, TX, Manufactured housing produced in four facilities located in northern Texas; Palm Harbor Homes, Inc., Dallas, TX, Manufactured housing produced in nine plants located in Arizona, Florida, Texas, North Carolina and Georgia; Pandick, Inc., New York, NY, Financial, legal, corporate, and commercial printing; Pharmacy Practice Group, Inc., Dallas, TX, Management of hospital pharmacies; The Rectorseal Corp., Houston, TX, Chemical specialty products; Repligen Corp., Cambridge, MA, Development of biologically derived products utilizing genetic engineering technology; Shippan Transportation Corp., Madison, WI, Common carrier trucking company; Skylawn Corp., Hayward, CA, Cemeteries, mausoleums, and mortuaries located in northern California; Tele-Communications, Inc., Denver, CO, Cable television systems with over 3.9 million subscribers; The Whitmore Manufacturing Co., Rockwell, TX, Specialized lubricants for heavy mining and industrial equipment; Worldwide Energy Corp., Denver, CO, Oil and gas exploration and production

CAPWEST CAPITAL SERVICES LTD.
1102, 10080 Jasper Avenue
Edmonton, Alberta T5J 1V9
Canada
(403) 426-7117

M. A. Miles
E. H. Millar
E. Pechet
J. R. Groves

Average Size of Investment	$750K
Size of Fund	Undisclosed
Investment Criteria	Undisclosed
Portfolio Companies	Undisclosed

CARIBANK CAPITAL CORP./CARIBANK VENTURE CORP.
255 East Dania Beach Boulevard
Dania, FL 33004
(305) 925-2211

Michael E. Chaney
Harold F. Messner
Elaine E. Healy

Average Size of Investment	$300K
Size of Fund	Caribank Capital: $4M Caribank Venture: $2M
Investment Criteria	Second- and third-stage electronics, health care, telecommunications
Portfolio Companies	Undisclosed

DIRECTORY AND BIOGRAPHIES

CAROLINA VENTURE CAPITAL CORP.
14 Archer Road
Hilton Head Island, SC 29928
(803) 842-3101

Thomas H. Harvey III
President

Directorships

Calibogue Broadcasting Company, Radio
Hilton Head Broadcasting Corp., Radio
Hotel Securities, Inc.

Prior Positions

Real estate salesman, Sea Pines Plantation
Vice President, Marketing, Professional Services, Inc.

Education

MBA, University of North Carolina, 1972
BA, Economics, University of North Carolina, 1970

Joe Harden
Thomas E. Harvey, Jr.
Jim Herring
Fred Hohage

Average Size of Investment	$100K
Size of Fund	Undisclosed
Investment Criteria	Communications, construction, hotels, recreation, diversified
Portfolio Companies	Undisclosed

CATALYST VENTURES, LTD.
1287 Lawrence Station Road
Sunnyvale, CA 94089
(408) 745-1110

Nolan K. Bushnell
Chairman of the Board

Directorships

Axlon, Inc., Electronic toys
ByVideo, Inc., Interactive video disk
Etak, Inc., Vehicle navigation
ACTV, Inc., Interactive cable television
I'RO, Inc., Computerized color analysis
Magnum Microwave Corp., Microwave telecommunications

Prior Positions

Chairman of the Board, Pizza Time Theatre, Inc.
Chairman of the Board, Atari, Inc.

Education

BSEE, University of Utah, 1968

Lawrence Calof
President

Directorships

Etak, Inc., Vehicle navigation
I'RO, Inc., Color analysis
Axlon, Inc., Electronic toys
ACTV, Inc., Interactive cable television
Phase 2 Automation, Automation systems
Vidium, Inc., Hi-Res television
Pizza Time Theatre, Inc., Restaurant chain

Prior Position

Attorney/Partner, Gibson, Dunn & Crutcher

Education

JD, Stanford University Law School, 1969
BA, Stanford University, 1966

John B. Anderson
Executive Vice President

Directorships

Axlon, Inc., Toys and games
I'RO, Inc., Computerized color analysis
Vidium, Inc., Hi-resolution TV
Greenbourne, Ltd., Trading company

Prior Positions

Director of Finance, Pizza Time Theatre, Inc.
Vice-President—Administration, Atari, Inc.

Education

MBA, University of Santa Clara, 1972
BS, San Jose State University, 1965

Perry D. Odak
Partner

Directorships

ByVideo Inc., Electronic retailing
Etak, Inc., Car navigation
I'RO, Inc., Color analysis

Prior Positions

President/Consumer Products Group, Atari, Inc.
Senior Vice President, Jovan, Inc.
Senior Vice President, Armour-Dial, Inc.

Education

MS, Economics, Cornell University, 1969
BS, Economics, Cornell University, 1968

Average Size of Investment	$500K
Size of Fund	$8.25M
Investment Criteria	Seed capital
Portfolio Companies	ACTV, Inc., Sunnyvale, CA, Interactive cable television; Androbot, Inc., Sunnyvale, CA, Robotics; ByVideo, Inc., Sunnyvale, CA, Interactive video disk; Etak, Inc., Sunnyvale, CA, Vehicle nagivation; I'RO, Inc., Sunnyvale, CA, Color analysis

CATERPILLAR VENTURE CAPITAL, INC.
100 N.E. Adams Street
Peoria, IL 61629-6170
(309) 675-5503

Robert L. Powers
President

Directorships

Advanced Technology Services, Inc.
C D High Technology, Inc.
Fared Robot Systems, Inc.
Industrial Lasers, Inc.

Prior Position

Caterpillar, Finance

Education

BA, Economics, Quincy College, 1967

Jack W. Dennis
Technical Manager

Prior Position

Caterpillar, Engineering/research

Education

MSME, University of Wisconsin, 1972
BSME, Purdue, 1959

William B. Heming
Venture Manager

Directorships

Industrial Lasers, Inc.

Prior Position

Caterpillar, Patents

Education

JD, University of Nebraska, 1977
BSME, University of Nebraska, 1974

Average Size of Investment	$2M
Size of Fund	Undisclosed
Investment Criteria	Product differentiation, large and growing markets, outstanding management team
Portfolio Companies	Advanced Technology Services, Inc., Computer repair, East Peoria, IL; C D High Technology, Inc., Asphalt reprocessing, Georgetown, TX; Fared Robot Systems, Inc., Factory automation, Fort Worth, TX; Industrial Lasers, Inc., Carbon dioxide lasers, Albuquerque, NM

DIRECTORY AND BIOGRAPHIES

CEDC-MESBIC, INC.
106 Main Street
Hempstead, NY 11550
(516) 292-9710

John L. Kearse

Average Size of Investment	$150K
Size of Fund	$1M
Investment Criteria	Manufacturing companies are of interest as well as other diversified areas; start-ups; geographic proximity is important
Portfolio Companies	Undisclosed

CEDCO CAPITAL CORP.
180 North Michigan Avenue
Chicago, IL 60601
(312) 984-5950

Frank B. Brooks
President

Directorships

Chicago Economic Development Corp.
CEDCO Commercial Credit

Prior Positions

President, Chicago Economic Development Corp., 1976–present
Executive Director, Combined Opportunities, Inc., 1973–76

Education

MBA, Keller Graduate School of Management
BA, Northwestern University

Webster Daniels
Executive Vice President

Directorship

YMCA

Prior Position

Finance Director, McKee, Burger, Mansueto, Inc., 1975–79

Education

MBA, Roosevelt University, 1977
MS, Mathematics, City College of New York, 1964
BS, Mathematics, City College of New York, 1962

Average Size of Investment	$100K
Size of Fund	$1M
Investment Criteria	Diversified preferences; geographic proximity important; start-ups; will act as lead investor
Portfolio Companies	Undisclosed

CENTENNIAL BUSINESS DEVELOPMENT FUND, LTD.
1999 Broadway
Suite 2100
Denver, CO 80202
(303) 298-9066

David Bullwinkle
Managing General Partner

Prior Position

Vice President and Department Head, Securities Investment Department, Mutual of New York

Education

MBA, University of Michigan, 1963
BA, The Principia College, 1962

William D. Stanfill
Managing General Partner

Prior Position

General Partner, Murrill Stanfill Company

Education

BA, University of Colorado, 1961

George J. Still, Jr.
General Partner

Directorships

Moritz Mining Co., Inc.
Intelligent Medicine, Inc.

Prior Position

Senior Accountant, Ernst & Whinney

Education

MBA, Amos Tuck School of Business Administration, Dartmouth College
BS, Pennsylvania State University

Average Size of Investment	$1M
Size of Fund	$20M
Investment Criteria	Later stage, venture capital backed companies

THE CENTENNIAL FUNDS
1999 Broadway
Suite 2100
Denver, CO 80202
(303) 298-9066

Steven C. Halstedt
General Partner

Directorships

Comlinear Corp.
PageAmerica Group, Inc.
Orion Satellite Corp., Inc.
Cencom Cable Associates, Inc.
Teloc, Inc.

Prior Positions

Executive Vice President, Daniels & Associates, Inc.
Investment Manager, Travelers Insurance Co.

Education

MBA, Amos Tuck School of Business Administration
University of Connecticut School of Law
BS, Worcester Polytechnic Institute

G. Jackson Tankersley, Jr.
General Partner

Directorships

Moritz Mining Company
Applied Spectrum Technologies, Inc.
Delta Systems, Inc.
Dowden Communications, Inc.
Informed Corp.

Prior Position

Second Vice President, Continental Illinois Bank

Education

MBA, Amos Tuck School, Dartmouth College
BA, Denison University

Dr. Mark Dubovnoy
General Partner

Directorships

Teloc, Inc.
Waveframe Corp.
Com Linear Corp.
Sadel Corp.

Prior Position

General Partner, Norwest Venture Capital Management

Education

PhD, University of California, Berkeley
MA, National University of Mexico
BS, National University of Mexico

Average Size of Investment	$1M
Size of Fund	$60M–$80M
Investment Criteria	Areas in which individuals have proven expertise; early stages in growth companies in Rocky Moutain region, and in telecommunications nationwide
Portfolio Companies	American Home Alert Corp., Denver, CO, Operates and markets on a wholesale basis the monitoring of home and business security systems; Applied Spectrum Technologies, Inc., Minneapolis, MN, Designs, manufactures, and markets products permitting more information to be transmitted over a given frequency spectrum; Breit International, Inc., Boulder, CO, Developing computer-based instruction software tools that are machine independent and employ state-of-the-art artificial intelligence methodologies; Cencom Cable Associates, Inc., St. Louis, MO, Raises capital to acquire and operate cable TV systems; Centennial Business

DIRECTORY AND BIOGRAPHIES 167

Development Co., Denver, CO, The general partner of The Development Fund, Ltd., an investment fund in formation; Comlinear Corp., Loveland, CO, Designs, manufactures, and markets to OEM customers a family of low-cost, high-performance video amplifier products; Communications Office Machines, Inc., Denver, CO, Developing a new communication product to supplement existing fixed-cost private communications networks; Connecting Point of America Holdings, Inc., Denver, CO, Operates and franchises Connecting Point and Team Electronic Stores, a chain of computer and advanced consumer electronic stores; Delta Systems, Inc., Westminster, CO, Manufactures and markets a proprietary adapter that permits CDC computers to utilize IBM-compatible peripherals; Dowden Communications, Inc., Atlanta, GA, Franchises, constructs, and manages cable television systems primarily in rural markets; Ford/Higgins, Ltd., Boulder, CO, Manufactures and markets variable architecture multiuser, multitasking computers; Infomed Corp., Englewood, CO, Developing a nationwide communication system to provide physiological diagnosis; International Technology Systems, Inc., Denver, CO, Publishes and distributes microcomputer software for selected vertical markets including the medical and agricultural industries; McCaw Cellular Communications, Inc., Bellevue, WA, Development stage company applying to FCC for cellular telephone licenses in 18 markets; McDATA Corp., Boulder, CO, Manufactures and markets proprietary hardware and software for IBM-compatible business systems; MiniScribe Corp., Longmont, CO, Manufactures and markets to OEM customers a family of low-cost Winchester disk drives; Moritz Mining Co., Inc., Englewood, CO, Fully integrated gold mining, milling, and refining company that has developed a proprietary refining process; One Point Walnut Creek, CA, Markets microcomputer software and peripherals to large corporations and on-line information services to corporations and computer retailers; Orion Satellite Corp., Washington, DC, Applying to the FCC for permission to launch, market, and operate private trans-Atlantic satellite communications facility on K band; PageAmerica Group, Inc., New York, NY, Operates a national communications network serving the paging industry as well as its own multicity operations; Prime Cable Corp., Austin, TX, Owns and operates cable television systems in New York, Georgia, and Massachusetts; Private Satellite Network, Inc., New York, NY, Sells satellite-based private video networks principally to Fortune 1000 corporations; Republic Telcom Corp., Minneapolis, MN, Provides long-distance telephone and private-line services to businesses in 10 states; Rocky Mountain Oilfinders, Inc., Englewood, CO, Oil and gas exploration company generating drilling prospects and developing them through industry partners; Skylink Corp., Boulder, CO, Applying to the FCC for permission to provide for the development and operation of a mobile and thin-route satellite communications service on U & L bands; Teloc, Inc., Van Nuys, CA, Designs, manufactures, and markets a proprietary two-way distributed intelligence infrared telecommunications device

CENTRAL CAPITAL CORP.
1097 Commercial Avenue
P.O. Box 3959
Lancaster, PA 17604
(717) 569-9650

Robert A. Rupel

Average Size of Investment	$200K
Size of Fund	Undisclosed
Investment Criteria	Manufacturing companies are of interest, as well as other diversified areas
Portfolio Companies	Undisclosed

CENTRAL N.Y. SBIC, INC.
351 South Warren Street
Syracuse, NY 13202
(315) 478-5026

Albert Wertheimer

Average Size of Investment	$100K
Size of Fund	Undisclosed
Investment Criteria	Undisclosed
Portfolio Companies	Undisclosed

CENTRAL VALLEY VENTURE CAPITAL CORP.
3621 Tina Place
Stockton, CA 95205
(209) 931-2505

Thomas M. Gibbs, III
President

Education

MBA, Cornell Graduate School of Business
MS, Cornell Graduate School of Nutrition
BA, Ithaca College

Newell Jackson, Vice Chairman

Average Size of Investment	$100K–$200K
Size of Fund	Undisclosed
Investment Criteria	Undisclosed
Portfolio Company	Undisclosed

CERTO CAPITAL CORP.
6150 McKee Road
Madison, WI 53711
(608) 271-4500

Donald Watzke

Average Size of Investment	$100K
Size of Fund	Undisclosed
Investment Criteria	Undisclosed
Portfolio Companies	Undisclosed

CFB VENTURE CAPITAL CORP.
530 B Street
Second Floor
San Diego, CA 92112
(619) 230-3304

Richard J. Roncaglia
Vice President

Prior Position
Vice President, California First Bank, International Trust Dept., 1980

Education
JD, University of San Diego, 1976
BA, University of San Diego, 1972

Piet Westerbeek
Yoji Anzai

Average Size of Investment	$200K
Size of Fund	Undisclosed
Investment Criteria	Undisclosed
Portfolio Companies	Undisclosed

CHAMBERS FINANCIAL CORP.
720 South Colorado Boulevard
Suite 940
Denver, CO 80222
(303) 759-4869

Brad C. Ayers
President

Directorship
Aspen Child Development Centers, Inc., Day care centers

Prior Positions
President, Ayers & Co.
Corporate Controller, Unirad, Technicare, Johnson & Johnson, 1976–80
Accounting Manager, Beckman Instruments, 1967–76

Education
MBA, University of Denver, 1978
BA, University of California at Long Beach, 1961

Robert S. Froug
Vice President and Director

Directorships
Consumer Health Services, Inc., Medical information service
Venture Capital International, Venture capital

Prior Position
President, Venture Capital International, 1982–85

Education
BS, University Northern Arizona, 1971

Average Size of Investment	$300K
Size of Fund	$3M
Investment Criteria	Joint venture financing for corporate marketing, domestic and international
Portfolio Companies	AMS Realstar; Denver, CO, Software; Charger Corp., Portland, OR, Athletic shoes; Consumer Health Services, Boulder, CO, Info technology; Rentech, Inc., Denver, CO, Energy

DIRECTORY AND BIOGRAPHIES

R. H. CHAPPELL COMPANY
One Lombard Street
San Francisco, CA 94111
(415) 397-5094

Robert H. Chappell
Chairman and President

Directorships

Matrix Corp., Video image recorders
Baccarat Teledex, Inc., Telecommunications
Counterpoint Computers, Inc., Supermicrocomputers
Pentron Industries, Inc., Automotive electronics

Prior Positions

President, Churchill International
Director/General Partner, Shuman, Agnew & Co., Inc.

Education

BA, University of Southern California

N. Colin Lind
Vice President

Directorship

Tekna, Underwater equipment

Prior Positions

Vice President, Davis, Skaggs & Co., Inc.
Vice President, Wheat, First Securities, Inc.

Education

B. Bus. Sc., University of Cape Town, 1978
Honors Finance, University of Cape Town, 1978

Average Size of Investment	$1M
Size of Fund	Undisclosed
Investment Criteria	Early-stage preference; experienced management team; high growth potential per dollar invested; all industries
Portfolio Companies	Currently 8 companies in portfolio

CHARLES RIVER VENTURES
67 Batterymarch Street
Boston, MA 02110
(617) 482-9370

Richard M. Burnes, Jr.
General Partner

Directorships

Bytex Corp.
Candela Electronics
ChipCom Corp., Communications-related products using digital signal processing
Exploration Production & Equipment Co., Piping, pumps, compressors, and trucking services for oil drilling sites
Seragen, Inc.
Summa Four, Inc.
Teledex

Prior Positions

Vice President and Analyst, Federal Street Capital Corp.
Credit Analyst, National Shawmut Bank

Education

MBA, Boston University, 1970
AB, Harvard College, 1963

Donald W. Feddersen
General Partner

Directorships

Network Systems Corp.
Policy Management Systems Corp., Software supplier to property and casualty insurance companies

Prior Positions

President and Chief Executive Officer, Applicon Inc., a Schlumberger Co.
President and Chief Executive Officer, Entrex, Inc.

Education

MBA, University of Chicago, 1969
BSME, Purdue University, 1956

Robert F. Higgins
General Partner

Directorships

National Healthcare, Inc., Rural hospital management
New England Critical Care, Home health care provider
Flextronics
Cadmus Computer, Supermicrocomputers

Prior Positions

Executive Director, John A. Hartford Foundation
Executive Director, Robert Sterling Clark Foundation

Education

MBA, Harvard Business School, 1970
AB, Harvard College, 1968

John T. Neises
General Partner

Directorships

Autographix
VIA Systems
Shared Financial Systems
Scott Systems, Inc.
Saddlebrook Corp.
Multiplications Software

Prior Positions

General Manager, Copier Division, Dennison Manufacturing
Division Controller and Head of Planning, Xerox Corp.

Education

MBA, Harvard Graduate School of Business Administration, 1956
BBA, University of Cincinnati, 1952

Paul A. Maeder
General Partner

Prior Positions

Chief Engineer, Synemed, 1978–82
Mechanical Engineer, Novacor, 1977–78

Education

MBA, Harvard Business School, 1984
MS, Stanford University, 1977
BS, Princeton University, 1975

Average Size of Investment	Undisclosed
Size of Fund	$14M
Investment Criteria	No oil, gas or real estate
Portfolio Companies	American Management Systems, Arlington, VA, Computer services; AMGen, Newbury Park, CA, Biotechnology; Applicon, Burlington, MA, Computer-aided design; Autex, Wellesley, MA, Financial computer services; Autographix, Waltham, MA, Computer-generated slides; Avantek, Santa Clara, CA, Microwave systems; Bytex, Newton, MA, Data communications switch; Candela, Sunnyvale, CA, Telephone automation equipment; Comprehensive Care, Newport Beach, CA, Alcoholism treatment; Concentric Data Systems, Inc., Westboro, MA, Data mangement for IBM PC; Consolidated Video, Santa Clara, CA, Broadcast equipment; Continental Cable, Boston, MA, Cable television; Cytogen, Princeton, NJ, Monoclonal antibodies; Data Electronics, San Diego, CA, Magnetic tape drives; Data Recording, Melville, NY, Laser printers; Delmed, Canton, MA, Medical supplies; Dest, San Jose, CA, Optical character recognition machines; DMA, Santa Barbara, CA, Winchester disk drives; Dysan, Santa Clara, CA, Computer memory media; Enter Computer, Inc., San Diego, CA, Graphics plotter for minicomputer systems; Entrex, Burlington, MA, Data entry; Flextronics, Newark, CA, Board level computer assemblies; Gradco Systems, Santa Ana, CA, Paper-handling devices; Henco, Waltham, MA, Software; Interactive Training Systems, Inc., Cambridge, MA, Interactive video training services and products; International Microelectronic Products, San Jose, CA, Custom VLSI; Kaye Instruments, Bedford, MA, Process measurement instruments; Materials Progress Corp., Santa Rosa, CA, Substrates for rigid disks, laser rods, and bubble memories; MCI, Washington, DC, Telephone common carrier; Multiplications, Cambridge, MA, Software; National Micronetics, San Diego, CA, Disk drive heads; Network Systems, Brooklyn Park, MN, High-speed data communication; New England Critical Care, Inc., Framingham, MA, Home health care; Park City Communications, Bridgeport, CT, Radio station operator; Pizza Time Theatres, Sunnyvale, CA, Restaurants; Polymer Technology, Wilmington, MA, Contact lenses; Priam, San Jose, CA, Winchester disk drives; Saddlebrook, Cambridge, MA, Computer systems; Scientific Systems Services, Melbourne, FL, Computer systems; Scott Systems, Inc., Marlborough, MA, Computer terminals and systems; Seragen, Boston, MA, Antibody serum; Shared Financial Systems, Inc., Dallas, TX, Software products; Storage Technology, Lewisville, CO, Tape drives; Stratus, Natick, MA, Nonstop computer; Summa Four, Inc., Manchester, NH, Telephone equipment; Syntrex, Eatontown, NJ, Word processors; National Healthcare, Inc., Dothan, AL, Owns, manages hospitals in Southeast; Ateq Corp., Beaverton, OR, Designs and manufactures laser-driven semiconductor

manufacturing; Axiom Technology Corp., Newton, MA, Produces test equipment for linear and mixed technology semiconductor components; Caddex, Woodlinville, WA, Develops and will market corporate electronic publishing software; Community Health Systems, Inc., Houston, TX, Owns and manages hospitals and nursing homes; Celerity Computing, San Diego, CA, Manufactures and markets high performance computer for engineering and scientific purposes; Consumer Health Systems, Inc., Boulder, CO, Healthcare marketing and information services company; Imagitex Inc., Nashua, NH, High resolution scanners for converging images into digital data for processing and storage; Interactive Video Systems, Inc., Concord, MA, Developing a digital microscope to measure line width on semiconductor masks or wafers; Ion Beam Systems Inc., Beverly, MA, Developing semiconductor wafer inspection and repair system; Medivision, Inc., Houston, TX, Medical service company that specializes in the development, acquisition and management of eye surgery centers; Sybase, Inc., Berkeley, CA, Relational database software which runs on standard mini-computers, and workstation networks; United Health Care, Inc., Nashville, TN, Healthcare management company that owns and operates psychiatric and acute care hospitals in the Southeast; Teledex, Santa Clara, CA, "Smart" telephones; Telequest, Inc., Burbank, CA, Designer telephones; VIA Systems, North Billerica, MA, Computer-assisted design systems; WUTV, Buffalo, NY, TV station operator; Zentec, Santa Clara, CA, Computer terminals; Zylin, Oakland, CA, Plasma etching equipment

CHARLESTON CAPITAL CORP.
P.O. Box 328
Charleston, SC 29402
(803) 723-6464

Thomas M. Ervin
Henry Yaschik

Average Size of Investment	$100K
Size of Fund	$4.5M
Investment Criteria	Diversified company interests; will act as lead investor; geographic proximity is important
Portfolio Companies	Undisclosed

CHARTER VENTURES
525 University Ave., Suite 1500
Palo Alto, CA 94301

Johnson M.D. Cha
Managing Director/CHAVENCAP Ltd., General Partner

Education

MBA, Stanford University, 1976
BS, Carnegie Mellon, 1973

A. Burr Dolan
General Partner

Education

MBA, Stanford University, 1976
BA, Cornell University, 1971

Average Size of Investment	$300–500K
Size of Fund	Undisclosed
Investment Criteria	Experienced management team; $50M+ in sales in five years; protectable market position
Portfolio Companies	Metricom, Communications, Cupertino, CA; Vasocor, Biotechnology, Mountain View, CA; Aspen Diagnostics, Biotechnology, Mountain View, CA; Data Technology, Data Storage, Santa Clara, CA

CHERRY TREE VENTURES
1400 Northland Plaza
3800 West 80th Street
Minneapolis, MN 55431
(612) 893-9012

Gordon F. Stofer
General Partner

Directorships

Datamyte Corp., Statistical quality control
Motion Research, Inc., Manufacturing automation
National Information Systems, Diversified information systems
Ringer Corp., Lawn care products
Springboard Software, Inc., Educational software
VEE Corp., Entertainment

Prior Positions

Vice President, Northwest Growth Fund, Inc.
Market Manager, Honeywell, Inc.

Education

MBA, Harvard Business School, 1975
BS, Cornell University, 1969

Tony J. Christianson
General Partner

Directorships

Jonathan Health Services, Retail dental care
Varitronics Systems, Inc., Graphics processor
Computer Petroleum Corp., Petroleum pricing information
Derata Corp., Diabetic health care
Genesis Labs, Inc., Bio-engineered diagnostics
Microtechnology Sources, Ltd., Manufacturing software
Republic Telcom Systems, Long distance enhancements

Prior Position

Vice President, Norwest Growth Fund, Inc.

Education

MBA, Harvard Business School, 1978
BA, Accounting, St. John's University, 1974

John Bergstrom
Investment Analyst

Education

MBA, University of Minnesota, 1985
BA, Gustavus Adolphus College, 1982

Average Size of Investment	$500K
Size of Funds	Cherry Tree Ventures I: $10M
	Cherry Tree Ventures II: $30M
Investment Criteria	Prefers Minnesota based; start-up first- or second-stage equity participation in technology-based companies in health care, communications, software, and retail
Portfolio Companies	Buffets, Inc., Minneapolis, MN, Restaurant; CNS, Inc., Minneapolis, MN, PC-driven EEG; Arbor Health Care, Inc., Lima, OH, Long-term health care; FSI, Inc., Minneapolis, MN, Semiconductor industry; Jiffy Lube International, Baltimore MD, Automotive service centers; Kronos, Inc., Waltham, MA, Computerized timekeeping systems; McClain Airlines, Phoenix, AZ, Commercial airlines; Motion Research, Inc., Minneapolis, MN, Manufacturing automation; National Information Systems, Minneapolis, MN, Diversified information services; Ringer Corp., Minneapolis, MN, Lawn care products; Computer Petroleum Corp., Minneapolis, MN, Petroleum pricing information; DataMyte Corp., Minneapolis, MN, Statistical quality control; Derata Corp., Minneapolis, MN, Diabetic health care; DLS, Inc., (The Connection), Minneapolis, MN, Consumer information; Edge Computer Corp., Minneapolis, MN, Supermicrocomputer; Genesis Labs, Inc., Minneapolis, MN, Bio-engineered diagnostics; Interpore, International, Irvine, CA, Artificial bone substitute; Jonathan Health Services, Minneapolis, MN, Retail dental care; MSL, Ltd., Minneapolis, MN, Manufacturing software; Republic Telcom Corp., Minneapolis, MN, Long distance enhancements; Springboard Software, Inc., Minneapolis, MN, Educational software; Telenova, Inc., San Francisco, CA, Digital voice/data; Truffles Group, Inc., Minneapolis, MN, Gourmet candies; United Healthcare Corp., Minneapolis, MN, HMO management company; Varitronic Systems, Inc., Minneapolis, MN, Graphics processor; XTAL Corp., Minneapolis, MN, Computer-aided machining

CHICAGO COMMUNITY VENTURES, INC.
104 South Michigan Avenue
Suite 215
Chicago, IL 60603
(312) 726-6084

Phyllis George, President

Average Size of Investment	$300K
Size of Fund	Undisclosed
Investment Criteria	Diversified company interests; start-ups; geographic proximity important
Portfolio Companies	Undisclosed

CHICKASAW CAPITAL CORP.
67 Madison Avenue
P.O. Box 387
Memphis, TN 38147
(901) 523-6404

Thomas L. Moore

Average Size of Investment	$100K
Size of Fund	$1M
Investment Criteria	Diversified interests; geographical location important
Portfolio Companies	Undisclosed

CHURCHILL INTERNATIONAL
444 Market Street
25th Floor
San Francisco, CA 94111
(415) 398-7677

9 Riverside Road
Weston, MA 02193
(617) 893-6555

Louis L. Davis
Chairman, Chief Executive Officer, CA

Prior Positions

President, Emerging Economies Corp., 1976–78
President, LEX Systems, Inc., 1970–76
Director, Management Systems, Engineering and Computing Sciences, Space Division, North American Rockwell, to 1970

Education

MBA, University of Southern California
BS, Industrial Technology, California State University at Long Beach

Robert C. Weeks
President and Chief Financial Officer, CA

Directorship

Oceanic Capital Corp.

Prior Position

Vice President, LEX Systems, Inc.

Education

MBA, Stanford University
BA, Stanford University

Janet G. Effland
Managing Director, CA

Directorship

CIN Investment Company

Prior Positions

Vice President, Corporate Planning, Qume Corp.
Vice President, General Counsel, ITT Courier Terminal Systems, Inc.

Education

Program for Management Development, Harvard Business School
JD, Arizona State University
BS, Arizona State University

Christopher Spray
Managing Director, MA

Directorship

Van Gogh, Ltd.

Prior Positions

Investment Manager, CIN Industrial Investments, Ltd., London
Management Consultant, Biss Lancaster, London
Management Consultant, Michael Rice & Co., London

Education

MBA, Insead, Fountainebleau
Bachelors, Exeter College, Oxford

Franz Helbig
Managing Director
c/o TIG
GmbH & Co. KG
Kurfurstenann 209
D-1000 Berlin 15
West Germany
30-882-7201

Prior Positions

Managing Director, Johnson & Johnson, Belgium and Holland
General Director, Johnson & Johnson, Austria
Director of European Sales, Gould, Inc.
Executive Vice President and General Manager, Gentron, Inc.

Education

Masters of Economics and Political Science, University of Pennsylvania
Bachelors, Texas Technological University

Average Size of Investment	$750K–$1.5M
Size of Fund	$107M under management
Investment Criteria	Specific areas of high technology differ according to requirements of each pool
Portfolio Companies	American Robot Corp., Pittsburgh, PA, Apiary/Gold Hill, Computers, Inc., Cambridge, MA; Applied Data Systems, Inc., Scottsdale, AZ; Bio Diagnostics, Inc., Arlington, TX; Computer* Thought, Plano, TX; Dalsat, Inc., Plano, TX; Data Group Corp., Lexington, MA; Doelz Networks, Inc., Irvine, CA; Dolch Logic Instruments, Inc., San Jose, CA; Electronic Systems Products, Inc., Titusville, FL; Explosive Fabricators, Inc., Louisville, CO; Integrated Office Systems, Inc., Cupertino, CA; Koltron, Inc., Sunnyvale, CA; Kronos, Inc., Waltham, MA; Logisticon, Inc., Santa Clara, CA; Logos Computer Systems, Inc., Waltham, MA; Maxitron Corp., Corte Madera, CA; Prentice Corp., Sunnyvale, CA; Robinton Products, Inc., Sunnyvale, CA; Saber Technology Corp., San Jose, CA; Thinking Machines Corp., Cambridge, MA; Xicor, Inc., Milpitas, CA

CIRCLE VENTURES, INC.
20 N. Meridian Street
Indianapolis, IN 46204
(317) 636-7242

Samuel B. Sutphin II

Average Size of Investment	$100K
Size of Fund	$1M
Investment Criteria	Undisclosed
Portfolio Companies	Undisclosed

CITICORP VENTURE CAPITAL, LTD.
Citicorp Center
153 East 53rd Street
28th Floor
New York, NY 10043
(212) 559-1127

2 Embarcedero Place
2200 Geng Road, Suite 203
Palo Alto, CA 94303
(415) 424-8000

717 North Harwood
Suite 2920, LB 87
Dallas, TX 75201
(214) 880-9670

David A. Wegmann
Vice President, CA

Directorships

Telco Systems, Inc.
Compression Labs, Inc.
Vicom Systems, Inc.
Technology for Data Acquisition
MMI Medical, Inc.
Grid Systems

Prior Positions

Vice President, Marsh & McLennan, 1977–79
Vice President, Citibank, 1976–77
Vice President, Kuhn Loeb & Co., 1969–76

Education

MBA, Northwestern University, 1969
BS, Northwestern University, 1968

Larry J. Wells
Vice President, CA

Directorships

Cogensys Corp.
Identix Inc.
Lisp Machines, Inc.
Personics Corp.
Prentice Corp.
Tecstor Inc.

Prior Position

President, Creative Strategies International, 1969–83

Education

MBA, Stanford University, 1965
BA/BS, Stanford University, 1963

DIRECTORY AND BIOGRAPHIES

William T. Comfort
Chairman, NY

Peter G. Gerry
President, NY

Directorships

American Exploration Co.
Burkhart Petroleum Corp.
Display Data Corp.
Intellitek Computer Corp.
Ion Beam Systems, Inc.
Pond Hill Homes Ltd.

Prior Position

Vice President, Citicorp Venture Capital, Ltd., 1978–83

Education

MBA, Harvard Business School, 1973
AB, Harvard College, 1968

Richard M. Cashin
Vice President, NY

Directorships

Levitz Furniture
Keller Industries
Auto Style
G. P. Technologies
Hoover Group
American Technologies
Dynamic Technologies

Prior Position

Jardine Matheson, Hong Kong, 1976–78

Education

Harvard Business School, 1980
Harvard College, 1975

Scott G. Fossel
Vice President, NY

Directorships

Pamida Inc.
Conductron Corp.
Papercraft Corp.
Autotote Corp.
Servo-Tek

Prior Position

Vice President, Continental Illinois Bank, 1978–84

Education

MBA, Amos Tuck School, Dartmouth College, 1977
BA, Lake Forest College, 1975

Stephen C. Sherrill
Vice President, NY

Directorships

HealthStar Corp.
American PsychManagement, Inc.
Quantum Computer Services, Inc.
Milk Specialties Co.

Prior Position

Associate, Paul, Weiss, Rifkind, Wharton & Garrison, 1979–83

Education

JD, Columbia Law School, 1978
BA, Yale College, 1975

Thomas C. Darling
Assistant Vice President, N.Y.

Prior Positions

Vice President, Wertheim & Co., 1982–86
Associate, Becker Communications/Becker Ventures, 1980–82

Education

MBA, Harvard Business School, 1979
AB, Princeton University, 1975

Kilin To
Vice President, NY

Directorships

Proteon Inc.
Netlink Inc.
Audio Visual Laboratories
American Matrix Inc.

Prior Positions

Group Manager, Digital Equipment Corp., 1982–84
Product Manager, AT&T, 1971–81

Education

MBA, Wharton School, 1979
MSc, Princeton University, 1970

John R. Whitman
Vice President, NY

Directorships

Universal Electric Co.
Sav-A-Stop, Inc.
A&W Brands, Inc.
Price Communications Corp.
TVX Corp.
Beverage Canners International

Prior Positions

Vice President, Citicorp Institutional Recovery Management, 1978–80
Vice President, Citicorp International Bank, London, 1976–78

Education

MBA, Harvard Business School, 1971
BA, Yale University, 1966

Richard E. Mayberry
Assistant Vice President, NY

Prior Position

Vice President, Merrill Lynch, 1978–84

Education

MBA, Amos Tuck, 1978
AB, Dartmouth College, 1975

David F. Thomas
Vice President, NY

Directorships

Brintec Corp.
Devon Group
Mid-Atlantic Coca-Cola Bottling Co., Inc.
Papercraft Corp.
People Express Airlines

Prior Positions

Vice President, Citibank Transportation Finance, 1978–80
CPA, Arthur Andersen & Co., 1974–78

Education

BS, University of Akron, 1972

James J. Paulos
Texas

Directorships

J&L Specialty Products Co.
Horizon Savings & Loan

Prior Position

Executive Vice President, LTV Corp. 1956–86

Education

BBA, University of Michigan, 1952

Allen G. Rosenberg
Vice President, CA

Directorship

Magnesys

Prior Position

Manager, Boston Consulting Group, 1976–83

Education

MBA, Stanford University, 1976
AB, Stanford University, 1968

DIRECTORY AND BIOGRAPHIES

Thomas F. McWilliams
Vice President, TX

Directorships

Lomax Oil & Gas
Underwater Engineering
Shirco Infrared Systems, Inc.
Gascard Club, Inc.

Prior Positions

President, Chief Operating Officer, Shelter Resources Corp., 1978–83
Vice President, Citicorp/Citibank, 1976–78

Education

MBA, Wharton School of Finance, 1967
AB, Brown University, 1965

Newell V. Starks
Vice President, TX

Directorships

Earth Resource Data Corp.
Advanced Mineral Technology

Prior Positions

Manager, Strategic Marketing, Texas Instruments, 1982–84
Subsidiary President, Everett Charles, 1981–82

Education

MBA, University of Michigan, 1978
BSEE, Rutgers University, 1973

Bruce C. Bruckmann
Vice President, NY

Directorships

J & L Specialty Products Corp.
Dunbarton Corp.
BGD Corp.
Hancor, Inc.

Prior Positions

Attorney, Patterson, Belknap, Webb & Tyler, 1980–83
Law Clerk, Hon. John J. Gibbons, U.S. Court of Appeals for the Third Circuit, 1979–80

Education

JD, Harvard Law School, 1979
BA, Harvard College, 1976

Stanley Nitzburg
Vice President, NY

Directorships

Applied Spectrum Technologies
Language Technology, Inc.
Shape, Inc.

Prior Positions

Vice President, Citibank, 1973–83
Various, Tax Department, Financial Control, Capital Markers Group, 1982

Education

LLM, Taxation, New York University, 1965
JD, Columbia, 1955

Average Size of Investment	$1M+
Size of Fund	$250M
Investment Criteria	Varies
Portfolio Companies	Accountants Microsystems, Inc., Bellevue, WA, Produces and distributes vertical market software and turnkey systems primarily for the accounting market; American Cablesystems Corp., Boston, MA, Owns and operates cable TV systems in Massachusetts, New York, Virginia, Florida, and California; American Exploration Co., New York, NY, Engages in acquisition and management of oil and gas production in Texas and Louisiana; American Healthcorp, Nashville, TN, Owns and operates acute-care hospitals and substance abuse treatment centers; Amnet, Inc., Watertown, MA, Manufactures packet switches for private data networks; Applitek Corp., Wakefield, MA, Manufactures a family of local area network products which allow for contention and token passing devices to run on the same network; Audio Visual Laboratories, Inc., Tinton Falls, NJ, Manufactures and markets computer systems for creating and controlling high-resolution slide or video presentations; A & W Brands, Inc., White Plains, NY, Franchisor of regular and sugar-free A & W Root Beer; Beverage Canners International, Inc., Miami, FL, Independent bottler and canner of soft

drinks; Brintec, Willimantic, CT, Diversified producers of specialty engineered wire, cable, electronic connectors, and interconnection components for the computer, telecommunications, industrial, and military/aerospace markets; Bridge Communications, Inc., Cupertino, CA, Manufacturer of internetwork gateways and communication servers for local area networks; Burkhart Petroleum Corp., Tulsa, OK, Engages in oil and gas exploration in the midcontinent area of the U.S.; Combined Cable Corp. Chicago, IL, Owns and operates cable TV systems in the Midwest and Texas; Commterm, Inc., Bedford, MA, Manufactures and develops a family of digitized voice messaging products; Compression Labs, Inc., San Jose, CA, Manufactures compression devices for video teleconferencing; Conductron Corp., Leominster, MA, Manufactures wire and cable primarily used by utilities; Contemporary Communications, New Rochelle, NY, Owns and operates communications networks used for the digital transmission of voice, data, and video; Cosco, Columbus, IN, Manufacturer of folding household furniture and juvenile accessories; CTI Data Corp., Raleigh, NC, Manufactures IBM-compatible intelligent controllers with personal computer capability and local area network functionality; Data Electronics Inc, San Diego, CA, Manufactures tape drives and cartridge for data collection, data storage, and backup to disk drives; Datamedia Corp., Pennsauken, NJ, Manufactures and markets general-purpose display terminals and multiuser supermicrocomputers; Data Recording Systems, Inc., Melville, NY; Manufactures and markets laser paper printers; Davox Communication Corp., Merrimack, NH, Manufactures computer terminals providing IBM 3270, asynchronous, personal computer and telephone capabilities; Dest Corp., San Jose, CA, Manufactures page readers for the capture of text and graphics for use in word processing and electronic filing systems; Devon Holding Corp., Stamford, CT, Markets computer-based graphic arts services and distributes wines and spirits in Colorado; Display Data Corp., Hunt Valley, MD, Provides turnkey microcomputer and minicomputer systems to automobile dealers, beverage distributors, and lumber and building supply dealers for accounting and management information; Doelz Networks, Inc., Irvine, CA, Designs and produces equipment to support communication between multiple electronic devices over standard telephone lines; Dunbarton Corp., Dothan, AL, Manufactures and markets steel door frames, bi-fold steel doors, and other building products; Earth Resource Data Corp., Kansas City, KS, Provides computer modeling for crop management services based partially on remotely sensed data; Express Messenger, Inc., Calgary, Alberta, Provides intracity courier services operating in 13 major cities in the U.S. and Canada; Gascard Club, Inc., Del Mar, CA, Retail gasoline point-of-sale information, control and transaction processing services; Geodyne Resources, Inc., Tulsa, OK, As co-general partner with major brokerage firm, operates public oil and gas income programs, and explores for oil and gas; Grid Systems Corp., Mountain View, CA, Manufacturer of high-performance computer systems based on portable computers; Houdaille Holdings, Fort Lauderdale, FL, Machine tool, pump, and industrial equipment manufacturer; Identix, Inc., Mountain View, CA, Manufactures and markets a fingerprint verification system for use in physical access control and data security applications; Interactive Training Systems, Inc., Cambridge, MA, Interactive training and point of sale systems employing video disk, personal computer, and touch screen technology; International Microelectronic Products, Inc., San Jose, CA, Provides custom design and manufacture of MOS-integrated circuits; Kaiser Aerospace and Electronics/K-Systems, Inc., Oakland, CA, Subcontractor and systems supplier to the military and commercial aviation industries; KCR Technologies, Inc., Hartford, CT, Manufactures and markets high-speed nonimpact printer; Keller Holdings, Inc., Miami, FL, Manufactures aluminum building products and lawn furniture; LAM Research Corp., Santa Clara, CA, Manufactures high-end semiconductor plasma etching devices; Language Technologies, Inc., Salem, MA, A software service company which automatically converts unstructured COBOL programs into structured programs through license sales or inhouse service; Life Technologies, Inc., Gaithersburg, MD, Produces and markets genetic engineering products, based primarily on recombinant DNA technology; Lisp Machines, Inc., Culver City, CA, Manufactures and markets specialized processors and software for use in artificial intelligence and expert systems applications; Lomax Oil & Gas, Inc., Houston, TX, Explores for oil and gas primarily in the Uinta Basin in northeastern Utah; Merrimack Laboratories, Inc., Hudson, MA, Manufactures and markets surgical lasers; Microcom, Inc., Norwood, MA, Manufactures a family of modems which have a multivendor-supported protocol (MNP) enabling personal computers to exchange data; Mid-Atlantic Coca-Cola Bottling Co., Inc., Richmond, VA, Regional Coca-Cola and other soft drinks bottling company servicing Virginia, Maryland, and Washington, DC; MMI Medical, Pomona, CA, Provides shared diagnostic imaging services; National Demographics Ltd., Denver, CO, Develops and markets segmented mailing lists and demographic data; Netlink, Inc., Raleigh, NC, Manufactures and markets interfaces to IBM's SNA network; Nuclear Assurance Corp., Norcross, GA, Provider of nuclear fuel transportation and consulting services; Omni Cable TV Corp., Mahwah, NJ, Owns and operates cable TV systems in the eastern United States; Advanced Mineral Technologies, Golden, CO, Proprietary services for the treatment of heavy metal toxic wastes; ALC Communications Corp., Birmingham, MI, Operates a specialized common carrier system offering discounted long distance telephone rates and other services; American Matrix, Inc., Knoxville, TN, Manufactures specialized ceramic materials and high temperature furnaces; American Psychmanagement, Inc., Washington, DC, Provides prepaid mental health plans and cost containment services; American Technologies, Inc., Detroit, MI, Diversified manufacturer of specialized gears, building products, and other industrial products for the aerospace industry; Applied Spectrum Technologies, Inc., Minneapolis, MN,

Manufactures telecommunication devices which permit digital data and voice to be sent simultaneously over twisted pare using spread spectrum technology; Auto Style, Inc., Grand Rapids, MI, Manufactures and sells stylistic automotive components; Baker Communications, Inc., Rolling Hills Estates, CA, Publisher of local newspapers on the West Coast; Canaan Computer Corp., Trumbull, CT, Manufactures departmental computer systems capable of running the library of IBM mainframe software programs; Cogensys Corp., La Jolla, CA, Provides expert systems to the financial services industry; Curaflex Health Services, Inc., Houston, TX, Provides program based home healthcare services; Dynamic Technologies, Inc., Westport, CT, Diversified manufacturer of mobile and transportation products, including industrial wheels, heavy equipment traction aided devices and specialized engine components; Faircom, Inc., Old Brookville, NY, Owns and operates radio broadcasting properties; Hancor, Inc., Findlay, OH, Manufactures plastic pipe and other industrial goods; Healthsouth Rehabilitation Corporation, Birmingham, AL, Owns and operates national network of comprehensive outpatient rehabilitation facilities (CORFs); Healthstar Corporation, Houston, TX, Owns and operates national network of freestanding ambulatory surgery centers and rehabilitation hospitals; Hoover Group, Inc., Roswell, GA, Diversified manufacturer of industrial products and consumer hardgoods; Infocel, Inc., Raleigh, NC, Provide turnkey computer systems for governments, schools, and other public institutions; Intellitek Computer Corporation, Lexington, KY, Provides computerized services for the CATV industry and computer systems and service for specialized distributors; Ion Beam Systems, Inc., Beverly, MA, Manufacturer of focused ion beam systems for semiconductor mask generation and repair; J&L Specialty Products, Pittsburgh, PA, Manufactures specialty stainless steel products; Levitz Furniture, Inc., Boca Raton, FL, Retailer of home furniture; Magnesys Corporation, San Jose, CA, Manufactures fully engineered storage memory subsystems for industrial and other harsh environment applications; Metro General Communications, Inc., Greenwich, CT, Owns and operates radio broadcasting properties; Milk Specialties Company, Dundee, IL, Processor of milk-based specialty animal feeds; Pamida, Inc., Omaha, NE, Leading discount retailer in upper Midwest; dominant in small towns; Papercraft Corporation, Pittsburgh, PA, Manufactures gift wrap, tape, Christmas trees, kitchen textiles, toilet detergents, and shoe polish; Personics Corporation, Menlo Park, CA, Manufactures electronic systems for the flexible distribution of prerecorded music; Proteon, Inc., Natick, MA, Manufactures token ring local area network for data communication; Quantum Computer Services, Inc., Vienna, VA, Provides computer based teleservices to home computer users; R&R Broadcasting, Inc., New York, NY, Owns and operates radio broadcasting properties; Sav-A-Stop, Inc., Jacksonville, FL, Brokers and distributes consumer merchandise; Shape, Inc., Biddleford, ME, Contract manufacturer of compact disks, VHS and audio cassettes, automated assembly lines, computer storage products, and injection molded specialty products; Shirco Infrared Systems, Inc., Dallas, TX, Manufactures waste incineration systems for toxic sludge; Technology for Data Acquisition, Fremont, CA, Manufactures test equipment for application specific semiconductor circuits; Tigon Corporation, Stamford, CT, Operates national and international voice messaging service for corporate accounts; Tootje California, Inc., Redwood City, CA, Markets Tootje Dutch Anytime dessert; Vitarine Pharmaceuticals, Inc., Springfield Gardens, NY, Manufacturer of generic drugs; Wolfdata Corporation, Chelmsford, MA, Manufacturer of high capacity, multi-function networking devices and other data communication equipment; Pencept, Inc., Waltham, MA, Manufactures and markets hand-generated character recognition input devices; People Express Airlines, Inc., Newark, NJ, Provides scheduled, low-cost short- and medium-haul jet passenger services primarily in the eastern United States; Prentice Corp., Sunnyvale, CA, Manufactures and markets modems and multiplexers; Price Communications Corp., New York, NY, Owns and operates broadcasting, publishing and outdoor media properties; Prime Cable Corp., Austin, TX, Acquires, rehabilitates, and operates cable TV systems; Read-Rite, Inc., Santa Clara, CA, Manufactures thin-film heads for magnetic disk drives; Servo-Tek Products Co., Hawthorne, NJ, Designs and manufactures tachometer generators and servo motors for industrial control applications; Silvar-Lisco, Menlo Park, CA, Develops and markets a broad range of computer software products that assist engineers in the design of integrated circuits; Skantek Corp., New York, NY, Manufactures optical fiber-based systems for inputting engineering drawings to CAD systems; Specialty Packaging, Richmond, VA, Manufacturer of plastic spray closures for consumer product packagers; Syntro Corp., San Diego, CA, Utilizes biotechnology to develop products for agriculture, food processing, and specialty chemicals; Tartan Laboratories, Inc., Pittsburgh, PA, Develops compilers for multiple processors and languages; Tecstor, Inc., Huntington Beach, CA, Produces digital image memory systems; Telco Systems, Inc., Mountain View, CA, Manufactures private-line equipment and fiber-optic systems for telephone operating companies; The Television Corp. Stations (TVX), Norfolk, VA, Owns or controls and operates five UHF Independent Television Stations in the Southeast; Tennessee Chemical Co., Copperhill, TN, Manufacturer of sulfuric acid and copper-based specialty chemicals; Teradata Corp., Los Angeles, CA, Manufactures and markets large-scale intelligent data base management systems; Underwater Engineering, Inc., Houston, TX, Provides underwater welding services for the construction and repair of subsea pipelines and offshore oil and gas production platforms; Universal Electric Co., Owasso, MI, Manufactures and markets a complete line of fractional-horsepower electric motors and sophisticated manufacturing systems based on rotary die stamping technology; Vicom Systems, Inc., San Jose, CA, Manufactures and markets image processing equipment

CLAFLIN CAPITAL MANAGEMENT, INC.
185 Devonshire Street
Boston, MA 02110
(617) 426-6505

Thomas M. Claflin II
General Partner

Directorships

Altron, Inc.
Churchill Coatings, Inc.
Sturges Publishing, Inc.
National Demographics, Ltd.
ZMI, Inc.

Prior Positions

Founder, Claflin Capital Management, 1978
Vice President and General Partner, Paine, Webber, Jackson & Curtis, Inc., 1973–78
Vice President, T. A. Associates, 1967–73

Education

MBA, Harvard Graduate School of Business Administration, 1967
Cum Laude, American History, Harvard College, 1963

Lloyd C. Dahmen
General Partner

Directorships

Ensonig Corp.
Frequency Devices, Inc.
Isoreg Corp.
Liberty Square Investors
XyPlex, Inc.

Prior Positions

Consultant, Claflin Capital Management, Inc., 1978
Vice President and Director, Franklin Management Corp., 1975–78
Founder, Dahmen Associates, Inc., 1969
Portfolio Manager, Scudder Stevens & Clark, 1965–69

Education

MBA (with distinction), Harvard Graduate School of Business Administration, 1965
AB, Chemistry, Harvard College, 1962

Joseph Stavenhagen
General Partner

Directorships

Altertept, Inc.
Computer Solutions, Inc.
Data Acquisition Systems, Inc.
Greystone Technology Corp.
Xydex Corp.
Vortech Corp.

Prior Positions

Executive Vice President, Director, Shear Development Corp., 1980
Chief Financial Officer, President, Chief Executive Officer, Education Development Center, Inc., 1972–80

Education

MBA, Harvard Graduate School of Business Administration, 1954
BA, Economics, Ohio Wesleyan University, 1952

John O. Flender
General Partner

Directorships

Alto-Tronics Corp.
PMC/BETA Corp.

Prior Positions

Treasurer, President, Transatlantic Capital Corp., 1979–86
Treasurer, Surftech Corp., 1977–79
Treasurer, MIT Development Foundation, Inc., 1971–77

Education

BS, Massachusetts Institute of Technology, 1954

Average Size of Investment	$300K
Size of Fund	$30M
Investment Criteria	Start-up and early-stage companies in New England
Portfolio Companies	Undisclosed

CLARION CAPITAL CORP.
35555 Curtis Blvd.
Eastlake, OH 44094
(216) 953-0555

Morton A. Cohen
President

Directorships

Voicemail, Voice messaging
FDRL, Contract research testing
Childers Products, Coatings, adhesives manufacturing
Monitek, Instrumentation manufacturing
IGI Biotechnology, Industrial microbiology

Education
MBA, Wharton School, 1960

Michael L. Boeckman
Roger Eaglen

Average Size of Investment	$250K
Size of Fund	$20M
Investment Criteria	Experienced management team; proprietary product; internal growth rate in the 30–40% range
Portfolio Companies	Childers Products, Cleveland, OH, Coatings, adhesives manufacturing; Food & Drug Research Labs, Waverly, NY, Contract research testing; Monitek, Hayward, CA, Instrumentation manufacturing; Multi-Planar Diagnostic Imaging, Torrance, CA, Diagnostic imaging service; Tacoma Boat, Tacoma, WA, Contract boat building; Western Agricultural Publishing Co., Fresno, CA, Vertical magazine publishers; Masstor Systems, Santa Clara, CA, Mass data storage; Glas-Craft, Indianapolis, IN, Industrial equipment

CLINTON CAPITAL CORP.
419 Park Avenue South
New York, NY 10016
(212) 696-4334

Alan Leavitt

Average Size of Investment	$700K
Size of Fund	Undisclosed
Investment Criteria	Diversified interests; will act as lead investor; interested in start-ups
Portfolio Companies	Undisclosed

CLOVER TECHNOLOGY
Box 4500
Davis, CA 95617
(916) 756-5206

Richard Dorf
Partner
(916) 752-7395

Directorships

Adaptive Technologies, Inc., Robot manufacturer
Westwind, Inc., Wind machines

Education
PhD, United States Naval Postgraduate School, 1961

Barbara Purdy

Average Size of Investment	Undisclosed
Size of Fund	Undisclosed
Investment Criteria	Technology-based products; past R&D stage
Portfolio Companies	Undisclosed

CMNY CAPITAL COMPANY, INC.
77 Water Street
New York, NY 10005
(212) 437-7078

Robert Davidoff
Vice President

Directorships

Instanet, Financial information automated execution of security trades
Delta Data Systems Corp., Manufacturer of CRT terminals
Audio/Video Affiliates, Inc., Chain of retail video and appliance stores
Hubco Exploration Inc., Oil and gas producer
Transmagnetics, Inc., Manufacturer of electronic products
Milgray Electronics, Inc., Distributor of electronic products

Education

BBA, City College of New York, 1948

Average Size of Investment	$250K
Size of Fund	$30M
Investment Criteria	Various
Portfolio Companies	Undisclosed

COASTAL CAPITAL CO.
16 Midtown Park East
Mobile, AL 36606
(205) 476-0700

David C. DeLaney

Average Size of Investment	$300K
Size of Fund	Undisclosed
Investment Criteria	Construction and real estate companies are of interest; geographic proximity is important
Portfolio Companies	Undisclosed

WILLIAM M. COCKRUM
666 Sarbonne Road
Los Angeles, CA 90077
(213) 552-6115

William M. Cockrum
Principal

Directorships

Transcon, Inc., Trucking
KCC, Publishing

Prior Position

Vice Chairman, A. G. Becker

Education

MBA, Harvard University, 1961
BA, DePauw University, 1959

Average Size of Investment	$500K
Size of Fund	Several: $10M
Investment Criteria	Will look at all ventures
Portfolio Companies	Undisclosed

COLEMAN VENTURES, INC.
5909 Northern Boulevard
East Norwich, NY 11732
(516) 626-3642

Gregory S. Coleman
President

Directorships

Dionics, Inc., Integrated circuits
Solid Power Corp., Power transistors
Circuit Technology, Hybrid circuits

Education

MA, Fordham University, New York, 1952
BA, Fordham University, New York, 1950

Roger V. Coleman

Average Size of Investment	$350K–$500K
Size of Fund	$5M
Investment Criteria	Propositions must be accompanied by at least an informal business plan
Portfolio Companies	Circuit Technology, Inc., Farmingdale, NY; Dionics, Inc., Westbury, NY; Solid Power, Inc., Farmingdale, NY

COLLEGE VENTURE EQUITY CORP.
1501 Second Avenue
Tampa, FL 33605
(813) 248-3878

Frances M. Williams, President
Albert Elia, Chief Financial Officer

Average Size of Investment	Undisclosed
Size of Fund	Undisclosed
Investment Criteria	Undisclosed
Portfolio Companies	Undisclosed

COLLIER ENTERPRISES
655 Madison Avenue
New York, NY 10021
(212) 752-0771

Miles Collier

Average Size of Investment	$100K
Size of Fund	$40M
Investment Criteria	Technology-based companies are of interest, as well as start-ups; will act as lead investor
Portfolio Companies	Undisclosed

COLORADO GROWTH CAPITAL, INC.
1600 Broadway
Suite 2125
Denver, CO 80202
(303) 831-0205

Nicholas H. C. Davis
Chairman and President

Education

MBA, Stanford University, 1963
BA, Princeton University, 1961

Debra J. Chavez

Average Size of Investment	$100K
Size of Fund	$2M
Investment Criteria	Operating manufacturing company; patented/proprietary product; annual sales $500K
Portfolio Companies	Unavailable

COLORADO VENTURE CAPITAL CORP.
4735 Walnut Street
Boulder, CO 80301
(303) 449-9018

Paul D. Whittle
Chairman of the Board and Chief Executive Officer

Directorships

Novan Energy, Solar-energy-device manufacturer
Dual Systems Corp., Computer manufacturer
Healthwatch, Family health care clinics
Colorado Venture Capital (Chairman), Investments

Prior Positions

President, Chairman of the Board, Synergetics, Intl., Inc.
President, Davis Whittle Co.

Education

MBA, University of Colorado, 1972
BBA (magna cum laude), Midwestern University, 1971

Clifford C. Thygesen
President

Directorships

Synergetics, Data-acquisition equipment
DBS, Inc., Manufacturing office equipment, desks

Prior Positions

President, Alpine Designs
Vice President, Ithaca Gun Co.

Education

BS, Industrial Administration, University of Illinois, 1961

Patrick J. Sweeney
Vice President

Directorships

Cyberlynx Computer Products, Computer add-on equipment for personal computers for home control and security
Milburn Technology, Manufactures and develops products based on new displacement technology

Prior Position

Private Consultant

Education

BS, Mathematics Education, State University of New York at Potsdam, 1967

Average Size of Investment	$250K
Size of Fund	$4M
Investment Criteria	Undisclosed
Portfolio Companies	Mobot, Houston, TX, Design and implementation of automated manufacturing systems; Cyberlynx Computer Products, Boulder, CO, Computer add-on equipment for home control and security; Drever Business Systems, Boulder, CO, Business furniture manufacturer; Dual Systems Corp., Berkeley, CA, Computer manufacturer; Healthwatch, Inc., Boulder, CO, Family health care clinics; Milburn Stirling Corp., Boulder, CO, Pump manufacturer; Synergetics Intl., Inc., Boulder, CO, Satellite communications manufacturer; Therapeutic Recreation Systems, Boulder, CO, Development and manufacture of prosthetic devices

COLUMBIA CAPITAL CORP.
419 Park Avenue South
New York, NY 10016
(212) 696-4334

Alan Leavitt

Average Size of Investment	$100K
Size of Fund	Undisclosed
Investment Criteria	Diversified interests, MESBIC
Portfolio Companies	Undisclosed

COLUMBIA VENTURES
1828 L Street, N.W.
Washington, DC 20036
(202) 659-0033

Richard Whitney
President

Directorships

Columbia Ventures, Inc.
Whitney & Co., Inc.
Interand Corp.
Color Custom, Inc.
Votrax, International
Welbac Cable TV Corp.

Prior Positions

President, Horizon Communications, 1978–81
Executive Vice President, Narrangansett Capital Corp., 1973–74
President, Whitney Financial Management, 1974–present

Education

BA, Brown University, 1959

Average Size of Investment	$200K
Size of Fund	$6M
Investment Criteria	Diversified interests
Portfolio Companies	Undisclosed

COLUMBINE VENTURE FUND, LTD.
5613 DTC Parkway
Suite 510
Englewood, CO 80111
(303) 694-3222

Mark J. Kimmel
General Partner

Directorships

Athens, Inc.
American International Communication Inc.
Colorado Small Business Council
Maxim Jeries Fund Inc.
Stolar, Inc.
Chairman, Venture Capital Assoc. of Colorado
Krysalis Corp.

Prior Positions

President, Enervest Inc.
Manager, New Business Development, Motorola, 1970–75
Evaluation Capacities, 3M Co., 1963–68

Education

MBA, University of Southern California
BS, Electrical Engineering, University of Colorado
BS, Business, University of Colorado

Duane D. Pearsall
General Partner

Directorships

Colorado Alliance of Business
AeroQuest, Aircraft instruments
Basis Medical Products, Health care products
Vice-Chairman, Colorado Association of Commerce & Industry

Prior Position

President, Statitrol Corp., 1963–78

Education

BSBA, University of Denver, 1947

Sherman J. Muller
General Partner

Directorships

Intelligent Medicine
Microtech Medical Photometrics

Prior Position

Vice President, Enervest, Inc.

Education

MBA, Tulane University, 1977

Terry E. Winters
General Partner

Directorships

Creative Biomolecules
Evans R & D
Microgenics
Wacon Corp.

Prior Position

Vice President, Diamond Shamrock Ventures

Education

PhD, Chemistry, 1968

Bryan Mitchell
Associate, Denver

Prior Position

Co-founder, Sundex Software Corp., 1981–85

Education

MBA, Harvard Business School, 1982
BS, Mechanical Engineering, Texas A & M University, 1978

Average Size of Investment	$500K
Size of Fund	$35M
Investment Criteria	Early stage; high technology; Rocky Mountain area
Portfolio Companies	Microgenics, Concord, CA, Homogeneous immunoassay diagnostics; Intelligent Medicine, Denver, CO, Advanced drug delivery systems; Saxpy Computers, Sunnyvale, CA, Supercomputers; Lawrence Medical, Redmond, WA, Non-invasive cardiac output monitors; American International Communications, Boulder, CO, Microframe software; Creative Biomolecules, So. San Francisco, CA, Biotechnology; Photometrics, Tucson, AZ, Electronic image processing

COMERICA CAPITAL CORP.
30150 Telegraph Road
Suite 245
Birmingham, MI 48010
(313) 258-5800

John D. Berkaw
President

Directorships

NASTEC Corp., Software productivity tools
Irwin Magnetic Systems, Peripheral company

Prior Positions

President, Comerica Financial Services
Vice President, Comerica Inc.
President, OBT Financial, 1979–82

Education

MBA, University of Michigan, 1966
BA, Kalamazoo College, 1965

Debra A. Ball

Average Size of Investment	$400K
Size of Fund	Undisclosed
Investment Criteria	Undisclosed
Portfolio Companies	Undisclosed

COMMERCE CITY INVESTMENTS LTD.
1645 Russel Road-Unit #2
Ottawa, Ontario K1G 4G5
Canada

Average Size of Investment	Undisclosed
Size of Fund	Undisclosed
Investment Criteria	Undisclosed
Portfolio Companies	Undisclosed

COMMUNITY EQUITY CORP. OF NEBRASKA
6421 Ames Avenue
Omaha, NE 68104
(402) 455-7722

Herbert M. Patten
Manager

Average Size of Investment	$100K
Size of Fund	Undisclosed
Investment Criteria	Diversified companies are of interest
Portfolio Companies	Diversified

CONCORD PARTNERS
535 Madison Avenue
New York, NY 10022
(212) 906-7000

600 Montgomery Street
San Francisco, CA 94111
(415) 362-2400

John P. Birkelund
General Partner, NY

Directorships

Cooperweld Corp.
Kramer Capital Corp.

Prior Positions

Chairman and Chief Executive Officer, New Court Securities Corp., 1967–81
Director and Officer, Amsterdam Overseas Corp., 1956–67
Consultant, Booz, Allen & Hamilton

Education

Princeton University, 1952

Charles L. Lea, Jr.
General Partner, NY

Directorships

Burkhurt Petroleum Corp.
Damon Corp.
Monolithic Memories, Inc.
George Moody, Inc.
Oximetrix, Inc.
Rome Group, Inc.

Prior Positions

Managing Director, New Court Securities Corp., 1970–81
Partner, F. S. Smithers & Co., 1961–70
Assistant to President, Bessemer Securities Corp., 1953–61

Education

BA, Cornell University, 1952

Edgar A. Miller
General Partner, NY

Directorships

Microwave Technology, Inc.
Private Satellite Network, Inc.

Prior Positions

Partner, McKinsey & Co., 1968–82
Assistant to the Director of Integrated Circuit Operations, Fairchild Camera and Instrument, 1966–67
Process Development Engineer, Texas Instruments, 1961–66

Education

MBA, Harvard Business School
MSEE, Massachusetts Institute of Technology
BSES, University of Texas

Thomas L. Piper III
General Partner, NY

Directorship

Medical Care International, Inc.

Prior Positions

Managing Director, New Court Securities Corp.
Senior Vice President and Director, Hayden Stone

Education

University of Virginia

Roland Underhill
General Partner, NY

Prior Position

Partner in Charge of Finance, Crowell, Weedon & Co.

Education

BS, Finance, University of California at Los Angeles, 1960

E. Payson Smith, Jr.
General Partner, SF

Directorships

Cadlinc, Inc.
George Moody, Inc.
Read-Rite Corp.
Rocky Mountain Oilfinders, Inc.
U. S. Windpower, Inc.

Prior Position

Vice President, First Chicago Capital Corp., 1976–82

Education

MM, Management, Northwestern University, 1976
BA, Business Administration, Monmouth College, 1971

John B. Clinton
General Partner, NY

Directorships

Medical Resources, Inc.
American Company for Property and Casualty Insurance

Prior Positions

Assistant Vice President, New Court Securities Corp., 1979–82
Senior Accountant, Peat, Marwick, Mitchell & Co., 1977–79

Education

MBA, New York University, 1982
BA, Amherst College, 1977

Peter A. Leidel
Associate, NY

Prior Position

Senior Financial Analyst, Mobil Corp., 1980–83

Education

MBA, Wharton School, University of Pennsylvania, 1980
BBA, University of Wisconsin, 1978

Marilyn G. Breslow
Associate, NY

Prior Positions

Director of Worldwide Marketing Services, Polaroid Corp., 1973–84
Consultant, Peat, Marwick, Mitchell & Co.

Education

MBA, Harvard Business School
BA, Barnard College

Stephen M. Wilson
Associate, SF

Prior Positions

Finance Director, U.S. Senate Campaign, 1982
Teacher, Harvard School in Los Angeles, 1979–81

Education

AB, Princeton University, 1979

Average Size of Investment	$1M
Size of Fund	$100M paid-in-capital
Investment Criteria	All stages from start-ups to leveraged buy-outs; U.S. only; telecommunications, computer-related, electronic components and instrumentation, energy-natural resources, genetic engineering, medical/health-care related, industrial products and equipment
Portfolio Companies	Undisclosed

CONTINENTAL CAPITAL VENTURES
3000 Sand Hill Road
Building 1, Suite 135
Menlo Park, CA 94025
(415) 854-6633

555 California Street
Suite 5070
San Francisco, CA 94104
(415) 989-2020

Frank G. Chambers
General Partner, S.F.

Directorships

Advanced Input Devices
BaronData Systems
Compumotor
Dataproducts
Guardian Packaging
Optical Coating Laboratories, Inc.

Prior Position

Founding Partner, Continental Capital Corp.

Education

MBA, Harvard Business School, 1939
BS, University of Utah

Lawrance A. Brown
General Partner, Menlo Park

Directorships

Biodiagnostics
Oncolab
Orange Medical Instruments
VLI
Weico

Prior Positions

President, SmithKline Diagnostics
Vice President, SmithKline Corp.

Education
BA, University of Pennsylvania

William A. Boeger
General Partner, Menlo Park

Directorships
Diagnostic Networks, Inc.
Kidron Digital Laser Systems

Prior Positions
Marketing Manager, Infomedia
Vice President, Crocker National Bank

Education
MBA, Harvard Business School
BA, Williams College

Donald R. Scheuch, Ph.D.
Partner, Menlo Park

Directorships
Communications Intelligence Corp.
Marcus Systems
MNR Technologies
Speech Plus

Prior Position
Senior Vice President, SRI International

Education
PhD, Electrical Engineering, Stanford University
BSEE, University of California at Berkeley

Average Size of Investment	$500K
Size of Fund	$10M and $20M
Investment Criteria	First-stage or early-stage high-technology and medical (to a limited degree)
Portfolio Companies	Caddex, Wodinville, WA, Computer engineering workstations; Chang Laboratories, San Jose, CA, Integrated productivity software; Compumotor, Petaluma, CA, Electronically driven motors; Orange Medical Instruments, Costa Mesa, CA, Critical care products

CONTINENTAL ILLINOIS VENTURE CORP.
231 South LaSalle Street
Chicago, IL 60697
(312) 828-8021

John L. Hines
President

Directorships
American Healthcorp, Inc., Health care
Filtration Sciences, Inc., Soft-goods manufacture

Education
BA, Economics, Stanford University, 1951

William Putze
Senior Vice President

Directorships
Early Winters, Inc.
Combined Cable Corp., Owns and operates cable TV systems
Skantek Corp., Manufactures and sells automatic digitizers
Wilkins Lumber Co.
Gyrodata, Inc.

Prior Position
Credit Officer, Citibank, 1974–77

Education
MBA, Columbia University Graduate School of Business, 1979
BS, Babson College, 1974

Seth L. Pierrepont
Vice President

Directorships
III-V Semiconductor, Inc.
Identification Devices, Inc., Identification systems
Siri Vail Corp., Mail order

Prior Positions
Consultant, Booz Allen Hamilton, 1980
Assistant Treasurer, Morgan Guaranty Trust Co., 1978

Education

MBA, Columbia University, 1979
BA, University of Pennsylvania, 1974

Judith Bultman Meyer
Vice President

Prior Position

Analyst, Continental Bank, 1977–78

Education

MBA, Northwestern University
BA, Political Science, Northern Illinois University

Samuel C. Freitag
Vice President

Directorships

Advanced Aluminum Products, Inc.
The Oakmark Corp.

Prior Position

Continental Illinois Bank

Education

MBA, University of Iowa, 1979
BA, Coe College, 1977

Scott E. Smith
Vice President

Directorship

General Power Corp.

Prior Position

Continental Illinois Bank

Education

MBA, University of Indiana, 1979
BS, University of Missouri, 1977

Edward K. Chandler
Investment Officer

Directorship

Barcus Berry Electronics, Audio processing technology

Prior Position

Associate, Boston Consulting Group, 1980–82

Education

MBA, Harvard University, 1984
BA, Yale University, 1980

Burton E. McGillivray
Investment Officer

Directorship

RAM Integrated Systems Corp.

Prior Positions

Assistant to the President, Hearst Cable, 1982–84
Assistant Treasurer, Chase Manhattan Bank, 1979–81

Education

MBA, Harvard Business School, 1984
BA, Economics, Harvard College, 1979

Average Size of Investment	$1M
Size of Fund	Undisclosed
Investment Criteria	Undisclosed
Portfolio Companies	Undisclosed

CONTINENTAL INVESTORS, INC.
2020 K Street, N.W.
Washington, DC 20006
(202) 466-3709

Lac Thantrong

Average Size of Investment	Undisclosed
Size of Fund	Undisclosed
Investment Criteria	Undisclosed
Portfolio Companies	Undisclosed

DIRECTORY AND BIOGRAPHIES

CONTROL DATA CAPITAL CORP.
8100 34th Avenue South
Minneapolis, MN 55440
(612) 853-5421

R. W. Bender

Average Size of Investment	$500K
Size of Fund	Undisclosed
Investment Criteria	Technology-based companies are of interest
Portfolio Companies	Undisclosed

CORNELL CAPITAL CORP.
2049 Century Park East
Twelfth Floor
Century City, CA 90067
(213) 277-7993

230 Park Avenue
Suite 3440
New York, NY 10169
(212) 490-9198

Alan Newman
Barry Bloom

Average Size of Investment	Undisclosed
Size of Fund	Undisclosed
Investment Criteria	Undisclosed
Portfolio Companies	Undisclosed

CORNING PARTNERS
125 Pearl Street
Boston, MA 02110-2417
(617) 451-6722

E. J. Stewart
N. E. Corning

Average Size of Investment	$250K–$500K
Size of Fund	Undisclosed
Investment Criteria	Diversified company interests including technology-based and medical companies; geographic location is important
Portfolio Companies	Teradata; Aeonic; Microtouch; Business Research

CORPORATE GROWTH ASSISTANCE LIMITED
19 York Ridge Road
Willowdale, Ontario M2P 1R8
Canada
(416) 222-7772

Millard S. Roth
President

Directorships

A-Cubed Inc.
Aim Zytron Corp.
Business Ventureco Inc.
Gemini Food Corp.
Inniskillin Wines Inc.
Swing Stage Ltd.
Two Futures Investment Corp.

Prior Positions

Partner, Hecker & Roth Associates
Corporate Controller, Levy Industries Limited
Consultant, VRSK Management Consultants
Assistant to the General Manager, Production, Electric Reduction Company of Canada, Ltd.

Education

MS, Industrial Management, Purdue University
Bachelor, Management Engineering, Rensselaer Polytechnic Institute

Average Size of Investment	$750K
Size of Fund	Undisclosed
Investment Criteria	Can act as either principal or intermediary; will negotiate investment in businesses which have the following characteristics: capable management and technical team in place or available; strong business concept, technical position, market segment, product strength, and purpose; comparative advantage such as market share, technology, proprietary process, or product; favorable industrial outlook, competitive position, regulatory climate, and product

Portfolio Companies — acceptance, with significant growth potential; existing presence in, or relatively easy entry to, appropriate U.S. and international markets; ability to achieve liquidity within reasonable time frame

Aim Zytron Corp., Weston, Ontario, Manufacturer of speciality chemicals, pressure sensitive labels, carton sealing tape; Gemini Food Corp., Bradford, Ontario, Processor, packer, and distributor of fresh fruit and vegetables; A-Cubed Inc., Mississauga, Ontario, Geophysical instruments; Swing Stage Limited, Scarborough, Ontario, Manufacturer of suspended scaffold systems

CORPORATION FOR INNOVATION DEVELOPMENT
One North Capitol
Suite 520
Indianapolis, IN 46204
(317) 635-7325

Marion C. Dietrich
President and Chief Executive Officer

Directorships

Corporation for Innovation Development, Venture capital
Corporation for Science & Technology, Research and development grants
White River Capital Corp., SBIC
Synthetic Diamond Technology, Industrial diamonds
MidAmerica Cellular, Inc., Cellular telephone

Prior Positions

Executive Vice President, Cummins Engine Company, Inc.
International and Domestic General Sales Manager, Kiekhaefer Corp.

Education

MBA, Harvard Business School, 1947
BA, Yale University, 1944

M. Archie Leslie
Vice President

Directorship

Equity Resource Co., SBIC
Indiana Railroad Co., Shortline RR
SciCor, Inc., Clinical laboratory testing

Prior Positions

Consultant, Bessire & Co.
Various Positions, Treasury Division, Cummins & Engine Co., Inc.
Investment Banker, Williams, GLYN & Co., London

Education

MA, Law, Cambridge University
MBA, Insead, France, 1976

Donald K. Taylor
Vice President

Directorships

Stratojac Corp., Men's outerwear manufacturer
SEA Group, Inc., Computer systems and peripherals
The Wholesale Club, Discount warehouse
1st Source Capital Corp., SBIC
Glas-Craft, Inc., Fiberglass resin spraying equipment
Benchmark Press, Inc., Publishes books in HPER fields

Prior Positions

Executive Vice President, MorAmerica Capital Corp.
Corporate Private Placement Investment Specialist, Northwestern National Life Insurance Co.

Education

MBA, Indiana University, 1972
BSEE, University of Louisville, 1970

Average Size of Investment	$400K
Size of Fund	$10M
Investment Criteria	Start-ups, first stage, expansion, leveraged buy-outs; must be located in Indiana
Portfolio Companies	Twelve companies located in Indiana and of various backgrounds

CR INVESTMENTS
Three First National Plaza
Suite 2725
Chicago, IL 60602
(312) 346-6038

Edward J. Roberts

Average Size of Investment	$500K
Size of Fund	$100M
Investment Criteria	Technology-based companies are of interest as well as start-ups; will act as lead investor
Portfolio Companies	Undisclosed

CRITERION VENTURE PARTNERS
333 Clay Street
Suite 4300
Houston, TX 77002
(713) 751-2400

David O. Wicks, Jr.
Senior Partner

Directorships
Intelligent Medicine, Inc.
Matrix, Inc., Holding company for cable television companies

Prior Positions
Managing Director, A. G. Becker Paribas Inc., 1968–83
Chemical Bank, 1963–66

Education
MBA, Darden Graduate School of Business, University of Virginia, 1968
BA, History, Trinity College, 1963

M. Scott Albert
Partner

Directorships
Microbot, Inc.
The Software Express, Inc.

Prior Positions
Associate, Golder, Thoma & Cressey, 1984
Associate, Booz, Allen & Hamilton, 1983

Education
MBA, University of Chicago, 1979
BSE, Duke University, 1977

Crichton W. Brown
Associate

Directorship
Bromar Distributors, Marketers of industrial water pollution control systems for use at geographically remote sites

Prior Positions
Associate, Seed Ventures, Ltd., 1982–84
Senior Consultant, Ernst & Whinney MCS, 1980–82

Education
MBA, Wharton School of Finance, 1983
BAS, Engineering Management, Stanford University, 1979

Average Size of Investment	$500K–$1M
Size of Fund	$20M
Investment Criteria	Experienced management team, rapid-growth market/industry, unique product and/or service, liquidity prospects in selected industry categories: life sciences, computer sciences, telecommunications, and special situations
Portfolio Companies	Columbia Universal Corp., Houston, TX, Life insurance; Intelligent Medicine, Inc., Englewood, CO, Drug delivery devices; Prime Ventures I, Inc., Austin, TX, Cable television; The Software Express, Houston, TX, Computer software; Wyndham Foods, Inc., Houston, TX, Specialty foods; McData Corp., Boulder, CO; IBM-compatible controller equipment; Megatest Corp., San Jose, CA, Automatic testing semiconductor materials; Microbot, Inc., Mountain View, CA, Light assembly robots; ProNet, Inc., Dallas, TX, Telecommunications and paging services; Republic Telcom, Minneapolis, MN, Long-distance reseller of telephone services; Teknowledge, Inc., Menlo Park, CA, Expert systems/artificial intelligence

CROCKER CAPITAL
111 Sutter Street
Suite 600
San Francisco, CA 94104
(415) 399-7889

Charles Crocker
William R. Dawson

Average Size of Investment $500K
Size of Fund   Undisclosed
Investment Criteria   Manufacturing
Portfolio Companies   Undisclosed

CROSSPOINT VENTURE PARTNERS
1951 Landings Drive
Mountain View, CA 94043
(415) 964-3545

4600 Campus Drive
Suite 103
Newport Beach, CA 92660
(714) 852-1611

John B. Mumford
Managing General Partner, Mt. View

Directorships

CXC Corp.
INMAC
Personal CAD Systems, Inc.
Conversant Software Corp.
LaserPath Corp.
Protolite Corp.
I-SCAN Corp.
Motion Analysis Systems, Inc.
Electron Beam Memories
Digital Appliance Controls
DigiRad Corp.
Office Club

Prior Positions

President, Crosspoint Financial Corp.
Founder and officer of 12 start-up companies.

Education

MBA, Stanford University, 1969
BS, Arizona State University, 1967

James F. Willenborg
Managing General Partner, Mt. View

Directorships

INMAC Corp.
Atron Corp.
Cubicomp Corp.
Precision Visuals Corp.
Norm Thompson Corp.

Prior Positions

Founder, Director, Officer, INMAC Corp.
Branch Sales Manager, Data General Corp.
Marketing Manager, Rolm & H.P.

Education

MBA, Stanford University
BSEE, Iowa State University

Roger J. Barry
General Partner, Mt. View

Directorships

LaPine Technology Corp.
SenSym Corp.
Sierra Monitor Corp.
Quadtree

Prior Positions

Partner, Manager, Peat Marwick Mitchell & Co.
Director of Taxes, Castle & Cook, Inc.

Education

MBA, Pace University
BS, Pace University

Frederick J. Dotzler
General Partner, Mt. View

DIRECTORY AND BIOGRAPHIES

Directorships

Neurocare
Vitaphore Corp.
BankPro Systems Corp.
Estabrooks Digital Graphics Corp.
Microfield Graphics Inc.

Prior Positions

Vice President, Marketing, Sales, Merrimack Laboratories
Director of Marketing, Millipore

Education

MBA, University of Chicago
Masters, Economics, University of Louvain (Belgium)
BS, Industrial Engineering, Iowa State University

William P. Cargile
General Partner, Mt. View

Directorships

Gordian Corp.
Precision Image Corp.

Prior Positions

Founder, President, Ausone Corp.
Engineering Manager, Basic Timesharing, Inc., and Biomation/Gould

Education

Graduate Courses, Computer Science, Stanford University
BSEE, Princeton University

Robert A. Hoff
General Partner, Newport Beach

Directorships

Studio Software Co.
Infusion Systems Corp.
Fashion Management Systems
Aspen Peripherals Corp.
Athens Inc.

Prior Positions

President, Marwit Capital Corp.
President, The Southern Pacific Regional Association of SBICs

Education

MBA, Harvard University
BS, Bucknell University

David J. Blecki
Associate, Mt. View

Directorship

I-SCAN Corp.

Prior Positions

President, Regis McKenna Marketing and Public Relations
President, Biomation/Gould

Education

MSEE, Rutgers University, 1964
BSBA, Management, University of Colorado, 1962
BSEE, University of Colorado, 1962

Neal Douglas
Associate, Mt. View

Prior Positions

Associate, Oxford Partners
Project Manager, AT&T Information Systems
Design Engineer, Raytheon

Education

MBA, University of California, Los Angeles
MS, Stanford University
BS, Cornell University

Walter Kortschak
Associate, Newport Beach

Prior Position

Marketing Manager, PDA Engineering

Education

MBA, University of California, Los Angeles
MS, California Institute of Technology
BS, Oregon State University

Average Size of Investment	$800K
Size of Fund	$65M
Investment Criteria	Start-up high-technology business in U.S.
Portfolio Companies	Aspen Peripherals, Longmont, CO, 3480-Compatible tape drive system; Atron Corp., Saratoga, CA, PC debugging tools; BankPro Systems, Inc., San Francisco, CA, Funds transfer system; Conversant Software Corp., Dallas, TX, Vertical market software; The Office Club, Concord, CA; Cubicomp Corp., Berkeley, CA, 3-D solid molding; DigiRad Corp., Palo Alto, CA, Digital filmless X rays; Digital Appliance Controls, Schaumburg, IL, Digital appliance control systems; Electron Beam Memories, Chicago, IL, Mass storage devices; Estabrooks Digital Graphics Corp., Lawrence, MA, High-speed printheads; Quadtree Software Corp., Bridgewater, NJ; Gordian Systems, Palo Alto, CA, Software protection; Infusion Systems, Irvine, CA, Infusion devices; I-SCAN Corp., Beaverton, OR, Optical input technology; LaPine Technology Corp., Milpitas, CA, Ruggedized disks; LaserPath Corp., San Jose, CA, Customized semiconductors; Neurocare, Mt. View, CA; Motion Analysis Systems, Inc., Santa Rosa, CA, Motion analysis systems; Personal CAD Systems, Los Gatos, CA, Architect and engineering CAD; Precision Image Corp., Palo Alto, CA, Color electrostatic plotters; Protolite Corp., San Jose, CA, Projection screens; SenSym Corp., Sunnyvale, CA, Pressure transducers; Athens, Inc., Oceanside, CA; Sierra Monitor Corp., Sunnyvale, CA, Gas detection systems; Studio Software Corp., Irvine, CA, Page processing software; Vitaphore Corp., San Carlos, CA, Medical biomaterials; Fashion Management Systems, Los Angeles, CA; Microfield Graphics, Beaverton, OR

CROYDEN CAPITAL CORPORATION
45 Rockefeller Plaza
New York, NY 10111
(212) 974-0184

Victor L. Hecht
President

Directorships

Circle Machine Company
The Belmont Group, Inc.
Health Management Inc.

Prior Positions

Vice President, Atlanta Investment Co.
Vice President/Controller, Excello, Inc. (subsidiary of G & W Industries)
Public Accountant

Education

MBA, Baruch College, 1976
BBA, University of Miami (FL), 1974

Average Size of Investment	$250K
Size of Investment	$8M
Investment Criteria	Second stage, third stage, leveraged buyouts
Portfolio Companies	Undisclosed

W. J. P. CURLEY
Rockefeller Plaza
Suite 1401
New York, NY 10020
(212) 582-1232

Walter J. P. Curley
Principal

Directorships

American Exploration Co., Oil and gas exploration and production
Bank of Ireland, Banking
Crane Co., Construction industry products, air frame accessories
Dowmar Securities Inc., Real Estate syndications
Fiduciary Trust Co. of New York, Money management
Curley Land Co., River barges and foreign real estate

Prior Positions

Ambassador to Ireland, United States government
Partner, J. H. Whitney and Co., New York
Caltex Petroleum Co.

Education

LLD (Hon.), Trinity (Dublin), 1976
MBA, Harvard University, 1948
BA, Yale University, 1944

Average Size of Investment	$100K
Size of Fund	Undisclosed
Investment Criteria	No service industries, no consumer goods
Portfolio Companies	Undisclosed

CURTIN & CO., INC.
2050 Houston Natural Gas Building
Houston, TX 77002
(713) 658-9806

John D. Curtin, Jr.
President

Directorship

Modar, Inc.

Prior Positions

Vice President, Corporate Finance, Rauscher Pierce Securities Corp.
Vice President, Corporate Finance, First of Texas, Inc.

Education

MBA, Harvard Graduate School of Business Administration, 1956
BA, Yale University, 1954

Stewart Cureton, Jr.
Vice President

Prior Position

Vice President, Rotan Mosle Inc., 1973–78

Education

MBA, Harvard University Graduate School of Business Administration, 1973
BA, Stanford University, 1967

Charles A. Armbrust
Vice President

Prior Positions

Vice President, Atlantis Corp., 1976–79
Corporate Finance Officer, First National Bank of Chicago, 1973–76

Education

MBA, Harvard Graduate School of Business Administration, 1973
BS, Yale University, 1969

Average Size of Investment	$500K
Size of Fund	Undisclosed
Investment Criteria	Undisclosed
Portfolio Companies	Undisclosed

CW GROUP, INC.
1041 Third Avenue
New York, NY 10021
(212) 308-5266

Walter Channing, Jr.
General Partner

Directorships

Sterivet Laboratories, Ltd.
Gabrielli Medical Information Systems, Inc.

Prior Positions

Founder, Channing, Weinberg and Co., Inc.
President, Merrimack Laboratories

Education

MBA, Harvard Business School
Harvard College

Barry Weinberg
General Partner

Directorships

Biomatrix, Inc.
Diamond Sensor Systems, Inc.
Photec Diagnostics
Intertherapy, Inc.

Prior Positions

Founder, Channing, Weinberg & Co., Inc.
Chairman and Chief Executive Officer, General Computer Systems

Education

MBA, New York University
Engineering, Massachusetts Institute of Technology

Charles M. Hartman
General Partner

Directorships

Queue Systems, Inc.
Phortran, Inc.
Genprobe
Business Research Corp.
Membrex, Inc.

Prior Position

Director, Acquisition and Licensing, Johnson & Johnson

Education

MBA, University of Chicago, 1969
BS, Notre Dame, 1963

Average Size of Investment	$1M
Size of Fund	$50M
Investment Criteria	Medical and biological fields; investments range from seed funding to $2M
Portfolio Companies	Columbia Corp., Nashville, TN, Provider of health care services to the elderly, whose management has many years of experience in the direction of multi-unit health care companies; Cooper Laseronics, Santa Clara, CA, World's leading supplier of surgical lasers for use in ob/gyn, neurosurgery otolaryngology, general surgery and other medical specialties; Gen-Probe, Inc., San Diego, CA, RNA probe technology with early emphasis on infectious disease diagnostic products; Glenn, Nyhan & Associates, Inc., San Francisco, CA, Specializing in malpractice insurance for doctors and other suppliers of health care services; Healthsouth, Inc., Birmingham, AL, Comprehensive medical rehabilitation services for patients with otherwise debilitating conditions; Medinet, Inc., Purchase, NY, Products for viewing and manipulating high resolution medical images; National Rehabilitation Centers, Nashville, TN, Rehabilitation services for individuals suffering debilitating conditions of the musculo-skeletal system; T Cell Sciences, Inc., Cambridge, MA, Immunodiagnostic and immunotherapeutic products; Membrex, Inc., NJ, Start-up company developing both devices and associated membranes to separate biologically active materials; Phortran, Inc., Mountain View, CA, Start-up company developing an automated 2-D gel electrophoresis system; Intertherapy, Inc., New York, NY, Start-up company developing vascular access devices to provide real-time images of vessel geometry and tissue characteristics while the device is in the patient's body; IDEC, Inc., La Jolla, CA, Biologicals company developing vaccine and therapeutic products from a particular group of antibodies, termed Anti-Ideotypes (Anti-Ids); Biomatrix, Inc., Ridgefield, NJ, Uses the natural materials found in the intercellular matrix of body tissues to develop artificial organs and products to repair and enhance damaged human tissue; Business Research Corp., Boston, MA, Information services company offering computerized data bases for use by the business and financial communities; Computers in Medicine, Cambridge, MA, Early stage company supplying a computer-based system for managing group practices and medical clinics; Diamond Sensor Systems, Inc., Ann Arbor, MI, Specializes in sensor technology with applications in patient monitoring, diagnostics, and artificial organs; Gabrieli Medical Information Systems, Paoli, PA, Processing and data base formation of medical records in their English-language form; Gambro, AB, Lund, Sweden, Leader in the field of renal care and dialysis; Photec Diagnostics, Inc., Little Falls, NJ, Early stage company with a proprietary method of tagging antigens and antibodies with dye markers; Quantum Medical Systems, Inc., Seattle, WA, Applies radar processing techniques used in aerospace applications to ultrasonic diagnostic imaging; Queue Systems, Inc., Parkersburg, WV, Manufacturer and marketer of innovative products for the fast-growing biotechnology field; Sterivet Laboratories, Ltd., Mississauga, Ontario, Canada, Veterinary company specializing in pharmaceuticals, feed supplements, and related products for the equine market

DCS GROWTH FUND
P.O. Box 740
Old Greenwich, CT 06870
(203) 637-1704

DIRECTORY AND BIOGRAPHIES

Donald C. Seibert
Owner

Directorships

Cambridge Robotics
Cleveland-St. Lawrence Fluorspar, Inc.
Marine Mining (Cornwall) Ltd.
Seibert Associates
Straight Line filters
Testsystems, Inc.
South County Vineyards

Prior Positions

Manager, Special Investments, Bessemer Securities Corp., 1963–68
Vice President, Eastern Region, Electronics Capital Corp., 1960–63

Education

MBA, Industrial Management, Wharton School, University of Pennsylvania, 1951
SBEE, Massachusetts Institute of Technology, 1948

Average Size of Investment	$50–100K
Size of Fund	$4M
Investment Criteria	Applied physics technology, turnaround management, leveraged buy-out deals; hardrock mining, oil and gas, real estate
Portfolio Companies	Cambridge Robotics, Watertown, MA, Vision inspection systems; Earthsearch, Inc., Golden, CO, Mineral prospecting; Cleveland-St. Lawrence Fluorspar Co., Cleveland, OH; Fluorspar drying and sales; Marine Mining Ltd., Cornwall, UK, Offshore tin mining; Straight Line Filters, Inc., Wilmington, DL, Filtration equipment; Testsystems, Inc., Tempe, AZ, In circuit electrical testing

DEARBORN CAPITAL CORP.
P.O. Box 1729
Dearborn, MI 48121
(313) 337-8577

Stephen M. Aronson
President

Prior Positions

Manager of Portfolio Administration, Ford Motor Credit Co.
Manager of Real Estate Financing, Ford Motor Credit Co.

Education

MBA, Michigan State University, 1979
BA, University of Rhode Island, 1963

Michael L. Lamanes

Average Size of Investment	$120K
Size of Fund	Undisclosed
Investment Criteria	Suppliers of parts or services to the automotive industry
Portfolio Companies	Undisclosed

DELTA CAPITAL, INC.
227 Tryon Street
Suite 201
Charlotte, NC 28202
(704) 372-1410

A. B. Wilkins, Jr.
William F. Lane

Average Size of Investment	$300K
Size of Fund	$5M
Investment Criteria	Manufacturing companies are of interest, as are other diversified companies; will act as lead investor; geographic location is important
Portfolio Companies	Undisclosed

DEMUTH, FOLGER & TERHUNE
One Exchange Plaza at 55 Broadway
New York, NY 10006
(212) 509-5580

Donald F. DeMuth
General Partner

Prior Position

Vice President/Director, Kidder, Peabody & Co., 1969–83

Education
MBA, Harvard University, 1968
BA, BSEE, Rutgers University, 1966

Thomas W. Folger
Partner
(212) 509-5717

Directorships
Telenex, Data communications equipment
Visionetics, Automatic optical inspection

Prior Position
Vice President, Kidder Peabody & Co., Inc., 1959–83

Education
MBA, Harvard University, 1953
BS, MS, Massachusetts Institute of Technology, 1949

J. Michael Terhune
General Partner
(212) 509-5629

Directorships
Control Key Corp.
Simtronics, Inc.

Prior Positions
Director, Corp. Diversification, Emerson Electric, 1981–83
Director, Commercial Business Development, General Dynamics, 1978–81

Education
MBA, Harvard University, 1968
BS, Purdue University, 1965

Average Size of Investment	$1.0M–$1.5M
Size of Fund	$50M
Investment Criteria	Undisclosed
Portfolio Companies	Undisclosed

DESOTO CAPITAL CORP.
60 North Third Street
Memphis, TN 38103
(901) 523-6894

Rudy Holmes

Average Size of Investment	$100K
Size of Fund	Undisclosed
Investment Criteria	Manufacturing, construction, real estate, and technology-based companies are of interest; geographic location is important
Portfolio Companies	Undisclosed

DEVELOPERS EQUITY CAPITAL CORPORATION
1880 Century Park East
Suite 311
Los Angeles, CA 90067
(213) 277-0330

Larry Sade, President

Average Size of Investment	$300K
Size of Fund	Undisclosed
Investment Criteria	Geographic location is important
Portfolio Companies	Undisclosed

DEVEREAUX CAPITAL CORPORATION
760 Market Street, Suite 315
San Francisco, CA, 94102
(415) 781-8390

David Younge
President

Average Size of Investment	Under $100K
Size of Fund	$1.5M
Investment Criteria	San Francisco area only; no computer related companies
Portfolio Companies	Undisclosed

DIEHL & COMPANY
1201 Dove Street
Suite 570
Newport Beach, CA 92660
(714) 955-2000

Russell R. Diehl
Managing Partner

Prior Positions

Vice President, Union Bank, 1975–78
Assistant Treasurer, The Bank of New York, 1972–75

Education

MS, American Graduate School, 1972
BA, Lake Forest College, 1968

Michael D. Henton
Partner

Prior Position

Analyst, Paine Webber, 1979–82

Education

MBA, University of Southern California, 1978
BA, University of California at Los Angeles, 1976

Average Size of Investment	$300K
Size of Fund	Undisclosed
Investment Criteria	Various types of industry preference; all stages of financing
Portfolio Companies	Undisclosed

DIXIE BUSINESS INVESTMENT CO.
P.O. Box 588
Lake Providence, LA 71254
(318) 559-1558

Jerry Donahoe

Average Size of Investment	$100K
Size of Fund	Undisclosed
Investment Criteria	Construction and real estate companies are of interest, geographic location is important
Portfolio Companies	Undisclosed

DOAN RESOURCES LIMITED PARTNERSHIP
333 East Main Street
Third Floor
P.O. Box 1431
Midland, MI 48641
(517) 631-2471

350 Second Street
Suite 7
Los Altos, CA 94022
(415) 941-2392

10 Fairmont Avenue
Suite E
Chatham, NJ 07928
(201) 635-3520

Herbert D. ("Ted") Doan
Chairman and Director, MI, Doan Resources, Limited Partnership
Limited Partner, MI, MBW Venture Partners LP

Directorships

Dow Chemical Co.
Dow Corning Corp.
Chemical Bank & Trust Co.
Noegen Corp.
Xycom, Inc.
Irwin Magnetics
Michigan Bell Telephone Co.

Prior Position

Dow Chemical Co.

Education

BChE, Cornell University, 1949

Ian R. N. Bund
Managing General Partner, MI, MBW Venture Partners Limited Partnership
President and Director, MI, Michigan Investment Fund L.P.
President and Director, MI, Doan Resources Limited Partnership

Directorships

Attache Software, Inc., Accounting software
LifeScan, Inc., Blood glucose monitoring device
Innovative Hearing Corp., Hearing enhancement for mild hearing loss
Sensormedics, Physiological, noninvasive measurement equipment monitoring head, heart and lung functions
Sequoia Turner Corp., Clinical hematology analyzers

Prior Positions

President, Sea Life, Inc.
Associate, Morgan Stanley & Co.
Senior Accountant, Price Waterhouse & Co.

Education

MBA, Harvard, 1968
BEc, University of Sydney, 1964

Philip E. McCarthy
Managing General Partner, NJ
MBW Venture Partners Limited Partnership
Senior Vice President, Director, NJ
Michigan Investment Fund, L.P.
Senior Vice President, Director, NJ
Doan Resources Limited Partnership

Directorship

Oximetrix Corp., Hospital supplies

Prior Position

Vice President, INCO Limited

Education

JD, Law, Cornell, 1965
BS, Cornell, 1960

Average Size of Investment	Undisclosed
Size of Fund	Undisclosed
Investment Criteria	Fund is in a maturing phase, no longer actively seeking new investment
Portfolio Companies	Undisclosed

DOUGERY, JONES & WILDER
2003 Landings Drive
Mountain View, CA 94043
(415) 968-4820

Two Lincoln Center
Suite 1100
5420 LBJ Freeway
Dallas, TX 75240
(214) 960-0077

John R. Dougery

Directorships

Compression Laboratories
Excelan
Kaiser Aerospace and Electronics
Magnesys
Printronix
VG Systems
Vicom Systems

Prior Positions

Vice President, General Manager, Western Region, Citicorp Venture Capital, Ltd.
Vice President, Finance, Diablo System, Inc.
Certified Public Accountant, Price Waterhouse & Co.

Education

MBA, Stanford University
AB, University of California, Berkeley

David A. Jones

Directorships

MAZE Exploration
Exploration Systems
Strategic Energy Services

Prior Positions

Vice President, Citicorp Venture Corp., Ltd.
Officer, affiliates of Citicorp, Citibank, N.A.

Education

MA, Memphis State University
Bachelors, Northeast Louisiana University

Henry L. B. Wilder

Directorships

CHEC Medical Centers
Caddex Corp.
Support Technology
Microgenics Corp.
Syntro Corp.

Prior Positions

Senior Investment Officer, Citicorp Venture Capital, Ltd.
Corporate Development, Finnigan Instruments

Education

MBA, Stanford University
BS, Physics, U.S. Naval Academy

A. Lawson Howard

Directorships

Advanced Business Communications

Prior Positions

Vice President, Marketing and Sales, Universal Computing Co.
Senior Vice President, Sales, United Computing Systems
Design Engineer, LTV

Education

MBA, University of Texas (Dallas)
MS, Southern Methodist University
BS, Texas A & M

Gerald R. Schoonhoven

Directorships

Aptec Computer Systems
High Yield Technology
Saratoga Semiconductor Corp.
Telematic Products

Prior Positions

General Manager, Optoelectronics Division, Fairchild Semiconductor

Education

MBA, Harvard University
BS, University of Illinois

Average Size of Investment	$250K–2.5M
Size of Fund	$85M+
Investment Criteria	Will act as lead investor and considers start-ups; prefers high-tech, biotechnology and medical, semi-conductor and advanced materials companies in the West and Southwest only
Portfolio Companies	Advanced Business Communications, Dallas, TX, Advanced switching technology; Ambulatory Hospitals of America, Houston, TX, Rehabilitation care hospitals; Aptec Computer Systems, Inc., Portland, OR, I/O Computer systems; Caddex Corp., Seattle, WA, Electronic publication system integrating text and graphics; California Devices, Inc., Milpitas, CA, Channelless Applications Specific Integrated Circuits; Cdex Intellisance Corp., San Jose, CA, Computer aided instruction market; CHEC Medical Centers, Inc., Seattle, WA, Medical health care clinics; Compression Labs, Inc., San Jose, CA, Video teleconfrencing signal compression; Excelan, Inc., San Jose, CA, Local Area Networking (LAN); Exploration Systems, Inc., Sausalito, CA, Vertical market computer and software systems for exploration geology, geophysics, reservoir engineering and land management; Filenet Corp., Orange County, CA, Laser disk technology; High Yield Technology, Mountain View, CA, Products addressing problems created by sub-micron semiconductor processing; Lawrence Medical Systems, Inc., Seattle, WA, Cardiovascular monitoring systems; Magnesys, San Jose, CA, Subsystem memory peripherals using proprietary bubble memory technology; MAZE Exploration, Inc., Englewood, CO, Oil and gas exploration and production; Microgenics Corp., Concord, CA, Biotechnology; Micropolis Corp., Chatsworth, CA, High capacity disk drives for minicomputers; Saratoga Semiconductor Corp., Cupertino, CA, Advanced semiconductor circuits; Strategic Energy Services, Inc., Bakersfield, CA, Innovative and proprietary equipment for increasing the productivity of oil wells in CA; Support Technologies, Inc., Portland, OR, Products for automated test equipment market in computer and electronics manufacturing; Syntro Corp., San Diego, CA, Biotechnology; Telematic Products, Inc., Seattle, WA, Telecommunication management equipment; VG Systems, Woodland Hills, CA, Interactive graphic displays used in CAD/CAM systems; Vicom Systems, Inc., San Jose, CA, Digital image processing of naturally produced images; Attain,

Inc., Milpitas CA, Linear automatic test equipment; Communications Transmission Holdings, Inc. (Transcon), Austin, TX, Microwave transmission service to common and private carriers of voice and data communications; DBC Capital Corp., Dallas, TX, Commercializes biomedical research done at University of Dallas; Medina Broadcast Group, Inc., Bellevue, WA, Acquires stations in the Western U.S., each developed with the aim of becoming a market leader serving a specific demographic group; Republic Telecom Systems, Boulder, CO, Telephone communication products

DREXEL BURNHAM LAMBERT INC.
The Lambda Funds
55 Broad Street
15th Floor
New York, NY 10004
(212) 480-5160

Anthony M. Lamport
Managing Director
(212) 480-6011

Directorships

Alinabal, Inc.
Powertec, Inc.
Great Southwest Industries Corp.
Votan
Giordano Associates Inc.
Quest Biotechnology, Inc.

Education

MBA, Harvard University, 1959
BA, Harvard University, 1957

Richard J. Dumler
First Vice President
(212) 480-8308

Directorships

BioLogicals, Inc.
Logos Corp.
Pencept, Inc.
Kronos, Inc.
Link Data, Inc.

Prior Positions

Partner, Bessemer Venture Partners, 1980–83
Investment Manager, Bessemer Securities Corp., 1979–80
Private Placement Department, Allstate Insurance Co., 1968–79

Education

MBA, University of Michigan, 1968
BA, Georgetown University, 1964

Frank R. Kline, Jr.
Vice President, Corporate Finance
(212) 480-3125

Directorships

Morrison Computer Corp.
Carlyle Systems, Inc.

Prior Positions

President and Managing Director, Pacific Technology Venture Fund, 1981–84
Computer Analyst, Drexel Burnham Lambert Inc., 1979–81

Education

MSBA, University of Massachusetts, 1974
BS, Commerce, Rider College, 1972

Alexandra Mahnken
Analyst

Education

BS, Wharton School, University of Pennsylvania, 1985

Average Size of Investment	$750K
Size of Fund	$40M
Investment Criteria	No real estate; no start-ups
Portfolio Companies	40 companies

DSV PARTNERS
221 Nassau Street
Princeton, NJ 08542
(609) 924-6420

DIRECTORY AND BIOGRAPHIES

Morton Collins
General Partner

Directorships

Kopin, Inc., Advanced semi-conductors
Applitek Corp., Local area network systems
The Liposome Co., Drug delivery systems
Summation, Inc., Instrumentation company using personal computer to integrate modular electronic instruments
Tandem Computers, Inc., Computer systems for on-line transactions processing
Theta-J Corp., Solid-state relays
Sea Pharm, Inc., Pharmaceuticals for marine organisms

Prior Positions

President, Data Science Ventures
General Partner, DSV Associates

Education

MA, PhD, Chemical Engineering, Princeton University, 1960, 1963
BS, ChE, Chemical Engineering, University of Delaware, 1958

James R. Bergman
Robert S. Hillas
John K. Clarke
James J. Millar

Average Size of Investment	$1M
Size of Fund	Over $100M
Investment Criteria	Start-up or early-stage high-technology companies
Portfolio Companies	Undisclosed

D. S. VENTURES, INC.
P.O. Box 152300
Irving, TX 75015-2300
(214) 659-7000

M. G. White
F. Briden

Average Size of Investment	$0.5M
Size of Fund	Undisclosed
Investment Criteria	Specialty materials, chemical specialties, electronics materials
Portfolio Companies	Undisclosed

DURKEE SHARLIT INDUSTRIES
680 Langsdorf Drive
Fullerton, CA 92631
(714) 992-5445

16714 Monte Alto Pl.
Pacific Palisades, CA, 90272
(213) 459-9929

Bruce G. Rossiter
Principal, Fullerton

Directorships

Standard Logic Inc.
Compucable Corp.

Prior Positions

President, Director, Bank of Boston
Senior Vice President, Director, Security Pacific National
Associate, McKinsey & Company

Education

JD, University of Oklahoma, 1970
MBA, Amos Tuck School of Business Administration, Dartmouth, 1968

Marshall C. Whitfield
Principal, Fullerton

Prior Positions

President, Cableshows
President, Green Tree Productions
President, Yasney Productions

Education

BS, University of Colorado, 1958

William C. Clapper
Principal, Fullerton

Prior Positions

President, Guardian Acceptance Corp.
Senior Vice President, Guardian Savings and Loan
Vice President/Manager, Home Federal
Vice President, Lloyds Bank of California

Education

BA, Hiram College, 1964

Average Size of Investment	$750K
Size of Fund	$15M
Investment Criteria	Turnaround companies, $15–100M in sales, not losing more than 3% of sales (pretax); must have 51% or greater stock control; not interested in real estate, financial companies, entertainment, agriculture, oil and gas, companies highly dependent on government regulation or sales highly volatile due to fashions
Portfolio Companies	Undisclosed

EAB VENTURE CORP.
90 Park Avenue
New York, NY 10016
(212) 437-4182

Richard C. Burcaw
Mark Littell

Average Size of Investment	$300K
Size of Fund	$15M
Investment Criteria	Diversified company preferences including technology-based companies, start-ups; will act as lead investor
Portfolio Companies	Undisclosed

THE EARLY STAGES COMPANY
244 California Street
Suite 300
San Francisco, CA 94111
(415) 986-5700

William P. ("Bill") Lanphear, IV
Partner

Directorships

Epyx, Software
Homestead Provisions, Snack food

Prior Position

General Manager, Duraflame

Education

MBA, Harvard University, 1972
MS, University of Illinois, 1970
AB, Albion College, 1969

Frank W. ("Woody") Kuehn
Partner

Directorship

Thomas E. Wolfe, Apparel

Prior Position

New Products Manager, Duraflame

Education

MS, University of Michigan, 1973
BS, Colorado State University, 1969

Morton Miller
Partner

Directorships

Synergex, Drug distribution
Jamboree, Retail clothing chain

Prior Positions

President, Castle & Cook Merchandising Corp.
President, Thriftom Drug
President, Skillern Drug

Education

MBA, Harvard University, 1947
BS, Wharton School, University of Pennsylvania, 1943

DIRECTORY AND BIOGRAPHIES

Average Size of Investment	$500K
Size of Fund	$12.75M
Investment Criteria	Technology as it's expressed in the mass marketplace; prefer companies in the expansion stage of their growth
Portfolio Companies	Undisclosed

EAST BOSTON COMMUNITY DEVELOPMENT CORPORATION
72 Marginal Street
East Boston, MA 02128
(617) 569-5590

Salvatore Colombo, Business Development Director

Albert F. Caldarelli, Executive Director

Average Size of Investment	$300K
Size of Fund	Undisclosed
Investment Criteria	Leveraged buy-outs are of interest and geographic location is important
Portfolio Companies	Undisclosed

EASTECH MANAGEMENT CO.
One Liberty Square
Boston, MA 02109
(617) 338-0200

G. Bickley Stevens, II
General Partner

Directorships

Automated Insurance Resource Systems
Autographix, Inc.
Pilot Executive Software, Inc.
Software Research Corp.
Interactive Training Systems, Inc.
Think Technologies

Prior Positions

Vice President, Paine Webber (Corporate Finance)
General Partner, Interdevelopmental Associates

Education

MBA, Harvard Business School, 1969
BS, Georgia Tech, 1967

Fontaine K. Richardson
General Partner

Directorships

Business and Professional Software, Inc.
Metagraphics, Inc.
Mentor Graphics
Aries Technology, Inc.
Banyan Systems, Inc.

Prior Position

Vice President and Founder, Applicon, Inc.

Education

PhD, Computer Science, University of Illinois
BS, MS, University of Arkansas

Michael H. Shanahan
Partner

Directorships

Computer Controls Corp.
Navigation Sciences, Inc.

Prior Position

Research Associate, Paine Webber Corporate Finance, 1978–80

Education

MBA, Harvard Business School, 1982
AB, Holy Cross College, 1978

Average Size of Investment	$600K
Size of Fund	$34.4M
Investment Criteria	Early-stage high technology in New England area
Portfolio Companies	Aries Technology, Inc., Lowell, MA, Integrated CAE system for mechanical engineers; Autographix, Inc., Waltham, MA, Computer-generated 35mm slides; Interactive Training Systems, Cambridge, MA, Interactive computer-based learning systems; Metagraphics, Woburn, MA, CAD/CAM data base creation; Pilot Executive Software, Boston, MA,

Mainframe access software; Software Research Corp., Natick, MA, Network management software; Think Technologies, Danvers, MA, Interactive Pascal for microcomputers; Xyvision, Inc., Woburn, MA, Computer-aided publishing and makeup systems

EAST WEST UNITED INVESTMENT CO.
6723 Whittier Avenue
McLean, VA 22101
(703) 821-6616

Doug Bui

Average Size of Investment	Undisclosed
Size of Fund	Undisclosed
Investment Criteria	Undisclosed
Portfolio Companies	Undisclosed

EATON CORPORATION
Eaton Center
Cleveland, OH 44114
(216) 523-5000

Robert P. Crease

Average Size of Investment	$1M
Size of Fund	Undisclosed
Investment Criteria	Technology-based and manufacturing companies of interest
Portfolio Companies	Undisclosed

EBERSTADT FLEMING VENTURE CAPITAL
1270 Avenue of the Americas
New York, NY 10020
(212) 713-7700

Jack W. Lasersohn
Managing Director

Directorships

Numerous

Prior Position

Cravath, Swaine & Moore

Education

JD, Yale, 1978
MA, Economics, Fletcher School of Law & Diplomacy, 1975
BS, Physics, Tufts University, 1975

Michael E. Norton
Vice President

Directorships

Numerous

Prior Positions

U.S. Attorney, Southern District, NY
Cravath, Swaine & Moore

Education

JD, Columbia University School of Law, 1975
AB, University of California, 1971

Andrew H. Chapman
Vice President

Directorships

Numerous

Prior Position

Vice President, Blyth, Eastman, Paine, Webber

Education

MBA, Wharton School, University of Pennsylvania, 1979
BA, Yale University, 1976

Average Size of Investment:	$1-2M
Size of Fund:	$70M
Investment Criteria:	Seed, early stage, later stage and leveraged buyouts; technology and health care
Portfolio Companies:	Daisy Systems, CAE, Sunnyvale, CA; Imed Corp., Medical equipment, CA; Support Systems International, Medical equipment, NC

ECI VENTURES
Leith House
47/57, Gresham Street
London EC2V 7EH
England
(01) 606-1000
Telex 892-528
Fax [01] 606-0247

Tony Lorenz
Managing Partner

Directorships

Health and Leisure Ltd., Health and leisure group
Leisure Development Ltd., Health and leisure group
Darnaway Venture Capital, Scottish venture capital fund
Polymill Investments Ltd., Offshore investment company
Dubilier, plc, Manufacturer of electronic components

Education

Business Degree, Dublin, 1962–66
2 Class Hons., Trinity College
5 'A'/2 'S' Levels, Stamford School, 1954–62

David Wansbrough
Jonathan Baker

Average Size of Investment	£400K
Size of Fund	£60M
Investment Criteria	To achieve a high growth in capital value over the longer term; invest in listed/unlisted companies in all sectors (excluding property and finance) amounts between £300,000 and £3,000,000 (more via syndication)
Portfolio Companies	Currently over 80 portfolio companies in areas such as biotechnology, telecommunications, venture capital funds, computer, etc.

EDELSON TECHNOLOGY PARTNERS
Park 80 West, Plaza Two
Saddle Brook, NJ 07662
(201) 843-4474

Harry Edelson
Managing Partner

Directorships

Nexa, Diversified information systems
Comptronix, Electronics manufacturer

Prior Positions

Vice President, Research, First Boston, 1981–84
President, Edelson Technology, Inc., 1980–81
Vice President, Research, Drexel Burnham Lambert, 1974–80
Vice President, Research, Merrill Lynch, 1973–74

Education

MBA, New York University Graduate School of Business, 1965
BS, Physics, Brooklyn College, 1962

Raymond J. Bosso
Partner
(201) 843-4761

Prior Position

Managing Director, L. F. Rothschild, Unterberg Towbin, 1969–84

Education

MBA, Fairleigh, Dickinson University, 1971
BBA, Iona College, 1964

Anthony Buffa
Partner

Directorships

Catalina Marketing Corp., Electronic coupon distribution
Mosaic Systems Inc., Electronics packaging
Triplex Inc., Programmable controller
Republic Telecom Systems, Telco network expansion products

Prior Positions

Vice President, Michigan Capital, 1983–85
Associate, Rothschild Inc., New Court Securities Corp., 1980–83
Assistant Treasurer, Chase Manhattan Bank, 1977–80

Education

BA, University of Michigan, 1977

Average Size of Investment	$750K
Size of Fund	$36M
Investment Criteria	Information systems and other high tech
Portfolio Companies	Amerinex, Saddle Brook, NJ, Diversified information systems; Aquanautics, San Francisco, CA, Oxygen extraction and generation; AT&E, San Francisco, CA, Telecommunications; Comptronix, Guntersville, AL, Electronics manufacturing; Nexa, Ottawa, Canada, Diversified information systems; Perception Technology, Canton, MA, Voice answerback systems

EDICT INVESTMENT CORP.
2908 South Carrollton Avenue
New Orleans, LA 70118
(504) 861-2364

Gregory B. Johnson

Average Size of Investment	$100K
Size of Fund	Undisclosed
Investment Criteria	Diversified company interests including start-ups; geographic location important
Portfolio Companies	Undisclosed

EDWARDS CAPITAL CORP.
215 Lexington Avenue
New York, NY 10016
(212) 686-2568

Edward H. Teitlebaum

Average Size of Investment	$100K
Size of Fund	Undisclosed
Investment Criteria	Transportation industry of interest
Portfolio Companies	Undisclosed

EG&G VENTURE PARTNERS
700 East El Camino Real
Suite 270
Mountain View, CA 94040
(415) 967-2822

John J. Rado, Managing General Partner
C. Gerald Diamond, General Partner
Andres Buser, General Partner
John A. Blaeser, General Partner

Average Size of Investment	$500–$2.5M
Size of Fund	$50M
Investment Criteria	Technology products
Portfolio Companies	Undisclosed

ELECTRO SCIENCE MANAGEMENT CORP.
1600 Aurora Road
Suite 214
Melbourne, FL 32935
(305) 242-8267

H. R. Denius
J. W. Boone
G. A. Herbert
President

Directorships

Electronic Systems Products Inc., Large-screen video displays
Trustee, Denius Cattle Co.

Prior Positions

Vice President, Corporate Development, Radiation, Inc.
Vice President, Long Range Planning, Harris Corp.

Education

MBA, Harvard University, 1956
BSE, United States Naval Academy, 1947

Average Size of Investment	$200K
Size of Fund	$7M–$10M
Investment Criteria	Proprietary products to growth markets; capable management team; balanced and well thought-out business plans
Portfolio Companies	Undisclosed

EMC II VENTURE PARTNERS
8950 Villa La Jolla Drive
Suite 2132
La Jolla, CA 92037
(619) 455-0362

Ray W. McKewon
General Partner

Directorships

Immunetech Pharmaceuticals, Health care firm engaged in development of therapeutic drugs for treatment of human allergies, rheumatic and infectious diseases, and cancer
Impulse Enterprise, Manufacturer of subsea electrical connectors and cable assemblies used in offshore oil and gas exploration
Cytotech, Inc., Health care firm engaged in the development and marketing of human diagnostics
McKewon & Timmins, Investment banking firm
Intelligent Images, Inc., Development and marketing of medical training systems utilizing interactive medical simulation device

Prior Positions

Naval Officer, United States Navy
Director of Program Development, Pepperdine University
Account Executive, Bache & Co. (now Prudential Bache)

Education

MBA, Pepperdine University, 1975
BS, Mathematics, University of Oklahoma, 1970
BA, English, University of Oklahoma, 1970

Bradley B. Gordon
General Partner

Prior Positions

Manager, Training Supervisor, Market Researcher, The May Company
Director, Housing Energy Mgt. Program, University of Southern California

Education

MBA, University of Southern California, 1981
Bachelor of Business, New Mexico State University, 1976

Hans W. Shoepflin
General Partner

Directorship

The Price Company, Specialty retailing

Prior Positions

CFO, SABA GmbH
Assistant to Chairman/Special Projects, MANN GmbH
Executive Vice President, President, The FedMart Corp.
Executive Vice President, The Price Company

Education

MA, University of Wisconsin, 1966
BA, University of Wisconsin, 1965

Alan J. Grant
General Partner

Directorships

International Rotex, Manufacturer and distributor of labeling systems
Linear Instruments Corp., Manufacturer of precision laboratory strip chart recorders

Prior Positions

Chairman and President, ATASI Corp.
Executive Vice President, Aerojet General Corp.
Group Vice President and Director, Fairchild Camera & Instrument Corp.
President, Lockheed Electronics Co.
President, Lockheed Aircraft Corp.
Vice President and General Manager, Autonetics' Computer & Data Systems Division

Education

Adjunct Professor of Managerial Sciences, University of Nevada at Reno, 1974
Graduate, Northwestern University's Institute for Management, 1961
BS, EE, MSEE, Illinois Institute of Technology, 1946, 1948

Paul J. Donnelly
Associate

Prior Positions

Intern, L. F. Rothschild, Unterberg, Towbin
Research Analyst, McKewon Securities

Education
BS, Business Administration, San Diego State University, 1984

Average Size of Investment	$250K–$750K
Size of Fund	$30M
Investment Criteria	Request business plan detailing product/services concept, marketing opportunity, qualifications of management team, and 3–5 years projected profit and loss and cash flow
Portfolio Companies	Intelligent Images, Inc., San Diego, CA, Development and marketing of medical training systems utilizing interactive medical simulation device

EMERGING GROWTH PARTNERS
400 East Pratt Street
Baltimore, MD 21202
(301) 332-1021

Howard P. Colhoun
Managing Partner

Directorship
Arnold Graphics, Business forms

Prior Positions
President, T. Rowe Price, New Era Fund, 1966–82
Senior Staff, Arthur D. Little, 1961–66

Education
MBA, Harvard Business School, 1961
Fulbright School, University of Trondheim, Norway, 1958
Engineering, Princeton University, 1957

Robert E. Hall
Peter S. Welles
W. Andrew Grubbs

Average Size of Investment	$1M
Size of Fund	$100M
Investment Criteria	Undisclosed
Portfolio Companies	Undisclosed

EMPRISE MANAGEMENT
1333 Lawrence Expressway, #150
Santa Clara, CA 95051
(408) 246-5500

Donald de Renne, General Partner
Patrick W. Latta, General Partner
J. Michael Loscavio, Partner
William H. Rusher, Jr., Partner

Average Size of Investment	Undisclosed
Size of Fund	Undisclosed
Investment Criteria	Prefer role as deal originator; seed and startup financing, research and development partnerships; prefer within two hours of Santa Clara
Portfolio Companies	Undisclosed

ENERGY ASSETS, INC.
1800 South Tower
Pennzoil Place
Houston, TX 77002
(713) 236-9999

L. E. Simmons

Average Size of Investment	$300K
Size of Fund	Undisclosed
Investment Criteria	Oil development companies preferred, geographic proximity important
Portfolio Companies	Undisclosed

ENERGY CAPITAL CORP.
953 Esperson Building
Houston, TX 77002
(713) 236-0006

Herbert F. Poyner

Average Size of Investment	$100K
Size of Fund	$11.5M
Investment Criteria	Oil development companies of interest as well as technology-based companies; geographic location is important
Portfolio Companies	Undisclosed

ENGLE INVESTMENT CO.
135 West 50th Street
New York, NY 10020
(212) 757-9580

35 Essex Street
Hackensack, NJ 07601
(201) 489-3583

Murray Hendel

Average Size of Investment	$200K
Size of Fund	Undisclosed
Investment Criteria	Interested in manufacturing companies and other diversified areas; will act as lead investor; geographic location important
Portfolio Companies	Undisclosed

ENTERPRISE CAPITAL CORPORATION
3501 Allen Parkway
Houston, TX 77019
(713) 521-4401

Fred S. Zeidman
Chief Operating Officer

Directorships

Synergetics International Inc.
Advanced Manufacturing, Inc.
Medication Services, Inc.
Pancretec, Inc.

Prior Positions

President/Chairman of the Board, Petrolith, Inc.
Vice President, Alliance Business Investment Co.

Education

MBA, New York University, 1970
BS, Washington University, 1968

Fiore P. Talarico Jr.

Directorship

Diversa Marketing, Inc.

Prior Positions

CFO, Signet Corporation
Manager, Peat Marwick Mitchell & Co.
In-charge Accountant, Fox & Co.

Education

MBA, University of Detroit, 1981
BS, University of Dayton, 1974

Average Size of Investment	$400K
Size of Fund	$16M
Investment Criteria	Co-investors preferred, second and third round financing; strong management, good profit potential, innovative product, investment in $400–600K range
Portfolio Companies	Undisclosed

EQUAL OPPORTUNITY FINANCE
420 Hurstbourne Lane
Louisville, KY 40222
(502) 423-1943

Frank Justice, Jr.

Average Size of Investment	$100K
Size of Fund	$2M
Investment Criteria	Diversified company interests, start-ups welcome, will act as lead investor; geographic proximity is important
Portfolio Companies	Undisclosed

EQUICO CAPITAL CORPORATION
1290 Avenue of the Americas
Suite 3400
New York, NY 10015
(212) 397-8600

Duane E. Hill
President, Chief Executive Officer

Prior Positions

Vice President, Morgan Guarantee Trust Co.
First Lieutenant, U.S. Air Force

Education

MBA, University of Chicago, 1973
BSEE, University of Illinois, 1968

Average Size of Investment	$300K
Size of Fund	$10.5M
Investment Criteria	Diversified investments; early stage, buyouts, and expansion financings
Portfolio Companies	Connection Communications Corp., Newark, NJ, Cable television; Essence Communications, Inc., New York, NY, Publishing/broadcasting; Unity Telecommunications, Inc., New York, NY, Cellular rapid

EQUITABLE CAPITAL CORP.
855 Sansome Street
San Francisco, CA 94111
(415) 434-4114

James C. Lee

Average Size of Investment	$50K–$150K
Size of Fund	$2M
Investment Criteria	Diversified
Portfolio Companies	Undisclosed

EQUITY CAPITAL CORPORATION
231 Washington Avenue, Suite 2
Sante Fe, NM 87501
(505) 988-4273

Jerry A. Henson
President

Directorships

Bank of Albuquerque
Santa Fe Economic Development, Inc.
New Mexico Business Development Corp.
Numerous portfolio concerns

Prior Positions

President, Bank of Santa Fe

Average Size of Investment	$100–150K
Size of Fund	$1.5M
Investment Criteria	Profitable companies in the Southwestern or Western U.S., in manufacturing and wholesale industries seeking expansion capital or in need of bridge financing
Portfolio Companies	Martin Development Corp., Home building, Albuquerque/Santa Fe, NM; Santa Fe Laminates, Inc., Manufacturing, Santa Fe, NM; Bagdad Plastics, Inc., Manufacturing, Grants, NM; The Synergistic Group, Inc., Distributor, Los Gatos, CA; Zwan Magnetics, Inc., Manufacturing, Los Angeles, CA

EQUITY DYNAMICS, INC.
2116 Financial Center
Des Moines, IA 50309
(515) 244-5746

John Pappajohn
Owner, Manager

Directorships

Caremark, Inc.
Bion Corp., Ultrasound imaging
Infrasonics, Inc.
Continental Healthcare Systems
Lasermed, Inc., Laser technology in medical area
Medical Imaging Centers of America
Coratomic, Inc.
Pancretec, Inc.
Asbestec Industries
Hemacare Inc., Blood filtration
Women's Health Centers of America

Education

BS, University of Iowa, 1952

Average Size of Investment	$500K
Size of Fund	$20M
Investment Criteria	Diversified company interests including health care and technology-based companies, start-ups; will act as lead investor
Portfolio Companies	Asbestec Industries, Training schools, et al in asbestos abatement training; Caremark Inc., Home health care; Continental Healthcare Systems Inc., Hospital information systems; Coratomic Inc., Pacemakers; Infrasonics Inc., Respirators; Medical Imaging Centers of America, Diagnostic imaging centers; Pancretic Inc., Insulin, chemotherapy, fertility pump manufacturers; Women's Health Centers of America, Free standing clinics for women patients

ESLO CAPITAL CORP.
2401 Morris Avenue
Suite 220, East Wing
Union, NJ 07083
(201) 687-4920

Leo Katz
President

Average Size of Investment	$100K
Size of Fund	Undisclosed
Investment Criteria	Diversified company interests including start-ups; will act as lead investor; geographic location is important
Portfolio Companies	Undisclosed

EUCLID PARTNERS CORP.
50 Rockefeller Plaza
New York, NY 10020
(212) 489-1770

Milton J. Pappas
Partner

Directorships

Applied Biotechnology, Inc.
Physical Acoustics Corp.
RTC Systems Inc.
Gyneco, Inc.
Itron, Inc.

Education

LLB, Cleveland Marshall Law School, 1956
BBA, Case Western Reserve University, 1950

A. Bliss McCrum, Jr.
Partner

Directorships

RTC Systems, Inc.
Lawrence Medical Systems
Conferex Corporation
Logisticon, Inc.

Education

MBA, Wharton School, University of Pennsylvania, 1958
AB, Princeton University, 1954

Jeffrey T. Hamilton
General Partner

Directorships

Cambridge Robotics Systems, Inc.
Zwan Magnetics, Thin-film media

Prior Positions

Vice President, Solar Thermal System, 1962–77
Vice President, Rothschild in Exxon Enterprises, 1962

Education

MS, Massachusetts Institute of Technology, 1976
BSME, University of Notre Dame, 1962
AB, University of Notre Dame, 1960

Average Size of Investment	$500K
Size of Fund	$22M
Investment Criteria	High technology
Portfolio Companies	Undisclosed

EURO/AMERICA TECHNOLOGY INVESTMENTS, INC.
2121 South El Camino Real
Suite 605
San Mateo, CA 94403
(415) 345-8523

Flemming Fischer
President
(415) 573-0800

Education
MBA, University of Copenhagen

Allan F. Robb
Vice Chairman

Education
BS, Oregon State University

Walter Rhiner
Vice Chairman

Education
MS, Federal Institute of Technology (Zurich)
BS, Federal Institute of Technology (Zurich)

Average Size of Investment	$350K
Size of Fund	Undisclosed
Investment Criteria	Undisclosed
Portfolio Companies	Undisclosed

EXIM CAPITAL CORP.
290 Madison Avenue
New York, NY 10017
(212) 683-3375

Victor Chun

Average Size of Investment	$100K
Size of Fund	Undisclosed
Investment Criteria	Diversified company interests including manufacturing
Portfolio Companies	Undisclosed

EXXON ENTERPRISES
1251 Avenue of the Americas
New York, NY 10019
(212) 398-2560

T. M. Castagna

Average Size of Investment	$1M
Size of Fund	Undisclosed
Investment Criteria	Technology-based companies are of interest; start-ups welcome; will act as lead investor
Portfolio Companies	Undisclosed

FAIRFIELD EQUITY CORP.
200 East 42nd Street
New York, NY 10017
(212) 867-0150

Matthew A. Berdon
Samuel L. Highleyman
Alfred L. Hollender

Average Size of Investment	$100K
Size of Fund	$3M
Investment Criteria	Secured lending; second-tier financing; debt or equity
Portfolio Companies	Undisclosed

FAIRFIELD VENTURE PARTNERS
1275 Summer Street
Stamford, CT 06905
(203) 358-0255

650 Town Center Drive
Suite 810
Costa Mesa, CA 92626
(714) 754-5717

DIRECTORY AND BIOGRAPHIES

Pedro A. Castillo
Randall R. Lunn
Oakes Ames
Edmund M. Olivier
Eugene E. Pettinelli
Thomas D. Berman
Lawrence A. Bock

Average Size of Investment	$1M
Size of Fund	$100M
Investment Criteria	Diversified company interests, especially technology based
Portfolio Companies	Undisclosed

FANEUIL HALL ASSOCIATES
One Boston Place
Boston, MA 02108
(617) 723-1955

David T. Riddiford

Average Size of Investment	$500K
Size of Fund	$6M
Investment Criteria	Diversified company preferences including start-ups; will act as lead investor
Portfolio Companies	Undisclosed

FBS VENTURE CAPITAL COMPANY
6900 East Camelback Road
Suite 452
Scottsdale, AZ 85251
(602) 941-2160

7515 Wayzata Boulevard
Minneapolis, MN 55426
(612) 544-2754

3000 Pearl Street, #206
Boulder, CO 80301
(303) 442-6885

William B. McKee
President and Chief Executive Officer, AZ

Directorships

Comven, Inc., Communication services
CerProbe Corp., Manufactures ceramic probe cards
Immuno Nuclear, Medical diagnostic test kits
Renal Systems, Equipment, devices, and supplies for kidney dialysis treatment
International Electronics, ATE networking
General Laser, Inc., Industrial laser equipment

Prior Position

Vice President, The Arizona Bank, 1978

Education

MA, University of California at Los Angeles, 1969
BS, United States Air Force Academy, 1968

W. Ray Allen
Executive Vice President, MN

Directorships

Flame, Drill rod, pipe tool joints, and air heaters for oil and gas, mining, and water well industries.
Northwest Teleproductions, Video productions
Ciprico, Control equipment for disk and tape memory storage devices

Prior Position

Planning and Acquisitions for Fortune 500 Companies

Education

MBA, University of Kentucky
BS, University of Kentucky

Brian Johnson
Vice President, CO

Directorships

andrew alexander, inc., Greeting card, gift, and fine stationery retail stores
Thermo-Serv, Inc., Plastic beverage and food storage containers
Mizar, Inc., Control cards and systems based on VME bus specifications

Prior Position

International Multifoods Corp.

Education

MBA, College of St. Thomas, 1977
BSBA, University of South Dakota, 1971

R. Randy Stolworthy
Vice President, AZ
(602) 941-2160

Directorship

Advanced Fiberoptics, Manufactures system components that convert digital and analog signals for optical transmission

Prior Positions

Senior Auditor, General Host, 1981
Senior Auditor, Touche Ross, 1977

Education

BBA, Washburn University, 1977

John H. Bullion
Vice President, MN

Prior Positions

Craig Hallum, 1984
Vice President, International Multifoods Corp.

Education

MBA, University of Minnesota
BA, Carleton College

Stephen W. Buchanan
Vice President, MN

Prior Position

Assistant Vice President, Valley National Bank, 1984

Education

BS, Virginia Polytechnic, 1976

Average Size of Investment	$250K
Size of Fund	$20M
Investment Criteria	Quality of management, sustainable uniqueness, opportunity for profitable growth; invest only in states where there is an FBS office (Arizona, Minnesota, or Colorado)
Portfolio Companies	Advanced Fiberoptics Corp., Tempe, AZ, Manufactures system components that convert digital and analog signals for optical transmission; andrew alexander, inc., Plymouth, MN, Retail stores carrying greeting cards, gifts, and fine stationery with locations in regional shopping malls; Applied Spectrum Technologies, Inc., Minneapolis, MN, Communications products based on spread spectrum technology; Audiobionics, Inc., Eden Prairie, MN, Hand-held communications terminals for hearing-impaired people and other applications; Cerprobe Corp., Tempe, AZ, Ceramic probe cards—devices used to test the quality of integrated circuits during their manufacture; Ciprico, Inc., Plymouth, MN, Control equipment for disk and tape memory storage devices; Comlinear Corp., Ft. Collins, CO, Manufactures DC-coupled operational amplifiers; Computer Designed Systems, Inc., Minneapolis, MN, Turnkey, interactive data processing systems; Comven, Inc., Phoenix, AZ, Communication services in paging, two-way radio, and data transmission; Deltak Corp., Minneapolis, MN, Equipment for the recovery and use of waste heat in oil refineries, petrochemical and natural gas processing plants; General Laser, Inc., Scottsdale, AZ, Laser-based manufacturing equipment for industrial applications; Immuno Nuclear Corp., Stillwater, MN, Medical diagnostic test kits for clinical reference laboratories and hospitals; Konan Corp., Phoeniz, AZ, Disk and tape controllers to enhance the storage capacity of microcomputers; Lucht Engineering, Inc., Bloomington, MN, Photograph-printing equipment for professional photo finishing labs; Mate Electronics, Inc., Denver, CO, Franchisor of retail electronic stores throughout the U.S.; Mizar, Inc., St. Paul, MN, Control cards and systems based on the VME bus specification; Northwest Teleproductions, Inc., Minneapolis, MN, Video productions and producer services for television commercials and educational and industrial markets; R & D Systems, Inc., Minneapolis, MN, Blood control products for hematology laboratories; Renal Systems, Inc., Minneapolis, MN, Equipment, devices, and supplies for kidney dialysis treatment; Sentech Medical Corp., Arden Hills, MN, Designs, manufactures, and markets diagnostic medical instrumentation systems and biosensors; Stanford Letterpress, Inc., Minneapolis, MN, Designs and markets rotary ultraviolet letterpresses for the label and flexible package printing industry; Thermo-Serv, Inc., Anoka, MN, Plastic beverage and food storage containers; Vertimag Systems Corp., Minneapolis, MN, Vertical recording technology for increasing storage capacity of flexible computer disks

FEDERATED CAPITAL CORP.
20000 West 12 Miles Road
Southfield, MI 48076
(313) 559-0554

DIRECTORY AND BIOGRAPHIES

Louis P. Ferris
Jack Takala

Average Size of Investment	$100K
Size of Fund	Undisclosed
Investment Criteria	Diversified company preferences
Portfolio Companies	Undisclosed

FERRANTI HIGH TECHNOLOGY, INC.
515 Madison Avenue
New York, NY 10022
(212) 688-9828

Sanford R. Simon
Keith C. Langworthy
Vice President

Prior Position
Vice President, American Corp. Services, 1981–present

Education
MBA, New York University, 1981
BS, New York University, 1978

Michael R. Simon
Vice President

Directorships
Aptec Computer Systems, I/O computers
Laser Corporation of America, High-power CO_2 lasers

Prior Position
Engineer, Systems Group, Inc., 1981–82

Education
BSBA, University of Pennsylvania

Average Size of Investment	$350K
Size of Fund	$3M
Investment Criteria	Ferranti High technology is owned 80% by Ferranti plc.—British Electronics Company; wish to invest in compatible high technology
Portfolio Companies	Aptec Computer, Portland, OR, I10 computers; Digital Pathways, Palo Alto, CA, Dial-up modems; Inference, Los Angeles, CA, Artificial intelligence; Laser Corporations of America, Wakefield, MA, Lasers—CO_2; Telematics, Ft. Lauderdale, FL, X.25 packet switching

FIDELITY VENTURE ASSOCIATES
82 Devonshire Street
Boston, MA 02109
(617) 570-7000

Thomas F. Stephenson
William R. Elfers
Donald R. Young
Samuel Bodman
Gordon F. Kingsley

Average Size of Investment	$800K
Size of Fund	$50M
Investment Criteria	Technology-based companies are of interest; will act as lead investor
Portfolio Companies	Undisclosed

FINANCIAL OPPORTUNITIES
981 South Third Street
Louisville, KY 40203
(502) 584-1281

Gary Duerr

Average Size of Investment	$100K
Size of Fund	$1M
Investment Criteria	Interested in convenience store operations; geographic location important
Portfolio Companies	Undisclosed

FINANCIAL RESOURCES
2800 Sterick Building
Memphis, TN 38103
(901) 527-9411

Milton Picard

Average Size of Investment	$100K
Size of Fund	Undisclosed
Investment Criteria	Diversified company interests including manufacturing areas
Portfolio Companies	Undisclosed

FIRST AMERICA-ISRAEL TECHNOLOGY L.P. (FAIT)
685 Fifth Avenue
New York, NY 10022
(212) 486-6670

Arie Genger
Partner

Directorship
Rapid American, Diversified retail and manufacturing

Prior Position
President, McCrory Corp., 1979–82

Education
MBA, City University of New York, 1972

Thomas Hardy
Partner

Prior Position
Principal, McKinsey & Co., 1969–84

Education
MBA, Wharton School, University of Pennsylvania, 1969
BA, Economics, University of Sydney, Australia, 1966

S. A. Spencer

Average Size of Investment	$250K–$1M
Size of Fund	Undisclosed
Investment Criteria	(1) Situation must have some relationship with Israel; (2) product(s) already developed so that funds are needed for marketing and manufacturing; (3) strong management team
Portfolio Companies	Undisclosed

FIRST AMERICAN LENDING CORP.
401 North Lakes Boulevard
North Palm Beach, FL 33408
(305) 848-0611

G. M. Caughlin

Average Size of Investment	$300K
Size of Fund	Undisclosed
Investment Criteria	Manufacturing companies are of interest
Portfolio Companies	Undisclosed

FIRST CALIFORNIA BUSINESS & INDUSTRIAL DEVELOPMENT CORP.
3931 MacArthur Boulevard
Suite 212
Newport Beach, CA 92660
(714) 851-0855

130 Montgomery Street
San Francisco, CA 94104
(415) 392-5410

Richard R. Heath
Chairman and Chief Executive Officer, San Francisco

Directorship
United Business Ventures, MESBIC

Prior Positions
Vice President, Marketing, AIS, Inc., 1981–84
Director, San Francisco International Airport, 1977–81

Education
LLB, University of Colorado, 1954
BA, University of Colorado, 1951

Leslie R. Brewer
President, Newport Beach

Directorship
United Business Ventures, Inc., Venture capital

Prior Positions
Vice President, Marwit Capital Corp., 1979
Credit Officer, Union Bank, 1971

Education
MBA, University of Southern California, 1974
BA, University of Washington

William G. Willson

Average Size of Investment	$250K
Size of Fund	$6M
Investment Criteria	Good product or service, strong experienced management team, personal and financial commitment of principals, excellent growth potential
Portfolio Companies	Approximately 25 companies, privately located in California in wide variety of businesses

FIRST CAPITAL CORP. OF CHICAGO
One First National Plaza
Suite 2628
Chicago, IL 60670
(312) 732-4000

Marshall L. Greenwald
Mary Helen Blakeslee
Thomas E. Galuhn
Andrew Beaurline
Daniel W. O'Connell

Average Size of Investment	$500K
Size of Fund	$25M
Investment Criteria	Technology-based companies and other diversified areas of interest; will act as lead investor; start-ups are also welcome
Portfolio Companies	Undisclosed

FIRST CENTURY PARTNERSHIPS
1345 Avenue of the Americas
New York, NY 10105
(212) 698-6000

350 California Street
San Francisco, CA 94104
(415) 955-1605

David S. Lobel
General Partner, NY

Education
MBA, MS, Stanford, 1977, 1978

Michael J. Myers
General Partner, NY

Education
MBA, Harvard

John S. Dulaney
General Partner, NY

Education
MBA, Harvard

C. Sage Givens
Vice President, CA

Education
MBA, Stanford

Steven Bird
Associate, CA

Education
MBA, Stanford

Geoffrey Y. Yang
Associate, NY

Education
MBA, Stanford, 1985

Lisa Roumell
Associate, NY

Education

MBA, Harvard, 1985

Average Size of Investment	$1.5M
Size of Fund	$100M
Investment Criteria	Strong management; potentially large emerging markets; proprietary products; modest competition; attractive operating economics
Portfolio Companies	Integrated Measurement Systems, Test equipment, Portland, OR; Glacial Confections, Frozen desserts, CT; Concord Data Systems, Map lans, MA; Healthsouth, Health services, AL; Marine Medical, Health services, CA; Waferscale Integration, Semiconductors, CA

FIRST CHICAGO INVESTMENT ADVISORS
Three First National Plaza
Chicago, IL 60670
(312) 732-4154

A. Bart Holaday
Vice President, Managing Director

Prior Positions

Vice President, Principal, InnoVen Venture Capital Group
Founder, Tenax Oil and Gas Corp.
Vice President, Gulf Oil Corp.

Education

JD, George Washington Law School
MA, Economics, Oxford University (Rhodes Scholar)
BS, Engineering, Air Force Academy

Michael Gallie
Vice President

Directorships

Chicago Capital Fund

Prior Positions

President, Fort Dearborn Paper Company
Vice President, Urban National Corp.

Education

MBA, Stanford University
BS, Engineering, University of California

David S. Timson
Vice President

Prior Positions

Vice President, Microelectronic Packaging
Director of Venture Management, Greyhound Capital Corp.

Education

MS, Finance, University of Illinois
BS, Finance, University of Illinois

Patrick A. McGivney
Vice President
(312) 732-4919

Prior Position

Head of a closely held business unit, First National Bank of Chicago

Education

CPA, 1981
MBA, Finance, University of Chicago, 1979
BS, Management, Purdue University, 1975

T. Bondurant French
Vice President, Senior Venture Capital Advisor
(312) 732-6743

Prior Position

Senior Portfolio Manager, Connecticut General Insurance Co., 1976–80

Education

MBA, Northwestern University, 1976
BA, Northwestern University, 1975

Average Size of Investment	$1M
Size of Funds	$150M
Investment Criteria	Start-up, late-stage private financing; preferences: information processing, communications and health care; investment size: $500K to $1.5M

Portfolio Companies

Amcodyne, Inc., Longmont, CO, High-performance disk drives; Arete Systems Corp., San Jose, CA, Transaction-processing computer systems; CCTC, Santa Barbara, CA, Magnetic read/write heads; Comarc Systems, Inc., San Francisco, CA, Geographical information software; ComDesign, Goleta, CA, Advanced communication products; Dest Corp., San Jose, CA, Optical character readers; Explosive Fabricators, Inc., Louisville, CO, Advanced materials processing; Genigraphics Corp., Saddlebrook, NJ, Color graphics, slide systems; Harley Industries, Inc., Tulsa, OK, Oil and construction equipment distributor; Intelligent Storage, Inc., Longmont, CO, Intelligent controllers for high-end storage systems; Pacer Corp., Bellevue, WA, Computerized point-of-sale system; Peak Systems, Inc., Fremont, CA, Rapid thermal processing equipment; Ovabloc, Stamford, CT, Sterilization procedure for women; Smith Laboratories, Inc., Northbrook, IL, Synthetic drug for back disorders; Sun Guard Data Corp., Wayne, PA, Software and computer backup centers; Mattison Instruments, Madison, WI, Fourier transform infrared spectrometer; MicroBeam, Inc., Newbury Park, CA, Focused ion beam systems; National Healthcare, Inc., Dottian, AL, Hospitals in non-urban areas; Texet, Arlington, MA, Computer-aided publishing systems; Thermedics, Woburn, MA, Biomedical products and systems; Transimage, Menlo Park, CA, Optical character readers; Tetra Resources, Inc., Houston, TX, Oil and gas service products; Redicare, Encinitas, CA, Medical treatment centers; VG Systems, Inc., Woodland Hills, CA, Interactive graphics terminals; Wall Data, Inc., Redmond, WA, Communication controller

FIRST CHICAGO VENTURE CAPITAL

Three First National Plaza
Suite 1330
Chicago, IL 60670-0501
(312) 732-5400

133 Federal Steet
Sixth Floor
Boston, MA 02110
(617) 542-9185

John A. Canning, Jr.
President, IL

Directorships

Ackerley Inc., Nationwide outdoor and airport advertising company
AEA Investors, Inc., Private placement and leveraged buyout activities
ReRokkor Corp., Manufactures industrial and aerospace products
CasChem, Inc., Manufacturers of motor oil and urethane products
Shaughnessy Holdings, Inc., Chain of budget motels located in western and southwestern U.S.

Prior Positions

Senior Vice President, The First National Bank of Chicago, 1982–present
Law Department, The First National Bank of Chicago, 1969–80

Education

JD, Duke University, 1969
AB, Denison University, 1966

Kent P. Dauten
Kevin M. McCafferty
Vice President/Partner, MA

Directorships

Autographix, Inc., Turnkey systems—35mm slides
Aries Technology, Mechanical CAE
Computers in Medicine, Turnkey system—medical market
Pilot Software, Executive information software
Envoy Systems, Software sales and marketing
Laserdata, Interactive videodisk

Prior Positions

Vice President, Finance, Goeken Systems, Inc., 1979–80
Investment Manager, First Chicago, 1976–79

Education

MBA, University of Chicago, 1979
BA, Harvard University, 1976

Paul R. Wood
William J. Hunckler, III
Samuel M. Mencoff
Randall S. Sturges
Investment Manager, IL
(312) 732-5408

Prior Position

Investment Banking, Corporate Finance, Shearson, Loeb Rhoades, Inc. 1977–81

Education

MBA, Harvard University, 1983
BA, Williams College, 1977

Robert A. Compton
Investment Analyst, MA

Prior Positions

Director of Marketing, ZOOM Telephonics, 1984–85
Marketing/Sales, IBM Corp., 1978–83

Education

MBA, Harvard University, 1984
BA, The Principia College, 1978

Gary J. Little
Vice President, IL
(312) 732-5414

Directorship

Letisse, Inc., Manufacturer of ladies' handbags and belts

Education

MBA, Illinois Institute of Technology, 1981
BS, University of Illinois, 1974

Paul J. Finnegan
Benjamin D. Chereskin
Investment Manager, IL
(312) 732-5115

Education

MBA, Harvard University, 1983
AB, Harvard College, 1981

David F. Mosher
Darius G. Nevin
Thomas R. Reusché
Investment Manager, IL
(312) 732-8036

Prior Positions

General Manager, L. Reusche & Co., 1980–81
Bond Salesman, Northern Trust, 1977–80

Education

MBA, Harvard University, 1983
BA, Brown University, 1977

James N. Perry, Jr.
Investment Manager, IL
(312) 732-5416

Education

MBA, University of Chicago, 1985
BA, University of Pennsylvania, 1982

Justin S. Huscher

Average Size of Investment	$5M
Size of Fund	$410M
Investment Criteria	Strong management team, a unique market opportunity, attractive economics and returns
Portfolio Companies	Currently over 140 companies in portfolio in the communications, health care, manufacturing, software and systems, technology, real estate, and retail areas

FIRST CITY TECHNOLOGY VENTURES
35555 Curtis Blvd.
Eastlake, OH 44094
(216) 953-0555

Morton A. Cohen
President

Directorships

Voicemail, Voice messaging
FDRL, Contract research testing
Childers Products, Coatings, adhesives manufacturing
Monitek, Instrumentation manufacturing
IGI Biotechnology, Industrial microbiology

Education

MBA, Wharton School, 1960

DIRECTORY AND BIOGRAPHIES

Average Size of Investment	$250K
Size of Fund	$20M
Investment Criteria	Experienced management team, proprietary product, internal growth rate in the 30–40% range
Portfolio Companies	ADAC Laboratories, San Jose, CA, Diagnostic imaging; Diasonics, Inc., Milpitas, CA, Diagnostic imaging; Igene Biotechnology, Columbia, MD, Industrial microbiology; Voicemail, Santa Clara, CA, Voice messaging; American Telecommunications, Dallas, TX, Telecommunications

FIRST CONNECTICUT SMALL BUSINESS INVESTMENT CO.
177 State Street
Bridgeport, CT 06604
(203) 366-4726

James M. Breiner
Chairman

Directorships

Valley Bank and Trust
Emson Manufacturing Co.
Charter Arms Co.
Alclaire Corp.

Education

LLB, Boston University, 1941

David Engelson
President

Directorship

Valley Bank & Trust Co., Banking

Education

BSE, Wharton School, University of Pennsylvania, 1941

Lawrence Yurdin
Steven Breiner

Average Size of Investment	Undisclosed
Size of Fund	$38M
Investment Criteria	Undisclosed
Portfolio Companies	Undisclosed

FIRST DAKOTA CAPITAL CORP.
52 Broadway
Fargo, ND 58102
(701) 237-0450

David L. Johnson

Average Size of Investment	$100K
Size of Fund	Undisclosed
Investment Criteria	Manufacturing and technology-based companies are of interest; geographic location is important
Portfolio Companies	Undisclosed

FIRST DALLAS FINANCIAL CO.
3302 Southland Center
LB 268
Dallas, TX 75201
(214) 231-1777

John T. McGuire
President
(214) 922-0070

Directorships

American Oil & Gas Co., Gas gathering and oil field services
May Financial Corp., Investment banking
Loop Cold Storage Co., Public refrigerated warehousing

Prior Positions

Vice President, Investment Banking, Rauscher, Pierce Retsues, Inc., 1975–80
Vice President, Investment Banking, Eppler Guerin & Turner, Inc., 1972–75
Vice President, Investment Banking, Kuhn Loeb & Co., Inc., 1967–72

Education

MIA, Columbia University, 1961
BA, Brandeis University, 1959

C. Thomas May

Average Size of Investment	$1M
Size of Fund	Undisclosed
Investment Criteria	Profitable company with excellent management and located in the Southwest
Portfolio Companies	Undisclosed

FIRST IDAHO VENTURE CAPITAL CO.
P.O. Box 1739
Boise, ID 83701
(208) 345-3460

Dennis Clark

Average Size of Investment	$150K
Size of Fund	$2M
Investment Criteria	Diversified areas of interest including service companies; geographic proximity important
Portfolio Companies	Undisclosed

FIRST INTERSTATE CAPITAL CORP.
707 Wilshire Boulevard
Los Angeles, CA 90017
(213) 614-5904

David Jones
John Funk
Kenneth M. Deemer

Average Size of Investment	$500K
Size of Fund	$10M
Investment Criteria	Diversified areas of interest, manufacturing companies included; will act as lead investor; start-ups considered
Portfolio Companies	Undisclosed

FIRST MARYLAND CAPITAL
107 West Jefferson Street
Rockville, MD 20850
(301) 251-6630

Joseph Kenary
Chairman/President

Education
LLB, Georgetown Law School, 1963
AB, Harvard, 1960

Average Size of Investment	$75K
Size of Fund	$600K+
Investment Criteria	Early stage companies (some start up) on East Coast
Portfolio Companies	Precision Media, Radio station, CT; Toledo Inv., L.P., TV station, Toledo, OH; Intercontinental Comm./Cellular Inc., Washington, D.C.; Spa Lady Inc., Women's health spas, VA, MD; Martek, Inc., Biotechnology, MD

FIRST MIDWEST CAPITAL CORP.
1010 Plymouth Building
12 South Sixth Street
Minneapolis, MN 55402
(612) 339-9391

Alan K. Ruvelson
Walter L. Tiffin

Average Size of Investment	$400K
Size of Fund	Undisclosed
Investment Criteria	Diversified areas of interest including technology-based companies; will act as lead investor
Portfolio Companies	Undisclosed

FIRST MISSOURI DEVELOPMENT FINANCE CORP.
P.O. Drawer 1745
1411 Southwest Boulevard
Jefferson, MO 65102
(314) 635-0138

Richard Jeffrey
Jerry Stegall
Sue Thompson

Average Size of Investment	$200K
Size of Fund	Undisclosed
Investment Criteria	Diversified areas of interest in companies; geographic locale of importance
Portfolio Companies	Undisclosed

DIRECTORY AND BIOGRAPHIES

FIRST OKLAHOMA INVESTMENT CAPITAL CORP.
120 North Robinson
Suite 880C
Oklahoma City, OK 73102
(415) 272-4693

David H. Pendley
President

Prior Positions
Senior Vice President, First Asset-Based Lending Group, Inc., 1981–83
Various positions, General Electric Credit Corp., 1965–81

Education
Stonier Graduate School of Banking, Rutgers University
BS, Business Administration, Washington University, 1971

Average Size of Investment	$350K
Size of Fund	$20M
Investment Criteria	Leveraged buy-outs, manufacturing, wholesaling, distributing, and retailing
Portfolio Companies	Undisclosed

FIRST PUERTO RICO CAPITAL, INC.
52 McKinley Street
Box 816
Mayagüez, PR 00708
(809) 832-9171

Eliseo F. Font

Average Size of Investment	Undisclosed
Size of Fund	Undisclosed
Investment Criteria	Undisclosed
Portfolio Companies	Undisclosed

FIRST SBIC OF ALABAMA
16 Midtown Park East
Mobile, AL 36606
(205) 476-0700

David C. Delaney

Average Size of Investment	$300K
Size of Fund	Undisclosed
Investment Criteria	Diversified areas of interest; start-ups are welcome; will act as lead investor; geographic proximity important
Portfolio Companies	Undisclosed

FIRST SBIC OF ARKANSAS, INC.
1400 Worthen Bank Building
Little Rock, AR 72201
(501) 378-1876

Fred C. Burns

Average Size of Investment	$100K
Size of Fund	Undisclosed
Investment Criteria	Diversified areas of interest; geographic proximity is important
Portfolio Companies	Undisclosed

FIRST SBIC OF LOUISIANA
2852 Carey Street
P.O. Box 1336
Slidell, LA 70459
(504) 561-0017

N. Gorman Hooper

Average Size of Investment	$300K
Size of Fund	Undisclosed
Investment Criteria	Diversified areas of interest; will act as lead investor; start-ups are welcome; geographic proximity important
Portfolio Companies	Undisclosed

FIRST SOUTHERN CAPITAL CORP.
6161 Perkins Road
Baton Rouge, LA 70808
(504) 769-3004

Charest D. Thibaut, Jr.
Carol S. Perrin

Average Size of Investment	$300K
Size of Fund	$6M
Investment Criteria	Diversified industry preferences, manufacturing companies considered; leveraged buy-outs of interest; will act as lead investor; geographic proximity is important
Portfolio Companies	Undisclosed

FIRST VALLEY CAPITAL CORP.
640 Hamilton Mall
8th Floor
Allentown, PA 18108
(215) 867-6760

Matthew W. Thomas
President

Directorships

Various charitable and nonprofit organizations
HCS Enterprises, Inc., Hospital co-op servicing company
Regional Vice President, First Valley Bank

Prior Positions

Regional Representative, SullieMae, 1982
Corporate Banking Officer, American Security Bank, 1980

Education

Masters, Finance (50% completed), American University, 1982
BS, Penn State, 1965

Average Size of Investment	$60K
Size of Fund	$600K
Investment Criteria	Start-up or later stage, limit $100K
Portfolio Companies	Undisclosed

FIRST VENTURE CORP.
Venture Building
The Quarters
Bartlesville, OK 74006
(918) 333-8820

Jon R. K. Tinkle
James G. Thompson
Ralph B. Finkle, Jr.

Average Size of Investment	$250K
Size of Fund	Undisclosed
Investment Criteria	General
Portfolio Companies	Undisclosed

FLEET VENTURE PARTNERS
111 Westminster Street
Providence, RI 02903
(401) 278-6770

666 Third Avenue
22nd Floor
New York, NY 10017

60 State Street
Boston, MA 02109
(617) 367-6700

Robert M. Van Degna
Managing Partner, RI

Directorships

Health Data Resources, Healthcare
N.H.C. Envelope Manufacturing Co., Commercial envelopes
Bedinghaus Business Forms, Printing
Randwal Instrument, Health care
Chicago Transparent, Plastics
Lawless Container Corp., Corrugated containers

Prior Position

Vice President, Fleet National Bank

Education

MBA, Harvard University, 1971
BS, Cornell University, 1966

DIRECTORY AND BIOGRAPHIES

James Saalfield
General Partner, MA

Directorships
KVH, Inc., Marine electronic compasses
Logicraft, Inc., Computer software

Prior Positions
President, James A. Saalfield and Company

Education
MBA, Harvard Business School
BA, Oberlin School

Habib Y. Gorgi
General Partner, NY

Directorship
Lawless Container Corp., Corrugated containers

Prior Position
Investment Banker, specializing in mergers and acquisitions

Education
MBA, Columbia Business School
BA, Brown University

Average Size of Investment	$500K
Size of Fund	$40M
Investment Criteria	Emerging growth companies and leveraged buy-outs
Portfolio Companies	Undisclosed

FLORISTS' CAPITAL CORP.
11260 Playa Court
Culver City, CA 90230
(213) 390-9781

Christopher M. Conroy

Average Size of Investment	$1M
Size of Fund	Undisclosed
Investment Criteria	Construction and real estate industry are of interest as well as other diversified areas
Portfolio Companies	Undisclosed

FLUID CAPITAL CORP.
8421-B Montgomery, N.E.
Albuquerque, NM 87111
(505) 292-4747

George T. Slaughter

Average Size of Investment	$300K
Size of Fund	$5M
Investment Criteria	Manufacturing companies considered as well as other diversified areas; start-ups welcome; geographic location important
Portfolio Companies	Undisclosed

FOSTER DYKEMA CABOT & CO., INC.
50 Milk Street
Boston, MA 02109
(617) 423-3900

Jere H. Dykema
Robert E. Gibbons
Frank H. Foster

Average Size of Investment	Undisclosed
Size of Fund	Undisclosed
Investment Criteria	Act as agent or investment bankers for new or emerging companies
Portfolio Companies	Undisclosed

FOSTER MANAGEMENT COMPANY
437 Madison Avenue
New York, NY 10022
(212) 753-4810

John H. Foster
President

Directorships

CHEC Medical Centers, Inc., Freestanding emergency center chain
Hearing Ventures, Inc., Retail hearing aid distribution
Chartwell Group, Ltd., Home furnishings

Prior Position

Vice President, Morgan Guaranty

Education

MBA, Dartmouth College, 1965
BA, Williams College, 1963

Michael J. Connelly
Executive Vice President

Directorships

Heritage Health Systems, HMO management company
Sky Communications, Radio broadcasting group
Babylon Communications, Radio station owner/operator
Tri-Ex Development Co., Oil and gas
Omni Cable TV Corp., Cable television MSO

Prior Position

Partner, Casey, Lane & Mittendorf

Education

JD, Columbia University, 1975
BA, Michigan State University, 1971

Timothy E. Foster
Vice President

Directorships

Medac, Inc., Freestanding emergency centers
Hercules Offshore Drilling Co., Oil service

Prior Positions

Vice President, General Electric Venture Co.
Internal Auditor, General Electric Co.

Education

BA, Union College, 1972

Average Size of Investment	$1.5M
Size of Fund	$75M
Investment Criteria	Undisclosed
Portfolio Companies	Babylon Communications, Babylon, NY, Radio station; Chartwell Group, Ltd., Carlstadt, NJ, Home furnishings; CHEC Medical Centers, Seattle, WA, Primary health care centers; Hearing Ventures, Inc., New York, NY, Retail hearing aid distribution; Heritage Health Systems, Miami, FL, HMO management; Medac, Inc., Cleveland, OH, Freestanding emergency center chain; Sky Communications, New York, NY, Radio broadcasting group

FOSTIN CAPITAL CORP.
681 Andersen Drive
Pittsburgh, PA 15220
(412) 928-8900

William F. Woods
President
(412) 928-8901

Directorships

PGS, Inc., Mail-order pharmaceuticals
Formative Technologies, Inc., CAD/CAM
The Sero Company, Mens/womens apparel

Prior Position

Vice President, INA Capital Management Company

Education

MBA, Duquesne University, 1963
BBA, University of Pittsburgh, 1960

Thomas M. Levine
Executive Vice President
(412) 928-8913

Directorship

DMI Furniture, Inc., Furniture manufacturing
Suprex Corporation

Prior Position

Partner, Berkman, Ruslander, Pohl, Leiber & Engel

Education

JD, University of Chicago Law School, 1974
BA, Colgate University, 1971

David M. Martin
Secretary/Treasurer
(412) 928-8907

Prior Position

Supervising Senior Accountant, KMG Main Hurdman

Education

BA, Robert Morris College, 1977

Joel P. Adams
Associate

Prior Positions

Chief Nuclear Test Engineer, General Dynamics
Assistant Chief Nuclear Test Engineer, General Dynamics
Shift Test Engineer, General Dynamics

Education

MSIA, Carnegie-Mellon University, 1986
BS, SUNY at Buffalo, 1979

Average Size of Investment	$250K–$500K
Size of Fund	$20M
	$30M jointly
Investment Criteria	Communications, computer related, consumer, electronic components/instrumentation, genetic engineering, industrial products/equipment, medical
Portfolio Companies	Cyborg Corp., Newton, MA, Scientific workstations based on personal computers; Formative Technologies, Inc., Pittsburgh, PA, Low-end CAD/CAM workstation providing scanning, drafting and plotting capabilities; Identix Inc., Palo Alto, CA, Fingerprint identification terminals which permit controlled access to computers; Finial Technology and Innovation, Sunnyvale, CA, Turntable system which uses laser-based optical pick-up instead of mechanical cartridge and stylus; Kurzweil Applied Intelligence, Inc., Waltham, MA, Speech recognition technology for voice writers, voice work stations, and telecommunications; Kurzweil Music Systems, Waltham, MA, Electronic keyboard instrument that recreates the sound quality of acoustic instruments including the grand piano; Laserscope Biomedical Corp., Medical surgical laser based upon a unique product design concept and proprietary crystal technology; Lisp Machine Inc., Cambridge, MA, Artificial intelligence for commercial application; Suprex, Pittsburgh, PA, Supercritical fluid chromatograph; Perceptron, Inc., Farmington Hills, MI, Machine vision systems; International Microelectronic Products, San Jose, CA, Custom VLSI semiconductors; Lightwave Technologies, Inc., Van Nuys, CA, Single-mode optical fibers, single- and multimode optical fiber cables; Medrad, Inc., Pittsburgh, PA, Medical diagnostic products; developers of an automatic implantable defibrillator; Pharmaceutical Group Services, Inc., Lewisburg, PA, Mail-order prescription drugs for employee benefit plans; VG Systems, Woodland Hills, CA, Interactive graphic display equipment; XYVision, Inc., Woburn, MA, Advanced computer workstations with integrated text and image processing and pagination systems

FOUNDERS EQUITY, INC.
200 Madison Avenue
New York, NY 10016
(212) 953-0100

Warren H. Haber
Chairman

Directorships

Campanelli Industries
Kenai Corp.
Fluid Components, Inc.
Lundy Electronics, Inc.

Prior Positions

Corporate Finance/Account Executive, Bear Stearns & Co., 1967–69
Junior Executive Trainee/Account Executive, Merrill Lynch Pierce Fenner & Smith, 1963–67

Education

BBA, Finance, Bernard M. Baruch School, 1962

Joel Friedman
Vice President

Directorships

Campanelli Industries
Kenai Corp.
Founders Communications, Inc.
Fluid Components, Inc.

Prior Positions

Corporate Finance/Account Executive, Bear Stearns & Co., 1967–69
Junior Executive Trainee/Account Executive, Merrill Lynch Pierce Fenner & Smith, 1961–67

Education

BA, Columbia College, 1961
London School of Economics and Political Sciences, 1960

John L. Teeger
President

Prior Positions

Vice President, Corporate Finance, Bear Stearns & Co., 1976–81
Group Financial Executive, Anglovaal Ltd. (South Arica), 1974–76
Corporate Finance Officer, Union Acceptances, Ltd. (South Africa), 1970–74
Chartered Accountant, Schwartz, Fine & Co., 1962–70

Education

MBA, Finance, Columbia University, 1969
B. Com., University of Witwatersrand, 1968
CASA, University of Witwatersrand, 1966

Donn L. Hartley
Vice President, Corporate Development

Prior Positions

Vice President Corporate Development, MacMillan, Inc., 1982–83
Vice President Corporate Development, Thomas Tilling Inc., 1977–82
Senior Investment Analyst, Teachers Insurance and Annuity Association, 1975–77

Education

MBA, Finance and International Business, Columbia University, 1975
BS, Business Administration, University of Arizona, 1968

Kevin B. McCollum
Vice President

Prior Positions

Morgan Stanley & Co., 1981–85
Davis Polk & Wardwell, 1977–81

Education

MBA, Columbia University, 1977
BA, Cambridge University, 1974

Average Size of Investment	$10M
Size of Fund	Undisclosed
Investment Criteria	Undisclosed
Portfolio Companies	Founders Communications, Publisher of community newspapers, Houston, TX; Fluid Components, Inc., Distributor of hydraulic components, Tulsa, OK; Kenai Corp., Oil and gas field services, New York, NY; SPORT Magazine Associates, Publish SPORT Magazine, New York, NY; Wine Masters International, Inc., Market and distribute wine with single custom labels, Los Angeles, CA

FOWLER, ANTHONY & CO.
20 Walnut Street
Wellesley Hills, MA 02181
(617) 237-4201

John A. Quagliaroli
President

Prior Positions

Vice President, Corporate Development, Dynatech Corp.
Marketing/Sales, Data Processing Division, IBM Corp.
Marketing/Product Management, Citicorp

Education

PMD, Harvard Business School, 1975
MBA, Syracuse University, 1965
BSEE, Worcester Polytechnic Institute, 1961

Average Size of Investment	$50K–$250K
Size of Fund	N/A
Investment Criteria	New England-based company; high technology preferred
Portfolio Companies	Undisclosed

THE FRANKLIN CORP.
1185 Avenue of the Americas
New York, NY 10036
(212) 719-4844

DIRECTORY AND BIOGRAPHIES

Alan L. Farkas
Executive Vice President and Treasurer

Directorships

Kent Electronics Corp.
Vanzetti Systems, Inc.
Mycro-Tek, Inc.
Oliver's Stores, Inc.

Prior Position

Attorney, CPA, Main Hurdman

Education

LLM, NYU Law School, 1970
LLB, Brooklyn Law School, 1966
BS, Economics, University of Pennsylvania, 1963

Average Size of Investment	$500K
Size of Fund	$26M
Investment Criteria	"Small businesses" in continental U.S.
Portfolio Companies	Kent Electronics Corp., Houston, TX, Specialty distributor of electronic connectors, wire and cable, electronic components, and interconnect assemblies; Oliver's Stores, Inc., Ridgefield, NJ, Off-price retailer of women's and children's clothing; Mycro-Tek, Inc., Wichita, KS, Designs, manufactures, and distributes microprocessor-based computer systems; Vanzetti Systems, Inc., Stoughton, MA, Innovative laser/INSPECT system performs high-speed inspection of solder joints on printed circuit boards

FREEPORT FINANCIAL SERVICES, INC.
10200 East Girard Avenue
Suite 210-A
Denver, CO 80231
(303) 755-1991

James D. Holmes
President

Directorships

Freeport Financial Services, Venture capital, Mergers and acquisitions
Recreational Leisure Services, Inc., Concessions
Farmer Brown's, Inc., Restaurant franchises
Carson Capital Management, Inc., Investments

Prior Positions

President, Barron Industries
Controller, Bio-Rad Labs

Education

MBA, Golden Gate University
BS, California State University

Kevin L. Novotney
Vice President

Directorship

Diamond Hill Industries, Real estate, computer peripheral, oil and gas

Prior Positions

Business Administrator, Queen of Peace Church, 1982–present
Registered Representative, Wall Street West, 1982

Education

BS, Finance, Metropolitan State College, 1983

Ann K. Holmes
Secretary and Treasurer

Directorships

Margate Ventures, Inc.
Carson Capital Management, Inc.

Prior Position

President, Shoshoni, Inc., 1983–84

Education

Casper College

Average Size of Investment	$150K
Size of Fund	$5M
Investment Criteria	General and various
Portfolio Companies	Arthur Treachers, Inc., Ohio, Fast food (fish and chips); Desktop Broker, Inc., California, Computer Software; Gold Ring Development Inc., Illinois, Natural resources; Recreation & Leisure Services, Inc., Illinois, Concessions

FRESHSTART VENTURE CAPITAL CORP.
313 West 53rd Street
New York, NY 10019
(212) 265-2249

Zindel Zelmanovitch
President

Directorships

East Coast Venture Capital Corp.
Wayne Smith Realty Corp.

Education

MBA, Long Island University, 1978
MS, LVOV Institute, 1959

Michael L. Moskowitz
Treasurer

Prior Positions

CPA, Pepper, Goldbert & Roth

Education

CPA, Baruch College

Neil Greenbaum
Secretary

Average Size of Investment	$35K
Size of Investment	$2.75M
Investment Criteria	Undisclosed
Portfolio Companies	Undisclosed

FRONTENAC VENTURE COMPANY
208 South LaSalle
Chicago, IL 60604
(312) 368-0044

Martin J. Koldyke
Partner

Directorships

American Healthcorp.
Acme-Cleveland Corp.
Rand McNally
Sunrise Medical, Inc.
Hutchinson Technology, Inc.

Education

BS, Purdue University, 1954

David A. R. Dullum
General Partner

Directorships

Duffy Broadcasting Co.
McCullough Cartwright Pharmaceutical Corp.
Anatel Instrument Corp.
Comlinear Corp.
Newtrend, Inc.
Reference Technology, Inc.
Thumbscan, Inc.

Prior Position

Associate, First National Bank of Chicago

Education

MBA, Stanford Graduate School of Business, 1971–73
Mechanical Engineering, Georgia Institute of Technology, 1966–70

Rodney L. Goldstein
General Partner

Directorships

Consolidated Stores, Inc.
Nutrition Technology Corp.
Bradley Printing Co.
Bulk Logistics, Inc.
Intermarket Publishing Co.

Prior Position

Management Consultant, Booz, Allen & Hamilton, Inc., 1978–81

Education

MBA, Wharton School, University of Pennsylvania, 1978
AB, Princeton University, 1974

Average Size of Investment	$1.5M
Size of Fund	$100M
Investment Criteria	Undisclosed
Portfolio Companies	Anatel Instrument Corp., Boulder, CO, Instrumentation for process and contamination control in manufacturing; Bradley Printing Company, Des Plaines, IL, Commercial printing; Comlinear Corp., Fort Collins, CO, Precision electronics components; Consolidated Stores Corp., Columbus, OH, Specialty retail company; Duffy Broadcasting Corp., Dallas, TX, AM/FM radio stations; Heico, Inc., Mendota, IL, Furnace draft controls and computerized inventory control systems; Homex Healthcare Corp., Milwaukee, WI, Medical equipment; Intermarket Publishing Corp., Chicago, IL, Publisher of magazine for financial securities industry; Intravascular Surgical Instruments, Inc., Chicago, IL, Micro-surgical instruments; Lasertrak Corp., Boulder, CO, Computerized delivery system; Newtrend, Inc., Oak Brook, IL, Proprietary software systems; Nutrition Technology Corp., Cincinnati, OH, High-nutrition consumer food products; Prestolite Electric Inc., Toledo, OH, Motors and ignition systems; Reference Technology, Inc., Boulder, CO, Computer peripheral products; Thumbscan, Inc., Champaign, IL, Computer recognition peripheral device; American Healthcorp., Inc., Nashville, TN, Health care facilities; Cadnetix Corp., Boulder, CO, Computer/electronic systems; Genderm, Inc., Chicago, IL, Dermatology products; Hutchinson Technology, Inc., Hutchinson, MN, Electronic components; McCullough Cartwright Pharmaceutical Corp., Barrington, IL, Veterinary products; Sunrise Medical, Inc., Torrance, CA, Health care equipment

FULCRUM VENTURE CAPITAL CORP.
2021 K Street, N.W.
Washington, DC 20006
(202) 833-9590

Divakar R. Kamath

Average Size of Investment	$300K
Size of Fund	Undisclosed
Investment Criteria	Diversified industry preferences
Portfolio Companies	Undisclosed

FUNDEX CAPITAL CORP.
525 Northern Boulevard
Great Neck, NY 11021
(516) 466-8550

Howard F. Sommer
President

Directorship

U. S. Capital Corp., Asset-based lending

Prior Positions

President, U. S. Capital Corp., 1973–present
Vice President, Drake-Beam & Assoc., 1972
National Sales Manager, Xerox Learning Systems, 1966–72
Marketing/Systems, IBM Data Processing Division, 1962–66

Education

MBA, New York University, 1969
BEE, City College of New York, 1962

Martin Albert

Average Size of Investment	$150K
Size of Fund	Undisclosed
Investment Criteria	General, diversified
Portfolio Companies	Undisclosed

GABELLI VENTURES, INC.
655 Third Avenue
New York, NY 10017
(212) 599-4770

Francine Sommer
General Partner

Prior Positions

Founding General Partner, Communication Ventures
Vice President and Principal, Research & Science Investors, Inc.

Education

MBA, Columbia University, 1976
BA, Goucher College, 1971

General Partner

Average Size of Investment	Undisclosed
Size of Fund	Undisclosed
Investment Criteria	Diversified
Portfolio Companies	Undisclosed

GENERAL ATLANTIC, INC.
120 East 55th Street
New York, NY 10022
(212) 888-9191

Steven Denning
Steve Reynolds
Ed Cohen
Alex Cranberg
David Hodgson

Average Size of Investment	$500K
Size of Fund	$80M
Investment Criteria	Technology-based companies are of interest; will act as lead investor
Portfolio Companies	Undisclosed

GENERAL ELECTRIC VENTURE CAPITAL CORP.
3135 Easton Turnpike
Fairfield, CT 06431
(203) 373-3333

33 Riverside Avenue
Westport, CT 06880
(203) 373-3238

3000 Sand Hill Road
Building Four, Suite 230
Menlo Park, CA 94025
(415) 854-8092

Exchange Place
Floor Fourteen
Boston, MA 02109
(617) 227-7922

Harry T. Rein
President and Chief Executive Officer, Fairfield
(203) 373-3356

Prior Positions

Manager of Strategic Planning and Development, General Manager, General Electric, 1979–83
Director of Corporate Planning, Gulf Oil Company, 1976–79
Vice President, Transaction Systems, Inc., 1973–76

Education

MBA, University of Virginia Darden School of Business Administration, 1973
BA, Oglethorpe College, 1968

James J. Fitzpatrick
Senior Vice President, Westport

Directorships

Gigabit Logic
Canaan Computer Corp.
Commstream, Inc.

Prior Positions

25 years in various engineering and management positions throughout General Electric Company

Education

MSEE, University of Connecticut, 1953
BSEE, University of Missouri, 1951

Preston H. Abbott
Secretary and Counsel, Fairfield
(203) 373-2429

Prior Positions

Commercial Equipment Leasing Operation, General Electric Credit Corp., 1979
Corporate Counsel, Components, General Electric Company
Associate, Wiggin & Dana (law firm), 1975–79

DIRECTORY AND BIOGRAPHIES

Education

JD, Harvard Law School, 1975
BA, honors, Economics, Harvard College, 1970

Lane C. DeCamp
Vice President, Westport

Directorships

Applied Immune Sciences, Inc.
OmniFlow, Inc.

Education

MBA, Finance, University of Texas, 1983

Dr. Robert W. McVicar
Senior Vice President, Menlo Park

Directorships

MegaTape Corp.
Computer-Aided Design Group

Prior Positions

Director of Corporate Research and Development, Anheuser-Busch, 1980–85
Vice President, Anheuser-Busch Wines, 1983–85
Director, New Product Development, Anheuser-Busch, 1977–80

Education

PhD, Industrial Engineering, Oregon State University, 1975
MSIE, Georgia Institute of Technology, 1967
BSIE, California State Polytechnic University (SLO), 1965

Eric A. Young
Vice President, Menlo Park

Directorships

Laserpath Corp.
Saber Technology Corp.
I-SCAN Corp.
Kurta Corp.

Prior Positions

Shop Manager Trainee, GE Apparatus Service Div.
Product Specialist, GE Transportation Systems Div.

Education

Master of Management, Finance, Northwestern University, 1980
BS, Mechanical Engineering (with distinction), Cornell University, 1978

Andrew C. Bangser
Vice President, Boston

Directorships

Medical & Scientific Designs, Inc.
Corporate Software Inc.

Prior Positions

Program Manager, General Electric Credit Corp., 1981–84

Education

MBA, Finance, Wharton School, University of Pennsylvania, 1979
BS, Physics (with honors), Brown University, 1976

David Nierenberg
Senior Vice President, CA

Directorships

Vitalink Communications Corp.
Tootje California, Inc.
Brooke & Mack, Inc. (DBA Souplantation)

Prior Positions

Vice President, Bain & Co., 1982–85
Manager, Bain & Company, 1980–82
Consultant, Bain & Company, 1978–80

Education

JD, Yale Law School, 1978
BA, Yale College, 1975

Gregory P. Stapleton
Senior Vice President, CA

Prior Positions

Operations Manager, Factory Automation Products Div., GE
Manager, Manufacturing, Appliance Motion Products Dept., GE
Plant Manager, Speciality Motor Products Dept., GE

Education

BS, Aerospace Engineering, Pennsylvania State University, 1968

Stephen L. Waechter
Vice President, Treasurer, Fairfield

Directorships

Hercules Offshore Drilling Co.
Arlington Cable Partners

Prior Positions

Financial Analyst, Corp. Financial Planning & Analysis, GE, 1984–85
Manager, Financial Operations Analysis, Electomaterials Business Dept., GE, 1982–84
Auditor, GE, Corp. Audit Staff, 1978–79

Education

MBA, Xavier University, 1974
BA, Christian Brothers College, 1971

Average Size of Investment	$500K–$1.5M
Size of Fund	Greater than $300M
Investment Criteria	Early-stage, high-technology
Portfolio Companies	Anadigics, Inc., Morristown, NJ, Gallium arsenide monolithic integrated circuits; Applied Information Memories, Milpitas, CA, High-performance vertical and horizontal recording media; Applied Materials, Inc., Santa Clara, CA, Chemical vapor deposition and dry plasma etch systems; Arlington Cable Partners, Arlington, VA, Leveraged buy-out of cable television franchise; Analogic Corporation, Peabody, MA, Measurement, signal translation, and data manipulation equipment; Applied ImmuneSciences, Inc., Menlo Park, CA, Specialized Protein A filters and monoclonal-based devices; Axiom Computers, Inc., Milpitas, CA, High performance system for numerically intensive computation; Brooke & Mack, Inc. (D.B.A. Souplantation), San Diego, CA, Self-service buffet restaurant specializing in soup, salad, and muffins; Cadre Technologies, Inc., Providence, RI, Computer aided analysis and design tools for system design and software development; Computer Aided Design Group, Santa Monica, CA, Facilities management software system for large building complexes; ComStream Corporation, San Diego, CA, Radio frequency modems for applications in ground stations in Kuband satellite communication systems; Corporate Software Incorporated, Canton, MA, Low-cost distribution of IBM-PC compatible software with value-added services; Crop Genetics International N.V., Dorsey, MD, Disease-free cloned sugar cane, microbial vectors, and automated can planting service; EnMasse Computer Corporation, Acton, MA, Multi-microprocessor computer system for on-line transaction processing; Glacial Confections, Inc., Westport, CT, Mousse de Jour, a pudding/frozen dessert competing with super-premium ice creams; I-Scan Corporation, Beaverton, OH, Hand-held and desk top scanners for business PC applications; Laserpath Corporation, San Jose, CA, Quick turnaround semicustom integrated circuits; Morris Decision Systems, Inc., New York, NY, Regional microcomputer hardware/software value-added reseller; Omniflow, Inc., Wilmington, VA, Four-line, fully programmable infusion pump, and disposable IV products; Perceptron, Inc., Farmington Hills, MI, Machine vision inspection systems; Scientific Computer Systems, Inc., Wilsonville, OR, High performance, low cost, Cray compatible 64-bit scientific computer; Tootje California, Inc., Redwood City, CA, All natural low calorie milk-based purable pudding dessert; Avanti Communications Corp., Newport, RI, High-speed multiplexing modems; Biological Energy Corp., Valley Forge, PA, Biomass reduction technologies for lignin and pulp production; Canaan Computer Corp., Trumbull, CT, High-performance workstations operating IBM 370-class software; CGX Corp., Acton, MA, CAD/CAM graphics workstations; Commterm, Inc., Billerica, MA, Digital voice messaging products; Computer*Thought Corp., Plano, TX, ADA tutorial products, interpreter and educational systems; Galileo Electro-Optics Corp., Sturbridge, MA, Fiber-optic and electro-optical components; Gigabit Logic, Inc., Newbury Park, CA, Ultra-high-speed gallium arsenide integrated circuits; Health Stop Medical Management, Inc., Wellesley, MA, Freestanding ambulatory medical care centers; Hercules Offshore Drilling Co., Houston, TX, Offshore workover oil rig contractors; Ibis Systems, Inc., Westlake Village, CA, High-capacity real-time storage subsystems; Koala Technologies, Santa Clara, CA, Personal computer data entry devices; Kurta Corp., Phoenix, AZ, Graphic digitizer products; Masstor Systems Corp., Santa Clara, CA, Mass storage subsystems and high-speed networking products; Medical and Scientific Designs, Inc., Rockland, MA, Automated clinical laboratory assay hardware; MegaTape Corp., Duarte, CA, Streaming tape backup storage; Mobile Satellite Communications Corp., King of Prussia, PA, Satellite-based mobile radio communications and location finding; Multiflow Computer, Branford, CT, 64-bit minisupercomputer; Nellcor, Inc., Hayward, CA, Noninvasive fetal blood gas oximeter and related products; Netra Corp., Mountain View, CA, Precision specialty plastics products; Octel Communications Corp., San Jose, CA, Digital voice messaging products; Raster Technologies, Inc., North Billerica, MA, High-performance color graphics displays; Saber Technology Corp., San Jose, CA, High-performance graphics

workstations; SEEQ Technology Corp., San Jose, CA, EEPROMs and a family of single-chip controller and processor designs; Silicon Compilers, Inc., Los Gatos, CA, VLSI design software; Stratus Computer, Inc., Marlboro, MA, Fault-tolerant computer systems; Sydis, Inc., San Jose, CA, Integrated office voice/data terminals; Symbolics, Inc., Cambridge, MA, LISP workstations; TeleSoft, San Diego, CA, ADA compilers and program support systems; UTI Instruments Company, Sunnyvale, CA, Mass analyzers, thermographic devices, laboratory instrumentation; Vitalink Communications Corp., Mountain View, CA, Point-to-point satellite communications services; Ztel, Inc., Wilmington, MA, Integrated digital PBX/local area network

GENESIS CAPITAL CORP.
20813 Stevens Creek Boulevard
Suite 101
Cupertino, CA 95014
(408) 446-9690

Gerald S. Casilli
President

Directorships

Identix, Inc.
NTX Communications Corp.
LISP Machine, Inc.
Quarterdeck Office Systems

Prior Positions

Co-founder, Chief Executive Officer, Millennium Systems, Inc., 1973–81

Education

BSEE, University of Pittsburgh, 1961

David E. Kratter

Average Size of Investment	$750K
Size of Fund	Undisclosed
Investment Criteria	Start-ups, second and third rounds; preferred areas: communications, computer hardware/software, electronic data processing, medical equipment, computer-aided design, office automation
Portfolio Companies	CAE Systems, Sunnyvale, CA, Computer-aided design; Identix, Palo Alto, CA, Fingerprint identification; Lightwave Tech., Los Angeles, CA, Fiber optics; LISP Machine, Inc., Los Angeles, CA, Artificial intelligence; NTX, Sunnyvale, CA, Communications; Quarterdeck, Santa Monica, CA, Office automation software

GENESIS SEED FUND, LTD.
Suite 227, 5 Great Valley Parkway
Malvern, PA 19335
(215) 648-3950

Two Penn Center Plaza #410
Philadelphia, PA 19102
(215) 988-0010

Thomas A. Penn
President, Malvern

Education

JD, University of Pennsylvania
MBA, Stanford University
BS (s), Massachusetts Institute of Technology

Joel S. Lawson, III
Chairman, Philadelphia

Education

MBA, Wharton School/University of Pennsylvania
BA, Yale University

Average Size of Investment	$200–500K
Size of Investment	$7M
Investment Criteria	Location: Pennsylvania; early stage or start-up companies that are primarily technology based; new microprocessor applications, industrial automation, telecommunications, and medical technology; no retail, restaurant, real estate, oil or gas
Portfolio Companies	Undisclosed

THE GENESIS VENTURE CAPITAL GROUP, INC.
100 Fifth Avenue
Waltham, MA 02154
(617) 890-4499

Arnold L. Mende
President

Directorships

General Ship Corp., Repair and overhaul naval combatants
Genesis Knitting Mills, Inc., Domestic sweater knits manufacturing company
Genesis Retail Stores, Inc., Chain of factory sweater stores
Logos Corp., Artificial intelligence (automatic language transmission systems)
Genesis Group International, Venture financing of non-U.S. major projects

Education

MBA, Harvard University, 1959
ILR, Cornell University, 1955

Average Size of Investment	$1M
Size of Fund	$160M
Investment Criteria	Undisclosed
Portfolio Companies	Undisclosed

GEOCAPITAL VENTURES
655 Madison Avenue
New York, NY 10021
(212) 935-0111

Stephen J. Clearman
Partner

Directorships

Xyvision, Inc., Computer-aided publishing
Panoramic Technology, Inc., System software
Education Systems Technology Corp., Computer-aided instruction
Acufex Microsurgical, Inc., Microsurgical instruments
Resource Dynamics, Inc., Facilities management software

Prior Position

Partner, Adler & Company

Education

JD, Harvard Law School, 1978
MS, Columbia University, 1974

Irwin Lieber
Partner

Directorships

LeaRonal, Specialty chemicals for electronics industry
S-P Drug, Drug distribution
Xyvision, Inc., Computer-aided publishing

Prior Positions

Partner, First Manhattan Co.
Partner, Nazem & Lieber

Education

MS, Syracuse University, 1963
BS, City College of New York, 1961

Walter C. Teagle, III
Associate

Prior Position

Investment Manager, Brown Brothers Harriman

Education

MBA, Wharton School, University of Pennsylvania, 1976
BA, University of Maryland, 1972

Average Size of Investment	$500K
Size of Fund	$20M
Investment Criteria	Early-stage projects in data communications, high-value software, and health care
Portfolio Companies	Undisclosed

GIRARD CAPITAL, INC.
4320 La Jolla Village Drive
Suite 210
San Diego, CA 92122-1233
(619) 457-5114

Sam Gudmundson
R. B. Woolley, Jr.
W. Creighton Gallaway

DIRECTORY AND BIOGRAPHIES

Average Size of Investment $500K
Size of Fund $10M
Investment Criteria Leveraged buy-outs are of interest; geographical location is important; will act as lead investor and considers start-ups; prefers technology-based companies
Portfolio Companies Undisclosed

GLENCO ENTERPRISES
1464 East 105th Street
Cleveland, OH 44106
(216) 721-1200

Lewis F. Wright

Average Size of Investment $150K
Size of Fund Undisclosed
Investment Criteria Diversified areas of interest including manufacturing; will act as lead investor; geographic location of importance
Portfolio Companies Undisclosed

GLENWOOD MANAGEMENT
3000 Sand Hill Road
Building One, Suite 230
Menlo Park, CA 94025
(415) 854-8070

Dag Tellefsen
Managing General Partner

Directorships

KLA Instruments
Arete Systems Corp.
Octel Communications Corp.
Adaptive Intelligence
Peak Systems

Prior Positions

Partner, Continental Capital Ventures, 1977–82
Executive Vice President, Oceanroutes, 1975–77
Director of Corporate Planning and Control, Raychem Corp., 1971–75
Associate, McKinsey & Co., 1969–71

Education

MBA, Stanford University, 1969
BS, Princeton University, 1966

John Hummer
Partner

Directorships

Conect Hospitality Systems
Opus Systems
Natural Language Products
Imperial Automation
Multivision Products, Inc.

Prior Position

President, Niederhoffer, Cross and Zechkeuser, Inc.

Education

MBA, Stanford University, 1980
BA, Princeton University, 1970

Doug Broyles
Partner

Directorships

Opus Systems
Arete Systems Corp.
Multivision Products, Inc.

Prior Positions

Vice President of Special Projects, Corvus Systems, 1980
President, Onyx Systems, Inc., 1980
Vice President, Zilog, 1978

Education

Electrical Engineering, California Polytechnic College

Victor Wei-Teh Long
Associate

Prior Positions

Assistant to the President, David Murdock, 1985
Associate, Concord Partners, 1983

Education

MBA, Stanford University, 1985
BA, Yale University, 1977

Average Size of Investment	$750K
Size of Fund	$17M
Investment Criteria	Sustainable unfair advantage in emerging technologies
Portfolio Companies	MultiVision Products, Inc., San Jose, CA, Designers of the circuitry that creates picture-within-a-picture television screens; Inova Microelectronics Corporation, Campbell, CA, Producers of monolithic multichip integrated circuits (integrated wafer scales); Opus Systems, Cupertino, CA, Producer of UNIX-based 32-bit board that allows mainframe-sized programs to run on microcomputer at mainframe speeds; Adaptive Intelligence Corp., Milipitas, CA, Manufacturer of computer-controlled industrial robots for lightweight applications; Aion Corp., Palo Alto, CA, Low-cost expert systems; Arete Systems Corp., San Jose, CA, Manufacturer of computers for transaction-oriented applications; Conect Hospitality Systems, Inc., Walnut Creek, CA, Turnkey computer systems for the hotel industry; Imperial Automation, Inc., Costa Mesa, CA, Provider of teller terminals and data processing systems for medium-size banks; Natural Language Products, Portola Valley, CA, Programs to access very large data bases, based on artificial intelligence; Octel Communications Corp., San Jose, CA, Manufacturer of voice messaging systems; The Palantir Corp., Santa Clara, CA, Developer of optical character readers for word processing systems; Peak Systems, Inc., Fremont, CA, Developer of processing equipment for the semiconductor industry; Saber Technology Corp., San Jose, CA, High-performance graphics workstation with ulta-high-resolution monitor

GLOBUS GROWTH GROUP
44 West 24th Street
New York, NY 10010
(212) 243-1000

Stephen E. Globus
Chairman

Directorships

CitiPostal, Inc., Courier service
Computer Doctor, Computer repair
Dental Technologies, Dental products, R&D

Education

BA, Lehigh University, 1969

Richard D. Globus

Average Size of Investment	Undisclosed
Size of Fund	Undisclosed
Investment Criteria	Seed capital, management, service industry
Portfolio Companies	Undisclosed

GLOVER CAPITAL CORP.
199 South Los Robles Avenue
Suite 625
Pasadena, CA 91101
(818) 795-6910

Malcolm D. Glover
President

Directorships

Astromec, Inc., Manufacturer precision motors
Glover Leasing Corp., Leasing aircraft hangars
Glover Properties, Property development
Glover Enterprises, Inc., Parent corporation
Cybergen Systems Corp.

Prior Positions

Account Executive, E. F. Hutton & Co.
General Manager, Convenience Service Corp.

Education

BA, Economics, University of California at Santa Barbara, 1978

M. D. Glover, Sr.

DIRECTORY AND BIOGRAPHIES

Average Size of Investment	$100K
Size of Fund	Undisclosed
Investment Criteria	Second-tier expansion, profitable
Portfolio Companies	Advanced Data Systems, San Jose, CA, Hardware, miniframe; Climatron, Costa Mesa, CA, Climate control system; Studio Software, Irvine, CA, Software; Cybergen Systems Corp., Santa Clara, CA, Hardware, static control device

GOLD COAST CAPITAL CORP.
3550 Biscayne Boulevard
Suite 601
Miami, FL 33137
(305) 576-2012

William I. Gold
President

Harry Hart
Chairman of the Board

Directorship

Hart Restaurant

Shelley R. Marrero

Average Size of Investment	$100K
Size of Fund	$3M
Investment Criteria	Direct loans to businesses
Portfolio Companies	Undisclosed

GOLDEN GATE INVESTMENTS, INC.
2121 South El Camino Real, Suite 605
San Mateo, CA 94403
(415) 345-9900

A. Larry Lindsey

Education

PhD studies, University of California at Los Angeles
MS, University of California at Los Angeles
MBA, University of Southern California
BSBA, Duquesne University

Average Size of Investment	$400K
Size of Fund	Undisclosed
Investment Criteria	Undisclosed
Portfolio Companies	Undisclosed

GOLDER, THOMA & CRESSEY
120 South LaSalle Street
Suite 630
Chicago, IL 60603
(312) 853-3322

Stanley C. Golder
Carl D. Thoma
Bryan C. Cressey
Bruce V. Rauner

Average Size of Investment	$1M
Size of Fund	$160M
Investment Criteria	Diversified interests, especially technology based; will act as lead investor; leveraged buyouts considered
Portfolio Companies	Undisclosed

ARTHUR P. GOULD & CO.
One Wilshire Drive
Lake Success, NY 11020
(516) 773-3000

74 Trinity Place
New York, NY 10006

Arthur P. Gould
President

Average Size of Investment	Principal: $100–500K; Agent: $2–15M
Size of Fund	Undisclosed
Investment Criteria	Niche technologies, new products and inventions, strong management
Portfolio Companies	Undisclosed

GRACE VENTURES CORPORATION
20300 Stevens Creek Blvd.
Suite 330
Cupertino, CA 95014
(408) 725-0774

Dr. Christian Horn
President

Directorships

W. R. Grace & Co., Multiproduct company
Anicon, Inc., Chemical vapor deposition equipment used for semiconductor manufacturing
Zoran Corporation, systems oriented, high performance specialty digital signal processing integrated circuits
ACCESS Medical Systems, Inc., Distributor of specialty diagnostic products, instruments and services for the physician's office market

Prior Positions

Vice President, Corporate Office for Operations, W. R. Grace & Co.
President, Polymer Technology, Inc.

Education

PhD, Technical University of Aachen, West Germany, 1958
MS, Technische Hochschule, Dresden, 1951

Dr. Charles A. Bauer
Vice President

Directorships

Omni Technology Corporation, high reliability semiconductor device testing services
Luxtron Corporation, fiber optic temperature sensors for industrial and medical applications

Prior Positions

Internal Management Consultant, W. R. Grace & Co.
Management Consultant, Theodore Barry & Associates

Education

MBA, Wharton School, University of Pennsylvania, 1972
PhD, Ohio State University, 1971
BS, Loyola Los Angeles, 1965

Robert E. Pedigo
Executive Vice President

Directorship

Marine Culture Enterprises, technology advanced intensive shrimp aquaculture

Prior Positions

President, Dearborn Utilities Services
Vice President, Finance, Chemed Corporation

Education

MBA, George Washington University, 1971
BA, University of California, 1954

Susan A. Woods
Assistant Vice President

Directorship

Omni Technology Corporation, High reliability semiconductor device testing services

Prior Position

Business Development, W. R. Grace & Co.

Education

MBA, Amos Tuck School, Dartmouth College, 1981
BA, Colby College, 1977

William B. Wittmeyer
Assistant Vice President

Directorships

Protolite Corporation, Special purpose reflective and transmissive optical materials for flight simulators, screens, and anti-glare devices
TransImage Corporation, Hand-held optical character recognition systems

Prior Position

Senior Analyst, Exxon Enterprises

Education

MBA, Columbia University, 1979
BS, United States Coast Guard Academy, 1972

Average Size of Investment	$750K
Size of Fund	$35M

DIRECTORY AND BIOGRAPHIES

Investment Criteria	Management quality; proprietary advantage; technical field
Portfolio Companies	ACCESS Medical Systems, Inc., Branford, CT, Distributor of specialty diagnostic products, instruments, and services for the physician's office market; Anicon, Inc., San Jose, CA, Chemical vapor deposition equipment used for semiconductor manufacturing; Concord Data Systems, Inc., Waltham, MA, Medium- and high-speed, full-duplex, dial-up modems and local area networks; Data Recording Systems, Inc., Melville, NY, High-speed laser printers that produce typeset-quality text and graphics on plain paper; EDA Systems, Inc., Cupertino, CA, Electronic design automation systems for custom integrated circuit design semiconductor manufacturers; Gen-Probe, Inc., San Diego, CA, DNA probe in-vitro diagnostics and related instrumentation; Integrated Measurement Systems, Inc., Beaverton, OR, Test and verification equipment for prototype application specific integrated circuits; IXYS Corporation, San Jose, CA, High performance standard, semi-custom and custom power semiconductors; Luxtron Corp., Mountain View, CA, Fiber-optic temperature sensors for industrial and medical applications; Micro Linear Corp., San Jose, CA, Semicustom linear and digital integrated circuits; Microwave Modules & Devices, Inc., Mountain View, CA, Radio frequency and microwave components for commercial and military communications equipment; Network Equipment Technologies, Inc., Menlo Park, CA, Telecommunications equipment to manage and control integrated voice and data networks; Omni Technology Corporation, Fremont, CA, High reliability semiconductor device testing services; Protolite Corp., San Jose, CA, Precision optical surface for exceptional image quality in front-and-rear projection audiovisual screens; Saxpy Computer Corp., Sunnyvale, CA, Digital optical supercomputers; Support Technologies, Inc., Tigard, OR, Portable, intelligent diagnostic equipment to field-test computers and printed circuit boards; Thesys Memory Products Corp., Scottsdale, AZ, Solid-state peripheral and plug-in memory systems for microcomputers; TransImage Corporation, Menlo Park, CA, Hand held optical character recognition systems; Zoran Corporation, Sunnyvale, CA, Systems oriented, high performance specialty digital signal processing integrated circuits

GRAYROCK CAPITAL, INC.
36 Grove Street
New Canaan, CT 06840
(203) 966-8392

Wolfgang J. Gluck
President

Directorships

Cangene Ltd., Biotechnology
Exercycle Corporation
Lancore Technologies, Inc.

Prior Position

Vice President, Corporate Development, The Molson Companies Ltd.

Education

MBA, University of St. Gall, Switzerland
BS, Federal Institute of Technology, Zurich, Switzerland

Donald P. Driscoll
Vice President

Prior Positions

Director, Business Development, The Molson Companies, Ltd.
Vice President, Strategic Planning, Chubb Holding, N.A.

Education

MBA, University of Western Ontario, 1966
BSc (honors), St. Francis Xavier, 1962

Average Size of Investment	$300K
Size of Fund	Undisclosed
Investment Criteria	Communications, health care, biotechnology, consumer products, specialty retailing
Portfolio Companies	Internet Systems, Chicago, IL, Bank software; Exercycle Corporation, Rhode Island, Exercise bike manufacturer; Lancore Technologies, Inc., California, Local area networks; Eyecare USA, Inc., California, Discount optomotrist retail chain; Loredan Biomedical, Inc., California

GRAYSTONE CAPITAL, LTD.
1600 Stout Street
Suite 1920
Denver, CO 80202
(303) 573-8866

Gregory Pusey
Special Limited Partner and Managing Director

Directorships

Applied Medical Devices, Medical sales, blood coagulants
Jones Optical Co., Sports optical wear manufacture and sales
U.S. Minerals Exploration Co., Precious metals exploration
GenTrac, Inc., Biomedical manufacture, blood coagulants
Grayhill Exploration, Mining

Prior Positions

Registered Representative, Hanifen Imhoff
President, Applied Medic Devices, Inc.

Education

BS, Finance, Boston College, 1974

Average Size of Investment	$200K
Size of Fund	$2M
Investment Criteria	High growth, Rocky Mountain region, various industries
Portfolio Companies	Allertech, Inc., Engelwood, CO, Allergy testing; Capfilm, Inc., Lee, MA, Dielectric films; Pasta Via International, Evergreen, CO, Pasta restaurant; Applied Medical Devices, Englewood, CO, Medical sales; Emery Datagraphic, Englewood, CO, Computer graphics; Enertrac, Inc., Cedar Rapids, IA, Communications systems; Gentrac, Inc., Madison, WI, Biomedical manufacturing; Jones Optical, Boulder, CO, Sports optical wear; Net Air International, Denver, CO, Executive air travel; U.S. Minerals, Arvada, CO, Precious metals mining and exploration

GREAT AMERICAN CAPITAL INVESTORS, INC.
1006 Holiday
Wichita Falls, TX 76301
(817) 322-5554

Albert Dillard

Average Size of Investment	$100K
Size of Fund	Undisclosed
Investment Criteria	Diversified areas of interest including manufacturing companies, geographic location is important
Portfolio Companies	Undisclosed

GREATER PHILADELPHIA VENTURE CAPITAL GROUP, INC.
225 South 15th Street
Philadelphia, PA 19102
(215) 732-3415

Martin Newman

Average Size of Investment	$300K
Size of Fund	Undisclosed
Investment Criteria	Diversified areas of interest including manufacturing companies; geographic location is of importance
Portfolio Companies	Undisclosed

GREATER WASHINGTON INVESTORS, INC.
5454 Wisconsin Avenue
Chevy Chase, MD 20815
(301) 656-0626

Don A. Christensen
President and Treasurer

Directorships

CENTEC Corp., Computer graphics
Data Plus, Inc., Communications products
National Demographics and Lifestyles, Inc., Demographically segmented mailing lists
Powertec, Inc., Electronic power supplies
Software Renovation Technology, Computer program maintenance software
Voice Computer Technologies, Inc., Voice response computer systems
UHR Corp., Residential energy systems
ZMI Corp., External cardiac pacemaker
Chisholm, Portable computer
Mastersoft

Education

MBA, Harvard Business School, 1958
BS, Chemical Engineering, Massachusetts Institute of Technology, 1952

Martin S. Pinson
Senior Vice President

Directorships

Automation Unlimited, Inc., Automated workstations for electronic assemblies
Computer Solutions, Inc., Computer software
General Health, Inc., Health risk management
Irwin Magnetic Systems, Inc., Manufacturer of magnetic tape drives
PC Technologies, Inc., Multiuser microcomputer systems
Process Engineering, Inc., Cryogenic equipment
Vortech Corp., Semiconductor testing services

Prior Position

Associate, Shaw, Pittman, Potts & Trowbridge

Education

JD, Georgetown University Law School, 1971
BA, American Studies, Union College, 1967

Cyril W. Draffin, Jr.
Vice President

Directorships

Allied Data Communications Group, Installation of local area networks
MIT Enterprise Forum of Washington-Baltimore, Regional entrepreneurial development

Prior Positions

Director, Solar Industrial Marketing, U.S. Department of Energy, 1982
Chief, Gas Production, U.S. Department of Energy, 1980

Education

MS, Massachusetts Institute of Technology, 1973
BS, Massachusetts Institute of Technology, 1972

Elizabeth S. Davies
Barbara L. Shaw

Average Size of Investment	$400K
Size of Fund	$28.5M (total assets)
Investment Criteria	Early-stage technology-oriented companies, principally computer-related, medical technology, and communications industries
Portfolio Companies	Allied Data Communications Group, Inc., Norcross, GA, Installers of local area networks; Automation Unlimited, Inc., Woburn, MA, Automated workstations for electronic assemblies; CENTEC Corp., Reston, VA, Computer graphics/process engineering; Chisholm, Milpitas, CA, Portable computer products; Computer Associates, Intl., Inc., Jericho, NY, Computer software products; Computer Solutions, Inc., Burlington, MA, Computer software for high-technology manufacturers; Concord Management Systems, Inc., Greenbelt, MD, Computer software for the construction industry; Data Plus, Inc., Lorton, VA, Communications products; DesignPak, Inc., Marlboro, MA, Printing and packaging; Display Data Corp., Hunt Valley, MD, Computer systems for selected vertical markets; Dixie Yeast Corp., Gastonia, NC, Bakers' yeast manufacturer; General Health, Inc., Washington, DC, Health-risk estimation products; Irwin Magnetic Systems, Inc., Ann Arbor, MI, Manufacturer of microcomputer tape drives; Mastersoft, Inc., Phoenix, AZ, Computer software for marketing managers; The Math Box, Inc., Rockville, MD, Computer retailing; National Computer Systems, Inc., Minneapolis, MN, Optical mark readers/computer software; National Demographics & Lifestyles, Inc., Denver, CO, Demographically segmented mailing lists; PC Technologies, Inc., Ann Arbor, MI, Multiuser microcomputer systems; Powertec, Inc., Chatsworth, CA, Electronic power supplies; Process Engineering, Inc., Plaistow, NH, Cryogenic equipment/specialty fabrication; Sentinel Computer Corp., Cincinnati, OH, Computer systems for distributors; Software Renovation Technology, Phoenix, AZ, Software to automate computer program maintenance; Systems Technology Associates, Inc., Sterling, VA, Telecommunications switching systems; UHR Corp., Springfield, VA, Development of residential energy systems; United Fiberglass, Inc., Woodbridge, VA, Manufacturer of fiberglass insulation; Voice Computer Technologies Corp., Norcross, GA, Voice response computer systems; Vortech Corp., Portland, ME, Semiconductor testing services; ZMI Corp., Cambridge, MA, External cardiac pacemaker

THE GREENHOUSE MANAGEMENT CORP.
4 Cedar Swamp Road
Glen Cove, NY 11542
(516) 759-1188

Solomon Manber
Chairman
(516) 759-1982

Directorships

Anaren Microwave, Microwave systems
Lasercad, Reprographics, Ltd., CAD services
Vanguard Ventures, Inc., Investments
Trac Line, Inc., Computer software
Telebyte Technology, Inc., Computer peripherals
Primages, Inc., Computer peripherals
Cullinet Software Corp., Computer software
Software Synergy, Inc., Computer software
DCS Controls Corp., Computer systems
Philon, Inc., Computer software

Evelyn Berezin
President
(516) 759-1982

Directorships

Philon, Inc., Software
Analytix, Inc., Blood test instruments
DCS Controls Corp., Lighting controls and energy management
DNAP, Plant Technology
LOCATE, Communications bypass
Primages, Inc., Printers
Software Synergy, Software

Prior Position

President, Potech Corp.

Education

AB, New York University, 1946

John Labiak

Average Size of Investment	$550K
Size of Fund	$18.2M
Investment Criteria	Research and development partnerships, start-up financing, communications, computer services, software applications and systems, electronic components and instruments, genetic engineering, diagnostic equipment
Portfolio Companies	Undisclosed

GREYHOUND CAPITAL MANAGEMENT CORP.
Greyhound Tower, MS 1408
Phoenix, AZ 85077
(602) 222-8816

Eight New England Executive Park
Burlington, MA 01803
(617) 272-8110

E. Allen Henson
President, AZ
(602) 222-8226

Directorships

Fortune Systems, Multiuser microcomputer
Companion Technologies, Converts CRT to desktop computer
Votan, Voice recognition

Prior Positions

Marketing/Executive, Greyhound Capital Corp., 1973–present
Marketing/Executive, RCA Corp., 1966–72

Education

Blackburn College
University of Illinois

David A. Bays
Vice President, AZ
(602) 222-8227

Directorships

AMBI Corp., Integrated voice data terminals
Microelectronic Packaging, Inc., Ceramic package
Multi-Systems, Inc., Telemarketing software
Studio Software, Page layout software
Companion Technologies, Converts CRT to desktop computer; point-of-sale terminal

Prior Positions

Var. Marketing/Management, Greyhound Computer Corp., 1972–80
Var. Marketing/Management, RCA Corp., Data Processing Division, 1964–72

Education

BS, Purdue University, 1959

DIRECTORY AND BIOGRAPHIES

John B. Schroeder

Average Size of Investment	$500K
Size of Fund	$25M
Investment Criteria	Equity investment opportunities in high technology; will provide seed, start-up, and subsequent round financing
Portfolio Companies	Aeonic Systems, Billerica, MA, Sensor-based computer integrated manufacturing system; AMBI Corp., Stamford, CT, Integrated voice data terminals; Companion Technologies Corp., Phoenix, AZ, Converts CRT to desktop computer; Point-of-sale terminals; DMA Systems Corp., Goleta, CA, Manufactures and markets 5¼" Winchester disk drives; Envoy Systems, Inc., Waltham, MA, Develops and markets sales management systems software; Fortune Systems Corp., Redwood City, CA, Multiuser microcomputer; Insurance Systems, Inc., Irvine, CA, Insurance agency software system; Kurta Corp., Phoenix, AZ, Graphic tablets and drawing board digitizers; Linear Technology Corp., Milpitas, CA, Linear-integrated circuits; Massachusetts Computer Corp., Littleton, MA, 32-bit scientific and technical computer systems; Microelectronic Packaging, Inc., Scottsdale, AZ, Ceramic package; Multi-Systems, Inc., Phoenix, AZ, Telemarketing software; Raster Technologies, Inc., North Billerica, MA, High-performance graphic display; Studio Software Corp., Irvine, CA, Page layout software; Votan, Fremont, CA, Voice recognition

GREYLOCK MANAGEMENT CORP.
One Federal Street
Boston, MA 02110
(617) 423-5525

William W. Helman
Howard E. Cox, Jr.
Daniel S. Gregory
Robert P. Henderson
Henry F. McCance
David N. Strohm
Charles P. Waite

Average Size of Investment	$1M
Size of Fund	$100M
Investment Criteria	Technology-based companies are of interest; start-ups welcome; will act as lead investor; interested in leveraged buy-outs
Portfolio Companies	Undisclosed

GRIES INVESTMENT COMPANY
720 Statler Office Tower
Cleveland, OH 44115
(216) 861-1146

Robert D. Gries
President

Directorships

Cleveland Browns, Football
Sulcus Computer Corp. Real estate closing and law office turnkey systems

Education

BA, Yale University, 1951

Richard F. Brezic
Vice President

Prior Positions

Controller, Allied Steel & Tractor Products, Inc.
CPA, Touche Ross & Co.

Education

JD, Cleveland State University, 1970
BBA, Case Western Reserve University, 1962

Average Size of Investment	$100K–$250K
Size of Fund	$3M
Investment Criteria	Diversified
Portfolio Companies	Undisclosed

GROCERS SBIC
3131 East Holcombe Boulevard
Houston, TX 77021
(713) 747-7913

Milton Levit

Average Size of Investment	$250K
Size of Fund	$3M

Investment Criteria   Grocer-type companies considered; start-ups welcome; will act as lead investor; geographic location is important

Portfolio Companies   Undisclosed

GRUBB & COMPANY
1500 Tower Place
3340 Peachtree Road
Atlanta, GA 30026
(404) 237-6222

Stephen B. Grubb
Managing Director

Directorships

Credit Card Software, Banking software

Prior Positions

President, Stephen B. Grubb & Co., 1979–82
Executive Vice President, Roe, Martin & Neiman, Inc., 1976–79

Education

MBA, Emory University, 1980
JD, University of South Carolina, 1974
BA, The Citadel, 1967

David E. Thomas, Jr.
Director

Education

JD, Emory University, 1983
MBA, Emory University, 1980
BS, University of Richmond, 1979

Average Size of Investment	Undisclosed
Size of Fund	Undisclosed
Investment Criteria	Undisclosed
Portfolio Companies	Undisclosed

GULF & WESTERN INC.
One G & W Plaza
New York, NY 10023
(212) 333-2720

James E. Parent

Average Size of Investment	$500K
Size of Fund	$36M
Investment Criteria	Technology-based companies are of importance, as are manufacturing companies; start-ups considered; will act as lead investor
Portfolio Companies	Undisclosed

GULFSTREAM CAPITAL CORP.
616 First National Bank Building
Augusta, GA 30902
(404) 722-5584

J. Thomas Jones

Average Size of Investment	$200K
Size of Fund	Undisclosed
Investment Criteria	Diversified interest areas; geographic locale of importance
Portfolio Companies	Undisclosed

GUNTHER, TALCOTT & BENSON, INC.
190 Godwin Avenue
Midland Park, NJ 07432
(201) 447-6021

Stephen Janick

Average Size of Investment	$100K
Size of Fund	$2M
Investment Criteria	Diversified companies are considered; start-ups welcome; will act as lead investor
Portfolio Companies	Undisclosed

HAMBRECHT & QUIST VENTURE PARTNERS
235 Montgomery Street
San Francisco, CA 94104
(415) 576-3333

One Hollis Street
Suite 102
Wellesley, MA 02181
(617) 237-2099

2655 LeJeune Road
Suite 500
Coral Gables, FL 33134
(305) 447-0423

William R. Hambrecht
Robert J. Kunze
Managing Partner, CA

Directorships

Advanced Genetics Research Institute, Vaccines for veterinary use
Calgene, Plant biotechnology
EXAC, Precision mass flow meters for process control
Luxtron, Fiber-optic temperature sensors and laboratory instruments
Orient Capital, Japanese-based investment company
Read-Rite Corp., High-performance thin-film recording heads
BBH&Q, London-based investment company
Visic, Inc., High-performance CMOS memory devices

Prior Positions

Chief Technical Officer, Senior Vice President, Group Executive, W. R. Grace & Co., 1974–83
President and Managing Director of G.E. Plastics & Chemicals, Europe General Electric, 1961–74

Education

BS, Chemistry, Bates College, 1957

John G. Balletto
David P. Best
General Partner, CA
(415) 576-3655

Directorships

Xilinx, Inc., Semiconductors
Optotech, Inc., Optical memory
Northwest Instrument Systems, Personal instruments
Telequest, Residential telephones
Seattle Silicon Technology, Silicon compilers

Prior Positions

Marketing Manager, Intel Corp.
Group Manager, Digital Equipment Corp.

Daniel H. Case III
General Partner, CA
(415) 576-3300

Directorships

Exac Corp., High-performance mass flowmeters
Harper S.I.D., Electronics distributor
Oriole Software, Inc., On-line, real-time manufacturing software
Read-Rite Corp., Thin-film recording heads for data storage

Prior Positions

Vice President, Hambrecht & Quist
Associate, Hambrecht & Quist

Education

Rhodes Scholar, Oxford University, 1981
BA, Princeton University, 1979

Bob O. Evans
Kenneth L. Guernsey
General Partner, CA
(415) 576-3495

Prior Positions

Vice President and General Counsel, Hambrecht & Quist Group
Attorney, Cooley, Godward, Castro, Huddleson & Tatum

Education

JD, MBA, University of California at Los Angeles, 1978
BA, University of California at Los Angeles, 1974

Theodor H. Heinrichs
General Partner, CA

Prior Positions

Chairman and Chief Executive Officer, Miles Laboratories
Chairman and Chief Executive Officer, Cutter Laboratories

Clifford H. Higgerson
Managing Partners, Communications, CA
(415) 576-3631

Directorships

Digital Microwave, Digital microwave radios
Kevex, Analytical instruments
Network Research, Local area networks

Education

MBA, University of California at Berkeley, 1966
BSEE, University of Illinois, 1962

John R. Johnston
General Partner, CA
(415) 576-3439

Prior Position

Vice President and General Manager, Inter-Asia Management Co., Ltd., 1977–81

Education

MBA, Harvard University, 1983
AB, Princeton University, 1975

Ta-Lin Hsu
General Partner, CA
(415) 576-3481

Directorships

MiniScribe, Disk drives
Kongene Automation, Turnkey control systems

Prior Positions

Manager, Storage Systems and Technology, IBM, 1973–85
Scientist, Materials Research Center, Allied, 1970–73

Education

PhD, Electrical Engineering, University of California at Berkeley, 1970
BS, Physics, National Taiwan University, 1964

Modesto A. ("Mitch") Maidique
General Partner, FL

Directorships

Automation Intelligence, Factory automation
Collaborative Research, Genetic engineering
Data Innovations, Computer graphics
DataNet, Factory data collection
Electronic Systems Products, Color projection systems
Finial Technology, High-end consumer electronics

Prior Positions

Professor of Management and Director of the Innovation and Entrepreneurship Institute of the University of Miami, 1984–present
Coordinator of the Engineering Management Program, Stanford University
Associate Professor, Stanford University, 1981–84
Assistant Professor, Harvard Business School, 1976–81

Education

PMD, Harvard Business School, 1975
PhD, Solid State Physics, Massachusetts Institute of Technology, 1970
EE, Electrical Engineering, Massachusetts Institute of Technology, 1966
MS, Electrical Engineering, Massachusetts Institute of Technology, 1964
BS, Electrical Engineering, Massachusetts Institute of Technology, 1962

Robert M. Morrill
Senior Investment Partner, MA

Directorships

Intecom, Inc.
Stratus Computer
Applix, Inc.
Celerity Computing
Health First, Inc.
Cognex Corp.
Javelin Software Corp.
V-Mark Computer
Applitek Corp.

Prior Position

Vice President, Marketing, Prime Computer, Inc.

Education

BS, Ohio Wesleyan

DIRECTORY AND BIOGRAPHIES

Thomas J. O'Rourke
W. Denman Van Ness
General Partner, CA
(415) 576-3550

Directorships

Accutest Corp.
ASI Teleprocessing
ATEX, Inc.
Computer Controls Corp.
Computer Corp. of America
Data Instruments Corp.
Stewart-Riess Laboratories, Inc.
Western Association of Venture Capitalists

Prior Positions

Consultant, New England Regional Commission, 1976–77
Assistant Treasurer, Inforex, Inc., 1975–76
Assistant Vice President, State Street Bank and Trust Co., 1971–75

Education

MBA, Harvard University, 1971
BA, Williams College, 1964

Charles P. Waite, Jr.
General Partner, CA

Directorships

VISIC, Inc., High-performance semiconductor memory
EAN, Inc., Point-of-sale marketing

Prior Position

Cardiovascular Specialist, Cobe Laboratories, Inc., 1977–81

Education

MBA, Harvard University, 1983
BA, Kenyon College, 1977

Allan M. Wolfe, M.D.
General Partner, CA
(415) 576-3455

Directorships

Neodontics Inc., Coating for dental and orthopedic prosthesis
Verax, Inc., Process technology to enhance and economize manufacture of molecular biologicals and fine chemicals
Infusion Systems, Inc., "Non" powered IV drug delivery systems

Prior Positions

Independent Consultant, 1980–85
Chairman, Business Development, New Products and Strategic and Operating Planning, McGaw Labs (Division of American Hospital Supply), 1975–80

Education

MD, New York School of Medicine, 1962
AB, American Civilization, Cornell University, 1958

George M. Drysdale
Partner, CA
(415) 576-3642

Directorships

Speech Recognition Systems
Xenotech Labs

Prior Position

Attorney, Davis, Polk & Wardwell

Education

JD, Stanford Law School, 1980
MBA, Stanford Business School, 1980
BS, Engineering, Harvey Mudd College, 1976

Kenneth B. Hart
Associate, CA
(415) 576-3629

Prior Position

National Accounts Division, IBM, 1978–83

Education

MBA, University of California at Berkeley, 1978
BSEE, University of California at Berkeley, 1973

Patrick J. Sansonetti
General Partner, MA

Directorships

VIA Systems, Inc., CAE software
1st Seminars, Inc., Telemarketing
Interleaf, Inc., Computer-aided publications

Prior Positions

Vice President, Business Development, Fidelity Systems, 1982–83
Director, International Marketing, Prime Computer, 1976–81

Average Size of Investment	$750K
Size of Fund	Over $450M
Investment Criteria	U.S. high technology
Portfolio Companies	H & Q has invested in over 275 companies since 1970

HAMBRO INTERNATIONAL VENTURE FUND
17 East 71st Street
New York, NY 10021
(212) 288-7778

One Boston Place
Suite 923
Boston, MA 02106
(617) 722-7116

Edwin A. Goodman
General Partner, NY

Directorships

Platt Music Corp., Consumer electronics
Staples, Discount office supplies
A. Howard Wholesale, Wholesale club
Founders Communications, Regional newspapers

Prior Positions

Vice President, Alan Patricof Associates

Education

MS, Graduate School of Business, Columbia University, 1979
BA, Yale, 1962

Anders Brag
General Partner, NY

Directorships

Prentice, Modems, data com products
Rivendell, Psychiatric care hospital management company
Nat Health Care, Small community hospital management company
Omnicad, CAD/CAM software

Prior Position

Consultant, Boston Consulting Group

Education

MBA, Harvard, 1979
BA, IECE (France), 1975

Richard A. D'Amore
General Partner, MA

Directorships

Corporate Software, Inc., Software distribution
Dalsat Inc., Satellite systems
Solectron, Contract manufacturing

Prior Positions

Consultant, Bain & Co.
CPA, Arthur Young Co.

Education

MBA, Harvard University, 1980
BS, Northeastern University, 1975

Robert S. Sherman
General Partner, MA
(617) 722-7055

Directorships

Strato-Medical Corp.
Techmedica
Multi-Planar Diagnostic Imaging
Secur-Image Technologies

Prior Position
Assistant Vice President, Bank of Boston, 1974–79

Education
MBA, Harvard Business School, 1974
AB, Amherst, 1968

Arthur Spinner
General Partner, NY

Directorships
Telematics International, Communications processors
Crystal Technologies, Secretarial workstations
KOMAG, Sputtered disk media
Enmasse Computer, Transaction processing computers

Prior Positions
Vice President, AXA Capital, 1975–81
Associate, Loeb, Rhoades & Co., 1973–75

Education
MBA, Harvard Business School, 1973
BA, Claremont-McKenna College, 1971

Frances Janis
Peter Santeusanio

Average Size of Investment	$500K
Size of Fund	$70M
Investment Criteria	Diversified investments in various industries and at various stages of financing
Portfolio Companies	Undisclosed

HAMPSHIRE CAPITAL CORP.
500 Spaudling Turnpike
P.O. Box 3010
Portsmouth, NH 03801
(603) 431-7755

Philip G. Baker
President

Directorships
Outlet Services Corp., Services/manufacturing firms wishing to enter "outlet" retailing
Capital Management Corp., Developer of commercial real estate
U.S. Trading Corp.
Business Opportunities Center Corp.
Capital Resources Inc.
Computer Exchange

Prior Positions
President, Business Investment Advisory Corp., 1979–present
Advisor to small venture funds and SBICs

Education
BS, Boston University, 1955

Lauren E. Wright
Harry F. Calaman

Average Size of Investment	$75K
Size of Fund	$2.5M
Investment Criteria	Service and franchise companies, selected real estate ventures
Portfolio Companies	Job Store, Inc., Clearwater, FL, Franchise company matches prospective employers to employees; Outlet Services Corp., Portsmouth, NH, Services to manufacturers of consumer goods wishing to enter retailing

JOHN HANCOCK VENTURE CAPITAL MANAGEMENT, INC.
200 Clarendon Street
Boston, MA 02114
(617) 421-6231

Edward W. Kane
Managing Director
(617) 421-6760

Directorship
Artificial Intelligence Corp., Natural language software

Prior Positions
Senior Investment Officer, John Hancock Mutual Life Insurance Co.
Assistant Vice President, New England Merchants Bank

Education

MBA, Harvard Business School, 1975
BA, University of Pennsylvania, 1971

William A. Johnston
Senior Investment Officer
(617) 421-5287

Prior Positions

Investment Officer, John Hancock Mutual Life Insurance Co.
Assistant Vice President, State Street Bank

Education

MBA, Syracuse University, 1975
BA, Colgate University, 1973

Nancy C. Raulston
Investment Officer
(617) 421-6854

Prior Positions

Security Analyst, Aetna Life & Casualty
Associate Engineer, McDonnell-Douglass

Education

MBA, Amos Tuck School, Dartmouth College, 1982
AB, Occidental College, 1979

D. Brooks Zng
Managing Director
(617) 421-6350

Directorship

Access Technology, Inc., Management decision software

Prior Positions

Senior Investment Officer, John Hancock Mutual Life Insurance Company
Senior Investment Analyst, Sun Life
Senior Investment Analyst, Paine Webber

Education

MBA, Harvard University, 1970
BS, Lehigh University, 1967

Robert J. Lepkowski
Investment Officer
(617) 421-6852

Prior Positions

Investment Analyst, Massachusetts Technology Development Corp.
Manager, Strategic Planning, Unimation, Inc.

Education

MS, Massachusetts Institute of Technology (Sloan School), 1982
BSME, Massachusetts Institute of Technology, 1976

Laurie J. Thomsen
Assistant Investment Officer
(617) 421-3562

Prior Positions

Assistant Investment Officer, John Hancock Mutual Life
Assistant Vice President, Loan Officer, United States Trust

Education

BA, Williams College, 1979

Average Size of Investment	$1M
Size of Fund	$225M
Investment Criteria	Proprietary technology, large market, strong management, good growth potential, potential for 5× return in 5 years
Portfolio Companies	Undisclosed

HANOVER CAPITAL CORP.
150 East 58th Street
New York, NY 10155
(212) 355-3111

Daniel J. Sullivan

Average Size of Investment	$250K
Size of Fund	Undisclosed
Investment Criteria	Diversified areas of interest; will act as lead investor
Portfolio Companies	Undisclosed

DIRECTORY AND BIOGRAPHIES

HAPP VENTURES
444 Castro Street
Suite 400
Mountain View, CA 94041
(415) 961-1115

William D. Happ
Principal

Directorship
Venture Administration, Inc.

Prior Position
Vice President, Kidder Peabody & Co., Inc., 1976–82

Education
MBA, Stanford University, 1956
BS, University of California, 1950

Average Size of Investment	$300K
Size of Fund	Undisclosed
Investment Criteria	Undisclosed
Portfolio Companies	Investments have been made in companies involved in software development tools, software data base system, visual image scanner, medical instrumentation, and digital X-ray imaging

HARBOUR FINANCIAL COMPANY
357 Fox Hill Street
Westwood, MA 02090
(617) 461-0460

John R. Schwanbeck
President

Directorships
Independent Cable, Inc., Electronic cable
Data Plus, Inc., Computer software
Lund International Corporation

Prior Position
Vice President, Blyth Eastman Paine Webber, Inc.

Education
MBA, Harvard Business School, 1968
BS, Massachusetts Institute of Technology, 1966

Average Size of Investment	$1M
Size of Fund	Undisclosed
Investment Criteria	Undisclosed
Portfolio Companies	Undisclosed

HARRISON CAPITAL, INC.
2000 Westchester Avenue
White Plains, NY 10650
(914) 253-7845

William T. Corl
John J. Huntz
Robert A. Backer
Margaret S. Johns

Average Size of Investment	$500K
Size of Fund	Undisclosed
Investment Criteria	Technology-based companies are of interest, as well as start-ups; will act as lead investor
Portfolio Companies	Undisclosed

HARVARD VENTURE CAPITAL
(an affiliate of The Harvard Group)
P.O. Box 746
27 Loop Road
Merrimack, NH 03054
(603) 429-0858

412 Beacon Street
Boston, MA 02135

Michael G. Angel
Managing Partner

Directorships
American Medical Plan
The Harvard Group

Education

MBA, Harvard Business School, 1983

John D. Keith
General Partner

Directorship

The Harvard Group

Education

Architecture, Harvard Design School, 1981

Average Size of Investment	$250K–1M
Size of Fund	$20M
Investment Criteria	Finance, real estate, health care medical products, special opportunities, small businesses, motion pictures, and entertainment
Portfolio Companies	American Medical Plan, Brentwood, TN

HARVEST VENTURES, INC.
767 Third Avenue
New York, NY 10017
(212) 838-7776

3000 Sand Hill Road
Menlo Park, CA 94025
(415) 854-8400

Harvey Mallement
Managing Director, NY

Directorships

CAE Systems, Inc., Manufactures CAE workstation for design of complex integrated circuits
Control Automation, Inc., Manufactures robotic and vision products for electronics and telecommunications
Elcam, Inc., CAD/CAM systems for mechanical manufacturing market
Ferrofluidics Corp., Manufactures products for semiconductor and computer industry using magnetic field technology
Symbol Technologies, Inc., Designs and manufactures Bar Code laser scanning devices for data entry

Prior Positions

Senior Vice President, The JLS Group, Inc.
Managing Partner, MASCO Associates

Education

MBA, City College of New York, 1968
CPA, New York State University, 1966

Harvey Wertheim
Managing Director, NY

Directorships

Account-A-Call Corp., Service company providing computerized analysis of telephone use for corporations
Keystone Camera Products Corp., Manufacturer of pocket-size cameras
O.K. Industries, Inc., Manufactures wire wrapping tools and equipment for electronics and hobby industries
Wolfdata Inc., Designs and manufactures communications products for microcomputers

Prior Position

Vice President and Director, Research & Sciences Investors, Inc.

Education

MBA, St. John's University, 1968
BBA, City College of New York, 1962

Cloyd Marvin
Managing Director, CA

Directorships

Ferix Corp., Manufactures high-speed, nonimpact printer based on thin-film technology
Gemini Magnetics, Inc., Manufactures thin-film recording disks
Optigraphics Corp., Manufactures system for capturing, storing, and manipulating graphics
ViewTech, Inc., Workstation system which combines text and graphics

Prior Positions

Founder, Four Phase Systems
Founder, Compression Labs, Inc.

Education

Graduate Studies, Applied Math, University of California at Los Angeles
BSEE, University of Colorado, 1958

Cydney Meltzer
Andrew Rachleff
Associate, CA

Prior Positions
Financial Analyst, Blyth Eastman Paine Webber
Associate, Lamoreaux & Associates

Education
MBA, Stanford University, 1984
BS, Wharton School, 1980

Average Size of Investment	$1M
Size of Fund	$80M
Investment Criteria	Proprietary technology, start-up, later stage; lead investor or follow-on
Portfolio Companies	Account-A-Call Corp., Burbank, CA, Service company providing computerized analysis of monthly telephone utilization for major corporations; Advanced Technology Laboratories, Inc., Seattle, WA, Manufacturer of ultrasound medical diagnostic equipment; Atlas Minerals & Chemicals, Inc., Mertztown, PA, Manufactures specialty chemicals for industry use; B & R Land Holdings, Ltd., Denver, CO, Purchases proven energy prospects for further development and sale; CAE Systems, Inc., Sunnyvale, CA, Manufactures a computer-aided engineering workstation for the design of complex integrated circuits; Callan Data Systems, Westlake Village, CA, Produces a 68000-based, scientific application workstation featuring the UNIX operating system; Comstron Corp., Freeport, NY, Designs and manufactures filter systems and frequency synthesizers for the electronic warfare and communications markets; Control Automation, Inc., Princeton, NJ, Manufacturer of robotic and vision products for the electronics and telecommunications market; CSP, Inc., Billerica, MA, Manufactures multiarray signal processing equipment for the computer industry; Discovery Oil, Ltd., Los Angeles, CA, Oil and gas exploration and production company; Dynabyte, Inc., Menlo Park, CA, Designs and manufactures small business microcomputer systems; Elcam, Inc., Woburn, MA, Produces CAD/CAM systems for the mechanical manufacturing market; Electro-Oxide Corp., West Palm Beach, FL, Manufactures conductive and resistive paste materials for the semiconductor market; Evans & Sutherland Computer Corp., Salt Lake City, UT, Manufactures CAD/CAM computer systems for engineering design and for simulation applications; Ferix Corp., Sunnyvale, CA, Manufactures a high-speed, nonimpact printer based on thin-film semiconductor technology; Ferrofluidics Corp., Nashua, NH, Manufactures a line of products for the semiconductor and computer industries using its proprietary magnetic fluid technology; Gemini Magnetics, Inc., San Jose, CA, Developing thin-film recording disks using advanced plating and sputtering technologies; Hurco Manufacturing Co., Indianapolis, IN, Designs and manufactures microprocessor-controlled machine tool systems; Intec Corp., Trumbull, CT, Manufacturer of laser scanning inspection systems for web process industries; Intercontinental Energy Corp., Denver, CO, Natural resource exploration and production company; International Microelectronic Products, Inc., San Jose, CA, Designs and manufactures custom MOS, LSI, and VLSI semiconductor devices; Interpore International, Irvine, CA, Developing implantable medical devices using a proprietary porous technology; Keystone Camera Products Corp., Clifton, NJ, Manufactures low-cost, easy-to-use cameras for the consumer market; Microtest Systems, Inc., Sunnyvale, CA, Designs and manufactures semiconductor burn-in test equipment; MRW, Inc., Wichita, KS, Owns and operates cold-storage food warehouses throughout the U.S.; National Computer Communications Corp., Stamford, CT, Distributes terminals, printers, and other computer-related products for sale and lease; Navidyne Corp., Newport News, VA, Designs and manufactures microprocessor-based navigation equipment for the marine industry; NCA Corp., Sunnyvale, CA, Develops standard application software systems for manufacturing and financial controls and for integrated circuit design analysis; O.K. Industries, Inc., Bronx, NY, Manufactures wire-wrapping tools and related equipment for the electronics and hobby industry; Optigraphics Corp., Scottsdale, AZ, Developing a processing system for capturing, storing, and manipulating graphic images; The Palantir Corp., Mountain View, CA, Engaged in the development of a low-cost optical character recognition device for office automation applications; Pyramid Technology Corp., Palo Alto, CA, Manufactures a high-performance 32-bit superminicomputer optimized for the UNIX operating system; Repligen Corp., Cambridge, MA, Biotechnology company developing "natural" additives for various commercial products such as food, cosmetics, and insecticides; Software Connections, Inc., Santa Clara, CA, Develops and markets multiuser DBMS networking software systems; Solo Systems, Inc., Sunnyvale, CA, Manufactures an intelligent workstation for programmers; Sutter Biomedical, Inc., San Diego, CA, Manufacturer of surgical instruments including soft skeletal implants for the hand and foot; Sykes Datatronics, Inc., Rochester, NY, Manufactures microcomputer-systems-based data communications and information processing equipment; Symbol Technologies, Inc., Bohemia, NY, Designs and manufactures bar code laser scanning devices for automatic distributed data entry; Systeme Corp., Orlando, FL, Manufacturers of computer systems for the savings and loan and commercial banking industry; Telesis Corp., Chelmsford, MA, Designs and manufactures CAD/CAM equipment for the design of printed circuit boards; Venus Scientific, Inc., Farmingdale, NY, Manufactures miniaturized high-voltage power supplies; ViewTech, Inc., Santa Clara, CA, Produces a distributed workstation system for use in in-house publication applications which combine both text processing and

graphics; Wolfdata, Inc., Chelmsford, MA, Designs and manufactures communications products for microcomputers; ZTEL, Inc., Andover, MA, Manufactures a fourth-generation proprietary LAN/private branch exchange (PBX) digital communications network for both data and voice

HAWAII-PACIFIC VENTURE CAPITAL CORP.
2121 South El Camino Real
Suite 605
San Mateo, CA 94403
(415) 573-0806

Raymond Y. C. Ho
Chairman of the Board

Education

JD, Yale Law School
BA, University of Hawaii

Tony H. Heo
Executive Vice President

Education

BS, University of California at Berkeley

Average Size of Investment	$500K

HEALTH/MEDICAL INVESTMENTS, INC.
2121 South El Camino Real
Suite 605
San Mateo, CA 94403
(415) 345-8500

Dr. Linda L. Mak
Senior Vice President

Education

MBA, University of California at Berkeley
PhD, University of California at Berkeley
MS, Arizona State University
AB, University of California at Berkeley

Average Size of Investment	$200K

HEALTH/MEDICAL VENTURES
2121 South El Camino Real
Suite 605
San Mateo, CA 94403
(415) 345-8500

K. L. Cerrone
Senior Vice President

Education

JD, Hastings College
MBA, University of San Francisco
MS, New York University
BS, University of Illinois

Average Size of Investment	$200K

HELLER CAPITAL SERVICES, INC.
200 Park Avenue
New York, NY 10166
(212) 880-7198

Jack A. Prizzi

Average Size of Investment	$200K
Size of Fund	$2M
Investment Criteria	Diversified areas of interest including technology-based and manufacturing companies; leveraged buy-outs are also of interest; will act as lead investor
Portfolio Companies	Undisclosed

HENRY & COMPANY
9191 Towne Centre Drive
Suite 230
San Diego, CA 92122
(619) 453-1655

Albert J. Henry
F. David Hare
President

Directorships

Raytel Systems Corp.
Spectragraphics Corp.
Motion Analysis Corp.

Prior Positions

Vice President, Irving Trust Co., 1969–83
Lieutenant, United States Navy, 1963–69

Education

MBA, New York University, 1975
BA, University of South Carolina, 1963

June M. Knaudt

Average Size of Investment	$1M
Size of Fund	$22M
Investment Criteria	Second-stage equity investments in unique or proprietary technology
Portfolio Companies	Motion Analysis Corp., Santa Rosa, CA, Motion analysis software; Scientific Computer Systems Corp., San Diego, CA; Portland, OR, Cray compatible mini-super computers; Etak, Inc., Menlo Park, CA, Electronic navigation equipment; Molecular Design Ltd., San Leandro, CA, Database management for chemical and pharmaceutical labs; American Cimflex Corp., Pittsburgh, PA, Computer-integrated manufacturing; Megatest Corp., San Jose, CA, IC test equipment; Raytel Systems Corp., San Jose, CA, Medical image management; Silicon Compilers, Inc., San Jose, CA, IC design tools; Spectragraphics Corp., San Diego, CA, CAD/CAM; Teknowledge, Inc., Palo Alto, CA, Expert Systems

HERITAGE CAPITAL CORP.
2290 First Union Plaza
Charlotte, NC 28282
(704) 334-2867

Herman B. McManaway
President

Directorships

Scope, Inc., Electronic countermeasures, scanners
Versa-Technologies, Inc., Hydraulic cylinders, silicone rubber products
Burris Industries, Furniture
Dixie Belle Textiles, Lingerie
Dumas Corp., Dried pea processor
S & W Inc., Auto engine rebuilders
Carolina Pump & Supply, Wholesale distributor of water pumps
Jordan Graphics, Business forms
Harris-Teeter Supermarkets, Food distribution

Prior Position

Vice President, Finance, Ruddick Corp.

Education

MBA, University of Pennsylvania, 1949
BS, University of South Carolina, 1947

William R. Starnes
G. Kinsey Roper

Average Size of Investment	$250K
Size of Fund	$6.5M
Investment Criteria	Industry: diversified; area of preference: Southeast; first or second stage; equity oriented
Portfolio Companies	Undisclosed

HERITAGE VENTURE GROUP, INC.
2400 One Indiana Square
Indianapolis, IN 46204
(317) 635-5696

Arthur A. Angotti
President, Chairman of the Board

Directorships

Heritage Venture Group, Inc., SBIC
Heritage Management, Inc., Financial consulting
Heritage Broadcasting Co., Inc., Operates radio stations
MidAmerica Cellular Corp., Cellular telephone
United States Auto Club, Sanctioning of auto races across USA
Pinebrook Recording Studios, Recording studio
Kittle's, Retail home furnishings

Prior Positions

Founding President, Indianapolis Cablevision Co., Cable television
Director and Executive Vice President, Syndicate Systems, Inc., Manufacturing store fixtures
Director, Noblesville Cablevision, Cable television

Education

MBA, Finance, Indiana University, 1969
BS, Indiana University, 1965

Average Size of Investment	$150K–$600K
Size of Fund	$3M
Investment Criteria	Emerging growth and mature companies, some start-up, acquisitions
Portfolio Companies	Undisclosed

HILL & KIRBY
885 Arapahoe Avenue
Boulder, CO 80302
(303) 442-5151

John G. Hill
Paul J. Kirby
Thomas G. Washing

Average Size of Investment	$1M
Size of Fund	$51M
Investment Criteria	Start-ups are desirable, will act as lead investor; prefer technology-based companies located nearby
Portfolio Companies	Undisclosed

HILLCREST GROUP
9 South 12th Street
Richmond, VA 23219
(804) 643-7358

A. Hugh Ewing
General Partner

Directorships

Jarvis Corp., Telephone interconnect
Riverton Corp., Cement manufacturer
Miller Manufacturing, Wood products

Prior Position

Vice President, Wheat, First Securities, 1971–78

Education

MBA, University of Virginia, 1971
BS, Civil Engineering, Virginia Military Institute

James B. Farinholt, Jr.
Partner

Directorships

Auto-Trol Technology, CAD/CAM manufacturer
Burke-Parsons-Bowlby Corp., Wood products
Owens & Minor, Inc., Distributing drugs and hospital supplies
Richmond Cold Storage, Inc., Warehousing
Major League Bowling, Bowling centers
Pearson Yachts, Sailing yacht manufacturer

Prior Positions

Assistant Secretary, Corporate Services, Chemical Bank, 1959–67
Senior Vice President, Corporate Finance, Wheat, First Securities, Inc., 1968–78

Education

BS, Hampden-Sydney College, 1957

John P. Funkhouser
General Partner

Directorships

dbo Corp., Manufacturer of air handling equipment
Do It Yourself, Inc., Educational video tapes
Franchise Enterprises, Inc., Hardee's franchise
CSVa, Inc., Specialty retail chain

Prior Positions

Partner, Isaacs & Funkhouser
Assistant Vice President, Wheat, First Securities
Associate, Chemical Bank

Education

MBA, University of Virginia, 1982
BA, Princeton University

Average Size of Investment	$500K
Size of Fund	$11.2M
Investment Criteria	Geographic proximity important; leveraged buy-outs of interest, technology-based companies considered; will act as lead investor
Portfolio Companies	Undisclosed

HILLMAN COMPANY
2000 Grant Building
Pittsburgh, PA 15219
(412) 281-2620

Steven J. Banks
Catherine C. Long
Carl G. Grefenstette

Average Size of Investment	$1M
Size of Fund	$100M
Investment Criteria	Technology-based companies are of interest; start-ups are welcome; will act as lead investor
Portfolio Companies	Undisclosed

HOEBICH VENTURE MANAGEMENT, INC.
5770 Croy Road
Morgan Hill, CA 95037
(408) 778-6271

Christian Hoebich
President

Directorships

Xebec, Winchester disk controller and subsystem manufacturing
Current Network
Premisys

Prior Positions

Partner, Hiller Investment Co., 1968–71
General Manager, Tymac Tracer, 1962–67

Education

MBA, Harvard University, 1962
BS, Mechanical Engineering, Stanford University, 1957

Average Size of Investment	$10K–$50K
Size of Fund	Undisclosed
Investment Criteria	Talented and motivated people; 20 minutes from office; early start-up
Portfolio Companies	AI Mentor, Palo Alto, CA, Expert knowledge; Current Network, Mountain View, CA, Office communications; Formaster, San Jose, CA, Software duplication equipment; Individual Software, Foster City, CA, Tutorial software; Vitalink, Mountain View, CA, Satellite communications; Xebec, San Jose, CA, Computer peripherals; Premisys, Foster City, CA, Service for Telecom

HOWARD, LAWSON & CO./VENTURE ASSOCIATES/GENESIS SEED FUND
Two Penn Center Plaza
Suite 410
Philadelphia, PA 19102
(215) 988-0010

Joel S. Lawson III
Managing Partner

Directorships

Datacap Systems, Inc.
Urban Outfitters, Inc.
Saladalley Restaurants, Inc.

Prior Position

Principal, Lawson Enterprises

Education

MBA, Wharton School, 1980
BA, Yale University, 1969

Graeme K. Howard, Jr.
Partner

Directorship

CBIT Corp.

Prior Position

Partner, Corporate Finance, Butcher & Singer

Education

LLB, Yale University Law School, 1960
BA, Amherst College, 1954

T. Patrick Hurley, Jr.
Partner

Prior Position

Asst. Portfolio Manager, Wood's Index, Inc.

Education

MBA, Drexel University, 1981
BBA, Temple University, 1979

Michael A. Cuneo
Partner

Prior Positions

Manager of Advanced Business Development, Leeds & Northrup
Manager, Corporate Planning, Catalytic, Inc.

Education

MBA, Wharton School, 1978
MSME, Northwestern University, 1972
BES, Johns Hopkins University, 1970

Average Size of Investment	$300K
Size of Fund	Undisclosed
Investment Criteria	Prefer early stage; will help entrepreneurs assemble team and complete business planning
Portfolio Companies	CBIT Corp., Computer-image inspection systems; Sechan Electronics, Inc., Military electronics; Urban Outfitters, Inc., Specialty retailers; Datacap, Inc., Electronic point-of-sale terminals; ENSONIQ Corp., Electronic music instruments; Saladalley Restaurants, Restaurant chain; Applied Business Technologies, Inc., Software systems for non-profit organizations

HUB ENTERPRISES, LTD.
5874 Doyle
Emeryville, CA 94608
(415) 653-5707

Jack M. Atkin

Average Size of Investment	$100K
Size of Fund	Undisclosed
Investment Criteria	Diversified areas of interest; geographic locale important; start-ups welcome
Portfolio Companies	Undisclosed

HUTTON VENTURE INVESTMENT PARTNERS INC.
1 Battery Park Plaza, Suite 1801
New York, NY 10004
(212) 742-3722

James E. McGrath
President

Directorships

Perception, Inc.
Kent Highlands, Inc.
IntelliTech, Inc.
American Reserves, Inc.

Prior Position

Chief Executive Officer, private investment firms

Education

MBA, Harvard Business School, 1979
AB, Harvard College, 1977

Timothy E. Noll
Vice President

Directorships

Gascard Club, Inc.
Amerlux Inc.

Prior Position

Investment Manager, E. F. Hutton Technology Group

DIRECTORY AND BIOGRAPHIES

Education

AB, Stanford University

James F. Wilson
Vice President

Directorships

Arkansas Modification Center, Inc.
Barcus-Berry Electronics
Corporate Technology Information Services

Prior Position

Investment Manager, Alan Patricof Associates

Education

MBA, Harvard Business School, 1982
AB, Dartmouth College, 1980

Average Size of Investment	$500K
Size of Investment	$25M
Investment Criteria	Early stage technology based companies
Portfolio Companies	Perception, Inc., Farmington Hills, MI, Vision systems; American Reserves Inc., Atlanta, GA, Private land reserves; IntelliTech, Inc., Northfield, IL, Noise suppression; Microcom, Inc., Norwood, MA, Data communication; Motion Analysis, Santa Rosa, CA, Image processing

IAI VENTURE PARTNERS
1100 Dain Tower
P.O. Box 357
Minneapolis, MN 55440
(612) 371-7780

Noel P. Rahn
Chief Executive Officer
(612) 371-7850

Prior Positions

Senior Vice President and National Sales Manager, Paine, Webber, Jackson & Curtis, 1972
National Training Director, Paine, Webber, Jackson & Curtis, 1971
Sales Manager, Paine, Webber, Jackson & Curtis, 1968

Education

BA, University of Southern California, 1962

Richard C. Pflager
Senior Vice President
(612) 371-2940

Prior Positions

Vice President, International Ventures, Control Data Corp., 1982
President, Control Data Capital Corp., and Vice President, Corporate Ventures, Control Data Corp., 1979
General Manager, Contracts and Licensing, Control Data Corp., 1975
Director, Contracts and Licensing, Control Data Corp., 1971

Education

JD, George Washington University National Law Center, 1967
BA, Lawrence University, 1960

Mitchell Dann
Partner
(612) 371-7740

Prior Position

Regional Analyst, Investment Advisers, Inc., 1982

Education

BS, Engineering and Management, University of Vermont, 1982

Stephen P. Weisbrod
Partner
(612) 371-2897

Prior Positions

Senior Vice President, Test Systems & Circuit Assembly Divisions, Micro Component Technology, 1979
Founder President, NWW Micro Systems, 1978
Biomedical Engineering Management, Medtronic, Inc., 1970
Department Manager, API Instruments, 1964
Project Engineer, Addressograph Multigraph Corp., 1963

Education

BS, Case Institute of Technology, 1962

Average Size of Investment	Undisclosed
Size of Fund	$120M
Investment Criteria	Manage $120M in venture capital, investing throughout the country in new businesses ranging from start-ups to more developed private businesses; invest in many industries with an emphasis in health care, telecommunications, and electronics
Portfolio Companies	Endotherapeutics Corp., Developing new generation of surgical tools that allow less invasive surgical procedures; First Western Health Corp., Provides medical evaluation services in litigated workers compensation matters through network of high quality physicians performing services at the company's outpatient facilities; Pacific Monolithics, Inc., Designs, manufactures, and markets gallium arsenide microwave integrated circuits; Syntelligence, Inc., Develops expert systems software that is used in the banking and insurance industry to assist in commercial loan evaluation and insurance rating; Xcat, Inc., Designs, manufactures, and markets logic and fault simulator accelerator for the integrated circuit design marketplace; Zoran Corporation, Develops and markets families of proprietary processors and peripherals specifically targeting the needs of Digital Signal Processing (DSP) applications; Celerity Computing, Inc., Designs, manufactures and markets a proprietary, network-based, high-performance, 32-bit, engineering workstation; Digital Microwave Corp., Designs, manufactures and markets point-to-point short-haul communication systems utilizing microwave and other technologies; Ecolaire Prime, Inc., Manufacturer of engineered capital equipment for the electric power utility industry and markets products for materials handling, pollution control, and fluid flow transfer; International Healthcare Corp., National Health maintenance organization and provider of addiction recovery services; Mycogen Corp., Develops and markets biologically safe pesticides and soil enhancement products; Performance, Semiconductor Corp., Develops high-performance CMOS very high-scale integrated circuits; Raycom Systems, Inc., Develops and markets low-cost data communication equipment, utilizing fiber optics; Resonex, Inc., Developing a specialized magnetic resonance imaging system to image blood vessels

IBERO-AMERICAN INVESTORS CORP.
Chamber of Commerce Building
55 Saint Paul Street
Rochester, NY 14604
(716) 262-3440

Emilio L. Serrano

Average Size of Investment	$100K
Size of Fund	$2.5M
Investment Criteria	Start-ups are considered along with other diversified company interests; will act as lead investor
Portfolio Companies	Undisclosed

IDANTA PARTNERS
201 Main Street
Suite 3200
Fort Worth, TX 76102
(817) 338-2020

David J. Dunn
Managing Partner

Directorships

Chairman, American Medical Plan
Chairman, Prime Computer, Inc.
Chairman, Iomega Corp.
Chairman, Western Yarns, Inc.

Prior Position

Partner, J. H. Whitney & Co.

Education

MBA, Harvard University, 1961
BS, Naval Academy, 1955

Dev Purkayastha
General Partner

Directorships

American Medical Plan
Western Yarns, Inc.

Prior Positions

Auditor, Price, Waterhouse and Company
Financial Accounting, Guest, Keen, Williams Ltd.

Education

MBA, Harvard Business School, 1977
Chartered Accountant, 1971
BA (honors), Ganhati University, 1967

Steven B. Dunn
General Partner

Prior Position

Associate, Corporate Finance, Bear Stearns

Education

MBA, Harvard Business School, 1983
BS, Economics, University of California at Berkeley, 1979

Average Size of Investment	$2M
Size of Fund	$100M+
Investment Criteria	Invest in start-ups and early-stage companies that have potential to become major corporations
Portfolio Companies	American Medical Plan, Nashville, TN, Health maintenance organizations; Iomega Corp., Ogden, UT, Flexible media disk drive; Prime Computer, Boston, MA, Minicomputers; Western Yarns, Inc., Los Angeles, CA, Spinner of carpet yarn

IEG VENTURE MANAGEMENT, INC.
401 North Michigan Avenue
Suite 2020
Chicago, IL 60611
(312) 644-0890

Francis I. Blair
President

Directorships

AeroQuest Corp.
Cell Analysis Systems, Inc.
Foster Airdata Systems, Inc.
Pride-Tech, Inc.
Pride-Tech, Inc., Develops, installs and modifies software for companies in the life insurance industry
Cell Analysis, Medical expert system

Prior Positions

Vice President, Business Development and Treasurer, Heizer Corp., 1979–82
Assistant to the Secretary, U.S. DOE and EPA, 1973–79
Fighter Pilot, U.S. Navy, 1966–71

Education

MPA, Decision Analysis and Quantitative Methods, Kennedy School of Government at Harvard University, 1973
BA, Political Science and Economics, Yale University, 1966

Marian M. Zamlynski

Average Size of Investment	$200K–$500K
Size of Fund	Over $3M
Investment Criteria	IEG invests primarily in technology-based start-up companies in the Midwest
Portfolio Companies	AeorQuest Corp., Wichita, KS, Technology for aircraft operations; CD High Technology, TX, Machinery for recycling asphalt using microwaves; Cell Analysis Systems, Inc., Lombard, IL, Software for medical diagnostics; Foster Airdata Systems, Inc., Columbus, OH, Avionics systems for general aviation aircraft; Pride-Tech, Inc., Chicago, IL, Develops, installs, and modifies software for companies in the life insurance industry

III
520 Madison Avenue
32nd Floor
New York, NY 10022
(212) 715-4988

Philippe Cerf

Average Size of Investment	$300K
Size of Fund	Undisclosed
Investment Criteria	Technology-based companies of interest; start-ups are welcome
Portfolio Companies	Undisclosed

IMPERIAL VENTURES
P.O. Box 92991
Los Angeles, CA 90009
(213) 417-5600

Donald Prell

Average Size of Investment	$400K
Size of Fund	Undisclosed
Investment Criteria	Diversified areas of interest including manufacturing industries; will act as lead investor
Portfolio Companies	Undisclosed

INCO VENTURE CAPITAL MANAGEMENT
One New York Plaza
New York, NY 10004
(212) 612-5620

Stuart F. Feiner
A. Douglas Peabody
George M. Middlemas

Average Size of Investment	$750K
Size of Fund	$125M
Investment Criteria	Diversified areas of interest including technology-based companies; start-ups are considered with first- and second-stage and buy-outs; will act as lead investor
Portfolio Companies	Undisclosed

INDIANA CAPITAL CORP.
5612 Jefferson Boulevard, West
Fort Wayne, IN 46804
(219) 432-8622

Samuel A. Rea

Average Size of Investment	$300K
Size of Fund	Undisclosed
Investment Criteria	Manufacturing companies are of interest along with other diversified areas; geographic locale is important
Portfolio Companies	Undisclosed

INDOSUEZ TECHNOLOGY GROUP
3000 Sand Hill Road
Building 4, Suite 130
Menlo Park, CA 94025
(415) 854-0587

Philippe Sevin
Partner

Prior Positions

Vice President, Banque INDOSUEZ
Director, Institute Industrial Development, France
Assistant Controller, Honeywell Bull

Education

MBA, INSEAD (Fontainebleau), 1976
MSc, University of Paris, 1970

David E. Gold
Partner

Prior Positions

President, David E. Gold Corp.
IBM Corp.

Education

PhD, University of Illinois, 1972
MS, University of Illinois, 1969
BSEE, University of Illinois, 1967

Average Size of Investment	$500K–$750K
Size of Fund	$34M
Investment Criteria	Highly competent, experienced and dedicated management team—the strength of the management team is the most important consideration in the investment decision; superior proprietary product or service which enables the company to achieve significant competitive advantage and meaningful market share; market sufficiently large to allow a substantial revenue base and sustained growth; well thought-out strategy for penetration of targeted market
Portfolio Companies	American Semiconductor Equipment Technologies, Woodland Hills, CA, Semiconductor capital equipment; Aptec, Portland, OR, Data I/O processors; Biotrack, Sunnyvale, CA, Therapeutic control systems; Command Data Systems, Dublin, CA, Turnkey systems; Covalent Systems, Sunnyvale, CA, Turnkey systems; International Marketvision, Los Gatos, CA, Turnkey Systems; Lin Data, Santa Clara, CA, Thin film media; Precision Image, Redwood City, CA, Electrostatic plotters; Relational Database Systems, Menlo Park, CA, Database software; Rugged Digital Systems, Sunnyvale, CA, Field hardened computers; Snapps Fine Fresh Produce, Cupertino, CA, Retail produce stores; Syntelligence, Sunnyvale, CA, Expert systems; Test Systems Strategies, Beaverton, OR, Semiconductor testing; Touch Distributed Systems, Scotts Valley, CA, Communications; Viewtech, Mountain View, CA, Vertical market software; David Systems, Sunnyvale, CA, Information management network; Protype, Inc., Sun Valley, CA, Word processor; Sierra Semiconductor, San Jose, CA, Application specific integrated circuits

DIRECTORY AND BIOGRAPHIES

INNOVEN GROUP
Park 80 Plaza West-One
Saddle Brook, NJ 07662
(201) 845-4900

Gerald A. Lodge
Chairman, Chief Executive Officer

Directorships

California Devices, Inc.
American Nucleonics Corp.
August Systems, Inc.
Emerson Electric Co.
Physical Acoustics Corp.
Telesis Corp.
Precision Connecter Designs, Inc.
Pure Water Technologies, Inc.
Digital Appliance Controls, Inc.
Weitek Corp.
Xylogics, Inc.

Prior Position

G. H. Walker and Co., 1959–72

Education

MBA, Harvard University, 1959
BS, West Point Military Academy, 1954

Raun J. Rasmussen
President

Directorships

Azonix Corp.
American Nucleonics Corp.
EOTec Corp.
Microdynamics, Inc.
Phoenix Digital Corp.
Sigma Design, Inc.
White Hat Systems, Inc.

Prior Position

G. H. Walker & Co.

Education

MBA, Harvard University
BS, United States Naval Academy

Harry Lambert
Vice President

Directorships

Voice Industries Corp.
Queue Systems, Inc.

Prior Positions

President, Chester Cablewaves Corp., 1983–85
Executive Vice President, Phelps Dodge Communications Corp., 1978–83

Education

AMP, Harvard Business School, 1979
BS, United States Military Academy, 1960

Robert C. Oliver
Vice President

Prior Positions

Vice President, L. F. Rothschild, Unterberg, Towbin, 1982–86
Associate, Merrill Lynch, Pierce Fenner & Smith, 1979–82

Education

MBA, New York University, 1982
BS, University of Virginia, 1979

Average Size of Investment	$750K
Size of Fund	Undisclosed
Investment Criteria	Start-ups and early-stage high technology and consumer; leveraged buy-outs; will act as lead investor
Portfolio Companies	Undisclosed

INNOVEST GROUP, INC.
1700 Market Street
12th Floor
Philadelphia, PA 19103
(215) 564-3960

Richard E. Woosnam
President

Directorships

Modern Video Productions, Inc., Videotape editing, audio production
Skyworks, Inc., Manufacture and marketing of a computer-controlled, mobile, aerial suspension system
Northern Lites, Ltd., D'Lites of America, fast-food franchise for PA, NJ and DE
Visionaire Communications, Inc., Feature film and television productions

Prior Position

Vice President, Capital Management Corp.

Education

MBA, Indiana University Graduate School of Business, 1968
JD, Indiana University School of Law, 1967
BS, Indiana University, 1964

Nila K. Sendzik
Vice President

Education

BA, Villanova University, 1974

Average Size of Investment	$500K–$1M
Size of Fund	N/A
Investment Criteria	Primarily start-up and first-stage companies
Portfolio Companies	Modern Video Productions, Philadelphia, PA, Videotape editing, audio production; Northern Lites, Ltd., Philadelphia, PA, D'Lites of America—fast-food franchise for Pennsylvania, New Jersey, and Delaware; Skyworks, Inc., Philadelphia, PA, Manufacture of a computer-controlled, modile, aerial suspension system; Visionaire Communications, Inc., New York, Feature film and television productions

INSTITUTIONAL VENTURE PARTNERS
3000 Sand Hill Road
Building 2, Suite 290
Menlo Park, CA 94025
(415) 854-0132

Reid W. Dennis
Managing General Partner

Directorships

Impres, Inc., Engineering document automation products
Collagen Corp., Manufacturer of biomedical products
GRiD Systems Corp., Manufacturer of portable personal computers
Reference Technology, Inc., Manufacturer of rapid-access archival data storage systems
Seagate Technology, Manufacturer of computer disk drives
Sequent Computer Systems, Inc., Manufacturer of multiprocessing microcomputer systems
Cemax, Inc., Medical 3-D imaging equipment

Prior Positions

President, American Express Investment Management Co., 1973–74
Investment Manager, Fireman's Fund Insurance Co., 1952–73

Education

MBA, Stanford University, 1952
BS, Electrical Engineering, Stanford University, 1950

John K. Poitras
Partner

Directorships

Archive Corp., 1/4″ streaming tape
Impres, Inc., Engineering document automation products
Pragmatic Test Systems, Inc., ATE (semiconductor test)
Visual Engineering, UNIX software
Cdex Corp., Training systems
Mindset Corp., Graphics computers

Prior Position

Associate Manager, Technology Licensing, Stanford University, 1975–80

Education

MBA, Stanford University, 1969
BA, Claremont Mens College, 1967
BS, Stanford University, 1967

Mary Jane Elmore
General Partner

Directorships

Analog Design Tools, Inc., CAE workstations for analog/linear integrated circuit design
Cydrome, Inc., Medium-priced supercomputer

Imperial Automation, Inc., Specialized computer terminals for bank tellers
Shiva Multisystems Corp., Simulation tools for integrated circuit designers

Prior Position

Product Manager, Microcomputer Systems Division, Intel Corporation, 1968–82

Samuel D. Colella
General Partner

Directorships

Reference Technology, Inc., Optical disk storage devices
Cygnet Systems, Inc., Optical disk storage, retrieval system
Focus Semiconductors Systems, Inc., Semiconductor equipment
Therma-wave, Inc., Thermal-accoustic surface inspection products (semiconductor test equipment)

Prior Positions

President, Chief Operating Officer and Director, Spectra Physics, 1971–84
Senior Manager, Corning Glass, 1964–71

Education

MBA, Stanford University
Business and engineering degrees, University of Pittsburgh

T. Peter Thomas
General Partner

Directorships

Altera Corp., Erasable CMOS programmable logic devices
Cirrus Logic, Inc., Turn-key supplier of OSIC semiconductors
Inova Microelectronics Corp., Static RAM memory modules
Menlo Care, Inc., Intravenous catheters

Prior Positions

Associate, Technology Venture Investors, 1982–85
Marketing Manager, Intel, 1975–82

Education

MSCS, University of Santa Clara, 1975
BSEE, Utah State University, 1968

Mark J. Bronder
Chief Financial Officer

Prior Positions

Division Controller, Rolm Corp., 1979–83
Management Consultant, Booz, Allen & Hamilton, 1978–79
Systems Analyst, Inland Steel Company, 1975–78

Education

MBA, University of Minnesota
BS, Computer Sciences, University of Minnesota

Average Size of Investment	$600K–$2M
Size of Fund	$150M
Investment Criteria	Seed, start-up, or first-stage financing; prefer role as deal originator but will also invest in deals created by others; prefer West Coast, within two hours of office
Portfolio Companies	See directorships

INTECH GROUP INC.
130 S. Bemiston, Suite 703
St. Louis, MO 63105
(314) 863-3888

William W. Canfield
President

Directorship

Intech Group Inc.

Prior Positions

President, Financial Data Systems, Inc.
Manager, Systems and Programming, Centerre Bank, N.A.
Systems Engineer, IBM Corporation

Education

MBA, Washington University, 1962
BSEE, Purdue University, 1961

Average Size of Investment	$200K
Size of Fund	$1.5M
Investment Criteria	Sales volume exceeding $1M; positive operating income, or which shows ability to be positive within reasonable period; experienced management team with strong desire to

Portfolio Companies   participate in ownership and demonstrated ability to grow with the company; Midwestern U.S.; growth potential within the company's current area of expertise
Electronic Keyboarding Inc., Computer service and software, St. Louis, MO; Langenbacher Data Systems, Inc., Computer service and software, St. Louis, MO, Noetic Technologies Corp., Engineering (FEA) software, St. Louis, MO

INTERCAPCO, INC.
1701 North Market
Suite 200
Dallas, TX 75202-1807
(214) 748-5893

Richard H. Collins
Linda G. Wilson

Average Size of Investment	$500K
Size of Fund	$13.5M
Investment Criteria	Diverse areas of interest, manufacturing, oil and gas, and technology-based companies included; will act as lead investor (fees)
Portfolio Companies	Undisclosed

INTERCAPCO, INC.
7800 Bonhomme
St. Louis, MO 63105
(314) 863-0600

Thomas E. Phelps
Mark J. Lincoln

Average Size of Investment	$1M
Size of Fund	Undisclosed
Investment Criteria	Diversified preferences; will act as lead investors; leveraged buy-outs; central time zone geographical preference
Portfolio Companies	Undisclosed

INTERCITY CAPITAL ACCESS CENTER INC.
1505 Woodward Avenue
Suite 700
Detroit, MI 48226
(313) 961-2470

Walter McMurtry

Average Size of Investment	$300K
Size of Fund	$2M
Investment Criteria	Diversified areas of interest including technology-based companies; start-ups are considered; will act as lead investor; geographic proximity is important
Portfolio Companies	Undisclosed

INTERCOASTAL CAPITAL CORP.
380 Madison Avenue
New York, NY 10017
(212) 986-0482

Herbert Krasnow

Average Size of Investment	$300K
Size of Fund	Undisclosed
Investment Criteria	Diversified areas of interest; will act as lead investor; geographic proximity important
Portfolio Companies	Undisclosed

INTERFIRST VENTURE CORP.
901 Main Street, 10th Floor
Dallas, TX 75283-0644
(214) 977-3160

James A. O'Donnell
President

Directorships

Houston Wire and Cable International, Distributors of wire and cable
Society Brands, Inc., Manufacturer of men's slacks
Contemporary Constructors, Inc., Construction
Gardiner Communications, Inc., Electronic components
Euless Aero Components, Inc.
Hoker Broadcasting, Inc., Radio Broadcasting co.
Mayfield Building Supply Co.
PUPCO, Inc., Commercial woodworking equipment
Storehouse, Inc., Furniture and accessories

DIRECTORY AND BIOGRAPHIES 273

Prior Positions

Vice President, Manager of Corporate Finance Dept., InterFirst Bank, Dallas, NA
Investment Manager, Equitable Life Assurance Co.

Education

MBA, Wharton School, University of Pennsylvania, 1978
BA, Rhodes College, 1974

Mark C. Masur
Vice President
(214) 977-3166

Directorships

Gigabit Logic Corp.
ProNet, Inc., Medical communications
Riverton Investment Corp., Cement
HMSS, Inc., Home health care

Education

MBA, University of Denver, 1979

Frank L. Young
Assistant Vice President
(214) 977-3170

Directorships

Data Net Corp., Factory data collection systems
Optical Data Systems, Fiber optics
Varix Corp., PROM programming equipment

Education

MBA, Millsaps College School of Management, 1981

Sallee L. McDermitt
Investment Officer

Directorships

Hoker Broadcasting, Inc., Radio broadcasting co.
Universal Cable Holdings, Inc., Cable systems operator

Education

MBA, University of Texas, 1982

Wendy H. Stanley
Investment Officer

Education

MBA, University of Texas Graduate School of Business, 1983

P. F. Whelan
Investment Officer
(214) 977-3167

Prior Position

Systems Engineer, IBM, 1980–82

Education

MBA, Wharton School, University of Pennsylvania, 1984
BS, Vanderbilt University, 1980

Average Size of Investment	$1.15M
Size of Fund	$40M
Investment Criteria	Venture capital and leveraged buy-outs
Portfolio Companies	Duffy Broadcasting Corp., Dallas, TX, Radio broadcasting company with stations in Denver, Sacramento, Daytona/Orlando, and San Antonio; Euless Aero Components, Inc., Euless, TX, Manufactures critical replacement parts for military and commercial helicopters; Gigabit Logic, Inc., Newbury Park, CA, Gallium arsenide digital semiconductors; Mayfield Building Supply, Dallas/Ft. Worth, TX, Wholesaler of lumber and other building products; Xilinx, Inc., San Jose, CA, Programmable logic semiconductors and related software development tools

INTERGROUP VENTURE CO.
230 Park Avenue
New York, NY 10169
(212) 661-5428

Ben Hauben

Average Size of Investment	$100K
Size of Fund	Undisclosed
Investment Criteria	Diversified areas of interest; start-ups are welcome; geographic proximity is of importance; will act as lead investor
Portfolio Companies	Undisclosed

INTERNATIONAL BUSINESS SPONSORS, INC.
765 Bridgeway Boulevard
Sausalito, CA 94965
(415) 331-2262

Mel L. Bacharach
President

Directorships

IMSI
IBSI Capital Corp., Venture capital
International Business Sponsors, Inc., Venture capital
ECS Microsystems
Roos Bros., Retail clothing stores
Farah Manufacturing Co., Apparel

Prior Position

Executive Vice President, Levi Strauss & Co.

Education

BS, University of California, 1948

Vernon O. Heyman
Treasurer

Prior Position

CPA, self-employed, 1948–83

Education

BS, University of California at Berkeley, 1942

Average Size of Investment	$250K
Size of Fund	$6.8M
Investment Criteria	Do not invest in movies, entertainment, publications, extracting industries, and most service industries
Portfolio Companies	Britton Lee, Data-based management; Command Data System, Software for police departments; DNI, Diagnostic Imaging; ECS Microsystems; Orient Trust, Offshore venture capital; Sytek, Broad-band network; International Microsoftware, Inc., Software publishing company

INTERNATIONAL FILM INVESTORS
595 Madison Avenue
New York, NY 10022
(212) 310-1500

Roland W. Betts

Average Size of Investment	$250K
Size of Fund	Undisclosed
Investment Criteria	Preference for movie industry; will act as lead investor
Portfolio Companies	Undisclosed

INTERSCOPE INVESTMENTS
10900 Wilshire Blvd., Suite 1400
Los Angeles, CA 90024
(213) 208-8636

J. Murray Hill II
Executive Vice President/Chief Financial Officer

Average Size of Investment	$1M
Size of Fund	$100M+
Investment Criteria	General
Portfolio Companies	Undisclosed

INTERSTATE CAPITAL CORP.
701 East Camino Real
Suite 9A
Boca Raton, FL 33432
(305) 395-8466

William C. McConnell, Jr.
President

Directorships

Interstate Capital Corp., Venture capital
IMI, Inc., Printed circuit boards
Sports Management Services, Inc., Indoor racquet sports
Protective Coatings Systems, Inc., Chemical coatings systems

DIRECTORY AND BIOGRAPHIES

Prior Positions

President, Servomation of New England, Inc.
President, Federated Vendors, Inc.
President, Interstate Finance Corp.

Education

BS, Harvard College, 1942

Average Size of Investment	$75K
Size of Fund	$5M
Investment Criteria	High technology, second stage, electronics, medical, computer suppliers, leveraged buy-outs
Portfolio Companies	Delta Education, Affiliates, Inc., Kansas City, MO, Education; IMI, Inc., Andover, MA, Printed circuit boards; Protective Coatings Systems, Longwood, FL, Chemical coatings; Sports Management Services, Winchester, MA, Indoor racquet sports

INTERVEN PARTNERS, INC./INTERVEN II, L.P.
445 South Figueroa St.
Suite 2940
Los Angeles, CA 90071
(213) 622-1922

227 S.W. Pine Street
Suite 200
Portland, OR 97204
(503) 223-4334

David B. Jones
Partner, CA

Directorships

Gigabit Logic, Inc., Gallium arsenide integrated circuits
Sensor Medics Corp., Medical instrumentation

Prior Position

President, First Interstate Capital, 1979–85
Vice President, Union Venture Corp., 1972–78
Attorney, Hufftedler, Miller, Carlson & Beardsley, 1970–72

Education

MBA, JD, University of Southern California, 1967, 1970
AB, Dartmouth College, 1965

Jonathan E. Funk
Partner, CA

Directorships

CR Technology, Inc., Machine vision systems
Sunward Technologies

Prior Positions

Vice President, First Interstate Capital, 1983–85
Sales Manager, United Western Newspapers, Inc.
Civil Engineer, Fluor Arabia Ltd.

Education

MBA, University of Southern California, 1981
BS, University of California at Berkeley, 1977

Keith R. Larson
Partner and Vice President, OR

Prior Positions

Controller, First Interstate Capital, Inc., 1983–85
CPA, Senior Accountant, Peat, Marwick, Mitchell & Co., 1980–83

Education

BS, Business Administration, University of Southern California, 1980

Wayne B. Kingsley
Partner, OR

Directorships

Gray & Company, Food processing
BiPolar Integrated Technology, Bipolar semiconductors

Prior Positions

Executive Vice President, First Interstate Capital, 1983–85
Vice President, Manager, Norwest Venture Capital, 1978–83
Chief Operating Officer, Cascade Capital Corp., 1972–78

Education

MBA, University of Virginia, 1971
AB, Miami University (Ohio), 1964

Kenneth M. Deemer
Partner, CA

Directorships

DayFlo, Inc., Microcomputer software
Trilog, Inc., Line printers

Prior Positions

Vice President, First Interstate Capital, 1982–85
Marketing Manager, Data Systems Design, Inc.
(Now Qualogy, Inc.)
Systems Engineer, Hughes Aircraft Corp.

Education

MBA, Carnegie-Mellon University, 1979
BS, Massachusetts Institute of Technology, 1975

Average Size of Investment	$2M
Size of Fund	$50M
Investment Criteria	Early-stage, technology-oriented, or growth buyouts in western U.S.
Portfolio Companies	BiPolar Integrated Technology, Portland, OR, BiPolar semiconductors; GigaBit Logic, Los Angeles, CA, Gallium arsenide semiconductors; Gray & Company, Portland, OR, Food processing; SensorMedics Corp., Anaheim, CA, Medical instruments; Sequent Computer Systems, Portland, OR, Computers

INTERWEST PARTNERS
3000 Sand Hill Road
Building 3, Suite 255
Menlo Park, CA 94025-7112
(415) 854-8585

Eugene F. Barth
General Partner

Prior Positions

Vice President, General Manager, Citicorp Venture Capital, Ltd.
First Chicago Investment Corp.
Member, Chicago Board of Trade

Education

MBA, Harvard, 1966
BA, Brown University, 1963

Harvey B. Cash
General Partner

Prior Positions

Vice President, Marketing, Mostek Semiconductor Corp.
Marketing Consultant, Apple Computer and InteCom

Education

MBA, Western Michigan University, 1964
BS, Electrical Engineering, Texas A & M, 1961

Philip T. Gianos
General Partner

Prior Positions

Project Manager, Analog IC design group, others, IBM

Education

MBA, Harvard, 1982
MS/BS, Electrical Engineering, Stanford, 1973

Wallace R. Hawley
General Partner

Prior Positions

President, SHV North America Holding Corp.
McKinsey & Co., Inc., international management consultants

Education

MBA, Harvard, 1963
BA, Stanford, 1960

W. Scott Hedrick
General Partner

Prior Positions

Partner, American-Euro Interfund
Small Business Enterprises Co., Bank of America

Education

MBA, University of Southern California, 1970
BA, University of California at Santa Barbara, 1968

Charles J. McMinn
General Partner

Prior Positions

Director of Marketing, Director of Engineering, Megatest Corp.
Product Line Manager, Marketing Manager, Intel Corp.

Education

MBA, Harvard, 1976
MS, Electrical Engineering, Syracuse University, 1976
BS, Electrical Engineering, Brown University, 1974

Robert R. Momsen
General Partner

Prior Positions

General Manager, Chief Financial Officer, Life Instruments Corp.
Operations Manager, Vail Associates, Inc.

Education

MBA, Stanford, 1972
BS, Stanford, 1968

Glenn A. Norem
General Partner

Prior Positions

Manager, Texas Instruments' Corporate Development Organization
Development Engineer, IBM

Education

MBA, Chicago, 1983
BS, Electrical and Systems Engineering, Southern Illinois University, 1978

Average Size of Investment	$1M
Size of Fund	$165M
Investment Criteria	No real estate, gas, or oil; minimum investment: $500K
Portfolio Companies	Northwest Instrument Systems, Inc., Portland, OR, CAE/Test & measurement; Valid Logic Systems, Inc., Mountain View, CA, CAE/Test & measurement; Convex Computer Corp., Dallas, TX, Computer and peripherals; Priam Corp., San Jose, CA, Computer and peripherals; Seagate Magnetics (Grenex), Scotts Valley, CA, Computer and peripherals; Silicon Graphics, Inc., Mountain View, CA, Computer and peripherals; HBO & Co., Atlanta, GA, Health care; Health Management Associates, Inc., Naples, FL, Health care; Menlo Care, Inc., Menlo Park, CA, Health care; Bridge Communications, Cupertino, CA, Network products; Network Systems Corp., Minneapolis, MN, Network products; Crystal Semiconductor, Austin, TX, Semiconductor products; Lam Research Corp., Fremont, CA, Semiconductor products; Saratoga Semiconductor, Cupertino, CA, Semiconductor products; Xilinx, Inc., San Jose, CA, Semiconductor products; ComDesign, Inc., Goleta, CA, Telecommunications; L.P. Com, Inc., Cupertino, CA, Telecommunications; Teling, Inc., Dallas, TX, Telecommunications; Burnham Service Corp., Columbus, GA; Businessland, Inc., San Jose, CA; Merit Technology, Dallas, TX; Southern Tool, Inc., Anniston, AL; Stamping Technology Corp., Milpitas, CA; Tetra Resources, Inc., Houston, TX

INVESAT CAPITAL CORP.
317 East Capitol Street
Suite 101
Jackson, MS 39201
(601) 969-3242

John R. Bise, IV
President

Directorships

CARE Systems, Inc., Medical monitoring devices
FMI, Inc.

Prior Positions

Assistant Vice President, Deposit Guaranty National Bank, 1978–80
Assistant Banking Officer, Citizens & Southern Bank of Georgia, 1973–76

Education

MBA, Harvard University, 1978
BA, Economics, Vanderbilt University, 1973

Average Size of Investment	$350K
Size of Fund	Undisclosed
Investment Criteria	Generally prefer second stage or later
Portfolio Companies	Undisclosed

INVESTECH, L. P.
515 Madison Avenue
New York, NY 10022
(212) 308-5811

Sheldon F. Claar
Sy L. Goldblatt
Carl S. Hutman
Tancred V. Schiavoni

Average Size of Investment	$500K
Size of Fund	$28M
Investment Criteria	Technology-based companies are of interest as well as start-ups; will act as lead investor
Portfolio Companies	Undisclosed

INVESTMENT CAPITAL, INC.
300 North Harrison
P.O. Box 1071
Cushing, OK 74023
(918) 225-5850

James J. Wasson

Average Size of Investment	$100K
Size of Fund	Undisclosed
Investment Criteria	Diversified areas of interest; start-ups considered; geographic proximity important; will act as lead investor
Portfolio Companies	Undisclosed

INVESTMENT SECURITIES OF COLORADO, INC.
4605 Denice Drive
Englewood, CO 80111
(303) 796-9192

Vern D. Kornelsen
President

Directorships

Total Logic Corp., Logic analyzers manufacturer
Tienet, Inc., Local area networking systems
Montech, Inc., Manufacturer of microprocessor based devices
Engineering Measurements Co., Manufacturer of flow meters

Prior Positions

President and Treasurer, Micromedex, Inc., 1979–84
Founder, accounting practice, now merged into McGladrey & Pullen, 1962–67
Assistant to Treasurer, O. K. Tire Co., 1961–62
Staff Accountant, Arthur Andersen & Co., and Arthur Young & Co., 1957–61

Education

Postgraduate work, University of Denver Law School CPA, 1959
BS, Business, University of Kansas, 1957

Average Size of Investment	$100K–$300K
Size of Fund	Varies
Investment Criteria	Venture should be a money-maker and be a candidate for public offering
Portfolio Companies	Montech Systems, Inc., Boulder, CO, Microprocessor-based device to monitor and report crude oil produced and sold; Tienet, Inc., Boulder, CO, Computer communications equipment; Total Logic Corp., Fort Collins, CO, Computer test instruments

INVESTOR'S EQUITY, INC.
2629 First Atlanta Tower
Atlanta, GA 30383
(404) 523-3999

Marian K. Pline

Average Size of Investment	$250K
Size of Fund	$5M
Investment Criteria	Manufacturing industries considered as well as other diversified areas; start-ups welcome; will act as lead investor; geographic proximity important
Portfolio Companies	Undisclosed

THE IOWA VENTURE CAPITAL FUND, L.P.
800 American Building
Cedar Rapids, IA 52401
(319) 363-8249

Suite 2724, Commerce Tower
911 Main Street
Kansas City, MO 64105
(816) 842-0114

600 East Mason Street
Milwaukee, WI 53202
(414) 276-3839

Donald E. Flynn, IA
David R. Schroder, IA
Kevin F. Mullane, MO
Steven J. Massey, WI

Average Size of Investment	$200–500K
Size of Fund	$10.6M
Investment Criteria	Manufacturing and service businesses from start-up through later stage, will act as lead investor
Portfolio Companies	Undisclosed

IRVINE TECHNOLOGY FUND
4600 Campus Drive
Newport Beach, CA 92660
(714) 852-9000

Walter Cruttenden
General Partner

Prior Positions

Shearson, Lehman American Express
Security Pacific National Bank

Directorships

Barcus Berry Electronics, Inc.
Micro General Corp.
Velie Circuits, Inc.
Exeters Corp.

H. D. Thoreau
General Partner

Prior Position

President, Hale Brothers Associates

Average Size of Investment	$200K
Size of Fund	$10M
Investment Criteria	Primarily interested in financing young companies in health care, medical devices, peripheral or specialty retailing business; like unusual businesses but will only invest in Southern California area
Portfolio Companies	Barcus Berry Electronics, Audio signal processing, Huntington Beach, CA; Exeters Corp., Mail order catalog, Costa Mesa, CA; Velie Circuits, Inc., Printed circuit boards, Costa Mesa, CA; Micro General Corp., Office Equipment, Irvine, CA; Total Pharmaceutical Care, Home infusion therapy, Hermosa Beach, CA; Gynex; Point Four Data Corp.; Kennedy Technology; Plant Genetics

IRVING CAPITAL CORP.
ITC Capital Corp.
1290 Avenue of the Americas
3rd Floor
New York, NY 10104
(212) 408-4800

J. Andrew McWethy
President

Directorships

ITC Capital Corporation, Venture capital firm
Irving Capital Corporation

Prior Positions

Vice President, Security Pacific Capital Corp., 1969–78
Assistant Manager, First Western Bank, 1963–67

Education

MBA, University of Southern California, 1969
BA, Pomona College, 1963

Barry A. Solomon
Vice President

Prior Position

Investment Manager, Prudential Insurance Co.

Education

MBA, University of Pennsylvania, 1973
BA, University of Pennsylvania, 1971

Stephen A. Tuttle
Vice President

Prior Positions

Vice President/General Manager, Eastern Regional Office, Pru Capital, 1983–85
Vice President, Pru Capital, 1979–83

Education

MBA, Rutgers Graduate School of Business, 1971
BA, Assumption College, 1962

Kathleen M. Snyder

Average Size of Investment	$1M
Size of Fund	$25M
Investment Criteria	Revenues of $2M or more and company must be in business a minimum of two years
Portfolio Companies	Undisclosed

IVANHOE VENTURE CAPITAL, LTD.
737 Pearl Street
Suite 201
La Jolla, CA 92037
(619) 454-8881

Alan R. Toffler
Managing General Partner

Directorship

La Jolla Rotary

Prior Positions

Brigadier General, United States Army (retired)
Executive Vice President, National University
Executive Vice President, EMA
Director, Ean Tech, ASSE, San Diego Civic Light Opera Association

Education

MA, International Relations, George Washington University
Army War College, PA (graduate)
BA, Psychology, University of Missouri

P. Frederick Wulff
General Partner
(619) 454-8882

Education

MSME, Industrial Management, Technological University, Delft, Holland
BS, Mechanical Engineering, Technological University, Delft, Holland

Average Size of Investment	$100K
Size of Fund	$1M
Investment Criteria	Five-year proven track record; high tech, R & D or expansion use; convertible debentures
Portfolio Companies	ATV Systems, Los Angeles, CA, Point-of-sale cash registers/computers; Climatron, Los Angeles, CA, Environmental control systems; Gradco Systems, Los Angeles, CA, Sorters for copiers; Home Communications, Oakhurst, CA, Cable TV; Primarius, San Diego, CA, Educational interactive computer/video; Sage Technology; San Diego, CA, Non-silver-based film

JAFCO AMERICA VENTURES
2180 Sand Hill Road, #320
Menlo Park, CA 94025
(415) 854-0746

Shunsuke Fukunda
President

William Shelander
Manager

Average Size of Investment	$1M
Size of Fund	Undisclosed
Investment Criteria	Track record of increasing sales
Portfolio Companies	Undisclosed

DIRECTORY AND BIOGRAPHIES

RICHARD JAFFE & COMPANY
7318 Royal Circle
Dallas, TX 75230
(214) 739-1845

Richard R. Jaffe
President

Directorships

Wagner-Jaffe Development Co., Real Estate
Beauty Mart, Beauty-care chain
Mondell Productions, Film company
Austin Leasing Co., Leasing equipment

Prior Positions

President, Sci-Tex Corp.
Executive Vice President, Camsco, Inc.
President, Transmodal Corp.

Education

MBA, New York University, 1965
BS, Trinity College, 1959

Average Size of Investment	$100K–$300K
Size of Fund	$3M+
Investment Criteria	Early funding of new technology companies; will invest with others
Portfolio Companies	Austin Leasing Co., Dallas, TX, Equipment leasing; Teledata Communications, Dallas, TX, Satellite communications; Wagner-Jaffe Development, Dallas, TX, Retirement apartment developers

J & D CAPITAL CORP.
12747 Biscayne Boulevard
North Miami, FL 33181
(305) 893-0303

Jack Carmal

Average Size of Investment	$250K
Size of Fund	Undisclosed
Investment Criteria	Diversified areas of interest, will act as lead investor, geographic location is of importance
Portfolio Companies	Undisclosed

JAPANESE AMERICAN CAPITAL CORP.
19 Rector Street, 35th Floor
New York, NY 10006
(212) 344-4588

Jack Sun, President

Average Size of Investment	$150K
Size of Fund	Undisclosed
Investment Criteria	Diversified
Portfolio Companies	Undisclosed

L. J. JOHNSON & CO.
2705 Lowell Road
Ann Arbor, MI 48103
(313) 663-5113

L. J. Johnson
President

Directorships

Arbor Valley Listing
Machine Vision International, Machine vision
Servo Kinetics, Electronic and hydraulic sales and replacement service
Word Processing Exchange, Electronic office equipment

Prior Position

Chief Financial Officer, Booth Newspapers, 1978

Education

BBA, Accounting, St. John's University, 1957

Average Size of Investment	Undisclosed
Size of Fund	Undisclosed
Investment Criteria	Undisclosed
Portfolio Companies	Undisclosed

JOHNSON & JOHNSON DEVELOPMENT CORP.
One Johnson & Johnson Plaza
New Brunswick, NJ 08933
(201) 524-6407

Charles M. Anderson
President
(201) 524-6405

Education

BS, Industrial Management, Georgia Institute of Technology, 1949

Linda A. Cahill
Vice President
(201) 524-8396

Prior Position

Manager, Corporate Development, Merck & Co., 1978–81

Education

MBA, Columbia University, 1981
BS, New York University, 1971

W. Ben Deibler
Vice President
(201) 524-6441

Education

MBA, Fairleigh Dickinson, 1980
BS, Drexel University, 1970

Average Size of Investment	Undisclosed
Size of Fund	Undisclosed
Investment Criteria	Health care field (not services), no minimum investment
Portfolio Companies	Undisclosed

JOHNSTON ASSOCIATES, INC.
181 Cherry Valley Road
Princeton, NJ 08540
(609) 924-3131

Robert F. Johnston
President

Directorships

Genex Corp., Genetic/protein engineering
Cytogen Corp., Monoclonal antibodies
Ecogen, Inc., Microbial pesticides
Sepracor, Inc., Bioactive membranes
Integrated Ionics, Inc., Electrochemical sensors
SPEX Group, Spectroscopic instruments

Prior Positions

F. S. Smithers & Co.
Smith Barney & Co.

Education

MBA, New York University, 1960
BA, Princeton University, 1958

Robert B. Stockman
Vice President, Mergers and Acquisitions

Prior Positions

Investment Analyst, Narrangansett Capital Corp.
Auditor, Price Waterhouse & Co.

Education

MBA, Amos Tuck School, Dartmouth College, 1981
AB, Harvard University

Richard G. Horan
Vice President

Prior Positions

Vice President, Mergers & Acquisitions, Bank of America

Education

MBA, Amos Tuck School, 1980
AB, Dartmouth College, 1976

Average Size of Investment	$500K
Size of Fund	$20M
Investment Criteria	Medical instrumentation, health care, biotechnology
Portfolio Companies	Cytogen Corp., Princeton, NJ, Monoclonal antibodies; Ecogen, Inc., Langhorn, PA, Microbial pesticides; Genex Corp., Gaithersburg, MD, Genetic engineering, protein engineering;

Integrated Ionics, Inc., Dayton, NJ, Electrochemical sensors; Sepracor, Inc., Marlborough, MA, Bioactive membranes; SPEX Group, Edison, NJ, Spectroscopic instruments

THE JORDAN COMPANY
315 Park Avenue South
New York, NY 10010
(212) 460-1910

John W. Jordan II
Managing Partner

Directorships

Bench Craft, Inc.
Cardiff Equities, Inc.
Imperial Electric Co.
David B. Lilly Co.
Carmike Cinemas, Inc.
Leucadia National Corp.
Industrial Sales Co., Inc.
Cape Craftsmen, Inc.

Prior Position

Vice President, Carl Marks & Co., Inc.

Education

MBA program, Columbia University, 1971–73
Business Administration, University of Notre Dame, 1970

David W. Zalaznick
Partner
(212) 460-1912

Directorships

Bench Craft, Inc.
Cardiff Equities, Inc.
Carmike Cinemas, Inc.
Imperial Electric, Inc.
Cape Craftsmen, Inc.
Thos. D. Murphy, Inc., Advertising specialties
Jones Mfg. Co., Inc., Plumbing specialties
Industrial Sales Co., Inc.
David B. Lilly Co., Inc.
Parson Precision Products, Inc., Defense products
Coronet Manufacturing Co., Inc., Lamp manufacturing
House of Ronnie, Inc., Apparel
Roanna Togs, Inc., Apparel
Hantscho, Inc., Printer press manufacturing
Marisa Christina, Inc., Apparel
Cal-Style Furniture Manufacturing Co., Furniture
The Dize Company

Prior Positions

Vice President, Carl Marks & Co., Inc., 1980–82
Associate, Merrill Lynch White Weld, 1978–80

Education

MBA, Columbia Business School, 1978
BA, Cornell University, 1976

Jonathan F. Boucher
Jack R. Lowden

Average Size of Investment	$5M
Size of Fund	$100M
Investment Criteria	Historically profitable, well-managed companies with pre-tax earnings of at least $2M
Portfolio Companies	Bench Craft, Inc., Blue Mountain, MS, Manufacturer and distributor of upholstered furniture; Cape Craftsmen, Inc., Elizabethtown, NC, Manufacturer and retailer of American decorative items, including wood, ceramic, brass, and candle products; Cardiff Equities, La Jolla, CA, Manufacturer of vanities for "do-it-yourself" market and electrical cord sets; Imperial Electric Company, Akron, OH, Manufacturer and distributor of motor generators and drives; Industrial Sales Co., Inc., Baltimore, MD, Manufacturer and distributor of marine and industrial wire rope, cable, and related products; Leucadia National Corp., New York, NY, Financial services company, primarily engaged in consumer finance business; David B. Lilly Co., Wilmington, DE, Manufacturer of defense-related items; Carmike Cinemas, Inc., Columbus, GA, Owner and operator of 420 movie screens in 9, principally southern, states

JULIAN, COLE AND STEIN
11777 San Vincente Boulevard
Suite 522
Los Angeles, CA 90049
(213) 826-8002

James M. Julian
General Partner

Directorships

Level One Communications
LaserCom, Inc.
Triconex Corp.
MicroBeam, Inc.
Paragon Network Int'l.

Prior Positions

Vice President, First Interstate Capital
Investment Officer, Union Ventures

Education

MBA, University of California at Los Angeles, 1976
BA, Stanford, 1970

Charles R. Cole
General Partner

Directorships

Level One Communications
Advanced Power Technology
Triconex Corp.
UniStructure, Inc.

Prior Positions

Chief Executive Officer, Tratec, 1968–80
Vice President, Sales, Scientific Data Systems, 1963–68

David L. R. Stein
General Partner

Directorships

Paragon Network Int'l
Advanced Power Technology
MicroBeam, Inc.
LaserCom, Inc.

Prior Position

Executive Vice President/Chief Operating Officer, Gartner Group

Average Size of Investment	$500K–$5M
Size of Fund	$40M
Investment Criteria	Prefer role as deal originator, seed, start-up, or first stage; Southern California first preference; communications, computer-related, electronic, industrial, medical/health-related; will not consider real estate, oil, gas, minerals exploration, or microcomputers
Portfolio Companies	LaserCom, Inc., Chatsworth, CA; Paragon Network International, San Diego, CA; Level One Communications, Folsom, CA; UniStructure, Inc., Chatsworth, CA; Advanced Power Technology, Bend, OR; MicroBeam, Inc., Newberry Park, CA; Triconex Corp., Irvine, CA

KANSAS VENTURE CAPITAL, INC.
One First National Bank Tower
1 Townsite Plaza
Topeka, KS 66603
(913) 233-1368

George L. Doak

Average Size of Investment	$100K
Size of Fund	Undisclosed
Investment Criteria	Manufacturing companies are of interest
Portfolio Companies	Undisclosed

KARMAL VENTURE CAPITAL
610 Plaza West Building
Little Rock, AR 72205
(501) 661-0010

Thomas Karam

Average Size of Investment	$100K
Size of Fund	Undisclosed
Investment Criteria	Diversified areas of interest; will act as lead investor; geographic location is of importance
Portfolio Companies	Undisclosed

KENTUCKY HIGHLANDS INVESTMENT CORP.
P.O. Box 628
London, KY 40741
(606) 864-5175

DIRECTORY AND BIOGRAPHIES

L. R. Moncrief

Average Size of Investment	$200K
Size of Fund	$4.5M
Investment Criteria	Interested in manufacturing and other diversified areas; geographic proximity is of importance
Portfolio Companies	Undisclosed

KEYSTONE VENTURE CAPITAL MANAGEMENT COMPANY
211 South Broad Street
Philadelphia, PA 19107
(215) 985-5519

G. Kenneth Macrae
President

Directorships

AM Communcations
Mini Base Systems
U.S. Restaurants

Prior Positions

Senior Advisor, Orange Nassau Companies
Division Director, Allstate Venture Division

Education

University of Toronto
Queens University, Kingston, Ontario

Timothy W. Cunningham
Vice President

Directorships

ICS, Inc.
Link Data, Inc.

Prior Positions

General Manager, Bucyrus Chile Ltd.
Sales Manager, Bucyrus-Erie Co.

Education

Masters, International Management, AGSIM, 1976
BA, Williams College, 1974

Average Size of Investment	$500K
Size of Fund	$12.5M
Investment Criteria	Post-start up; must have sales, need not be profitable; growth potential to $20M in approximately five years; proprietary products or services preferred; no real estate; prefer Mid-Atlantic region
Portfolio Companies	AM Communications, Telecommunications, Quakertown, PA; ICS Inc., Integrated circuits, King of Prussia, PA; Mini Base Systems, Natural gas measurement instruments, Houston, TX; AVL, Inc., Computer graphics, Tinton Falls, NJ; U.S. Restaurants, Operator of 51 restaurants, Norristown, PA

KITTY HAWK CAPITAL, LTD.
2030 One Tryon Center
Charlotte, NC 28284
(704) 333-3777

Walter H. Wilkinson, Jr.
General Partner

Directorships

Tangram Systems, Inc.
Indigo Press, Inc.

Prior Position

Vice President, Delta Capital

Education

MBA, Harvard, 1974
BS, North Carolina State, 1968

W. Chris Hegele
Vice President

Directorships

Indigo Press, Inc., Publishing
Premier Press, Inc., Publishing
Learning Resources, Inc.

Prior Position

Manager, Small Business Group, Arthur Andersen & Co., 1984

Education

MBA, University of North Carolina, Chapel Hill, 1977
BS, Economics, University of North Carolina, Wilmington, 1975

Average Size of Investment	$250K
Size of Fund	$5.5M
Investment Criteria	Diversified
Portfolio Companies	Undisclosed

KLEINER PERKINS CAUFIELD & BYERS
4 Embarcadero Center
Suite 3520
San Francisco, CA 94111
(415) 421-3110

Thomas J. Perkins
Brook H. Byers
Frank J. Caufield
John Doerr
James P. Lally
E. Floyd Kvamme
Regis McKenna

Average Size of Investment	$3M
Size of Fund	$380M
Investment Criteria	Technology-based companies; will act as lead investor; start-ups
Portfolio Companies	Undisclosed

JAMES B. KOBAK & COMPANY
774 Hollow Tree Ridge Road
Darien, CT 06820
(203) 655-8764

James B. Kobak
President

Directorships

Gifted & Talented
Human Resource Services, Inc.
The Robbins Company, Jewelry manufacturers
National Student/Parent Mock Election
Teachers Guide to Television Family Institute
Miller Communications, Inc.

Prior Position

International Administrative Partner, Lasser, Harmood, Banner & Dunwoody

Education

BS, Harvard College, 1942

Hope M. Kobak

Average Size of Investment	$100K or less
Size of Fund	Undisclosed
Investment Criteria	Publishing; start-ups; first-stage mail order
Portfolio Companies	Undisclosed

KOPVENCO, A SUBSIDIARY OF KOPPERS CO., INC.
Koppers Building
Pittsburgh, PA 15219
(412) 227-2608

James A. Harris
President

Directorships

MotorTech, Inc.
Ceramatec, Inc.
DNA Plant Technology

Prior Positions

Vice President, Engineering and construction division, 1982
Vice President, Executive department, 1980
Koppers Co.

Education

MBA, University of Pittsburgh, 1965
Bachelors Mechanical Engineering, Auburn, 1956

Average Size of Investment	$500K initially
Size of Fund	$38M
Investment Criteria	Prefers early stage, start-up businesses; related to Koppers Co. technical and marketing skills if at all possible; does not prefer consumer product or health care related firms requiring extensive government approval
Portfolio Companies	Advanced Refractory Technologies, Inc., Buffalo, NY, Ceramics; American Cimflex Corp., Pittsburgh, PA, Robotics; Ceramatec, Salt Lake City, UT, Ceramics; DNA Plant Technology, Mt. Kisco, NY, Life sciences; Ecogen, Lawrenceville, NJ, Biological pesticides; Engenics, Lexington, MA, Life sciences; EOTec, West Haven, CT, Fiber optics; Formative Technologies, Pittsburgh, PA, Advanced engraved graphics; Genex, Rockville, MD, Life sciences; Inspiration Systems, Sewickley, PA, Software; Metcal, Menlo Park, CA, Advanced materialurgical; MotorTech, Daytona Beach, FL, High efficiency automotive equipment; Oxford Partners, Stamford, CT, fund; Pharmaceutical Group Services, Inc., Lewisburg, PA, Mail order prescriptions

LAMOREAUX PARTNERS
650 California Street
San Francisco, CA 94108
(415) 781-5858

Phillip A. Lamoreaux

Average Size of Investment	$500K
Size of Fund	$30M
Investment Criteria	Technology-based companies and diversified companies
Portfolio Companies	Undisclosed

LANDMARK MANAGEMENT CO.
119 East 55th Street
New York, NY 10020
(212) 371-8210

Michael Monier

Average Size of Investment	$5M
Size of Fund	$100M+
Investment Criteria	Technology-based and manufacturing companies are of interest
Portfolio Companies	Undisclosed

LASUNG INVESTMENT & FINANCE CO., INC.
3600 Wilshire Boulevard
Suite 1410
Los Angeles, CA 90006
(213) 384-7548

Jung S. Lee

Average Size of Investment	$100K
Size of Fund	$2M
Investment Criteria	Diversified areas of company interest including manufacturing; geographic locale of importance
Portfolio Companies	Undisclosed

LATIGO VENTURES
23410 Civic Center Way
Suite E-2
Malibu, CA 90265
(213) 456-5539

Donald Peterson
General Partner

Directorship

Inner City Law Center

Prior Positions

Partner, Montgomery Securities
Partner, White, Weld & Co.

Education

Masters, Columbia, 1967
AB, Colorado College, 1965

Robert A. Peterson

Average Size of Investment	$250K
Size of Fund	$15M
Investment Criteria	Second stage
Portfolio Companies	Intran Corp., Bloomington, MN, Text input; Zycad Corp., Arden Hills, MN, Special-purpose computer

LAWRENCE VENTURE ASSOCIATES
515 Madison Avenue
29th Floor
New York, NY 10022
(212) 826-9080

3401 West End Avenue
Suite 680
Nashville, TN 37203
(625) 383-0982

Larry J. Lawrence
Managing Partner, NY

Directorships

Dedicated Dental Systems
HealthStar Corp.
Health Stop Medical
ImmunoMed Corp.
Tennessee Chemical Co.

Prior Positions

President and Chairman, Citicorp Venture Capital, Ltd.

Education

MBA, Columbia Graduate School of Business, 1971
BA, Columbia University, 1969

Richard W. Smith
Partner, NY

Directorships

Data Recording Systems, Inc.
Sawtek, Inc.
Xyvision, Inc.

Prior Positions

Senior Investment Manager, Citicorp Venture Capital Ltd., 1979–81
Assistant Treasurer, Morgan Guaranty Trust Co., 1974–79

Education

BA, Harvard University, 1974

Philip B. Smith
Partner, NY

Prior Positions

Executive Vice President, Irving Trust Co., 1981–84
President, Citicorp Venture Capital, Ltd., 1967–72
Citibank, N. A., 1963–77

Education

MBA, Harvard University, 1963
BSE, Princeton University, 1958

Jack Tyrell
Partner, TN

Directorships

Oxford Health Plan

Prior Positions

President, Prudential-Bache Health Care Group, 1982–85
Vice President, Finance, Hospital Corp. of America, 1976–82

Education

MBA, Harvard University, 1972
BS, University of Tennessee, 1969

W. Patrick Ortale III
Partner, TN

Prior Positions

First Vice President, Prudential-Bache Health Care Group, 1983–85
Vice President, J. C. Bradford & Co., 1979–83
Stock Option Trader, J. C. Bradford & Co., 1975–79

Education

BA, Hanover College, 1975

Thomas A. Gallagher
Associate, TN

Prior Positions

Associates, Prudential-Bache Health Care Group, 1983–85
CPA-Consultant, Thomas A. Gallagher, 1982–83
Senior Auditor, Touche Ross & Co., 1980–82

DIRECTORY AND BIOGRAPHIES

Education
MBA, Vanderbilt University, 1984
BS, University of Tennessee, 1980

Brian T. Horey
Associate, NY

Prior Positions
Analyst, Smith Barney, Harris Upham & Co.

Education
MBA, Harvard University, 1986
BA, Colgate University, 1982

Average Size of Investment	$1–1.5M
Size of Fund	$70M
Investment Criteria	Experienced management, proprietary idea or technology; potential to be a $50–100M revenue company with high profit margins in three to five years
Portfolio Companies	Autotote Systems, Newark, DE, Data processing; HealthStar Corp., Houston, TX, Health care management; ImmunoMed Corp., Tampa, FL, Biotechnology; Oxford Health Plans, Darien, CT, HMO; SCOA Investment Corp., Columbus, OH, Retailing

LENDMAN CAPITAL ASSOCIATES, L. P.
Five Piedmont Center
Suite 320
Atlanta, GA 30305
(404) 233-9003

William M. Lendman
General Partner

Directorships
National Bank of Georgia, Banking
ByCom Systems, Inc., Installation and maintenance to telecommunications industry
Horizon Industries, Inc., Carpet manufacturing
Integrated Computer Graphics, Inc., CAD/CAM software
The System Works, Inc., Maintenance software
Graphics Research Corp., Graphics software

Prior Position
President and Chief Executive Officer, Glasrock Home Health Care, Inc.

Education
New York University, School of Commerce
Syracuse University

Loren J. Rivard
General Partner

Directorship
Integrated Computer Graphics, Inc., CAD/CAM software

Prior Position
President, Sonitrol Security Systems, Inc., of Baltimore

Education
BS, University of Wisconsin, 1968

Average Size of Investment	$250K
Size of Fund	$10M
Investment Criteria	High technology or low technology, super growth opportunities
Portfolio Companies	Graphics Research Corp., Norcross, GA, Computer-aided engineering programs for automated mapping facilities applications; Integrated Computer Graphics, Inc., Atlanta, GA/Corte Madera, CA, Computer-aided design program for the wood frame construction industry; The System Works, Inc., Atlanta, GA, Integrated computer software system for maintenance planning and control functions at industrial and manufacturing facilities; United Asset Management Corp., New York, NY, Holding company acquiring firms in the investment management business

LENZINI & CO., INC.
847 Sherman Street
Denver, CO 80203
(303) 832-1922

Michael Lenzini, Jr.
President

Directorships
Business Programming Inc., Specialized software
Gray International Forwarding, Freight forwarder

Education

BA, University of Colorado, 1968

Lance Buchner

Average Size of Investment	Undisclosed
Size of Fund	Undisclosed
Investment Criteria	Start-ups; first-phase financing; almost all industry categories; generally $100,000 or more fund requirement; assist client as consultant in most cases with contingency fee upon raising funds
Portfolio Companies	Undisclosed

LEONG VENTURES
146 Atherton Avenue
Atherton, CA 94025
(415) 327-1169

Helen C. Leong
Managing Partner

Directorship

Advanced Polymer Systems, Inc., Specialty chemicals

Prior Position

Management Consultant, Matteson Investment Corp.

Education

MA, Stanford University, 1949
BA, Stanford University, 1948

George F. Leong
Partner
(415) 327-8970

Prior Positions

Owner/Consultant, GFL-en Consultants, 1974–present
Deputy Director for Scientific Activities, Officer of Scientific Evaluation, Bureau of Drugs, Food and Drug Administration, 1970–74
Special Assistant to Assistant Secretary for Health and Scientific Affairs, Department of Health, Education & Welfare, 1969–70
Various positions, U.S. Naval Radiological Defense Laboratory, 1951–60

Education

PhD, Physiology, Stanford University, 1951
MA, Physiology, Stanford University, 1947
BA, Biology, Stanford University, 1946

Average Size of Investment	$300K
Size of Fund	Undisclosed
Investment Criteria	Biomedical technology; plant and food technology
Portfolio Companies	Advanced Polymer Systems, Inc., Redwood City, CA, Specialty chemicals; Datastream, Inc., Mountain View, CA, Telecommunications; IPRI, California, Plant technology

ARTHUR D. LITTLE ENTERPRISES, INC
20 Acorn Park
Cambridge, MA 02140
(617) 864-5770

Paul J. Ballantine
Walter J. Cairns

Average Size of Investment	Up to $600K
Size of Fund	$15M
Investment Criteria	Technologies and markets that correspond to areas of expertise at Arthur D. Little, Inc.
Portfolio Companies	Venture fund commenced operation 9/1/84

LLOYD CAPITAL CORP.
77 State Highway 5
Edgewater, NJ 07020
(201) 947-6000

Joseph Scharf
Solomon Scharf

Average Size of Investment	$100K
Size of Fund	Undisclosed
Investment Criteria	Diversified areas of interest; start-ups are welcome; will act as lead investor
Portfolio Companies	Undisclosed

DIRECTORY AND BIOGRAPHIES

LONGWORTH VENTURES
135 South LaSalle Street
Suite 616
Chicago, IL 60603
(312) 372-3888

Lawrence G. Sucsy
General Partner

Directorships

Sucsy, Fischer & Co., Investment bankers
Fertility and Genetics Research, Inc., Human infertility treatment
Systems Management, Inc., Software systems
Wagner Castings Co., Castings
Occu-Med, Inc., Occupational medical system

Prior Positions

Founder, Sears, Sucsy Investment Bankers
Management Consultant, Booz, Allen & Hamilton

Education

MBA (with distinction), Harvard University
BE, Electrical Engineering, Yale University

Thomas E. Galuhn
General Partner

Prior Position

Assistant Vice President, Institutional Venture Capital, First National Bank of Chicago, 1973–83

Education

MBA, University of Chicago
BS, Finance, Notre Dame

Andrew A. Beaurline
General Partner

Prior Positions

Investment Officer, Institutional Venture Capital, First National Bank of Chicago
Tax and Audit Senior, CPA, Arthur Andersen & Co., Minneapolis

Education

MBA, University of Chicago, 1981
BS, Accountancy (with honors), University of Illinois, 1974

Average Size of Investment	$300K
Size of Fund	Undisclosed
Investment Criteria	Health-care related, computer related, communications, other technology; basic industry leverage buy-out
Portfolio Companies	Undisclosed

LOUISIANA EQUITY CAPITAL CORP.
P.O. Box 1511
Baton Rouge, LA 70821
(504) 389-4421

Melvin L. Rambin
Jack McDonald

Average Size of Investment	$250K–$500K
Size of Fund	$8M
Investment Criteria	Undisclosed
Portfolio Companies	Undisclosed

LUBAR & CO. INCORPORATED
777 East Wisconsin Avenue
Suite 3060
Milwaukee, WI 53202
(414) 291-9000

Sheldon B. Lubar
President

Directorship

National Venture Capital Association

Prior Positions

Assistant Secretary, Housing Production and Mortgage Credit; Commissioner of Federal Housing Administration, Dept. of Housing and Urban Development, 1973–74
Chairman, Chief Executive Officer, Mortgage Associates, Inc., 1966–73

Education

BA, University of Wisconsin, 1951

David J. Lubar

Prior Position

Assistant Vice President, Manufacturing and Electronics Lending Division, Northwestern National Bank of Minneapolis, 1977–82

Education

MBA, University of Minnesota, 1982
BA, Bowdoin College, 1977

James C. Rowe

Directorships

Chicago Gear Works, Inc.
Evans Food Products Co.

Prior Position

Tax Department, Arthur Andersen & Co., 1970–72

Education

CPA
BBA, University of Wisconsin

William T. Donovan

Directorships

A. L. Gebhardt Co., Inc.
Process Equipment Corp.

Prior Position

Manufacturers Hanover Trust, 1976–80

Education

MBA, University of Notre Dame, 1976
BS, University of Notre Dame, 1974

Average Size of Investment	$500K
Size of Fund	Undisclosed
Investment Criteria	Leveraged buy-outs are of interest; will act as lead investor; diversified preferences
Portfolio Companies	Undisclosed

LUBRIZOL ENTERPRISES, INC.
29400 Lakeland Boulevard
Wickliffe, OH 44094
(216) 943-4200

Donald L. Murfin
President

Directorships

Primus Capital Fund

Education

BS, University of Iowa, 1965

Bruce H. Grasser
Vice President

Prior Positions

Senior Process Development Engineer, Lubrizol Corp., 1968–82
Department Head, Process Development Dept., Goodrich-Gulf Chemicals, Inc., 1964–68

Education

MBA, Case Western Reserve University, 1971
BS, Iowa State University, 1964

David R. Anderson
Vice President

Prior Postions

Manager, International Seed Sales, Cargill Grain Co., 1980–82
Director, International Seed Sales, Anderson Clayton & Co.
DeKalb Agricultural Research, Inc.

Education

MBA, University of Santa Clara, 1972
MS, University of Minnesota
BS, Utah State University, 1972

Edward M. Kiggins
Director of Licensing & Technology

Prior Positions

Director, Biotechnology, SDS Biotechnology, 1979–85
Director, Research and Development, Rhone-Poulenc, Inc., 1975–79
Abbot Laboratories

Education

PhD, Microbiology, University of Connecticut, 1958
MBA, Advanced Management Institute, Lake Forest College, 1968

James R. Glynn
Vice President, Finance/Treasurer

Prior Positions

Manager of Audits and Financial Controls, Lubrizol Co.
Audit Manager, Price Waterhouse

Education

BBA, Cleveland State University

Arthur J. Chatroo
Secretary/General Counsel

Prior Positions

Corporate Counsel, Tax and Finance, Lubrizol Corp., 1982–85
Halcon SD Group, 1975–82
Chemical engineer, Standard Oil Co. of Ohio

Education

MBA, New York University, 1982
JD, New York Law School, 1979
BE, City College of New York, 1968

Average Size of Investment	$600K
Size of Fund	$84M
Investment Criteria	Interested in specialty and fine chemistry—biology, chemistry and material sciences
Portfolio Companies	Agrigenetics Corp., Boulder, CO, Genetically improved plants; Lynnville Seed Co., Lynnville, IA, Proprietary soybean planting seed; Sigco Research, Inc., Breckenridge, MN, Hybrid sunflower planting seed; Altus Corp., San Jose, CA, Advanced electrochemical battery systems; Catalytica Associates, Mountain View, CA, Advanced catalytic processes; ChemDesign Corp., Fitchburg, MA, Custom specialty and fine chemicals; Creative BioMolecules, Inc., Hopkinton, MA, Engineered protein products and processes; Genentech, Inc., So. San Francisco, CA, Genetically engineered pharmaceuticals; GLC Associates, Wickliffe, OH, Specialty and fine chemicals produced via biocatalysis; Greenwich Oil Corp., Dallas, TX, Thermally enhanced oil recovery; Intera Company, Ltd., Cleveland, TN, Processes to improve the surface properties of polymers; Mycogen Corp., San Diego, CA, Genetically engineered microbial pesticides and mycoherbicides; Sungene Technologies Corp., Palo Alto, CA, Plant genetics; SVO Enterprises Corp., Columbus, OH, Specialty vegetable oils and derivatives; Syntro Corp., San Diego, CA, Genetically engineered systems for production of specialty chemicals

DONALD L. LUCAS
3000 Sand Hill Road
Building 3, Suite 210
Menlo Park, CA 94025
(415) 854-4223

Donald L. Lucas
Owner

Directorships

Oracle, Software data base management systems
Tri-Data Corp., Electronic networking products
Data Card Corp., Identification systems
HBO & Co., Hospital information systems
ICOT Corp., Data communication products
Liconix, Lasers

Prior Positions

General and Limited Partner, Draper, Gaither & Anderson
Corporate Finance Dept., Smith Barney & Co., New York

Education

MBA, Stanford University, 1953
BA, Stanford University, 1951

Average Size of Investment	$500K
Size of Fund	Undisclosed
Investment Criteria	Undisclosed
Portfolio Companies	Pacific Monolithics, Inc.; SDA Systems, CAD/CAE tools; Tri-Data, Electronic networking products; Westworld Community Healthcare, Rural health care facilities

THE LUKEN COMPANY
135 South LaSalle Street
Chicago, IL 60603
(312) 263-4015

Donald Luken
President

Directorships

Education & Information Systems, Inc., Computer products
Suppliers On Line Systems, Computer service

Prior Positions

Director for Venture Capital and Chief Financial Officer, Altorfen, Podesta, Wooland & Co.
Commercial Lending Officer, Continental Illinois National Bank

Education

MBA, University of Wisconsin, 1969
BBA, St. Norbert College, 1967

Average Size of Investment	$500K–$1M
Size of Fund	Undisclosed
Investment Criteria	Beyond start-up stage
Portfolio Companies	Undisclosed

MAC MANAGEMENT ASSOCIATES, INC.
35555 Curtis Blvd.
Eastlake, OH 44094
(216) 953-0555

Morton A. Cohen
President

Directorships

Voicemail, Voice messaging
FDRL, Contract research testing
Childers Products, Coatings, adhesives manufacturing
Monitek, Instrumentation manufacturing
IGI Biotechnology, Industrial microbiology

Education

MBA, Wharton School, 1960

Average Size of Investment	$250K
Size of Fund	$3M
Investment Criteria	Experienced management team; proprietary product; internal growth rate in the 30–40% range
Portfolio Companies	ADAC Laboratories, San Jose, CA, Diagnostic imaging; Diasonics, Inc., Milpitas, CA, Diagnostic imaging; Igene Biotechnology, Columbia, MD, Industrial microbiology; Voicemail, Santa Clara, CA, Voice messaging; American Telecommunications, Dallas, TX, Telecommunications

MAIN CAPITAL INVESTMENT CORP.
426 Essex Street
Suite J
Hackensack, NJ 07601
(201) 489-2080

Sam Klotz

Average Size of Investment	$100K
Size of Fund	Undisclosed
Investment Criteria	Diversified preferences, will consider oil and construction; geographic proximity important; will act as lead investor
Portfolio Companies	Undisclosed

MAINE CAPITAL CORP.
Seventy Center Street
Portland, ME 04101
(207) 772-1001

Albert W. Moore, Chairman
David M. Coit
President

Directorships

Maine Science, Technology Board, State advisory group
Vortech Corp., Semiconductor test lab
Maine Post & Beam Co., Home construction
Mowatt Sporting Goods, Accessories

DIRECTORY AND BIOGRAPHIES

Prior Position
Assistant Vice President, Bank of Boston, 1981

Education
MBA, Harvard Business School, 1975
BA, Economics, Yale University, 1969

Average Size of Investment	$100K
Size of Fund	$1
Investment Criteria	Undisclosed
Portfolio Companies	Undisclosed

M&I VENTURES CORP.
770 North Water Street
Milwaukee, WI 53202
(414) 765-7910

Daniel P. Howell
Vice President
(414) 765-7912

Directorships
AQS, Inc.
Office Solutions, Inc.

Prior Position
Investment Officer, MorAmerica Capital Corp., 1980–83

Education
MBA, Finance, University of Wisconsin, 1980
BA, Government, Lawrence University, 1974

John J. Riley
Vice President

Prior Positions
Manager, Financial Analysis, Newell Companies, Inc., 1982–83
Vice President, Katy Cable Television, Inc., 1980–82
Financial Analysis, Blount, Inc., 1978–80

Education
BBA, Finance, University of Notre Dame, 1978

Average Size of Investment	$500K
Size of Fund	Undisclosed
Investment Criteria	Prefer financings with right to acquire stock interests; geographic preference; Midwest, but will consider other; industry preferences: communications, computer related, electronics related, genetic engineering, medical/health related, industrial automation, diversified
Portfolio Companies	Undisclosed

M & T CAPITAL CORP.
One M & T Plaza
Buffalo, NY 14240
(716) 842-5881

Joseph V. Parlato
President

Directorships
Comptek Research Inc., Defense-related computer systems
Terrano Corp., Laboratory and hospital computer systems
Barrister Information Systems Corp., Computer systems for the legal profession

Prior Positions
Vice President, Manufacturers & Traders Trust Co., 1976–81
Vice President, M & T Capital Corp., 1969–76
CPA, Price Waterhouse & Co., 1967–69

Education
MBA, University of Michigan, 1965
BS, University of Buffalo, 1964

Norma E. Gracia

Average Size of Investment	$350K
Size of Fund	$20M
Investment Criteria	Second- or later-stage financing preferred; no geographical limitations with U.S.
Portfolio Companies	Currently 23 companies in portfolio

MANNING AND COMPANY
29438 Quailwood Drive
Rancho Palos Verdes, CA 90274
(213) 377-4335

Christopher A. Manning, M.D.
President

Education

PhD, University of California at Los Angeles, 1981
MBA, Northwestern University, 1971

Average Size of Investment	$100K
Size of Fund	$1M+
Investment Criteria	Technology-based companies of interest as well as start-ups; will act as lead investor
Portfolio Companies	Undisclosed

MANUFACTURERS HANOVER VENTURE CAPITAL CORP.
140 East 45th Street
New York, NY 10017
(212) 808-0109

Thomas J. Sandleitner
President
(212) 808-0107

Directorships

Astrex, Electronics
Congoleum, Defense

Prior Position

Vice President, Manufacturers Hanover Trust

Education

PMD, Harvard, 1978
MBA, Iona Graduate School, 1973
BA, Manhattan College, 1964

Edward L. Koch III
Vice President
(212) 808-0105

Directorship

International Healthcare Corp., HMOs

Education

MBA, Wharton School, University of Pennsylvania, 1981
BS, Business Administration, Colorado State University, 1975

Kevin P. Falvey
Bryan J. Carey

Average Size of Investment	$1M
Size of Fund	$110M
Investment Criteria	Leveraged buy-outs; diversified company areas of interest; will act as lead investor
Portfolio Companies	Undisclosed

MANUFACTURERS SBIC
310 Main Street
East Haven, CT 06512
(203) 469-7901

Louis W. Mingione

Average Size of Investment	$500K
Size of Fund	$1.6M
Investment Criteria	Diversified areas of interest; will act as lead investor; start-ups are encouraged; geographic proximity is of importance
Portfolio Companies	Undisclosed

MAPLELEAF CAPITAL CORPORATION
55 Waugh Drive
Suite 710
Houston, TX 77007
(713) 880-4494

Edward M. Fink
President

Directorships

Allied Comprehensive Health, Inc., Diversified health care services company
National Entertainment Corp., Specialty retailing

DIRECTORY AND BIOGRAPHIES

Prior Positions
General Manager, 15 syndicated real estate partnerships, Houston, TX
Management Consulting Group, Tax Department, Arthur Anderson & Co.
Tax Specialist, Peat Marwick

Education
BBA, CPA, University of Texas, 1977

Bernadette Obermeier, Corporate Secretary

Average Size of Investment	$500K
Size of Fund	$5M
Investment Criteria	Diversified, including communications, computer ware, distribution, electronics, manufacturing, and medical products, services, and distribution
Portfolio Companies	Undisclosed

MARCON CAPITAL CORP.
49 Riverside Avenue
Westport, CT 06880
(203) 226-7751

Martin Cohen

Average Size of Investment	$200K
Size of Fund	$4M
Investment Criteria	Diversified areas of interest; geographic proximity important; will act as lead investor
Portfolio Companies	Undisclosed

MARINE VENTURE CAPITAL, INC.
111 East Wisconsin Avenue
P.O. Box 2033
Milwaukee, WI 53201
(414) 765-2274

H. Wayne Foreman
President

Directorships
International Electronics Corp.
Gleason Reel Corp.
Gander Mountain, Inc.
Panef Corp.
Industrial Data Terminals Corp.
Automated Industrial Systems, Inc.

Prior Position
Vice President, MorAmerica Capital Corp.

Education
MBA, University of Wisconsin, 1975
BBA, University of Wisconsin, 1974

Average Size of Investment	$400K
Size of Fund	$3M
Investment Criteria	Diversified; all stages of development except seed; particular interest in leveraged buy-outs
Portfolio Companies	Automated Industrial Systems, Inc., Austin, TX, Manufacturer of computerized systems to automate numerically controlled machine tools; Gleason Reel Corp., Mayville, WI, Manufacturer of cable and hose control devices for industrial machines; International Electronics Corp., Tucson, AZ, Manufacturer of MNET, a proprietory network for communication between non-compatible computerized test equipment; Shoreland Medical Marketing, Inc., Wauwatosa, WI, Marketing service company serving physician, medical clinic, and hospital markets; Industrial Data Terminals, Columbus, OH, Industrial control color graphics terminals; Gander Mountain, Inc., Wilmot, WI, Catalog retailer outdoor recreation; Panef Corp., Milwaukee, WI, Manufacturing lubricants and custom packaging; Servlite, Inc., Madison, WI, Franchise of D'Lites restaurants

MARKET CAPITAL CORP.
P.O. Box 22667
Tampa, FL 33630
(813) 248-5781

E. E. Eads

Average Size of Investment	$100K
Size of Fund	Undisclosed
Investment Criteria	Construction, real estate, grocery, manufacturing industries considered; start-ups are welcome
Portfolio Companies	Undisclosed

MARKETCORP VENTURE ASSOCIATES, L.P.
285 Riverside Avenue
Westport, CT 06880
(203) 222-1000

E. Bulkeley Griswold
General Partner

Directorships

Spectrascan, Medical diagnostics
Medplus, Freestanding emergency care chain

Prior Positions

Executive Vice President, General Electric Investment Co.
Vice President, Phoenix Mutual Life

Education

MBA, University of Connecticut, 1966
BA, University of Maryland, 1961

Michael J. Feldman
General Partner

Directorships

Fire Control Technologies, Home safety products
Glacial Confections, Specialty food products

Prior Positions

Director of Marketing, Pepsico, 1980–81
Consultant, McKinsey & Co., 1977–80
Marketing Manager, Procter & Gamble, 1973–77

Education

MBA, Michigan State University, 1973
BA, Michigan State University, 1972

James W. Larson
General Partner

Directorships

Computerworks, Computor retailing
Au Bon Pain, Manufacturing and retail chain of French bakery cafes
Glacial Confections, Manufacturer and distribution of frozen dessert products

Prior Positions

President, Westport Restaurants, Inc. (Marketing Corp. of America)
Vice President, Product Management, Quaker Oats

Education

MBA, Michigan State University, 1967
BS, Valparaiso University, 1966

Frederick H. Kurz
General Partner

Directorships

Co-optics of America, Marketing services to optometrists
Pioneer Medical Systems, Personal emergency communications

Prior Positions

Consultant, Marketing Corp. of America
President, Somerset Wine Co. (NSI)

Education

Advanced Management, Wharton School, University of Pennsylvania, 1968
BS, Washington and Lee University, 1962

Average Size of Investment	$250K–$1.5M
Size of Fund	$65.6M
Investment Criteria	Consumer-oriented products and companies in the following categories; retailing, both specialty and restaurants; packaged goods, both food and nonfood; health care, communications, and consumer electronics
Portfolio Companies	Au Bon Pain, Inc., Chain of bakery-cafés specializing in the preparation and sale of high-quality, authentic French food items; Computerworks, Inc., Chain of retail centers which sell microcomputer products primarily to business; Co-optics of America, Products and services for the eye care market; Fire Control Technologies, Fire suppression products for home and other consumer markets; Glacial Confections, Inc., Frozen specialty dessert products; Medplus, Inc., Freestanding health care centers; Pioneer Medical Systems, Inc., Medical products and monitoring services for the in-home market; Rabbit Systems, Inc., Home audio/visual electronics

MARWIT CAPITAL CORP.
180 Newport Center Drive
Newport Beach, CA 92660
(714) 640-6234

Martin W. Witte
Robert A. Hoff

Average Size of Investment	$200K
Size of Fund	$5M
Investment Criteria	Diversified areas of interest including manufacturing; geographic location is important
Portfolio Companies	Undisclosed

MASSACHUSETTS CAPITAL RESOURCE CO.
545 Boylston Street
Boston, MA 02116
(617) 536-3900

William J. Torpey
Richard W. Anderson
John W. Burgess
Kenneth J. Lavery
Ben Bailey III
Joan A. Creamer

Average Size of Investment	$300K
Size of Fund	$100M
Investment Criteria	Technology-based and manufacturing companies are of interest; geographic location is important
Portfolio Companies	Undisclosed

MASSACHUSETTS COMMUNITY DEVELOPMENT FINANCE CORP.
131 State Street
Suite 600
Boston, MA 02109
(617) 742-0366

Charles T. Grigsby
President

Directorships

Steering Committee, Chamber of Commerce, Boston
2000
Urban League of Eastern Massachusetts
Massachusetts Venture Capital Corp.
ICA Revolving Loan Fund
Advisory Committee, Neworld Bank for Savings

Prior Positions

President, Massachusetts Venture Capital Corp.
Partner, Lee-Grisby Associates

Education

BA, Harvard College, 1961

Nancy Nye
Vice President

Directorships

Industrial Cooperative Association, Business consulting for worker ownership
ICA Revolving Loan Fund, Investments in worker cooperatives
Women's Institute for Housing and Economic Development, Consulting for women's organizations

Prior Positions

Development Specialist, Massachusetts Commmunity Development Assistance Corp.
Real Estate Underwriter, National Consumer Cooperative Bank

Education

MPPM, Yale School of Management, 1980
BA, Radcliffe University, 1971

Judith Cranna
Investment Officer

Prior Positions

Financial Analyst, Boston Financial Technical Group
Assistant Treasurer, Picnique Corp.

Education

MBA, Simmons College, 1981

Average Size of Investment	$75K–$300K
Size of Fund	$10M
Investment Criteria	Economically distressed areas of Massachusetts
Portfolio Companies	Undisclosed

MASSACHUSETTS TECHNOLOGY DEVELOPMENT CORP.
84 State Street
Boston, MA 02109
(617) 723-4920

William F. Aikman

Average Size of Investment	$100K
Size of Fund	Undisclosed
Investment Criteria	Diversified areas of interest; geographic location is important
Portfolio Companies	Undisclosed

MASSEY BURCH INVESTMENT GROUP, INC.
One Park Plaza
Suite One
Nashville, TN 37203
(615) 329-9449

Jack C. Massey
Lucius E. Burch III
President

Directorships

Intermedics, Inc., Implantable medical devices
QMS, Inc., Laser print systems
Barrister Information Systems, Law office automation
OnLine Software, Computer software/service
Surgical Care Affiliates, Outpatient surgical centers
International Transtech, Chain of automotive repair shops
Monoclonal Antibodies, Biotechnology diagnostics

Prior Position

Vice President, Massey Investment Co., 1968–81

Education

BA, University of North Carolina, 1963

Donald M. Johnston

Average Size of Investment	$1M+
Size of Fund	$30M
Investment Criteria	Seed, second round; no industry restrictions
Portfolio Companies	In the portfolio there are currently companies in the medical, technological, service, and communications industries

THE MASTERS FUND
1426 Pearl Street, Suite 211
Boulder, CO 80302
(303) 443-2460

Carl D. Carman
General Partner

Directorships

American International Communications
Aspen Peripherals
Aweida Systems Corp.
Cubicomp Corp.
Optotech Inc.
Palantir
Symantec
WaveFrame
Video TeleCom Corp.
Alliant Computers
Cadnetix
CXC Corp.

Prior Positions

Vice President, Engineering/Technology, NBI
Vice President, Engineering, Data General

Education

BS, Electrical Engineering, University of Kentucky, 1960

Martin J. Chizzick
Partner

DIRECTORY AND BIOGRAPHIES

Directorships

Exabyte Corp.
Shannon Systems
Unisyn Inc.

Prior Positions

Corporate Vice President of Corp. Program Management, StorageTek
Corporate Vice President of International Operations, StorageTek
Vice President, Controller, StorageTek

Education

BS, Accounting, University of Colorado, 1969

Average Size of Investment	$500K–1M
Size of Fund	$12M
Investment Criteria	Return on Investment
Portfolio Companies	American International Communications Corp., CO, Software; Aspen Peripherals, CO, 3480-type tape drive; Aweida Systems Corp., CO, Marketing and service of computer peripheral and related equipment; Cubicomp Corp., CA, Manufacture micro-computer based solids modeling system; Exabyte Corp., CO, Manufacture high capacity tape back-up systems; Optotech, Inc., CO, Manufacture 5¼″ optical disk drive; Palantir Corp., CA, Manufacture optical/scanning recognition equipment; Shannon Systems, CA, Digital communications security equipment; Symantec, CA, Productivity software; Unisyn, Inc., CO UNIX-based manufacturing software; WaveFrame, CO, Computer based audio equipment; Video TeleCom Corp., TX, Video image transmission between PCs

MATRIX PARTNERS, L.P.
One Post Office Square
Boston, MA 02109
(617) 482-7735

224 Airport Parkway
San Jose, CA 95110
(408) 298-0270

Paul J. Ferri
Managing Partner, MA

Directorships

BancTec, Inc., Electronic check-processing equipment for banking industry
Paradyne Corp., Communications equipment
Stratus Computer, Inc., Fault-tolerant computers
Applix, Inc., Office automation software
Bytex Corp., Communications equipment
Ferretec, Inc., Microwave components

Prior Positions

General Partner, Hellman, Ferri Investment Associates
General Partner, Western Investment Associates

Education

MBA, Columbia University, 1968
MSEE, Polytechnic Institute, 1964
BEE, Cornell University, 1960

Frederick K. Fluegel
Managing Partner, CA

Directorships

Aspect Telecommunications Corp., Modular telephone call distribution system
Applied MicroCircuits Corp., ECL gate array manufacturer
ComDesign, Inc., Data communications equipment
ELXSi International, Inc., Supercomputer
LP Com, Inc., Telephone test equipment
Saratoga Semiconductor, Inc., Specialty semiconductors

Prior Positions

General Partner, Western Investment Associates II
General Partner, Western Investment Associates

Education

MS, University of California at Irvine, 1968
BS, United States Naval Academy, 1961

F. Warren Hellman
General Partner
c/o Hellman & Friedman
One Bush Street
Suite 1107
San Francisco, CA 94104

Directorships

Acton Computer, Inc., Ferrite heads for disk storage devices
Il Fornaio (America) Corporation, Specialty retailer of Italian bread, pasta, pastry
Shaughnessy Holdings, Regional operator of budget motels

Prior Positions

General Partner, Hellman, Ferri Investment Associates
President, Partner, Lehman Brothers Kuhn Loeb & Co.

Education

MBA, Harvard Graduate School of Business Administration, 1959
BA, University of California at Berkeley, 1955

W. Michael Humphreys
General Partner, MA

Directorships

Medivision, Inc., Ophthalmic surgery centers
Axiom Technology Corp., Semiconductor test equipment
New England Critical Care, Inc., Home health care

Prior Position

General Partner, Hellman, Ferri Investment Associates

Education

MBA, Harvard Graduate School of Business Administration, 1979
BS, University of Oregon, 1974

David L. Douglass
General Partner, CA

Directorships

CEMAX Medical Products, Inc., Workstations for 3-D anatomical imaging and prosthetic modeling
Covalent Systems Corp., Computerized data collection/shop floor management systems for the publishing industry
Menlo Care, Inc., Specialty peripheral and central venous catheters for intravenous therapy

Prior Positions

Founder, Chief Operating Officer, Paladin Software Corp.
Vice President, Finance and Administration, Collagen Corp.

Education

MA, Stanford University, 1979
MBA, Stanford University, 1978
BA, Amherst College, 1974

Timothy A. Barrows
General Partner, MA

Directorships

Omnirel Corp., Power hybrid devices for defense electronics

Prior Positions

Associate, Merrill Lynch Capital Markets, 1981–82
Analyst, Merrill Lynch Capital Markets, 1979–80

Education

MBA, Stanford Graduate School of Business, 1984
BA, Williams College, 1979

Average Size of Investment	$1.5M
Size of Fund	$115M
Investment Criteria	No real estate or oil and gas
Portfolio Companies	Undisclosed

MAYFIELD FUND
2200 Sand Hill Road
Menlo Park, CA 94025
(415) 854-5560

Thomas J. Davis, Jr.
General Partner

Directorships

Catalytica Associates
Compression Labs
Equatorial Communications
Tandem Computers

Prior Position

Founding Partner, Davis & Rock Venture Capital

DIRECTORY AND BIOGRAPHIES

Education

JD, Harvard Law School
BA, Harvard University

F. Gibson Myers, Jr.
General Partner

Directorships

Adept Technology
Amcodyne
Grid Systems
MIPS Computer Systems
Cadnetix Corp.
Dest Corp.
International Power Technology
3Com Corp.

Prior Position

Manufacturing Manager, Hewlett-Packard

Education

MBA, Stanford Graduate School of Business
Engineering, Dartmouth College

Glenn M. Mueller
General Partner

Directorships

Integrated Measurement Systems
Masstor Systems
Megatest Corp.
Silicon Graphics
Aehr Test Systems, Inc.
Eldec Corp.
Linear Technology Corp.
Quantum Corp.
USX TELECENTERS Corp.

Prior Positions

Founder, California Northwest Fund (now Menlo Ventures)
Manufacturing Engineering, Hewlett-Packard

Education

MBA, Stanford Graduate School
BEE, Rensselaer Polytechnic

A. Grant Heidrich, III
General Partner

Directorships

Adept Technology
Catalytica Associates, Inc.
MIPS Computer Systems
Silicon Graphics

Prior Positions

Vice President, Wood River Capital
Analyst, McGraw-Hill

Education

MBA, Columbia University
BA, Human Biology, Stanford

Norman A. Fogelsong
General Partner

Directorships

Counterpoint Computers
Lam Research Corp.
Aspect Telecommunications Corp.
Automated Technology Products
Codesmith Technology, Inc.
Tricom Automobile Dealer Systems, Inc.

Prior Positions

Management Consultant, McKinsey & Co.
System Analyst Corp., Finance, Hewlett-Packard

Education

JD, Harvard Law School
MBA, Harvard Business School
BS, Industrial Engineering, Stanford University

Michael J. Levinthal
Partner

Directorships

Epyx, Inc.
Onset
Presentation Technologies, Inc.

Prior Positions

Partner, New Enterprise Associates
Marketing Manager, Orion Research, Inc.

Education

MBA, Graduate School of Business, Stanford University
BS, MS, Engineering, Stanford University

William D. Under
Partner

Prior Positions

Founder, President, Positek

Education

BA, Special Education, University of Illinois, 1971

Average Size of Investment	$1M
Size of Fund	In excess of $200M
Investment Criteria	Undisclosed
Portfolio Companies	Undisclosed

MBW VENTURE PARTNERS LIMITED PARTNERSHIP
333 East Main Street
Third Floor
P.O. Box 1431
Midland, MI 48641
(517) 631-2471

350 Second Street
Suite 7
Los Altos, CA 94022
(415) 941-2392

10 Fairmont Avenue
Suite E
Chatham, NJ 07928
(201) 635-3520

Ian R. N. Bund
Managing General Partner, MI, MBW Venture Partners Limited Partnership
President and Director, MI, Michigan Investment Fund L.P.
President and Director, MI, Doan Resources Limited Partnership

Directorships

Attache Software, Inc., Accounting software
LifeScan, Inc., Blood glucose monitoring device
Innovative Hearing Corp., Hearing enhancement for mild hearing loss
Sensormedics, Physiological, noninvasive measurement equipment monitoring head, heart and lung functions
Sequoia Turner Corp., Clinical hematology analyzers

Prior Positions

President, Sea Life, Inc.
Associate, Morgan Stanley & Co.
Senior Accountant, Price Waterhouse & Co.

Education

MBA, Harvard, 1968
BEc, University of Sydney, 1964

Philip E. McCarthy
Managing General Partner, NJ
MBW Venture Partners Limited Partnership
Senior Vice President, Director, NJ
Michigan Investment Fund, L.P.
Senior Vice President, Director, NJ
Doan Resources Limited Partnership

Directorship

Oximetrix Corp., Hospital supplies

Prior Position

Vice President, INCO Limited

Education

JD, Law, Cornell, 1965
BS, Cornell, 1960

DIRECTORY AND BIOGRAPHIES

James R. Weersing
Managing General Partner, CA
MBW Venture Partners Limited Partnership
Senior Vice President and Director, CA
Michigan Investment Fund, L.P.

Directorships

Amber Systems, Software company
Innovative Hearing Corp., Hearing-device manufacturer
LifeScan, Inc., Blood glucose monitoring system manufacturer
Rigi Systems, Inc., Care products for elderly
Sequoia Turner Corp., Clinical products manufacturer
SensorMedics Corp., Physiological monitoring device manufacturer

Prior Positions

President, JRW Technology, Inc., 1980–present
President, Royco Instruments, 1967–79

Education

MBA, Stanford, 1962
BS, Mechanical Engineering, Stanford, 1960

Herbert D. ("Ted") Doan
Chairman and Director, MI, Doan Resources, Limited Partnership
Limited Partner, MI, MBW Venture Partners LP

Directorships

Dow Chemical Co.
Dow Corning Corp.
Chemical Bank & Trust Co.
Noegen Corp.
Xycom, Inc.
Irwin Magnetics
Michigan Bell Telephone Co.

Prior Position

Dow Chemical Co.

Education

BChE, Cornell University, 1949

Average Size of Investment	$500K
Size of Fund	Undisclosed
Investment Criteria	Seed, start-up, buy-outs in life sciences, communication and information systems, industrial automation, computer hardware and peripherals, software products and data base services, semiconductor products and equipment, advanced materials
Portfolio Companies	Undisclosed

MCA NEW VENTURES, INC.
100 Universal City Plaza
Universal City, CA 91608
(213) 508-2933

W. Roderick Hamilton

Average Size of Investment	$500K
Size of Fund	$12M
Investment Criteria	Interested in entertainment ventures; start-ups are welcome; will act as lead investor
Portfolio Companies	Undisclosed

MCCOWN DE LEEUW & CO.
3000 Sand Hill Road
Building 2, Suite 220
Menlo Park, CA 94025
(415) 854-0850

900 3rd Avenue, 28th Floor
New York, NY 10022
(212) 418-6539

George E. McCown
Managing Partner, CA

Directorships

Cobe Labs
Western Lumber Co., Inc.
Stanford Children's Hospital
Coast Gas, Inc.

Prior Positions

Chairman, Boise Construction Co., 1980–84
Senior Vice President, Boise Cascade Building Materials Group, 1976–80
President, Boise Cascade Home & Land Corp., 1974–79

Education

MBA, Harvard, 1962
BS, Stanford, 1957

David E. De Leeuw
Managing Partner, NY

Directorships

Universal Die Casting, Inc.
Western Lumber Co., Inc.
Coast Gas, Inc.

Prior Positions

Vice President, Citibank, 1978–84
Assistant Treasurer/Manager, Corporate Finance Dept., W. R. Grace & Co., 1975–78
Vice President, Paine Webber & Co., 1969–74

Education

MBA, Columbia, 1969
BA, Lafayette College, 1967

Average Size of Investment	$1.5M
Size of Fund	$27.5M
Investment Criteria	Leveraged buyout fund, focusing on divisions or subsidiaries of public companies, in size range of $20–75M purchase price; particularly divisions with strong traditional product base but serve high growth industries, and service companies with strong market positions

Portfolio Companies

Universal Die Casting Inc., Custom aluminum and zinc die casting; Western Lumber Co., Inc., Building materials distribution, San Diego, CA; FIserv, Inc., Administrator of private self-directed retirement plans; Coast Gas, Inc., LP Gas distributor, Fresno, CA

MCGOWAN LECKINGER BERG

10 Forbes Road
Braintree, NY 02184
(617) 849-0020

1350 Avenue of the Americas, #500
New York, NY 10019
(212) 315-0360

Robert T. Leckinger
General Partner, MA

Directorships

Hip Pocket (CSVa., Inc.)
Bin & Barrel

Prior Position

President, Apparel Retail Corp.
Senior Vice President, Commonwealth Trading Corp.

Education

MBA, Xavier University, 1967
BBA, University of Cincinnati, 1966

James A. McGowan
General Partner, MA

Directorships

Sterling, Inc.
Countdown, Inc.

Prior Positions

Senior Vice President, The Trump Group, 1982–84
Executive Vice President, Raxton Corp., 1978–82
Senior Vice President, Bond Industries, 1975–78

Education

MBA, Suffolk University, 1966
BSBA, Boston University, 1965

Stanley A. Berg
General Partner, NY

Directorships

Hip Pocket (CSVa., Inc.)
Bin & Barrel, Inc.

Prior Positions

Executive Vice President, The Trump Group
General Manager, Metro Cash & Carry Holdings

Education

Chartered Accountant (SA), University of Witwatersrand, Johannesburg, 1965

Average Size of Investment	$2.9M
Size of Investment	$49M
Investment Criteria	Retail companies with valid merchandise concept in place; management with merchandising and marketing expertise; commitment to build professional management team; commitment to growth; ability to work with investors to develop and execute strategic plan
Portfolio Companies	Sterling, Inc., Akron, OH, Retail jewelry store chain; Hip Pocket (CSVa., Inc.), Charlotte, NC, Retail young men's apparel; Countdown, Inc., Bridgeport, CT, Retail off-price children's apparel; Bin & Barrel, Pompano Beach, FL, Retail gourmet snacks and gifts; Home Express, Inc., San Francisco, CA, Retail home furnishings and accessories

MEDICAL INDUSTRIAL CAPITAL, INC.
1201 Marquette Avenue, Suite 400
Minneapolis, MN 55403
(612) 332-5130

Timothy I. Maudlin
President, Chief Operations Officer, Secretary, Treasurer

Prior Positions

Audit Manager, Arthur Anderson & Co., 1975–82
Consultant, G. D. Searle & Co., 1974–75

Education

MM, Northwestern University Graduate School of Management
BS, St. Olaf College, 1973

Jeffrey E. Figgatt
Vice President, Investment Officer

Prior Positions

First National Bank of Minneapolis, 1980–85
The First National Bank of Cincinnati, 1973–80

Education

MBA, University of Cincinnati, 1979
BA, International Relations, Denison University, 1973

Average Size of Investment	Undisclosed
Size of Fund	Undisclosed
Investment Criteria	Makes seed, start up, and a limited number of first stage investments in innovative medical technology and health care companies located in MN and selected other major medical centers in the U.S.
Portfolio Companies	CuraTech, Inc., Minneapolis, MN, Research, development, commercial exploitation of core technologies involving the manipulation of cells; Bactex, Inc., PA, Development of vaccines, immunotherapeutics, and diagnostics tests for bacterial diseases; Home Diagnostics, Inc., Eatontown, NJ, Manufacture, market medical diagnostic products and systems for home and professional markets; Labelco Co., Minneapolis, MN, Medical products distribution to healthcare providers; Mediqual, Inc., Boston, MA, Software company, database management to measure clinical quality, cost, efficiency

MED–TECH VENTURES, INC.
201 Tabor Road
Morris Plains, NJ 07950
(201) 540-3457

Fred G. Weiss
President
(201) 540-3562

Prior Positions

Vice President, Planning, Investment and Development, Warner-Lambert Co.
Vice President, Treasurer, Warner-Lambert Co.

Education

MBA, University of Chicago, 1967
BA, University of Pennsylvania, 1963

H. Kirk Merritt
Vice President
(201) 540-4794

Prior Positions

Director of Business Development, Deseret Medical Products, 1981–82
Director of Market Development, Hospital Products Division, Warner-Lambert, 1980–81

Education

BS, University of Colorado, 1962

Owen W. McGillicuddy

Average Size of Investment	$500K
Size of Fund	$25M
Investment Criteria	Med-Tech will invest in most health-care-related businesses that have the appropriate quality of management and sufficient proprietary products and services sold in markets large enough to grow at least $100 million
Portfolio Companies	Cistron, New Jersey, Rapid diagnostic tests; Health Stop, Boston, Emergency medical centers; Luxtron, California, Fiber-optic sensors; Sensym, California, Pressure transducers; XOMA, California, Biotechnology

MELCHOR VENTURE MANAGEMENT, INC.
170 State Street
Suite 220
Los Altos, CA 94022
(415) 941-6565

Jack L. Melchor
President

Prior Positions

Founder, Chairman, Chief Executive Officer, Palo Alto Investment Co.
General Manager, Palo Alto Division, Hewlett-Packard
Co-founder, President, Hewlett-Packard Assoc.
Co-founder, President, Melabs, 1956–61
Sylvania Electric Products, 1953–56

Education

PhD, Physics, Notre Dame
BS, MS, Physics, University of North Carolina

Richard H. Frank

Prior Positions

Chairman of the Board, Sorcim Corp.
Founder, Chief Executive Officer, Sorcim Corp., 1979–83
Control Data Corp.

Gregory S. Young

Prior Positions

Corporate Finance Specialist, Salomon Bros. Inc.
Wells Fargo Bank, 1976–79

Education

BA, Economics, University of California at Berkeley
Stanford Graduate School of Business

Average Size of Investment	$350K–$500K
Size of Fund	$17M
Investment Criteria	Seed or first stage only
Portfolio Companies	Abekas Video Systems, Inc., Foster City, CA, Manufactures high-performance, low-cost digital video products for broadcasting and postproduction markets; Amlyn, Inc., San Jose, CA, Manufactures low-cost ultra-high-density 5¼" floppy disk storage devices for microcomputers; Anfield Systems, Inc., Penn Valley, CA, Designing a low-cost business management system for small, distribution-oriented businesses; AZ Technology, Inc., Palo Alto, CA, Produces a portable data projector for use in presenting CRT information on a large screen for group presentations; California Devices, Inc., San Jose, CA, Builds semicustom CMOS gate arrays and sells them on a worldwide basis; Control Video Corp., Campbell, CA, Manufactures video tape editing and control equipment; Direct, Inc., Santa Clara, CA, Manufactures computer terminals that offer advanced editing, display, and computation features; Dynabyte, Inc., Milpitas, CA, Manufacturer of single- and multiuser small-business computers sold through domestic and multinational distributors; FutureNet, Inc., Canoga Park, CA, Manufactures a low-cost schematic capture workstation; GraphOn Corp., Santa Clara, CA, Manufactures a lines of low-cost graphics terminals; Interactive Research Corp., Santa Clara, CA, Offers interactive training systems for a variety of computer applications; Interactive Technology, Inc., Portland, OR, Supplies standard software for the minicomputer marketplace; The Learning Co., Menlo Park, CA, Designs and produces interactive educational software for children ages 4 to 14, which operates on popular microcomputers; Megatest Corp., Santa Clara, CA, Provides sophisticated, cost-effective, high-volume production test equipment for semiconductor manufacturers and volume users; Newspaper Systems, Inc., Culver City, CA, Provides turnkey business management computer systems for small- and medium-size newspapers and magazines; Octagon Computer Systems, Inc., San Jose, CA, Developing a line of single- and multiuser microcomputers; Osborne Computer Corp., Hayward, CA, Manufactures low-cost, portable computer systems which are sold worldwide; Redwood Software, Inc., Santa Clara, CA, Provides manufacturing management software that operates on Tandem and Stratus computers; Santek, Inc., Milpitas, CA, Develops and manufactures thin-film thermal printing heads; Software Components Group,

Inc., Santa Clara, CA, Company licenses a real-time operating system in silicon for the Motorola 68000 microprocessor; Software Publishing Corp., Mountain View, CA, Develops and publishes software for popular microcomputers; Sorcim Corp., San Jose, CA, Develops and markets applications software for most popular microcomputers; Strobe, Inc., Mountain View, CA, Manufactures low-cost intelligent graphic plotters for use with all popular brands of microcomputers; Summit Information Systems Corp., Corvallis, OR, Provides turnkey business management systems for credit unions and other financial institutions; Systel, Inc., San Jose, CA, Manufactures low-cost word-processing attachment for electronic typewriters; Telesys, Inc., Fremont, CA, Designs and markets software and peripherals for the home computer market; 3COM Corp., Mountain View, CA, Develops and manufactures Ethernet-based communications hardware and software; Zitel Corp., San Jose, CA, Manufactures custom memory systems for OEM Manufacturers and volume end-users of computer equipment

MEMHARD INVESTMENT BANKERS, INC.
P.O. Box 617
Old Greenwich, CT 06870
(203) 637-5494

Richard C. Memhard
President

Directorships

Greenwich News, Inc., Weekly/local newspaper
Cape Pond Ice Co., Inc., Ice manufacturer
Crisafulli Pump Co., Inc., Pump manufacturer

Prior Positions

Senior Vice President and Director of Corporate Finance, G. H. Walker & Co., Inc., 1971–72
General Partner, Hornblower & Weeks—Hemphill, Noyes, 1959–68

Education

MBA, Golden Gate College, 1957
BA, Yale University, 1951

R. Scott Memhard
Vice President

Directorship

Cape Pond Ice Co., Ice manufacturer

Education

BA, Amherst College, 1978

Laura M. Fleming Memhard
Treasurer

Education

Peking Languages Institute, 1981
BA, Stanford University, 1980

Average Size of Investment	$500K
Size of Fund	$1M
Investment Criteria	Undisclosed
Portfolio Companies	Cape Pond Ice Co., Inc., Gloucester, MA, Ice manufacturer; Crisafulli Pump Co., Inc., Glendive, MT, Pump manufacturer; C. R. Fleming Associates, Wilton, CT, Residual construction

MEMORIAL DRIVE TRUST
Acorn Park
Cambridge, MA 02140
(617) 864-5770

Jean E. deValpine
Administrator and Chief Executive Officer

Directorships

Continental Cablevision, Inc.
Display Components, Inc.
Foster Medical Corp.
Helix Technology Corp.
North American Management
Realty Income Trust
Symbolics, Inc.
Terradex Corp.

Education

JD, Harvard Law School
BA, Harvard University, 1943

Jay V. Senerchia
Paul D. Shuwall
Schoor Berman

Average Size of Investment $1M
Size of Fund $300M
Investment Criteria Technology-based companies; will act as lead investor; start-ups
Portfolio Companies Undisclosed

MENLO VENTURES
3000 Sand Hill Road
Menlo Park, CA 94025
(415) 854-8540

H. DuBose Montgomery
General Partner

Directorships

Data Electronics, Inc.
International Microelectronic Products
Masstor Systems Corp.
Valid Logic Systems
Assyst Technologies
Via Visuals, Inc.
Code Smith Technology, Inc.
American Semiconductor Equipment Technologies

Prior Positions

Wang Laboratories, Inc.
Computer Signal Processors, Inc., 1972–73
Researcher, Bell Telephone Laboratories, 1969–71

Education

MBA, Harvard University
BS, MS, Massachusetts Institute of Technology

Ken E. Joy
General Partner

Directorships

Accountants Microsystems
Innovative Hearing Corporation
MMI Medical
Sanmina Corporation
Sensor Medics Corporation

Prior Positions

State Street Bank & Trust Co.
United States Navy, Supply officer

Education

MBA, Harvard University, Graduate School of Business Administration
BA, Economics, Amherst College

Richard P. Magnuson
General Partner

Directorships

Innovative Concepts, Inc., Stamping Technology Corp., IKOS Systems

Prior Positions

Tandem Computers, Inc.
Atari, Inc.
Wilson, Sonsini, Goodrich & Rosati

Education

JD, Stanford Law School
MBA, Stanford School of Business
AB, Economics, Stanford University

Douglas C. Carlisle
General Partner

Directorships

Enter Computer, Inc.
Silicon Design Labs, Inc.
Sunward Technologies
Lin Data Corporation

Prior Positions

General Motors Corporation
ROLM Corporation
Orrick, Herrington & Sutcliffe
Brobeck, Phleger, & Harrison

Education

JD, Stanford Law School
MBA, Stanford School of Business
BS, Electrical Engineering, University of California, Berkeley

Thomas H. Bredt
General Partner

Directorship

Astra Communications, Inc.

Prior Positions

Dataquest
Hewlett-Packard
Bell Laboratories

Education

PhD, Computer Science, Stanford University
Master's, Electrical Engineering, New York University
BS, Science Engineering, University of Michigan

Denise M. O'Leary
Associate

Prior Positions

Spectra-Physics, Inc.
Bechtel Investments

Education

MBA, Harvard University Graduate School of Business Administration
BS, Industrial Engineering, Stanford University

John W. Jarve
Associate

Prior Positions

Charles Stark Draper Laboratory
Harvard Medical School
Booz, Allen & Hamilton
Intel Corporation

Education

MBA, Stanford University Graduate School of Business
MS, BS, Electrical Engineering, Massachusetts Institute of Technology

Average Size of Investment	$1.5M
Size of Fund	$140M
Investment Criteria	Will act as lead investor in start-ups; technology-based and other diversified companies, also leveraged buy-outs
Portfolio Companies	Undisclosed

MERIDIAN CAPITAL CORP.
Blue Bell West
Suite 222
Blue Bell, PA 19422
(215) 278-8907

Knute C. Albrecht
President and Chief Executive Officer

Directorship

Meridian Capital Corp.
U.S. Airgas, Inc., Industrial gasses
Delaware Valley Venture Group
Meridian Commercial Credit Corp., Commercial finance

Education

MBA, Drexel University, 1967
BA, Finance, Temple University, 1964

Jay M. Ackerman

Average Size of Investment	$250K
Size of Fund	Undisclosed
Investment Criteria	Later-stage and leveraged buy-outs
Portfolio Companies	Undisclosed

MERIDIAN VENTURES
21 West Road
Towson, MD 21204
(301) 296-1000

Earl L. Linehan
Managing Partner

Directorships

Meridian Healthcare, Nursing homes
Hospital Group of America, Psychiatric hospitals
McCulloch Corp., Outdoor power equipment
Mill Creek Lumber, Building supply company
Meridian Properties, Real estate development

Prior Position

President, MSC Corp., 1974–82

Education

MBA, Harvard Business School, 1967
BSME, University of Notre Dame, 1962

Average Size of Investment	$500K
Size of Fund	$5M
Investment Criteria	Healthcare Co., start-up or existing; leveraged buy-out of manufacturing company
Portfolio Companies	Hospital Group of America, Virginia, Psychiatric hospitals; McCulloch Corp., Los Angeles, Outdoor power equipment

MERRILL LYNCH VENTURE CAPITAL
717 Fifth Avenue
New York, NY 10022
(212) 980-0410

Stephen J. Warner
George L. Sing
George Kokkinakis
R. Stephen McCormack

Average Size of Investment	$5M–$200K
Size of Fund	$60M
Investment Criteria	Technology-based companies of interest as well as start-ups; will act as lead investor; leveraged buy-outs considered
Portfolio Companies	Undisclosed

MERRILL, PICKARD, ANDERSON & EYRE
Two Palo Alto Square
Suite 425
Palo Alto, CA 94306
(415) 856-8880

Steven L. Merrill, General Partner
James C. Anderson, General Partner
Chris A. Eyre, General Partner
W. Jeffers Pickard, General Partner
Stephen E. Coit, General Partner
Andrew S. Rachleff, Associate

Average Size of Investment	$750K
Size of Fund	$90M
Investment Criteria	Technology-based companies and start-ups are of interest; will act as lead investor
Portfolio Companies	Undisclosed

MESBIC FINANCIAL CORP. OF DALLAS
Allied Bank Plaza
12655 N. Central Expressway
Suite 814
Dallas, TX 75243
(214) 991-1597

Donald R. Lawhorne
President

Prior Positions

President, Captronics, Inc.
Division Head, Brookhaven College

Education

MBA, Pepperdine University, 1976
BBA, Southern Methodist University, 1972

Thomas G. Gerron
Vice President and Controller

Education

CPA, State of Texas, 1964
BBA, University of Texas, 1961

DIRECTORY AND BIOGRAPHIES

Ira D. Harrison
Business Development Manager

Prior Positions

General Manager, Captronics
Regional District Distribution Manager, Frito-Lay, Inc.
Marketed Commodities Coordinator, 3M Company

Education

MBA, Management, University of Dallas, 1972
BA, St. Mary's University, 1968

Average Size of Investment	$100K
Size of Fund	$4M
Investment Criteria	Start-ups and second-round financings
Portfolio Companies	Advanced Image Systems, Inc., Dallas, TX, Ricoh & Panasonic copiers; Amistad Electronics, Dallas, TX, Printed circuit boards; BGE & C., Inc., Dallas, TX, Electronic and electro mechanical components; De La Torre Sheet Metal Manufacturing Co., Inc., Dallas, TX; First Tuesday Productions, Dallas, TX, Commercial video production company; H-R Industries, Inc., Dallas, TX, Printed circuit boards; Image Industries, Inc., Dallas, TX, Industrial coatings and silk screening; Robins Landscape, Inc., Dallas, TX, Landscaping, retaining walls, irrigation systems; CareTeam Management Services, Inc., Dallas, TX, Home health care; Civic Communications, Jackson, MS, TV station; KESS, Fort Worth, TX, Radio station; Ninfa's, Houston, TX, Restaurant chain; Sivakumar, Inc., Dallas, TX, Photographic supplies manufacturing; Star/Adair Insulation, Houston, TX, Insulation construction

MESBIC FINANCIAL CORP. OF HOUSTON
1801 Main Street
Suite 320
Houston, TX 77002
(713) 228-8321

Richard Rothfeld
President, Tulsa

Directorships

Energy Minerals, Inc.
First Development Corp.
Titan Rig Corp.

Education

BBA, Corporate Finance

$100K
Size of Fund	Undisclosed
Investment Criteria	Diversified areas of interest considered; will act as lead investor and leveraged buy-outs are of interest; location important
Portfolio Companies	Undisclosed

MESIROW VENTURE CAPITAL
350 North Clark Street
Chicago, IL 60610
(312) 670-6000

James C. Tyree
Executive Vice President

Directorships

Techtron Graphic Arts
Birdview Satellite
U. S. Robotics
Chicago South Shore & South Bend Railroad
Fender Musical Instruments

Education

MBA, Illinois State University
BS, Illinois State University

William P. Sutter, Jr.
Vice President

Directorships

The Chuckles Company
Now Products
Symacon

Prior Position

Corporate Finance, Smith Barney Harris Upham & Co.

Education

MBA, Stanford University
BA, Yale University

Michael Barrett

Average Size of Investment	$1M
Size of Fund	$75M
Investment Criteria	Diversified
Portfolio Companies	18 companies

METROPOLITAN CAPITAL CORP.
2550 Huntington Avenue
Alexandria, VA 22303
(703) 960-4698

S. W. Austin, Vice President/Treasurer

Average Size of Investment	$100K
Size of Fund	Undisclosed
Investment Criteria	Interested in technology-based and manufacturing companies; geographical preference is Washington, DC, metro area; no start-ups
Portfolio Companies	Undisclosed

METROPOLITAN VENTURE CO., INC.
5757 Wilshire Boulevard
Suite 670
Los Angeles, CA 90036
(213) 938-3488

Esther Rose Lowy
President

Directorships

DICO National, Insurance company
Pacific States Casualty, Insurance company
RELCO Industries, Real estate development
Atlas Capital, Mortgage banking

Education

MBA, University of California at Los Angeles, 1984
PhD, New York University, 1973
MS, New York University, 1971
BS, Brooklyn College, 1969

Rudloph J. Lowy
Chairman of the Board

Directorships

DICO National, Insurance company
Pacific States Casualty Co., Insurance company
RELCO Industries, Real estate development
Atlas Capital City Corp., Mortgage banking

Prior Position

President, Lesny Development

Education

MBA, University of California at Los Angeles, 1972
BS, University of California at Los Angeles, 1969

Average Size of Investment	$100K
Size of Fund	$2M
Investment Criteria	Real estate, financial services, leveraged buy-outs
Portfolio Companies	Undisclosed

MIAMI VALLEY CAPITAL, INC.
131 North Ludlow Street
Suite 315
Dayton, OH 45402
(513) 222-7222

Everett F. Telljohann
President

Directorships

Benchmark Communities, Inc., Modular homes
Cad Cam, Inc., CAD/CAM services and equipment
Lion Apparel, Inc., Industrial uniforms
Venture Manufacturing, Inc., Couplers and jacks
Measuray Corp., X-ray measurement gages
Paperplains, Inc., Custom-designed gift wrap
Advanced Assembly Automation, Inc., Automated assembly equipment
Supafine Products, Inc., Abrasive media
The Ohio Art Company (ASE)

DIRECTORY AND BIOGRAPHIES

Prior Positions

Vice President, Finance, and Treasurer, Copeland Corp.
Vice President, Finance, and Treasurer, Philips Industries, Inc.

Education

BBA, University of Cincinnati, 1956

W. Walker Lewis, Jr.
Chairman of the Board

Directorships

Vulcan Tool Company
Lion Uniform, Inc.
Queen City Leasing Corp., Car leasing
Gem City Leasing, Inc.
Supafine Products, Inc.

Prior Positions

General Counsel, The Mead Corp., 1958–75
Attorney, Smith & Schnacke, 1945–75
Chairman of the Board, Master Consolidated, Inc., 1950–67
Secretary, The Mead Corp., 1952–64

Education

JD, Harvard University, 1939
AB, Dartmouth College, 1936

Average Size of Investment	$150K
Size of Fund	$2.7M
Investment Criteria	Manufacturing or marketing companies with proprietary products
Portfolio Companies	Advanced Assembly, Automation, Inc., Dayton, OH, Automated assembly equipment; Ameripak, Inc., Middletown, OH, Vacuum forming and packaging; Burjon Steel Service, Inc., Springboro, OH, Steel warehouse and service center; Deraspan Corp., Dayton, OH, Panels for refrigerated buildings; Magnum Development, Englewood, OH, Breast health clinics; Magnum Electronics, Inc., Englewood, OH, Cancer detection bra; Measuray Corp., Dayton, OH, X-ray measurement gages; Paperplains, Inc., Cincinnati, OH, Custom-designed giftwrap; QMI Corp., Centerville, OH, Photographic developing, printing, and enlarging equipment; Supafine Products, Inc., Xenia, OH, Abrasive media for deburring and polishing

MICHIGAN CAPITAL AND SERVICE, INC.
500 First National Building
201 South Main Street
Ann Arbor, MI 48104
(313) 663-0702

Joseph F. Conway
President

Directorships

Emkay, Inc., Computer-based program of controlling fleet costs by reporting and identifying the exceptions in a particular fleet
Current Networks, Intraoffice communications system
Irwin Magnetic, Designs, manufactures, and sells small tape drives for Winchester disk backup market
Timberjack Holding Inc.

Prior Positions

Principal Consultant, First Ann Arbor Corp.
Director of Marketing, Bendix Systems Division

Education

BSEEE, Newark College of Engineering, 1941

Mary L. Campbell
Vice President/Treasurer/Director

Directorships

PC Technologies Inc.
Boris Systems Inc.

Prior Positions

Credit Officer, National Bank of Detroit
Real Estate Lending and Management, Percy Wilson Mortgages & Finance Corp.

Education

MBA, University of Michigan, 1979
MA, Fairfield (CT) University, 1972
BA, University of Michigan, 1967

Carlene D. Dettleff
Assistant Secretary/Assistant Treasurer/Administrative Manager

Prior Positions

Administrative Coordinator, Michigan Savings & Loan Association
Administrative Manager, Health Systems Group
Office Coordinator, Chi Systems, Inc.

Philip G. Waldrop
Investment Associate

Prior Positions

Assistant Vice President, Commercial Loans, NBD Bancorp, Inc.
Credit Analyst, NBD Bancorp, Inc.
Regional Planner, Great Lakes Basin Commission

Education

MBA, University of Michigan, 1982
MRP (Regional Planning), University of Michigan, 1976
AB, University of Michigan, 1974

Average Size of Investment	$750K
Size of Fund	$29M
Investment Criteria	High tech, computer related, manufacturing, communications, automation; start-up, first, second, and third stage and leveraged buy-outs; equity capital or subordinated debt with equity features; prefer participations with other venture capital firms; greater Midwest or nationwide
Portfolio Companies	Advanced Aluminum Products, Inc., Hammond, IN, Aluminum alloy sheets; Applied Spectrum Tech., Inc., Minneapolis, MN, Data communications over existing telephone lines; Arete Systems Corp., San Jose, CA, High-performance computers capable of intensive input/output utilization; Autographix, Inc., Boston, MA, Computerized color slide production service; Current Networks, Mountain View, CA, Message communication via AC power lines; Emkay, Inc., Chicago, IL, Auto fleet leasing and management services; Epyx, Inc., Sunnyvale, CA, Home computer entertainment and educational software; Falco Data Products, Inc., Sunnyvale, CA, Computer terminals; Four Star Corp., Troy, MI, Fabricated parts for auto OEM and aftermarkets; Houston Oil Fields Co., Houston, TX, Oil and gas exploration, development and production; IBIS Systems, Inc., Westlake, CA, 14" high-capacity disk drives; Infomed Corp., Englewood, CO, Remote diagnoses of pulmonary test data; Internet Systems, Inc., Sunrise, FL, LAN applications software; Irwin Magnetic Systems, Inc., Ann Arbor, MI, High-density cartridge magnetic tape system; Kronos Inc., Waltham, MA, Electronic time clocks; ALC Comm. Corp., Birmingham, MI, Long-distance telephone communications; Machine Intelligence Corp., Sunnyvale, CA, Factory vision automation systems; Mager Scientific, Inc., Dexter, MI, Nationwide distribution of metallographic equipment and supplies; Margaux Controls, Inc., San Jose, CA, Energy management control systems; Maxtor Corp., San Jose, CA, High-capacity Winchester disk drives; Medical Resources, Inc., Englewood Cliffs, NJ, Diagnostic ambulatory care centers; Mosaic Systems, Inc., Troy, MI, Developing advanced computer chips; Mountain Computer, Inc., Scotts Valley, CA, Diskette copiers, certifiers, storage devices; NASTEC Corp., Southfield, MI, Software productivity workstations; PC Technologies, Inc., Ann Arbor, MI, IBM PC multiuser expansion product; Peak Systems, Inc., Fremont, CA, Develops, manufactures, and markets capital equipment for semiconductor industry; Prab Robots, Inc., Kalamazoo, MI, Manufactures industrial robots (OTC); Printek, Inc., Benton Harbor, MI, Dot matrix computer printer; Boris Systems, Inc., Lansing, MI, Computerized real estate systems; SensorMedics Corp., Anaheim, CA, Noninvasive physiological measurement equipment; Sentinel Computer Corp., Cincinnati, OH, Computer equipment software for small distributors; Syntellect Inc., Phoenix, AZ, Hardware/software automation of telephone reception, operator, and remote data entry; Systeme Corp., Orlando, FL, Bank and S & L computer systems; Telematics Intl., Ft. Lauderdale, FL, High-speed data communications processors; Telenova, Inc., Los Gatos, CA, Fully digital voice and data telecommunications sytems; Timberjack Holding Inc., Woodstock, Ontario, Canada, Logging equipment; Universal Semiconductor Inc., San Jose, CA, Manufactures gate array computer chips

MICHIGAN INVESTMENT FUND L.P.
2000 Hogback Road
Suite 2
Ann Arbor, MI 48105
(313) 971-3100

350 Second Street
Suite 7
Los Altos, CA 94022
(415) 941-2392

365 South Street
Morristown, NJ 07960
(201) 285-5533

Ian R. N. Bund
Managing General Partner, MI, MBW Venture Partners Limited Partnership
President and Director, MI, Michigan Investment Fund L.P.
President and Director, MI, Doan Resources Limited Partnership

Directorships

Attache Software, Inc., Accounting software
LifeScan, Inc., Blood glucose monitoring device
Innovative Hearing Corp., Hearing enhancement for mild hearing loss
Sensormedics, Physiological, noninvasive measurement equipment monitoring head, heart and lung functions
Sequoia Turner Corp., Clinical hematology analyzers

Prior Positions

President, Sea Life, Inc.
Associate, Morgan Stanley & Co.
Senior Accountant, Price Waterhouse & Co.

Education

MBA, Harvard, 1968
BEc, University of Sydney, 1964

James R. Weersing
Managing General Partner, CA
MBW Venture Partners Limited Partnership
Senior Vice President and Director, CA
Michigan Investment Fund, L.P.

Directorships

Amber Systems, Software company
Innovative Hearing Corp., Hearing-device manufacturer
LifeScan, Inc., Blood glucose monitoring system manufacturer
Rigi Systems, Inc., Care products for elderly
Sequoia Turner Corp., Clinical products manufacturer
SensorMedics Corp., Physiological monitoring device manufacturer

Prior Positions

President, JRW Technology, Inc., 1980–present
President, Royco Instruments, 1967–79

Education

MBA, Stanford, 1962
BS, Mechanical Engineering, Stanford, 1960

Philip E. McCarthy
Managing General Partner, NJ
MBW Venture Partners Limited Partnership
Senior Vice President, Director, NJ
Michigan Investment Fund, L.P.
Senior Vice President, Director, NJ
Doan Resources Limited Partnership

Directorship

Oximetrix Corp., Hospital supplies

Prior Position

Vice President, INCO Limited

Education

JD, Law, Cornell, 1965
BS, Cornell, 1960

Richard M. Goff
Robert J. Harrington
Dr. Thomas Rice

Average Size of Investment	$500K
Size of Fund	$32.3M
Investment Criteria	Start-up; early stage; buy-outs
Portfolio Companies	Undisclosed

MICHIGAN TECH CAPITAL CORP.
1414 College Avenue
Houghton, MI 49931
(906) 487-2643

Edward J. Koepel
Clark L. Pellegrini

Average Size of Investment	$100K
Size of Fund	$600K
Investment Criteria	Technology-based companies are of interest along with other diversified areas; geographic location is important
Portfolio Companies	Undisclosed

MICROTECHNOLOGY INVESTMENTS, LTD.
46 Red Birch Court
Danville, CA 94526
(415) 838-9319

3400 Comserv Drive
Eagan, MN 55122
(612) 681-7580

M. M. Stuckey
Chairman, CA

Directorship

M.S.L., Chairman, Microsoftware development and marketing company

Prior Position

President, Computer Peripherals, Inc.

Education

BS, Southern Methodist University, 1960

Average Size of Investment	$250K
Size of Fund	Confidential
Investment Criteria	Microsoftware-related products
Portfolio Companies	Undisclosed

MIDDLEWEST VENTURES
20 North Meridian Street
Indianapolis, IN 46204
(317) 631-8822

Charles L. Rees
Managing General Partner

Directorships

Delta Data Systems Corp.
Hurco Manufacturing Co., Inc.
Profitwatch, Inc.

Prior Positions

Investment Manager/Director, Allstate Insurance Co., 1978–84
Chief Executive Officer, Greater Springfield Investment Co. and Pioneer Valley Business Development Center, 1974–78
Stockbroker, Edelstein, Campbell, & Co., 1971–74
Founder, Positron, 1970–71
Stockbroker, Reynolds and Co., 1967–70

Education

BA. Lehigh University, 1966

Joseph H. Broecker
General Partner

Directorship

Ash Medical, Inc.

Prior Positions

President/Chief Executive Officer, Seragen Diagnostics, Inc.; Vice President/Director, Seragen, Inc., 1983–85
Founder, Technology Statagies, Ltd., 1982
President, Bio-Dynamics Home Healthcare, Inc./Environmental Systems Division, 1976–82
Directors/Vice President, Bio-Dynamics, Inc., 1973–76
Ernst & Ernst, 1967–73

Education

Indiana University Executive Program, 1981
MS, Purdue University, 1972
BBA, University of Notre Dame, 1967

Thomas A. Hiatt
General Partner

Directorship

Vaser, Inc.

Prior Positions

President/Director, Sungene Technologies Corp., 1982–84
Director of Marketing, International Plant Research Institute, 1981
Manager, Business Planning/Asst. to the Vice President, Elanco Products Co., 1976–81
Assistant to the Representative, The Ford Foundation, Pakistan, 1972–75

Education

MSc, Alfred P. Sloan School of Management, MIT, 1972
BA, Wabash College, 1970

Average Size of Investment	$500–750K
Size of Investment	Undisclosed
Investment Criteria	Product or service must be unique, enjoy lead time on competitors; medical products and instrumentation, information management, data communications, artificial intelligence, industrial automation, and biotechnology; must be able to generate $30M+ in five years; strong management team
Portfolio Companies	Hurco Companies, Indianapolis, IN, Computer controls for machine tools; Vaser, Inc., Indianapolis, IN, Laser angioplasty; Profitwatch, Fort Wayne, IN, Software for food service industry; Stewart & Lloyd, Indianapolis, IN, Microcomputer systems distribution

MIDLAND BANK EQUITY GROUP
47 Cannon Street
London EC4M 5SQ
England
01-638-8861

J. R. Beevor, F.C.A.
Managing Director

Prior Positions

Development and Venture Capital, Charterhouse Developments
Development and Venture Capital, The Spey Group
Finance Director, Conran Group
Accountant, Robson Rhodes

Education

F.C.A.

David Hutchings
Marketing Director

Prior Positions

Investors in Industry
Research physicist, Various companies

Education

MBA, Cranfield Business School
BA, (Honors)

Roger Heath
Executive Director

Prior Positions

Draymont Securities, Ltd., Samuel Montagu Co.
Special Projects Manager, Telecommunications Group, Plessey

Education

MBA, Marketing and Finance, Manchester University
BSc

Hugh de Quervain
Exeuctive Director

Prior Positions

Chief Executive, Company group with property, construction interests
Managing Director, Major steel stockholding group
Marketing Director, a GKN company
Head, Research & Development Group, Comino-Dexion International Ltd.
Consultant Engineer, Various companies

Education

BSc (English); PhD; CEng; MICE; MIStructE; FIMH

B. C. J. Warnes, F.C.A.
Managing Director
(01) 638-8861 ext. 1599

Prior Positions

Deputy Divisional Director, National Enterprise Board
Senior Executive, Spey Investments Ltd.
Executive, Commonwealth Development Corp., 1964–72
New Business Development, Chartered Accountant, Peat Marwick Mitchell
Temporary Assistant Principal, Foreign Office, Southeast Asia Department

Education

MA (honors), Natural Sciences (Physics), St. Peters College, Oxford, 1959

Ian C. Taylor
Executive Director

Prior Positions

Managing Director, Corruplast Ltd.
Managing Director, British Rayophane (Overseas) Ltd.

Education

MA (honors), Cambridge University, 1961
Diploma, Sorbonne, Paris, 1957

Average Size of Investment	£350,000
Size of Fund	Unlimited
Investment Criteria	Predominantly equity investors with loan finance only as part of a package; investments made between £20,000/£2,000,000 for development situations, shareholders' needs, and management buy-outs
Portfolio Companies	£54M invested in more than 150 companies, all investments to date are U.K. domiciled

MID-SOUTHERN FINANCIAL CORP.
One Perimeter Way, N.W.
Suite 501
P.O. Box 723355
Atlanta, GA 30339
(404) 952-2500

George H. Naterman
President

Directorships

Rilco Development Corp., Real estate development
New South Enterprises, Investments
Students' Financial Services, Educational consulting

Prior Positions

President, Master Mortgage Corp.
President, Computer Credit Systems

Education

MBA, Wharton School, University of Pennsylvania, 1955
BA, University of Pennsylvania, 1953

Average Size of Investment	$300K
Size of Fund	Undisclosed
Investment Criteria	We act as intermediaries for small and middle-size firms
Portfolio Companies	Undisclosed

MILLER & LAHAYE
606 Wilshire Boulevard
Suite 602
Santa Monica, CA 90401
(213) 458-1441

20885 Stevens Creek Boulevard
Cupertino, CA 95014
(408) 996-7212

Gene Miller
Partner, Santa Monica

Directorships

Formaster Corp.
Axonics
Microvertics
Kurzweil Music Systems
Lexocorp

Prior Position

Principal, Xerox Development Corp.

Education

MBA, Harvard University, 1969
JD, New York University, 1966
BS, New York University, 1963

Frank LaHaye
Partner, Cupertino

Directorships

Metheus
Quarterdeck Office Systems
Fisher Imaging
Parkview Centers

Prior Position

Principal, Xerox Development Corp.

Education

BS, Stanford University, 1951

DIRECTORY AND BIOGRAPHIES 321

John C. Spence
Limited Partner, Santa Monica

Directorships
Catheter Technology Corp., Medical disposable products
Raytel Systems Corp., Medical image management systems

Prior Position
Group Executive, Teledyne, Inc.

Education
BS, Business Administration, Ohio State University, 1952

Average Size of Investment	$750
Size of Fund	$44M
Investment Criteria	Undisclosed
Portfolio Companies	Undisclosed

MINNESOTA SEED CAPITAL, INC.
1660 South Highway 100
Suite 146
Minneapolis, MN 55416-1519
(612) 545-5684

Richard C. Gottier
President, Chief Executive Officer, and General Partner

Directorships
Applied Spectrum Technologies, Inc., Spread spectrum technology
Magnetic Data, Inc., Refurbishment and recertification of magnetic disk media
Polymer Composites, Inc., Advanced polymer composite material

Prior Positions
Senior Vice President, Control Data Corp.
General Manager, Magnavox Co.

Education
BS, Ohio State University

Thomas M. Neitge
Vice President and Limited Partner

Directorships
Applied Vision Systems, Inc., Automated optical inspection equipment
BlueLine Software, Inc., IBM mainframe software
Mizar, Inc., Board level computers and peripherals

Prior Positions
President, First Midwest Capital Corp.
Vice President, Eagle Ventures, Inc.

Education
JD, William Mitchell College of Law, 1968
BS, Iowa State University

Dr. Thomas K. Rice
Vice President

Directorships
Lemna Corp., Acquaculture for waste water treatment and animal feed

Prior Positions
Technology Assessment Coordinator, 3M Company

Education
PhD, University of Oklahoma, 1971

Average Size of Investment	$50K–$250K
Size of Fund	$12M+
Investment Criteria	New start-up entities involved in the creation of or creative use of new technologies or technical processes that provide potential for growth and a significant return; must be located in or agree to locate in Minnesota
Portfolio Companies	Undisclosed

MINORITY BROADCAST INVESTMENT CORP.
1220 19th St., N.W.
Suite 501
Washington, DC 20036
(202) 293-1166

Larry Edler
President

Directorship

American Association of MESBICs

Prior Positions

Venture Capital Vice President, Fulcrum Venture Capital, 1978–82
Senior Accountant, Arthur Anderson & Co., 1974–78

Education

MBA, Stanford University, 1981
BBA, Howard University, 1975

Minta D. Branham
Walter L. Threadgill
President/Chief Executive Officer
1820 Jefferson Place, N.W.
First Floor
Washington, D.C. 20036

Prior Positions

Vice President, Storer Communications, Inc., 1982–85
President, Minority Broadcast Invest. Corp., 1979–81

Education

MBA, Long Island University
MA, Antioch School of Law
BBA, Baruch College (CCNY)

Average Size of Investment	
Size of Fund	$3.2M
Investment Criteria	Communications: radio, TV, cellular radio, MDS, etc.; start-ups, acquisitions and working capital financings
Portfolio Companies	BENI, Philadelphia, PA, Radio and TV; ETTN, Houston, TX, TV; ITS, Denver, CO, Cable distribution; Marr Broadcasting, Houston, TX, Radio; RTC Broadcasting, Palm Springs, CA, Radio; Sanders Communications, Washington, DC, Radio

MINORITY EQUITY CAPITAL CO., INC.
275 Madison Avenue
New York, NY 10016
(212) 686-9710

Donald F. Greene
Clarence W. Arrington

Average Size of Investment	$300K
Size of Fund	$5M
Investment Criteria	Diversified company preferences
Portfolio Companies	Undisclosed

ML VENTURE PARTNERS I, L.P.
717 Fifth Avenue
New York, NY 10020
(212) 980-0410

George Kokkinakis
Partner and Chairman

Directorships

Cygnet Technologies, Inc., Voice data communication systems for personal computers
Qubix Graphic Systems, Inc., Electronic publishing workstations
ImagiTex, Inc., Image scanners and processors
Data Recording Systems, Inc., Electrostatic laser printers

Prior Positions

Partner, Advanced Technology Ventures, 1979–81
Venture Capital Advisor, Exxon Enterprises, Inc., 1971–79
Senior Consultant, Peat, Marwick, Mitchell & Co., 1967–71

Education

MBA, Xavier University, 1963
Aeronautical Engineer, University of Cincinnati, 1960

R. Stephen McCormack
Vice President
(212) 980-0420

Directorships

Optigraphics Corp., Automatic graphics data capture and processing systems
Bytel Corp., Software productivity tools

Prior Positions

Investment Officer, The Bank of New York
Product Manager, Interactive Data Corp.
Senior Investment Analyst, Massachusetts Technology Development Corp.

Education

MBA, University of Michigan, 1976
AB, Dartmouth, 1974

George L. Sing
Partner, Vice President
(212) 980-0428

Directorships

Charlton Associates, Rigid media
Inference Corp., Artificial intelligence
Carcinex, Monoclonal antibodies

Prior Position

General Partner, Advanced Technology Ventures

Education

MBA, Harvard Business School, 1976
BE, Stevens Institute of Technology, 1971

Stephen J. Warner
President

Directorships

United AgriSeeds, Inc., Agribusiness
Visidata Corp., Data terminals

Prior Positions

Managing Director, Merrill Lynch Capital Markets
Consultant, Arthur D. Little, Inc.
Associate, Laird Systems, Inc.

Education

LLB, Blackstone School of Law, 1967
MBA, Wharton School, University of Pennsylvania, 1966
BS, Massachusetts Institute of Technology, 1962

Robert Finzi
Associate
(212) 980-0438

Prior Positions

Associate, Menlo Ventures
Manager, Management Information Consulting
Division, Arthur Anderson & Co.

Education

MBA, Harvard Business School, 1983
MS, Industrial Engineering, Lehigh, 1976
BS, Industrial Engineering, Lehigh, 1975

Average Size of Investment	$1M
Size of Fund	$60M
Investment Criteria	Management team, market potential, and innovative/proprietary technology
Portfolio Companies	Behaviortech, Inc., Lawrence, KS, Artificial Intelligence training/learning systems for microcomputers; Bytel Corp., Berkeley, CA, Software for COBOL and DBase III software languages; California Devices, San Jose, CA, Channelless CMOS Gate Arrays; Data Technology Corp., Santa Clara, CA, Peripheral Controllers and flexible cartridge drives; Imagitex, Inc., Nashua, NH, Image Scanners and processors; Itran Corp., Manchester, NH, Computer visions systems; Network Equipment Technologies, Menlo Park, CA, Telecommunications for high-speed digital networks; Silicon Design Labs, Liberty Corner, NJ, Silicon compiler software for CAE industry; The Systems Center, Inc., Irving, TX, Data transfer of software between mainframes; Twyford Plants Laboratories, Santa Paula, CA, Plant technology industry; Viewlogic Systems, Inc., Marlboro, MA, Integrated CAE/CAD software systems; American Cimpflex Corp., Pittsburgh, PA, Industrial robots; Inter-Diagnostics, Burlingame, CA, Monoclonal antibody based diagnostic reagents; Charlton Associates, Inc., Irvine, CA, Rigid disk media; Contemporary Communications Corp., Telecommunications; Cygnet Technologies, Inc., Sunnyvale, CA; Voice/data communications systems for personal computers; Dallas Semiconductor Corp., Dallas, TX, Modifiable CMOS-integrated circuits; Data Recording Systems, Inc., Electrostatic laser printers; Higher Order Software, Inc., Computer software development tools; ImagiTex, Inc., Nashua, NH, Image scanners and processors; Inference Corp., Los Angeles, CA, Artificial intelligence software and expert systems; Optigraphics Corp., San Diego, CA, CAD/CAM digitizing systems; Private Satellite Network, Inc., New York, NY, Satellite-based video networks; Qubix Graphic Systems, Inc., Electronic publishing workstations; Signode Industries, Inc.,

Strapping materials and systems; United AgriSeeds, Inc., Illinois, Seed distribution and agricultural genetics research; Valid Logic Systems Inc., San Jose, CA, Computer-aided engineering systems

MONMOUTH CAPITAL CORP.
P.O. Box 335
Eatontown, NJ 07724
(201) 542-4927

Eugene W. Landy
President and Director

Directorships

United Mobile Homes, Inc.
Monmouth Real Estate Investment Trust
Attorney at Law, Eugene W. Landy, P.C.

Education

LLB, Yale Law School, 1958
BS, United States Merchant Marine Academy, 1955

Ralph B. Patterson
Executive Vice President
Chief Operational Officer

Education

BS, Fairleigh Dickinson University, 1971

Ernest V. Bencivenga

Average Size of Investment	$250K
Size of Fund	$10M
Investment Criteria	Undisclosed
Portfolio Companies	Undisclosed

MONTGOMERY SECURITIES
235 Montgomery Street
San Francisco, CA 94104
(415) 989-2050

Thomas W. Weisel
Allan L. Stein
Robert S. Washburn
Robert W. Greer

Average Size of Investment	$500K
Size of Fund	$15M
Investment Criteria	Technology-based companies are of interest; start-ups are welcome; will act as lead investor
Portfolio Companies	Undisclosed

MORAMERICA CAPITAL CORP.
800 American Building
Cedar Rapids, IA 52401
(319) 363-8249

Commerce Tower
911 Main St.
Suite 2724
Kansas City, MO 64105
(816) 842-0114

600 E. Mason St.
Milwaukee, WI, 53202
(414) 276-3839

Donald E. Flynn, IA
David R. Schroder, IA
Kevin F. Mullane, MO
Steven J. Massey, WI

Average Size of Investment	$500K
Size of Fund	$22M
Investment Criteria	Manufacturing, technology-based, and other diversified areas are of interest; start-ups considered; will act as lead investor
Portfolio Companies	Undisclosed

MORGAN, HOLLAND VENTURES CORP.
One Liberty Square
Boston, MA 02109
(617) 423-1765

DIRECTORY AND BIOGRAPHIES

James F. Morgan
Chairman

Directorships

ADRA Systems, Inc., CAD workstation systems
Champion Software Corp., Accounting software for microcomputers
Xylogics, Intelligent controllers for computer data storage peripherals

Prior Positions

Senior Vice President, American Research and Development
Lecturer, Faculty Member, Harvard Graduate School of Business Administration

Education

MBA, Harvard University, 1964
B. Mgmt. E., Rensselaer Polytechnic Institute, 1958

Daniel J. Holland
President

Directorships

ImagiTex Inc., Image processing
Medplus, Inc., Immediate-care clinics
Sphere Technology, Inc., Voice recognition
Wolfdata Inc., Data communications

Prior Positions

President, Massachusetts Capital Resource Co.
Vice President, American Research & Development Corp.
Vice President, First Chicago Corp.
Industrial Liaison, Massachusetts Institute of Technology

Education

MBA, Harvard Business School, 1962
BS, Massachusetts Institute of Technology, 1958

Edwin M. Kania, Jr.
Associate

Prior Positions

Investment Officer, First Capital Corp. of Boston, 1983–85
General Manager, J. Cunningham, Inc., 1978–80

Education

MBA, Harvard Business School, 1982
AB, Dartmouth College, 1979

Jay A. Delahanty
Vice President

Directorships

CTiData Corp., IBM 3274–compatible terminal controllers
Axiom Technology Corp., Automatic test equipment for electronic components and printed circuit boards
Netlink Technology, Inc., IBM SNA–compatible communication gateways

Prior Positions

American Research & Development
Arthur D. Little, Inc.

Education

MBA, Stanford University, 1976
BS, MS, Massachusetts Institute for Technology, 1971

Robert L. Rosbe, Jr.
Vice President
(617) 423-1712

Directorship

TSC Corp., Consulting engineering

Prior Positions

Vice President, Sippican Corp.
Vice President, KeydataCorp.
Vice President, DPD Division, Itel Corp.
McKinsey & Co.
Arthur Andersen & Co.

Education

MIA, Yale University, 1965
BS, Northwestern University, 1963

Average Size of Investment	$500K–$2.5M
Size of Fund	$58.5M
Investment Criteria	None

Portfolio Companies   ADRA Systems, Inc., Lowell, MA, CAD workstations; Axiom Technology Corp., Newton, MA, Automatic test equipment for electronic components and printed circuit boards; Champion Software Corp., Golden, CO, Accounting software for microcomputers; CTiDATA Corp., Raleigh, NC, IBM 3274-compatible terminal controllers; ImagiTex Inc., Nasua, NH, High-speed, high-resolution image scanners; Intech, Inc., Cambridge, MA, CAD for EDP systems analysis and development; Medplus, Inc., Dallas, TX, Freestanding, immediate-care medical clinics; Multiflow Computer, Inc., Branford, CT, High-performance, parallel processing computer systems; Netlink Technology, Inc., Raleigh, NC, IBM SNA-compatible communication gateways; Sphere Technology, Inc., Providence, RI, Speech recognition systems; Système Corp., Orlando, FL, Turnkey computer systems for the thrift and commercial banking industries; Visic, Inc., San Jose, CA, High-performance, high-density CMOS HRAM semiconductors; Wolfdata Inc., Chelmsford, MA, Communication interface boards for microcomputers and terminals; Xylogics, Inc., Burlington, MA, Intelligent controllers for computer data storage peripherals

MORGAN STANLEY & CO., INC.
1633 Broadway
New York, NY 10019
(212) 974-4000

Robert Walkingshaw

Average Size of Investment	$500K
Size of Fund	Undisclosed
Investment Criteria	Diversified areas of interest; start-ups are welcome; leveraged buy-outs considered also (fees)
Portfolio Companies	Undisclosed

MORGENTHALER VENTURES
700 National City Bank Building
Cleveland, OH 44114
(216) 621-3070

David T. Morgenthaler
Robert D. Pavey
Paul S. Brentlinger
Robert C. Bellas, Jr.

Average Size of Investment	$1M
Size of Fund	$100M
Investment Criteria	Technology-based companies; start-ups welcome; will act as lead investor
Portfolio Companies	Undisclosed

MOTOR ENTERPRISES
3044 West Grand Boulevard
13-152 GM Building
Detroit, MI 48202
(313) 556-4273

James Kobus

Average Size of Investment	$100K
Size of Fund	$5M
Investment Criteria	Diversified areas of interest including manufacturing; geographic proximity of importance
Portfolio Companies	Undisclosed

MSI CAPITAL CORP.
People Bank Building
6510 Abrams Road
Suite 650
Dallas, TX 75231
(214) 341-1553

Nick Stanfield
President

Directorships

Able Enterprises, Inc., Van windows
Near Space Communications, Telephone switching equipment
Palindromics Systems, Software company
Kirby Mortgage Company, Mortgage company

Prior Positions

Chairman of the Board, Metal Services, Inc.
Vice President, Eppler, Guerin & Turner
Vice President, Rotan Mosle, Inc.

Education

BBA, North Texas State University, 1963

DIRECTORY AND BIOGRAPHIES

Average Size of Investment	$50K–$500K
Size of Fund	$14M and $1M
Investment Criteria	Texas-based, small fund will do start-ups but the large fund looks for management to be in place, developed product and benchmark sales
Portfolio Companies	Able Enterprises, Inc., Ennis, TX, Van windows; DiFlo, International, Houston, TX, Fuel monitoring; Key Concepts, Inc., Houston, TX, Key boards; Near Space Communication, Dallas, TX, Telephone switching equipment; New England Monthly, Haydenville, MA, Monthly magazine

MULTI-PURPOSE CAPITAL INVESTMENT CO.
31 South Broadway
Yonkers, NY 10701
(914) 963-2733

Eli B. Fine

Average Size of Investment	$400K
Size of Fund	$6M
Investment Criteria	Diversified areas of interest; start-ups are encouraged; will act as lead investor; geographic locale important
Portfolio Companies	Undisclosed

MVENTURE CORP.
P.O. Box 662090
Dallas, TX 75266-2090
(214) 741-1469

Joseph B. Longino, Jr.
Chief Operating Officer

Directorships

Ennis Asphalt Co.
Hicks Communications, Inc.
Maindata, Inc.

Prior Position

Executive Vice President, MVenture Corp.

Education

MBA, Finance, College of William and Mary
BBA, University of Texas at Austin

J. Wayne Gaylord
Executive Vice President
(214) 698-6573

Directorship

MVenture Corp.
Texas Wholesale Grocery, Inc.

Prior Position

Vice President, Mercantile National Bank at Dallas, 1959–79

Education

Graduate, Southwestern Graduate School of Banking, Southern Methodist University, 1967
BA, Wheaton College, 1955

Michael D. Brown
Vice President
(214) 698-1256

Prior Position

Investment Officer, MVenture
Banking Officer, MBank Dallas, N.A.

Education

MBA, University of Texas at Austin, 1982
BBA, University of Georgia, 1980

Thomas F. Bartlett
Investment Officer
(214) 698-1253

Prior Position

Investment Associate, MVenture

Education

BBA, Baylor University, 1983

Erin A. Tierney
Investment Officer

Prior Positions
Investment Associate, MVenture
Credit Analyst, MBank Dallas
Assistant Marketing Representative, IBM
Owner, Micrographics, Inc.

Education
BBA, University of Texas at Austin, 1984

Average Size of Investment	$1M
Size of Fund	$60M
Investment Criteria	Diversified areas of interest including manufacturing; leveraged buy-outs are also of interest; geographic locale important
Portfolio Companies	Undisclosed

MYRIAD CAPITAL, INC.
113 E. Savarona Way
Carson, CA 90746
(213) 327-7539

Chuang-I Lin
President

Directorships
General Bank, Bank
Western Underwriters Insurance Co., Insurance company

Prior Position
MTS, TRW, 1972–75

Education
PhD, Duquesne University, 1970

Average Size of Investment	$300K
Size of Fund	$6M
Investment Criteria	(1) Minority; (2) small business (after-tax income smaller than $2M); (3) potential ROI greater than or equal to 3.0 for next 5 years
Portfolio Companies	Chen-Tech Industries, Inc., Irvin, CA, Forging of special alloys; General Bank, Los Angeles, CA, Bank; Microscience International Corp., Mountain View, CA, Computer component manufacturing; Simon, Li & Associates, Fort Collins, CO, Engineering consulting; Western Underwriter Insurance Co., Huntington Beach, CA, Insurance company

NARRAGANSETT CAPITAL CORP.
40 Westminster Street
Providence, RI 02903
(401) 751-1000

Arthur D. Little
Chairman of the Board and Chief Executive Officer

Directorships
Bevis Industries, Inc., Stainless-steel pressure tubing for heat exchangers and industrial pumps and blowers
Burro Crane, Inc., Manufactures self-propelled track-mounted railroad cranes and material-handling equipment
Chicago Transparent Products, Inc., Extrudes, prints, and markets low-density polyethylene bags
Photo Systems, Inc., Processes film for professional photographers; manufactures and sells darkroom equipment supplies
Selecterm, Inc., Data communication terminal devices
U.S. Broach and Machine Co., Broach tools and machines
Western-Cullen-Hayes, Inc., Signaling, communications, and maintenance-of-way equipment for the railroad industry
Century Electric, Inc.

Education
BA, History, Stanford University, 1966

Robert D. Manchester
President and Chief Operating Officer

Directorships
Chicago Transparent Products, Inc., Extrudes, prints, and markets low-density polyethylene bags
Clay Video, Inc., Cable TV system operator
FNI Management Corp.
K.T.I., Inc., Cable TV system operator
Lincoln Cablevision, Inc., Cable TV system operator
Lyndon Color Labs, Inc., Professional photographic color lab
Main Line Fashions, Inc., Specializes in ladies' coats
Michigan Cable Associates, L.P.

Monona Wire Corp., Electrical harnesses used in construction of vehicles, farm equipment, and tractor-trailor refrigeration units
Narragansett Capital Corp. of Alabama
NVC Holdings, Inc.
RICAP Co.
Sound Color Corp., Processes film, provides proofing service and quality enlargements for professional photographers
Russel Taylor, Inc., Ladies' fashion apparel of man-made furs and cloth
WBC Management Corp.

Prior Positions

Vice President, Narragansett Capital Corp.
Plant Manager, North American Pharmacal, Inc.

Education

MBA, Amos Tuck School, Dartmouth College, 1976
BSBA, Boston University, 1974

William P. Lane
Vice President and Treasurer

Prior Positions

Vice President, Finance, Bevis Industries, Inc.
Treasurer, Business Development Co. of Rhode Island

Education

BSBA, Boston College, 1961

Gregory P. Barber
Vice President

Directorships

Meenan Oil Co., Fuel oil distributor
Dowden Communications, Inc., Cable television

Prior Position

Vice President, Fleet National Bank

Education

BA, Boston College, 1969

Roger A. Vandenberg
Vice President

Directorships

Broadcast Electronics, Inc., Manufacturer of radio broadcasting equipment
CPM Inc., Specialty paper manufacturer
Carolina Pump & Supply Corp., Independent distributor of equipment for water and sewage systems
Cissell Manufacturing Co., Manufacturer of commercial dry-cleaning equipment
Decor Gravure Corp., Manufacturer of vinyl laminated paneling
Forenta, Inc., Manufactures and sells commercial laundry and dry-cleaning equipment
MD Pneumatics, Inc., Manufacturer of industrial pumps and blowers
Universal Fasteners, Inc., Manufacturer of various apparel closures

Prior Positions

Assistant to the President, Amtel, Inc.
Captain, United States Army

Education

MBA, Finance, Amos Tuck School of Business Administration, 1976
BS, Engineering, U.S. Military Academy at West Point, 1969

Paul A. Giusti
Vice President

Directorships

Lytron Inc., Heat transfer equipment manufacturing
TechMark, Inc., Process control equipment manufacturing
Chas. Gilman & Sons, Distributor

Prior Position

United Brands, 1976–78

Education

MBA, Boston University, 1976
AB, Boston University, 1968

Average Size of Investment	$2M
Size of Funds	Narragansett Capital Corp.—$112M; Narragansett First Fund—$75M
Investment Criteria	Leveraged buy-outs and early-stage high technology
Portfolio Companies	Amron Corp., Houston, TX, Diversified holding company; Bevis Industries, Inc., Providence, RI, Stainless-steel pressure tubing for heart exchangers and industrial pumps and blowers; Broadcast Electronics, Inc., Quincy, IL, Manufacturer of radio broadcasting equipment; Burro

Crane, Inc., Chicago, IL, Manufactures self-propelled track-mounted railroad cranes and materials-handling equipment; Carolina Pump & Supply Corp., Charlotte, NC, Independent distributor of equipment for water and sewage systems; Charter Supply Co., Inc., Philmont, NY, Manufactures custom blow-molded plastic bottles and containers and injection-molded items for the chemical, pharmaceutical, cosmetic, food, and houseware industries; Chicago Transparent Products, Inc., Chicago, IL, Extrudes, prints, and markets low-density polyethylene bags for industrial and consumer use; Cissell Manufacturing Co., Louisville, KY, Manufacturer of a broad range of equipment in the dry-cleaning, laundry, and garment care industries; Clay Video, Inc., Orange Park, FL, Cable television system operator; Cytogen Corp., Princeton, NJ, Biotechnology company specializing in the commercial application of monoclonal antibodies; Dowden Communications, Inc., Atlanta, GA, Cable television system operator; Emulogic, Inc., Norwood, MA, Manufacturer of computer systems used to test microprocessor software and circuits; Engineering Automation Systems, Inc., Kensington, CT, Manufacturer of computer-aided design systems; Forenta, Inc., Morristown, TN, Manufactures and sells commercial laundry and dry-cleaning finishing equipment; Fugua Industries, Inc., Atlanta, GA, Diversified company specializing in the recreation field; Chas. Gilman & Sons, Inc., Medford, MA, Liquor distributor; Gil's, Inc., Monroeville, PA, Operates a discount health and beauty chain; K.T.I., Inc., Fulton, MO, Cable television system operator; Lincoln Cablevision, Inc., Ruidoso, NM, Cable television system operator; Lyndon Color Labs, Inc., Dexter, MI, Professional photographic color lab; Lytron Inc., Woburn, MA, Designs, develops, and manufactures sophisticated heat transfer equipment for military and industrial applications; Main Line Fashions, Inc., New York, NY, Specializes in ladies' coats; Marley Plastics (U.S.A.), Inc., New York, NY, Worldwide interests in the plastics industry; Monona Wire Corp., Decorah, IA, Manufacturer of electrical harnesses used in construction vehicles, farm equipment, and tractor-trailer refrigeration units; Old Fox Chemical, Inc., East Providence, RI, Chemical fertilizer business; Oxwall Tool Co., Inc., Flushing, NY, Manufactures, imports, and distributes nonpower hand tools; Photo Systems, Inc., Dexter, MI, Processes films for professional photographers; manufactures and sells darkroom equipment and supplies; Plasti-Kote Co., Inc., Medina, OH, Manufactures, markets, and distributes aerosol paints, chemicals, and lubricants; Pru-Lesco, Inc., Providence, RI, Picture frames and displays; Reuter-Stokes, Inc., Cleveland, OH, Leading manufacturer of nuclear detection devices for reactors, safety, gauging, and oil well logging; Russel Taylor, Inc., New York, NY, Designs, markets, and distributes better-priced ladies' fashion apparel of man-made furs and cloth; Second Foundation, Inc., Rancho Cordova, CA, Manufacturer of medical diagnostic equipment in the ultrasonic imaging field; Selecterm, Inc., Danvers, MA, Leases and services a variety of data communication terminal devices; Sound Color Corp., Edmonds, WA, Processes film, provides proofing service and quality enlargements for professional photographers; Spectrum Fabrics Corp., New York, NY, Converter of fabric for the home furnishings and home decorative industries; SWF Machinery, Inc., Sanger, CA, Manufacturer of packaging forming equipment serving the corrugated paper industry; TCI Growth, Inc., Denver, CO, Wholly owned subsidiary of TeleCommunications, Inc., which owns and operates CATV systems and microwave video service to CATV systems, television stations, and broadcast networks; Techmark Corp., Newport, RI, Consultant and equipment supplier to the pulp and paper industry and developer of an industrial energy pump capable of generating high-pressure steam from low-temperature waste heat; Tilton & Cook Co., Leominster, MA, Manufactures and markets barrettes, bandeaux, dress and side combs, and other hair care products; U.S. Broach and Machine Co., Detroit, MI, Manufacturer of broach tools and machines; West Boca Cablevision, West Boca Raton, FL, Cable television system operator; Western-Cullen-Hayes, Inc., Chicago, IL, Manufacturer of signaling, communications, and maintenance-of-way equipment for the railroad industry

NATIONAL CITY CAPITAL CORP.
623 Euclid Avenue
Cleveland, OH 44114
(216) 575-2491

Martha A. Barry
John B. Naylor
Michael Sherwin

Average Size of Investment	$300K
Size of Fund	$5M
Investment Criteria	Diversified areas of interest; geographic proximity important; will act as lead investor; leveraged buy-outs of importance
Portfolio Companies	Undisclosed

NAUTILUS FUND, INC.
24 Federal Street
Boston, MA 02110
(617) 482-8260

Landon T. Clay
Richard A. Spillane, Jr.
Portfolio Manager (Vice President)

DIRECTORY AND BIOGRAPHIES

Prior Position

Project Engineer, Union Carbide (Linde Division)

Education

MBA, Harvard Business School, 1977
BS, Chemical Engineering, Rensselaer Polytechnic Institute, 1972

James B. Hawkes

Average Size of Investment	$500K
Size of Fund	$19M
Investment Criteria	Small growth companies in high-technology areas
Portfolio Companies	Camex, Inc., Boston, MA, CAD systems; Carleton Corp., Cambridge, MA, Software; Concentric Data Systems, Westboro, MA, Software; Teradata, Inc., Los Angeles, CA, Data base management computers

NAZEM & COMPANY
600 Madison Avenue
New York, NY 10022
(212) 644-6433

Fred F. Nazem
Peter G. Imperial
Philip E. Barak
Edward F. Hummer
Ramon V. Reyes

Average Size of Investment	$750K
Size of Fund	$50M
Investment Criteria	Technology-based companies are of interest; will act as lead investor; start-ups are welcome
Portfolio Companies	Undisclosed

NEIGHBORHOOD FUND, INC.
1950 East 71st Street
Chicago, Ill 60649
(312) 684-8074

James Fletcher
President

Directorship

South Shore Bank of Chicago

Prior Position

Senior Vice President, Urban Fund of Illinois, 1976–78

Education

BS, Northern Illinois University, 1958

Shirley A. Kyle
Vice President

Prior Positions

Investment Manager, Tower Ventures, Inc., 1983–present
Training Coordinator, Sears, Roebuck & Co., 1980–83
Buying Assignments, Sears, Roebuck & Co., 1975–80
Merchandising Management Trainee, Sears, Roebuck & Co., 1973–75
Administrative Assistant, St. Paul Federal Bank, 1971–72

Education

MBA, Roosevelt University, 1979
Illinois Institute of Technology, 1976–78
BA, Psychology and Education, Macalester College, 1971

Average Size of Investment	$150K
Size of Fund	$1M
Investment Criteria	Diversified company preferences; geographic proximity important
Portfolio Companies	Undisclosed

NELSON CAPITAL CORP.
591 Stewart Avenue
Garden City, NY 11530
(516) 222-2555

10000 Santa Monica Boulevard
Los Angeles, CA 90067
(213) 556-1944

8550 Bryn Mawr Avenue
Chicago, IL 60631
(312) 693-5990

Irwin B. Nelson

Average Size of Investment	$100K
Size of Fund	Undisclosed
Investment Criteria	Interested in workouts and diversified areas of interest
Portfolio Companies	Undisclosed

NEPA VENTURE FUND, L.P.
125 Goodman Drive
Bethlehem, PA 18015
(215) 865-6550

Frederick J. Beste III
President, Chief Executive Officer

Directorships

Delex Systems, Inc.
Foam Design, Inc.
Churchill Weavers, Inc.

Prior Positions

President, Kentucky Highlands Investment Corp.
Vice President, Greater Washington Investors, Inc.

Education

BA, Stetson University, 1968

Glen R. Bressner
Assistant Fund Manager

Prior Positions

Investment officer, Key Venture Capital Corp.
Loan officer, Baybank Harvard Trust Co.

Education

MBA, Babson College, 1984
BSBA, Boston University, 1981

Average Size of Investment	$400K
Size of Fund	$10M
Investment Criteria	All stages; virtually all industries; primary interest in PA- and NJ-based firms
Portfolio Companies	Metech Corp., Elverson, PA, Electronics materials manufacturer; CMV Associates, Ltd., Allentown, PA, Transportation services; CALAN Inc., Dingman's Ferry, PA, CATV instrumentation; Maintenance Systems, Inc., Allentown, PA, Inventory services

NEWBURY, ROSEN & CO., INC.
One State Street
Suite 1250
Boston, MA 02109
(617) 227-2707

Francis W. Newbury, Jr.
Chairman

Directorship

Compo Industries, Textiles and footwear

Prior Position

Senior Vice President, State Street Bank & Trust Co., Boston

Education

BA, Economics, Harvard University, 1960

Marguerite A. Piret
President

Directorships

Pioneer Fund, Inc., Mutual fund
Pioneer II, Inc., Mutual fund
Pioneer Three, Inc., Mutual fund
Pioneer Bond Fund, Inc., Mutual fund

Prior Positions

Managing Director, Kridel Securities Corp.
Loan Officer, Bank of New England

Education

MBA, Harvard University, 1974
AB, Radcliffe College, Harvard University, 1969

DIRECTORY AND BIOGRAPHIES 333

Howard J. Gordon
Edward S. Perry

Average Size of Investment	$1M
Size of Fund	Undisclosed
Investment Criteria	Profits and positive cash flow
Portfolio Companies	Undisclosed

NEW ENGLAND CAPITAL CORP.
One Washington Mall
Boston, MA 02108
(617) 722-6400

Z. David Patterson
Executive Vice President

Prior Position

Vice President, Bank of New England

Education

MBA, Boston College, 1967
University of London, 1962
BS, Babson College, 1961

Thomas C. Tremblay
Vice President

Prior Position

Senior Consultant, Technology Consulting Group

Education

MS, Manufacturing Engineering, Boston University, 1981
MBA, Boston University, 1979
BSEE, Lafayette College, 1974

Average Size of Investment	$400K
Size of Fund	$10M
Investment Criteria	Good managements in good businesses
Portfolio Companies	Undisclosed

NEW ENGLAND MESBIC, INC.
50 Kearney Road
Suite 3
Needham, MA 02194
(617) 449-2066

Dr. Etang Chen
President
(617) 769-5148

Directorships

ENK Electric, Computer OEM
ENK/Six Tau, Engineering design

Prior Positions

President, ENK Electric
President, ENK/Six Tau

Education

PhD, Mathematics, Physics, University of Marburg, West Germany, 1966
BS, Electrical Engineering, National Taiwan University, Taiwan, 1958

Dr. San-Lang Lien
Treasurer and Loan Officer

Prior Position

Engineering, Stone & Webster Engineering Corp., 1980–85

Education

PhD, University of Wisconsin at Madison, 1973

Tong K. Wong

Average Size of Investment	Small, medium
Size of Fund	Undisclosed
Investment Criteria	High tech, diversified
Portfolio Companies	Undisclosed

NEW ENTERPRISE ASSOCIATES
235 Montgomery Street
Suite 1025
San Francisco, CA 94104
(415) 956-1579

1119 St. Paul Street
Baltimore, MD 21202
(301) 244-0115

3000 Sand Hill Rd., Bldg. 2, Suite 210
Menlo Park, CA 94025

Southwest Enterprise Associates
1266 Lincoln Centre
5420 LBJ Freeway
Dallas, TX 75240
(214) 991-1620

119 East 55th Street
New York, NY 10022
(212) 371-8210

Spectra Enterprise Associates
31194 La Baya Drive
Westlake Village, CA 91362
(818) 991-8540

C. Richard Kramlich
Managing General Partner, San Francisco

Directorships

Dallas Semiconductor, CMOS products using late implantation technique
ForeThought, Inc., Microcomputer software for Apple's MacIntosh
GigaTronics, Inc., Telecommunications instrumentation
Devices for Vascular Intervention
Sherpa Corp., CAE/CAM database systems
Immunex Corp., Biotechnology R & D of immune system
Microsource, Inc., Microwave components
North Star Computers, Inc., Microcomputer manufacturer
NTX Communications, Corp., Communications processor for intercomputer communications
Personal CAD Systems, Inc., CAD software
Republic Geothermal, Inc., Geothermal exploration and development
Sierra Monitor Corp., Gas and water monitoring and control equipment
Silicon Graphics, Inc., Intelligent graphics workstations and terminals
Silicon Systems, Inc., Custom integrated circuits
Syquest Technology, Inc., 100-millimeter Winchester disk drives
Telebit Corp., High-performance, low-cost modem
3Com Corp., Hardware and software for digital communications
Virtual Imaging

Prior Positions

General Partner, Arthur Rock & Associates, 1969–80
Executive Vice President, Gardner and Preston Moss, Inc., 1964–69

Education

MBA, Harvard, 1960
BS, Northwestern University, 1957

Cornelius C. Bond, Jr.,
General Partner, San Francisco

Directorships

Evans Rents
GigaTronics, Inc., Telecommunications instrumentation
Microwave Technology, Inc., Amplifiers and oscillators based on gallium arsenide hybrid
Resonex, Inc.

Prior Position

Vice President and Director, T. Rowe Price Associates, Inc., 1960–82

Education

BSEE, Princeton, 1956

C. Woodrow Rea, Jr.
General Partner, Menlo Park

Directorships

Bowers Impact Graphics
Cirrus Logic, Inc., Improved design method of integrated circuit development
Diamon Images, Electron beam imaging services for the semiconductor industry
Genesis Electronics Corp., Markets voice mail equipment
Micro MRP, Inc., Computer turnkey systems
Onset Partners, Prototype development outlet for those seeking engineering, management, or financial assistance
Presentation Technology, Inc., Products that support the use of 35mm slides for business presentations
Tele-Learning Systems, Inc., Products enabling instruction via personal computers
Telestream
Telmos, Semiconductor integrated circuits using CMOS and DMOS technologies
Virtual Imaging

DIRECTORY AND BIOGRAPHIES

Prior Positions

President, Ultratech Stepper, 1981–84
Director Corp. Development/Counsel, General Signal Corp., 1977–81

Education

MBA, New York University, 1980
JD, George Washington University, 1973
BA, University of Rochester, 1970

Thomas C. McConnell
Associate, San Francisco

Directorship

Graphic Software Systems

Prior Positions

Product Manager, Apple Computer, 1982–84
Independent Consultant, Texas Instruments, 1981–82

Education

MBA, Stanford University, 1979
AB, Dartmouth College, 1976

Frank A. Bonsal, Jr.
General Partner, Baltimore

Directorships

Concept Systems, Inc., Turnkey computer systems to specialty retailing and food service installations
Data Language Corp., Application generators for the computer software industry
Digital Communications Associates, Inc., Supplier of data communications networking equipment
Medical & Scientific Design
TCS Software, Integrated business software

Prior Position

General Partner, Alex. Brown & Sons, 1965–77

Education

Columbia School of Advanced International Studies, 1960–61
AB, Princeton, 1959

Charles W. Newhall, III
General Partner, Baltimore

Directorships

Healthsouth Rehabilitation Corp., Rehabilitation services through outpatient centers and rehabilitation hospitals
Crop Genetics International, N.V., Improved plant products based on proprietary tissue culture technology
Dallas Biomedical
Queue Systems, Inc., Instrumentation for medical and life sciences industries
Zymark Corp., Laboratory automation systems that combine robotics and laboratory stations to automate laboratory procedures
Sepracor, Inc.

Prior Positions

Vice President, T. Rowe Price Associates, Inc., 1971–77
United States Army, 1967–69

Education

MBA, Harvard University, 1971
BA, University of Pennsylvania, 1967

Arthur J. Marks
General Partner, Baltimore

Directorships

Lisp Machine Corp.
Network Switching Systems, Inc., Digital switching equipment used with wideband digital transmission media
Private Satellite Network, Provides communications between a headquarters location and many branches
Quantum Medical Systems, Ultrasound equipment for human blood flow imaging
Resonex, Inc., Nuclear magnetic resonance equipment for screening the arterial system
Soft-Switch, Inc., Office automation software
Spinnaker Software

Prior Positions

Senior Vice President, GEISCO, 1980–84
General Manager, X-Ray Products, G. E. Medical Systems, 1978–80

Education

MBA, Harvard University, 1971
BSIE, University of Michigan, 1967

Curran W. Harvey
Special Partner, Baltimore; General Partner, Westlake Village

Directorship

Star Microwave, Traveling wave tubes for the electronic counter-measures, radar, and commercial and military communications markets

Prior Position

President, Chief Executive Officer, T. Rowe Price Associates, Inc., 1961–84

Education

BE, Yale University, 1951

Howard D. Wolfe
Senior Vice President

Prior Position

Chief Executive Officer, Cielo Food Service Inc.

Education

BA, University of California at Santa Barbara, 1972

Raymond L. Bank
Associate, Baltimore

Directorship

Joshua Slocum Ltd.

Prior Positions

Vice President, Joseph A. Bank Clothiers, 1979–82
Associate, Weinberg & Green, 1978–79

Education

MBA, Wharton School, 1985
JD, University of Baltimore, 1978
AB, Vassar College, 1975

C. Vincent Prothro
Special Partner/General Partner, Dallas

Directorships

Image Data Corp.
Dallas Semiconductor, CMOS products using late implantation technique
Silicon Systems, Semiconductor
Dallas Biomedical Corp.

Prior Position

Chief Executive Officer, Mostek Corp., 1969–82

Education

MBA, Harvard University, 1966
BSIE, Stanford University, 1964

Leland Murphy
Associate, Dallas

Prior Positions

Senior Vice President, Republic Bank of Dallas, 1970–85

Education

MBA, Indiana University, 1970
AB, Drury College, 1968

James A. Cole
General Partner, Westlake Village

Directorships

Microsource, Inc.
Microwave Modules & Devices
Eesof, Inc.

Prior Positions

Executive Vice President, Amplica, Inc., 1972–84
Director of Marketing, E & M Laboratories, 1967–72

Education

University of California Graduate School of Management, Los Angeles, 1981
San Fernando Valley (CA) Community College, 1965

John W. Glynn, Jr.
Special Partner, Menlo Park

Directorships

Molecular Design Ltd., Software for chemists in research laboratories
The Learning Company, Educational microcomputer software for the home and school market
International Marketvision

Prior Position
General Partner, Lamoreaux, Glynn Associates, 1974–83

Education
MBA, Stanford, 1970
JD, University of Virginia, 1965
BS, Notre Dame, 1962

Average Size of Investment	$1M
Size of Funds	NEA I—$16.45M; NEA II—$45.5M; NEA III—$125M; SEA—$25.5M; Spectra—$25M
Investment Criteria	A company must have (1) a unique product or service; (2) a chance to dominate a large and growing market; and (3) quality experienced professionals
Portfolio Companies	Currently over 100 companies in such diversified areas as: computer turnkey systems; packaged software for mainframes, minicomputers, and microcomputers; biotechnology; health care services and products; computers and peripherals; telecommunications; office communications; semiconductors; specialty retailing; energy/alternative energy, etc.

NEW MEXICO CAPITAL CORP.
2900 Louisiana Boulevard, N.E.
Albuquerque, NM 87110
(505) 884-3600

Richard A. Price

Average Size of Investment	$60K
Size of Fund	$600K
Investment Criteria	Diversified company interest areas including manufacturing; geographic location of importance
Portfolio Companies	Undisclosed

NEW MEXICO RESEARCH AND DEVELOPMENT INSTITUTE
Pinon Building, Suite 358
1220 S. St. Francis Drive
Santa Fe, NM 87501
(505) 827-5886

NM Research and Development Institute Communications Office
457 Washington, S.E. Suite M
Albuquerque, NM 87131
(505) 277-3661

Larry Icerman
Director, Santa Fe

Prior Positions

Director, New Mexico Energy R&D Institute, 1984–86
Director, New Mexico State University Energy Institute, 1980–84
Associate Professor, Washington University, 1978–80

Education

Ph.D., Engineering Sciences, University of CA at San Diego, 1976
MBA, San Diego State University, 1976
BS, Massachusetts Insitute of Technology, 1967

Emily Miller
Business Analyst, Sante Fe

Prior Positions

Business Analyst, NM Energy R&D Institute, 1982–86
Energy Consultant, NM Energy and Minerals, 1979–81
Research Associate, Denver Research Institute, 1975–79

Education
MA, Economics, University of Denver, 1979
BA, University of Denver, 1975

Average Size of Investment	$250K
Size of Fund	$6M
Investment Criteria	Advanced-technology-based products, processes, or services close to commercialization; support provided only for R & D activities; company must be in New Mexico or willing to relocate
Portfolio Companies	Stolar Inc., Mine instrumentation, Albuquerque and Raton, NM; Gattlin Research Co., Inc., Oil and gas wellhead processing equipment, Albuquerque, NM; Pneumatic Turbine Partnership, Advanced well drilling equipment, Santa Fe, NM; Hot Hole Instruments, Advanced well logging tools, Los Alamos, NM; Bacchus Industries, Inc., Residential evaporative cooling units, Sunland Park, NM; Brother Sun, Inc., Prefabricated sunspaces, Santa Fe, NM

NEW OASIS CAPITAL CORP.
114 Liberty Street
New York, NY 10006
(212) 394-2804

James J. H. Huang

Average Size of Investment	$100K
Size of Fund	$1M
Investment Criteria	Diversified company interests including restaurant industry; geographic proximity is important
Portfolio Companies	Undisclosed

NEWTEK VENTURES
500 Washington Street
Suite 720
San Francisco, CA 94111

Peter J. Wardle
General Partner
(415) 986-5711

Directorships

Prometrix, Automated systems for characterizing the equipment used in semiconductor manufacturing
Phase 2 Automation, Automated products for the disk media industry

Prior Positions

Managing Partner, Henry F. Swift & Co.
Investment Banker, Reynolds Securities

Education

BA, Economics and Business Administration, Dartmouth College, 1957

Barry M. Weinman
General Partner
(415) 986-5711

Directorships

InterTest Corp., Environmental test equipment for semiconductor industry
Phase 2 Automation, Automation products for disk media industry

Prior Positions

Acting President/Chief Executive Officer, Battery Systems
Founder, Vice President Marketing, President, Chief Executive Officer, Interactive Applications

Education

MA, International Relations, London School of Economics, 1968
BS, Industrial Engineering, Clarkson College of Technology, 1961

Average Size of Investment	$500K
Size of Fund	$20M
Investment Criteria	Undisclosed
Portfolio Companies	Cadnetix Corp., Boulder, CO, Low-cost, next-generation CAD/CAE workstations for the electronics industry; Colorado Venture Management, Boulder, CO, CVM is a seed-capital venture partnership operating in the Colorado Front Range area; Cypress Semiconductor Corp., San Jose, CA, Advanced CMOS products; International Power Technology, Palo Alto, CA, Cheng Cycle Cogeneration engines, producing steam energy and electrical power; Intertest Corp., Santa Clara, CA, Semiconductor environmental test equipment, including fine and gross leak detection and centrifuges; Phase 2 Automation, Inc., Palo Alto, CA, Automation products for the disk media industry; Prometrix Corp., Santa Clara, CA, Automated systems for characterizing the equipment used in semiconductor manufacturing; Sutter Biomedical, Inc., San Diego, CA, Computerized orthopedic knee devices for postoperative care and rehabilitation; Xoma Corp., San Francisco, CA, Bioengineering products for cancer diagnosis and therapy, bone marrow transplantation, and infectious diseases

NEW VENTURE PARTNERS
119 East 55th Street
New York, NY 10022
(212) 371-8210

Howard D. Wolfe, Jr.
General Partner, New York

Directorships

Convex Computer Corp., 32-bit supermicrocomputer
Concept Systems, Inc., Turnkey computer systems to specialty retailing and food service installations

Prior Positions

Principal, Landmark Management, Inc., 1972–present
Vice President, White, Weld & Co., 1965–72

Education

New York University Graduate School of Business
BA, Yale University, 1963

Average Size of Investment	$400K
Size of Funds	$20M
Investment Criteria	Early-stage technology: communications, computers, software, specialty retailing, medical products and devices
Portfolio Companies	Undisclosed

NEW WEST VENTURES

4350 Executive Drive
Suite 206
San Diego, CA 92121
(619) 457-0722

Tim Haidinger
Partner

Directorships

Decom Systems, Communications
Giltronix, Computers

Prior Positions

Partner, Arthur Young & Co.
Manager, Collins Radio

Education

BA, Naval P.G. School, 1967
MBA, Stanford University, 1965
BS, Notre Dame, 1963

Average Size of Investment	$500K
Size of Fund	$15M
Investment Criteria	No start-up
Portfolio Companies	Undisclosed

NEW YORK SECURITIES CO., INC.

Two Rocaton Road
Darien, CT 06820
(203) 655-7488

F. Kenneth Melis
Chairman

Directorships

Marevex Corp., Oil and gas
Associated Mortgage Investors

Prior Positions

Managing Trustee, Associated Mortgage Investors, 1973–84
Partner, F. Eberstadt & Co., Inc., 1945–62

Education

Corporate Finance, New York University Graduate School, 1951
BS, Accounting, New York University, 1948

Average Size of Investment	$100K
Size of Fund	$500K
Investment Criteria	High growth potential public offering candidate
Portfolio Company	American Computer Resources, Inc., Stamford, CT, Computer distributor

NORFOLK INVESTMENT CO.

100 West Plume Street
Suite 208
Norfolk, VA 23510
(804) 623-1042

Kirk W. Saunders

Average Size of Investment	$100K
Size of Fund	Undisclosed
Investment Criteria	Diversified company interests including manufacturing; geographic proximity is important
Portfolio Companies	Undisclosed

NORO-MOSELEY PARTNERS
Suite 1240, 100 Galleria Parkway
Atlanta, GA 30339
(404) 955-0020

Charles Moseley
General Partner

Prior Position
Senior Vice President, Robinson-Humphrey

Education
MBA, Harvard

Russell French
General Partner

Prior Position
Partner, King & Spaulding

Education
Dr. of Law, University of Virginia

Jack Kelly
General Partner, Atlanta

Prior Position
Executive Vice President, Scientific Atlanta

Education
Bachelor of Physics, Georgia State

Average Size of Investment	$1M
Size of Investment	$43.5M
Investment Criteria	Generally established companies, located in the Southeast, diverse industries
Portfolio Companies	Undisclosed

NORSTAR VENTURE CAPITAL
One Norstar Plaza
Albany, NY 12203
(518) 477-5170

Stephen Puricelli
Associate

Joseph L. Reinhart
Associate

Raymond A. Lancaster
President

Average Size of Investment	$600K
Size of Fund	$20M
Investment Criteria	Invest very selectively at seed stage, all other later stages of venture financing; also operate leveraged buyout fund; Northeastern U.S. only
Portfolio Companies	Undisclosed

NORTH AMERICAN COMPANY LTD.
111 East Las Olas Boulevard
Fort Lauderdale, FL 33301
(305) 463-0681

Charles L. Palmer
President

Directorships
Barnett Bank of South Florida, Bank
Rycoline Products, Inc., Specialty chemical
Heizer Corp., Venture capital
Sea Ranch Properties, Inc., Real estate

Prior Position
Vice President, Finance, Heizer Corp., 1972

Education
MBA, Northwestern University, 1965
BSBA, Georgetown University, 1964

Average Size of Investment	Minimum investment $300K; preferred investment $1M
Size of Fund	Undisclosed
Investment Criteria	Private firm investing own capital prefers start-up, second-stage, or buy-out financing; geographical preference; East Coast, Midwest, Southeast and Southwest
Portfolio Companies	Undisclosed

NORTH AMERICAN INVESTMENT CORP.
P.O. Box 1831
Isato Rey Station
San Juan, PR 00919
(809) 754-6177

Santiago Ruiz-Bentancourt

Average Size of Investment	$100K
Size of Fund	Undisclosed
Investment Criteria	Diversified areas of company interest; goegraphic proximity important
Portfolio Companies	Undisclosed

NORTH AMERICAN VENTURE GROUP, LTD.
55 W. Monroe
Suite 3500
Chicago, IL 60603
(312) 236-6800

Jeffrey E. Grossman
Chairman

Directorship
North American Group, Ltd.

Prior Position
President, Eurisco Industries, Inc.

Education
BS, Loyola University, 1964

Gregory I. Kravitt
President

Directorship
North American Group, Ltd.

Prior Position
Commercial Banking Officer, Continental Illinois National Bank, 1976–80

Education
MBA, Northwestern, 1975
BA, University of Denver, 1972

Jeffrey G. Naylor
Vice President

Prior Positions
Consultant, Deloitte Haskins & Sells, 1982–86

Education
MBA, Northwestern University, 1982
BA, Northwestern University, 1980

Average Size of Investment	$1M
Size of Fund	Undisclosed
Investment Criteria	Strong management, economically justified product/service, existing market
Portfolio Companies	Undisclosed

NORTHEASTERN CAPITAL CORP.
61 High Street
East Haven, CT 06512
(203) 469-7901

Louis W. Mingione

Average Size of Investment	$500K
Size of Fund	$1.6M
Investment Criteria	Diverse areas of interest, start-ups, will act as lead investor, geographic proximity important
Portfolio Companies	Undisclosed

NORTHERN BUSINESS CAPITAL CORP.
20 Sasqua Road
East Norwalk, CT 06855
(203) 866-1000

Joseph Kavanewsky

Average Size of Investment	$100K
Size of Fund	Undisclosed
Investment Criteria	Interested in real estate, financial services, and manufacturing industries
Portfolio Companies	Undisclosed

NORTHERN COMMUNITY INVESTMENT CORP.
P.O. Box 396
St. Johnsbury, VT 05819
(802) 748-5101

Stephen C. McConnell

Average Size of Investment	$100K
Size of Fund	Undisclosed
Investment Criteria	Diverse areas of interest including manufacturing; start-ups; will act as lead investor; geographic proximity important
Portfolio Companies	Undisclosed

NORTHERN PACIFIC CAPITAL CORP.
Suite 608, Century Tower
1201 Southwest 12th Avenue
Portland, OR 97205
(503) 241-1255

John J. Tennant, Jr.

Average Size of Investment	$150K
Size of Fund	$1.5M
Investment Criteria	Manufacturing industry of interest as well as construction and real estate; geographic location of importance
Portfolio Companies	Undisclosed

NORTHLAND CAPITAL CORP.
613 Missabe Building
227 West First Street
Duluth, MN 55802
(218) 722-0545

George G. Barnum, Jr.
President

Directorships
Northland Capital Corp., SBIC
Norwest Bank, Duluth NA, Banking

Prior Position
Vice President, Norwest Bank, Duluth NA, 1949–66

Education
BA, Business, Hamilton College, 1947

John C. Andersen
R. N. McGiffert
Conrad M. Fredin
Elizabeth J. Barnum
David C. Barnum

Average Size of Investment	$100K
Size of Fund	Undisclosed
Investment Criteria	Diversified
Portfolio Companies	Undisclosed

NORTH STAR VENTURES
100 South 5th Street
Suite 2200
Minneapolis, MN 55402
(612) 333-1133

Keith Eastman
David W. Stassen
Terrence W. Glarner

Average Size of Investment	$3M–$6M
Size of Fund	Undisclosed
Investment Criteria	Technology-based and manufacturing companies of interest; start-ups are encouraged; geographic location is not important
Portfolio Companies	Undisclosed

NORTH STREET CAPITAL CORP.
250 North Street
White Plains, NY 10625
(914) 335-7901

DIRECTORY AND BIOGRAPHIES

Ralph L. McNeal, Sr.

Average Size of Investment	$250K
Size of Fund	$1.7M
Investment Criteria	Diversified company interests; geographic location is of importance
Portfolio Companies	Undisclosed

NORTHWEST BUSINESS INVESTMENT CORP.
West 929 Sprague Avenue
Spokane, WA 99204
(509) 838-3111

Paul Sandifur, Sr.
Paul Sandifur, Jr.

Average Size of Investment	$100K
Size of Fund	Undisclosed
Investment Criteria	Diversified companies, especially real estate; perfer those in the Northwest
Portfolio Companies	Undisclosed

NORTHWOOD VENTURES
420 Madison Avenue
13th Floor
New York, NY 10017
(212) 935-4679

Peter G. Schiff
General Partner

Directorships

EMS Development Corp., Mine warfare countermeasure equipment
Cincinnati Coca-Cola Acquisition, Inc., Coca-Cola
American Exploration Company, Oil and gas
Cafe Concepts Corp., Restaurants
Republic Broadcasting Corp., Radio stations
Universal Paging Corp., Paging company

Prior Positions

E. M. Warburg, Pincus & Co.
Chemical Bank

Education

MBA, University of Chicago, 1976
BA, Lake Forest College, 1974

Average Size of Investment	Varies
Size of Fund	Undisclosed
Investment Criteria	Leveraged buy-outs and venture capital
Portfolio Companies	Undisclosed

NORWEST VENTURE CAPITAL
Northwest Growth Fund
2800 Piper Jaffray Tower
222 South Ninth
Minneapolis, MN 55402
(612) 372-8770

1300 Southwest Fifth Avenue
Suite 3018
Portland, OR 97201
(503) 223-6622

8777 E. Via De Ventura
Suite 335
Scottsdale, AZ 85258
(602) 483-8940

Timothy A. Stepanek
Vice President, MN

Directorships

Aeronca Electronics, Inc.
Concord Computing Corp.
D'Lites of America, Inc.
Datakey, Inc.
Morgan Products, Ltd.

Prior Position

Dain Bosworth, Inc., 1973–81

Education

MBA, University of Minnesota School of Business, 1973
BA, College of St. Thomas, 1971

Robert F. Zicarelli
Chairman, AZ

Directorships

Ault, Inc.
Bemis Corp.
Community Pacific Broadcasting Corp.
Cray Research, Inc.
Detector Electronics Corp.
EMC Corp.
Famous Restaurants, Inc.
International Hairgoods, Inc.
National Computer Systems Corp.
Pacer Corp.
Spartanics, Ltd.
VanRich Casting Corp.
VEE Corp.

Prior Position

Allstate Insurance Co., 1956–61

Education

MBA, Northwestern University, 1953
BS, Northwestern University, 1948

John P. Whaley
Vice President, MN

Directorships

C & G Associates, Inc.
The Kartridg Pak Co.
Pinstripes Petites, Inc.

Prior Position

Norwest Corp.

Education

MBA, College of St. Thomas, 1980
BSB, University of Minnesota, 1974

Dale J. Vogel
Vice President, OR

Directorships

Agricultural Genetic Systems, Inc.
Pensa, Inc.
S. R. Smith Co., Inc.
Seattle Silicon Technology, Inc.
Van Rich Casting Corp.
Support Technologies, Inc.

Prior Position

President, K2 Corp.

Education

MBA, Harvard School of Business, 1968
BS, San Jose State College, 1966

Douglas E. Johnson
Vice President, MN

Directorships

CAMAX Systems, Inc.
EDGE Computer Corp.
FSI Corp.
NASTEC Corp.
Systeme Corp.
Zycad, Corp.

Prior Position

Vice President, Dain Bosworth, Inc., 1977–81

Education

MBA, College of St. Thomas, 1977
BA, Mathematics, University of Minnesota, 1966

Daniel J. Haggerty
President, MN

Directorships

Management Graphics, Inc.
Network Systems Corp.

DIRECTORY AND BIOGRAPHIES

Prior Position
Prudential Insurance Company, 1963–72

Education
BA, College of St. Thomas, 1962

Leonard J. Brandt
Vice President, MN

Directorships
Applied Intelligent Systems, Inc.
Curatech, Inc.
PERQ Systems Corp.
National Psychiatric Centers, Inc.

Education
MBA, Harvard School of Business, 1980
BS, University of Illinois, 1978

Tony J. Miadich
Vice President, OR

Directorships
August Systems, Inc.
Centigram Corp.
McData Corp.
MMR Technologies, Inc.
Pacific Nuclear Systems
Phaze Information Machines Corp.
RPC Industries, Inc.

Prior Positions
Chief Financial Officer, TRW Semiconductor Division
Mergers and Acquisitions, TRW Defense and Energy Group

Education
MBA, University of California at Los Angeles, 1970
MSEE, University of Southern California, 1967
BSEE, University of Southern California, 1965

Average Size of Investment	$750K
Size of Fund	$270M
Investment Criteria	Diverse areas of interest including technology-based leveraged buy-outs; start-ups; geographic proximity important; will act as lead investor
Portfolio Companies	Undisclosed

NOVACAP INVESTMENTS, INC.
1981 McGill College
Suite 380
Montreal, Quebec H3A 3A9
Canada
(514) 282-1383

Marc Beauchamp
President

Directorships
Taurus Computer
Volcano, Inc.
Stablex Canada Inc.
R.C.R. International Inc.
Memotec Data Inc.
Novacap Investments Inc.
Gestion Deucap Inc.

Prior Positions
Investment Officer, Innocan Investments Inc.
Vice President, Westhill Industries, Inc.

Education
MBA, Columbia University, 1969

Jacques Tousignant
Vice President

Directorships
R.C.R. International Inc.
Mansion Bakeries Inc.
Volcano Inc.
International Boiler Works Co.
Security Chimneys Ltd.
Armtex Fibers, Inc.
Gestion Devcap Inc.
Agence Quebecoise de Valorisation de la Recherche (AQUIR)
Sofati Pharmaceutical Canada Inc.

Prior Positions

Vice President, Finance, Coronet Housewares Inc.
Executive Vice President, Imperial Mops & Brooms Ltd.
Vice President, Finance, John Lewis Industries Inc.

Education

CGA, Ecole Hautes Etudes Commerciales (HEC), 1966

Jean-Pierre Chartrand
Vice President, Operations

Directorships

RCR International Inc.
Mark Hot Inc.
Mansion Bakeries
Cascades Technologies

Prior Positions

Vice President, General Manager, Denis Equipment
President, Devcom Ltd.
Vice President, BCP Advertising

Education

MBA, York University, 1969
Bachelor of Commerce, University of Montreal, 1967

Average Size of Investment	$1M Cdn.
Size of Fund	$20M Cdn.
Investment Criteria	Experienced management, proprietary product, export potential
Portfolio Companies	Human Computing Resources Corp., UNIX operating software; Armtex Fibers Inc., Industrial synthetic fibers; Mansion Bakeries Inc., Frozen dough; Stablex Canada Inc., Waste management; Cascade Technologies, Air purification; Memotec Data Inc., Data communication processors; RCR International, Inc., Hardware products; Taurus Computer Products, Inc., Data acquisition computers; Volcano, Inc., Industrial boiler

NOVATECH RESOURCE CORP.
103 East 37th Street
New York, NY 10016
(212) 725-2555
Telex 236 491 NRC UR

Reynald G. Bonmati
Gerald J. Iannone
Charles H. Weight

Average Size of Investment	$1M
Size of Fund	$50M
Investment Criteria	Technology-based companies (life sciences, ie. agribusiness, biotechnology, health care; new materials and processes; information systems); clear focus on
Portfolio Companies	Undisclosed

NYBDC CAPITAL CORP.
41 State Street
Albany, NY 12207
(518) 463-2268

Marshall R. Lustig
John D. Wasson
Robert W. Lazar

Average Size of Investment	$500K
Size of Fund	$15M
Investment Criteria	Diversified company interests including manufacturing; start-ups encouraged; will act as lead investor; geographic location important
Portfolio Companies	Undisclosed

OAK INVESTMENT PARTNERS
257 Riverside Avenue
Westport, CT 06880
(203) 226-8346

Edward F. Glassmeyer
Stewart H. Greenfield
Ginger M. More
Jeffrey D. West
Michael D. Kaufman

Average Size of Investment	$1.5M
Size of Fund	$100M
Investment Criteria	Technology-based companies are of interest; will act as lead investor; start-ups are welcome
Portfolio Companies	Undisclosed

DIRECTORY AND BIOGRAPHIES

O'BRIEN INDUSTRIES
4350 East Camelback
Suite 120 B
Phoenix, AZ 85018
(602) 840-6070

Wm. Howard O'Brien
President

Directorships

Founder and first President, The Jojoba Growers Association
Former director and secretary, National Association Small Business Investment Companies
Former director, Phoenix Chamber of Commerce

Prior Positions

Founder and President, First Southwest Small Business Investment Co.
Founder, Security Savings and Loan, Nogales, AZ
Founding Director, Sunup Transportation (trucking)
Founding Director, John Gardiner's Tennis Ranch

Education

BS, Agriculture, University of Arizona

A. George Rice
Edgar C. Park
John C. Hughes
Edwin Q. Barbey
L. Salvatore

Average Size of Investment	$200K
Size of Fund	$2M
Investment Criteria	Economic crops for arid lands
Portfolio Companies	Undisclosed

OMEGA CAPITAL CORPORATION
755 S. 11th Street
Beaumont, TX 77701
(409) 835-5928

P.O. Box 2173
Beaumont, TX 77704

Frank Ryan
General Manager

Prior Positions

Controller, Texas Oil & Chemical Co.
Assistant Treasurer, Good Hope Industries
CPA, Haskins & Sell

Education

BS, Accounting, Fairleigh Dickenson University, 1973

Average Size of Investment	$50–100K
Size of Fund	$500K
Investment Criteria	Open
Portfolio Companies	Undisclosed

ONSET, A CALIFORNIA LIMITED PARTNERSHIP
151 University Avenue
Palo Alto, CA 94301
(415) 327-5470

Terry L. Opdendyk
General Partner

Directorships

Presentation Technologies, Inc., Telestream Corporation

Prior Positions

President, VISICORP, 1980–84
Manager, Microprocessor Systems, ITEL, 1973–80
Product Manager, Hewlitt-Packard, 1970–73

Education

MS, Stanford University, 1972
BS, Michigan State University, 1970

David M. Kelley
General Partner

Directorship

David Kelley Design, Inc., Product design firm

Prior Positions

Assistant Professor of Product Design, Stanford University
Consultant, Chemetric Corp., 1975–77
Design Engineer, NCR, 1974–75
Engineer, Boeing, 1973–74

Education

MS, Stanford University, 1977
BS, Carnegie-Mellon University, 1973

Average Size of Investment	$200K–$600K
Size of Fund	$5M
Investment Criteria	Seed-level investments in technology companies in Northern California. Specialize in "incubating" new technology companies by providing direct management, engineering, and marketing assistance as well as seed financing. Affiliated with Kliener Perkins Kaufield and Byers, Mayfield, and New Enterprise Associates funds.
Portfolio Companies	Presentation Technologies, Inc., Santa Clara, CA, Presentation Graphics Equipment; Telestream Corporation, Mt. View, CA, Telecommunications; Biometrics, Inc., Palo Alto, CA, Recognition Equipment

OPPORTUNITY CAPITAL CORP.
50 California Street
Suite 2505
San Francisco, CA 94111
(415) 421-5935

J. Peter Thompson

Average Size of Investment	$150K
Size of Fund	Undisclosed
Investment Criteria	Diverse areas of interest including manufacturing; geographic proximity important
Portfolio Companies	Undisclosed

ORANGE NASSAU
260 Franklin Street
Suite 1501
Boston, MA 02110
(617) 439-6160

One Galleria Tower
13355 Noel Road
Suite 635
Dallas, TX 75240
(214) 385-9685

Westerly Place, Suite 540
1500 Quail Street
Newport Beach, CA 92660-2737
(714) 752-7811

25 Nassauplein
P.O.B. 85578
2508 cg, The Hague
The Netherlands
011-31-70-469-670

Dallas Pacific Ltd.
14th Floor
88 Gloucester Rd.
Hong Kong
852-5-893-1838

Alpha Associes S.A.
Bureaux de Parc du Griffon
513 Route de la Sèds
13127 Vitrolles, France
(42) 79-5777

89 Rue Taitbout
75009 Paris
France
(42) 85-3000

John W. Blackburn
Orange Nassau, CA/General Partner

Directorships

Datametrics, Defense Electronics
Orange Coast Venture Group

Prior Position

International Lending Representative, Philadelphia National Bank

DIRECTORY AND BIOGRAPHIES

Education
MBA, Wharton School
BS, Lehigh University

F. Daniel Blanchard
Orange Nassau, TX/Associate

Prior Positions
Office Manager, Golder, Thoma & Gressey
InterFirst Venture Corp.

Education
MBA, University of Chicago
BS, Louisiana State University

Paul A. Deiters
Orange Nassau, The Netherlands General Partner

Prior Positions
Unilever, Ltd.
Assistant Manager, Amsterdam-Rotterdam Bank N.V.

Education
MBA, University of Delft, The Netherlands
BS, University of Rotterdam

Guy R. Eugene
Orange Nassau, France, General Partner

Education
MBA, University of Paris
MBA, Wharton School

Herve LeGoupil
Orange Nassau, France
General Partner

Linda S. Linsalata
Orange Nassau, MA

Directorships
Unisource Inc.
Logos Corp.
Scientific Micro Systems Inc.
Software Distribution
Artificial Intelligence
Peripheral Products

Prior Positions
Marketing Manager, Systems Engineering Manager and Product and Systems Management, IBM

Education
MBA, Harvard University, 1982
BA, Mathematics, Vassar College, 1966

Gregory B. Peters
Orange Nassau, MA

Martin J. Silver
Orange Nassau, TX
Associate

Prior Positions
Product Marketing Manager, Hewlett-Packard
General Dynamics

Education
MBA, Wharton School
BS, Purdue University

Rene Smits
Orange Nassau, The Netherlands
Managing Director

Richard D. Tadler
Vice President, MA
General Partner

Directorships
Microdynamics, CAD
Microelectronic Packaging, Inc., Ceramic technology
EXPRO, Oil service

Prior Position
Assistant to the President, ARMCO, Inc.

Education

MBA, Wharton School, University of Pennsylvania, 1982
BS, University of Virginia, 1978

Joost E. Tjaden
President, MA

Directorships

Alpha Associates, S.A.
Bever Investments I & II
China Vest Management Ltd.
Orange Nassau Electronics, Inc.
Robotics, Inc.
Sigma Design, Inc.
XTEL Computer International B.V.

Prior Positions

Vice President, Orange-Nassau Group B.V., The Hague, Netherlands, 1981
Staff Member, Orange-Nassau Group B.V., The Hague, Netherlands, 1976–80

Education

MBA, University of Delft, Netherlands, 1974
Graduate, Business Economy, Rotterdam University, 1972

Paul Versluis
Orange Nassau, The Netherlands
General Partner

Alexander S. McGrath
Analyst, MA

Prior Positions

Corporate Finance Dept., Prudential-Bache Securities

Education

BA, Princeton

Robert Theleen
General Partner, Hong Kong

Average Size of Investment	$1.5M
Size of Fund	$100M
Investment Criteria	$500K minimum investment at any stage; diversified preferences including technology-based companies; no oil and gas exploration or real estate
Portfolio Companies	Undisclosed

ORIANS INVESTMENT COMPANY
529 Southwest Third Avenue
Portland, OR 97204
(503) 224-7885

Orians Entertainment Co.
700 Third, #850
Seattle, WA 98104
(206) 467-0880

Robert J. Orians, President
James M. Key, Vice President
J. H. Seeley, Jr., Vice President, Corp. Finance

Average Size of Investment	$300K
Size of Fund	$10M
Investment Criteria	High technology, medical technology, telecommunications
Portfolio Companies	Graphic Software Systems, Inc., Wilsonville, OR, Computer graphics; Northwest Instrument Systems, Inc., Beaverton, OR, Instruments; Saber Technology, Inc., San Jose, CA, CAE, CAD, CAM

OSCCO VENTURES
3000 Sand Hill Road
Building 4, Suite 140
Menlo Park, CA 94025
(415) 854-2222

James G. Rudolph
General Partner

Directorships

Cydrome, Minisupercomputers
DAVID Systems, Telecommunications
Krysallis, Semiconductor materials

Prior Positions

Partner, Booz Allen & Hamilton
President, Gnostic Systems & Technology

Education

PhD, Syracuse University, 1966
MS, New York University, 1959
BS, University of Illinois, 1955

F. Ward Paine
Partner

Directorships

Adaptive Intelligence, Manufacturing robotics
Command Data Systems, Software systems
Information Design, Microfilm equipment
Silverking Oceanic Farms, Anadromous fisheries
Peak System, Semiconductor materials

Prior Positions

Founder, KRS Electronics
Engineer, Joy Manufacturing Co.

Education

BS (ME), Princeton University, 1956

Stephen E. Halprin
General Partner

Directorships

Information Design, Microfilm equipment
Conect Hospitality Systems, Software systems
Seatek International, Stabilization systems for the oil industry

Prior Positions

Researcher, Stanford Business School, 1965–67
Industrial Engineer, Port Murray Dairy, 1961–63

Education

MBA, Stanford University, 1965
BS, Massachusetts Institute of Technology, 1960

Average Size of Investment	$750K
Size of Fund	$25M
Investment Criteria	Seed through second round; West and Southwest; proprietary technology
Portfolio Companies	Undisclosed

OSHER CAPITAL CORP.
Wyncote House
Township Line Road and Washington Lane
Wyncote, PA 19095
(215) 624-4800

L. Cantor

Average Size of Investment	$300K
Size of Fund	Undisclosed
Investment Criteria	Manufacturing and other diversified areas including construction and real estate; workouts
Portfolio Companies	Undisclosed

OXFORD PARTNERS
Soundview Plaza
1266 Main Street
Stamford, CT 06902
(203) 964-0592

233 Wilshire Boulevard
Suite 730
Santa Monica, CA 90401
(213) 458-3135

Francis X. Driscoll
General Partner, CT

Directorships

Adra Systems
Cray Research, Inc.
LNR Communications, Inc.
Immunetech Pharmaceuticals

Prior Positions

President, Francis X. Driscoll Associates, Inc.
Venture Capital Dept. Head, Rothschild, Inc.

Education

MBA, St. John's University, 1969
MSEE, New York University, 1958
University of Notre Dame, 1952

William R. Lonergan
General Partner, CT

Directorships

Zitel
Celerity Computing
Faraday Electronics
Kurzweil Applied Intelligence
Kurzweil Music
Saxpy

Prior Positions

Vice President, Business Development, Xerox Corp.
Director, Corporate Development, Burroughs Corp.

Education

MA, Philosophy, University of Pennsylvania

Kenneth W. Rind
General Partner, CT

Directorships

Theta-J Corp.
California Devices, Inc.
Applied Spectrum Technologies, Inc.
Diplomat Electronics
Baillie Gifford Technology Fund

Prior Positions

Principal, Xerox Development Corp.
Vice President, Corporate Finance, Oppenheimer (Partner, New York Plaza Associates)

Education

PhD, Columbia University
MA, Columbia University
BA, Cornell University

Cornelius T. Ryan
General Partner, CT

Directorships

Photec Diagnostics, Inc.
Micro General
Esprit Systems, Inc.
Diamond Electro-Tech
Access Technologies
Leasing Technologies International
Cognitive Systems
Hospital Efficiency Corp.

Prior Positions

President, GTE New Ventures, and Vice President, Corporate Development, GTE
Founder and President, Randolph Computer Corp.

Education

MBA, Wharton School, University of Pennsylvania
BE, University of Ottawa

Steven A. Birnbaum
General Partner, CA

Directorships

Innovus
Micro General

Prior Positions

Partner, Hohenberg & Associates
Principal, Xerox Corp.

Education

MBA, Harvard Business School
BS, Engineering, University of California at Los Angeles

Average Size of Investment	$1M
Size of Fund	$83.35M
Investment Criteria	High-technology area; 10× return in 5–10 years
Portfolio Companies	Access Technologies, Inc., South Natick, MA, Develops decision support software; Applied Spectrum Technologies, Inc., Minneapolis, MN, Manufactures spread spectrum communications equipment; Astech, Inc., Bedford, MA, Manufactures AC wire-connected extension telephones; Businessland, San Jose, CA, Retailer of advanced office equipment and computer systems; California Devices, Inc., San Jose, CA, Manufactures customized gate array semiconductors; Celerity Computing, San Diego, CA, Manufactures high-performance 32-bit networked-based engineering workstations; EnMasse Computer Corp., Acton, MA,

Manufacture transactional data processing system; Photec Diagnostics Inc., Little Falls, NJ, Diagnostic tests for clinical labs, doctor's offices, and home testing; Nastec Corp., Southfield, MI, Supply computer-aided engineering products and services; Athens, Oceanside, CA, Chemical cleaning process for reducing particles and trace impurities for sub-micron wafer fabrication; Adra Systems, Lowell, MA, Computer-aided design/drafting systems; Cohesive Network Corp., Campbell, MA, Digital switch for data and voice communications; Cogensys, La Jolla, CA, Non-rule based expert systems for vertical market; Hospital Efficiency Corp., Boston, MA, Specialize in hospital energy conservation projects; Immunetech Pharmaceuticals, San Diego, CA, Proprietary technology for identifying new immunologically active peptides; Leasing Technologies International, Darien, CT, Leases high technology equipment to young growth-oriented companies; Cognitive Systems, New Haven, CT, Developer of artificial intelligence software; Diamond Electro-Tech, Ann Arbor, MI, Manufactures blood gas and ion analyzers; Diplomat Electronics, Melville, NY, Distributes electronic components; Esprit Systems, Inc., Melville, NY, Supplies video display terminals; Faraday Electronics, Palo Alto, CA, Manufactures micro-CPUs; Saxpy, Sunnyvale, CA, Developer of optical computers; Innovus, Fremont, CA, Manufactures gas-flow controllers for the semiconductor industry; Kurzweil Applied Intelligence, Inc., Waltham, MA, Developer of a voice-activated typewriter; Kurzweil Music System, Inc., Waltham, MA, Developer of musical synthesizers using artificial intelligence; Metcal, Inc., Menlo Park, CA, Manufactures self-limiting heating elements; Micro General, Irvine, CA, Manufactures digital postal scales; Queue Systems, Parkersburg, WV, Manufactures equipment for biotechnology; RF Monolithics, Dallas, TX, Manufactures surface acoustic wave (SAW) devices used as filters and oscillators; Telesis Corp., Chelmsford, MA, Manufactures CAD/CAM systems; Theta-J Corp., Wakefield, MA, Manufactures optical solid-state relays and single-chip power supplies; Vitelic, Los Altos, CA, Developer of CMOS memory; Zitel, San Jose, CA, Manufactures semiconductor memory systems and memory-intensive microcomputer systems

PACIFIC VENTURE CAPITAL LTD.
1405 North King Street
Suite 302
Honolulu, HI 96817
(808) 847-6502

Dexter J. Taniguchi

Average Size of Investment	$100K
Size of Fund	$1.4M
Investment Criteria	Diversified areas of interest; geographic location is of importance; will act as lead investor
Portfolio Companies	Undisclosed

PACIFIC VENTURE PARTNERS
3000 Sand Hill Road
Building 4, Suite 175
Menlo Park, CA 94025
(415) 854-2266

James C. Balderston
General Partner

Directorship

Imagen, Raster image processors to merge text and graphics

Prior Position

General Manager, Searle Ultrasound, 1980

Education

MCS, Amos Tuck School, 1952
BA, Dartmouth College, 1951

Ridgon Currie
General Partner

Directorships

BDS Corp.
Lucid Corp.
MoneyCare, Inc.
Synergy Computer Graphics Corp.
Triconex Corp.

Prior Positions

Vice President, Diablo (Xerox), 1981
Director Special Business, Xerox, 1976

Education

MBA, Harvard University, 1956
BIE, Georgia Tech, 1951

Anthony T. Ellis
General Partner

Directorship

MoneyCare, Inc.

Prior Positions

Executive Vice President, American Security Bank, N.A., 1979–81
Vice President, Finance, and Treasurer, Kennecott Copper Corp., 1970–79

Education

MBA, Harvard Business School, 1956
BS, University of California at Berkeley, 1951

Average Size of Investment	$500K
Size of Fund	$15.2M
Investment Criteria	Start-up and early-stage technology companies with products or services which address large and rapidly growing markets; prefer investments in California
Portfolio Companies	BDS Corp., Mountain View, CA, Independent plug-compatible, value-added computer printer supplier selling directly to end users; David Systems, Inc., Sunnyvale, CA, Developed integrated voice/data add-on products for existing analog PBXs such as AT&T's Dimension or Centrex; Biotrack, Inc., Sunnyvale, CA, Test systems for drug monitoring; Imagen Corp., Santa Clara, CA, Manufactures intelligent page printer systems; Lucid, Inc., Palo Alto, CA, Developing a Portable Common Lisp environment and Lisp runtime systems as delivery vehicles for general-purpose computers; Moneycare, Inc., Mountain View, CA, Developing personal financing microsoftware and related services; By Video, Inc., Sunnyvale, CA, Interactive video terminals, customer activated retail transaction systems; Synergy Computer Graphics Corp., Sunnyvale, CA, Manufactures CAD/CAM output devices; Triconex, Corp., Irvine, CA, Developing fault-tolerant process control computer systems

PAINE WEBBER VENTURE MANAGEMENT CO.
265 Franklin Street
Suite 1501
Boston, MA 02110
(617) 439-8300

Richard A. Charpie
Managing General Partner

Directorships

Ceramics Process Systems Corp.
Axiom Technology Corp.
Aseco Corp.

Education

PhD, Management, Massachusetts Institute of Technology, Sloan School of Management, 1979
MS, Physics, Massachusetts Institute of Technology, 1975
BS, Physics, Massachusetts Institute of Technology, 1973

William C. Mills, III
Managing General Partner

Directorships

Material Progress Corp.
Cytogen Corp.
Tegra, Inc.

Education

Masters, Management, Massachusetts Institute of Technology, Sloan School of Management, 1981
Masters, Chemistry, Massachusetts Institute of Technology, 1979
BA, Chemistry, Princeton University, 1977

Merlin D. Schulze
Managing General Partner

Directorship

Paine Webber Development Inc.

Prior Position

Director of Corporate Development, Xerox Corp.

Education

MBA, Northwestern University
AB, Willamette University

Marcia J. Hooper
Charles D. Yie

Average Size of Investment	$750K
Size of Fund	Undisclosed
Investment Criteria	Technology-based companies of interest; will act as lead investor
Portfolio Companies	Undisclosed

DIRECTORY AND BIOGRAPHIES

PALMER PARTNERS
300 Unicorn Park Drive
Woburn, MA 01801
(617) 933-5445

William H. Congleton
General Partner

Directorships

Advanced Electronics Design, Inc., Computer peripherals
Cintas Corp., Corporate uniforms
Datamedia Corp., Computer peripherals
Great Lakes Chemical Corp., Chemicals
Vestar Research, Inc., Biotechnology

Prior Positions

Senior Vice President, American Research and Development Corp.
Group Leader, Standard Oil Company (Indiana)

Education

MBA, Harvard University, 1948
MS, Princeton University, 1943
BS, Princeton University, 1942

John A. Shane
General Partner

Directorships

Abt Associates, Inc., Consulting
AVIV Corp., Computer peripherals
Boston Biotechnology Corp., Biological products
Darling Associates, Computer software
Provident Capital Corp., Real estate development
Provident Institution for Savings, Bank
Sensor Diagnostics, Inc., Biotechnology
United Asset Management Corp., Financial service
Summa Four, Telephone equipment

Prior Positions

Senior Vice President, American Research and Development Corp.
Research Assistant, Harvard Business School

Education

MBA, Harvard University, 1960
BA, Princeton University, 1954

Stephen J. Ricci
General Partner

Directorships

Advanced Circuit Technology, Inc., Industrial components
AMNET, Inc., Telecommunications
Cambridge Tool and Manufacturing Co., Inc., Machine tools
Kaye Instruments, Inc., Industrial equipment
New England Venture Capital Association, Venture capital organization
Summa Four, Inc., Telecommunications
Vac-Hyd Corp., Turbine engine repair
Support B.V., Dutch venture firm
Iris Graphics, Inc., High resolution ink-jet printer

Prior Positions

Chief Engineer, Cambridge Tool & Manufacturing Co., Inc.
Process Engineer, E. I. DuPont de Nemours & Co.

Education

MBA, Harvard University, 1974
BS, Tufts University, 1967

Karen S. Camp
Partner

Directorship

Sensor Diagnostics, Inc., Biotechnology

Prior Positions

Assistant Vice President, State Street Bank and Trust Co. International Officer, Texas Commerce Bank
Advisor, La Banque Rothschild
Management Trainee, Federal Reserve Bank of New York

Education

MA, Middlebury College, 1971
AB, Smith College, 1969

Michael T. Fitzgerald
Partner

Directorship

Distribution Management Systems, Inc., Application software

Prior Position

Marketing Representative, IBM

Education

MBA, Harvard University, 1981
BA, Amherst College, 1975

Alison J. Seavey
Partner

Prior Positions

Administrator, Children's Hospital Medical Center
Engineering Assistant, Jackson & Moreland, Inc.

Education

M.Ed., Boston University, 1971
BA, Beaver College, 1968

Average Size of Investment	$500K
Size of Fund	$52.5M
Investment Criteria	Quality of management key
Portfolio Company	Undisclosed

PAPPAJOHN CAPITAL RESOURCES
2116 Financial Center
Des Moines, IA 50309
(515) 244-5746

John Pappajohn
Owner, Manager

Directorships

Caremark, Inc.
Bion Corp., Ultrasound imaging
Asbestec Industries
Infrasonics, Inc.
Continental Healthcare Systems
Women's Health Centers of America
Lasermed, Inc., Laser technology in medical area
Medical Imaging Centers of America
Coratomic, Inc.
Pancretec, Inc.
Hemacare, Inc., Blood filtration

Prior Position

President, Equity Dynamics, Inc., Corporate finance

Education

BS, University of Iowa, 1952

Average Size of Investment	$500K
Size of Fund	$20M
Investment Criteria	Interested in health care and technology-based companies along with other diversified areas; start-ups and will act as lead investor
Portfolio Companies	Asbestec Industries Inc., Training schools et al in asbestos abatement training; Caremark Inc., Home health care; Continental Healthcare System, Hospital information systems; Coratomic Inc., Pacemakers; Infrasonics Inc., Respirators; Medical Imaging Centers of America, Diagnostic imaging centers; Pancretec Inc., Insulin, chemotherapy, fertility pump manufacturers; Women's Health Centers of America, Free standing clinics for women patients

PATHFINDER VENTURE CAPITAL FUNDS
One Corporate Center
7300 Metro Boulevard
Suite 585
Minneapolis, MN 55435
(612) 835-1121

Jack K. Ahrens, II
Partner

Directorships

VG Systems, Inc.
Micro Business Applications, Inc.
American Medical Plan, Inc., Health maintenance organization (HMO) management company

Prior Positions

Officer, United Capital Corp. of Illinois
President, United Venture Capital, Inc.

DIRECTORY AND BIOGRAPHIES

Education

Certified Financial Analyst
BS, Indiana University, 1971

Marvin Bookin
Partner

Prior Positions

Founder and Vice President, DATA 100
Data Display Division, Control Data Corp.

Education

BS, Iowa State University, 1957

Norman Dann
Founding Partner

Directorships

CNS, Inc.
Loredan
EdenTec
LyphoMed, Inc., Critical care micronutrients
Cardiometrics, Inc.
Innoventions Biomedical, Inc.
Controlled Release Technologies, Inc.
Spectro Sonex, Inc.
Microgon, Inc.

Prior Positions

Principal, Pathfinder Consultants
Senior Vice President, Medtronic, Inc.
Owner, Dann Co.

Education

BS, Industrial Engineering, Pennsylvania State University, 1949

Andrew J. Greenshields
Founding Partner

Directorships

Intran Corp.
AET, Chip-handling equipment

Prior Positions

Senior Contract Negotiator, Honeywell
Senior Vice President, First Midwest Capital Corp.

Education

BA, University of Minnesota, 1962

Todd Johnson
Associate

Prior Positions

Controller, Centennial Group, Inc.
Auditor, Touche Ross & Co.

Education

BA, University of Wisconsin, 1980
CPA, 1980

Kenneth H. Levin
Associate

Prior Positions

Investment Officer, The Hillman Company

Education

MBA, University of Chicago, 1980
PhD, Biochemistry, University of California, 1983

Gary A. Stoltz
Founding Partner

Directorships

Central Data Corp.
Disk-Tek, Inc.
Intran Corp.
Microdynamics
BlueLine Software, Inc.

Prior Positions

Principal, Pathfinder Consultants
Founder and Vice President, DATA 100

Education

MBA, Northwestern University, 1956
BS, Case Institute of Technology, 1955

Average Size of Investment	$750K
Size of Fund	$73M
Investment Criteria	All stages from start-ups to leveraged buy-outs; U.S. only; medical, computer and data communications industries
Portfolio Companies	ADL, Inc., St. Paul, MN, Intravenous volumetric infusion pumps and disposable administration sets; Advanced Cardiovascular Systems, Inc., Mountain View, CA, Coronary dilatation catheter systems; American Medical Electronics, Inc., Dallas, TX, Electronic bone growth stimulation equipment; The Anderson Cornelius Company, Eden Prairie, MN, Computerized environmental and facility control systems; Autographix, Inc., Waltham, MA, Computer systems for generating color graphic 35mm slides; Automated Electronic Technology, Inc., North St. Paul, MN, Handling equipment for surface mounted electronic chips; BlueLine Software, Inc., Minneapolis, MN, Productivity software for IBM (and compatible) computers; Cardiometrics, Inc., Palo Alto, CA, Cardiac output measurement systems; Central Data Corp., Champaign, IL, Commercial and industrial grade microcomputer boards, subsystems and systems; Controlled Release Technologies, Inc., Batavia, IL, Drug delivery systems; Cordata Technologies, Inc., Thousand Oaks, CA, Portable and desktop microcomputers and laser printers that are compatible with IBM PC; Cryo2 Corp., Fort Pierce, FL, Liquid oxygen systems for home medical care; Disk-Tec, Inc., Champaign, IL, Computer disk media for 5¼" and 3½" Winchester hard disk drives; EdenTec Corp., Eden Prairie, MN, Sudden Infant Death (SIDS) monitoring equipment; IBIS Systems, Inc., Westlake Village, CA, High performance disk drives; ImmunoMed Corp., Tampa, FL, Pharmaceuticals for veterinary (and potential human) use; Innoventions Biomedical, Inc., Indianapolis, IN, Laser catheter systems for coronary angioplasty; Loredan Biomedical, Inc., Davis, CA, Sports medicine and rehabilitation systems; Medinet, Inc., Purchase, NY, Medical image processing and networking equipment; Micro Business Applications, Inc., Burnsville, MN, Business software for microcomputers; Microgon, Inc., Laguna Hills, CA, Hollow fibre microfiltration systems; Raycom Systems, Inc., Boulder, CO, Fiberoptic interconnection devices for computer systems; Resonex, Inc., Sunnyvale, CA, Magnetic Resonance (MR) imaging machines for cardiac diagnosis; Smith Laboratories, Inc., Northbrook, IL, Orthopedic rehabilitation devices and drugs; SpectroSonex, Inc., Van Nuys, CA, Medical ultrasonic imaging systems; Stearns Computer Systems Corp., Eden Prairie, MN, Office automation systems; VG Systems, Inc., Woodland Hills, CA, Computer graphic workstations for CAD/CAM and command and control; CNS, Inc., Eden Prairie, MN, Computer systems which provide graphic reproduction of EEG responses for medical monitoring; Comlinear Corp., Fort Collins, CO, High-performance electronic operational amplifiers used in defense, communications, and computer products; Intran Corp., Minnetonka, MN, Computer/workstation system for electronic publishing and graphics; Microdynamics, Inc., Dallas, TX, CAD/CAM and automated sewing systems for footwear and apparel industry; VIA Systems, Inc., North Billerica, MA, Computer-aided system for the design of electronic integrated computer-aided systems circuits

ALAN PATRICOF ASSOCIATES, INC.
545 Madison Avenue
New York, NY 10022
(212) 753-6300

1245 Oakmead Parkway
Suite 105
Sunnyvale, CA 94086
(408)737-8788

24 Upper Brook Street
London W1Y 1PD
England
493-3633

67 rue de Monceau
75008 Paris
France
563-3513

Alan J. Patricof
Chairman, NY

Directorships

Datascope Corp., Medical electronics manufacturer
Harman International Industries, Inc., Manufactures home and auto speakers
Kings Road Productions, Inc., Film producer
Cellular Communications, Inc.
Cinecom International Films
Orbis Communications, Inc.

Prior Positions

Assistant to the Chairman, Northwest Industries, Inc., 1968–69
Founder, Lin Broadcasting Corp.

DIRECTORY AND BIOGRAPHIES

Founder, Datascope Corp.
Founder, New York Magazine Co.
Assistant Vice President and Vice President, Central National Corp., 1960–68
Lambert & Co., 1958
Schroeder, Naess & Thomas

Education

MS, Finance, Columbia University Graduate School of Business, 1957
BS, Finance, Ohio State University, 1955

Robert G. Faris
President, NY

Directorships

Bioassay Systems Corp.
Plains Resources, Inc., Oil and gas drilling
Liposome Technology, Inc.
Syntro Corp., Expands biotechnological and genetic engineering advances into commercial applications
VSC, Inc., Video display devices, monitors, and cameras
Creative Biomolecules, Inc.
Protein Databases, Inc.
SCP Communications, Inc.

Prior Positions

McKinsey and Company, 1969–70
Amoco Chemicals Division, Standard Oil of Indiana, 1960–68

Education

MBA, Finance and Economics, University of Chicago, 1964
BS, Chemistry, Pennsylvania State University, 1960

Lewis Solomon
Executive Vice President, NY

Directorships

Anadigics, Inc., Electronic circuits manufactured using gallium arsenide material
Canaan Computer Corp., Designs, manufactures, and services a family of multiuser mainframe computers
Cybernetic Data Products Corp., Electronic moving message signs
Microelectronic Packaging, Inc., Supplies ceramic hermetically sealed packages used by the semiconductor industry
Multiflow Computer, Inc., Designs and builds a 64-bit general-purpose computer
Ontologic, Inc., Object-oriented data base management system

Prior Positions

Senior Vice President and Executive Assistant to the Chairman, General Instrument Corp., 1980–83
Vice President, Marketing and General Manager, Microelectronics Division, General Instrument Corp., 1968–80
Director of Marketing, Teledyne Corp.
Director of Marketing, Fairchild Semiconductor Corp.
Design Engineering, Univac Corp.

Education

Stanford University Graduate School of Business, 1975
Temple University Graduate School of Industrial Engineering
BS, Physics, St. Joseph's College of Philadelphia, 1954

W. R. Bottoms, PhD
Senior Vice President, CA

Directorships

California Devices, Inc., Semicustom integrated circuits
Dominion Venture Partners
Ion Beam Systems, Inc.
Semiconductor Test Solutions, Inc., Automatic test equipment for the digital LSI/VLSI segment of the market
Superwave Technology, Inc., Advanced processing of equipment for semiconductor and microelectronics industry

Prior Positions

Vice President of Corporate Development, Varian Associates
President of the Semiconductor Equipment Group, Varian Associates, 1982
General Manager, Varian Associates, 1977
Manager of Research and Development, Varian Associates, 1976
Professor of Electrical Engineering, Princeton University, 1969–76
Research Physicist, Exxon Corp., 1969

Education

PhD, Solid State Physics and Chemistry, Tulane University, 1969
MS, Physics, Tulane University, 1967
BS, Physics, Huntington College, 1965

John C. Baker
Vice President, NY

Directorships

Optical Data, Inc., Optically erasable storage
Skylink Corporation, mobile satellite system

Prior Positions

Research Econometrician, Data Resources, Inc.
Marketing Management, GFI/Knoll
Vice President of Marketing/Europe, Knoll International

Education

MBA, Marketing and Finance, Harvard Business School
BS, Mathematics and Economics, Harvard College

Jonathan Ben-Cnaan
Vice President, NY

Directorships

Inspiration Systems, Inc., Software products
Market Vision Corp., Computer software and systems for securities traders
The Langer Biomechanics Group, Inc., Foot and gait related products
Transform Logic Corporation, software and maintenance systems for IBM mainframes

Prior Positions

Founder and General Manager, Ben-Cnaan Marketing and Distribution
Circulation and Distribution Manager, *Monitin Magazine*
Assistant Product Manager, Braun Appliances Division of Gillette Corp.
Financial Consultant, Northern Energy Corp.

Education

MBA, Finance, Marketing and Business Policy, Boston University Graduate School of Business Administration, 1981
BA, Economics, Hebrew University of Jerusalem, 1979

Charles Leonard
Vice President, NY

Prior Positions

Vice President, Business Information Group, Dun & Bradstreet, 1985–86
General Manager, Technical Data Resources, Dun & Bradstreet, 1980–85
Director, Marketing Information Services Development, Dun & Bradstreet, 1976–80

Education

MBA, The Wharton School, 1961
BS, Massachusetts Institute of Technology, 1958

Charles Cheskiewicz
Managing Director, NY

Prior Position

Development Engineer/Systems Analyst, Eastman-Kodak Company

Education

MBA, Management and Finance, Wharton School, 1979
BS, Engineering, Pennsylvania State University, 1984

Camilla Jackson
Associate, CA

Prior Positions

Product Manager, Becton-Dickinson Consumer Products
Senior Sales Forecast Analyst, Johnson & Johnson Personal Products

Education

MBA, Marketing, Fairleigh Dickinson University, 1980
BS, Microbiology, University of Maryland, 1975

Paige A. Meili
Associate, NY

Prior Positions

Associate, Chemical Venture Capital Corp., 1985–86
Associate Director, Baxter Travenol Laboratories, Inc., 1980–85
Consultant, McKinsey & Company, Inc., summer 1979

Education

MBA, Harvard Graduate School of Business Administration, 1980
BA, Princeton University, 1976

William Cross
Associate, NY

DIRECTORY AND BIOGRAPHIES

Prior Positions

Associate, Westchase Morgan Incorporated, summer 1985
Freelance Journalist, India Afghanistan, Pakistan, 1984
Business Development Analyst, Corning Glass Works, 1981–84

Education

MBA, Harvard University Graduate School of Business Administration, 1986
BA, Yale University, 1981

Ronald M. Cohen
Executive Chairman, London

Directorships

My Kinda Holdings Ltd., Specialty theme restaurants
Package Programs Ltd., Financial software for mainframe computers
Sinclair Research Ltd., Consumer electronics products

Prior Positions

Consultant, McKinsey & Co., Great Britain and Italy
Associate, Institut de Développment Industriel, France

Education

Harvard Business School
Oxford

Peter Troughton
Director, United Kingdom

Prior Positions

Managing Director, British Telecom Enterprises, 1984–86
Director, British Telecom/London, 1982–84
General Manager, British Telecom/City Telephone Area, 1978–82

Education

BSE, First Class Honors, Electrical Engineering, London University
PhD, Integrated Circuits at Microwave Frequency, University College London

Peter Englander
Director, London

Directorships

Encotel Systems Ltd.
Information Technology Ltd., Minicomputers and office automation systems
Integrated Power Semiconductors Ltd., Integrated circuits for power control applications
Sphinx Ltd., Utility and applications software compatible with UNIX
Systematics International Group of Companies, Ltd., Financial software for microcomputers

Prior Positions

Financial Analyst, Air Products Ltd.
Financial Consultant, Boston Consulting Group

Education

MS, Management, Massachusetts Institute of Technology, 1976
Chemical Engineering, University of Manchester, 1973

Adrian Beecroft
Director, London

Prior Position

Financial Consultant, Boston Consulting Group (London)

Education

MBA, Harvard University, 1976
Physics, The Queen's College, Oxford, 1968

Jonathan Stuart
Assistant Director, United Kingdom

Directorships

Video Data Systems, Ltd., computer graphics systems
Metropolis Studios, sound studios

Prior Positions

Senior Vice President, LF Rothschild, Unterberg, Towbin International, 1983–85
Director, Hambros Advanced Technology Trust, 1981–83
Chief Engineer, Laser Scan Laboratories, Ltd. 1975–81

Education

BSE, Engineering and Electrical Sciences, Cambridge University, 1975

Maurice Tchénio
Managing Director, Paris

Directorships

Toupargel, S.A., Retail chain
Kalamazoo, S.A., Business systems distributor

Prior Positions

Associate, Institut de Développement Industriel
Teacher, École des Hautes Études Commerciales de Paris

Education

Harvard Business School, with top awards
École des Hautes Études Commerciales de Paris

Eric Adjoubel
Associate, Paris

Prior Positions

Director of Export, CGCT (division ITT), France
Manager of Export Sales, CIT, France

Education

MBA, International Business, Harvard Business School, 1977
Management, Ecole Nationale Superieure des Mines, 1975
International Economics, Faculte de Sciences
Economiques, 1975

Patrick DeGiovanni
Associate, Paris

Prior Positions

Engineer, COFROR (France)
Administrative Director, The Neiman Group
Consultant, Société Générale
Joint Managing Director, Private industrial equipment manufacturer

Education

Engineering, L'École Polytechnique, 1965

Average Size of Investment	Undisclosed
Size of Fund	Total U.S. capital: $240M; France: FF 400M; United Kingdom: £40M
Portfolio Companies	Acrian, Inc., Cupertino, CA, Designs, develops, manufactures, and markets an extensive line of advanced semiconductor devices, principally microwave and radio frequency power transistors, and higher-level assemblies; Anadigics, Inc., Morristown, NJ, Manufactures electronic circuits using gallium arsenide material; Applied Intelligent Systems, Inc., Ann Arbor, MI, Develops and manufactures machine vision and seed analyzer systems; Bioassay Systems Corp., Woburn, MA, Biological testing laboratory; California Devices, Inc., San Jose, CA, Designs and manufactures semicustom integrated circuits; Camex, Inc., Boston, MA, Develops, manufactures, sells and services computer graphics systems for the newspaper, printing and publishing industries; Canaan Computer Corp., Trumbull, CT, Designs, manufactures, and services a family of economical, time-shared, multiuser mainframe computers; Cellular Communications, Inc., New York, NY, Construction and operation of cellular mobile radiotelephone service; CIMCO, Austin TX, Numerically controls upgrade systems to the machine tool industry; Cinecom International Films, New York, NY, Acquires and distributes independently produced, high quality English language films targeted at highly educated, adult audiences, aged 25–40, in urban markets; Creative Biomolecules, Inc., Woburn, MA, Develops processes for production of biologically active proteins and peptides using advanced techniques of nucleic acid, protein, and organic chemistry; Cybernetic Data Products Corp., Chatsworth, CA, Designs and manufactures electronic moving message signs utilizing LED displays and microcomputer controls; Cygnet Systems, Inc., Sunnyvale, CA, Designs, develops, and markets an electronic storage and retrieval system; Datametrics Corporation, Chatsworth, CA, Supplies military qualified, high speed and high resolution digital printers and printer plotters; Diagnon Corp., Westport, CT, Produces and markets clinical test kit which incorporates monoclonal antibodies to diagnose certain human illnesses; Docupro Corporation, Santa Clara, CA, Develops a modular, ethernet networked, automated composition system for inplant publishing groups; Dollar Dry Dock Savings Bank, White Plains, NY, A New York chartered savings bank; Dominion Venture Partners, Inc., San Francisco, CA, Leases equipment to venture capital companies; Emmis Broadcasting Corporation, Indianapolis, IN, Acquires broadcasting properties; Harman International Industries, Inc., North Ridge, CA, Leading manufacturer of consumer high fidelity speakers for home and automotive use; Image Storage/Retrieval Systems, Inc., West Trenton, NJ, Develops and markets a proprietary information delivery system; Immunotech Corp., Allston, MA, Develops diagnostics reagents for the hospital and clinical laboratory markets; Incepts, Inc., Dallas, TX, Provides proprietary software products, consulting and data processing services for the life insurance industry; Inspiration Systems, Inc., Sewickley, PA, Develops, markets, and supports a state-of-the-art set of software products; International Biotechnologies, Inc., New Haven, CT, Manufactures and markets restriction and modifying enzymes, ultrapure and fine chemicals for the molecular biology research and development community; International Software Database Corp., Fort Collins, CO, An international clearing center for obtaining computer software information as well as for the sale of software products; Ion Beam Systems, Inc., Beverly, MA, Develops and markets products utilizing focused ion beam technology employed in materials characterization and semiconductor device production; Kings Road Productions, Inc., Los Angeles, CA, Develops

and produces moderately budgeted films; The Langer Biomechanics Group. Inc., Deer Park, NY, Design, development, manufacture, and sale of foot- and gait-related products; LAN.TEL, Inc., Orleans, MA, Produces a low-cost PABX business communication system with voice and high-speed data PBX; Lanx Corp., San Jose, CA, Manufactures sputtered magnetic media in rigid 5¼" and 8" diameter disks for Winchester drive applications; Liposome Technology, Inc., Menlo Park, CA, Utilizes liposomes for human diagnostics and therapeutics in a drug delivery system; Lomax Oil and Gas Co., Inc., Houston, TX, Explores, develops, and produces oil and gas within the United States; Luxtron Corporation, Mountain View, CA, Develops and markets unique phosphor based fiberoptic temperature sensing devices to be used principally in electrically hostile environments; Market Vision Corp., New York, NY, Develops, markets, and services computer software and systems that provide securities traders with investment info; Microelectronic Packaging, Inc., Scottsdale, AZ, Supplies ceramic hermetically sealed packages called CERDIPS, which are used by the semiconductor industry; Middex Hospitality, Inc., New York, NY, Chain of "hometels" in the northwest region of the United States; Miniscribe Corp., Longmont, CO, Designs, develops, manufactures, and markets 5¼" Winchester technology disk drives; Multiflow Computer, Inc., Branford, CT, Designs and builds a high-speed 64-bit general-purpose computer for scientific and engineering applications; Network Equipment Technologies, Inc., Menlo Park, CA, Develops and markets an Integrated Digital Network Exchange, a "superswitch multiplexer"; Nimbus Medical, Inc., Rancho Cordova, CA, Develops and markets circulatory support medical devices; Ontologic, Inc. (formerly Mosaic Technologies, Inc.), Billerica, MA, Developing an object oriented database management system; Optical Data, Inc., Tigard, OR, Optically erasable storage; Orbis Communications, Inc., New York, NY, Television distribution and advertising sales company; PETS (Professional Expert Training Systems), New York, NY, Provides specialized investment services to the professional trading community; Plains Resources, Inc., Oklahoma City, OK, Exploratory drilling in oil and gas acreage; Porta-Printer Systems, Inc., Largo, FL, Develops, markets, and distributes a portable, computerized on-site meter-reading and billing system for electric, gas, and water utility industry; Protein Databases, Inc., Huntington, NY, Service laboratory; Protolite Corp., San Jose, CA, Develops, manufactures, and supplies imaging products for the visual communications industry; PSI Star Corp., Hayward, CA, New process for etching the pattern in copper foil on laminated circuit boards used in assembling electronic equipment; Quantronix Corp., Smithtown, NY, Laser company; Quantum Computer Services, Inc., Vienna, VA, Provides a computer network and on-line services for home computers; Quick Service Concepts, Inc., Cabin John, MD, Fast-food restaurants; SCP, Inc., New York, NY, Publishes surgical journals; SDA Systems; Santa Clara, CA, Develops, markets, and supports complete turnkey CAD systems for VLSI design; Semiconductur Test Solutions, Inc., Santa Clara, CA, Develops and manufactures automatic test equipment for the digital LSI/VLSI segment of the ATE market; Shared Financial Systems, Inc., Dallas, TX, Designs, develops and markets an on-line electronic financial transaction system for financial institutions; Skylink Corp., Boulder, CO, A company formed to promote, develop and launch a Mobile Satellite System (MSS) which would provide cellular-type communications to remote areas not serviced by standard telephone or cellular communications service; Stewart, Tabori & Chang, Inc., New York, NY, Publishes illustrated hardcover and paperback books; Superwave Technology, Inc., Santa Clara, CA, Develops and produces advanced processing equipment utilizing microwave energy for the semiconductor and microelectronics industry; Symbolics, Inc., Cambridge, MA, Develops, designs, and manufactures high-performance personal computing environments for artificial intelligence; Syntro Corp., San Diego, CA, Formed to expand biotechnological and genetic engineering advances into commercial applications; Transform Logic Corporation, Phoenix, AZ, Develops and markets a software and maintenance system to automate software design, programming, and implementing functions for IBM mainframe computers; VCS, Inc., Carol Stream, IL, Manufactures a range of video display devices, monitors, and cameras; Velo-Bind, Inc., Sunnyvale, CA, Business of document packaging using a unique bindery process; VMX, Inc., Richardson, TX, Develops a microprocessor and disk-based storage and switching system called Voice Message Exchange; Aberdeen Cable Services Ltd., United Kingdom, Operation of a cable network; Bellwinch Limited, United Kingdom, Building and marketing of private residential housing in London and South England; Computacenter Limited, United Kingdom, Nationwide organization for the sale and maintenance of microcomputer hardware and software to corporate customers; Damon Biotech Europe Limited, United Kingdom, Establishing a UK factory for the production of monoclonal antibodies; Efamol Holdings plc, United Kingdom, Markets Gamma linolinic Acid (GLA) to the health food retail sector under the brand name "Efamol" and is applying for product licenses for the use of GLA in medical applications; Filtronic Components Limited, United Kingdom, Development, manufacture and marketing of filters and other microwave components; Hy-Comp Limited, United Kingdom, Packaging and distribution of semi-conductors and passive components; Information Technology Ltd., United Kingdom, Development, manufacture, and marketing of minicomputers and office automation systems; Integrated Power Semiconductors, United Kingdom, Design, manufacture, and marketing of integrated circuits for power control applications; Metropolis Studio Limited, United Kingdom, Sound recording studios; Mnemos Limited, United Kingdom, Manufacture and marketing of computer graphics storage and display devices; My Kinda Holdings Ltd., United Kingdom, Specialty theme restaurants; National Telephones Limited, United Kingdom, Development and marketing of microcomputer enhancement products and telephone equipment, the production of which is subcontracted; Neurotech Limited, United Kingdom, Design, manufacture and marketing of a range of neuro-muscular stimulation equipment; Package Programs Ltd., United Kingdom, Development and marketing of financial applications software for mainframe computers; Rel Limited, United Kingdom, The production of defense power supplies and the provision of "Tempest" products and services; Rubygrove Ltd., United Kingdom, Development and marketing of microcomputer enhancement products and telephone equipment; Soundcraft Electronics Limited, United Kingdom, Design, manufacture and marketing of sound mixers and multi-track analogue tape recorders; Spinx Ltd., United Kingdom, Publishing and distribution of utility and applications software compatible with the UNIX operating system; The Sterling Publishing Group Ltd., United Kingdom, Publishing of annual reference books, buyers' guides, and journals; Structural Development Group plc, United Kingdom, Manufactures and markets a range of building products based on gypsum and polymer; Systematics International Group of Companies Ltd., United Kingdom, Development and marketing of financial software packages for microcomputers; Video Data Systems Limited, United Kingdom, Manufacture and distribution of computer graphics system for creative artists; Waterstone & Company Limited, United Kingdom, Nationwide book retail chain; A.T. Gigadisc, France, Designs, manufactures and markets digital optical discs (DOD) systems, both drives and media; Acte, S.A., France, Operates a network of business centers which provide a full range of services on an interim basis directly and through franchising; Bioetica, France, Develops and manufactures products extracted from connective tissues of animals for cosmetic, medical and food applications; Cofirad, France, Holding company of a network of FM local radio stations braodcasting under the name of FUN FM; Exxa Publication, France, Software magazine; FPH/CEPP, France, Publishes four professional directories; Icare France Assurances, SA, France, Provides services to the automotive market; Kalamazoo, S.A., France, Small-business systems distributor; Mitchell Sports, SA, France, Designs, manufactures and markets a line of fishing reels; Silent Radio, SA, France, Markets and operates a network of LED display panels used for communication of news programs and advertisement; Transgene, France, Genetic engineering company which develops products, organisms and processes for pharmaceutical and food applications; Unixsys, France, Markets mini- and microcomputer systems running with UNIX operating system; Valorga, SA, France, Produces energy from various types of waste products through a process of continuous fermentation

PCK TECHNOLOGY INVESTMENTS
Four Old Mill Road
Georgetown, CT 06829
(203) 544-9484

Roger A. Curtis

Average Size of Investment	$100K
Size of Fund	Undisclosed
Investment Criteria	Technology-based and manufacturing companies of interest; start-ups considered
Portfolio Companies	Undisclosed

PENNSYLVANIA GROWTH INVESTMENT CORP.
1000 RIDC Plaza
Suite 311
Pittsburgh, PA, 15238
(412) 963-9339

Wm. L. Mosenson
President

Directorships

Aerotech, Inc., Electromechanics
Zurex, Inc., Electronic weighing systems
Berkley Schools, Business school
Plum Manufacturing, Electronics

Prior Position

President, Homestead Diesel Electronics, 1956–61

Education

Law, Duke University, 1936
Business Administration, Duke University, 1934

M. G. Dell

Average Size of Investment	Financing preferences: $250K–$500K to $1M with participations, minimum investment $100K
Size of Fund	Undisclosed
Investment Criteria	Diversified; geographical preference: Middle Atlantic, Northeast
Portfolio Companies	Undisclosed

DIRECTORY AND BIOGRAPHIES

PEREGRINE ASSOCIATES
606 Wilshire Boulevard
Santa Monica, CA 90401
(213) 458-1441

Frank LaHaye
Eugene I. Miller

Average Size of Investment	$500K
Size of Fund	$20M
Investment Criteria	Diversified company interests including technology-based companies; will act as lead investor; interested in start-ups
Portfolio Companies	Undisclosed

PERMIAN BASIN CAPITAL CORP.
303 West Wall
P.O. Box 1599
Midland, TX 79702
(915) 685-2000

Wayne Merritt

Average Size of Investment	$200K
Size of Fund	Undisclosed
Investment Criteria	Interested in oil industry endeavors; geographic area important
Portfolio Companies	Undisclosed

P. R. PETERSON VENTURE CAPITAL CORP.
7301 Washington Avenue South
Edina, MN 55435
(612) 941-8171

P. R. Peterson

Average Size of Investment	$200K
Size of Fund	$2M
Investment Criteria	Technology-based companies are of interest; start-ups encouraged; geographic location important
Portfolio Companies	Undisclosed

PHILADELPHIA COMMERCIAL DEVELOPMENT CORP.
Suite 433
Sovereign Building
714 Market Street
Philadelphia, PA 19106
(215) 238-7676

Thomas J. Patterson, Chairman
Dean Rosencranz, President
Joseph J. James, Deputy Director of Commerce, Philadelphia
Robert A. Price, Secretary

Average Size of Investment	$100K
Size of Fund	$1.5M
Investment Criteria	Diversified areas of interest including technology-based and manufacturing companies; Philadelphia businesses only
Portfolio Companies	Undisclosed

PHILADELPHIA INDUSTRIES, INC.
1401 Walnut Street
Philadelphia, PA 19102
(215) 569-9900

John J. Murray
Jack Farber

Average Size of Investment	$200K
Size of Fund	Undisclosed
Investment Criteria	Leveraged buy-outs are considered; geographic proximity important
Portfolio Companies	Undisclosed

PIONEER INVESTORS
113 East 55th Street
New York, NY 10022
(212) 980-9094

R. Scott Asen
James G. Niven

Average Size of Investment	$500K
Size of Fund	$60M
Investment Criteria	Diversified company interests; leveraged buy-outs are of interest; will act as lead investor
Portfolio Companies	Undisclosed

PIPER JAFFRAY & HOPWOOD, INC.
Piper Jaffray Tower
222 South Ninth Street
P.O. Box 28
Minneapolis, MN 55440
(612) 342-6000

R. Hunt Greene
First-Vice President
(612) 342-6310

Prior Position

Director of Corporate Development, Cardiac Pacemakers, Inc.

Education

MBA, Harvard Business School, 1975
BA, Northwestern University, 1971

Frank Bennett
Associate
(612) 342-6314

Prior Position

Vice President, Mayfield Corp.

Education

BS, University of Oregon, 1980

Douglas R. Whitaker
Associate
(612) 342-6316

Prior Positions

Securities Analyst, First Bank Systems, Inc.
Securities Analyst, Mark Twain Bancshares

Education

MBA, Harvard Business School, 1984
AB, Duke University, 1980

Average Size of Investment	$500K
Size of Fund	Undisclosed
Investment Criteria	No preference
Portfolio Companies	Undisclosed

THE PITTSFORD GROUP, INC.
8 Lodge Pole Road
Pittsford, NY 14534
(716) 223-3523

Logan M. Cheek, III
Managing Principal

Prior Positions

Group Program Manager, Xerox Corp.
Associate, McKinsey & Co.

Education

AB, Cornell University, 1960

C. C. Hipkins, Jr.
Principal

Prior Position

Senior Venture Manager, Exxon Corp.

Education

MBA, Harvard Business School, 1957
BSME, Catholic University of America, 1953

William R. Rassman, M.D.
Principal
(808) 935-3928

DIRECTORY AND BIOGRAPHIES

Directorships

Renewable Energy Ventures, Inc., Windmills/alternative energy
R-P/R&D, Vertical market software
Medware, Inc., Medical software

Prior Position

Private Practice of Surgery, St. Johnsbury, VT, and Hilo, HI, 1973–83

Education

MD, Virginia Medical College, 1966
BS, Long Island University, 1962

Average Size of Investment	$500K
Size of Fund	$30M
Investment Criteria	Medical/health care; finance at all stages but developmental
Portfolio Companies	Undisclosed

PIVAN MANAGEMENT CO.
7840 North Lincoln Avenue
Skokie, IL 60077
(312) 677-1142

David B. Pivan
Richard L. Nelson

Average Size of Investment	$300K
Size of Fund	$4M
Investment Criteria	Manufacturing and technology-based companies are of interest; geographic location is important
Portfolio Companies	Undisclosed

PLANT RESOURCES VENTURE FUNDS
124 Mt. Auburn Street
Cambridge, MA 02138
(617) 492-3900

John R. Hesse
Plant Resources Venture Funds

Directorships

International Plant Laboratories
New World Bank
Twyford Laboratories, Ltd.
United AgriSeeds, Inc.

Prior Positions

Chairman and President, American Garden Products, Inc., 1971–80
President, Private Equity Group, Inc., 1967–71
Associate, Corporate Finance, C. J. Lawrence Inc., 1963–67
Associate, New Business, F. Eberstadt & Co., 1959–62

Education

MBA, Harvard University, 1959
BS, Yale University, 1956

Richard C. McGinity
Richard O. von Werssowetz

Average Size of Investment	$750K
Size of Funds	$58M
Investment Criteria	Will act as lead investor; start-ups are desirable; interested in technology including agriculture, horticulture, food processing, and waste treatment
Portfolio Companies	Agricultural Technology Ltd., Cambridge, England; Agris Corp., Roswell, GA; AgriTech Systems, Inc., Portland, MA; Biotrol, Inc., Minneapolis, MN; Calgene, Inc., Davis, CA; Concentrex, Inc., Andover, MA; Microbial Resources Ltd., Berkshire, England; Plant Genetics, Inc., Davis, CA; Safer Agro-Chem, Ltd., Victoria, British Columbia; Twyford International, Inc., Somerset, England; United AgriSeeds, Inc., Champaign, IL

PNC VENTURE CAPITAL GROUP
5th Avenue and Wood Street
Pittsburgh, PA 15222
(412) 355-2245

David Hillman
Executive Vice President

Directorships

Pacamor Bearings, Inc., Miniature ball bearings
Franchise Enterprise, Inc., Hardee's franchise

Prior Positions
Vice President, PNC Venture Capital
Commercial Banking Officer, Pittsburgh National Bank

Education
MBA, University of Virginia, 1982
BA, Williams College, 1976

Jeffrey H. Schutz
Vice President

Directorships
Bellefonte Lime Co., Limestone producer
Fabrication Specialties Co., Robotic positioners

Prior Positions
Consultant, The Synectics Group, Washington, D.C.
International Banking, First National Bank of Boston

Education
MBA, University of Virginia, 1983
BA, Middlebury College, 1974

Peter V. Del Presto
Vice President

Prior Positions
Partner, Interactive Medical System
Director, Federal Systems Division, Commonwealth Clinical Systems
Junior Research Scientist, Department of Toxology, E. R. Squibb & Sons

Education
MBA, University of Virginia, 1985
ME, Biomedical Engineering, 1976
BS, University of Notre Dame, 1972

Average Size of Investment	$500K
Size of Fund	$20M
Investment Criteria	Mid-Atlantic or Midwest geographic preference; later-stage and/or current return preferred
Portfolio Companies	Undisclosed

PORCARI, FEARNOW & ASSOC., INC.
3D/International Tower
1900 West Loop South
Suite 1150
Houston, TX 77027
(713) 840-7500

Arthur J. Porcari
Michael T. Fearnow

Average Size of Investment	$500K
Size of Fund	Undisclosed
Investment Criteria	Return on investment; management staff
Portfolio Companies	Undisclosed

PRIME CAPITAL L.P.
One Landmark Square
Suite 800
Stamford, CT 06901
(203) 964-0642

Theodore Elliott
General Partner

Directorships
Avanti
CDA
UTI
Xylogics

Prior Positions
Vice President, General Electric Co., 1976–81
Vice President, Clark Dodge & Co., Inc., 1960–74

Education
LLD, New York University School of Law
MBA, Harvard University, 1959
AB, Harvard College, 1957

Dean E. Fenton
General Partner

DIRECTORY AND BIOGRAPHIES

Directorships

International Biotechnology, Inc., Biotechnology
Intelligent Business Systems, Inc., AI
Master Software, Inc., IBM mainframe software
Cognex, AI, Vision systems for industrial applications plus three other companies

Prior Positions

General Partner, Sprout Capital Groups, 1972–80
Venture Capital Finance Director, Arthur D. Little, Inc., 1970–72
Investment Associate, Boston Capital, Inc., 1965–70

Education

MBA, Columbia University, 1961
AB, Harvard College, 1955

Thomas H. Gnuse
General Partner

Directorships

CTi Data Corp., IBM-compatible data communications equipment
Inspiration Systems, Inc., Integrated multiuser software products
Cadre Technologies, Inc., Software system design tools
Xylogics, Microprocessor-based peripheral controllers
Auragen Systems Corp., Fault-tolerant supermicrocomputer systems

Prior Position

General Manager, NCR Corp.

Education

MBA, Harvard University, 1967
MS, Engineering, University of California at Los Angeles, 1964
BSEE, Duke University, 1961

Average Size of Investment	$750K
Size of Fund	$27M
Investment Criteria	Technology-oriented fund
Portfolio Companies	21 companies currently in portfolio

PRIMUS CAPITAL FUND
1375 East Ninth Street
Suite 2140
One Cleveland Center
Cleveland, OH 44114
(216) 621-2185

Loyal Wilson
David A. DeVore

Average Size of Investment	$750K
Size of Fund	$30M
Investment Criteria	Primus will consider an investment in any industry, but prefers businesses compatible with the manufacturing, service, and technology base in the Midwest
Portfolio Companies	Undisclosed

PRINCETON/MONTROSE PARTNERS
101 Poor Farm Road
Princeton, NJ 08540
(609) 921-1590

2331 Honolulu Avenue
Suite G
Montrose, CA 91020
(818) 957-3623

Ronald R. Hahn
Managing General Partner, NJ

Directorships

Neogen Corp.
Ocean Products, Inc.
Protein Databases, Inc.

Prior Positions

First Vice President/Treasurer, Commodities Corp.
Vice President, Heizer Corp.

Education

MBA, University of California, Los Angeles, 1968
BA, Occidental College, 1966

Donald R. Stroben
Managing General Partner, CA

Directorships
Beard Oil Company
Etz Lavud, Ltd.
USPCI, Inc.
Laura Scudder's, Inc.
Plant Genetics, Inc.
Growers Transplanting, Inc.

Prior Positions
Executive Vice President, Hayden, Stone, Inc.
President, Acapulco Restaurants

Education
MBA, Harvard, 1954
BA, Knox College, 1952

Charles I. Kosmont
General Partner, CA

Directorships
Earth Resource Data Corp.
Growers Transplanting, Inc.

Education
MBA, University of Southern California, 1982
BS, State University of New York at Albany, 1979

Richard J. Defieux
General Partner, NJ

Prior Position
Project Manager, Environmental Research & Technology, Inc.

Education
MBA, Columbia University, 1984
MA, Boston University, 1976
BA, Boston University, 1973

Average Size of Investment	$700K
Size of Fund	$17.1M
Investment Criteria	Agribusiness/food, energy/natural resources, waste treatment
Portfolio Companies	Earth Resource Data Corp.; Neogen Corp.; Ocean Products, Inc; Plains Resources, Inc.; Plant Genetics, Inc.; Protein Databases, Inc.; Laura Scudder's, Inc.; Sungene Technologies Corp.; Twyford International, Inc.

PRIVATE CAPITAL CORP.
2160 Highland Avenue
Birmingham, AL 35205
(205) 933-4618

William W. Featheringill
President

Directorships
SEAKO, Computer marketing
Industrial Supplies, Industrial distribution

Education
MBA, Columbia University Graduate School of Business, 1970
JD, Columbia School of Law, 1969
BE, Vanderbilt University, 1964

William P. Acker, III
Vice President

Directorships
Metretek, Remote data collection and transmission
Computer marketing
SEAKO

Education
Postgraduate work, Finance, University of Alabama, 1965–66
AB, Vanderbilt University, 1965

Average Size of Investment	$500K
Size of Fund	Not disclosed
Investment Criteria	Generally prefer familiar industries
Portfolio Companies	Metretek, Melbourne, FL, Remote data collection and transmission; Seako, Birmingham, AL, Computer marketing

DIRECTORY AND BIOGRAPHIES

PRO-MED CAPITAL INC.
1380 Miami Gardens Drive N.E.
No. Miami Beach, FL 33179
(305) 949-5900

F. M. Rosemore
President

Directorships

Western Financial Capital Corp. (SBIC)
First Western SBLC Inc. (SBLC)
Pro-Med Investment Corp. (MESBIC)

Education

BS and OD

Average Size of Investment	$100–600K
Size of Fund	$20M
Investment Criteria	Second tier financing; no start-up; prefer marketing program in place; portfolio accounts seeking business expansion funds
Portfolio Companies	Undisclosed

PRUTECH RESEARCH AND DEVELOPMENT PARTNERSHIP
1290 Ridder Park Drive, Suite One
San Jose, CA 95131
(408) 293-0990

Average Size of Investment	$4M
Size of Fund	$82M
Investment Criteria	High technology investments in products which have an 18–30 month development cycle in identified growth markets with projected volume greater than $500M and in which the companies can capture a significant market share
Portfolio Companies	Biosis, Palo Alto, CA, Biological pest control; Forest Laboratories, Inc., New York, NY, Pharmaceutical; Marquest Medical Products, Inc., Boulder, CO, Medical equipment; Mesa Diagnostics, Inc., Albuquerque, NM, Medical diagnostics; Synrto Corp., San Diego, CA, Biotechnology; Bolt, Beranek and Newman, Inc., Cambridge, MA, Computers; Intelledex, Inc., Corvallis, OR, Robotics; Quintron Corp., Quincy, IL, Cellular mobile phones; Irvine Sensors Corp., Costa Mesa, CA, Military electronics; LaPine Technology Corp., Milpitas, CA, Computer products; Tridom Corp., Marietta, GA, Telecommunications; Advanced Computer Techniques, New York, NY, Computer systems; American Software Inc., Atlanta, GA, Computer software; Near Space Communications, Inc., Plano, TX, Telecommunications; Aydin Corp., San Jose, CA, Telecommunications

PRUTECH RESEARCH AND DEVELOPMENT PARTNERSHIP II
1290 Ridder Park Drive, Suite One
San Jose, CA 95131
(408) 293-0990

Richard E. Moser
President, San Jose

Directorships

Optical Specialties, Inc.
Hana Biologics
Synbiotics Corp.
Syntro Corp.
TurboEnergy Systems, Inc.
Silvar-Lisco, Inc.
Quintron Corp.

Prior Positions

President, Chief Executive Officer, Lefcourt Group, Inc.
Vice President, Corporate Development Arcata Corp.

Education

MBA, Stanford, 1971
BA, Yale, 1963

Patrick Owen Burns
Vice President, New York

Directorships

Essence Communications, Inc.
The Long Island College Hospital
Minority Equity Capital Company, Inc. (MECCO)

Prior Positions

Partner, Consumer Venture Group
President, MECCO

Education

LLB, Harvard Law School, 1962
AB, Dartmouth College, 1959

Louis C. Gerken
Vice President, San Francisco

Directorships

Masstron
Tridom Corp.
LaPine Technology Corp.
Ecogen, Inc.
Visiontech, Inc.
Boston Scientific Corp.

Prior Positions

Member, Investment Committee, Montgomery Securities
Vice President, Wells Fargo Capital Markets
President, TCG International

Education

MBA, Southwest Methodist University, 1974
BA, University of Redlands, 1971

Irving Weiman
Vice President, San Jose

Directorships

Biosis, Inc.
Mesa Diagnostics, Inc.
Reid-Ashman, Inc.
Aries Technology, Inc.
Seattle Silicon Technology

Prior Positions

Vice President, Southmark Corp.
President, Brentford Ventures, Inc.

Education

Master of Physics, University of Pennyslvania, 1955
BA, University of Pennsylvania, 1950
Certificate in Business, UCLA Graduate School of Management, 1967

Average Size of Investment	$6M
Size of Fund	$110M
Investment Criteria	High technology investments in products which have an 18–30 monthly development cycle in identified growth markets with projected volume greater than $500M and in which the companies can capture a significant market share
Portfolio Companies	Aries Technology, Computer Systems, Lowell, MA; Boston Scientific Corp., Medical treatment, Watertown, MA; Ecogen, Inc., Biological pest control, Langhorne, PA; Electro-Nucleonics, Inc., Medical diagnostics, Fairfield, NJ; Hana Biologics, Cell transplants, Berkeley, CA; Mesa Diagnostics, Inc., medical diagnostics, Albuquerque, NM; Optical Specialties, Inc., Semiconductor manufacturing, Fremont, CA; Reid-Ashman, Inc., Semiconductor manufacturing, Santa Clara, CA; Seattle Silicon, ECAD Software, Bellevue, WA; Silvar-Lisco, ECAD Software, Menlo Park, CA; Synbiotics Corp., Animal health care/monoclonal antibody technology, San Diego, CA; Syntro Corp., Biotechnology, San Diego, CA; Tridom Corp., Telecommunications, Marietta, CA; TurboEnergy Systems, Inc., Enhanced energy recovery, Los Altos, CA; VisionTech, Inc. Optical care products, Roswell, GA

QUESTEC ENTERPRISES INC.
328 Main Street
Huntington, NY 11743
(516) 351-1222

William P. Sharpe
President

Directorships

Vicor, Inc., Power supplies
Proconics, Clean room automation
Crystal Specialities, Gallium arsenide
Proto-Power Corp., Nuclear engineering

Prior Position

President, PCK—Kollmorgen

Education

MS, Dartmouth College
MBA, Boston University
AB, Williams College

Charles L. Lassen
Vice President

Directorships

PCK Elastomerics, Connectors
Innovus, Gas delivery systems

Prior Positions

Product Development Director, PCK—Kollmorgen
Project Manager, ITT

Education

MBA, Long Island University, 1983
BS, DIP Engineering, Kingston, 1962

Average Size of Investment	$2.5M
Size of Fund	$15M
Investment Criteria	Sustainable return on investment
Portfolio Companies	Crystal Specialities Inc., Portland, OR, Gallium arsenide; Innovus, Inc., Fremont, CA, Semi-gas systems; Proconics International, Wobuck, MA, Clean room automation; Vicor Corp., Andover, MA, Power supplies

QUINCY PARTNERS
Box 154
Glen Head, NY 11545
(516) 759-1752

Donald J. Sutherland
President

Directorships

Mark Controls Corp., Valves and building systems
Profit Systems, Inc., Freight forwarder
Will & Baumer, Inc.
Publix Shirt Corp.
Quincy Packaging Group
Quincy Spring Group, Springs

Education

MBA, Harvard Business School, 1958
AB, Princeton University, 1953

Average Size of Investment	Undisclosed
Size of Fund	Undisclosed
Investment Criteria	Undisclosed
Portfolio Companies	Publix Shirt Corp., New York, NY, Shirts; Lewis Spring & Mfg. Co., Chicago, IL, Springs; Quincy Packaging Group, Waterbury, CT, and Marlboro, MA, Boxes; Will & Baumer, Syracuse, NY, Candles; Muehlhausen Bros. Spring & Mfg. Co., Loganspond, IN, Springs

RAIN HILL GROUP, INC.
90 Broad Street
New York, NY 10004
(212) 483-9162

Richard A. Cawley
President

Prior Position

Vice President, First Boston, 1976

Education

BA, University of Virginia, 1968

Robin George
Vice President

Prior Position

Bankers Trust Company, 1979

Education

MBA, Columbia University, 1978
BS, University of Washington, 1962

Average Size of Investment	Undisclosed
Size of Fund	Undisclosed
Investment Criteria	Firms must show potential to become an operating group of a large industrial or consumer products firm
Portfolio Companies	Undisclosed

RAINIER NATIONAL BANK
1301 Fifth Avenue
Seattle, WA 98010
(206) 621-5418

James C. Pierce
Robert E. Karns

Average Size of Investment	$500K
Size of Fund	Undisclosed
Investment Criteria	Technology-based and manufacturing companies are of interest; will act as lead investor
Portfolio Companies	Undisclosed

RAINIER VENTURE PARTNERS
9725 Southeast 36th Street
Suite 30
Mercer Island, WA 98040
(206) 232-6720

One Lincoln Center
Suite 440
10300 Southwest Greenburg Road
Portland, OR 97223
(503) 245-5900

John L. Moser
Partner, WA

Directorships

Seattle Silicon Technology, Inc., Developer of silicon compilation tools for rapid design of electronic memories
Celerity Computing, Inc., Developing state-of-the-art engineering workstations
Graphic Software Systems, Developer of graphic software tools for microcomputers

Prior Positions

President, Cado Systems Corp.
Executive positions, Computer Machinery Corp.
Scientific Data Systems, Packard Bell, Stromberg Carlson

Education

BSEE, California Institute of Technology

George H. Clute
Partner, WA

Directorships

Quantum Medical Systems, Inc., Development stage company which intends to manufacture medical diagnostic equipment
Personal Scientific Corp., Developing test equipment for electronic manufacturing

Prior Positions

Executive and management positions, Rainier
Bancorporation, First National Bank of Chicago, Able Associates

Education

MBA, Finance, University of California at Los Angeles
AB, Economics, University of California at Los Angeles

Richard H. Drew
Partner, OR

Directorships

Support Technologies, Inc., Developing portable field test equipment
Photon Kinetics, Inc., Manufacturer of optical fiber instruments for laboratory and field test

Prior Positions

Executive and management positions, Tektronix, Inc., Computer Automation, Inc., Texas Instruments, Autonetics Data Systems Division of North American Rockwell

Education

MSEE, California Institute of Technology
BS, Physics, California Institute of Technology

Average Size of Investment	$250K–$1M
Size of Fund	$25.6M
Investment Criteria	Undisclosed
Portfolio Companies	Amcodyne, Inc., Longmont, CO, Manufacturer of 8" fixed and fixed/removable disk drives; Cadlinc, Inc., Elk Grove Village, IL, Manufacturer of CAD/CAM workstations that integrate the automated design and manufacture of mechanical products; Celerity Computing, Inc., San Diego, CA, Developing state-of-the-art engineering workstations; Graphic Software Systems, Inc., Wilsonville, OR, Developer of graphic software tools for microcomputers; Intelledex, Inc., Corvallis, OR, Manufacturer of high-precision assembly robots; Lam Research Corp., Fremont, CA, Manufacturer of plasma etching semiconductor manufacturing

equipment for VLSI circuitry; Northwest Instrument Systems, Inc., Beaverton, OR, Manufacturer of personal instruments for test and measurement applications; Personal Scientific Corp., Woodinville, WA, Developing test equipment for electronic manufacturing; Photon Kinetics, Inc., Beaverton, OR, Manufacturer of optical fiber instruments for laboratory and field test; Quantum Medical Systems, Inc., Issaquah, WA, Development stage company which intends to manufacture medical diagnostic equipment; Seattle Silicon Technology, Inc., Bellevue, WA, Developer of silicon compilation tools for rapid design of electronic memories; Support Technologies, Inc., Tigard, OR, Developing portable field test equipment; VISIC, Inc., San Jose, CA, Development stage company which intends to manufacture very high-speed CMOS semiconductor memory

RAND CAPITAL CORP.
1300 Rand Building
Buffalo, NY 14203
(716) 853-0802

George F. Rand, III
Donald Ross
Barbara Stack

Average Size of Investment	$300K
Size of Fund	$8M
Investment Criteria	Diversified company interests, will act as lead investor, start-ups, geographic location important
Portfolio Companies	Undisclosed

R & D PARTNERS, INC.
701 Welch Road, Suite 1119
Palo Alto, CA 94304
(415) 328-2525

Norman Smothers
President

Directorships

R&D Partners, Inc.
Axton, Inc.

Education

PhD, Business, University of California, Berkeley, 1981
MBA, University of California, Berkeley, 1980
Masters, Electrical Engineer, University of Kansas, 1978

Elliot MacLennan
Senior Vice President

Directorship

R&D Partners

Education

JD, Hastings College of Law, 1975
Master Law in Taxation, Golden Gate University, 1978
LLM, Taxation, Golden Gate University, 1981

Average Size of Investment	$200K–1M
Size of Fund	$1.2M invested to date
Investment Criteria	Structure and implement R&D Partnerships for any research and development project; prefer to only accept projects where contingent sale, licensing, or further funding is locked in contractually before beginning the R&D (contingent on the R&D meeting contract goals and specifications); also may act as General Partners on any sort of venture deal (providing management and limited liability to investors); also do consulting work (such as due diligence, turn-arounds, licensing, etc.)
Portfolio Company	Microinstruments, Palo Alto, CA, California limited partnership, R&D oriented

R & R FINANCIAL CORP.
1451 Broadway
New York, NY 10036
(212) 790-1400

Irme J. Rosenthal
Chester Solomons

Average Size of Investment	$100K
Size of Fund	Undisclosed
Investment Criteria	Diversified areas of interest including manufacturing; will act as lead investor
Portfolio Companies	Undisclosed

RED RIVER VENTURES, INC.
777 East 15th Street
Plano, TX 75074

Delwin W. Morton

Average Size of Investment	$200K
Size of Fund	Undisclosed
Investment Criteria	Diverse company interests
Portfolio Companies	Undisclosed

REEDY RIVER VENTURES
P.O. Box 17526
Greenville, SC 29606
(803) 297-9196

John M. Sterling, Jr.
General Partner

Directorships

Steel Heddle Corp., Textile accessories
NRUC Corp., Transportation
Aquaenergy Systems, Inc., Small-scale hydro developer
Modern Office Machines, Copier, computer, sales
Artcon Corp., Nonwoven products

Prior Position

General Manager, Sonoco Products Co., 1964–73

Education

MBA, Darden, University of Virginia, 1964
BS, Civil Engineering, The Citadel, 1960

Tee Hooper

Average Size of Investment	$200K
Size of Fund	$3.5M
Investment Criteria	Diversified
Portfolio Companies	Undisclosed

REGENT FINANCIAL CORP.
10 Commercial Wharf West
Boston, MA 02110
(617) 723-4820

Jason S. Rosenberg
President

Directorships

Research & Planning, Inc., Computer software/courseware
Care Management, Inc., Health care
Amervest, Inc., Financial

Prior Position

President, Prime Capital Corp., 1975

Education

Brown University, 1951

Average Size of Investment	$50K–$500K
Size of Fund	Undisclosed
Investment Criteria	General
Portfolio Companies	Undisclosed

REGULUS INTERNATIONAL CAPITAL CO., INC.
10 Rockefeller Plaza
New York, NY 10020
(212) 582-7715

Lee H. Miller
President

Directorships

Elitine Corp., Technology licensing
Spectramedic Network, Inc., Outdoor electronic advertising
Giesecke & Deurient Security Systems, Inc., Security printers, banknote paper and currency processing machine manufacturers
Indices-Pac Research Corp., Arbitrage computer systems

Prior Position

Associate, Alan Patricof Associates

Education

MBA, Stanford Business School, 1971
BA, Stanford University, 1969

Average Size of Investment	$250K
Size of Fund	$3M
Investment Criteria	Start-up, R&D and leveraged buy-outs
Portfolio Companies	Elitine Corp., New York, NY, Technology licensing; Indices Pac Research Corp., New York, NY, Arbitrage computer systems; Spectramedic Network, Inc., New York, NY, Outdoor electronic advertising

REPUBLIC VENTURE GROUP, INC.
Bryan and St. Paul Streets
P.O. Box 225961
Dallas, TX, 75265
(214) 922-5078

Robert H. Wellborn
President

Directorships

CECO, Radio communication units
SBI, Inc., Apparel manufacturer
Wiederkehr Wine Cellars, Manufacturer of wines
Mobile Radio Communications, Communications
Republic Venture Capital Corp.

Prior Positions

Vice President, Trust Investment Division, RepublicBank Dallas, 1970–79
General Partner, Goodbody & Co., 1962–70

Education

Banking and BBA, Finance, Southern Methodist University, 1959
Investment Banking Inst., Wharton School, University of Pennsylvania

William W. Richey
Investment Officer, Treasurer, and Vice President
(214) 922-7885

Directorships

CARE Systems, Inc., Manufacture and market intensive-care patient monitoring systems
Pharmacy Practice Group, Contract hospital pharmacy management and hospital pharmacy consulting

Prior Positions

Credit Analyst, Republic Bank Dallas, 1979
Assistant Manager, Cloth World, 1975

Education

MBA, University of Texas at Arlington, 1981
BBA, University of Texas at Arlington, 1975

Wayne C. Willcox
Vice President
(214) 922-6933

Prior Positions

Associate, International Finance, Parsons Corp., 1978–80
Corporate Analyst, First Interstate Bank, 1976–78

Education

MBA, Wharton School, University of Pennsylvania, 1982
AB, Princeton University, 1975

Bart A. McLean
Sherry L. Richardson
Investment Officer
(214) 922-4609

Prior Position

CPA, Ernst & Whinney, 1980–82

Education

MBA, Harvard Business School, 1984
BBA, University of Oklahoma, 1980

Average Size of Investment	$700K
Size of Fund	$35M
Investment Criteria	Complete business plan; minimum investment $250K; will invest nationally but prefer Southwest
Portfolio Companies	BancTec, Inc., Dallas, TX, Manufacturer of check processing equipment; International Microelectronics Inc., San Jose, CA, Custom semiconductors; Lexitel Corp., Birmingham, MI,

Long-distance telephone; Maze Petroleum, Denver, CO, Oil and gas exploration; Price Communications, Inc., New York, NY, Radio/TV station owner; SBI, Inc., St. Louis, MO, Apparel manufacturer

RESEARCH & SCIENCE INVESTORS
230 Park Avenue
New York, NY 10017
(212) 867-9535

John H. French, II
Francine Sommer

Average Size of Investment	$500K
Size of Fund	$15M
Investment Criteria	Technology-based companies and start-ups considered; will act as lead investor
Portfolio Companies	Undisclosed

RETAILERS GROWTH FUND, INC.
2318 Park Avenue
Minneapolis, MN 55404
(612) 872-4929

Cornell L. Moore, President

Average Size of Investment	$100K
Size of Fund	Undisclosed
Investment Criteria	Manufacturing and other diverse companies of interest; will act as lead investor; geographic locale important
Portfolio Companies	Undisclosed

REVERE AE CAPITAL FUND, INC.
745 5th Avenue, 19th Floor
New York, NY 10151
(212) 888-6800

Gregor Medinger
Chairman

Prior Positions

Officer/Director, Worms American Capital

Education

Doctorate, Law and Economics, University of Vienna, 1965

Clinton A. Reynolds
President

Directorships

Oxford First Corp.
Eaton Financial Corp.

Prior Positions

Vice President, Investments, Paul Revere Investment Management Corp.

Education

JD, Harvard Law School
BA, Dartmouth College

Average Size of Investment	Undisclosed
Size of Fund	$41,846,447 as of July 31, 1986
Investment Criteria	Debt instruments with equity kickers; generally engage in mezzanine financing; no dealings with companies in business less than three years
Portfolio Companies	Undisclosed

RIHT CAPITAL CORPORATION
One Hospital Trust Plaza
Providence, RI 02903-2449
(401) 278-8448

796 Huntington Building
Cleveland, OH 44115
(216) 781-3655

Peter D. Van Oosterhout
President and Chief Executive Officer, RI
(401) 278-8819
(216) 781-3655

Directorships

Alanco, Ltd., Precious-metals mining and milling
Allied Resinous Products, Inc., Custom plastic extruder

Alloy Metal Wire Works, Inc., Manufacturer of alloy wire
American Electro-Coatings, Inc., On-site refinisher of office metal furniture
Boston Distributors, Inc., Distributor of health and beauty aids
Carboride Corp., Coatings for hardening metal parts
Comfrey Intl. Inc., Food and drug processor and grower
Fort Barton Holdings, Inc., Silver reclamation and waste removal
Freshnet, Inc., Electronic produce network
Healthcare Technology, Inc., Physical therapy systems
Ken Mac Metals, Inc., Processor and slitter of metal sheet
L.A.P., Inc., Temporary medical help
Partners Petroleum, Inc., Oil and gas operator and syndicator
Portfolio Securities Transactions Corp., Discount brokerage
Suntron, Inc., Solar heating valves
Tennco Technologies, Inc., Custom plastic rotomolder
Venture II Land Corp., Real estate developments
Visual Graphic Services, Inc., Computer-generated graphics
Wellington Industrial Tire Co., Solid industrial tires

Prior Positions

President and Director, Clarion Capital Corp., 1972–82
Executive Vice President, Park-Ohio Industries, Inc., 1971–72
President, Growth International, Inc., 1960–66
Associate, Squire, Sanders & Dempsey, 1957–60

Education

JD, University of Iowa, 1955
BA, University of Iowa, 1953

Robert A. Comey
Vice President, RI

Directorships

A.M.D.G., Inc., Apply dehydration plant
Bridgeport Heat Treating Corp., Custom metal heat treating
Fort Barton Holdings, Inc., Chairman
Gurley-Ortman, Inc., Diesel repower and conversion
Micro Sensors, Inc., Instrumentation for gauging and consistency
Northeast Polydyne, Inc., Manufacturer of plastic bottles
Omni Resources Corp., Computer disk manufacturing and reproducer
Systems & Materials Intl. Ltd., Manufacturer of silver and other metal recovery equipment
Vision Communications Corp., Audio, visual and computer disk reproduction

Prior Positions

President, Tower Ventures, Inc., 1980–82
Vice President, General Manager, Tower Ventures, Inc., 1978–80
Investment Analyst, Tower Ventures, Inc., 1977–78
Buying; Factory Coordinator and Analyst; Asst. Controller; Asst. Buyer, Sears, Roebuck & Co., 1969–77

Education

MB, Finance, Fordham University Graduate School of Business, 1974
AB, Economics, Brown University, 1968

Peter C. Canepa
Vice President, RI
(401) 278-8815

Prior Positions

Assistant Vice President, RIHT Financial Corp.
Senior Accountant, Coopers and Lybrand
Staff Accountant, Deloitte Haskins & Sells

Education

BA, Accounting, Ohio Wesleyan University, 1980

Average Size of Investment	$250K–$750K
Size of Fund	$20M
Investment Criteria	Diversified
Portfolio Companies	Alanco, Ltd., Phoeniz, AZ, Precious metals mining and milling; Allied Resinous Products, Inc., Conneaut, OH, Custom plastic extruder; A.M.D.G., Inc., Sunnyside, WA, Apple dehydration plant; American Electro-Coatings, Inc., Shaker Heights, OH, On-site refinisher of metal office furniture; A.M.W. Corp., Prospect Park, PA, Manufacturer of alloy wire; The Book Peddler, Hendersonville, TN, Discount book store chain; Boston Distributors, Inc., Maple Heights, OH, Distribution of health and beauty aids; Brideport Heat Treating Co., Bridgeport, CT, Custom metal heat treating; California Silver, Inc., Minden, NV, Precious metal minc; Carboride Corp., Cleveland, OH, Coatings for hardening metal parts; Comfrey International, Inc., Woodburn, OR, Food and drug processor and grower; Decisions & Designs, Inc., McLean, VA, Computer software, telecommunications, and planning packages; Distribution Management Systems, Inc., Lexington, MA, Computer software; Fort Barton Holdings, Inc., Warwick, RI, Silver reclamation and waste disposal; Freshnet, Inc., Cleveland, OH, Electronic produce network; GSA Partners, New York, NY, Distribution of electronic golf swing analyzer; Gurley-Ortman, Inc., Elk Grove, IL, Diesel power and

conversion; Healthcare Technology, Inc., Solon, OH, PT systems; Ken Mac Metals, Inc., Middlebury Heights, OH, Processor and slitter of metal sheet; L.A.P., Inc. d/b/a Med. Personnel, Pool of Cleveland, Bedford Heights, OH, Temporary medical help; Leavens Awards, Inc., Attleboro, MA, Manufacture of precious metal awards; Micro Sensors, Inc., Holliston, MA, Instrumentation for gauging and consistency; Northeast Polydyne, Inc., Providence, RI, Manufacture of plastic bottles; Omni Resources Corp., Millbury, MA, Computer disk manufacturing and reproducer; Paramount Cards, Inc., Pawtucket, RI, Manufacturer of greeting cards; Partners Petroleum, Inc., Chagrin Falls, OH, Oil and gas operator and syndicator; Portfolio Securities Transactions Corp., Cleveland, OH, Discount brokerage; P.S.C., Inc., Fairfax, VA, Computer software and planning; Suntron, Inc., North Ridgeville, OH, Solar heating valves; Systems & Materials International, Ltd., Cranston, RI, Manufacturer of silver and other metal recovery equipment; Technick & Trade, Inc., Cleveland, OH, Distributor of imported industrial products; Tennco Technologies, Inc., Memphis, TN, Custom plastic rotomolder; Venture II Land Corp., Cleveland, OH, Real estate developments; Visual Graphic Services, Inc., Indianapolis, IN, Computer-generated graphics; Vision Communications Corp., Ridgefield, NJ, Audio, visual, and computer disk reproduction; Ward's Fine Candies, Inc., Memphis, TN, Manufacturer and distributor of candies; Wellington Industrial Tire Co., Wellington, OH, Solid industrial tires

ROBERTSON, COLMAN & STEPHENS

One Embarcadero Center
Suite 3100
San Francisco, CA 94111
(415) 781-9700

Sanford R. Robertson
Partner

Education

MBA, University of Michigan, 1954
BBA, University of Michigan, 1953

Paul H. Stephens
Partner

Prior Positions

General Partner, Robertson, Colman, Siebel & Weisel, 1972–78
Institutional Sales, Smith Barney & Co., 1969–72

Education

MBA, University of California at Berkeley, 1969
BS, University of California at Berkeley, 1967

Robert L. Cummings
Partner

Directorships

State of the Art
CXC Corp.
Sensym
Video Telecom

Prior Position

Senior Consultant, McKinsey & Co.

Education

MBA, Harvard University, 1976
BSME, Rensselaer Polytechnic Institute, 1969

Nywood Wu
Partner

Directorships

Metapath, Inc.
The Learning Co.
Aspen Peripherals, Inc.
Unisyn, Inc.

Prior Positions

President, L. H. Research, Inc.
Senior Consultant, McKinsey & Co.

Education

MBA, Wharton School, University of Pennsylvania, 1974
BS, Electrical Engineering, Stanford University, 1968

R. Lee Douglas, Jr.
Special Limited Partner

Directorships

Parallel Computers, Inc., Computer manufacturing
Test Systems Strategies, Inc.

DIRECTORY AND BIOGRAPHIES

Prior Position

Associate, Donaldson, Lufkin & Jenrette

Education

MCP, Harvard Graduate School of Design, 1980
MBA, Harvard Business School, 1980
BA, University of North Carolina at Charlotte, 1977

Gary W. Masner
Partner

Directorships

ALS Corp.
Advanced Minerals Technology, Inc.
The Palantir Corporation
Komag
Sensym

Prior Positions

Vice President, General Manager, Computer Products Division, Ampex 1983–85
Senior Vice President, Freightliner Corp., 1976–83

Education

MBA, Stanford University, 1972
BS, Rensselaer Polytechnic Institute, 1968

J. Matthew MacKowski

Directorships

Innovative Health Care
Healthsouth
Curaflex Health Services

Prior Positions

Vice President, Citicorp Venture Capital

Education

MBA, The Wharton School, 1980
BA, Duke University, 1977

David L. Goldsmith
Partner

Directorships

Tokos Medical Corporation

Prior Positions

Bank of America, 1978–81
Lehman Management, 1972–78

Education

MBA, Columbia University, 1972
BA, Occidental College, 1970

Vicki Haven
Venture Capital Controller

Education

BS, Michigan State University, 1980

Sy F. Kaufman
Partner

Directorships

Personal CAD Systems
DBMS
Internet Systems

Prior Positions

Senior Research Partner, Hambrecht & Quist

Education

MBA, University of Santa Clara, 1972
MSEE, San Jose State University, 1964
BEE, New York University, 1960

Susan W. Vican
Venture Administration Officer

Prior Position

Manager, Investments, Pacific Telesis Group, 1979–85

Education

MBA, University of California at Berkeley, 1978
BA, Portland State University, 1973

Average Size of Investment	$1M–$1.5M
Size of Fund	$250M
Investment Criteria	Primary emphasis on start-ups; areas of special interest include: computer-aided software engineering, software productivity tools; health care services; financial services; proprietary database services; hazardous waste and environmental control; other technology
Portfolio Companies	Undisclosed

ARTHUR ROCK & CO.
1635 Russ Building
San Francisco, CA 94104
(415) 981-3921

Arthur Rock
Marie Getchel

Average Size of Investment	Undisclosed
Size of Fund	Undisclosed
Investment Criteria	Undisclosed
Portfolio Companies	Undisclosed

THE ROCKIES FUND, INC.
100 Garfield St.
#200
Denver, CO 80206
(303) 320-0090

James H. Galbreath
President/Director

Directorships

The Rockies Fund, Expansion capital investment company
Howe Audio Productions, Inc., Manufacturer of audio equipment

Prior Positions

General Partner/Co-manager, Stephenson Merchant Banking
Special Partner, Stephenson Merchant Banking II

Education

Bachelor of Business Administration, University of Denver, 1969
Economics, University of Stockholm, 1966

Michael J. Scanlan
Vice President/Treasurer

Directorships

Vice President/Secretary, Galbreath Financial Investment Corp., Venture capital
Vice President/Secretary, Galbreath Financial Services Corp., Venture capital
Chairman, Scanlan, Cordes & Rieck, P.C., General accounting/business consulting
Director, Car Doctor, Mobile auto repair
Director, FAME, Video publishing for medical industry
Director, Touch Dialogues, Public access video advertising medium
Director, Team Marketing, Sales training/sales planning
Director, Gold C Enterprises, Discount coupon marketing

Prior Positions

Partner, Peat Marwick Mitchell & Co.
Manager, In business advisory service practice

Education

PhD, Business Administration/CPA, University of Texas, 1973
BA, Accounting, University of Missouri, 1964
BBA, University of Missouri, 1963

Edgar J. Pfohl
Vice President/Secretary

Directorships

Director, Newtek Communications Corp.
Director, First Image Corp.

Prior Positions

Vice President, CIT Commercial Finance Co.
Sales, Westinghouse Credit Corp.

Education

BA, Capital University, 1966

Average Size of Investment	$200K–$300K
Size of Fund	$3M
Investment Criteria	Later stage, break-even stage; Rocky Mountain region

Portfolio Companies	Biostar Medical Products, Boulder, CO, Diagnostics; Car Doctor USA, Inc., Colorado Springs, CO, Mobile auto repairs; CVM Equity Fund I, Ltd., Boulder, CO, Early-stage venture capital; Frye, Adamson & Marosits, Inc., Englewood, CO, Video publishing/medical specialties; Osprey, Inc., Fort Collins, CO, Construction/development; Value Molding Corp., Loveland, CO, Injection molded plastic parts; Satellink Corporation, Denver, CO, Cable television

H. DONALD ROSE INC.
P.O. Box 741924
Dallas, TX 75374
(214) 349-8811

H. Donald Rose
President

Directorship

Professional Group Services, Inc., Management services

Prior Positions

President and CEO, Banyan Corp., 1977–83
President and CEO, First Dallas Capital Corp., 1971–75

Education

MBA, Finance, Southern Methodist University, 1965
BSEE, Southern Methodist University, 1961

Average Size of Investment	$500K
Size of Fund	Undisclosed
Investment Criteria	New and emerging businesses in Southwest having potential of minimum 25% annual real growth
Portfolio Companies	The Cam Shack, Dallas, TX, Computer software; Magnetic Media, Dallas, TX, Video systems; Media Ventures, Dallas, TX, Publishing; Professional Group Services, Dallas, TX, Management services

ROSENFELD & CO.
1211 Southwest Sixth Avenue
Portland, OR 97204
(503) 228-3255

William W. Rosenfeld, Jr.
Principal

Directorships

NeuroCom International, Inc., Medical equipment manufacturer
Portco Corp., Flexible packaging manufacturer

Prior Positions

Vice President and Manager, Corporate Finance Dept., United States National Bank of Oregon, 1976–77
Senior Associate, Hornblower & Weeks-Hemphill, Noyes, 1970–73

Education

MBA, Harvard University, 1970
BA, Stanford University, 1967

Average Size of Investment	$1M
Size of Fund	Undisclosed
Investment Criteria	Third stage, buy-out, expansion, Pacific Northwest preferred
Portfolio Companies	Undisclosed

ROTHSCHILD, INC.
One Rockefeller Plaza
New York, NY 10020
(212) 757-6000

Jess L. Belser
Aniello A. Bianco
Douglas S. Luke
Ivan L. Wolff
James J. O'Neill
Patrick F. Latterell
Kathryn A. Minckler
Gary E. Stiller
Bruce A. Kaufman

Average Size of Investment	$750K–1.5M
Size of Fund	$250M
Investment Criteria	Diversified company interests; leveraged buy-outs are considered; start-ups encouraged; will act as lead investor
Portfolio Companies	Undisclosed

RUST VENTURES, L.P.
114 West Seventh Street
Austin, TX 78701
(512) 479-0055

Jeffrey Garvey
Kenneth DeAngelis
General Partner

Directorships

Gascard Club, Inc., Transaction processing
Pic Mount Corp., Manufacturing
The Oak'n Ark Corp., Health care

Prior Positions

Senior Vice President, Rust Capital, Ltd., 1981–84
Assistant Vice President, Bank of Boston, 1976–81

Education

MBA, Wharton School of Finance, 1976
AB, Harvard College, 1974

Joseph Aragona
William Wood

Average Size of Investment	$1M
Size of Fund	$28M
Investment Criteria	Undisclosed
Portfolio Companies	Automated Industrial Systems, Austin, TX, Factory automation; Edens Broadcasting, Phoenix, AZ, Radio; McData Corp., Boulder, CO, Programmable controller; Proteon, Inc., Boston, MA, Local area network; Aweri Suites, Inc., Austin, TX, Hotel

RUTGERS MINORITY INVESTMENT COMPANY
180 University Avenue
Newark, NJ 07102
(201) 648-5627

Oscar Figueroa
President

Directorships

Rutgers Minority Investment Co., MESBIC
Soccer Education Associates, Soccer education/promotion

Prior Position

Regional Manager, New Jersey Small Business Development Center, 1977–82

Education

MA, Economics, Pennsylvania State University, 1974

Average Size of Investment	$75K
Size of Fund	$2M
Investment Criteria	General; investment in minority businesses only
Portfolio Companies	Undisclosed

SAFECO CAPITAL, INC.
835 Southwest 37th Avenue
Miami, FL 33174
(305) 443-7953

Rene J. Leonard

Average Size of Investment	$300K
Size of Fund	Undisclosed
Investment Criteria	Diversified company interests; geographic locale important
Portfolio Companies	Undisclosed

SAN ANTONIO VENTURE GROUP, INC.
2300 West Commerce Street
San Antonio, TX 78207
(512) 223-3633

William A. Fagan, Jr.
Thomas F. Woodley

Average Size of Investment	$200K
Size of Fund	Undisclosed
Investment Criteria	Diversified company interests; geographic preference important; will do leveraged buy-outs
Portfolio Companies	Undisclosed

SAN JOAQUIN CAPITAL CORP.
1675 Chester Avenue
Suite 330
P.O. Box 2538
Bakersfield, CA 93303
(805) 323-7581

Chester W. Troudy
President

Directorship

Madera Broadcasting, Inc., Radio station

Education

MBA, University of Southern California, 1965
BA, University of California at Santa Barbara, 1950

Jimmie Icardo
Robert Sheldon, M.D.
David Cerrina
John E. Boydstun

Average Size of Investment	$200K
Size of Fund	$5M
Investment Criteria	Diversified preferences, manufacturing, technology-based companies preferred; geographic proximity important
Portfolio Companies	Undisclosed

SAN JOSE CAPITAL
100 Park Center Plaza
Suite 427
San Jose, CA 95113
(408) 293-7708

Robert T. Murphy
General Partner

Directorships

Satellite Information Services Corp., Satellite communications services
Mountain Computer, Computer peripherals
San Jose SBIC, Inc., Small business investment company
Celtic, Computer peripherals

Prior Position

President, Antekna, 1978

Education

MSEE, Stanford, 1959
BSEE, University of Illinois, 1956

Daniel Hochman
General Partner

Directorships

Advanced Imaging Devices, Inc., Graphics systems
Systel Computers, Inc., Data processing
Roconex Corp., Graphics devices

Prior Position

President, Dacom, Inc., 1966–76
Engineering Manager, Lockheed Missiles & Space Co.

Education

MSEE, University of Pennsylvania, 1956

Average Size of Investment	$300K
Size of Fund	Undisclosed
Investment Criteria	High-technology manufacturing, communications, equipment, computer peripherals, health care, instrumentation
Portfolio Companies	Undisclosed

SAN MARINO CAPITAL CORPORATION
57 Post Street
Suite 513
San Francisco, CA 94104
(415) 781-1313

Bruce Glaspell
President

Education

BA, St. John's College, New Mexico, 1971

Average Size of Investment	$250K
Size of Fund	Undisclosed
Investment Criteria	None
Portfolio Companies	Undisclosed

SANTA FE PRIVATE EQUITY FUNDS
524 Camino del Monte Sol
Santa Fe, NM 87501
(505) 983-1769

A. David Silver
Managing General Partner

Directorships

Mesa Diagnostics, Inc.
Pathfinder Corp.
Cipherlink Corp.
Fasco, Inc.
Gateway Computer Systems
One Point

Prior Positions

President, A. David Silver & Co., 1971–82
Associate, Kuhn, Loeb & Co., 1966–70

Education

MBA, University of Chicago, 1963
BA, University of Chicago, 1962

Jesse L. Acker
General Partner
8 Oswega Avenue
Rockaway, NJ 07866
(201) 625-3502

Directorships

NMR Imaging, Inc.
Sonostics Corp.
Mesa Diagnostics, Inc.
Preventacare, Inc.
PDT Systems Corp.

Prior Positions

Co-founder and Vice President, Engineering, Personal Diagnostics Inc.
Co-founder and President, Akro-Medic Engineering, Inc.

Education

MSEE, Columbia University, 1955
BSEE, Cooper Union Institute, 1950

Average Size of Investment	$750K
Size of Fund	$32M
Investment Criteria	Health care services preferred
Portfolio Companies	Preventacare, Inc., Louisville, KY, Operates HMO in Southeast; PDT Systems Corp., Boston MA, manufacturers of a new cancer therapy; Central Data Corp., Champaign, IL, Manufactures multibus boards and systems; Cipherlink Corp., Los Angeles, CA, Expert systems that link any computers; Fasco, Inc., Livingston, NJ, holding company for diverse businesses; Gateway Computer Systems, Huntington Beach, CA, Chain of computer systems houses; Mesa Diagnostics, Inc., Los Alamos, NM, Developer of medical diagnostic device; NMR Imaging, Inc., Houston, TX, Manufactures small NMR devices; One Point Corp., Walnut Creek, CA, Electronic distributor; Pathfinder Corp., Santa Fe, NM, holding company for diverse businesses; Sonostics Corp., Cleveland, OH, Operates mobile diagnostic ultrasound service

SAS ASSOCIATES
515 South Figueroa Street
6th Floor
Los Angeles, CA 90071-3396
(213) 624-4232

Bruce P. Emmeluth
Robert W. Campbell

Average Size of Investment	$200K
Size of Fund	Undisclosed
Investment Criteria	Diversified company interests including technology-based companies; will act as lead investor; geographic location important
Portfolio Companies	Undisclosed

DIRECTORY AND BIOGRAPHIES

SBI CAPITAL CORP.
6305 Beverly Hill
Houston, TX 77057
(713) 975-1188

William E. Wright
President

Prior Positions
Executive Vice President, Gulf Republic Financial
President, Home Savings

Education
MBA, University of Pennsylvania, 1962
Bachelor of Electrical Engineering, Rensselaer Polytechnic Institute, 1960

W. M. Wright
Paul W. Wright

Average Size of Investment	$1M–$2M
Size of Fund	Undisclosed
Investment Criteria	High technology; no seed capital; businesses within the state of Texas
Portfolio Companies	Undisclosed

SBIC OF CONNECTICUT
1115 Main Street
Bridgeport, CT 06604
(203) 367-3282

Ken F. Zarrilli

Average Size of Investment	$300K
Size of Fund	Undisclosed
Investment Criteria	Diversified company interests including manufacturing
Portfolio Companies	Undisclosed

SCHOONER CAPITAL CORP.
77 Franklin Street
Boston, MA 02110
(617) 357-9031

Vincent J. Ryan, Jr.
Cynthia C. Heller
Bernice E. Bradin
Garry B. Watzke

Average Size of Investment	$500K
Size of Fund	$31M
Investment Criteria	Interested in companies that can generate cash flow within first year; alternative energy, communications, particularly cable TV, other service companies
Portfolio Companies	Undisclosed

SCHRODER VENTURES
3000 Sand Hill Road
Building 2, Suite 130
Menlo Park, CA 94025
(415) 854-8833

One State Street
New York, NY 10004
(212) 269-6500

Michael A. Hentschel
Director, CA

Directorships
Telebit
Intelligent Images

Prior Positions
Senior Manager, Berkeley International
Treasury Manager, Rolm Corp.

Education
MBA, International Northwestern, 1977
BA, Archaeology/Economics, Yale University, 1975

Robert Gailus
Director, CA

Directorship
OpCom

Prior Positions

Assistant Vice President, Merrill Lynch Capital Markets Group, 1980–82
Account Officer, Manufacturers Hanover Leasing Corp., 1978–80

Education

MBA, Finance, Columbia University, 1978
BA, Columbia College, 1971

Jeffrey J. Collinson
Managing Partner, NY

Directorships

Action Auto, Inc.
Coca Cola Bottling Investment Group, Inc.
DNA Plant Technology Corp.
Midwest Employers Casualty Company
Moorco International, Inc.

Prior Positions

Chairman, J. Henry Schroder Corp., 1972–1985
Vice President, Drexed Firestone, Inc., 1968–72
Assistant to the Treasurer, Baxter Travenol, Inc., 1966–68

Education

MBA, Harvard University, 1966
BA, Yale University, 1963

Judith E. Schneider
Partner, NY

Directorship

Cotton Comfort, Inc.

Prior Positions

Principal, Hay Associates
Financial Planner, Corp. Finance, Joseph E. Seagram & Sons, Inc.
Marketing Representative, Leveraged Leasing, International Paper Credit Corp.
Official Assistant, Banker's Trust

Education

MBA, Columbia University, 1975
BA, Queens College, 1973

Average Size of Investment	$750K
Size of Fund	$37.5M
Investment Criteria	Seed start-up and later-stage financing for companies in a broad range of industries
Portfolio Companies	Navigation Sciences, Inc., Bethesda, MD, Systems for navigating harbors and waterways; Moorco International Inc., Houston, TX, Manufacturer of valves, meters and related equipment for the oil and petrochemicals industry; Cincinnati Coca-Cola Bottling, Cincinnati, OH, Soft drink bottling company; The Philadelphia Financial Group, Jenkintown, PA, Financial holding company; Action Auto, Flint, MI, Chain of automotive stores providing auto parts, gasoline and repair service; Scientific Computer Systems, Wilsonville, OR, Mini-supercomputer; Banyan Systems, Inc., Westboro, MA, Network servers; Micro Linear Corp., San Jose, CA, Semicustom linear semiconductors; Midwest Employers Casualty Co., Cincinnati, OH, Insurance; Cotton Comfort, Inc., Plano, TX, Retail of casual cotton apparel; Automation Technology Products, Campbell, CA, CAD/CAM software; Imagen Corp., Santa Clara, CA, Raster image processors; Intelligent Images, La Jolla, CA, Interactive educational systems for health; OpCom, Inc., Sunnyvale, CA, Voice mail; Raytel Systems Corp., San Jose, CA, Digitized x-ray image transmission and storage; Telebit Corp., Cupertino, CA, Manufactures 9600 Baud dial-up modems; Unlimited Processing, Jacksonville, FL, Multiuser microcomputer data base software; Viewtech, San Jose, CA, Computer-aided publishing; X-Cyte, Inc., Mountain View, CA, Remote sensing technology

SCIENTIFIC ADVANCES, INC.
601 West Fifth Avenue
Columbus, OH 43201
(614) 294-5541

Charles G. James
Thomas W. Harvey
Daniel J. Shea
Paul F. Purcell

Average Size of Investment	$500K
Size of Fund	$20M
Investment Criteria	Technology only; start up and later stage
Portfolio Companies	Undisclosed

SC OPPORTUNITIES, INC.
1112 Seventh Avenue
Monroe, WI 52566
(608) 325-3134

Robert Ableman

Average Size of Investment	$300K
Size of Fund	$2M
Investment Criteria	Diversified company interests; start-ups encouraged
Portfolio Companies	Undisclosed

SEAPORT VENTURES, INC.
770 B Street
Suite 420
San Diego, CA 92101
(619) 232-4069

Michael Stolper
Carole Rhoades

Average Size of Investment	$200K
Size of Fund	$7.5M (includes SBA leverage)
Private Capital	$1.5M
Investment Criteria	Technology-based companies preferred, manufacturing companies, diversified preferences; will act as lead investor
Portfolio Companies	Undisclosed

SECURITY FINANCIAL MANAGEMENT CORP.
100 Bush Street, #1905
San Francisco, CA 94104
(415) 981-8060

Byron G. Rouda
Thomas G. Hagins

Average Size of Investment	Undisclosed
Size of Fund	Undisclosed
Investment Criteria	Technology-based companies are of interest; start-ups; will act as lead investor
Portfolio Companies	Undisclosed

SECURITY PACIFIC CAPITAL CORP. and FIRST SBIC OF CALIFORNIA
50 Milk Street
Boston, MA 02109
(617) 542-7601

P.O. Box 512
Washington, PA 15301
(412) 223-0707

650 Town Center Drive
17th Floor
Costa Mesa, CA 92626
(714) 556-1964

155 N. Lake Avenue, #1010
Pasadena, CA 91109
(818) 304-3451

5 Palo Alto Square
Suite 1038
Palo Alto, CA 94304
(415) 424-8011

Tim Hay
Chairman and Chief Executive Officer, Costa Mesa

Education
MBA, Harvard University Graduate School of Business, 1957
BA, Pomona College, 1955

Al Brizzard
First Vice President, Costa Mesa

Education
M.Acc., University of Southern California
BS, University of Southwest, LA

Michael Cronin
First Vice President, Boston

Education
MBA, Harvard University Graduate School of Business, 1977

Greg Forrest
Executive Vice President, Costa Mesa

Education
MBA, University of Southern California

Brian Jones
Senior Vice President, Costa Mesa

James McGoodwin
Vice President, Costa Mesa

Education
MBA, Harvard University Graduate School of Business, 1983

Tony Stevens
First Vice President, Pasadena

Prior Position
Manager, Technical Development Capital, Ltd., London, 1968–78

Education
BSC (Eng.), University of Glasgow, 1952
Post Graduate Studies, Cornell and Stanford Universities

Dmitry Bosky
Vice President, Costa Mesa

Education
MBA, Harvard University Graduate School of Business, 1983

Everett Cox
Vice President, Costa Mesa

Education
MBA, University of Southern California, 1983

Daniel A. Dye
First Vice President, PA

Prior Positions
Management Consultant, Haskins & Sells, Los Angeles, CA
Director, Station Manager, Princeton Broadcasting, Princeton, NJ

Education
MBA, Harvard University, 1977
AB, Economics, Princeton University, 1975

John Geer
First Vice President, Costa Mesa

Prior Position
Senior Associate Attorney, Gendell, Raskoff, Shapiro & Quittner, Los Angeles, 1978–80

Education
AB, Union College, CT, 1967
JD, Boston University Law School, 1970

Jim McElwee
First Vice President, Palo Alto
(415) 424-8011

Education
MBA, Wharton School, University of Pennsylvania, 1976

John Padgett
Senior Vice President, Pasadena

Prior Position
Manager, Corporate Finance Dept., Lazard Bros. & Co., Ltd., London, 1973–76

Education
MBA, Stanford University Graduate School of Business, 1973
MA, Oxford University, 1968
BA, Oxford University, 1965

Robert Lunbeck
Senior Investment Analyst, Costa Mesa

Education
MBA, Stanford University Graduate School of Business, 1986

Ed Moss
Senior Investment Analyst, Costa Mesa

Education
MPPM, Yale School of Organization and Management, 1980
BA, Williams College, 1974

DIRECTORY AND BIOGRAPHIES

William Service
Senior Investment Analyst, Costa Mesa

Education

MVBA, Stanford University Graduate School of Business, 1986

Average Size of Investment	Approximately $2M
Size of Fund	$200M+
Investment Criteria	Broad portfolio and investment interest; no specific criteria
Portfolio Companies	120 companies (both SPCC and FSBIC)

SEIDMAN JACKSON FISHER & CO.
233 North Michigan Avenue
Suite 1812
Chicago, IL 60601
(312) 856-1812

David C. Seidman
Partner
(312) 856-1812

Prior Positions

Investment Manager, Venture Capital Group, Allstate
Management Consultant, McKinsey & Co.

Education

MBA, University of Chicago, 1962
BS, Babson College, 1960

Douglas L. Jackson
Partner

Prior Positions

Investment Manager, Venture Capital, Allstate
Loan Officer, Continental Illinois National Bank

Education

MBA, Wharton School, 1973
BSEE, University of Cincinnati, 1970

Margaret G. Fisher
Partner

Prior Positions

Investment Manager, Venture Capital, Allstate
Vice President, Continental Illinois National Bank

Education

MBA, University of Michigan, 1974
BA, University of Pennsylvania, 1970

Average Size of Investment	$1M
Size of Fund	$45M
Investment Criteria	Early stage to buy-outs/nonconsumer products
Portfolio Companies	Undisclosed

SEQUOIA CAPITAL
3000 Sand Hill Road
Building 4, Suite 280
Menlo Park, CA 94025
(415) 854-3927

Donald T. Valentine
Partner

Directorships

LSI Logic
Valid Logic
Sierra Semiconductor
Electronic Arts
Pyramid Technology

Prior Position

Founder, Vice President, Marketing and Sales, National Semiconductor

Gordon W. Russell
Partner

Directorships

Equatorial Communications, Small satellite earth stations
Datastream, Data communications equipment
Camino Laboratories, Physiological monitoring systems

Biotrack, Therapeutic drug monitoring systems
Interpore, Supplier of bone substitute material

Prior Position

Vice President, General Manager, Syntex Analytical and Medical Instrument Division

Pierre Lamond
Walter Baumgartner

Average Size of Investment	$1M
Size of Fund	Sequoia Capital IV: $90M
Investment Criteria	Computer related; semiconductor, medical
Portfolio Companies	Altos Computer, California; Apple Computer Corp., California; LSI Logic, California; Tandem Computer Corp., California; Tandon Computers, California; Valid Logic, California

SEVIN ROSEN MANAGEMENT CO.
1245 Oakmead Parkway
Suite 101
Sunnyvale, CA 94086
(408) 720-8590

L. J. Sevin
Ben M. Rosen
Stephen M. Dow
Jon W. Bayless
Roger S. Borovoy
General Partner

Directorships

Palantir
Ansa Corp., Personal computer software
SiScan Systems, Inc.

Prior Position

Vice President, Secretary and General Counsel, Intel Corp.

Education

JD, Harvard Law School, 1959
BS, Massachusetts Institute of Technology, 1956

Dennis Gorman

Average Size of Investment	$1M
Size of Fund	$60M
Investment Criteria	Management and product
Portfolio Companies	Acuson, Mountain View, CA, Ultrasound imaging systems; Amcodyne, Longmont, CO, 8" fixed-removable drives; Cadtec, San Jose, CA, Engineering data base; COMPAQ Computer, Houston, TX, Personal computers; Convex Computer, Richardson, TX, Affordable supercomputers; Crystal, Austin, TX, Analog/digital semiconductors; Cypress Semiconductor, San Jose, CA, CMOS-integrated circuits; Electronic Arts, San Mateo, CA, PC entertainment software; General Parametrics, Berkeley, CA, Business presentation systems; Intelledex, Corvallis, OR, High-precision assembly robots; Itran, Manchester, NH, Factory vision inspection system; Landmark Graphics, Houston, TX, Seismic analysis workstations; Lotus Development, Cambridge, MA, PC productivity software; Merit Technology, Dallas, TX, Military avionic systems; NW Instrument Systems, Beaverton, OR, PC-based test instruments; Palantir, Santa Clara, CA, Omni-font document reader; Pronet, Dallas, TX, Health industry paging systems; Proteon, Natick, MA, Local area network systems; Quarterdeck Office Systems, Santa Monica, CA, PC software window managers; Silicon Graphics, Mountain View, CA, High-performance workstations; SRX, Dallas, TX, Small business voice data PBXs; SiScan Systems, Inc., Los Gatos, CA, Laser microscopes

SHARED VENTURES, INC.
6550 York Avenue South
Edina, MN 55435
(612) 925-3411

Howard Weiner
Frederick L. Weiner

Average Size of Investment	$100K
Size of Fund	$2.0M
Investment Criteria	Diversified
Portfolio Companies	Undisclosed

SIERRA VENTURES MANAGEMENT COMPANY
3000 Sand Hill Road
Building One, Suite 280
Menlo Park, CA 94025
(415) 854-1000

Peter C. Wendell
President

Directorships

Environmental Testing Corp. (OTC—ETCC), Hazardous waste/toxic substance testing
Datacopy Corp. (OTC—DCPY), Electronic imaging systems
Laserscope, Inc., Surgical laser systems plus others
Contex Telecommunications, Inc., Telecommunication services

Prior Positions

IBM Corporation
McKinsey & Company

Education

MBS, Harvard Business School
AB, Princeton University

Vincent H. Tobkin
General Partner

Directorships

StrataCom, Inc.
Lab Support, Inc.

Prior Position

Partner, McKinsey & Co., 1976–85

Education

JD, Harvard Business School, 1977
MBA, Harvard Business School, 1977
BS, MS, EE, Massachusetts Institute of Technology, 1973

Jeffrey M. Drazan
Vice President

Directorships

Centex Telecommunications, Telecom service management
Perfect Data Corp., Computer aftermarket products

Prior Position

Manager, AT&T, 1980–84

Education

MBA, New York University, 1984
BSE, Princeton University, 1980

Average Size of Investment	$500K–$1M
Size of Fund	Three funds totaling approximately $75M
Investment Criteria	Early-stage companies with strong management teams capable of becoming at least $50M profitable companies within 5–7 years
Portfolio Companies	Centex Telecommunications Corp., California, Telecommunications services; Datacopy Corp., (OTC—DCPY), California, Electronic imaging; Environmental Testing, (OTC—ETCC); New Jersey, Toxic waste/hazardous substance testing; Strataway, Inc., CA, T-1 Telecom Systems; Terndata Corp., CA, Relational database processors

MARTIN SIMPSON & CO., INC.
115 Broadway
New York, NY 10008
(212) 349-7450

Martin Simpson
Robert S. Anderson
Frank Halpern

Average Size of Investment	$200K
Size of Investment	Undisclosed
Investment Criteria	Manufacturing, technology-based companies, and other diversified areas of interest considered; geographic proximity important
Portfolio Companies	Undisclosed

SITUATION VENTURES CORP.
502 Flushing Avenue
Brooklyn, NY 11205
(212) 855-1835

Sam Hollander

Average Size of Investment	$200K
Size of Fund	Undisclosed
Investment Criteria	Geographic proximity of importance; diversified areas of interest
Portfolio Companies	Undisclosed

SMALL BUSINESS ASSISTANCE CORP.
2612 West 15th Street
Panama City, FL 32402
(904) 785-9577

Charles S. Smith

Average Size of Investment	$300K
Size of Fund	$3M
Investment Criteria	Diversified areas of interest; start-ups, will act as lead investor; geographic proximity important
Portfolio Companies	Undisclosed

SMALL BUSINESS INVESTMENT CAPITAL, INC.
1003 New Benton Highway
Little Rock, AR 72203
(501) 455-2234

C. E. Toland

Average Size of Investment	$300K
Size of Fund	Undisclosed
Investment Criteria	Interested in construction and real estate areas
Portfolio Companies	Undisclosed

SMITH BARNEY VENTURE CORP.
1345 Avenue of the Americas
48th Floor
New York, NY 10105
(212) 399-6127

350 California Street
San Francisco, CA 94104
(415) 955-1671

Michael J. Myers
President, NY
(212) 698-6382

Directorships

Entre Computer Centers, Inc., Large computer retail chain
Floating Point Systems, Inc., Manufacturer of scientific computers
Iomega Corp., Manufacturer of disk data storage systems

Prior Position

Associate, J. H. Whitney & Co.

Education

MBA, Harvard Business School, 1969
JD, George Washington University, 1966
BA, University of Illinois, 1963

David S. Lobel
General Partner, NY
(212) 698-6688

Prior Position

Bain & Company, 1978–81

Education

MBA, Stanford University, 1979
MS, Stanford University, 1978
BSc (Honors), University of the Witwatersrand, 1975

C. Sage Givens
Vice President, CA
(415) 955-1605

Directorship

Healthsouth, Inc., Specialized medical services

Prior Positions

Director, Strategic Planning, Eantech, Inc., 1982
Consultant, Management Analysis Center, Inc., 1978–81

Education

MBA, Stanford University, 1984
BA, Georgetown University

John S. Dulaney
Steven P. Bird
Associate, CA
(415) 955-1672

DIRECTORY AND BIOGRAPHIES

Prior Positions

Consultant, Bain and Company
Senior Research Engineer, Battelle-Northwest Laboratories

Education

MBA, Stanford University, 1983
MS, Stanford University, 1977
BS, Stanford University, 1976

Lisa Roumell
Geoffrey Y. Yang

Average Size of Investment	$1M
Size of Fund	$100M
Investment Criteria	Good management and under $15 million valuation
Portfolio Companies	Undisclosed

SOFINNOVA, INC.
Three Embarcadero Center
San Francisco, CA 94111
(415) 362-4021

Jean Bernard Schmidt

Average Size of Investment	$400K
Size of Fund	$18M
Investment Criteria	Technology-based companies are of interest as well as other diversified areas; will act as lead investor; start-ups are considered
Portfolio Companies	Undisclosed

SI SOKOL & ASSOCIATES
50 West Broad Street
Suite 1006
Columbus, OH 43215
(614) 228-2800

Si Sokol

Average Size of Investment	Undisclosed
Size of Fund	Undisclosed
Investment Criteria	Undisclosed
Portfolio Companies	Undisclosed

SOUTH ATLANTIC VENTURE FUND
220 East Madison
Suite 530
Tampa, FL 33602
(813) 229-7400

Donald W. Burton

Directorships

Digital Transmission Systems, Inc.
Sawtek, Inc.

Prior Positions

General Partner, Fidelity Ventures Limited
Vice President, Fidelity Venture Associates

Education

MBA, Harvard University, 1971
BA, Yale University, 1966

Richard J. Brandewie
General Partner

Prior Positions

General Partner, MBW Venture Partners
Vice President, Michigan Investment Fund
Vice President, Doan Resources Corp.

Education

MBA, University of Michigan, 1980
BS, Bowling Green State University, 1976

Average Size of Investment	$625K
Size of Fund	$17.5M
Investment Criteria	Diversified company preferences, including manufacturing, medical; also leveraged buy-outs are of interest; geographic proximity is important
Portfolio Companies	Undisclosed

SOUTH CAROLINA FARM CORP.
c/o World Businessmen Credit Corp.
2174 West Foothill Boulevard
P.O. Box 2178
Upland, CA 91785
(714) 391-1883

Jimmy ("James") Nixon, PhD
Harold Millican
Larry McLaughlin

Average Size of Investment	Undisclosed
Size of Fund	$200K
Investment Criteria	Farm and small cattle ranches
Portfolio Companies	World Businessmen Credit Corp.

SOUTHERN CALIFORNIA VENTURES
9920 La Cienega Boulevard
Suite 510
Inglewood, CA 90301
(213) 216-0544

2102 Business Center
Suite 218
Irvine, CA 92715
(714) 752-9341

B. Allen Lay
General Partner, Inglewood

Directorships

FRS, Inc., Post sales computer peripherals servicing
Speech Systems, Inc., Continuous speech to text conversion system
Precision Image, High resolution printers for computer graphics

Prior Positions

President and Director, Cada Systems Corp.
Founder, Pertec Computer Corp.

Education

Industrial Engineering, Kansas University

Jay Raskin
General Partner, Inglewood

Directorships

Techmedica, Customized orthopedic implants
Computer-Aided Design Group, Software space management facilities
Multi-Planer Diagnostic Imaging, Medical diagnostic imaging enhancement
Medclone, Medical diagnostic test kit

Prior Positions

General Partner, The Foothill Group
President and Chief Executive Officer, Rotomaster

Education

BS, Allegheny College

Robert W. Johnson
General Partner, Irvine

Directorships

Computer Accessories, Accessories for PCs
Celerity Computing, High end engineering workstations
Oakwood Publishing, Inc., Microcomputer software publisher
ViaSat, Military telecommunications

Prior Positions

Project Engineer, Martin/Decker Co.
Melchor Venture Management

Education

MS, BS, Electrical Engineering
MS, BS, Business Administration

Lois Fisher
Principal

Prior Positions

Producer, WXIA TV, Altanta, GA
Associate Producer, Cable News Network, Atlanta, GA

Education

MBA, University of California, Los Angeles
BS, Journalism, University of Wisconsin, Madison

DIRECTORY AND BIOGRAPHIES

Average Size of Investment	$450K
Size of Fund	$15M
Investment Criteria	Seek high value-added proprietary products and services
Portfolio Companies	Undisclosed

SOUTHERN TIER CAPITAL CORP.
55 South Main Street
Liberty, NY 12754
(914) 292-3030

Milton Brizil

Average Size of Investment	Undisclosed
Size of Fund	Undisclosed
Investment Criteria	Undisclosed
Portfolio Companies	Undisclosed

SOUTHWEST CAPITAL INVESTMENTS
3500 East Comanche N.E.
Albuquerque, NM 87107
(505) 884-7161

Valerie Wetherill
Martin J. Roe

Average Size of Investment	$150K
Size of Fund	$2.5M
Investment Criteria	Interested in manufacturing, construction, real estate, technology-based, and other companies; will act as lead investor
Portfolio Companies	Undisclosed

SOUTHWEST ENTERPRISE ASSOCIATES, L.P.
5420 LBJ Freeway
Suite 1266/LB41
Dallas, TX 75240
(214) 991-1620

C. Vincent Prothro
Special Partner/General Partner, Dallas

Directorships

Image Data Corp.
Dallas Semiconductor, CMOS products using late implantation technique
Silicon Systems, Semiconductor
Dallas Biomedical Corp.

Prior Position

Chief Executive Officer, Mostek Corp., 1969–82

Education

MBA, Harvard University, 1966
BSIE, Stanford University, 1964

Dick Kramlich
Leland H. Murphy
Associate

Prior Position

Senior Vice President, Manager Special Industries Division, Republic Bank of Dallas, 1970–85

Education

MBA, Indiana University, 1970
AB, Drury College, 1968

Average Size of Investment	$250K
Size of Fund	$25M
Investment Criteria	High technology, computer, electronics related, biomed, optics, lasers with high potential for good return on investment; prefer first-round financing
Portfolio Companies	Convex Computer, Dallas, TX, Microcomputers; Dallas Semiconductor Corp., Dallas, TX, Semiconductor; Molecular Design Ltd., San Leandro, CA, Biomed; Photophone (Image Data), San Antonio, TX, Telecom; Resonex, Sunnyvale, CA, Biomed; RF Monolithics, Dallas, TX, SAW devices/telecom; Shared Resource Exchange, Dallas, TX, Personal PBX; Software Publishing Corp., Mountain View, CA; TCS Software, Houston, TX, Accounting software; Zaisan, Houston, TX, Integrated workstations

SOUTHWESTERN VENTURE CAPITAL OF TEXAS, INC.
P.O. Box 1719
Seguin, TX 78155
(512) 379-0380

James A. Bettersworth, President
Joe A. Mueller, Executive Vice President

Average Size of Investment $125K; Maximum $200K
Size of Fund $1M
Investment Criteria   Technology-based companies and other diversified areas of interest
Portfolio Companies   Undisclosed

SOUTHWEST VENTURE CAPITAL, INC.
2700 East 51st Street
Suite 340
Tulsa, OK 74105
(918) 742-3177

Donald J. Rubottom
President

Directorships

Rubottom, Dridash & Associates, Inc.
Investment Management, Inc.

Prior Positions

Executive Vice President and Trust Officer, F & M Bank, Tulsa, 1966–68
Head of Trust Investment Division, First National Bank, Tulsa, 1955–66
Representative, Harris Upham & Co.

Education

Chartered Financial Analyst
Certified Management Consultant
BS, Banking, Oklahoma State University, 1951
Graduate courses, Management

A. Lucille Hitch

Average Size of Investment $100K
Size of Fund $1.05M
Investment Criteria   Provides equity capital and long-term financing where potential exists for capital gains
Portfolio Companies   Currently there are companies in the high-technology, wholesale/retail/services, distribution, and light manufacturing areas in the portfolio

THE SOUTHWEST VENTURE PARTNERSHIPS
300 Convent
Suite 1400
San Antonio, TX 78205
(512) 227-1010

5080 Spectrum Drive
Suite 610 East
Dallas, TX 75248
(214) 960-0404

Michael Bell
J. Edward McAteer
C. D. Grojean

Average Size of Investment $500K
Size of Funds $62.5M
Investment Criteria   Technology-based companies important; will act as lead investor; start-ups considered
Portfolio Companies   Undisclosed

SPROUT GROUP
140 Broadway
48th Floor
New York, NY 10005
(212) 902-2492

One Center Plaza
Sixth Floor
Boston, MA 02108
(617) 570-8700

5300 Stevens Creek Boulevard
Suite 320
San Jose, CA 95129
(408) 554-1515

Richard E. Kroon
Managing Partner, NY

Directorships

FoxMeyer Corp., Drug wholesaling
Illinois Soil Spring Co., Springs and control manufacturing

DIRECTORY AND BIOGRAPHIES

Rob Roy, Inc., Boys' sportswear manufacturing
Nominated for Pantry Pride, Inc., Supermarkets and department stores

Prior Position

United States Department of Defense

Education

MBA, Harvard Business School
BA, Yale University

David L. Mordy
General Partner, NY
(212) 902-2513

Directorship

Belvedere Holdings Ltd., Reinsurance

Prior Positions

IBM World Trade Corp.
IBM Corp.

Education

BA, University of Kansas

Larry E. Reeder
General Partner, MA

Directorships

Angenics, Inc., Genetic engineering
Company Stores Development Corp., Manufacturer's outlet malls
Digitech Industries, Inc., Telecommunications test equipment
Network Switching Systems, Inc., Communications switches
S.A.Y. Industries, Inc., Specialty packaging systems manufacturing

Prior Positions

Keydata Corp.
G. S. Grumman & Associates, Inc.
RCA Corp.
IBM Corp.

Education

BA, Harvard College

Lloyd D. Ruth
General Partner, NY
(212) 902-2482

Directorships

Dest Corp., OCR scanners
DRG Funding Corp., Financial services
HomeClub, Inc., Home improvement centers
Kaiser-Crebs Management Corp., Captive insurance
Visual Intelligence Corp., Graphics software

Prior Positions

Progressive Casualty Insurance Co.
Supply Corps, United States Navy

Education

MBA, Stanford University
MS, Naval Postgraduate School
BS, Cornell University

Keith B. Geeslin
Associate, CA

Prior Positions

Tymnet, Inc.
United States Senate Commerce Committee

Education

MA, Oxford University
BS, MS, Stanford University

C. Edward Hazen
Associate, MA

Directorships

Cyborg Corp., Data acquisition system
Network Switching Systems, Inc., Communication switches

Prior Positions

American Express Co.
DLJ Investment Banking Group

Education

MBA, Harvard Business School
BA, Brown University

Russell B. Pyne
Associate, NY
(212) 902-2509

Directorship

Visual Intelligence Corp., Graphics software

Prior Position

Davis Polk & Wardwell

Education

JD, MBA, Stanford University
AB, Princeton University

Jon R. Stone
Associate, CA

Prior Positions

Intercapco Venture Capital Fund
Syndrill Co.
Telxon Corp.
General Foods Corp.
Warner Communications
B. Dalton Booksellers

Education

MBA, Columbia University School of Business
BA, Brandeis University

Average Size of Investment	$500K–$1M
Size of Fund	$200M
Investment Criteria	Early-round financings of emerging growth companies and well-conceived management buy-outs of profitable, established companies, high profit potential
Portfolio Companies	Aida Corp., Santa Clara, CA, CAE products; Amtron Corp., Santa Clara, CA, High-resolution monitors; Angenics, Inc., Cambridge, MA, Genetic engineering; Atasi Corp., San Jose, CA, Computer peripheral equipment; Babbage's Inc., Dallas, TX, Software retailer; Baldt, Inc., Chester, PA, Marine hardware manufacturing; Belvedere Holdings, Ltd., Hamilton, Bermuda, Reinsurance; Bullwinkle's Inc., Santa Clara, CA, Restaurant chain; Company Stores Development Corp., Brentwood, TN, Manufacturers' outlet malls; Cyberdisk, Orange, CA, Disk drive media; Cyborg Corp., Newton, MA, Data acquisition systems; Cygnet Technologies, Inc., Sunnyvale, CA, Graphics communications products; Dest Corp., Milpitas, CA, OCR scanners; Digitech Industries, Inc., Ridgefield, CT, Telecommunications test equipment; DRG Funding Corp., Washington, DC, Financial services; ECS Microsystems, Inc., San Jose, CA, Distributed processing systems; FoxMeyer Corp., Denver, CO, Drug wholesaler; HomeClub, Inc., Long Beach, CA, Home improvement centers; Illinois Coil Spring Co., McHenry, IL, Springs and controls manufacturing; InfoCorp, Cupertino, CA, Technology market research; Kaiser-Crebs Management Corp., Oakland, CA, Captive insurance; Landmark Graphics Corp., Houston, TX, Seismic interpretation workstations; Marline Oil Corp., Dallas, TX, Natural resources; Material Progress Corp., Santa Rosa, CA, Disk drive substrates; Molecular Genetics, Inc., Minnetonka, MN, Microbiological research; Network Switching Systems, Inc., Andover, MA, Communications switches; Pantry Pride, Inc., New York, NY, Supermarkets and department stores; Rob Roy, Inc., New York, NY, Boys' sportswear manufacturing; S.A.Y. Industries, Inc., Leominster, MA, Specialty packaging; Soltex Oil & Gas, Inc., Dallas, TX, Oil and gas exploration; TeleQuest, Inc., Burbank CA, Consumer telephones; Tennessee Chemical Co., Copperhill, TN, Industrial chemicals; Texas Gas Transport Co., Austin, TX, Compressed natural gas transportation; VdK Holding Corp., Austin, TX, Baker products manufacturing; Visual Intelligence Corp., Amherst, MA, Graphics software; VLI Corp., Costa Mesa, CA, Health care; White Hat Systems, Inc., Woburn, MA, Manufacturing software

SPURT INVESTMENT FUND I
26H, 411-1 Street S.E.
Calgary, Alberta T2G 4Y5
Canada
(403) 231-8269

Norman W. Clark
Vice President, Alta-Can Telecom, Inc.

Prior Positions

Principal, Touche Ross & Partners, Management Consultants, 1980–85

Education

Master's, Computer Science, University of Calgary, 1971
Certified Management Accountant, 1982
Certified Management Consultant, 1983

Average Size of Investment	$75–250K
Size of Fund	$3M, Limited Partnership
Investment Criteria	Advanced technology companies in Alberta, Canada at the seed or start-up stage of development
Portfolio Companies	Omara Systems, Inc., Edmonton, Alberta, Design and manufacture of electronic industrial controls; Information Dynamics Corp., Calgary, Alberta, Design and manufacture of petroleum retail site controllers

SRK MANAGEMENT CO.
126 East 56th Street
New York, NY 10022
(212) 371-0900

Sidney R. Knafel
Managing Partner
Chairman, Insight Communications, Inc.

Directorships

Advanced Refractory Technologies, High-purity ceramic powder
Personics, Inc., Personal software
Microbiological Associates, Inc., Biomedical/Diagnostics
Cellular Communications, Inc., Cellular telephone
Formative Technologies, Inc., CAD
Medical Imaging Centers of America, Freestanding diagnostics
Vivid Systems, Inc., Computer projection system
Igene Biotechnology, Inc.

Prior Positions

Chairman, Vision Cable Communications
Vice President, Loeb, Rhoades & Co.

Education

MBA, Harvard University, 1954
AB, Harvard University, 1952

Victoria Hamilton

Directorships

Personics, Inc., Personal software
Lucid Inc., Lisp/AI
Microbiological Associates, Inc., Biomedical/Diagnostics

Prior Position

Consultant, Charles River Associates

Education

MBA, Harvard, 1979
AB, Harvard/Radcliffe, 1975

Michael I. Willner

Average Size of Investment	$500K
Size of Fund	Undisclosed
Investment Criteria	Early stage; business plan; not retailing or real estate; interest in cable
Portfolio Companies	Undisclosed

STANDARD OIL COMPANY OF INDIANA
200 East Randolph Drive
P.O. Box 5910-A
Chicago, IL 60680
(312) 856-5348

Naaman G. Landers
Gordon McKeague
Barbara Young

Average Size of Investment	$500K
Size of Fund	Undisclosed
Investment Criteria	Technology-based companies of interest; will act as lead investor; start-ups
Portfolio Companies	Undisclosed

STANFORD UNIVERSITY—ENDOWMENT FUND
Office of Treasurer
209 Hamilton Avenue
Palo Alto, CA 94301
(415) 326-5782

Rodney H. Adams
Treasurer

Directorships

Capital Preservation Fund
Capital Preservation Fund II
Telesensory Systems, Inc.
Midway Premier Oil Co.
AICCU Financial Services Co.

Prior Positions

Director of Finance, Stanford University, 1974–81
Manager, Investments, Stanford University, 1970–74

Education

MBA, Stanford University, 1962
BS, Mechanical Engineering, Stanford University, 1960

Average Size of Investment	$500K (range $300K–$700K+)
Size of Fund	$100M allocated to venture capital
Investment Criteria	Product-oriented companies rather than service companies; require presence of lead investor
Portfolio Companies	Undisclosed

STEPHENSON MERCHANT BANKING
899 Logan Street
Denver, CO 80203
(303) 837-1700

A. Emmet Stephenson, Jr.
Senior Partner

Directorships

Satellink Corp., Cable TV
River Oaks Industries, Mobile homes
Panelvision Corp., Computer terminals
Martin Oil Co., EDP
General Communications Inc., Publishing

Education

MBA, Harvard, 1968
BS, Louisiana State University, 1966

Thomas Kent Mitchell
Director

Prior Position

Investment Officer, MVenture Corp. (formerly Mercantile Dallas Corp.)

Education

MIM, American Graduate School of International Management, 1980
BA, University of Illinois, 1978

Average Size of Investment	$750K
Size of Fund	$100M
Investment Criteria	Historically profitable, at least $250K pretax profits
Portfolio Companies	General Communications, Inc., Denver, CO, Publishing; River Oaks Industries, Denver, CO, Mobile home manufacturer; Satellink Corp., Denver, CO, Cable television; Telesis Corp., Chelmsford, MA, Computer-aided design

STERLING CAPITAL LTD.
60 Camperdown Way
P.O. Box 8931
Greenville, SC 29604
(803) 233-2374

John M. Sterling, Jr.

Average Size of Investment	$250K
Size of Fund	$2M
Investment Criteria	Construction, real estate, manufacturing, technology-based companies of interest; start-ups; will act as lead investor; geographic locale important
Portfolio Companies	Undisclosed

STUART & ASSOCIATES
2421 One Main Place
Dallas, TX 75202
(214) 744-0750

Daniel B. Stuart
President

Directorships

Nichols-Homeshield, Inc.
Transform Logic Corp.

Nova Graphics
Interfirst Bank Galleria

Prior Positions

Director, Omex Corp.
Director, Primefax
Director, Insurance Systems of America
Chairman, Director, National Sharedata Corp.

Education

PMD, Harvard University Graduate School of Business Administration, 1968
MBA, University of Texas, 1950
BBA, University of Texas

Average Size of Investment	$100–250K (venture cap)
	$1–50M (LBO)
Size of Fund	$15M
Investment Criteria	Deal originator or investor; seed, startup, LBO; computer software and services, industrial products and equipment, distribution
Portfolio Companies	Nichols-Homeshield Inc. (LBO), Aluminum building products manufacturing, Aurora, IL; Transform Logic Corp., Artificial intelligence, Phoenix, AZ; Nova Graphics Co., Computer graphics, Austin, TX

SUBURBAN CAPITAL CORP.
6610 Rockledge Drive
Bethesda, MD 20817
(301) 493-7025

Henry ("Pete") Linsert
President

Directorship

Entech, Optics/solar

Prior Position

Vice President, Inverness Capital Corp., 1980

Education

MA, George Washington University, 1979
BA, Duke University, 1963

Steve Dubin
Vice President

Directorship

Capital Systems Holdings, Inc., Cash management systems and value-added IBM dealer

Prior Position

Vice President, Suburban Bank, 1974–83

Education

JD, George Washington University, 1980
BS, University of Maryland, 1974

Average Size of Investment	$500K
Size of Fund	$8M
Investment Criteria	Diversified within 2 hours' travel of Washington, DC
Portfolio Companies	Undisclosed

SUMMIT VENTURES
One Boston Place
Suite 912
Boston, MA 02108
(617) 742-5500

E. Roe Stamps, IV
Managing Partner

Directorships

Healthdyne, Inc., Medical electronics
Nu-Med, Inc., Hospital management
Sunrise Medical, Inc., Durable medical equipment

Prior Positions

General Partner, TA Associates
Senior Investment Manager, First Chicago Investment Corp.

Education

MBA, Harvard Business School, 1974
BS, MS, Industrial Engineering, Georgia Institute of Technology, 1967, 1972

Gregory M. Avis
Senior Associate

Prior Positions

Financial Analyst, McDonald & Company
Corporate Finance Dept., Goldman, Sachs & Co.

Education

MBA, Harvard Business School, 1984
BA, Political Economy, Williams College, 1980

Stephen G. Woodsum
Managing Partner

Directorships

QMS, Inc., Graphics processors for printers
Radionics, Inc., Alarm communication equipment
Sky Computers, Inc., Array processors
Systech Corp., Data communication controllers

Prior Positions

General Partner, TA Associates
Investment Analyst, First Chicago Investment Corp.

Education

Masters, Management, Graduate School of Management at Northwestern University, 1979
BA, Psychology, Yale University, 1976

Lawrence W. Lepard
Senior Associate

Directorship

ProQuip, Inc., Rigid-media test equipment

Prior Positions

Investment Analyst and Investment Officer, Continental Illinois Venture Corp.
Financial Analyst, Smith Barney Harris Upham & Co.

Education

MBA, Harvard Business School, 1983
BA, Economics, Colgate University, 1979

Thomas A. Avery
General Partner

Prior Positions

Associate, Robinson-Humphrey/American Express
First Vice President, Robinson-Humphrey/American Express

Education

MBA, Harvard Business School, 1983
BS, Industrial Management, Georgia Institute of Technology, 1975

Craig Y. Lee
Associate

Education

BA, Economics, Williams College, 1984

Average Size of Investment	$1M–$5M
Size of Fund	$160M
Investment Criteria	Emerging technology-based growth companies, health care services; leveraged buy-outs
Portfolio Companies	Proquip, Inc., Santa Clara, CA, Rigid media test equipment; Sky Computers, Lowell, MA, Array processors; Systech Corp., San Diego, CA, Data communication controllers; VM Software, Inc., Vienna, VA, IBM systems software

SUN BELT FUNDING CORP.
P.O. Box 7006
Macon, GA 31298
(912) 474-5134

Charles J. Jones

Average Size of Investment	Undisclosed
Size of Fund	Undisclosed
Investment Criteria	Undisclosed
Portfolio Companies	Undisclosed

SUNWESTERN MANAGEMENT, INC.
6750 LBJ Freeway
Suite 1160
Dallas, TX 75240
(214) 239-5650

DIRECTORY AND BIOGRAPHIES

Floyd W. Collins
Tom H. Delimitros
Dan M. Krausse
James F. Leary
Thomas W. Wright

Average Size of Investment	$1M
Size of Fund	$45M
Investment Criteria	Diversified areas of interest; start-ups and will act as lead investor; geographic proximity important
Portfolio Companies	Undisclosed

SUTTER HILL VENTURES
Two Palo Alto Square
Palo Alto, CA 94306-0910
(415) 493-5600

William H. Younger
General Partner

Directorships

Adept Technology, Inc.
Celeritek, Inc.
Koch Systems
Relational Technology Inc.
Tesseract Corp.

Prior Positions

Cummins Engine Company, 1975–81
U.S. Public Health Service, 1972–73

Education

Stanford Graduate School of Business, 1975
BS, University of Michigan, 1972

David L. Anderson
General Partner

Directorships

Activision, Inc.
Apollo Computer, Inc.
Dionex Corp.
Hybritech, Inc.
Integrated Genetics, Inc.
Manufacturing Management, Inc.
Molecular Devices Corp.
Nelson Analytical, Inc.
Source 2 International

Prior Positions

Financial Administrator, Watkins Johnson Co., 1968–71

Education

MBA, Harvard Graduate School of Business, 1968
BS, Massachusetts Institute of Technology, 1966

G. Leonard Baker, Jr.
General Partner

Prior Positions

Director, Cummins Engine Co., 1973
General Manager, Delta Enterprises, Delta Foundation, 1970–72
Manager, Cummins Engine Co., 1966–70

Education

MBA, Stanford, 1966
BA, Yale, 1964

Paul M. Wythes
General Partner

Directorships

Acrian, Inc.
Gemini Research Inc.
Priam Corp.
Tellabs, Inc.
Teltone Corp.
Xidex Corp.
T. Rowe Price New Horizons Fund, Inc.
T. Rowe Price Growth & Income Fund, Inc.
T. Rowe, Price New America Growth Fund, Inc.

Prior Positions

Associate, Corporate Staff, SmithKline Beckman, Inc., 1963–64
Senior Sales Engineer, Honeywell, Inc., 1959–63

Education

MBA, Stanford, 1959
BS, Princeton, 1955

Average Size of Investment	Min.: $150K
	Max.: $2.0M
Size of Fund	$500M
Investment Criteria	Technology-based companies of interest; desire to be lead or seed investor; second and later rounds also considered
Portfolio Companies	43 companies

SWEDISH INDUSTRIAL DEVELOPMENT CORP.
600 Steamboat Road
Greenwich, CT 06830
(203) 661-2500

Tord Carmel

Average Size of Investment	$500K
Size of Fund	Undisclosed
Investment Criteria	Technology-based companies of interest; will act as lead investor; start-ups
Portfolio Companies	Undisclosed

SYNDICATED COMMUNICATIONS, INC.
1030 15th Street, N.W.
Suite 203
Washington, DC 20005
(202) 293-9428

Herbert P. Wilkins
President

Directorships

Syndicated Communications, Inc.
Syncom Capital Corp.
Stellar Communications, Inc.
OFC, Inc.
District Cablevision, Inc.
Stellar Continental Cablevision
Buenavision Telecommunications, Inc.
Harvard Community Health Plan
Black Entertainment Television

Prior Positions

Financial Consultant, 1975–77
Senior Vice President, Urban National Corp., 1973–75

Education

MBA, Harvard Business School, 1970
BS, Boston University, 1965

Terry L. Jones
Duane C. McKnight

Average Size of Investment	$300K
Size of Fund	$10M
Investment Criteria	Invests solely in minority telecommunications properties
Portfolio Companies	Connection Communication Corp., Newark, NJ, Cable; KBLE Ohio, Inc., Columbus, OH, Cable; National Group TV, San Jose, CA, TV; Newsystems, Inc., Indiana, Radio; Stellar Communications, Washington, DC, Cellular radio; Telecable Broadcast of America, East Cleveland, OH, Cable

SYSOREX INTERNATIONAL, INC.
10590 North Tantau Avenue
Cupertino, CA 95014
(408) 996-9363

A. Salam Qureishi
Chairman, President, Chief Executive Officer, CA

Directorships

Janus Dysc Co., Inc.

Prior Positions

President, Optimum Systems, Inc., 1967–71
Manager, Applications, IBM Service Bureau Corp., 1961–67

Education

MS, Patna University (India), 1957
BS, Aligarh University, 1954

James I. Murphy
Vice President, Falls Church, VA

Directorships

Janus Dysc Co., Inc.

Prior Positions

Western Region Software Sales Manager, Optimum Systems, 1970–72
Vice President, Information Systems Co., 1966–70
Section Head, Systems Development Corp., 1957–66

Education

BA, University of California, 1957

Joseph Papa
Vice President, CA

Directorships

Image Systems Inc.
Janus Dysc Co., Inc.

Prior Positions

Director, Optimum Systems, Inc., 1967–75
Engineer, Lockheed Missiles & Space Co., 1962–67

Education

MSE, University of California, Berkeley, 1963
BSE, Princeton University, 1958

Average Size of Investment	$500K
Size of Fund	Undisclosed
Investment Criteria	Start-ups are considered as well as technology-based companies; will act as lead investor
Portfolio Companies	Undisclosed

TA ASSOCIATES
45 Milk Street
Boston, MA 02109
(617) 338-0800

435 Tasso Street
Suite 200
Palo Alto, CA 94301
(415) 328-1210

Peter A. Brooke
Managing Partner, MA

Directorships

Damon Corp.
Ex-Cell-O Corp.
Guilford Mills, Inc.
Unitrode Corp.
Wang Laboratories, Inc.

Prior Positions

Manager, Venture Capital Dept., Bessemer Securities, 1961
Partner, Tucker, Anthony & R. L. Day, Inc., 1963

Education

MBA, Harvard Business School, 1954
AB, Harvard College, 1952

John L. Bunce, Jr.
Associate, MA
(617) 574-6785

Directorships

CEM Corp., Moisture analysis instrumentation
PTM Industries Corp., Precision tooling and machining parts
Sequence, Inc., Digital oscilloscopes and waveform digitizers

Prior Position

Analyst, Lehman Brothers Kuhn Loeb

Education

MBA, Harvard University, 1984
AB, Stanford University, 1980

Michael C. Child
Partner, CA

Directorships

Teltrend, Inc., Telecommunications supplier
AST Research, Inc., Microcomputer enhancement
DH Technology, Printhead
ECAD, Inc., IC design software
Magnum Microwave, Microwave components
State of the Art, Inc., Accounting software
SAMNA Corporation, Word processing software
Verilink, Inc., Telecommunications supplier

Prior Positions

Product Manager, Rolm Corp.
Consultant, Boston Consulting Group
Production Engineer, Hewlett-Packard

Education

MBA, Stanford University, 1980
BSEE, University of California at Davis, 1976

Jeffrey T. Chambers
General Partner, CA

Directorships

Insurance Systems, Computer systems for independent insurance agencies
Precision Visuals, Graphics software
Scientific Micro Systems, Microcomputers and disk drive subsystems
Telcom Technologies, Manufacturer of automatic call distributors
XEL Communications, Telecommunication products

Prior Positions

Associate, Meredith Associates

Education

MBA, Stanford University, 1980
BA, Harvard College, 1976

Nabil N. El-Hage
Associate, MA

Directorships

American Matrix, Inc., Hi-tech ceramics
Insurance Systems, Inc., Office automation software
I.P. Sharp Associates, Ltd., Software

Prior Positions

Finance Instructor, Harvard Business School
Management Consultant, McKinsey & Co., Inc.

Education

MBA, Harvard Business School, 1984
BS, Yale University, 1980

Henry Koerner
Associate, MA

Directorship

Electronic Designs, Inc., Semiconductor modules

Prior Position

Design Engineer, Hewlett-Packard

Education

MBA, Harvard Business School, 1985
MSEE, Stanford University, 1976
BSEE, Stanford University, 1975

Richard H. Churchill, Jr.
General Partner, MA
(617) 574-6723

Directorships

Massachusetts Communications, Cable T.V.
Masada Telecommunications, Cable television
MDS Acquisition Corp., Cable T.V.

Prior Position

Accountant, Coopers & Lybrand, 1974–76

Education

MBA, Harvard University, 1978
AB, Dartmouth College, 1974

William P. Collatos
General Partner, Boston
(617) 574-6721

DIRECTORY AND BIOGRAPHIES

Directorships

Nautilus Leasing Services, Container leasing
Wisconsin Cable Investors, Cable television

Prior Position

Assistant Vice President, Commercial Banking, Fleet National Bank, 1976–80

Education

AB, Economics, Harvard University, 1976

Brian J. Conway
Associate, Boston
(617) 574-6705

Directorships

Concord Data Systems, Inc., Data communications equipment
Netrix Corp., Communication switches

Prior Position

Financial Analyst, Merrill Lynch White Weld Capital Markets Group

Education

MBA, Graduate School of Business, Stanford University, 1984
BA, Economics, English Amherst College, 1980

David D. Croll
Managing Partner, MA
(617) 574-6719

Directorships

Numerous cable television, broadcasting, and other media communications companies

Prior Position

Loan Officer, First National Bank of Boston, 1973–76

Education

MBA, Harvard University, 1973
BS, Cornell University, 1970

Robert W. Daly
Partner, MA
(617) 574-6710

Directorships

Computer Petroleum Corp., Data lease for petroleum products trading
Quad Systems Corp., Surface-mount assembler
Home Diagnostics, Inc., Medical diagnostics
Scientific Computer Systems, Near-supercomputer
Electronic Design, Inc., Semiconductor modules
Mediqual Systems Inc., Medical software

Prior Positions

Partner, Adler & Co., 1983–84
Partner, Daly, Hutcheson & Co., 1981–83

Education

MBA, Harvard University, 1978
AB, Brown University, 1973

Stephen F. Gormley
General Partner, MA
(617) 574-6724

Directorships

Pipe Technology, Inc., Manufacturing
Federal Communication Corp., Radio broadcasting
Mass Communications Corp., Outdoor advertising
Pharmasol Corp., Specialty packaging

Prior Position

Loan Officer, Bank of Boston, 1972–76

Education

MBA, Columbia Graduate School of Business, 1978
BA, Bowdoin College, 1972

Donald J. Kramer
Partner, MA
(617) 574-6709

Directorships

Alpha Software, Business software publishers
Metra Instruments, Inc., Machine interface systems
Maxitron Corp., Programmable controllers
PTM Industries, Precision machine shop

Varitronic Systems, Inc., Manufacturer of electronic lettering machines
Seiberco, Inc., Manufacturer of motion control systems
Spinnaker Software Corp., Microcomputer software

Prior Positions

Chief Executive Officer, Hastech
Chief Executive Officer, MFE

Education

MBA, Boston University, 1965
BS, Northeastern University, 1959

C. Kevin Landry
Managing Partner, MA
(617) 574-6701

Directorships

Maxitron Corp., Programmable controllers
National Venture Capital Association
Standex International Corp., Diversified manufacturing
Softsel Corp. Products, Inc., Microcomputer software distribution

Education

MBA, Wharton School, University of Pennsylvania, 1968
BA, Harvard College, 1966

P. Andrews McLane
General Partner, MA
(617) 574-6704

Directorships

Sigmatron Nova, Inc., Flat EL displays
Emulex Corp., Communications and data storage controllers
Concord Communications, Inc., Modems and LAN systems
Aegis, Inc., Microelectronic packages
FiberCom, Inc., Fiber-optic communications products
Equinox Systems, Inc., Data PBXs
President, New England Venture Capital Association

Prior Position

Vice President, State Street Bank and Trust Co.

Education

MBA, Amos Tuck School, 1973
AB, Dartmouth College, 1969

Jacqueline C. Morby
General Partner, CA

Directorships

BMC Software, Inc., Mainframe utility software
Artificial Intelligence Corp., Mainframe software
Information Builders, Inc., Mainframe software
Datatel, Inc., Data communications equipment
Systems Software Associates, System 36-38 software
Spinnaker Software, Micro software

Education

Masters, Management Simmons Graduate Management School, 1978
AB, Psychology, Stanford University, 1959

James F. Wade
Associate, MA
(617) 574-6722

Prior Position

Foreign Exchange Trade, Harris Trust & Savings Bank, 1978–80

Education

MBA, Harvard University, 1982
BBA, University of Notre Dame, 1978

Linda C. Wisnewski
Associate, MA
(617) 574-6703

Directorships

Alpha Software, Microcomputer software
ImmunoGen, Inc. Drug delivery systems
Datamedia Corp., CRT terminals, microcomputers

Prior Position

Associate, New England Capital Corp.

Education

MA, Management, Simmons College Graduate School of Management, 1981

Average Size of Investment	$2M
Size of Fund	$500M capital at cost
Investment Criteria	Experienced management; large fast-growth markets; proprietary products or know-how
Portfolio Companies	Portfolio presently consists of investments in 120 companies, mainly in high-technology industries and media communications

TAMCO INVESTORS SBIC INC.
375 Victoria Road
P.O. Box 1588
Youngstown, OH 44501
(216) 792-3811

Nathan H. Monus

Average Size of Investment	Undisclosed
Size of Fund	Undisclosed
Investment Criteria	Undisclosed
Portfolio Companies	Undisclosed

TAPPAN ZEE CAPITAL CORP.
120 North Main Street
New City, NY 10956
(914) 634-8890

Jack Birnberg
Chief Operating Officer
201 Lower Notch Road
Little Falls, NJ 07424
(201) 256-8280

Directorships

Authenticolor, Inc., Photographic lab
BB Energy Corp., Oil and gas company
Employees Retirement Benefit Association, Benefit and consulting services
Ferdon Equipment Co., Distribution of materials handling equipment
U.S. Graphite, Manufacturer
Waldorf Group, Inc., Leasing

Prior Position

Chairman, Board of Directors, Alan Investment Planning

Education

BS, Fairleigh Dickinson University, 1959

Average Size of Investment	$150K
Size of Fund	$3M
Investment Criteria	Diversified areas of interest; will act as lead investor; geographic proximity important
Portfolio Companies	Undisclosed

TAROCO CAPITAL CORP.
19 Rector Street
35th Floor
New York, NY 10006
(212) 344-6690

David Chang, President

Average Size of Investment	$300K
Size of Fund	Undisclosed
Investment Criteria	Diversified; start-ups and lead investments considered
Portfolio Companies	Undisclosed

TAYLOR & TURNER
220 Montgomery Street
San Francisco, CA 94104
(415) 398-6821

Rotan Mosle Technology Partners
3800 Republic Bank Center
700 Louisiana Street
Houston, TX 77002
(713) 236-3180

VenWest Partners
Westinghouse Electric Building
Gateway Center
Pittsburgh, PA 15222
(412) 642-5858

Marshall C. Turner, Jr.
General Partner, CA

Directorships

Remanco, Restaurant systems
Magnesys, Bubble memory components
Raycom Systems, Fiber-optic communications components
KQED, Inc., Public television

Prior Positions

Chief Operating Officer, RPR, Inc., 1975–80
Associate, Crocker Capital, 1973–75
Environmental Protection Agency, 1971–73
White House Fellow, 1968–71

Education

MBA, Harvard University
BS, MS, Mechanical Engineering, Stanford

William H. Taylor, II
General Partner, CA

Directorships

Oncor, Inc., DNA probes
R.D. Percy & Co., Audience measurement systems

Prior Positions

Chief Executive Officer, BEI Electronics, 1979–82
Vice President, Crocker Capital, 1972–79
Principal, Data Science Ventures, 1968–72

Education

PhD, Solid State & Material Sciences, Princeton University
BS, Mechanical Engineering, John Hopkins University

John V. Jaggers
President, TX

Prior Position

Vice President, Corporate Finance, Rotan Mosle, 1979–83

Education

MBA, Harvard University, 1979
BA, MEE, Electrical Engineering, Rice University, 1973

John W. Brock, Jr.
President, PA

Directorship

Formative Technologies, CAD/CAE systems

Prior Position

Attorney and Corporate Development, Westinghouse

Education

Chemical Engineering and Law Degrees, University of Pennsylvania

Average Size of Investment	$500K
Size of Funds	$18.4M
Investment Criteria	Technology related; early stage
Portfolio Companies	Akashic Memories, Santa Clara, CA, Sputtered disk media for use in high performance Winchester memory systems; Formative Technologies, Pittsburgh, PA, CAE workstations for architecture, engineering and construction industries; The Genra Group, Dallas, TX, Nationwide retail computer store chain; Magnesys, San Jose, CA, Developing solid state memory subsystems based on magnetic bubble technology; R. D. Percy & Co., Seattle, WA, System for television audience behavior and market research measurement; TCS Software, Houston, TX, Leading supplier of financial and accounting software to single station and networked microcomputers; Consilium Associates, Palo Alto, CA, Factory shop floor software; Image Data Corp., San Antonio, TX, Video conferencing equipment; Oncor, Inc., Gaithersburg, MD, Assay and diagnostic oncogene products; Performance Semiconductor, Sunnyvale, CA, Logic, memory and microprocessor circuits; Raycom Systems, Boulder, CO, Fiber-optics communications components; Validec, San Carlos, CA, Restaurant systems

TDH CAPITAL CORP.
Two Radnor Corporate Center
P.O. Box 234
Radnor, PA 19087
(215) 293-9787

DIRECTORY AND BIOGRAPHIES

J. Mahlon Buck, Jr.
William C. Buck
Alexander K. Buck
J. B. Dougherty

Average Size of Investment $500K
Size of Fund   Undisclosed
Investment Criteria   Diversified areas of interest including manufacturing; will act as lead investor; geographic locale important
Portfolio Companies   Undisclosed

TECHNOLOGY PARTNERS
257 East Main Street
Barrington, IL 60010
(312) 381-2510

1550 Tiburon Boulevard
Suite A
Belvedere, CA 94920
(415) 435-1935

Peter J. Gillespie
Managing Partner, IL

Prior Positions

Vice President, Heizer Corp.
Vice President, Johnson & Johnson

Education

MBA, Amos Tuck School, Dartmouth College, 1967
BS, Chemical Engineering, New Jersey Institute of Technology, 1958

William Hart
Managing Partner, CA

Directorships

Akashic Memories Corp., Sputtered rigid-disk media
Genesis Electronics Corp., Low-cost voice mail
Skylink Corp., Mobile and remote satellite communications
Trimble Navigation, Ltd., Satellite navigation systems

Prior Positions

Vice President and Director, Cresap, McCormick and Paget, Inc.
Manufacturing and Sales, IBM Corp.

Education

MBA, Amos Tuck School, Dartmouth College, 1967
B.Mgt.E., Rensselaer Polytechnic Institute, 1962

Average Size of Investment $500K
Size of Fund $3M
Investment Criteria   People with significant experience in related field; identifiable market opportunity
Portfolio Companies   Akashic Memories Corp., Santa Clara, CA, Thin-film media Winchester drives; Amiga Computer, Santa Clara, CA, High-performance personal computer; Cadtec Corp., San Jose, CA, VLSI CAE System; Genesis Electronics Corp., Folsom, CA, Voice mail system; Optical Data, Portland, OR, Optical disk storage; Skylink, Boulder, CO, Mobile and remote satellite communication; Trimble Navigation, Mountain View, CA, Satellite nagivation systems

TECHNOLOGY VENTURE INVESTORS
3000 Sand Hill Road
Building 4, Suite 210
Menlo Park, CA 94025
(415) 854-7472

James J. Bochnowski
Robert C. Kagle
James A. Katzman
David F. Marquardt
Burton J. McMurtry
Pete Thomas

Average Size of Investment $1M
Size of Fund $155M
Investment Criteria   Technology-based companies; will act as lead investor; start-ups considered; geographic proximity important
Portfolio Companies   Undisclosed

TECHNO WORLD INVESTMENTS, INC.
2121 South El Camino Real
Suite 605
San Mateo, CA 94403
(415) 573-0800

Allan F. Robb
Vice Chairman

Education
BS, Oregon State University

Average Size of Investment	$200K
Size of Fund	Undisclosed
Investment Criteria	Undisclosed
Portfolio Companies	Undisclosed

TELESCIENCES CAPITAL CORP.
26 Broadway
New York, NY 10004
(212) 425-0320

Robert F. Anderson
Seymour Hernes
Vincent J. Petrozeo
Michael A. Petrozeo

Average Size of Investment	$250K
Size of Fund	$2M
Investment Criteria	Telecommunications industry of interest; will act as lead investor
Portfolio Companies	Undisclosed

TELPAR, INC.
P.O. Box 796
Addison, TX 75001
(214) 233-6631

Richard Hanschen

Average Size of Investment	$1K
Size of Fund	Undisclosed
Investment Criteria	Diversified areas of manufacturing; start-ups considered
Portfolio Companies	Undisclosed

TENNECO VENTURES INC.
1010 Milam
Houston, TX 77001

Richard L. Wambold
President

Directorship
Automated Industrial Systems

Prior Position
Assistant to the Chairman, Tenneco Inc.

Education
MBA, University of Texas, 1977
BA, University of Texas, 1974

Carl S. Stutts
Vice President

Directorships
J B Systems
Neogen Corp.
Maxell Hybrids

Prior Positions
Facilities General Manager, Tenneco Oil
Sales & Marketing Manager, Petro-Tex (A Tenneco subsidiary)
Planning Manager, Tenneco, Inc.
Engineering Manager, Tenneco Chemicals

Education
MBA, University of Houston, 1975
BS, ChE, North Carolina State University, 1968

Average Size of Investment	$500K–1M
Size of Fund	$30M
Investment Criteria	Technology based companies

DIRECTORY AND BIOGRAPHIES

Portfolio Companies Automated Industrial Systems (CIMCO), Factory automation, Austin, TX; J B Systems, Industrial software, Woodland Hills, CA; Neogen Corp., Biotechnology, Lansing, MI; Optigraphics Corp., CAD, San Diego, CA; Space Industries, Inc., Space commercialization, Houston, TX; Maxell Hybrids, Biotechnology, Reno, NV; CTC Corp., Factory automation, Cincinnati, OH; LifeCell Corp., Medical technology, Houston, TX

TESSLER & CLOHERTY, INC. (MANAGEMENT COMPANY)
Fifty-Third Street Ventures, L.P.
420 Madison Avenue
New York, NY 10017
(212) 752-8010

Daniel Tessler
Chairman, management company
General Partner, fund

Directorships

Fusion Systems
Production Technologies
Logisticon
Softworks
Others

Prior Positions

General Partner, Patricof, Tessler & Co.
Associate, Lazard Freres & Co.

Education

BS, Cornell University, 1964

Patricia Cloherty
President, management company
General Partner, fund

Directorships

Knowledge Engineering, Inc.
International House
New York City Partnership
Others

Prior Positions

Deputy Administrator, U.S. Small Business Admin.
Vice President, Partner, Alan Patricof Assoc., Inc.

Education

MIA, Columbia University, 1968
MA, Teachers College, Columbia University, 1968

Average Size of Investment $650K
Size of Fund $40M
Investment Criteria Balanced fund investing $250K to $1.5M at all venture capital stages; occasional leveraged buyouts and reorganizations; no real estate or finance, but otherwise no geographic or industry limitations
Portfolio Companies Cellular Communications, Inc., Cellular telephone operations, New York, NY; Computer Identics Corp., Bar code systems, Canton, MA; Fusion Systems Corp., Ultraviolet lamp systems, Rockville, MD; Harman International Industries, High fidelity equipment, Los Angeles, CA; Kings Road Entertainment, Inc., Theatrical films, Los Angeles, CA; Liposome Technologies, Inc., Biotechnology, Menlo Park, CA; Logisticon, Inc., Warehouse automation systems, Santa Clara, CA; Miniscribe, Inc., Winchester disk drives, Longmont, CO; Ontologic, Inc., Graphics data base management system, Billerica, MA; Plains Resources, Inc., Oil/Gas producer, Oklahoma City, OK; Production Technologies, Inc., Oilwell production systems, Houston, TX; Satellite Music Network, Inc., Radio programming services, Dallas, TX; Softworks, Inc., Software engineering tools, Palo Alto, CA; Symbolics, Inc., Symbolic computing, Cambridge, MA; Syntro Corp., Biotechnology, San Diego, CA; Vortec, Corp., Air handling equipment, Cincinnati, OH

TEXAS CAPITAL CORP.
1341 West Mockingbird
Suite 1250 East
Dallas, TX 75247
(214) 638-0652

Lawrence W. Schumann
David G. Franklin
Larry T. Marek
Tom L. Beecroft
Thomas M. Gaubert

Average Size of Investment $400K
Size of Fund $20M

Investment Criteria	Diverse areas of interest including technology-based and manufacturing companies; will act as lead investor
Portfolio Companies	Undisclosed

TEXAS COMMERCE INVESTMENT COMPANY
TexCom Venture Capital, Inc.
c/o Lummis, Hamilton & Co.
Texas Commerce Bank Bldg.
Suite 3100
712 Main Street
Houston, TX 77002
(713) 236-4719

Fred R. Lummis
Manager

Directorships

HyClone, Inc., Plant genetics
Equus Capital Corp., Leveraged buy-out fund
Interbevco, Inc., Soft-drink bottling
Fared Robot Systems, Inc., Automated systems

Prior Position

Assistant Vice President, Texas Commerce Bank

Education

MBA, University of Texas, 1978
BA, Vanderbilt University, 1976

Frederic C. Hamilton, Jr.
Manager

Directorship

Interbevco, Inc., Soft-drink bottling and distribution

Prior Position

Farm Management, Plantation services

Education

MBA, Babson College, 1982
BA, University of Denver, 1978

Average Size of Investment	$500K
Size of Fund	$15M
Investment Criteria	First, second, and later stage; leveraged buy-outs; all industries
Portfolio Company	Undisclosed

THRESHOLD VENTURES, INC.
430 Oak Grove Street, Suite 200
Minneapolis, MN 55403
(612) 874-7199

T. Denny Sanford
Chairman

Directorships

Scientific Computers

Prior Positions

President and CEO, Contech, Inc., 1968–82

Education

BS, University of Minnesota

John L. Shannon Jr.
Vice President

Directorships

United Phone Book Advertisers, Inc.
Serv-Eez Foods, Inc.

Prior Positions

Marketing Executive, SciMed Life Systems, Inc., 1984–85
Marketing Executive, The Toro Company, 1979–84

Education

MBA, Finance, School of Management, University of Minnesota, 1979
BS, University of Minnesota, 1975

Average Size of Investment	$100K
Size of Fund	$1M, SBIC/$5M, potential

Investment Criteria	Size of Investment from $50K to $250K; Upper Midwest; telecommunications, medical, consumer, low to medium technology companies
Portfolio Companies	Camax Systems, Inc., CAD/CAM, Minneapolis, MN; Central Data Corp., STD Bus computer manufacturer, Champaign, IL; Gascard Club, Fuel management, San Diego, CA; Impact Systems, Inc., Diagnostic imaging, Milwaukee, WI; Luther Medical Products, Medical catheters, Santa Ana, CA; Lemna Corp., Water purification, Minneapolis, MN; Micro Business Applications, Inc., Accounting software, Minneapolis, MN; Mizar, Inc., VME Bus computer manufacturer, St. Paul, MN; Sentech Medical Corporation, Blood chemistry analyzers, St. Paul, MN; Blue Line Software, Inc., IBM mainframe software, Minneapolis, MN; United Phone Book Advertisers, Inc., Yellow Pages, Lincoln, NE; Wholesale Club, Discount retail club, Indianapolis, IN; Serv-Eez Foods, Inc., Frozen foods, Minneapolis, MN

TIDEWATER SMALL BUSINESS INVESTMENT CO.
1106 Maritime Tower
234 Monticello Avenue
Norfolk, VA 23510
(804) 627-2315

Robert H. Schmidt

Average Size of Investment	$200K
Size of Fund	$2M
Investment Criteria	Diverse areas of interest including manufacturing; start-ups; will act as lead investor; geographic location of importance
Portfolio Companies	Undisclosed

TLC FUNDING CORP.
141 South Central Avenue
Hartsdale, NY 10530
(914) 683-1144

Philip G. Kass

Average Size of Investment	$100K
Size of Fund	$5M
Investment Criteria	Geographic proximity important; will act as lead investor; diversified areas of interest
Portfolio Companies	Undisclosed

TOMLINSON CAPITAL CORP.
3055 East 63rd Street
Cleveland, OH 44127
(216) 271-2103

H. F. Meyer
Donald R. Calkins
John A. Chernak

Average Size of Investment	$200K
Size of Fund	Undisclosed
Investment Criteria	Diversified interest areas; geographic location important
Portfolio Companies	Undisclosed

TOWER VENTURES INC.
Sears Tower-BSC 43-50
Chicago, IL 60684
(312) 875-0583

James M. Troka

Average Size of Investment	$250K
Size of Fund	Undisclosed
Investment Criteria	Diversified areas of interest; will act as lead investor
Portfolio Companies	Undisclosed

TRAMMELL CROW INVESTMENT CORP.
2002 Bryan Tower
Dallas, TX 75201
(214) 747-0643

Henry Billingsley

Average Size of Investment	$200K
Size of Fund	$1.5M
Investment Criteria	Real estate ventures of interest; geographic locale important
Portfolio Companies	Undisclosed

TRANSPORTATION CAPITAL CORP.
60 East 42nd Street
New York, NY 10165
(212) 697-4885

Melvin L. Hirsch
Chairman and Chief Executive Officer

Directorship

Lencadia National Corp., Consumer finance life insurance

Prior Positions

Counsel, Law Offices of Irving L. Gartenberg, 1977–84
Senior Vice President, A. J. Armstrong Co., Inc., 1954–74
General Counsel, United Factors, 1974–77

Education

JD, Harvard Law, 1948
BA, Cornell University, 1944

Robert H. Silver
Vice President

Directorship

Transportation Capital Corp.

Prior Positions

Vice President, Arnoff & Richline, Inc.
Vice President, International Trading & Commodities, Ltd.

Education

Accounting, St. John's University, 1943

Dorothy T. Hirsch, Treasurer

Average Size of Investment	$150K
Size of Fund	$30M
Investment Criteria	Transportation in New York City, Boston, and Philadelphia
Portfolio Companies	Undisclosed

TRIAD VENTURES LIMITED
4600 Post Oak Place, Suite 100
Houston, TX 77027
(713) 627-9111

P.O. Box 1987
Austin, TX 78767
(512) 472-7171

6510 Abrams Road, Suite 650
Dallas, TX 75231
(214) 341-1553

Lloyd M. Bentsen III
General Partner, Houston

Directorships

Trinity Computing
Cardiovascular Systems
Houston Metropolitan Ministries
Several family owned corporations

Prior Positions

Vice President, Rotan Mosle

Education

MBA, Stanford University, 1968
BA, Princeton University, 1966

Hobby Abshier, Jr.
General Partner, Austin

Directorships

Copeland Flame Spraying
Xanthus Corp.
Centex Communications

Prime Positions

Officer and Director, Rotan Mosle

Education

MBA, Harvard University, 1954
BBA, Rice University, 1952

Nick Stanfield
General Partner, Dallas

DIRECTORY AND BIOGRAPHIES

Directorships

Able Enterprises, Inc.
Ennis Automotive, Inc.
Kirby Mortgage & Investments, Inc.
Palindromic Systems, Inc.
Roy Stone Transfer Corp.

Prior Positions

Vice President, Rotan Mosle
Vice President, Eppler, Guerin & Turner

Education

BBA, North Texas State University, 1963

Average Size of Investment	$500K–1M
Size of Fund	$15M+
Investment Criteria	Texas based; two to three year track record; ability to go public, be acquired or merge upstream in five years; proprietary attributes
Portfolio Companies	Biomedical Research, Austin, TX, Medical; Cardiovascular Systems, Houston, TX, Medical; Centex Communications, Austin, TX, Telecommunications; CYB Systems, Austin, TX, Microprocessing; DiFlo International, Houston, TX, Fuel Management; Key Concepts, Inc., Houston, TX, Computer; Near Space Communications, Plano, TX, Telecommunications; New England Monthly, MA, Magazine; Nova Graphics, Austin, TX, Graphic software; Shakey's Pizza Restaurants, Dallas, TX, Food service; Trinity Computing, Houston, TX, Medical; Xanthus Corporation, Austin, TX, Computer software

TRIARCH CORPORATION LIMITED
120 Adelaide Street West
Suite 1120
Toronto, Ontario M5H 1V1
Canada
(416) 364-2271

James F. C. Stewart
Chairman and Chief Executive Officer

Education

MBA, McMaster University
B. Comm. & BA, Economics, University of Ottawa

Peter E. Roode

Average Size of Investment	Companies with sales over $5M annually
Size of Fund	Undisclosed
Investment Criteria	Outside investors must have control
Portfolio Companies	Undisclosed

TRICON FINANCIAL CORPORATION
20 Broad Street
New York, NY 10005
(212) 809-5928

Joseph Tricomi
President

Prior Positions

President, Fidenas Corporation
President, Feminique Products Corp.
Vice President, Aladdin Interstate Corp.
Vice President, Spencer International Corp.

William Marvin
E. Tricomi

Average Size of Investment	$1M
Size of Fund	Undisclosed
Investment Criteria	Undisclosed
Portfolio Companies	Undisclosed

TRINITY VENTURES
20813 Stevens Creek Boulevard, #101
Cupertino, CA 95014

Gerald S. Casilli
General Partner

Directorships

NTX Communications Corp., Communications
Cogensys Corp., Expert systems software

Prior Positions

President, Genesis Capital, 1982–present
Chief Executive Officer, Millenneum Systems, Inc., 1973–81

Education

BSEE, University of Pittsburgh, 1961

Noel J. Fenton
General Partner

Directorship

Personal Computing Tools, Computer equipment catalog for engineers

Prior Positions

President/Chief Executive Officer, Covalent Systems Corp., 1983–86
President/Chief Executive Officer, Acurex Corp., 1972–83

Education

MBA, Stanford, 1963
BS, Cornell, 1959

Average Size of Investment	Undisclosed
Size of Fund	Undisclosed
Investment Criteria	Undisclosed
Portfolio Companies	Undisclosed

TURNER REVIS ASSOCIATES
14 Union Wharf
Boston, MA 02109
(617) 227-9734

John G. Turner
General Partner

Prior Positions

Vice President, Teradyne, 1978–82
General Manager, Industrial consumer division, Teradyne, 1975–78
Chief Engineer, Mark Instruments (U.K.), 1965–75

Education

MBA, Boston University School of Management
BSEE, Middlesex Polytechnic (U.K.).

Kenneth J. Revis
General Partner

Prior Positions

Marketing Director, Industrial consumer division, Teradyne, 1981–82
Product Manager, Teradyne, 1976–81
Manager, Coopers & Lybrand, 1966–76

Education

MBA, Columbia Business School, 1966
AB, Brandeis University

Average Size of Investment	$500K
Size of Fund	$12M
Investment Criteria	Early stage ventures in the electronics industry, primarily in the Greater Boston area; particular areas of interest include hardware/software product companies in: semiconductor capital equipment information processing, computer aided design and manufacturing, manufacturing control and factor automation, office automation
Portfolio Companies	ASECO Corp., Semiconductor capital equipment, Marlboro, MA; AXIOM Technology Corp., Semiconductor capital equipment, Newton, MA; Custom Silicon, Inc., Semiconductor equipment, Lowell, MA; Digital Automation Corp., Semiconductor equipment, Peabody, MA; Interactive Video Systems, Semiconductor equipment, Concord, MA; Natural Microsystems Corp., Telecommunications products, Natick, MA; Semiconductor Test Solutions, Semiconductor equipment, Santa Clara, CA; Vermont Microsystems, Inc., Graphic subsystems, Winooski, VT; Visage, Inc., Vision products, Framingham, MA

ULIN, MORTON, BRADLEY & WELLING, INC.
75 Federal Street
Boston, MA 02110
(617) 423-0003

Peter A. Ulin
Managing Director

Directorships

SMD Industries, Manufacturer of consumer products
CTEC, Inc., Computer software, systems organization

DIRECTORY AND BIOGRAPHIES

Prior Position
Vice President, Director of Mergers and Acquisitions, E. F. Hutton & Co.

Education
AB, Harvard University, 1953

Perry Morton
W. Lambert Welling
Managing Director

Directorships
Broad Street Communications, Radio
Design Pak, Paperboard boxes

Prior Positions
Partner, Pace Consulting Group, 1980–82
Vice President, Federal Street Capital, 1972–80

Education
MBA, Columbia University Graduate School of Business, 1958
AB, Middlebury College, 1954

Average Size of Investment	$1M
Size of Fund	$25M
Investment Criteria	Established companies, must be breaking even or earning second stage or later
Portfolio Companies	Portfolio currently consists of consumer companies, high technology, etc.

UNC VENTURES
195 State Street
Suite 700
Boston, MA 02109
(617) 723-8300

Edward Dugger III
President

Directorship
Air Atlanta, Airline

Prior Position
Manager, Real Estate Group, Irwin Management Co., Inc.

Education
MPA-UP, Princeton University, 1973
AB, Harvard College, 1971

James W. Norton, Jr.
Vice President and Treasurer

Directorships
Infolink, Data collection
Xinix, Process control instrumentation

Prior Positions
Investment Banking, Corporate Finance, Morgan Stanley, 1979–83
Marketing, Data Processing Division, IBM Corp.
Program Director, Dept. of Health and Hospitals, Boston

Education
MBA, Stanford University
BA, Economics, Boston University

Ursula Z. Loucks
Laurence C. Morse, Ph.D.
Elaine Papadopoulos

Average Size of Investment	$500K
Size of Fund	$30M
Investment Criteria	Continental United States; companies substantially owned and/or managed by minorities
Portfolio Companies	Air Atlanta, Altanta, GA, Airline; Accent Hair Salons, OH, Retail chain hair salons; Broadcast Enterprises Natl., Philadelphia, PA, Radio stations; Cydrome Inc., Milpitas, CA, Computers; Optotech, Inc., Colorado Springs, CO, Optical disk drives; Xinix, Santa Clara, CA, Control instrumentation; WDG-III Post Medical Center, San Francisco, CA, Developing Post Medical Center

UNICORN VENTURES LTD.
6 Commerce Drive
Cranford, NJ 07016
(201) 276-7880

Frank P. Diassi
General Partner

Directorships

Intellitech, Inc.
Software Plus, Inc.
Hawkeye Chemical Co.
Amerlux, Inc.
Balco, Inc.
Pawnee Industries, Inc.
Procedyne Corp.
Steffen Dairy Foods Co.

Prior Positions

President, Darrill Associates, 1971–81
Division Manager, Continental Oil Co., 1960–67

Education

MBA, University of Chicago, 1960
BS, Rutgers University, 1954

Arthur B. Baer
Unicorn Ventures Ltd.

Directorships

American Reserves, Inc.
Leisure Market Radio, Inc.
American National Beverage Corp.
IntelliTech, Inc.
Software Plus, Inc.

Prior Positions

Security Analyst, E. F. Hutton & Co., 1978
Security Analyst, Faulkner, Dawkins & Sullivan, 1972–78

Education

MBA, Harvard University, 1958
BA, Harvard University, 1954

Average Size of Investment	$750K
Size of Fund	$35M
Investment Criteria	Interested in diverse companies, preferably technology based; will act as lead investor; leveraged buy-outs are of interest
Portfolio Companies	Undisclosed

UNION VENTURE CORPORATION
225 S. Lake Avenue
Suite 601
Pasadena, CA 91101
(818) 304-1989

18300 Von Karman Ave.
Irvine, CA 92715
(714) 553-7130

John W. Ulrich
Vice President, Irvine

Directorships

Microbeam, Inc., Focused ion beam systems
Novatech Corp., Manufacturer of solid-state data acquisition and recording systems
Bio Diagnostics, Inc., Development of proprietary fluorescent immunoassay test kits
Bipolar Integrated Technology, Inc., Digital signal processing bipolar VLSI

Prior Positions

Assistant Credit Manager, Union Bank, Los Angeles Regional Office
President, So. Pacific Reg. Assoc. of Small Bus. Investment Companies

Education

MBA, University of Denver, 1974
BA, Westminster College, 1970

Christopher L. Rafferty
Vice President, Pasadena

Directorships

Telegence Corporation, Manufactures and markets distributed, date over voice communication system
Carlyle Systems, Inc., Manufactures and markets turnkey computer system used in automating libraries
Triplex, Fault tolerant programmable controller manufacturer

Prior Positions

Vice President, Coronado Minerals Company (Houston)
Attorney, Bracewell & Patterson, Houston

Education

JD, Georgetown University, 1975
BA, Stanford University, 1970

Jeffrey A. Watts
Senior Investment Officer, Pasadena

Directorship

Syconex Corp., Designs and manufactures gas analysis instruments to improve combustion efficiency

Prior Positions

Loan Officer, Northern Trust Company, Illinois
Accountant and Consultant, Arthur Andersen & Co., Illinois
President, Western Region, Association of Small Business Investment Companies

Education

MBA, Finance and Accounting, University of Michigan, 1975
BS, Cellular Biology, University of Michigan, 1972

Lee R. McCracken
Investment Officer, Irvine

Prior Positions

Advertising Manager, NCR Comten
Advertising Manager, Microelectronics Division

Education

MBA, University of California at Los Angeles, Graduate School of Management, 1984
Master of Computer Science, University of Dayton, 1982
BS, University of Santa Clara, 1979

Thomas H. Peterson
Investment Officer, Pasadena

Prior Positions

Production Engineer, Hewlett-Packard, 1982–84
Product Assurance Engineer, Hewlett-Packard, 1980–82
Supervising Process Control Engineer, General Electric, 1978–80

Education

MBA, University of California at Los Angeles, 1985
BSEE, Iowa State University, 1978

Average Size of Investment	$750K
Size of Fund	$22M
Investment Criteria	Undisclosed
Portfolio Companies	Undisclosed

UNITED BUSINESS VENTURES, INC.
(Space Ventures Inc.)
3931 McArthur Boulevard
Suite 212
Newport Beach, CA 92660
(714) 851-0855

Leslie R. Brewer

Average Size of Investment	$250K
Size of Fund	$2.5M
Investment Criteria	Diverse areas of interest including start-ups, second stage, acquisitions, divestitures; will act as lead investor; California preferred
Portfolio Companies	Undisclosed

UNITED CAPITAL CORP. OF ILLINOIS
120 West State Street
United Center, 3rd Floor
Rockford, IL 61101
(702) 782-5114

Seth L. Atwood
Gregory Abbott

Average Size of Investment	$350K
Size of Fund	Undisclosed
Investment Criteria	Diverse areas of interest including manufacturing and technology-based companies
Portfolio Companies	Undisclosed

UNITED INVESTMENT GROUPS, INC.
508 North Second Street
Suite 302
Fairfield, IA 52556
(515) 472-8296

Clyde J. Cleveland
President

Directorships

United International Ventures
Cleveland Investment Management Corp.
Tetratech Building Services, Inc.

Prior Position

Executive Vice President, La Jolla Investment Groups

Education

BSc, Indiana State University, 1971

Mark Hanson
Marketing Representative

Prior Positions

President, Coherent Systems
Registered representative for a securities company

Education

Mankato Teachers College

Kevin T. Twohy
Senior Vice President

Prior Position

Chief Executive Officer, Cielo Food Service Inc.

Education

BA, University of California at Santa Barbara, 1972

Martin DelRe
Bryan K. Peterson
Vice President
Project Development

Directorship

United International Ventures, Venture capital

Prior Positions

Director, No. New Mexico Emergency Medical Services Council, 1978–79
Emergency Care Instructor/Coordinator, County of Maui, 1975–76

Average Size of Investment	$2.33M
Size of Fund	$20M+
Investment Criteria	Diversified technologies and products to high-growth industries
Portfolio Companies	United Communications Systems, Ltd., Fairfield, IA, Develop Japanese electronic typewriter; United Controller Technologies, Ltd., San Diego, CA, Develop controller for low-cost printers; United Fibertech, Ltd., Houston, TX, Improve manufacture of fused fiberboard; United Soil Technologies, Ltd., Fairfield, IA, Develop algae as soil fertilizer; United Wind Partners, Ltd., Southern California, Develop windfarm; United Yuma, Ltd., Yuma, AZ, Acquisition for resale, 2 mobile home parks

UNITY CAPITAL CORP.
4343 Morena Boulevard
Suite 3A
San Diego, CA 92117
(619) 270-1130

Frank W. Owen

Average Size of Investment	$100K
Size of Fund	Undisclosed
Investment Criteria	Diversified company preferences, will act as lead investor
Portfolio Companies	Undisclosed

U.S. MANAGEMENT CORP.
1500 Locust Street
Philadelphia, PA 19102
(215) 985-4468

Howard I. Green

Average Size of Investment	$200K
Size of Fund	Undisclosed
Investment Criteria	Diversified areas of interest including manufacturing
Portfolio Companies	Undisclosed

UST CAPITAL CORP.
40 Court Street
Boston, MA 02108
(617) 542-6300

Stephen R. Lewinstein
Arthur F. F. Snyder
C. W. Dick

Average Size of Investment	$200K
Size of Fund	$3M
Investment Criteria	Diversified areas of interest, geographic proximity important
Portfolio Companies	Undisclosed

U.S. VENTURE PARTNERS
2180 Sand Hill Road
Suite 300
Menlo Park, CA 94025
(415) 854-9080

William K. Bowes, Jr.
General Partner

Directorships

Amgen, Inc., Molecular genetics
Cydrome, Inc., Mini supercomputers
DVI, Devices for vascular intervention
Imperial Automation, Microprocessor-based teller systems for financial institutions
Resonex, Inc., MRI devices for cardiovascular diagnosis
Ross Stores, Inc., Off-price apparel stores
Siegen Corp., Diagnostic medical equipment
Surface Mounted Technology, Custom bipolar gate arrays
XOMA Corp., Monoclonal antibodies
Applied Biosystems, Inc., Analytical instruments for genetic engineering research
Institute for Biological Research & Development, Clinical research for pharmaceutical companies

Prior Position

Senior Vice President and Director, Blyth & Co., Inc., 1953–78

Education

MBA, Harvard Business School, 1952
BA, Stanford University, 1950

Stuart G. Moldaw
General Partner

Directorships

Ross Stores, Inc., Chain of department stores; off-price branded merchandise
Craft Mart
Home Express
Thomas E. Wolfe
Petite Concept, Ltd.
Casey & Osh

Prior Positions

Senior Vice President, Lucky Stores, Inc., 1977–79
Organized Operating Pic-a-Dilly, Atherton Industries, 1973 (later sold to Lucky Stores, Inc.)
Vice President, Melville Corp., 1970–73
Organized Operating Country Casual Stores, Stuart G. Moldaw Enterprises, 1959 (later sold to Melville Corp.)

Education

BA, Syracuse University, 1949

Robert Sackman
General Partner

Directorships

Microwave Technology Corp., Microwave components
Sun Microsystems, Inc., Scientific and engineering workstations
Telenova, Inc., Voice/data telephone systems
Surface Mounted Technology, Semiconductor device assembly

Prior Positions

U. S. Venture Partners, 1981–present
Venture Capitalist/Consultant, 1970–81
Director, Investor/Consultant, Vidar Corp., 1963–70
Vice President—General Manager, Ampex Corp., 1953–63
Manager, R & D, National Security Agency, 1946–53

Education

Electrical Engineering, George Washington University, 1953

Roderick C. M. Hall
General Partner

Directorships

F & C Enterprise Trust, Investment trust (U.K.)
U.S. Ventures, S.A., Venture capital company

Prior Positions

Associate Director, Wobaco Investments Ltd., 1974–78
General Partner, McMicking & Co., 1960–73

Education

AB, History, Stanford University, 1954

H. Joseph Horowitz
General Partner

Directorships

Avia
Epyx, Inc., Entertainment game software for microcomputers
Laura Scudder's

Prior Position

Venture Capital, Exxon Enterprises Inc., 1979–82

Education

MBA, Wharton School of Finance, 1979
BA, Columbia College, 1973

Bruce J. Boehm
General Partner

Directorships

StrataCom, Telecommunications network management
Cygnet Systems, Inc., Optical disk filing retrieval system
Synergy Computer Graphics, High-performance color hard-copy printer/plotters
X-Cyte, Inc., Proximity detection equipment

Prior Positions

Engineer, NorthStar Computers, Inc., 1980
Designer and Manager, Telesensory Systems, Inc., 1977
Analyst, Foster Miller Associates, 1975

Education

MBA, Stanford University, 1982
MS, Stanford University, 1977
BS, Massachusetts Institute of Technology, 1975

Jane H. Martin
General Partner

Directorships

Evans Rents, Furniture rental
Stylus
C. S. Brods

Prior Positions

All Venture of Delaware/Maryland, Cable TV franchise
All Venture of Vermont, Cable TV franchise
All Venture of New York, Cable TV franchise

Philip S. Schlein
General Partner

Directorships

Petite Concepts
Casey & Osh
Home Express
CraftMart
C.S. Brod's
Apple Computer

Prior Positions

President, Chief Executive Officer, Macy's CA, 1974–85
Senior Vice President, Director of Merchandising, Banberger's, NJ, 1964–74

Education

BS, Economics, University of Pennsylvania, 1954

Steven M. Krausz
Associate

Prior Positions

Product Manager, Daisy Systems, 1984
Product Manager, Direct Inc., 1981–83

DIRECTORY AND BIOGRAPHIES

Research and Development Engineer, BTI Computer Systems, 1978–81
Engineer, NASA Ames Research Center, 1976

Education

MBA, Stanford University, 1985
BSEE, Stanford University, 1977

Nancy E. Glaser
Associate

Prior Positions

Director of Retail and Franchise, Barton's Candy Corp., 1981–83
Managing Director, Lord & Taylor, 1978–81
Buyer, The Gap, Inc., 1973–78
Group Sales Manager, Macy's, 1968–73

Education

MBA, Stanford Graduate School of Business, 1985
BS, Marshall University, 1967

Average Size of Investment	$1M
Size of Fund	$160M
Investment Criteria	Industry preferences: high technology and consumer products/specialty retailing
Portfolio Companies	Undisclosed

UTECH VENTURE CAPITAL CORPORATION—UVCC FUND I
c/o Arete Ventures, Inc.
4330 East West Highway, Suite 916
Bethesda, MD 20814
(301) 951-4499

990 Hammond Drive, Suite 620
Atlanta, GA 30328
(404) 396-2480

711 W. 40th Street, Suite 420
Baltimore, MD 21211
(301) 243-5551

515 Madison Avenue
New York, NY 10022
(212) 826-9824

Robert W. Shaw
President, Bethesda, MD

Prior Positions

Senior Vice President, Booz, Allen & Hamilton, 1972–82
Research Scientist, Bell Laboratories, 1969–72

Education

Ph.D., Stanford University, 1968
MPA, American University, 1981
MSEE and BEP, Cornell University, 1964

Philip B. Smith
Consultant and Ltd. Partner, New York, NY

Prior Positions

Partner, Lawrence Venture Associates, 1985–present
Executive Vice President, Irving Trust, 1977–84
Vice President, Citibank, 1963–77
President, Citibank Venture Capital Ltd., 1968–72

Education

MBA, Harvard Business School, 1963
BSE, Princeton University, 1958

Michael T. Eckhart
Consultant and Ltd. Partner, Bethesda, MD

Directorships

Wormser Engineering, Inc.
RCG Technologies, Ltd.
Touch Technologies, Inc.

Prior Positions

Director, Arete Ventures, Inc.
Vice President, corporate marketing, Combustion Engineering
Manager, strategic planning, General Electric
Principal, Booz, Allen & Hamilton

Education

MBA, Harvard Business School, 1975
BSEE, Purdue University, 1973

George W. Levert
Secretary/Treasurer, Ltd., Partner, Altanta, GA

Directorships
Graphics Research Corporation

Prior Positions
Manager, planning, Oglethorpe Power Corp.
Consultant, Arthur Andersen & Co.

Education
MSIM, Georgia Tech, 1974
BSEE, Louisiana Tech, 1969

John C. Weiss, III
Limited Partner, Baltimore, MD

Directorships
Advanced Manufacturing Systems, Inc.
Chesapeake Biological Laboratories, Inc.
MIT Enterprise Forum of Washington-Baltimore, Inc.

Prior Positions
Senior Vice President, Baltimore Economic Development Corp.
Associate Vice President, Union Trust Company of MD

Education
MBA, Loyola College, 1979
BS, Towson State University, 1972

Average Size of Investment	$500K
Size of Fund	$20M
Investment Criteria	Portfolio companies must provide products or services that relate directly or the needs of electric and gas utilities
Portfolio Companies	Summagraphics Corp., Computer peripherals, Fairfield, CT; Kurzweil Applied Intelligence, Artificial intelligence, Waltham, MA; Applied Spectruc Technologies, Data communications, Minneapolis, MN; Graphics Research Corp., Computer mapping, Atlanta, GA; Artificial Intelligence Corp., Artificial intelligence, Waltham, MA; Advanced Manufacturing Systems, Factory automation, Sparks, MD; Skantek Corp., Scanners, Warren, NJ; Computer Technology Corp., Factory automation, Cincinnati, OH; Metricom, Inc., Utility metering, Cupertino, CA; Gold Hill Computers, Artificial intelligence software, Cambridge, MA

UTICA INVESTMENT CORP.
1924 South Utica
Tulsa, OK 74104
(918) 749-9976

David D. Nunneley

Average Size of Investment	$100K
Size of Fund	$500K
Investment Criteria	Manufacturing, oil and gas, real estate areas considered; will act as lead investor
Portfolio Companies	Undisclosed

VALLEY CAPITAL CORP.
Krystal Building
100 West M.L. King Boulevard
Suite 806
Chattanooga, TN 37402
(615) 265-1557

Lamar J. Partridge
President

Directorships
Alton Park Community Health Agency, Health care entity
Contin-U-Care Home Health, Inc., Health care entity
Southern Star Systems, Inc., Communications entity

Prior Positions
Manager, Tennessee Valley Authority, 1979–84
Audit Manager, Arthur Andersen & Co., 1972–78

Education
BS, Business Administration, University of Tennessee at Knoxville, 1972

Faye Munger

Average Size of Investment	$150K
Size of Fund	$1M

DIRECTORY AND BIOGRAPHIES

Investment Criteria   MESBIC—must qualify under SBA guidelines as a socially and/or economically disadvantaged entity; entity must be located in Southeastern U.S.
Portfolio Companies   Undisclosed

VANGUARD CAPITAL CORP.
5 Revere Drive
Suite 200
Northfield, IL 60062
(312) 272-3636

Kenneth M. Arenberg
President

Directorships

BYAD, Inc., Microcomputer software
Hospital Financial Corp., Medical equipment leasing

Education

MBA, Harvard Business School, 1954
BS, Brown University, 1952

Average Size of Investment	$100K
Size of Fund	Undisclosed
Investment Criteria	Seed capital; spin-off; marketing oriented
Portfolio Companies	Undisclosed

VANGUARD INVESTMENT CO.
308-A South Elm Street
Greensboro, NC 27401
(919) 378-0100

Lee D. Andrews
Chairman and President
(919) 378-0533

Directorships

A&M Fast Foods, Franchise food operation
JABOT, Inc., Design and marketing company
Guilford Tech Community College, Education
Guilford County Mental Health, Community service

Prior Positions

Vice President, Washington Business Development Corp.
Vice President, PIC, Inc.

Education

LLM, George Washington University, 1972
JD, Howard University, 1970

David H. Wagner

Average Size of Investment	$100K
Size of Fund	Undisclosed
Investment Criteria	Undisclosed
Portfolio Companies	Undisclosed

VEGA CAPITAL CORP.
720 White Plains Road
Suite 360
Scarsdale, NY 10583
(914) 472-8550

Victor Harz
Ronald A. Linden

Average Size of Investment	$200K–$400K
Size of Fund	$10M
Investment Criteria	Undisclosed
Portfolio Companies	Undisclosed

VENCAP EQUITIES ALBERTA LTD.
#816 Imperial Oil Building
10025 Jasper Avenue
Edmonton, Alberta T5J 1S6
Canada
(403) 420-1171

Derek Mather

Average Size of Investment	$2M
Size of Fund	$250M
Investment Criteria	Projects of interest to Alberta, excluding oil and gas exploration, real estate, and banking and finance
Portfolio Companies	Corod Manufacturing Ltd., Nisku, Alberta, Oil drilling equipment; D & S Petroleum Consulting Group Ltd., Calgary, Alberta, Technology including software, for petroleum industry; GEOTECHnical Resources Ltd., Calgary, Alberta, Lab and testing services for petroleum exploration and development; Hanson Materials Engineering, Edmonton, Alberta, Metallurgical engineering service; Idacom Electronics Ltd., Edmonton, Alberta, Data communications test equipment; Niart International Inc., St. Albert, Alberta, Traffic control products; P.T.I. Holdings (1983) Ltd., Edmonton, Alberta, Camp services including catering, camp leasing and oil field and general heavy transport; Synerlogic, Inc., Calgary, Alberta, Computer software consulting company

VENCON MANAGEMENT INC.
301 West 53rd Street
New York, NY 10019
(212) 581-8787

Irvin Barash
President

Directorship

Recticon Corp.

Prior Positions

Assistant to the President, Belco Petroleum Corp., 1972
Director of Corporate Planning, BASF Corp., 1969–72
Acquisitions Analyst, W. R. Grace Co., 1968
Planning Analyst, EBS Industries, 1964–68
Chemical Engineer, Catalytic, Inc., 1961–62

Education

MBA, Columbia University, 1964
BS, Chemical Engineering, Drexel University, 1961

H. Herman Zand

Average Size of Investment	$2M
Size of Fund	Undisclosed
Investment Criteria	Semiconductors, high technology, biotechnology, chemicals and allied products, plastics, electronics
Portfolio Companies	Undisclosed

VENGROWTH CAPITAL FUNDS
111 Richmond Street West
Suite 805
Toronto, Ontario M5H 2G4
Canada
(416) 947-9123

R. Earl Storie
Managing Partner

Directorships

Pension Finance Associates Ltd.
Pacific Northwest Equipment Leasing Corp.
Protein Foods Group, Inc.
Targa Electronics Systems, Inc.
Tuckahoe Leasing Corp.

Prior Position

President, TD Capital Group Ltd., 1977–82

Education

CA, British Columbia Institute of Chartered Accountants, 1969
B. Comm., University of British Columbia, 1964

Harry G. Mortimore
Managing Partner

Directorships

Innovative Concepts, Inc.
Prime Energy Ltd.
Physicians Radio Network, Inc.
Read-Rite Corp.
Time Air (1982) Ltd.
Teraca Communications Corp.

DIRECTORY AND BIOGRAPHIES 431

Prior Position

Vice President, TD Capital Group Ltd., 1979–82

Education

MBA, Queen's University, 1973

Andrew L. Gutman
Partner

Directorships

Capsule Technology, Pharmaceutical packaging
Daltons, Ltd., Food processor
Data Acquisition Systems, Process control
Resource Dynamics, Facilities management software
Thalamus Electronics, ATE
The Office Manager, Vertical market software

Prior Position

Associate, Dean Witter, 1983

Education

MBA, Massachusetts Institute of Technology, 1982
BA, University of Michigan, 1974

Mark H. Leonard
Investment Manager

Directorship

Konar Ltd., Printed circuit boards

Prior Position

International Banking, First National Bank of Chicago

Education

MBA, University of Western Ontario, 1982
BSc, Physics, University of Guelph, 1980

Average Size of Investment	$650K
Size of Fund	$34M
Investment Criteria	Canada and U.S.: start-up; turnaround; expansion; leveraged buy-outs
Portfolio Companies	Undisclosed

VENROCK ASSOCIATES
30 Rockefeller Plaza
Room 5508
New York, NY 10112
(212) 247-3700

Two Palo Alto Square
Suite 528
Palo Alto, CA 94306
(415) 493-5577

Peter O. Crisp
General Partner, NY

Directorships

Apple Computer, Inc., Personal computers
Evans and Sutherland Computer Corp., Computer graphics systems
Galileo Electro-Optics, Inc., Electro-optical and fiber-optic components
Thermedics, Inc., Biocompatible plastics-cardiac assist systems
Thermo Electron Corp., Energy conservation systems
Voluntary Health Enterprises, Health-care-related investments

Education

MBA, Harvard Business School, 1960
BA, American Studies, Yale University, 1955

Ted H. McCourtney
General Partner, NY

Directorships

AVX Corp., Passive electronic components, esp. capacitors
American Robot Corp., Robotic systems
Apollo Computer, Inc., Networked minicomputers
Cellular Communications, Inc., Cellular communications
Coherent, Inc., Lasers and optics
National Venture Capital Assoc.

Prior Position

Associate, McKinsey & Co.

Education

MBA, Harvard Business School, 1966
BS, Mechanical Engineering, Notre Dame, 1960

Anthony B. Evnin
General Partner, NY

Directorships

Centocor, Inc., Immunodiagnostics based on monoclonal antibodies
Genetics Institute, Inc., rDNA technology
The Liposome Co., Drug delivery systems
NPI, Plant technology

Prior Positions

Manager, Market Development, Story Chemicals
Scientific Group Leader, Union Carbide

Education

PhD, Organic Chemistry, Massachusetts Institute of Technology, 1966
BA, Chemistry, Princeton University, 1962

David R. Hathaway
General Partner, NY

Directorships

Mentor Graphics, CAE workstations
Mosaic Systems, Inc., Wafer scale integration
Palladian Software, Inc., Expert systems
Raster Technologies, Inc., Display technologies
Sequent Computer Systems, High-performance minicomputers

Prior Positions

Vice President, DLJ Company
Vice President, Corporate Development, Automatic Data Processing

Education

BA, American Studies, Yale University, 1966

Henry S. Smith
General Partner, NY

Directorships

Alliant Software Systems Corp., High-performance minicomputers
Caere Corp., Wand readers
Enterprise Systems, Hospital management software
Raster Technologies, Inc., Display processors

Prior Positions

Director, Microcomputer Systems Group, Intel Corp.
Product Marketing Manager, Fairchild Industries
Product Marketing Specialist, IBM

Education

MS, Electrical Engineering, Syracuse University, 1967
BS, Electrical Engineering, Rensselaer Polytechnic Institute, 1964

Anthony Sun
General Partner, CA

Directorships

Charlton Associates, Rigid media for disk drives
Saxpy Computer Corp., Optical array processors
Inference Corp., Knowledge-based systems
Komag, Inc., Sputtered media for disk drives
Telelogic, Inc., Telephone switching devices

Prior Positions

Design Engineer, Hewlett-Packard
Product Line Manager, TRW, Inc.
Engineering Manager, Caere Corp.

Education

MBA, Harvard Business School, 1979
EE, Electrical Engineering, Massachusetts Institute of Technology, 1975
BS, MS, Electrical Engineering, Massachusetts Institute of Technology, 1974

Average Size of Investment	$300K–$1.5M
Size of Fund	Undisclosed
Investment Criteria	Advanced technology companies in their early stage of development
Portfolio Companies	Undisclosed

VENTANA GROWTH FUND
1660 Hotel Circle North
Suite 502
San Diego, CA 92108
(619) 291-2757

F. Duwaine Townsen
Thomas O. Gephart
Kenneth B. Tingey

Average Size of Investment	$400K
Size of Fund	$6M
Investment Criteria	Undisclosed
Portfolio Companies	Brooktree Corp., San Diego, CA; Intelligent Images, San Diego, CA; Karyon Scientific, San Diego, CA; Master Care Corp., Dallas, TX; R2 Corporation, Chicago, IL

VENTECH PARTNERS, L.P.
30 Tower Lane
Avon Park South
Avon, CT 06001
(203) 677-0183

Samuel F. McKay
President and Chief Executive Officer

Directorships

Automatix, Inc., Robotics
Contrex, Inc., Automatic VLSI inspection equipment
Spartacus, Inc., Data networking products
HHB, Inc., Design simulation systems
Tower Capital Management, Inc., Specialized money management

Prior Position

Director of Venture Capital and Portfolio Manager, Connecticut General Insurance Co., 1973–81

Education

MBA, Finance, University of New Hampshire, 1972
BA, Physics, University of New Hampshire, 1966

Richard L. King

Average Size of Investment	$1M
Size of Fund	$29M
Investment Critiera	Technology oriented
Portfolio Companies	Contrex, Billerica, MA, Automatic LSI inspection; Cygnet, California, Voice/data terminals; Dallas Semiconductor, Texas, Late definition LSI; Excelan, California, Data networking products; HHB, New Jersey, Design simulation software; Lin Data, California, Sputtered magnetic media

VENTURE ASSOCIATES LTD.
1337 18th Street
Suite 300
Denver, CO 80202
(303) 297-8670

James B. Arkebauer
President

Prior Positions

Registered Representative, J. Daniel Bell & Co., 1976–80
President, Image, Inc., 1972–76

Education

University of Nebraska, 1962

Peter A. Thompson
Vice President

Directorship

Creative Publishing, Inc., Writing and publishing

Prior Positions

Senior Analyst, Solar energy research institute
Geologist Hixon Development Co.

Education

MBA, Finance, University of Colorado, 1984
BA, Geology, Trinity University, 1972

Stephen D. Replin
Vice President

Directorships

Matthews Inc.
Autographs International Ltd.
Nicholds Productions Inc.

Prior Positions

President, Apache Resources, 1980–85
Treasurer, Commonwealth Capital Ltd., 1982–85
President, Rainbow Equities Ltd., 1983–85

Education

JD, Law, University of Colorado, 1976
MS, Tax, University of New York, 1977
MBA, New York University, 1971
BS, Accounting, University of Colorado, 1969

Average Size of Investment	$250K
Size of Fund	Undisclosed
Investment Criteria	Immediate public offering
Portfolio Companies	Undisclosed

VENTURE CAPITAL FUND, INC.
777 East Wisconsin Avenue
Suite 3060
Milwaukee, WI 53202
(414) 291-9000

Sheldon B. Lubar
President

Directorship

National Venture Capital Association

Prior Positions

Assistant Secretary, Housing Production and Mortgage Credit; Commissioner of Federal Housing Administration, Dept. of Housing and Urban Development, 1973–74
Chairman, Chief Executive Officer, Mortgage Associates, Inc., 1966–73

Education

BA, University of Wisconsin, 1951

David J. Lubar

Prior Position

Assistant Vice President, Manufacturing and Electronics Lending Division, Northwestern National Bank of Minneapolis, 1977–82

Education

MBA, University of Minnesota, 1982
BA, Bowdoin College, 1977

William T. Donovan

Directorships

A. L. Gebhardt Co., Inc.
Process Equipment Corp.

Prior Position

Manufacturers Hanover Trust, 1976–80

Education

MBA, University of Notre Dame, 1976
BS, University of Notre Dame, 1974

James S. Vaughan
James C. Rowe

Directorships

Chicago Gear Works, Inc.
Evans Food Products Co.

Prior Position

Tax Department, Arthur Andersen & Co., 1970–72

Education

CPA
BBA, University of Wisconsin

Average Size of Investment	$250K–$750K
Size of Fund	Undisclosed
Investment Criteria	Technology-based companies preferred; geographic proximity important; will act as lead investor
Portfolio Companies	Undisclosed

THE VENTURE CAPITAL FUND OF NEW ENGLAND
100 Franklin Street
Boston, MA 02110
(617) 451-2575

Richard A. Farrell
General Partner
(617) 451-2577

Directorships

Allied Devices Corp., Precision electromechanical devices
Auburn Intl, Flow measurement instrumentation
Cadec Systems, Data acquisition and communications devices
Cape-Islands Broadcasting, WCIB-FM, Falmouth, MA
Dorman Bogdonoff Corp., Membrane keyboards
Dowden Communications, CATV MSO
Eljenn Intl. Corp., Hair-care products
Silicon Technology, Diamond blade saws for cutting silicon ingots
Termiflex Corp., Hand-held computer terminals

Prior Positions

President, First Capital Corp. of Boston, 1961–80
President, First Venture Capital Corp. of Boston (both subsidiaries of Bank of Boston)

Education

MBA, Boston University, 1962
BSBA, Boston University, 1954

Harry J. Healer, Jr.
General Partner
(617) 451-2576

Directorships

Concord Computing Corp., Electronic financial services
Cytogen Corp., Antibody modification technology
Data Language Corp., 4th Generation, supermicro, data base management systems
Firing Circuits, Inc., Microprocessor-based industrial battery chargers
Indata Corp., Industrial parts counting systems
Lion Precision Corp., Peripheral equipment for programmable controllers
Oil Recovery Systems, Inc., Products and services for pollution control and resource recovery
Perception Technology Corp., Computer voice response systems
The Stypher Corp., Microprocessor-based equipment for post-production editing of videotape

Prior Positions

Vice President, First Capital Corporation of Boston
Vice President, First Venture Capital Corp. of Boston (both subsidiaries of Bank of Boston)

Education

BSBA, Babson College, 1964

E. Janice Leeming
Associate
(617) 451-2578

Directorships

Altertext, Inc., Incompatible text conversion systems
Brattle Research Corp., Artificial intelligence
Xydex Corp., Sample preparation products used in analytical testing

Prior Positions

Research Analyst, Venture economics
Staff Accountant, Narragansett Capital Corp., 1964–72

Education

MBA, Babson College, 1980
BS, University of Rhode Island, 1978

Kevin J. Dougherty
Associate

Prior Positions

Vice President, Investors in Industry Capital Corp.
Vice President, Massachusetts Capital Resource Company
Vice President, First National Bank of Boston
Assistant Vice President, Bankers Trust Company

Education

BA, Williams College, 1968
Columbia University

Average Size of Investment	$450K
Size of Fund	$50M
Investment Criteria	Emphasis on early-stage high-technology investments in New England
Portfolio Companies	35 companies

VENTURE CAPITALISTS, INC.
1801 East 5th Street, Suite 210
Charlotte, NC 28204
(704) 333-5360

Fred W. Byrum
President

Directorships
Rainbow Media Corp.

Average Size of Investment	$100K
Size of Fund	$1M
Investment Criteria	Any business with large growth capacity
Portfolio Companies	Cinematronics, Inc., Electronic communication for shippers, Atlanta, GA; Zarkon Corp., Gold mining in Costa Rica, Atlanta, GA; Rainbow Media Corp., Cable TV programming, Charlotte, NC; Transtrak, Inc., New engines/generators, Charlotte, NC; Adcom Systems, Inc., Computer electronic services, Charlotte, NC

VENTURE FIRST, LTD.
2422 Reynolda Road
Winston-Salem, NC 27106
(919) 722-9600

M. Campbell Cawood
General Partner

Directorships
LanTel Corp.
Liposome Sciences, Inc.

Prior Positions
Co-founder, Salem Investment Counselors, 1978–84
Management division, Wachovia Bank-Capital, 1976–78
Securities, Analyst, Girard Band, 1971–76

Education
BS, University of Virginia, 1970

J. Douglas Mullins
General Partner

Directorships
Linus Technologies
Health Trends
Tangram

Prior Positions
Vice President, Mead Corp., 1980–84
Executive Vice President, Ronson Corp., 1974–80

Education
MBA, Harvard Business School
MA, Economics, Virginia Polytechnic Institute

B. Otto Wheeley
General Partner

Directorships
American Matrix
Liposome Sciences
Phyton Technologies

Prior Position
Chemical Engineer, President/Chief Executive Officer, The Koppers Co., Inc./Kopvenco, 1943–84

Education
BS, Chemical Engineering, University of Tennessee

Average Size of Investment	Undisclosed
Size of Investment	$13.5M
Investment Criteria	Entrepreneurism, leadership, superior and experienced management teams; distinctive, unique, or proprietary products; large growing markets; high growth potential in sales; long-term and sustainable profitability; seed and early stages of business development; compatible business philosophies including exit vehicle
Portfolio Companies	American Matrix, Knoxville, TN, Advanced ceramic materials; Codeworks, Washington, DC, Building code materials; LanTel Corp., Atlanta, GA, Broadban voice and data equipment; Liposome Sciences, Inc., Knoxville, TN, Diagnostics; Health Trends, Charlotte, NC, Physical, occupational and speech therapy clinics; Image Systems, Inc., Atlanta, GA, Thermography imagery; Phyton Technologies, Inc., Knoxville, TN, Plant tissue culture; Tangram, Inc., Cary, NC, Mainframe computer software; Linus Technologies, Inc., Reston, VA, Handwritten character recognition

VENTURE FOUNDERS CORP.
One Cranberry Hill
Lexington, MA 02173
(617) 863-0900

Alexander L. M. Dingee, Jr.
President, General Partner, Director

Directorships

BeneVenture Founders Risk Capital Fund, N.V. (Belgium)
Homeowners Equity
Venture Founders Florida Corp.
Venture Founders Investments Ltd. (U.K.)
Venture Founders of Canada, Ltd.
Venture Management Corp.
Venture Management, Ltd. Partnership

Prior Positions

Corporate Planner, EG & G, Inc.
Founder/President, Geodyne Corp., 1962–68
Founder/President, Massey Dickinson Co., Inc., 1956–62

Education

BS, Management, Massachusetts Institute of Technology, 1952

Edward H. Getchell
Vice President, General Partner

Directorships

ANA Tech Corp.
Metallurgical Instruments Group
Transaction Engineering L.P.
Inomed, Inc.
Venture Founders of Canada
Venture Management Corp.

Prior Positions

Manager, Electrical Design Dept., Signatron, Inc., 1970–74
Program Manager, Epsco, Inc., 1966–69

Education

MBA, Sloan Fellows' Program, Massachusetts Institute of Technology, 1975
MS, Electrical Engineering, Massachusetts Institute of Technology, 1961
BS, Electrical Engineering, Massachusetts Institute of Technology, 1959

Joseph M. Frye, Jr.
Director of European Operations and General Partner of Venture Capital Fund

Directorships

American Channels, Inc.
BeneVenture Founders Management N.V. (Belgium)
Softbridge Microsystems Corp.
V.F. (Europe) Ltd.
Venture Founders Investments Limited
Venture Founders Limited (U.K.)

Prior Position

Executive Vice President, Kentucky Highlands Investment Corp., 1974–80

Education

Master of Planning, University of Virginia, 1974
MA, Philosophy, University of Virginia, 1968
BA, Philosophy, University of Virginia, 1967

John O. Peterson
Vice President

Prior Position

Associate, T.A. Associates

Education

MBA, Harvard Business School, 1965
ScB, Brown University, 1951

Gregory A. Hulecki
Associate

Directorship

Transaction Engineering Corp.

Prior Positions

Investment Analyst, Jenney Oil Company, 1983–84
Quality Engineer II, Digital Equipment Corp., 1981–82

Education

MBA, Harvard Graduate School of Business
BEE, General Motors Institute

Leonard E. Smollen
Executive Vice President and General Partner

Directorships

Creare, Inc.
Disc Technology Corp.
Venture Founders Florida Corp.
Venture Founders Investment Limited (U.K.)
Venture Management Corp.
Visage, Inc.

Prior Positions

Program Manager, Chief Mechanical Engineering, EG&G, Inc., 1963–70
Director Customer Products and Program Management, EG&G, Inc., 1962–70
Engineering Manager, Allied Research Association, 1957–62

Education

Mechanical Engineering, Massachusetts Institute of Technology, 1962
MS, Civil Engineering, Columbia University, 1952
BS, Civil Engineering, Carnegie Institute of Technology, 1951

Ross M. Yeiter
Treasurer and General Partner

Directorships

AXIS Computer Systems Corp., Manufacturing software
Adelie Corp., Mainframe marketing software
Visage, Inc., Interactive video systems

Prior Positions

Vice President, Director of Information, Systems Group, ERT, Inc., Subsidiary of Comsat Corp., 1976–83
Vice President, Director, E G & G International, Inc.
President, BBN Geosciences Corp., 1970–76

Education

BS, EE, Bucknell University, 1946

David T. Riddiford
General Partner

Directorships

Allied Devices, Precision electromechanical components
CSA Financial, Computer leasing
Clinical Data, Medical services
Certiflex, Microcomputer software
Unity Broadcasting, Radio, cable, cellular
Viceo, Power supplies

Prior Positions

Director, Corporate Development, Kendall Co.
Consultant, McKinsey & Co.

Education

LLB, William Mitchell, 1962
BA, Yale University, 1957

Michael Zeldin
Investment Manager

Prior Positions

Program Manager, Higher Order Software, 1979–81
Research Fellow in Neurobiology, Harvard University, 1974–82

Education

PhD, Temple University, 1964
MA, Temple University, 1963
BS, Franklin and Marshall College, 1959

Average Size of Investment	$500K
Size of Fund	$70M
Investment Criteria	High technology; seed, start-up, or first stage; entrepreneur who has significant working experience in one field; the entrepreneur team should have previous profit and loss management experience; product of service must be sold on a national basis
Portfolio Companies	Adelie Corp., Newtonville, MA, Software systems for integrated sales and marketing management; Adra Systems, Inc., Lowell, MA, 2-D workstation for the mechanical CAD/CAM market; American Channels, Lexington, MA, Software for scientific engineering and software development markets; ANA Tech Corp., Littleton, CO, Systems which automatically convert paper-based graphics to CAD/CAM format; Axis Computer Systems L.P., Sudbury, MA,

Software products for manufacturing resource planning system; Ceramic Process Systems, Cambridge, MA, New integrated processing system for producing high-technology ceramics; Disc Technology Corp., Billerica, MA, 5¼" Winchester rigid magnetic disks for computer data storage; ImagiTex, Inc., Nashua, NH, Digital image document preparation system; Metallurgical Instruments Group, Lexington, MA, Metallurgical instrumentation; Navigation Sciences, Inc., Bethesda, MD, Display systems for marine navigation; Softbridge Microsystems, Cambridge, MA, Integrated microcomputer software tools for personal financial planners; Telesis Controls Corp., Chillicothe, OH, Microprocessor-based automation equipment applied to measuring, marking, identifying, and tracking products; Transaction Engineering L.P., Plymouth, MA, Microprocessor systems for physicians processing insurance claims; VICOR Corp., Westford, MA, Patented line of power supply devices; Visage, Inc., Natick, MA, Interactive video disk system for the industrial training market

VENTURE FRONTIERS CORP.
402 Barker Circle
Suite 5
West Chester, PA 19380
(215) 431-0660

Lawrence Murray
Chairman of the Board

Directorships

Financial Management Professional Corp., Tax planning centers
Norman Rockwell's America Museum, Theme attraction
Promotion Management Corp., Marketing

Prior Positions

Chairman of the Board, Creative Management Corp., 1982–84
Chairman of the Board, Century Management Corp., 1976–82

Education

MBA, University of Oklahoma Graduate School of Business, 1966
BA, Cornell University, 1961

Average Size of Investment	$200K
Size of Fund	$10M
Investment Criteria	Undisclosed
Portfolio Companies	Financial Management P.C., Pennsylvania; Princeton Geophysics, Inc., New Jersey; WorldWater, New Jersey

VENTURE INVESTORS OF WISCONSIN, INC.
102 State Street
Madison, WI 53703
(608) 256-8185

Roth S. Schleck
Chairman

Directorships

Video Monitors, Inc.
First Wisconsin National Bank
American Family Insurance Group
Madison Club
Madison Area Governmental Education Committee

Prior Positions

Chairman of the Board and Chief Executive Officer, First Wisconsin National Bank of Madison
President, First Wisconsin National Bank of Eau Claire
Chief Administration Assistant, State Department

Education

Central State School of Banking
BA, Accounting, University of Wisconsin at Madison, 1938

Roger H. Ganser
President & Chief Executive Officer

Directorship

Venture Investors of WI, Inc.

Prior Positions

President, Madison Development Corp.
Vice President, Sail Co. Ltd.
Director, Department of Development, Winona, MN

Education

MPA, University of New York, 1974
BED, UW Whitewater, 1967

John Neis

Average Size of Investment	$150K
Size of Fund	$3.0M
Investment Criteria	Businesses that will be profitable, significant growth potential, growing faster than the economy, basic/value added
Portfolio Companies	Office Solutions, Madison, WI, Computer software; Promega Corp., Madison, WI, Biological research products; Latitude Corp., Madison, WI, Marine electronic weather fax; Impact Systems, Milwaukee, WI, Diagnostic interface products

VENTURE MANAGEMENT ASSOCIATES INC.
SOUTHEAST VENTURE CAPITAL LTD. FUNDS
One Southeast Financial Center
Miami, FL 33131
(305) 375-6470

C. L. Hofmann
John H. Lamothe
James R. Fitzsimons, Jr.

Average Size of Investments	$600K
Size of Funds	$23M
Investment Criteria	Diverse areas of interest; start-ups; geographic proximity important; leveraged buy-outs important
Portfolio Companies	Undisclosed

VENTURE OPPORTUNITIES CORP.
444 Brickle Avenue
Suite 930
Miami, FL 33131
(305) 358-0359

A. Fred March

Average Size of Investment	$100K
Size of Fund	$3M
Investment Criteria	Technology-based, manufacturing, and other diverse areas of interest; will act as lead investor; start-ups are considered; geographic proximity important
Portfolio Companies	Undisclosed

VENTURES WEST TECHNOLOGIES, INC.
400-321 Water Street
Vancouver, B.C. V6B 1B8
Canada
(604) 688-9495

Michael J. Brown
President

Directorships

Human Computing Resources Corp., UNIX software systems
MacDonald Dettwiler & Assoc. Ltd., Remote sensing products, aviation systems and precision image recorders
Ventures West Management Inc., Management company
Pacific Microcircuits Ltd., Custom integrated circuits
Ventures West Minerals Ltd., Mineral exploration

Prior Positions

Founder and Executive Vice President, Ventures West Capital Ltd.
Founder and Partner, Brown, Farris & Jefferson Ltd.
Director, Odlum Brown & T. B. Read Ltd.

Education

BA (Honors in Politics, Philosophy and Economics), University of Oxford, 1960–62
BA (First Class Honors in Economics), University of British Columbia, 1956–60

J. Haig deB. Farris
Executive Vice President

Directorships

MacDonald Dettwiler & Assoc. Ltd., Remote sensing products, aviation systems and precision image recorders
New Media Technologies Ltd., Software-supported terminals using Videotex
Consumers Software Inc., Microcomputer software development
Dilor Industries Ltd., Computer-controlled lighting consoles

Prior Positions

Founder and President, Ventures West Capital Ltd.
Partner, Brown, Farris & Jefferson Ltd.

Education

LLB, University of Pennsylvania Law School, 1960–63
BA (honors), Economics and English, University of British Columbia, 1956–60

James M. Fletcher
Vice President

Directorships

Meiogenics, Inc., DNA probe technology
Myrias Research Corp., Computer design and development
Pacific Microcircuits Ltd., Custom integrated circuits
The Office Manager, Inc., Manufacturer and distributor of vertical business software
Ventures West Technologies Ltd., Investments
Ventures West Management Inc., Management company

Prior Positions

Director, Corporate Finance and Treasurer, MacMillan Bloedel Ltd.
Senior Associate, Morgan Stanley & Co., Inc.

Education

MBA, Harvard Business School, 1974–76
BSc, Engineering Physics, Queens University, 1966–72

Victor J. E. Jones
Vice President

Directorships

Ventures West Technologies Ltd., Investments
Ventures West Minerals Ltd., Mineral exploration
Westley Mines Ltd., Mineral exploration
Ventures West Management Inc., Management company
International Mobile Data Inc., Computer manufacturer

Prior Positions

President, Westley Mines Ltd.
President, MDI International Mobile Data Inc.
Manager, Coastal Shipping

Education

MBA, McGill University, 1975
BSc, McGill University, 1971

William J. Boden
Vice President, Finance and Administration

Directorships

Enertec Geophysical Services Ltd.
Dilor Industries Ltd.
Ventures West Management, Inc.
Westley Mines Ltd.

Prior Positions

Audit Manager, Coopers & Lybrand
Treasurer, Bethelehem Copper Corp.
Secretary/Treasurer, Whitehorse Copper Mines Ltd.

Education

CA, University of British Columbia & ICABC, 1968

Sam Znaimer
Senior Investment Officer

Directorships

Wavefront Technologies, Inc., Computer graphics animation
Starnav Corporation, Marine navigation technology

Prior Positions

Staff Engineer, International Coal Refining Co.

Education

MSc, MIT, 1981
AB, Harvard University, 1978

Average Size of Investment	$300K
Size of Fund	$22M
Investment Criteria	High technology
Portfolio Companies	Human Computing Resources Corp., Toronto, Ontario, UNIX software systems; MacDonald Dettwiler & Assoc. Ltd., Richmond, B.C., Remote sensing products, aviation systems and precision image recorders; MDI Mobile Data International Inc., Richmond, B.C., Data communications products (i.e., mobile data terminals); Meiogenics, Inc., Ottawa, Ontario, DNA probe technology; Myrias Research Corp., Edmonton, Alta., Development of computer for scientific and engineering applications; New Media Technologies Ltd., Burnaby, B.C., Software supported terminals using VIDEOTEX

VENTURETECH II, L.P.
Box 210
Gladstone, NJ 07934
(201) 234-2373

30092 Ivy Glen Road
Suite 230
Laguna Niguel, CA 92677
(714) 495-7151

Max Charlat
General Partner, NJ

Duff Meyercord
General Partner, NJ

Dave Costine
General Partner, CA

Average Size of Investment	$500K
Size of Fund	$10.6M
Investment Criteria	Innovative high technology, early stage
Portfolio Companies	Undisclosed

VERDE CAPITAL CORP.
255 Alhambra Circle
Suite 720
Coral Gables, FL 33134
(305) 444-8938

Jose Dearing
President and Chief Executive Officer

Directorships

Atlantis Financial Corp.
Samary Labes Shopping Centers

Prior Positions

Director, National Economic Development Agency, 1977–78
Executive Director, Planning, Southeast Banking Corp., 1973–77

Education

PhD, University of Florida, 1973
MS, University of Florida, 1971

Average Size of Investment	$300K
Size of Fund	$9.8M
Investment Criteria	Diversified preferences; geographic proximity important
Portfolio Companies	Undisclosed

VERMONT INVESTMENT CAPITAL, INC.
Route 14, Box 590
South Windsor Street
South Royalton, VT 05068
(802) 763-7916

Harold Jacobs

Average Size of Investment	$100K
Size of Fund	Undisclosed
Investment Criteria	Diversified areas of interest including manufacturing; start-ups considered; will act as lead investor; geographic proximity important
Portfolio Companies	Undisclosed

VERONIS, SUHLER & ASSOCIATES
515 Madison Avenue
New York, NY 10022
(212) 935-4990

John S. Suhler
President, Co-chief executive officer

Prior Positions

President, CBS Publishing Group, 1979–81
President, CBS Publications, 1974–79
Publisher, Corporate Vice President, Psychology Today Magazine, 1969–74
Publishing consultant, Benson Stagg & Associates, 1966–68

Education

BS, University of Kansas
William Allen White School of Journalism

DIRECTORY AND BIOGRAPHIES 443

John J. Veronis
Chairman, Co-chief executive officer

Prior Positions

President, JJV Publishing Co., Inc., 1979–81
President, Book Digest Magazine, 1973–79
President, Saturday Review Magazine, 1971–73
President, CRM, Inc., 1967–71
General Corporate Executive, Interpublic Group of Companies, 1965–67
President, Curtis Magazine Division, Curtis Publishing Co., 1958–64

Education

BA, Lafayette College
Graduate School of Business, NYU

Average Size of Investment	Undisclosed
Size of Fund	Undisclosed
Investment Criteria	Media, entertainment, and communications companies; business information services, databases, personal computer software, advertising
Portfolio Companies	Undisclosed

VIMAC CORP.
12 Arlington Street
Boston, MA 02116
(617) 267-2785

Max J. Steinmann
President

Directorship

ISC Systems Corp., Banking terminals

Prior Positions

Vice President International, AB Dick Co., 1980–81
Executive Consultant, Control Data Corp., 1978–79
General Manager, Sperry Corp., Zurich, 1961–77

Education

Business Diploma, Cantanal School Soleure, Switzerland, 1945

Average Size of Investment	$300K
Size of Fund	$1.5M per year
Investment Criteria	Start-up companies; computer vertical solutions favored
Portfolio Companies	Undisclosed

VISTA CAPITAL CORPORATION
701 B Street
Suite 760
San Diego, CA 92101
(619) 236-1900

Fred J. Howden, Jr.
Chairman

Prior Positions

Founder, President, and Chief Executive Officer, Commercial Computers, Inc.
Management, IBM Corporation

Education

BS, Thermodynamics, Massachusetts Institute of Technology

William W. Otterson
Vice President

Prior Positions

Chairman and Chief Executive Officer, Cipher Data Products, Inc., and Lexorcorp

Education

MBA, Stanford Business School
BA, Stanford University

Average Size of Investment	$100K
Size of Fund	Undisclosed
Investment Criteria	Undisclosed
Portfolio Companies	Undisclosed

VISTA TECHNOLOGY VENTURES, INC.
2410 Long Ridge Road
Stamford, CT 06903
(203) 322-0091

Irwin Rudich
President

Directorship

Seniority Magazine, Specialty publishing

Prior Positions

Investment Banking Associate, Kuhn Loeb & Co.
General Manager and Director, Corporate Planning, North American Phillips Co.

Education

MBA equivalent, New York University & Investment Institute, 1969
MS, Physics, Brooklyn Polytechnic, 1950
BEE, City College of New York, 1945

Rose Rudich

Average Size of Investment	$500K
Size of Fund	As required
Investment Criteria	Early stages; electronic, computer, and biomedical technology; specialty publishing; leveraged buy-outs
Portfolio Companies	ADI Electronics, Long Island, NY, Electronic components; Seniority Magazine, Syracuse, NY, Specialty publishing

VISTA VENTURES
36 Grove Street
New Canaan, CT 06840
(203) 972-3400

Gerald B. Bay

Directorships

InteCom
Concord Data Systems
International Microelectronics
Genesis Electronics

Prior Positions

President, Verbax Inc., 1979–80

Education

MBA, Xavier, 1965
BS, Electrical Engineering, Purdue University, 1962

John F. Tomlin

Directorships

Interactive Images
ALF Corporation
Focus Health Care
Managed Care

Prior Positions

Second Vice President, Continental Illinois Venture Corp., 1981–83
Director, JW Vaughan

Education

MBA, University of Chicago, 1981
BA, Vanderbilt University, 1978

Robert P. Cummins

Directorships

Automated Diagnostics
MTDI
Sigma Circuits
Strato Medical
Zoran Corp.

Prior Positions

Vice President, Continental Illinois Venture Corp., 1981–84

Education

MBA, University of Illinois, 1979
BA, Dartmouth, 1976

Robert C. Fleming

Directorships

Adaptive Data
Concord Data Systems

DIRECTORY AND BIOGRAPHIES

Prior Positions

Service Director, Gartner Group, 1983–85
Associate, Booz, Allen & Hamilton, 1982–83

Education

MBA, University of Pennsylvania, 1983
BA, Dartmouth, 1978

Gregory F. Zaic

Directorships

Biocom Inc.
Medical Resources

Prior Positions

Director, Cambridge Research & Development Group, 1983–84
Business Development Manager, American Can Co., 1979–83

Education

MS, Management, MIT, 1972
MS, Mechanical Engineering, MIT, 1971
BS, Princeton, 1969

Dr. Edwin Snape

Directorships

Airmac Technology Systems
Delpnian Corp.
Liposome Co.
Plant Genetics, Inc.
Sonobond Ultrasonics, Inc.

Prior Positions

Vice President, Inco Securities Corp., 1979–81
Vice President, MPD Technology Corp., 1977–79

Education

BSME, PhD, Leeds University, U.K.

Average Size of Investment	$1M
Size of Fund	$150M
Investment Criteria	Start-ups; technology-based; leveraged buy-outs and other diversified areas of interest; will act as lead investor
Portfolio Companies	Undisclosed

VK VENTURES
50 California Street, Suite 2350
San Francisco, CA 94111
(415) 391-5600

F. Van Kasper
General Partner

Directorships

Sunworld
The Exploratorium

Prior Positions

Vice President, Manager, Loeb Rhoades & Co., 1974–78
Manager, Shearson Hammill, 1969–74

Education

BS, Business Administration, California State University, Los Angeles, 1964
AA, Pasadena City College, 1959

Average Size of Investment	$250K; Access to more substantial capital if necessary
Size of Fund	$2M
Investment Criteria	Will consider medium to low technology companies with established management; prefer to provide growth capital rather than start-up financing; will consider management buy-outs
Portfolio Companies	Berkeley Glasslab, Pleasanton, CA; Business Research Corp., Boston, MA; Cooker Concepts, Inc., Louisville, KY; Collins Industries, Hutchinson, KS; Deep Ocean Technology, San Leandro, CA; Pro-Tech-Ion, Emeryville, CA; Quintel, Tempe, AZ; Slautterback Corp., Monterey, CA; Sunworld International, Las Vegas, NV; Airways, Inc.; U.S. Medical, Los Angeles, CA; VK Capital, San Francisco, CA

VNB CAPITAL CORPORATION
15 E. Monroe Street, Suite 1200
Phoenix, AZ 85004
(602) 261-1577

John M. Holliman III
Managing Director

Average Size of Investment $400K
Size of Fund $15M
Investment Criteria   Leveraged buyouts, later stage, expansionary working capital
Portfolio Companies   Undisclosed

WACHTEL & CO., INC.
1101 Fourteenth St., N.W.
Washington, DC 20005-5680
(202) 898-1144

Sidney B. Wachtel
Chairman

Prior Positions

Investment Advisory Dept. (Head), A. T. Brod & Co., 1960–61
Economist and Account Executive, Laidlaw & Co., 1959–60

Education

MA, Economics, New York University, 1941
BS, Economics, New York University, 1939

John D. Sanders
Vice President

Directorships

Radiation Systems, Inc., Antenna manufacturer
Daedalus Enterprises, Inc., IR scanning equipment
Tork, Inc., Energy management systems
Industrial Training Corp., Video training programs
Photo Data, Inc., Printing and composition
Temporaries, Inc., Temporary help
Information Analysis, Inc., Computer software
Vision Technology Corp., Law-enforcement computer systems
BioClinical Systems, Inc., Diagnostics products
Teledial Devices, Inc., Telephone dial equipment
RAMCOR, Inc., Government defense services
Data Measurement Corp., Industrial instruments
Waxie Maxie Music Co., Retail record stores

Prior Positions

Research Scientist, U. S. Central Intelligence Agency, 1964–68
Member of Technical Staff, RCA Research Labs, 1962

Education

PhD, Electrical Engineering, Carnegie-Mellon University, 1965
MS, Electrical Engineering, Carnegie-Mellon University, 1962
BEE, University of Louisville, 1961

Bonnie K. Wachtel
Vice President

Directorships

LFM, Inc., Legal and financial services
Anadac, Inc., Government defense services
Apogee Research, Inc., Engineering services
MIT Enterprise 70 RVM, Non-profit educational
National Press, Inc., Book publishing
MRC, Inc., Microcomputer training
Lightworks, Inc., Interior design

Prior Position

Attorney, Weil, Gotshal & Manges, 1980–84

Education

JD, University of Virginia, 1980
MBA, University of Chicago, 1978
BA, University of Chicago, 1977

Wendie L. Wachtel
Vice President

Directorships

Pubsat, Inc., Programming for television news
Florida Glass Ind., Inc., Distribution and installation of glass products
CVI Corp., Video production and equipment leasing
Valkyrie Finance Group, Ltd., Consulting and project management for financial institutions

Average Size of Investment	$125K
Size of Fund	$10M+
Investment Criteria	Start-up okay, but prefer to see six months to one year of actual operations; prefer non-capital-intensive industries, particularly data processing
Portfolio Companies	Undisclosed

WALDEN
12639 Northeast 5th Street
Bellevue, WA 98005
(206) 462-7248

303 Sacramento Street
San Francisco, CA 94111
(415) 391-7225

Arthur S. Berliner
General Partner, CA

Directorships

Codon, Genetic engineering
Cyborg, Instrumentation
Thomas E. Wolfe, Men's clothing manufacturer
Creative Biomolecules, Biotechnology
Optical Specialties, Semiconductor equipment manufacturing

Prior Position

Investment Banking, Sutro & Co., Inc.

Education

MBA, University of California at Berkeley, 1966
BS, University of California at Berkeley, 1964

George S. Sarlo
General Partner, CA

Directorships

Rugged Digital Systems, Computers
Elantec, Semiconductors
Mass Merchandising, Inc., Distribution

Prior Positions

President, Ashfield & Co.
Vice President, William D. Witter, Inc.

Education

MBA, Harvard Business School, 1963
BS, University of Arizona, 1959

Lip-Bu Tan
General Partner, CA

Directorships

Mouse Systems, Optical mice and graphics software
Walden International, Inc., Venture capital management company
Mulpha, U.S.A., Trading and manufacturing concern in Asia
Orient Capital & Technology Corp., Consulting and investment

Prior Positions

Vice President, Chapell & Co.
Financial Manager, Echo Energy Consultants, Inc.

Education

MBA, University of San Francisco, 1980–83
MS, Massachusetts Institute of Technology, 1979–80

Theodore M. Wight
General Partner, WA

Directorships

Inference Corp., Artificial intelligence
Dealer Information Systems, Software
Techmedica, Inc., Artificial joints

Education

MBA, University of Puget Sound, 1966
BS, University of Puget Sound, 1964

Average Size of Investment	$750K
Size of Fund	$35M
Investment Criteria	Invest at all stages, prefer West Coast
Portfolio Companies	Undisclosed

WALNUT STREET CAPITAL CO.
702 Cotton Exchange Building
New Orleans, LA 70130
(504) 525-2112

William D. Humphries
Managing General Partner

Directorships

GTS Corp., Seismic data
CUCOS, Inc., Mexican restaurant chain
Cartrex Corp., Computer peripherals
Integrated Energy Corp.
The Syconex Corp., Combustion control instrumentation
Delta Capital Corp., Venture capital

Prior Positions

Chief Financial Officer, Royal Street Corp., 1955–82
President and Director, Royal Street Development Co.
General Partner, Stanford Court Hotel
President, Royal Street Land Co., Controls Deer Valley Ski Area, Park City, UT
Salesman, Drug Products Division, Procter & Gamble, 1952–55

Education

BA, Foreign Affairs, University of Virginia, 1951

Alexander B. Wilkins

Average Size of Investment	$250K
Size of Fund	$7M
Investment Criteria	Balanced fund
Portfolio Companies	Automatix, Inc., Billerica, MA, Robotics; BYAD, Inc., Arlington Heights, IL, Computer workstations; Cartrex Corp., Grand Rapids, MI, Computer memory; Cucos, Inc., Metarie, LA, GTS Corp., Metarie, LA, Houston Oil Fields Co., Houston, TX, Oil and gas E & P; Medical Resources, Inc., Teaneck, NJ, Health care; MCO Resources Corp., Houston, TX, Oil and gas E & P; MWB Associates, Inc., Great Falls, VA, Health care; Sea Oats Associates, Inc., Wrightsville Beach, NC, Real estate; S.E.I., Inc., Rockhill, SC, Specialty foods and gifts; Syconex Corp., Duarte, CA; Technology Associates, Inc., Atlanta, GA, Office building development

WARBURG, PINCUS VENTURES INC.
466 Lexington Avenue
New York, NY 10017
(212) 878-0600

Lionel I. Pincus
Chairman and President

Directorships

Orion Pictures Corp.
Western Pacific Industries
SFN Companies
Mattel, Inc.

Education

MBA, Columbia University, 1956
BA, University of Pennsylvania, 1953

Christopher W. Brody
Managing Director

Directorships

National Venture Capital Association
Gartner Group
Ortel Corp.
Shaughnessy Holdings
Hypres, Inc.

Education

MBA, Harvard Graduate School of Business, 1968
BA, Harvard College, 1966

Rodman W. Moorhead III
Managing Director

Directorships

Symbion, Inc.
Centrafarm, N.V.
Synergen, Inc.
Vestar Research, Inc.
Medical Review Corp.

Education

MBA, Harvard Graduate School of Business, 1968
BA, Harvard College, 1966

Andrew Gaspar
Managing Director

Directorships

Page America Group, Inc.
Bridge Communications, Inc.
Private Satellite Network, Inc.

Prior Positions

Vice President, Strategic Planning RCA Communications, Inc., 1981–82
Vice President, Strategic Planning RCA Global Communications, Inc., 1980–81

Education

MBA, Harvard Graduate School of Business, 1973
MS, Northwestern University, 1971
BS, Columbia University, 1969

Barbara L. Manfrey
Managing Director

Directorships

Synergen, Inc.
Ingersoll Publications

Education

BA, Vassar College, 1976

Charles A. Steinberg
Managing Director

Education

BA, Hunter College, 1957

John L. Vogelstein
Vice Chairman

Directorships

Mattel, Inc.
DeVry, Inc.
SFN Companies

Education

Harvard College, 1954

Sidney Lapidus
Managing Director

Directorships

Allied Supermarkets
Dallas Media Investors Corp.
Ingersoll Publications
Mead Trucking

Education

LLB, Columbia University School of Law, 1962
AB, Princeton University, 1959

Stephen W. Fillo
Managing Director

Directorships

United States Health Care Systems
Foxmeyer, Inc.
Babbages, Inc.
Agridata Resources
MMR Technologies

Prior Position

General Partner, Quidnet Venture Capital Fund, 1974–81

Education

MBA, Harvard Graduate School of Business, 1963
BS, Cornell University, 1959

Nissan Boury
Managing Director

Directorships

Certified Collateral Corp.
Cdex Corp.
Hunter & Ready

Prior Positions

Assistant Director, Center for Strategic Studies, 1978–79
Assistant to Ambassador, Israel Mission to the UN Diplomatic Service, 1972–77

Education

MBA, New York Graduate School of Business, 1976
BS, New York College of Business and Public Administration, 1971

Dr. Henry Kressel
Managing Director

Directorships

Hypres, Inc.
Yeshiva University Research Institute

Prior Position

Vice President, RCA Laboratories, 1959–83

Education

PhD, University of Pennsylvania, 1965
MBA, Wharton School, 1959
MS, Harvard University, 1956
BS, Yeshiva University, 1955

Ernest H. Pomerantz
Managing Director

Directorships

Coastal Service Corp.
Dallas Media Investors Corp.
Four Star Broadcasting, Inc.
Babbage's, Inc.

Prior Positions

Vice President, Lehman Brothers Kuhn Loeb, 1977–78
Vice President, Kuhn Loeb & Company

Education

MBA, New York University Graduate School of Business, 1977
MA, University of South California (London School of Economics), 1968
BS, Rensselaer Polytechnic Institute, 1964

Reuben S. Leibowitz

Average Size of Investment	$1M
Size of Fund	$500M
Investment Criteria	Diversified preferences; leveraged buy-outs; start-ups are desirable; will act as lead investor
Portfolio Companies	Undisclosed

WASHINGTON CAPITAL CORP.
1417 Fourth Avenue
Seattle, WA 98111
(206) 682-5400

Jerry K. Weaver

Average Size of Investment	$100K
Size of Fund	Undisclosed
Investment Criteria	Diversified areas of interest; geographic location important
Portfolio Companies	Undisclosed

WASHINGTON NATIONAL INVESTMENT CORPORATION
1211 Connecticut Avenue, N.W.
Suite 402
Washington, DC 20036
(202) 452-9113

Richard S. Bodman
President and Director

Directorships

Emhart Corporation
Joyce Beverages, Inc.
SouthernNet, Inc.
Washington Bancorporation

DIRECTORY AND BIOGRAPHIES

Prior Positions

President, COMSAT General Corporation
Senior Vice President, Finance and Corporate Development, Communications Satellite Corporation
E. I. Du Pont de Nemours & Co.
Partner, Touche, Ross & Co.
Assistant Secretary, U.S. Department of the Interior

Education

MS, Massachusetts Institute of Technology, 1961
BS, Princeton University, 1959

Richard S. Trutanic
Director and Senior Vice President

Directorship

SouthernNet, Inc.

Prior Positions

President, National Telephone Systems
Chief Financial Officer, Universal Packers Corporation
Lawyer, Hogan & Hartson

Education

MS, Stanford University, 1978
JD, Stanford University, 1978
BA, Stanford University, 1974

Average Size of Investment	$2M
Size of Fund	Undisclosed
Investment Criteria	We specialize in direct equity investments: All situations and leveraged buy-outs
Portfolio Companies	Undisclosed

WASHINGTON TRUST EQUITY CORP.
Washington Trust Financial Center
P.O. Box 2127
Spokane, WA 99210
(509) 455-4106

Average Size of Investment	$500K
Size of Fund	Undisclosed
Investment Criteria	Diverse areas of interest; geographic location important
Portfolio Companies	Undisclosed

WATCHUNG CAPITAL CORP.
431 Fifth Avenue
New York, NY 10006
(212) 889-3466

Thomas S. T. Jeng

Average Size of Investment	Undisclosed
Size of Fund	Undisclosed
Investment Criteria	Undisclosed
Portfolio Companies	Undisclosed

NEAL WEHR & ASSOCIATES
108-I Seaside Avenue
Milford, CT 06460
(203) 874-4926

Neal Wehr
President

Prior Positions

Chairman of the Board, Winston Industries
President, Seilon, Inc.

Education

CPA, Pennsylvania
MA, University of Pittsburgh
BA, Allegheny College

Average Size of Investment	Undisclosed
Size of Fund	Undisclosed
Investment Criteria	Leveraged buy-outs only
Portfolio Companies	Undisclosed

WEISS, PECK & GREER
555 California Street, Suite 4760
San Francisco, CA 94104
(415) 622-6864

Philip Greer
General Partner

Directorships

Federal Express Corp., Air courier service, electronic document transmission service
Pentos plc, Industrial holding company
Bridge Communications, Inc., Computer networking equipment

Prior Position

Vice President, A. G. Becker & Co., 1966–70

Education

MBA, Harvard Business School, 1960
AB, Psychology, Princeton, 1957

Gunnar Hurtig, III
General Partner

Directorships

Data I/O, CAE
Silicon Solutions, CAE accelerators
Saratoga Semiconductor, Semiconductors

Prior Positions

Chief Executive Officer, Integrated office systems
Director, Marketing, Fairchild Camera Instrument Corp.

Education

MBA, Stanford University, 1976
MS, Cornell University, 1964
BEE, Cornell University, 1963

Robert J. Loarie
General Partner

Directorships

Micropolis Corp., Floppy/rigid disk drives for micro/minicomputers
Silicon Solutions Corp., CAE Accelerators
Spectragraphics Corp., Color graphics terminal systems for computer-aided design applications
Adaptec, Inc., Semiconductor (LSI) based controllers for Winchester disk drives
Bridge Communications, Inc., Computer network/internetwork equipment

Prior Positions

General Partner, Lawrence WPG Partners, L.P., 1981–present
Vice President, Chief Financial Officer, Siliconix, Inc., 1979–80
Treasurer, Four Phase Systems, Inc., 1974–79

Education

MBA, Harvard Business School, 1971
BSEE, Illinois Institute of Technology, 1964

John C. Savage
General Partner

Directorships

New West Technology Corp., Printed wiring boards
Cardiovascular Devices, Inc., Blood gas monitoring equipment
Interpore International, Bone substitute material
FileNet Corp., Optical disk storage filing systems
The Systems Center, Communications software
Exploration Systems, Inc., Turnkey systems for exploration analysis

Prior Positions

General Partner, Lawrence WPG Partners, L.P., 1981–present
Director, Corporate Planning, Four-Phase Systems, Inc., 1978–81
Various management, Envirotech Corp., 1974–78
Branch Chief, U.S. Environmental Protection Agency, 1972–74

Education

MBA, Harvard Business School, 1972
B. ChE., Georgia Institute of Technology, 1970

Eugene M. Weber
General Partner

Directorships

Shared Financial Systems, Transaction processing software
Stylus Inc., Manufactures and retails custom upholstered furniture
H L Capital Management Corp., Worker's compensation insurance and related services

DIRECTORY AND BIOGRAPHIES

Prior Positions
Senior Manager, McKinsey & Co., 1977–83
Product Specialist, Burroughs Corp., 1973–75
Design Engineer, Sealectro Corp., 1972–73

Education
MBA, Wharton School, University of Pennsylvania, 1977
BSEE, Cornell University, 1972

Average Size of Investment	$1–1.5M
Size of Fund	$230M
Investment Criteria	Undisclosed
Portfolio Companies	Undisclosed

WELSH, CARSON, ANDERSON AND STOWE
45 Wall Street
New York, NY 10005
(212) 945-2000

Patrick J. Welsh
Russell L. Carson
Bruce K. Anderson
Richard H. Stowe
Charles G. Moore
Andrew M. Paul
William W. Neal

Average Size of Investment	$1M–5M
Size of Fund	$325M
Investment Criteria	Technology-based and other diverse areas; will act as lead investor, start-ups; considers leveraged buy-outs
Portfolio Companies	Undisclosed

WESCOT CAPITAL CORPORATON
1601 North Seventh Street
Phoenix, AZ 85006

P O Box 5190
Phoenix, AZ 85010

Scott Eller
General Partner

Directorships
Kurta Corp.
Edens Broadcasting, Inc.
Immunetech Inc.
OMAC Inc.

Pamela Mason
Vice President

Education
MBA, Arizona State University
BS, Michigan Technological University

James G. Gardner
General Partner

Directorship
Safe Power, Computer UPS

Prior Position
Senior Vice President, Valley National Bank

Education
BS, Dartmouth, 1954

Karl Eller
General Partner

Average Size of Investment	$500K
Size of Fund	$20.6M
Investment Criteria	Media, communications, advertising, publishing, high technology
Portfolio Companies	Amcodyne, Diskdrives; Celerity Comp., Inc., High speed computer; Dallas-Smith Engineering, Robotics; Edens Broadcasting, Radio stations; Immunetech, Inc., Pharmaceuticals; Kurta Corp., Digitizers/graphics devices; Multi-Systems, Inc., Telemarketing software; OMAC, Inc., Canard aircraft; SAFE Power Systems, Computer power supplies; Syntellect, Inc., Voice response systems; Syntro Corp., Biotechnology; Viasoft, Inc., Mainframe maintenance software; VISIC, Inc., High performance CMOS device

WESTAMCO INVESTMENT CO.
8929 Wilshire Boulevard
Beverly Hills, CA 90211
(213) 652-8288

Leonard G. Muskin
Scott T. Van Every

Average Size of Investment	$100K
Size of Fund	Undisclosed
Investment Criteria	Construction, real estate, manufacturing, technology-based, and other diverse areas
Portfolio Companies	Undisclosed

WEST CENTRAL CAPITAL CORP.
440 Northlake Center
Suite 206
Dallas, TX 75238
(214) 348-3969

Howard W. Jacob
Barbara C. Evans

Average Size of Investment	Undisclosed
Size of Fund	Undisclosed
Investment Criteria	Undisclosed
Portfolio Companies	Undisclosed

WEST COAST VENTURE CAPITAL
5300 Stevens Creek Boulevard
San Jose, CA 95129
(408) 554-8744

Ralph Rodrigues

Average Size of Investment	$500K
Size of Fund	$10M
Investment Criteria	Technology-based companies of interest; start-ups; geographic locale important
Portfolio Companies	Undisclosed

WESTERN
One New York Plaza
New York, NY 10004
(212) 908-9553

Larry J. Lawrence
Richard W. Smith
Robert J. Loarie
Philip Greer
John C. Savage

Average Size of Investment	$500K
Size of Fund	$22M
Investment Criteria	Technology-based companies and other diverse areas of interest; start-ups; will act as lead investor
Portfolio Companies	Undisclosed

WESTERN FINANCIAL CAPITAL CORP.
1380 Miami Gardens Drive, N.E.
Suite 225
North Miami Beach, FL 33179
(305) 949-5900

Fredric M. Rosemore
Lance B. Rosemore

Average Size of Investment	$600K
Size of Fund	Undisclosed
Investment Criteria	Diversified areas of interest including manufacturing; interested in debt with equity
Portfolio Companies	Undisclosed

WESTERN VENTURE CAPITAL CORP.
P.O. Box 702680
Tulsa, OK 71470
(918) 744-6275

William B. Baker
President

DIRECTORY AND BIOGRAPHIES

Directorships

Sepratech Corp.
Prodek Inc.
Nusonics Inc.
Southwestern Porcelain Signs Inc.

Prior Position

President, ComputerLand of OK

Education

BS, Drake University, 1970

John M. Lare
Vice President, Chief Financial Officer

Directorships

Post Petroleum
Prodek Inc.

Prior Position

Vice President, Continental Trend Resources

Education

Graduate School of Business, University of California at Los Angeles, 1971
BS, Economics, University of California at Los Angeles, 1970

Average Size of Investment	$400K
Size of Fund	Undisclosed
Investment Criteria	Leveraged buy-outs are of interest; will act as lead investor; diversified company interests; Oklahoma and surrounding states
Portfolio Companies	Undisclosed

WEYERHAEUSER VENTURE CO.
21515 Hawthorne Boulevard
Suite 310
Torrance, CA 90503
(213) 543-2661

401 Parkplace
Suite 415
Kirkland, WA 98033
(206) 827-3878

1510 Fashion Island Blvd.
Suite 104
San Mateo, CA 94404
(415) 341-5663

23282 Mill Creek Road
Suite 200
Laguna Hills, CA 92653
(714) 742-2428

Donald E. Lange
Stephen M. Margolin
Daniel S. Fulton
Ronald S. Bliss
Robert J. Plavchak
Darla V. Norris
James D. Lawrence
Kevin W. Peters

Average Size of Investment	$1M
Size of Fund	Undisclosed
Investment Criteria	Real estate only
Portfolio Companies	Undisclosed

WHITE & CO.
15 North 21st Street
Steiner Building
P.O. Box 11633
Birmingham, AL 35203
(205) 252-3681

John A. Screws
James Milton Johnson
James H. White, III
Marvin B. Claige

Average Size of Investment	$300K
Size of Fund	Undisclosed
Investment Criteria	Diversified areas of interest including real estate; start-ups; will act as lead investor
Portfolio Companies	Undisclosed

WHITEHEAD ASSOCIATES
15 Valley Drive
Greenwich, CT 06830
(203) 629-4633

William E. Engbers
Joseph A. Orlando
Andrew M. Ziolkowski

Average Size of Investment	$500K
Size of Fund	Undisclosed
Investment Criteria	Start-ups of interest as well as technology-based companies; will act as lead investor
Portfolio Companies	Charlton Associates; Cyberdick, Inc.; Genesis Labs, Inc.; The Liposome Company; Plant Genetics, Inc.; Santa Clara Systems, Inc.; Seeq Technology, Inc.; T Cell Sciences, Inc.; Theta-J Corporation

WHITE RIVER CAPITAL CORP.
500 Washington Street
P.O. Box 929
Columbus, IN 47202
(812) 376-1759

David James Blair
President, Investment Manager

Directorship

Entek Scientific Corp., CAE software

Prior Position

Assistant Secretary, Manufacturers Hanover Trust Co.

Education

MBA, The Darden School, University of Virginia, 1982
BA, Economics, Williams College, 1976

Thomas D. Washburn
Vice Chairman/Director

Directorships

Inland Mortgage Corp., Mortgage subsidiary of Irwin Union Corp.
Irwin Union Credit Insurance Corp., Credit insurance subsidiary of IUC

Education

MBA, University of Virginia, 1976
BS, University of Virginia, 1970

Average Size of Investment	$100K
Size of Fund	$1.4M
Investment Criteria	Later stage; $500K minimum revenues; one to two years operating history; established management team; Midwest, Indiana for origination; always participate with two or more professional venture capital companies
Portfolio Companies	Enteck Scientific Corp., Ohio, CAE software; Riverton Investment Corp., Virginia, Cement manufacturer; Sentinel Computer Corp., Ohio, Profit control software; The Wholesale Club, Indiana, Wholesale consumer products; Glas-Craft, Inc., Indiana, Fiberglass and insulation spray equipment; Infortext Systems, Inc., Illinois, Office equipment cost control systems

WIND POINT PARTNERS
1525 Howe Street
Racine, WI 53403
(414) 631-4030

Arthur DelVesco
General Partner

Directorships

Somerset Pharmaceuticals, Inc.
American Cablesystems Corp.
Backe Communications, Inc.
Centigram Corp.
Physicians Radio Network, Inc.
Servlite, Inc.
Speech Plus, Inc.

Prior Position

Senior Investment Manager, First Chicago Corporation Equity Group

Education

MBA, Harvard University, 1979
BA, Rutgers University, 1975

James E. Daverman
General Partner

Directorships

Aspen Peripherals, Inc.
Universal Development Corp.
Hannover Healthcare, Inc.
Irwin Magnetic Systems, Inc.
NeoRx Corp.

Prior Positions

Vice President and Deputy Head, First Chicago Corp. Equity Group

Education

MBA, Wharton School, 1973
BA, University of Ann Arbor, 1971

S. Curtis Johnson
General Partner

Directorships

Effective Management Systems, Inc.
GenDerm Corp.
Somerset Pharmaceuticals, Inc.

Prior Position

President, Omnicom, Inc.

Education

MBA, Northwestern University, 1983
BA, Cornell University, 1977

Richard R. Kracum
Investment Manager

Directorships

International Laser Machines Corp.
Parallel Computers, Inc.
Speech Plus, Inc.

Prior Position

Senior Associate, Booz, Allen & Hamilton

Education

MBA, University of Chicago, 1980
MS, University of Chicago, 1978
BA, Carleton College, 1976

Average Size of Investment	$1M
Size of Fund	$36M
Investment Criteria	Strong management team, unique market opportunity, attractive economics and returns; will consider management buy outs
Portfolio Companies	Undisclosed

WINFIELD CAPITAL CORP.
237 Mamaroneck Avenue
White Plains, NY 10601
(914) 949-2600

Stanley Pechman
President

Directorship

McGregor Sporting Goods, Manufacturer and importer of sporting goods equipment

Education

BS, Wharton School, University of Pennsylvania, 1950

Martin Bring
Robert Fischer

Average Size of Investment	$250K
Size of Fund	$10M
Investment Critria	Established companies in business at least three years; turnaround or leverage buy-outs preferred
Portfolio Companies	Undisclosed

WINTHROP VENTURES
74 Trinity Place
New York, NY 10006
(212) 422-0100

Cyrus Brown
H. Trimble

Average Size of Investment $600K
Size of Fund   Undisclosed
Investment Criteria   Technology-based companies of interest; will act as lead investor; start-ups considered as well as leveraged buy-outs and other diverse areas of interest
Portfolio Companies   Undisclosed

WISCONSIN VENTURE CAPITAL FUND
c/o Lubar & Co., Inc.
3060 First Wisconsin Center
Milwaukee, WI 53202
(414) 291-9000

Sheldon B. Lubar
David J. Lubar
James C. Rowe
William T. Donovan
James S. Vaughan
Vice President

Directorships

W. H. Brady Co., Manufacturer of labels, nameplates, signs and wiremakers, membrane switches
Chicago Gear Works, Inc., Small cut gears
Teletech Resources Corp., Shared tenant telephone service

Prior Position

Vice President and Director of Manufacturing, Square D Co., 1977–82

Education

BS, CE, University of Wisconsin-Madison, 1938

Average Size of Investment $500K
Size of Fund $10.5K
Investment Criteria   Start-up; second- and third-stage financing
Portfolio Companies   The Bartsch Corp., Milwaukee, WI, Computer-aided manufacturing; The Business Journal Serving Greater Milwaukee, Milwaukee, WI, Weekly business newspaper; Gander Mountain, Inc., Wilmot, WI, Mail order retailer; Teletech Resources, Inc., Milwaukee, WI, Provider of shared tenant telecommunication services

WOODLAND CAPITAL COMPANY
3007 Skyway Circle North
Irving, TX 75038
(214) 659-9500

Stewart Siebens, President

Average Size of Investment $500K
Size of Fund $15M
Investment Criteria   Leveraged buy-outs are of interest; geographic proximity important; will act as lead investor, interested in diverse companies
Portfolio Companies   Attention Medical Co.

THE WOODLANDS VENTURE CAPITAL COMPANY
2201 Timberloch Place
The Woodlands, TX 77380
(713) 363-7136

Martin P. Sutter
Managing Partner

Directorships

Cardiovascular Systems, Inc.
Houston Biotechnology Inc.
LifeCell Corp.
The Macrophage Company

Prior Positions

Assistant to the President, Mitchell Energy & Development
Manager, NGI Marketing, Liquid Energy Corporation
Consultant, Peat, Marwick, Mitchell Co.

Education

MBA, University of Houston, 1981
BS, LSU, 1977

J. Michael Schafer
Investment Associate

Directorship

LifeCell Corporation

Prior Positions

Associate, Burr, Egan, Deleage & Co.
Research Associate, University of Michigan
General Manager, Stripe 3—Adidas

Education

MBA, University of Michigan, 1985
BA, Davidson College, 1980

Average Size of Investment	$400–500K
Size of Fund	$15M
Investment Criteria	Invest primarily in very early stage companies in medical/biomedical technology and healthcare services; aggressively pursue technology transfer ventures from academic institutions
Portfolio Companies	Cardiovascular Systems, Inc., Medical devices, The Woodlands, TX; Houston Biotechnology, Inc., Biotechnology, The Woodlands, TX; Intelligent Medicine, Inc., Medical devices, Denver, CO; LifeCell Corp., Cryobiology Services, The Woodlands, TX; The Macrophage Company, Biotechnology, Houston, TX

WOOD RIVER CAPITAL CORP.
645 Madison Avenue
New York, NY 10022
(212) 750-9420

Elizabeth W. Smith, President

Average Size of Investment	Approx. $600K
Size of Fund	$40M
Investment Criteria	Diversified, interested in technology-based companies; will act as lead investor and will consider start-ups
Portfolio Companies	Undisclosed

WOODSIDE FUND
850 Woodside Drive
Woodside, CA 94062
(415) 368-5545

699 Peter Street #C
Pleasanton, CA 94566
(415) 462-0326

Vincent M. Occhipinti, General Partner
Charles E. Greb, General Partner
E. Frank Mendicino, General Partner
Robert E. Larson, General Partner
Thomas R. Blakeslee, Partner
William Hassebrock, Partner

Average Size of Investment	$200–500K
Size of Fund	Undisclosed
Investment Criteria	Emphasize seed and early-stage opportunities; will consider later-stage; will consider non-high technology industries, provided there is a barrier to entry
Portfolio Companies	Undisclosed

WOODY CREEK CAPITAL, INC.
1375 Walnut Street
Suite 225
Boulder, CO 80302
(303) 444-6000

Joseph A. Zebrowski, Jr.
President

Directorships

Woody Creek Leasing, Inc.
Plowboy Partners, Ltd.

Prior Position

Venture Capitalist, Time, Inc., New York, 1975–78

Education
MA, Tufts University, 1971
AB, Lafayette College, 1966

Wayne W. Goss
Chairman

Directorships
Woody Creek Leasing, Inc.
Plowboy Partners, Ltd.

Prior Position
Consulting, Venture Capital, Goss Companies, Inc., 1980–82

Education
BA, Mathematics, University of Colorado

Regina Celi
Senior Associate

Directorships
Several companies in Brazil

Prior Positions
Several Brazilian companies

Education
MA, Yale University, 1975
BA, University of Kansas, 1972

Average Size of Investment	No restrictions on size
Size of Fund	Undisclosed
Investment Criteria	The company is engaged in venture capital private placements in natural-resource and high-technology companies; of particular interest is the application of technology to natural-resource development
Portfolio Companies	Undisclosed

WORLD BUSINESSMEN CREDIT CORP.
2174 West Foothill Boulevard
P.O. Box 2178
Upland, CA 91785
(714) 391-1883

Jimmy ("James") Nixon, Ph.D.
Chairman of the Board

Directorships
Westerns Financial Thrift & Loan, Financial institution
South Carolina Farm Corp., Farm
N & T Bonding Co., Insurance/bonding
The Nixon Co., Clothing
Nure Salaam Jean Manufacturing Corp.

Prior Position
President, American Financial Savings & Loan, 1969–73

Education
PhD, Technical University, Nova Scotia, 1976

V. Lynn ("Beauty") Nixon
Latisha M. Nixon
Eunice N. Solomon
Corporate Secretary and Vice President

Directorships
Ontario Acceptance Corp., Finance
World International, Inc.

Prior Position
Vice President, First Women Auto Leasing Inc.

Education
BS, Northeast Louisiana University, 1969

Average Size of Investment	Undisclosed
Size of Fund	$40M
Investment Criteria	Small and mid-size start-up companies
Portfolio Companies	World Businessmen Monecard Intl. Ltd., Upland, CA

DIRECTORY AND BIOGRAPHIES

XEROX VENTURE CAPITAL
800 Long Ridge Road
Stamford, CT 06904
(203) 329-8700

2029 Century Park East
Suite 740, Xerox
Los Angeles, CA 90067
(213) 278-7940

Richard J. Hayes
Senior Principal, CT

Directorship

Vice President, Corporate Business Development

Education

PhD, American University, 1967
MBA, George Washington University, 1964
MS, Massachusetts Institute of Technology, 1960
BS, Massachusetts Institute of Technology, 1954

Lawrence R. Robinson, III
Principal, CT
(203) 968-3994

Prior Positions

Senior Vice President, General Electric Venture Capital Corp.
Associate, Wm. Sword & Co.

Education

JD, Stanford Law School, 1976
MBA, Stanford Business School, 1976
MA, Princeton University, 1967
BS, United States Air Force Academy, 1964

Michael Y. Granger
Associate, CT

Prior Positions

Analyst, Cigna Capital
Project Chairman, AT & T
Telecommunications Consultant, Price Waterhouse

Education

MBA, Dartmouth, Amos Tuck School of Business Administration, 1985
BS, University of Massachusetts, 1981

Stephen P. Taylor
Associate, CA

Prior Positions

Consultant, Peat, Marwick, Mitchell & Co.
Senior Systems Analyst, Sperry Corp.
Consultant, Dayflo, Inc.

Education

MBA, University of California, Los Angeles, 1985
MS, University of California, Irvine, 1983
BS, University of California, Irvine, 1979

Alvin Talbot
Principal, CA

Average Size of Investment	$1M
Size of Fund	$55M
Investment Criteria	High technology, business systems, components, and applications
Portfolio Companies	Advanced Business Communications, Richardson, TX, Manufacturer and marketer of digital switching systems; California Devices, Inc., San Jose, CA, Designer and manufacturer of custom integrated circuits; Candela Electronics, Sunnyvale, CA, Telecommunications equipment; Cauzin Systems, Inc., Waterbury, CT, Optical data distribution and retrieval; Greyhawk Systems, Milpitas, CA, High resolution, large screen imaging system; Hunter & Ready, Palo Alto, CA, Standard system software for microprocessors used in embedded applications; Imagen, Santa Clara, CA, Image processors; Intelligent Business Systems, New Haven, CT, Natural language; Microlytics, Inc., E. Rochester, NY, Office automation software; Saxpy Computer Corp., Sunnyvale, CA, Very high-speed matrix processors; Synektron Corp., Portland, OR, Proprietary motors, actuators, and associated drive electronics; Theta-J Corp., Wakefield, MA, Solid-state relays and power supplies; Voice Industries Corp., Morristown, NJ, Word recognition, continuous speech recognition; Intran Corp., MInneapolis, MN, Electronic graphic workstations; Kurzweil Applied Intelligence, Waltham, MA, Voice recognition systems; Micro Linear Corp., San Jose, CA, Linear custom LSI chips; Raster Technologies, Billerica, MA, Graphics controllers; Sequent Computer Systems, Inc., Portland OR, Multimicroprocessors or computers

ZERO STAGE CAPITAL EQUITY FUND, L.P.
One Broadway
Kendall Square
Cambridge, MA 02142
(617) 876-5355

Paul M. Kelley
President and Managing Partner

Directorships

New Media Graphics, Inc.
Estabrook Digital Graphics, Inc.
Tech Financial Services, Inc.
Octocom Systems, Inc.
Data Innovations, Inc.

Prior Position

A Principal, Massachusetts Technology Development Corp.

Education

MBA, Northeastern University, 1969
BA, Harvard University, 1959

Gordon Baty
General Partner
c/o Wormser Engineering, Inc.
225 Merrimac Street
Woburn, MA 01888

Directorships

Mercury Computers, Inc., Array processors
Texet Corp., Text processing systems
Clinical Data Inc., Medical monitoring systems
Wormser Engineering, Inc., Coal combustion systems

Prior Positions

President, Wormser Engineering, Inc., 1981–present
Division Manager, Burroughs Corp., 1979–81
President, Context Corp., 1973–79

Education

PhD, Massachusetts Institute of Technology, Sloan School, 1967
MS, Massachusetts Institute of Technology, Sloan School, 1963
BS, Massachusetts Institute of Technology, 1961

Edward B. Roberts
General Partner

Directorships

Medical Information Technology, Inc., Hospital information systems
SofTech, Inc., Software
Pugh-Roberts Associates, Inc., Technology and strategy management consulting
Advanced Magnetics, Bioclinical diagnostics

Prior Positions

President, Pugh-Roberts Associates, Inc., 1963–present
David Sarnoff Professor of Management of Technology, Massachusetts Institute of Technology, Sloan School of Management, 1961–present

Education

SB, SM, Electrical Engineering; SM, Management; PhD, Economics; Massachusetts Institute of Technology, 1958, 1960, 1962

Joseph P. Lombard
Jerome Goldstein
General Partner

Directorships

Advanced Magnetics, Inc., Biotechnology
Medical & Scientific Designs, Immunodiagnostics
Eljenn International, Ltd., Personal care products

Prior Position

President, Clinical Assays (now Travenol-Genentech Diagnostics), until 1980

Education

SB, SM, MBA, Massachusetts Institute of Technology, 1964, 1965, 1967

Average Size of Investment	$50K–$300K
Size of Fund	$5M
Investment Criteria	Business plan; annual sale: nominal
Portfolio Companies	Estabrooks Digital Graphics, Dot-matrix printers; New Media Graphics, Computer graphics integration; Octocom Systems Network, communications; Technology Financial Services, Hi-

tech industry data base; Maze Technology, Full-custom IC design; Advanced Dielectric Technologies, Thin film applications

ZERO STAGE CAPITAL OF PENNSYLVANIA EQUITY FUND, L.P.
1308 Charles Street
State College, PA 16801
(814) 237-2551

Paul M. Kelley, General Partner
Gordon Baty, General Partner
Edward B. Roberts, General Partner
Joseph P. Lombard, General Partner
Jerome Goldstein, General Partner

Dennis R. Costello
General Partner

Prior Position

Executive Director, Colorado Advanced Technology Institute

Average Size of Investment	$50–250K
Size of Fund	$10M
Investment Criteria	Business plan; nominal sales/profit
Portfolio Companies	Undisclosed

INDEX

ABC Radio & Television, 19
ABS Ventures, 47
Adelson, Sheldon, 9
Adler, Fred R., 31
Adler & Co., 47
Advanced Micro Devices, Inc., 12
Advanced Technology Ventures, 47
Aeigis Fund Limited Partnership, 54
Affirmative Covenants, 81
AIDS, 48, 73
Airborne Freight, 76
Allen, Martin A., 9
Allen, Paul, 24–25
Allstate Insurance Co., 47
Alpert, Martin, 9
Alpha Partners, 54
AMERCO, 27
American Cancer Society, 75
American Discount Auto Parts, 11
American Medical Association, 31, 43
American Shared Hospital Services, 17
AmGen Corp., 45
Amos'n'Andy, 24
Analog Devices, Inc., 13
Anderson, J. Reid, 9
Apollo Computer, Inc., 12, 51
Apple Computer, Inc., 10, 49–50, 53
Aristera, 26
Ash, Mary Kay, 9, 22–23
Ash, Richard, 22
ASK Computer Systems, Inc., 11
AT&T, 31
Automatic Data Processing Corp. (ADP), 2, 13

Bagamery, Anne, 22
Bass Brothers Enterprises, 48
Battelle Memorial Laboratories, 70
Battery Ventures, 51
Bay Pacific Health Corp., 16
Ben Franklin Stores, 29
Benny, Jack, 98
Berkshire Hathaway, Inc., 9
Berry Cash Southwest Partnership, 51
Bessemer Venture Partnership, 91
Best Products Co., Inc., 11
Biogen, 75

Black, Charlie, 21
Bliss, E.W., 66
Block, Henry W., 9
Block, Richard A., 9
Blount, Winton Malcom, 9
Blount, Inc., 9
Bluhdorn, Charles, 66
Blumkin, Rose, 9
BMW, 45
Bobby McGee's U.S.A., Inc., 13
Boehringer Mannheim Corp., 41
Boettcher Venture Capital Partners, L.A., 51
Boyer, Herbert W., 13, 41
Browning-Ferris Industries, Inc., 9
Buffett, Warren, 9, 19
Bunnell, David, 25
Bunny-Hut, 55
Burr, Donald C., 9

Cable, Howse & Cozado, Inc., 47
Cambridge Venture Partners, 47
Cape, Ronald E., 9, 43, 48
Capital Cities Communications Corp., 12, 18–19
Capital Corporation of Wyoming, Inc., 54
Carlson, Chester, 4, 55, 70
Carlson, Curtis L., 9
Carlson Companies, 9
Carney, Frank L., 9
Carson, Johnny, 98
CAT Scan, 16
Celestial Seasonings, Inc., 13
Cetus Corp., 9, 41–48, 75
Chapter X Involuntary Bankruptcy, 61
Chapter XI, 61–63
Charles Schwab & Co., 13
Charter Medical Corp., 8–9, 14
Chef Boy-Ar-Dee, 21
Chevron, 44
Chiron Corp., 45
Chun King Corp., 18–21
Citicorp Venture Capital, Ltd., 41, 47
Cities Service, 48
City of Hope National Medical Center, 42

Clarion Capital Corp., 47
Colorado Venture Capital Corp., 51
Columbia Data, 53
Columbine Venture Fund, Ltd., 47
Commercial Bank, 94
Commercial Finance Co., 94
Common stock, 83–90
Community Psychiatric Centers, Inc., 8, 10, 14, 48
Computerland Corp., 11
Computervision Corp., 9
Continental Capital Ventures, 47
Continental Health Affiliates, 17
Continental Illinois Venture Corp., 47
Control Data Corp., 12
Cooper Laboratories, 12
Corporate achiever, 91
Country Notebook, 26
Crea, Robert, 42

Daisy Systems Corp., 10, 51
Damon Biotech, Inc., 11, 45
d'Arbeloff, Alexander V., 9
Data Products, 4
Day, Cecil B., 9
Day in the Life of Sam Walton, A, 29
Days Inns of America, Inc., 9
DEJ Factor, 2, 30–35, 55–56
Delmed, Inc., 11
DeLorean Motor Co., 56
De Wolf, Nicholas, 9
Digital Equipment Corp., 12
Dion, C. Norman, 9
Discovery Toys, 12
Disney, Walt, 23
Doc-in-a-Box Services, 8, 14–17
Dogfight, 22
Dotts, Richard, 9
Draper, William G., 6
Drucker, Peter F., 30
DuBose, Gibbs Jane, 27
Due-Diligence Process, 79–80
Dysan Corp., 9

Early Stages Co., The, 47
Electronic Data Systems Corp. (EDS), 2, 8, 12, 33–35
Elegant Solutions, 5, 54–56

Eli Lilly & Co., 41–42
Emery, 76
Entrepreneurial Megabucks: The 100 Greatest Entrepreneurs of the Last 25 Years, 14
Entrepreneurship and Innovation: Principles and Practice, 30
Export-Import Bank, 6

Fairchild Publications, 19
Fairfield Venture Partners, 47
Farley, Dr. Peter, 44
Farley, William Francis, 9
Farley Industries, Inc., 9
Fatjo, Tom J., Jr., 9
Federal Aviation Administration, 31, 34
Federal Drug Administration, 31
Federal Express Corp., 13, 71, 76
Federal Insurance Contributions Act (FICA), 64
Ferranti High Technology, Inc., 51
Fickling, William Arthur, Jr., 9
Fields, Debbi, 10
Finegold, Aryeh, 10
First National Bank of Maryland, 67
FlightSafety International, Inc., 13, 18, 21–22
FoxMeyer Corp., 13
Frankfort Flying School, 21
Franklin, Benjamin, 7, 54
Freidman, Milton, 40
Frierson, Lawrence, 27
Frist, Dr. Thomas F., Jr., 10
Frist, Dr. Thomas F., Sr., 10, 48
Frontenac Venture Co., 47
Fuqua, John Brooks, 10
Fuqua Industries, Inc., 10

Gates, William, 10, 24–25, 30
Genentech Corp., 6, 13, 41–42, 48, 75
General Motors Corp., 2, 8
General Nutrition, Inc., 13
Generic Entrepreneurial Opportunities (GEOs), 3–5, 47
Genex Corp., 45, 75
Gibbons, Fred, 10
Gibson's, 29
Gilder, George, 45
Glickstein, David, 49
Goldenson, Leonard S., 19
Golder, Thoma & Cressey, 47
Good Society, The, 3, 45–46
Government guarantor, 94
Graham, Reverend Billy, 98
Granite State Capital, Inc., 54
Grant, W.T., 53
Greater Washington Investor, 47
Green, Robert L., 10, 48
Greenmail, 47
Grove, Andrew, 10
Gulfstream Aerospace Corp., 12
Gulf & Western, 66

Haloid Corp., 70
Hambrecht, William, 10
Hambrecht & Quist, Inc., 10, 47
Hambro International Venture Fund, 47
Hanson, John K., 10

Hardymon, Felda G., 91
Harlem Globetrotters, 7
Harvard University, 19, 24
Haynes, Marques, 7
HealthAmerica Corp., 16
HealthGroup International, 16
Health Maintenance Organizations (HMOs), 14, 32–33
HealthWays Systems, Inc., 16
H.J. Heinz, 76–77
Hemingway, Ernest, 23
Heritage Capital Corp., 54
Hewlett-Packard, Inc., 12
High-Tech Start-Up Corp. (HTSU), 83–90
Hillman Co., The, 47
Hill Partnership, The, 51
Hirsch, Neil S., 10
Hollie, Pamela G., 19
Honda, Soichiro, 10
Honda Motor Co., Ltd., 10
Horchow, Roger, 10
Horchow Collection, The, 10
Hospital Corporation of America, 8, 10, 14, 48
H & R Block, Inc., 9
Hudson Valley Broadcasting Co., 19
Humana Corp., 8, 14, 48
Hutton Venture Investment Partners, Inc., 51
Hwang, K. Philip, 10

Ibuka, Masaru, 10
IBM, 25, 53, 72
Immunex Corp., 45
Impact Seven, Inc., 54
Intel Corp., 4, 10, 24, 49–51
Interface Group, Inc., 9
Internal Revenue Service, 63
International Data Group, Inc., 11
Interwest Partners, 47
Investech, L.P., 51
Investment Criteria of Venture Capitalists, 5, 69
Investments Orange Nassau, 51

Jackson, David, 10
J.C. Penney, 29
Jeanloz, Claude & Donna, 10, 25–26
Jeno's, Inc., 12, 20–21
Jobs, Steven, 10
John O. Butler Co., 17
J.R. Simplot Corp., 13

Kauffman, Ewing Marion, 10
Kelly, Thomas L., Jr., 11
Kemmons Wilson Companies, 14
Kenyon & Eckhardt, 19
Kessler, Richard C., 9
Khoury, Amin J., 11
Kleiner & Perkins, 41
Klein, Raphael, 11
K-Mart Corp., 29
Knight, Phillip H., 11
Knoware, Inc., 31
Korvette, E.J., 53
Kosowsky, David I., 11
Kroc, Raymond A., 11, 23–24

Kuhn, Loeb & Co., 27
Kurtzig, Sandra L., 11

LaBrecque, Francis, 11
Lambda Funds, The, 47
Land, Edwin H., 5, 55
Laundry list, 80–82, 91
Lautenberg, Frank, 2, 13
Law of the big P, 39
Law of the Hockey Stick, 6, 39–40, 77–79
Law of Risk Aversion, 38
Laws of Venture Capital, 38
Lazarus, Charles, 11
Lender's policies, 94–95
Lever Brothers, 19
Levy, Lawrence F., 11
Levy Organization, Inc., 11
Lewis, Sydney, 11
Link, 22
Lippman, Walter, 3, 45–46
Little, Royal, 11
Liz Claiborne, Inc., 12
Lockheed, 22
Lucas, George, 11
Lucasfilms, Inc., 11

McDonald Brothers, The, 24
McDonald Corp., 11, 18, 23
McDonnell Douglas, 22
McGill, Archie, 30–31
McGovern, Patrick J., 11
McGowen, William G., 11
McLean, Malcolm P., 11
Maine Capital Corp., 54
Manoogian, Alex, 11
Marion Laboratories, Inc., 10
Marketcorp Venture Associations, L.P., 47
Mary Kay Cosmetics Corp., 9, 18, 22–23
Masco Corp., 11
Masters Fund, The, 51
Matrix Partners, L.P., 47
Maxfield, Robert R., 12
Maxicare Health Plans, Inc., 16
Mayfield Fund, 51
MCI Communications Corp., 11
Medical Care International, 17
Megatrends: Ten New Directions Transforming Our Lives, 73
Mentor Corp., 45
Merck & Co., 43
Merns, Sy Syms, 11
Merrill Pickard Anderson & Eyre, 51
MESBIC, 94
Micron Technology, Inc., 12
Microsoft Corp., 10, 18, 24–25, 30, 49
Miles Laboratories, 41
Millard, William H., 11
MMI Medical, Inc., 17
Moffitt, Phillip, 11, 26–27
Molecular Genetics, 75
Monoclonal Antibodies, 45
Montgomery, Parker G., 12
Montgomery Ward, 53
Moore, Gordon, 10
Morita, Akio, 10

INDEX

Mozart, 18
Mr. K, 23
Mrs. Fields Cookies, Inc., 10
MSX, 25
Mundale, Susan, 20
Murdock, David, 48
Murdock, Rupert, 26, 48
Murphy, Charles, 18
Murphy, Thomas Sawyer, 12, 18–19

Naisbitt, John, 73
National Distillers, 44
National Medical Enterprises Corp., 8, 14
National Venture Capital Association, 6
Nazem & Co., 47
Nebraska Furniture Mart, 9
Neditch, Jean, 79
Negative covenants, 81
Nemeth, Lane, 12
New England Capital Corp., 51
New Enterprise Association, 47
New Jersey Zink, 66
New York Life Insurance Co., 49
New York Times, 19, 73–74
Nike, Inc., 11
Nissan Motor Corp., 26
NMR Image, 16
Norris, William C., 12
North American Capital Group, 54
Northland Foods, 20–21
Norwest Venture Capital Management, Inc., 47
Noyce, Robert, 10
Nu-West Group, 48

Oak Investment Partners, 47
Oak Management Corp., 47
Occidental Petroleum Corp., 48
Occupational Medical Corp., 17
Olsen, Kenneth H., 12
Ortenberg, Elisabeth Claiborne, 12
Osborne, 53
Oshman, M. Kenneth, 12

Packard, David, 12
Palmer Partners, 51
Pan American Airlines, 21–22
Pancretic, Inc., 17
Paramount Pictures, 66
Park, Roy Hampton, 12
Park Communications, Inc., 12
Parkinson, Joseph C., 12
Pathfinder Venture Capital Fund, 47
Paulson, Allen E., 12
Paulucci, Luigino F. "Jeno", 12, 20–21
PC World, 25
Pedus International, Inc., 9
Penney, James Cash, 29
Perkins, Tom, 41, 50
Perot, H. Ross, 2, 8, 12, 26, 33–35
Persha, David, 20
Petrie, Milton S., 12
Petrie Stores Corp., 12

Pine, Carol, 20
Pioneer Ventures Co., 47
Pizza Hut, Inc., 9
Plant Resources Venture Fund, 47
Play for Growth, 26
Poduska, John William, 12
Polaroid Corp., 4–5, 7, 55
Preferred Stock, 83–92
Price, Sol, 12
Price Company, The, 12
Primus Capital Fund, 54
Private Capital Corp., 54
Problems:
　big-P companies, 40–48, 73
　law of big-P, 39, 73–75
　problem formation, 55–56, 74
　problem size as function of valuation, 73–74
Proctor, Barbara Gardner, 12
Proctor & Gardner Advertising, Inc., 12
Professional Pharmaceutical Corp., 43
Purolator, 76

Quality of the Entrepreneurial Team, 78
Qume, 4

Ralston Purina Co., 26
"Ray Kroc Did It All For You," 24
R & D Ltd. Partnership, 44
Readicare, Inc., 17
Reedy River Ventures, Inc., 54
Regional Financial Enterprises, 47
Renovator's Supply, Inc., 18, 25–26
Reverend Ike, 98
R.J. Reynolds Industries, 21, 26
Robbins, Tom, 24
"Robert A. Swanson, Chief Generic Officer," 42
Roberts, Oral, 98
Robertson, Coleman & Stephens, 47
Rolm Corp., 12
Ronald McDonald House, 24
Rothchild's, Inc., 30
Rothenberg, Randall, 42
Rouse, James W., 12
Rouse Co., 12
Ruth, Babe, 4

Sanders, W. Jeremiah III, 12
Santa Fe Private Equity Fund, 47, 49, 51–53
SBIC, 94
Schwab, Charles, 13
Seagram Company, Ltd., 27
Sea-Land Services, Inc., 11
Self-Made, 20
Seneker, Harold, 29
Sevin Rosen Management Co., 51
Shakarian, David B., 13
Shearson Loeb Rhoades, 14
Shoen, Leonard Samuel "Sam", 13, 27–29
Siegel, Morris J., 13
Sikora, Robert F., 13

Sikorsky, 22
Silver, A. David, 14, 18
Silver, Herbert, 55
Simplot, Jack R., 13
Singer Co., 22
Sloan School of Management, 41
Smith, Frederick E., 2, 13
Software Publishing Corp., 10
Solutions:
　elegance of, 54–55, 75
　uniqueness of, 77–78
Sony Corp., 10
South Atlantic Capital Corp., 54
Southwest Venture Partners, 47
Sperry Corp., 7
Spiva, Tony, 27
Sprout Group, 47
Standard Oil of Indiana, 44
Stata, Raymond, 13
Steinberg, Saul, 48
Summit Partners, 97
Surgical Care Affiliates, 17
Sutter Hill Capital, 6, 47
Swanson, Robert A., 13, 41, 48
Syms Corp., 11

Tandem Computers, Inc., 13, 49–51
Tandon, Sirjang Lal, 13
Tandon Corp., 13
Tandy, Charles, 13
Tandy Corp., 13
Tatum, Goose, 7
Taub, Henry, 2, 13
Taub, Joseph, 2, 13
Tauscher, William Y., 13
Technology Venture Investors, 47
Tecmar, Inc., 9
Tektronix, Inc., 13
Teledyne, Inc., 13, 66
Telerate, Inc., 10
TeleVideo Systems, Inc., 10
Tennessee Venture Capital Corp., 54
Teradyne, Inc., 9
Term Sheet, 80–82
Texaco, 18, 48
Textron, Inc., 11
TG & Y Stores, 29
13-30 Corp., 11, 18, 26–27
TIE/Communications, Inc., 11
Toys'R'Us, Inc., 11
Treybig, James G., 13
Trippe, Juan, 21
Turner, Robert Edward, III, 13
Turner Broadcasting Systems, Inc., 13

Ueltschi, Albert L., 13, 21–22
U-Haul Systems, Inc., 12, 18, 27–29
U.S. Health Care Systems, Inc., 16
U.S. Medical Enterprises, Inc., 17
U.S. Postal Service, 76
United Technologies, 22
Up-Front Financing, 18

Valentine, Don, 50
Value Line, 48
Verbatim Corp., 9
Victor, 53

Vista Ventures, 47
Vollum, Howard, 13

Wakefield, Jerry, 21
Wall Street Journal, The, 67
Wal-Mart Stores, Inc., 8, 13, 18, 29–30, 53
Walt Disney Productions, 48
Walton, James, 29
Walton, Sam Moore, 8, 13, 29–30, 53

Wang, An, 14, 53
Wang Laboratories, Inc., 14, 53
Warner Communications, Inc., 48
Washington Post, 73
Wealth and Poverty, 45
Weight Watchers International, Inc., 76–77
Weill, Sanford I., 14
Western Health Plans, 16
Whitehead Associates, 47
White River Capital Corp., 54

Whittle, Christopher, 11, 26–27
Wilson, Charles Kemmons, 14
Winnebago Industries, Inc., 10
Woodland Venture Capital Co., 54
Wozniak, Steven, 10

Xerography, 4
Xerox Corp., 4, 7, 53, 70
Xicor, Inc., 11

You and Me, 28